Henry IV of Germany, 1056–1106

This is the first book in English devoted to the German king and emperor Henry IV (1056–1106), whose reign was one of the most momentous in German history and a turning-point in the history of the medieval empire (the kingdoms of Germany, Italy and Burgundy).

The reign was marked by continuous rebellions and fluctuating fortune. Earlier monarchs had also witnessed conflict between crown and aristocracy, but Henry IV's reign differed in that his conflicts could never be definitively resolved either by negotiation or by resorting to war. During the 1070s the young king, in strengthening his authority over the key province of Saxony, gained a reputation for tyranny which he could never afterwards shake off. Simultaneously his assertion of the crown's traditional rights over the imperial church aroused the opposition of the newly reformed papacy, implementing a programme of ecclesiastical liberty. The alliance between the German princes and the papacy haunted Henry IV for the rest of his life. He meanwhile, by turns a bold opportunist and a flexible compromiser, dedicated himself at all times to preserving the traditional rights of the monarchy.

I. S. ROBINSON is Associate Professor of Medieval History, Trinity College, Dublin. His previous publications include *The Papacy, 1073–1198: Continuity and Innovation* (Cambridge, 1990).

Henry IV of Germany
1056–1106

I. S. ROBINSON

CAMBRIDGE
UNIVERSITY PRESS

PUBLISHED BY THE PRESS SYNDICATE OF THE UNIVERSITY OF CAMBRIDGE
The Pitt Building, Trumpington Street, Cambridge, United Kingdom

CAMBRIDGE UNIVERSITY PRESS
The Edinburgh Building, Cambridge CB2 2RU, United Kingdom   www.cup.cam.ac.uk
40 West 20th Street, New York, NY 10011-4211, USA   www.cup.org
10 Stamford Road, Oakleigh, Melbourne 3166, Australia
Ruiz de Alarcón 13, 28014 Madrid, Spain

First published 1999

Printed in the United Kingdom at the University Press, Cambridge

Typeset in 11/13pt Abode Garamond in QuarkXPress™   [SE]

A catalogue record for this book is available from the British Library

ISBN 0 521 65113 1 hardback

CONTENTS

Acknowledgements   *page* vii

INTRODUCTION   I

THE YOUNG KING, 1056–1075   17
1   The minority, 1056–1065   19
2   Henry IV and Saxony, 1065–1075   63

THE CONFLICT WITH POPE GREGORY VII   105
3   Henry IV, the imperial Church and the reform
       papacy, 1065–1075   107
4   Worms, Canossa, Forchheim, 1076–1077   143
5   Civil war in Germany, 1077–1081   171
6   The second Italian expedition, 1081–1084   211

EMPEROR HENRY IV, 1084–1106   237
7   The pacification of Germany, 1084–1089   239
8   Henry IV, the imperial Church and the
       papacy: the third Italian expedition, 1090–1097   275
9   The restoration of royal authority in Germany,
       1097–1103   296
10   The end of the reign, 1103–1106   321

CONCLUSION   345
Bibliography   370
Index   397

ACKNOWLEDGEMENTS

In writing this introduction to the reign of Henry IV, king of the Germans and emperor, I have received the generous help and advice of many distinguished scholars. My grateful thanks are due to the Reverend Mr H. E. J. Cowdrey (Oxford), Professor Dr Horst Fuhrmann (Munich), Professor Dr Wilfried Hartmann (Tübingen), Dr Irmgard Höss, Professor Dr Rudolf Schieffer (Munich), Dr Wolfram Setz (Munich) and Professor Dr Tilman Struve (Cologne).

Mr William Davies of the Cambridge University Press has been unfailingly helpful and encouraging. The later stages of the research for this book were made possible by a grant from the Arts and Social Sciences Research Fund, Trinity College, Dublin, which I acknowledge with gratitude. The staff of the Library of Trinity College, Dublin, have been extremely generous with their time and their assistance and I must express my particular thanks to Roy Stanley, Anne Walsh and Mary Higgins. I am grateful also for the help of the librarians of the Monumenta Germaniae Historica, Munich, the Historical Seminar and the University Library of Bonn and the University Library of Freiburg im Breisgau. Important material was sent to me by friends working in other libraries: by Elizabeth Rublack-Diamond (Tübingen), Dr Virginia Davis and Dr John McLoughlin (London), Dr Benedikt Stuchtey and Henriette Stuchtey (Freiburg), Dr Niall O Ciosáin (Paris), Dr Mark Humphries (St Andrews), Douglas Carver (Washington and Rome) and by my nephew, Daniel Becker (Cologne).

I have been most fortunate in the encouragement of my friends in Dublin, Mary and Aidan Clarke and Margaret and Patrick Kelly; of my friends in Freiburg, Dr Ellen Gottlieb-Schramm and Professor Dr Gottfried Schramm; and of my family in Bad Godesberg and in Nassau, Waldi and Werner Becker and Dagmar and Walter Hammerstein. I wish to record my grateful thanks to them and above all to my wife, Dr Helga Robinson-Hammerstein, without whose patient help, encouragement and scholarly advice this book would *never* have been completed.

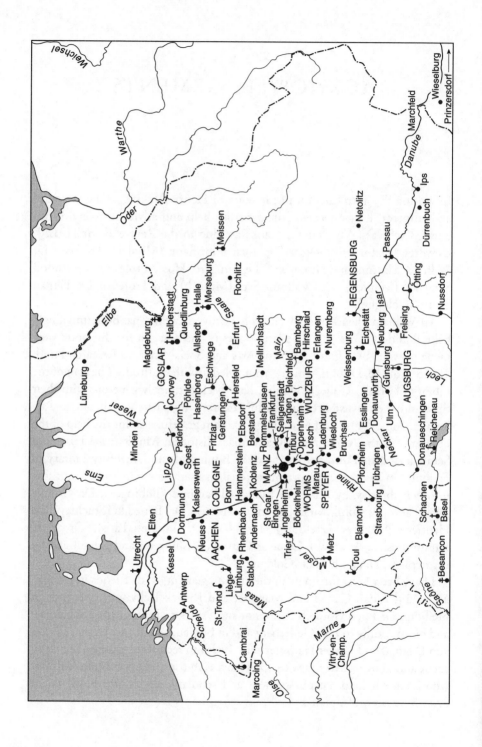

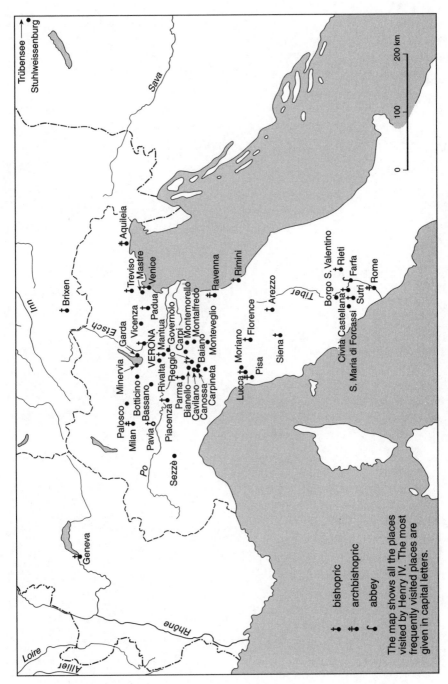

The kingdoms of Germany, Burgundy and Italy in the reign of Henry IV

Trübensee
Stuhlweissenburg

Sava

Inn

Brixen

Aquileia

Etsch

Treviso
Mastre
Venice

Garda
Vicenza
Padua

Minervia
Palosco
Botticino
Bassano
VERONA
Rivalta
Mantua
Parma
Governolo
Montemorello
Montalfredo
Ravenna

Milan
Pavia
Piacenza
Reggio
Carpi
Monteveglio
Rimini

Po
Bianello
Cavilano
Canossa
Baiano
Carpineta

Sezzè

Moriano
Florence
Arezzo

Lucca
Pisa
Siena

Tiber

Borgo S. Valentino
Rieti

Civitè Castellana
Farfa
S. Maria di Forcassi
Sutri
Rome

Geneva

Rhône

Loire

Allier

The map shows all the places
visited by Henry IV. The most
frequently visited places are
given in capital letters.

✝ bishopric

‡ archbishopric

⚓ abbey

0   100   200 km

Introduction

'Since he was a man born and brought up to rule, he always showed a royal spirit in adversity, as was fitting in one of such descent, whose ancestors had held such high office and enjoyed such renown, and he preferred to die rather than be conquered. He considered it a matter of irremediable shame to allow an injury to go unpunished.'[1] Thus Henry IV is portrayed in the chronicle of Lampert, monk of Hersfeld, the apologist of his Saxon enemies. According to this chronicler, Henry's 'royal spirit' deteriorated under the influence of low-born counsellors into a lust for power which threatened the property and the very freedom of his subjects. Another apologist of the Saxon rebels, Bruno, clerk of Merseburg, wrote that it was uncertain 'which was the greater infamy, that of his incestuous lust or that of his boundless cruelty'.[2] Most narrative sources for the reign of Henry IV were written from an anti-Henrician point of view. Many were composed by supporters of Pope Gregory VII and the reform papacy with which Henry was in conflict for the last thirty years of his reign. These Gregorian chroniclers echoed the language of the Saxon apologists, portraying a king who 'used to rage savagely against [his subjects] according to his whim'; whose 'thoughts turned to tyranny and [who] planned to hold the kingdom not by justice but by violence'.[3]

Henry IV 'wished there to be no lords in his kingdom, so that he might be the sole lord over all men'. He conceived 'a great design such as none of his predecessors had ever attempted': to deprive first the Saxons and later the rest of the nobility of their lands and their liberty.[4] These polemics prompted some twentieth-century scholars to adopt a strikingly positive view of Henry IV's regime in his German kingdom. He was 'a state reformer of genius', 'the great, unfortunate king who was left with the tragic duty of building a new state out of the breakdown of the imperial constitution dominated by the ecclesiastical hierarchy and the aristocracy'. This far-sighted statesman, wishing to found

[1] Lampert of Hersfeld, *Annales* 1076, p. 270.
[2] Bruno of Merseburg, *Saxonicum bellum* c. 10, p. 18. Cf. c. 5, p. 16.
[3] Berthold of Reichenau, *Annales* 1077, p. 298; Bernold of St Blasien, *Chronicon* 1077, p. 434.
[4] Bruno, *Saxonicum bellum* c. 60, p. 55; Lampert, *Annales* 1073, p. 147.

I

his 'new royal state' on a broader social basis, 'had recourse, in his struggle with the nobility and the Church, especially to the social strata of the unfree servants and the towns'.[5] The scholarship of the later twentieth century has become sceptical of this view of Henry IV as an enlightened centraliser of the German kingdom and 'a revolutionary attacking the old constitution'. Recent studies of the government of the western empire in the eleventh century have above all emphasised the extreme limitations of the powers of the crown.

The empire, created in the tenth century by the great warlord Otto I, had none of the centralising characteristics of a modern state. Its three main component parts were the German, Italian and Burgundian kingdoms, which possessed a common ruler but no common institutional framework. These kingdoms were collections of autonomous provinces governed by secular and ecclesiastical princes. The princes had performed homage and sworn fealty to the king, on the occasion of his election or coronation or on his ceremonial journey around the kingdom. The successful assertion of royal authority depended largely on the cooperation of the princes and the obligation of service which resulted from their homage and fealty. The king possessed no special administrative machinery to enforce his will on the kingdom. There is no evidence that eleventh-century kings and their advisers ever formulated the concept of centralisation: certainly they lacked the material resources to make it a reality. The empire of the Ottonian and Salian emperors 'was born particularistic'. 'From the start the nobles possessed lordship and powers in their own right, outside the king's reach.'[6] The rights of lordship exercised by the princes in their own localities were part of the divinely ordained scheme of terrestrial government which it was the special duty of the king to protect. 'We possess in the king and emperor the supreme defender on earth of our liberty', declared the princes in an idealised mid-eleventh-century portrait of kingship, the biography of Conrad II, Henry IV's grandfather.[7] Royal and princely power were regarded not as competing with, but as complementing each other. The German kingdom, like the Italian and Burgundian kingdoms, was a collection of parallel lordships, some exercised by secular princes, dukes, margraves and counts; some by ecclesiastical princes.[8]

The office of duke (*dux*), the most exalted of the princely dignities in the German kingdom, was still essentially military in character in the reign of Henry IV. The dukes were the military commanders of the nobility in the German duchies (Bavaria, Swabia, Carinthia, Saxony, Upper and Lower Lotharingia), with the duty of leading the nobles of their duchy and the

---

[5] Bosl (1950) 1:3, 12–16, 74–101. Cf. Hirsch (1922) 139–49, 150–7, 221–38.
[6] Leyser (1968) 32. Cf. Arnold (1991) 11–60.   [7] Wipo, *Gesta Chuonradi* c. 20, p. 40.
[8] Lintzel (1929) 233–63; Werle (1956) 225–99; Keller (1982) 74–128; Goetz (1991) 253–71; Arnold (1991) 88–132.

knights in their retinues on royal expeditions. Within their duchies they were responsible for the maintenance of peace and they held regular assemblies of the nobility in which the most important political and judicial business of the duchy was transacted. Their authority over the nobility of the province derived partly from the ducal office, partly from the feudal relationship (some of the counts and other noblemen were their vassals) and partly from being great landowners. Dukes who were natives of their duchies disposed of extensive family lands; 'foreign' dukes enjoyed the use of some of the crown lands in their duchies. The duke was the representative of the people of his province at the imperial court and he seems to have been regarded by the king as the agent of the imperial court among his own people. The king invested dukes with their office and they performed homage and swore fealty to him. Many dukes, however, seem to have owed their titles as much to hereditary succession as to royal designation. Of the eighteen dukes appointed during the reign of Henry IV, nine were the sons or the nearest male relatives of their predecessors. The office of duke of Saxony had been held uninterruptedly by members of the Billung dynasty since 936.[9] In designating dukes in the two Lotharingian duchies Henry respected the rights of the Châtenois (Upper Lotharingia) and the house of Verdun (Lower Lotharingia). It was in the south German duchies of Swabia, Bavaria and Carinthia that eleventh-century kings were able to appoint to ducal office newcomers who were not the hereditary successors of their predecessors. Of such newcomers in the reign of Henry IV two were kinsmen of the imperial dynasty: Conrad III and Liutold of Carinthia, respectively of the Ezzonid and Eppenstein families.[10] In the cases of Rudolf of Swabia and his successor, Frederick I, the new duke was permitted to marry into the imperial family.[11] The hereditary principle was reasserted in the final years of the reign, when in each of the south German duchies the ducal newcomer was succeeded by his own heir.[12]

The office of margrave (*marchio*), like that of duke, was military in origin, signifying the command of a frontier or march. During the later eleventh century the duties of those margraves stationed on the vulnerable eastern frontier of Saxony, Bavaria and Carinthia were still mainly military. The march of the Billungs, the most northerly of the Saxon marches, involved the duty of maintaining surveillance over the Obodrite Slavs (who were at this time being converted to Christianity). The march was in the hands of the Billung duke of Saxony and constituted the basis of his authority in the duchy. The neighbouring march was the Saxon Nordmark, which confronted the Slav military

[9] See below p. 70.
[10] Otto, duke of Bavaria, was married to an Ezzonid. See below pp. 35, 66 n. 10.
[11] See below pp. 33, 189.   [12] See below pp. 297, 331.

confederation of the Liutizi, hostile and resolutely pagan. The vulnerable character of this march was demonstrated one month before Henry IV's accession, when Margrave William was defeated and killed by the Liutizi. His march was conferred on a kinsman of the imperial dynasty, Count Luder-Udo I of Stade, whose family retained it for the rest of Henry IV's reign.[13] To the south of the Saxon Nordmark lay the march of Lower Lusatia and that of Meissen, bordering on the kingdom of Poland. In the early years of Henry IV's reign Lower Lusatia was in the hands of Dedi, a prince of the house of Wettin, while Meissen was held by the counts of Weimar-Orlamünde, firstly William and later his brother Otto. When Margrave Otto died, leaving three daughters (1067), the king conferred Meissen on his own kinsman, Count Ekbert I of Brunswick, of the dynasty of the Brunones.[14] Ekbert I was succeeded by his young son, Ekbert II, who proved the most implacable of Henry's enemies in Saxony. Both Dedi and Ekbert II took part in the Saxon rebellion of 1073. The king's victory over the Saxons in 1075 enabled him to withdraw the marches from the rebel margraves and confer them both on his loyal ally, Duke Vratislav II of Bohemia.[15] In 1088, however, Henry was reconciled with Dedi's son, Henry I of Eilenburg, who played a leading role in the campaigns against the lawless Ekbert II of Brunswick. Henry IV invested this valuable supporter not only with his father's march of Lower Lusatia but also with his enemy's march of Meissen.[16] Henry of Eilenburg was able to transmit both marches to his son. The margraves of south-eastern Germany, like those of Saxony, were drawn from local families and usually owed their office to hereditary succession. The march of the Bavarian Nordgau was held by the Diepolds, descendants of Count Diepold of Augstgau. The Bavarian Ostmark (the core of the twelfth-century duchy of Austria) had since the late tenth century been in the hands of the Babenberg family. The Carinthian march was held by the Otakars, counts of the Chiemgau and the Traungau (this march being the basis for the later duchy of Styria).

The most frequent princely title was that of count (*comes*). In the eighth and ninth centuries that title had denoted an influential royal agent, charged with administrative, military and judicial duties in the specific area of his jurisdiction (*comitatus*, 'county'). The count had been responsible for the administration of crown lands and for military leadership when the nobility of his county was summoned on a royal campaign. Above all he presided over the law court to which the free men of his county brought their cases. By the end of the eleventh century, however, much of the count's original role of royal agent had disappeared. The administration of the crown lands had been

---

[13] See below p. 74.   [14] See below p. 80.   [15] See below p. 102.
[16] See below p. 270.

placed largely in the hands of royal *ministeriales*, the unfree knights, servants of the crown who first come to prominence in the documents of the Salian period.[17] The counts' jurisdiction had been greatly diminished throughout the kingdom by the royal practice of creating alternative jurisdictions: notably by exempting the lands of the churches from the interference of any secular power. While in the tenth and eleventh centuries the crown had diluted the counts' governmental functions, the counts themselves had ceased to regard service to the crown as the principal source of their authority and status. They treated the countship as an hereditary dignity which reflected their local pre-eminence, which was based on their family lands, military followings and castles. A countship seemed now to be so much a piece of family property that it could be inherited even by a distant kinsman or by a minor.

The office of count palatine, which in the eighth and ninth centuries had been the most important judicial office in the Frankish royal palace, survived into the reign of Henry IV in the provinces of Bavaria, Saxony and Lotharingia. It is not clear whether this was merely an honorific title, conferred on a prince in acknowledgement of his local greatness, for, as in the case of margraves and counts, the title was held by a succession of members of the same great landowning family. It is possible that the count palatine, unlike the count, continued to regard himself as a royal official, perhaps with responsibility for the defence and administration of crown lands in his province. Certainly the Bavarian and Lotharingian counts palatine maintained close links with the court during Henry IV's reign. The Bavarian count palatine Rapoto, count of Cham and Vohburg, was conspicuously loyal.[18] In Lotharingia the title of count palatine belonged to the Hezelid dynasty, kinsmen of the imperial family. The count palatine Henry I [19] was succeeded by his son, Herman II, who was in turn succeeded by his nephew, Henry II, count of Laach, his closest kinsman. Count palatine Henry II was eventually succeeded by a stepson, the Saxon prince Siegfried of Ballenstedt.[20] In Saxony the title of count palatine was held for the first three decades of the reign by Count Frederick II of Goseck (brother of the great Archbishop Adalbert of Bremen). On his death the title was secured by his nephew, Count Frederick I of Sommerschenburg. Both played a prominent role in the Saxon rebellions against Henry IV, in marked contrast to their loyal Bavarian and Lotharingian counterparts.[21]

The administrative and judicial functions of secular princes throughout the kingdom had been eroded by granting immunity to the extensive lands of the

[17] See below pp. 322, 357–60. [18] See below p. 305.
[19] Considered a possible successor to Henry III in 1045: Steindorff (1874) 1:287.
[20] See below p. 314. [21] See below pp. 74, 181.

ecclesiastical princes, the archbishops and bishops and those abbots who were royal vassals. Since the tenth century the possession of an immunity had not only freed the immunist from the jurisdiction of the count but also permitted him to exercise the count's judicial and other powers within his own territories. In addition, from the reign of Emperor Otto III (983–1002) onwards kings conferred on churches whole counties with full comital rights. Fifty-four such grants are recorded between the reign of Otto III and that of Henry IV, nineteen of them in the reign of Henry IV himself.[22] This practice of delegating secular office to churchmen, considered in the light of the well-documented royal control over the appointment of bishops and royal abbots, has prompted the notion of an Ottonian–Salian 'imperial Church system'. Otto I and his successors allegedly 'set about systematically developing the Church as the central institution of the empire'. 'The bishops were entirely at the king's disposal: in return they received extensive political rights.' 'The ecclesiastical magnates were to participate in government throughout the empire according to the king's will', while the monarch 'largely dispensed with the participation of the secular nobility'. The 'Investiture Contest' in the reign of Henry IV challenged the royal right to invest bishops with their office and cast doubt on the 'sacral aura' which supposedly surrounded the king. By destroying the 'harmony of the ecclesiastical and secular spheres' the Investiture Contest 'deprived the system of its internal justification'.[23] The most recent studies of Ottonian–Salian government and of the imperial Church present a more complex picture. They show that, although kings might depose individual secular princes on the grounds of rebellion or incompetence, it was never possible for them to 'dispense with the participation of the secular nobility' in the government of the empire. Recent scholarship confirms that, especially from the early eleventh century onwards, kings both controlled episcopal appointments and endowed bishoprics with lands and rights of government. There is, however, no firm evidence of any 'system', according to which kings replaced secular princes with bishops as their agents in local government, in order to bring the provinces under closer royal supervision.[24]

It is indeed uncertain whether granting immunities and counties to bishoprics actually resulted in closer royal supervision of local government. Churchmen were forbidden by canon law to exercise criminal jurisdiction, because it involved bloodshed. Bishops who received immunities were, therefore, obliged to delegate their administration to advocates, who were members

---

[22] Santifaller (1964) 36, 105–15; Arnold (1991) 77–87.
[23] Mitteis (1959) 117–18; Santifaller (1964) 27–49.
[24] Reuter (1982) 347–74; Fleckenstein (1985) 83–98; Schieffer (1989) 291–301.

of the secular aristocracy. The surviving accounts of the conflicts between churchmen and their advocates reveal that many of the noblemen entrusted with this office were by no means under the control of their ecclesiastical lords and used their position to aggrandise themselves at the expense of the churches.[25] As with immunities, so also with the counties which the king conferred on bishoprics: the bishops derived financial benefits from the grant but they could not administer the counties in person and were obliged to delegate them to secular princes. In most cases the recipient was the same man who had held the county before it was granted to the bishop. When, for example, in 1063 Henry IV granted to Archbishop Adalbert of Bremen 'the county of Margrave Udo' in the territory between the lower Elbe and the lower Weser, the archbishop conferred the county on the prince, Udo II of Stade, who had previously held it from the king. Udo was now the vassal of the archbishop and owed him service, but what is known of his later conduct suggests that his lord exercised no effective control over him.[26]

Adam of Bremen, the historian of the archbishopric, described Adalbert's acquisition of Saxon and Frisian counties in a passage of particular importance for understanding the workings of the 'imperial Church system'. Adam wrote that the church of Bremen was so rich that the archbishop need not envy his colleagues of Cologne and Mainz. Nevertheless there was one bishop whom he envied. 'The bishop of Würzburg was the only prelate of whom it was said that he had no equal in his bishopric, since he himself holds all the counties of his diocese and, although a bishop, he governs the province as its duke. Our archbishop was moved to imitate him and he resolved to bring within the power of his church all the countships which appeared to involve any jurisdiction inside his diocese.'[27] The initiative in this acquisition of counties by the church came from the archbishop, not from a king anxious to replace secular princes with churchmen willing to serve as his agents in local government. There is no doubt that other prelates wished, like Adalbert, to strengthen their authority in their dioceses by the acquisition of rights of government and of the increased income which immunities and counties brought with them. Their petitions to the king were sympathetically received, because prelates performed for the crown valuable services which involved their churches in great expense.

The imperial government was, therefore, a partnership of many lords – dukes, margraves, counts palatine, counts, advocates representing ecclesiastical immunists – all performing governmental functions independently of the crown. The particular responsibility of the king himself was (according to the

---

[25] See below pp. 117, 313–14.   [26] *D H IV* 112. See below p. 74.
[27] Adam of Bremen, *Gesta* iii.146, p. 187. See below p. 58.

biographer of Conrad II) 'to give the land judgement, justice and peace', to protect the rights of his secular and especially his ecclesiastical subjects and to defend the kingdom itself from enemies.[28] The most important political and judicial business of the crown was transacted in assemblies of bishops and secular princes. These assemblies met at irregular intervals in different regions of the kingdom, whenever the king saw fit to summon them. It was here that questions of war and peace were discussed and vacancies in secular and ecclesiastical offices filled; here also the king acted as judge in important local cases. As long as he remained in a particular area, the king's authority as supreme judge took precedence over that of any local official. The records of royal judicial proceedings show, however, that on these occasions the king reached a decision with the assistance of local princes and of advisers from his own entourage. In most of these cases the king was called on to act as umpire in the disputes of members of the local aristocracy. Less frequently the king introduced judicial business of his own into the assembly: the judgement of rebels and the confiscation of their offices and property.

The kingdom of Henry IV possessed no capital city. An eleventh-century king was accustomed 'to pursue his high vocation by wandering about'.[29] The king spent his whole reign in a constant journey (*iter*) through the provinces of his kingdom, a progress interrupted only by the need to conduct military campaigns or to suppress rebellions. He remained in one place sometimes only for a few days, rarely for more than a few weeks. Given the immense size of the German kingdom and the independent attitude of the provinces, such rapid mobility was the only means of making royal government effective. Recent scholarship has identified the royal *iter* as 'the most essential . . . institution' of the kingdom because it gave 'the best cohesion possible' to political society.[30] The princes enjoyed no such mobility because they could not afford the great expense which it entailed. Consequently kings possessed 'a near-monopoly of long distance communications', which served to make them 'the principal binding agents' of the kingdom. The royal *iter* was the more remarkable in that it involved the provision of food and lodging for the several hundred persons who usually accompanied the king. The royal entourage could be accommodated in one of the 'palaces' (*palatia*) associated with certain of the crown lands.[31] The crown lands (or royal fisc) were not fixed units of property but constantly fluctuated in size. They were expanded by the confiscation of the lands of rebels and by the legal custom that the king inher-

---

[28] Wipo, *Gesta Chuonradi* c. 3, p. 23.   [29] Schulte (1935) 132.

[30] Leyser (1981) 746–7. Cf. Reinke (1987) 225–51; Reuter (1991) 208–11, 213, 214–15; Bernhardt (1993) 45–75.

[31] Notably Aachen, Goslar, Kaiserswerth and Nuremberg: Rieckenberg (1942) 99–103, 110; Brühl (1968) 134, 158–9.

ited the property of noble families when there was no heir. They were diminished by acts of royal generosity (particularly, in the case of the Salians, towards the church of Speyer, the mausoleum of their dynasty). The eleventh-century monarchy increasingly relied less on the income of the fisc and more on alternative resources. The king could claim hospitality (*gistum*) and the provision of food (*servitium*) from the archbishoprics, bishoprics and royal abbeys.[32] The heavy demands made by the royal *iter* on the material resources of the German churches serve to put into perspective the generosity of the eleventh-century kings towards the imperial Church. The transfer of land and profitable jurisdictional rights to bishoprics was in many cases the essential precondition for the increasing royal demands for *gistum* and *servitium*.

The kings of the first half of the eleventh century visited their palaces less and less frequently and put more and more pressure on the churches. During the reign of Henry IV this trend was intensified. The itinerary of Henry IV, the pattern of the king's journeys through the kingdom from year to year, at once reveals the crisis which overtook his government, forcing fundamental change on the regime. The royal journeys of the Ottonian kings had been concentrated in particular in eastern Saxony and northern Thuringia, the homeland of the Liudolfing (Ottonian) dynasty, where their lands and residences were most numerous. They had also often visited the Rhine and Main region and the Lower Lotharingian neighbourhood of Aachen, so closely associated with the Carolingian kingship. The royal journeys of their Salian successors, whose dynasty originated in the middle Rhineland and whose family lands were in the neighbourhood of Worms and Speyer, were rather more evenly spread over the whole kingdom. While the Ottonians preferred to celebrate the great Christian festivities and to hold their assemblies of princes within the triangular territory formed by Magdeburg, Ingelheim and Aachen, the Salians held their festive courts in Bavaria and Swabia, as well as Franconia, Lotharingia and Saxony. This change was made possible by demanding *gistum* and *servitium* from churches. The Salians preferred to celebrate the great festivals as the guests of their bishops. Nevertheless the first two Salian kings, Conrad II and Henry III, the grandfather and father of Henry IV, continued regularly to visit the old centres of Ottonian power in northeastern Germany.[33] The Salians seem to have inherited all the lands and rights of lordship of their Ottonian predecessors and consequently the material resources of the eleventh-century kingship remained heavily concentrated in eastern Saxony.

During the first two decades of the reign of Henry IV the pattern of the king's itinerary resembled that of the first two Salians. He perambulated all

---

[32] Brühl (1968) 132–9, 157–8; Metz (1971) 257–91; Bernhardt (1993) 75–84.
[33] Rieckenberg (1942) 32–154.

the provinces of the kingdom but showed a marked preference for eastern Saxony, or at least for one particular royal palace in eastern Saxony, which had also been the favourite residence of his father. This was Goslar, described by the chronicler Lampert of Hersfeld as 'the town which the German kings were accustomed to treat as their homeland and their private residence', a 'very wealthy place, always most dear' to Henry IV.[34] During the years of his minority (October 1056 – March 1065) the royal itinerary included eleven recorded visits to Goslar; in the first decade of Henry's personal rule (1065–75) there were nineteen visits.[35] This decade 1065–75 witnessed an attempt by Henry IV to consolidate his lordship in eastern Saxony.[36] The royal itinerary after 1075 changed dramatically. Apart from visits in January and March 1076, Goslar disappeared from the itinerary. The king was driven from his favourite palace by the Saxon princes who had rebelled in 1073, demanding that 'he should not spend all his life exclusively in Saxony in sloth and indolence but should sometimes leave Goslar and travel round his kingdom'.[37] After the Saxon war broke out again in 1076 Goslar became the residence of anti-kings elected by Henry's enemies. Henry now appeared in the province not as the acknowledged ruler on a royal *iter* but as a military commander campaigning against rebels. After making peace with the Saxon princes in 1089, Henry did not set foot in the province again. For the remaining years of the reign information about the royal itinerary becomes steadily sparser, but the general trend is clear. During these three decades the court usually resided in episcopal cities and lived at the expense of the imperial Church.[38] It is this dependence on the material resources of the Church that explains Henry IV's determination to control ecclesiastical appointments, despite the vigorous opposition of the reform papacy.

The royal *iter* is one of the two best-documented and most thoroughly researched institutions of the eleventh-century German monarchy, the other being the royal chancery. The chancery had not yet developed into a separate department of government with its own personnel. As in every other western European kingdom, the task of writing the king's letters and diplomas belonged to royal chaplains, who were also responsible for the conduct of divine service in the royal household. The title of arch-chancellor for the German kingdom belonged in the eleventh century to the archbishop of Mainz and that of arch-chancellor for the Italian kingdom to the archbishop of Cologne, but these were purely honorific dignities. The actual direction of chancery business was in the hands of the chancellors for the German and

---

[34] Lampert, *Annales* 1066, 1071, 1075, pp. 100, 117, 225. See below pp. 79–80.
[35] See below p. 79.   [36] See below pp. 84–7.
[37] Lampert, *Annales* 1074, p. 178. See below pp. 78–9.
[38] Kilian (1886) 144–52; Kottje (1978) 131–57.

Italian kingdoms, who were appointed by the king. The German chancellor, whose duties brought him regularly into close contact with the king, may well have enjoyed considerable influence as a royal adviser. The chancellors appointed during Henry IV's reign seem all to have been of the highest nobility. Gebhard, chancellor of the German kingdom (who later became archbishop of Salzburg) belonged to a noble Swabian family, perhaps that of the counts of Helfenstein. His successor Frederick (later bishop of Münster) was the son of the Wettin prince Margrave Theoderic of Lower Lusatia. He was succeeded by Sigehard (later patriarch of Aquileia), of the Bavarian comital family of the Sigehardings in Chiemgau. Subsequent holders of the office included the Saxon nobleman Pibo (later bishop of Toul), Gebhard-Jaromir, bishop of Prague, who was the brother of Duke Vratislav II of Bohemia, and Herman (later archbishop of Cologne) of the Lotharingian comital house of Hochstaden. The Italian chancellor Wibert of Parma (the future archbishop of Ravenna and one of Henry's most important adherents) was a kinsman of the dynasty of Canossa, which held the office of margrave of Tuscany.[39] The distinguished birth of these chancellors underlines the importance of the royal chapel in creating bonds between the king and the great aristocratic families from which almost all chaplains were recruited.

The drafting and writing of the royal diplomas was usually the work of the royal notaries. (In the case of perhaps a quarter of the extant diplomas of Henry IV the finished document was provided by the recipient himself and was the work of a scribe from outside the chancery.) One of the notaries of the Henrician chancery has attracted the special attention of modern scholarship: Gottschalk, provost of Aachen (and subsequently monk of Klingenmünster), one of the most remarkable of Henry IV's servants. There is evidence of his activity in the chancery over a period of thirty-three years, from December 1071 to February 1104. During these years Gottschalk was responsible for the production of perhaps as many as eighty of the surviving royal diplomas.[40] He also composed nine, or possibly eleven, of the forty-two extant letters issued in the name of the king, including the well-known polemics against Pope Gregory VII of 1076 and 1082.[41] Gottschalk of Aachen was the first royal supporter to formulate a theoretical defence of Henry IV's kingship. The arguments presented in his polemics of 1076 continued to influence 'state propaganda' for the rest of the century.[42]

---

[39] Gawlik (1978) xxi–lxxxii.
[40] Erdmann and von Gladiss (1939) 115–74; Gawlik (1978) lxi–lxviii. In earlier scholarship Gottschalk was identified as 'Adalbero C' (the notary responsible for writing the diplomas authenticated by the chancellor Adalbero, canon of Metz).
[41] Henry IV, *Letters* 6, 9, 10, 12, 13, 15, 17–19; perhaps also 32–3.
[42] Erdmann (1936a) 491–512.

The diplomas produced by the royal chancery recorded grants of land or governmental rights by the king to a favoured subject or else confirmed the existing possessions and rights of an institution. Diplomas were intended by the chancery to be impressive demonstrations of the unique legitimating authority of the monarch. The text begins with a solemn invocation of the Holy Trinity; it often includes a lengthy arenga, a preamble which moralises on the theme of the ruler's rights or duties; it ends with an anathema against anyone violating its terms. The document is authenticated by the names of the chancellor and arch-chancellor and by the seal of the monarch. These imposing documents have been described as 'the written counterpart of the ruler's ceremonial appearances on the great church feasts or at assemblies'.[43] Medieval rulers used the diploma not only as an instrument for recording a grant of land or rights but also as a medium of royal propaganda, for which it was particularly suitable. For the recipient of a diploma customarily 'published' the contents of the document in a public reading, frequently during a church service and perhaps with a vernacular translation of the Latin text for the benefit of the illiterate laity. Diplomas constitute the single most important source for the study of eleventh-century royal government. They provide evidence of the distribution of royal patronage and (in the arenga) of royal political theory and propaganda.[44] The dating clauses which conclude diplomas furnish the most important raw material for reconstructing the royal itinerary. No less important is the clause of the diploma which names the 'interveners' (*intervenientes*): that is, the persons who intervened to persuade the emperor to grant the diploma. Diplomas were usually issued, not on the initiative of the monarch himself, but as the result of a petition from a subject. The petitioner usually enlisted the support of persons whom he believed to have influence at court, 'interveners' whose lobbying would improve his chances of success. The 'intervention clause' in a diploma, therefore, is useful evidence for identifying the politicians currently believed to be enjoying royal favour.[45]

A little fewer than five hundred authentic diplomas survive from the fifty-year reign of Henry IV. The figure for the reign of his father, Henry III, is twenty-two per annum and for his grandfather, Conrad II, nineteen per annum. There is a steady decline in the numbers of surviving diplomas in the successive decades of Henry IV's reign. In the period of the minority (October 1056 – March 1065) diplomas survive at the rate of seventeen per annum. For the first decade of Henry's personal rule (March 1065 – December 1075) the survival rate is just under thirteen per annum. During the decade ending

[43] Reuter (1991a) 212.   [44] Fichtenau (1977) 2:22, 29–30; Struve (1982) 217–22.
[45] Gawlik (1970a).

December 1085 the rate falls to just under ten per annum and in the decade ending December 1095, to seven per annum. For the final decade of the reign the rate is four per annum. Since in most cases a diploma was issued as a result of a petition from a subject, the demand for diplomas may give us a rough indication of public confidence in the effectiveness of royal government. If so, the declining numbers of diplomas throughout Henry IV's reign signify a continual erosion of respect for royal authority (echoing the disloyal tone of most of the narrative sources for the reign).

The statement of the chronicler Bruno of Merseburg that Henry 'wished there to be no lords in his kingdom' except himself, was inspired by the king's hostility towards Duke Rudolf of Swabia in 1076.[46] The king indeed deposed Rudolf from his duchy in 1077, together with his allies, Dukes Welf IV of Bavaria and Berthold of Carinthia, and the imperial kinsman, Margrave Ekbert II of Meissen. The king's deposition of Otto of Northeim (the hero of Bruno's chronicle) from the duchy of Bavaria in 1070 was represented by Bruno as Henry's first open act of tyranny,[47] the beginning of the campaign which would make him 'the sole lord over all men'. In fact, after deposing rebel princes the king usually conferred their offices on other secular princes whom he considered more loyal. The king simply had no alternative means of providing for the government of his kingdoms. The freedom of action of the king's opponents was similarly limited. In March 1077 a faction of secular princes held an assembly in Forchheim in which they declared Henry IV to be deposed. They then 'decided for the good of the commonwealth' to elect a new king, Rudolf of Swabia.[48] He was to be the first of four anti-kings supported by Henry's opponents, his successors being Herman of Salm and Henry's own sons, Conrad and Henry V. Evidently the princes could no more dispense with a king than the king could dispense with the princes.

It was not only the adherents but also the enemies of Henry IV who accepted the notion of the king as a divinely ordained ruler, necessary to the good order of Christian society. Pope Gregory VII wrote to Henry in December 1074 to remind him of the responsibilities of one 'whom God has placed at the summit of the world, through whose agency many can either stray from the right path or observe the Christian religion'.[49] Archbishop Werner of Magdeburg, a leader of the Saxon rebellion against Henry IV, exhorted the king to 'remember that he has the name and is the representative of the heavenly king'.[50] This image of the king as 'the representative of Christ' (*vicarius Christi*) was of central importance in Ottonian–Salian royal

---

[46] Bruno, *Saxonicum bellum* c. 60, p. 55.   [47] *Ibid.* c. 19, p. 25. See below p. 68.
[48] See below p. 168.   [49] Gregory VII, *Registrum* II.31, p. 165.
[50] Bruno, *Saxonicum bellum* c. 48, p. 47.

theology. The image is found in the oldest German liturgical text for the consecration of the king (the Mainz coronation *ordo* of *c.* 960): the king is 'believed to bear the name and to be the representative' of Jesus Christ.[51] The idea of the king as Christ's deputy on earth was central to the rituals of kingship, the ceremonial processions and 'crown-wearings' on the great feast-days of the Christian year, and central to the liturgical celebration of kingship, the *laudes regiae*, the triumphal hymns applauding the victory of Christ and the victories of the king. It is the central idea in the royalist polemics composed after the outbreak of Henry IV's conflict with the reform papacy. Henry was 'the vicar of the Creator', 'the image of God', 'king and emperor after God', appointed by God 'to rule the whole world'.[52] Henrician polemicists cited the favourite scriptural text of Ottonian–Salian royal theology, the warning of the apostle Paul to the Romans: 'He who resists the authorities, resists what God has ordained and those who resist will incur judgement. . . .[The ruler] is God's minister to execute His wrath on the evildoer' (Romans 13:2, 4). Through all the vicissitudes of his reign Henry IV was sustained by a belief in his divine ordination to the kingship. It was he 'whom, although unworthy, God ordained even from his childhood to be king and every day shows that He has ordained him'.[53]

It was on the basis of his authority as the divinely ordained 'representative of Christ' that the king claimed to manage the affairs of the imperial Church and especially to appoint archbishops, bishops and royal abbots. An imperial adherent explained in 1085 that, although according to canon law 'the power to order ecclesiastical affairs was never conceded to any layman', this prohibition did not extend to kings. For 'the king is rightly separated from the number of the laity, since as one anointed with the oil of consecration, he is known to be a sharer in the priestly ministry.'[54] Gregory VII, rejecting the idea of the king as 'a sharer in the priestly ministry', offered a different interpretation, albeit a positive one, of the king's relationship with the Church. 'You rightly hold the royal power,' he wrote to Henry in December 1074, 'if you incline your high authority to Christ, the king of kings, for the restoration and defence of his churches.'[55] The king's role in the Church was that of a servant, not of a ruler. What Christian society needed, Gregory concluded in 1081, was 'a suitable king for the honour of holy Church'. 'Unless he is obedient, humbly devoted and useful to holy Church, just as a Christian king ought to be . . ., then beyond a doubt holy Church will not only not countenance him but will

[51] Kost (1962) 43–54.
[52] Benzo of Alba, *Ad Heinricum* I.7, 9, 17, 23, v.5, vi.7, pp. 122, 130, 154, 164, 468, 574. See Robinson (1978) 70–5.   [53] Henry IV, *Letter* 17, p. 25.
[54] Wido of Osnabrück, *Liber de controversia* p. 467.
[55] Gregory VII, *Registrum* II.30, p. 164.

oppose him.'[56] Already in 1065, the year of Henry IV's coming of age, the great reformer Peter Damian, cardinal bishop of Ostia, had lectured the young king on his obligations towards the Roman church. His letter is remarkable for its exposition of the text Romans 13:4, which ignores the Ottonian–Salian pre-occupation with the subject's duty of obedience and emphasises instead the duties of the king himself. 'If you are God's minister, why do you not defend God's Church? . . . You are not an avenger in wrath to the evildoer while you do not arise against the defilers of the Church . . . A king must be revered while he obeys the Creator, but when a king opposes the divine commands he is rightly held in contempt by his subjects.' The obedience owed by subjects to the king was conditional on his correct performance of the duties of the kingship. 'Whosoever is shown to rule not in God's interest but in his own', who fails to 'stand in the Church's defence in the day of battle', does not deserve obedience.[57] Kingship, as the most exalted secular office, capable of affecting the salvation of many Christians, should be in the hands only of a suitably qualified candidate. Henry IV's determination to be the master, rather than the servant, of the imperial Church eventually persuaded Gregory VII that he was unfit to be king. For the last thirty years of his reign Henry was to be involved in conflict with the reform papacy and its allies, as he strove to defend the customary rights of the German monarch over the Church.

[56] *Ibid.*, IX.3, p. 575.   [57] Peter Damian, *Letter* 120: *Briefe* 3, 389, 391.

The young king, 1056–1075

1

The minority, 1056–1065

Henry IV was born on 11 November 1050, perhaps in Goslar, the favourite palace of his father, Emperor Henry III. 'In the autumn the empress bore a son, thanks be to God!' wrote the chronicler of Niederaltaich, his pious exclamation underlining the importance of this long-awaited birth of a male heir.[1] Anxiety about the succession to the throne is already apparent in a report from 1047. Archbishop Herman II of Cologne, the emperor's trusted adviser, celebrating mass on 8 September, perhaps in the emperor's presence, called on the faithful to 'pray that divine mercy may give the emperor a son so that the peace of the kingdom may continue'. The urgency of this need had recently been underlined by an attempt on the emperor's life.[2] Henry III's first wife, Gunhild (daughter of Cnut the Great, king of Denmark and England), had borne him one daughter, Beatrice. (Henry appointed her abbess of Quedlinburg and Gandersheim when she was eight years old.) His second wife, Agnes of Poitou bore three more daughters – Matilda (1045), Judith (1047) and Adelaide (1048) – before bearing a son after seven years of marriage. The child was at first given the name of his grandfather, the first Salian king and emperor, Conrad II. When he was baptised in Cologne by Archbishop Herman on Easter day (31 March) 1051, the name Conrad was replaced by Henry, the name of his father and great-grandfather.[3] Henry IV's mother, Agnes of Poitou, was a French princess of illustrious lineage, claiming descent from the Carolingians on both her father and mother's side. (Carolingian blood was evidently an important qualification for a Salian consort: Gisela, wife of Conrad II, was of Carolingian descent, as was Henry IV's first wife, Bertha of Turin.) Agnes's father was Duke William V 'the Great' of Aquitaine and count of Poitou, a prince as devout as his predecessor,

---

[1] *Annales Altahenses* 1050, p. 47. Cf. Herman of Reichenau, *Chronicon* 1050, p. 129. Date of birth: Lampert, *Annales* 1051 (*sic*), p. 63. See Steindorff (1881) 2:117–18; Meyer von Knonau (1890) 1:4–5; Black-Veldtrup (1995) 10, 76.

[2] *Brunwilarensis mon. fundatorum actus* c. 27, p. 138; Adam of Bremen, *Gesta* III.8, p. 149.

[3] The name Conrad was given to a second son (autumn 1052), who lived for only two-and-a-half years: Steindorff (1881) 2, 219; Black-Veldtrup (1995) 10, 79.

William III 'the Pious', the founder of the abbey of Cluny. Marriage with the Poitevin princess brought Henry III into close contact with this great centre of monastic reform, so that when the emperor sought a godfather for his infant son in 1051, he called on Abbot Hugh I of Cluny to 'receive from the holy font the boy in whom you have so much rejoiced and, as a spiritual father, sign him with the gift of your blessing'.[4] It was not for her Cluniac connections, however, that Henry had married Agnes but for her maternal kindred, the family of Count Otto-William of Burgundy. The marriage was intended to conciliate this dangerous family and strengthen the Salian hold on the Burgundian kingdom. (The security of Burgundy was also one of the considerations that would determine the emperor's choice of a bride for his son in 1055.)[5]

At the time of his son's birth Henry III was thirty-three years old, in the twelfth year of his reign as king of the Germans, his fourth as emperor and at the height of his power. The most formidable rebel in his empire, Godfrey 'the Bearded' of Verdun, the deposed duke of Upper Lotharingia, had been defeated. On the eastern frontier King Andreas of Hungary had recently promised to acknowledge the emperor as his feudal superior, while King Casimir of Poland and Duke Bretislav of Bohemia had appealed to the emperor to adjudicate their territorial conflict. The Italian kingdom had submitted peacefully to Henry's government. His first Italian expedition (1046–7) culminated in his intervention in Rome, which freed the papacy from the control of the Roman aristocracy and introduced a reforming regime into the Roman church. Henry III appointed a series of German popes, the third of whom, Leo IX, was his kinsman and gave the emperor invaluable moral and diplomatic support. It was at this propitious moment that Henry was able to ensure the Salian succession. On Christmas day 1050 in the palace of Pöhlde 'he caused the princes of the kingdom to take an oath promising to be faithful to his son Henry, who had not yet been baptised'. The baptism had been postponed to the following Easter, to enable the godfather, Hugh of Cluny, to be present. Henry III would not, however, delay the ceremony in which the princes swore an oath of fidelity to his heir, even though the child was not yet two months old.[6]

Henry evidently regarded the oath-taking of 25 December 1050 as insufficient to ensure his son's succession to the throne. The child's not being baptised may have been seen as a difficulty, while the fact that the ceremony

[4] Henry III, Letter: von Giesebrecht (1890) 720. See Lynch (1985) 800–26.
[5] The opposition of the family of Otto-William to German rule: Steindorff (1874) 1:154; Bulst-Thiele (1933) 1–11. Agnes's lineage: Kimpen (1955) 72.
[6] Lampert, *Annales* 1052 (*sic*), p. 63; Herman, *Chronicon* 1051, p. 129. See Gericke (1955) 735–7; Scheibelreiter (1973) 2–3.

took place in the Saxon palace of Pöhlde may have meant that only Saxon and Thuringian princes were present. The second stage in securing Henry IV's succession was an election in an assembly of princes in November 1053. The chronicle of Herman of Reichenau contains the only account of this event. 'Emperor Henry held a great assembly in Tribur and caused his son of the same name to be elected by all and caused them to promise subjection to him after [the emperor's] death, if he was a just ruler.' There is an obvious contrast between this election in Tribur and the oath-taking in Pöhlde in December 1050. On the former occasion the emperor simply designated his son as his successor: there is no sign of the princes' participation. (It was in this way that Henry III himself had been designated by his father in 1026, when he was nine years old.) In the election of 1053, however, according to Herman of Reichenau, the princes assumed an active role, making Henry IV's succession conditional on his future conduct. He must prove himself 'a just ruler', pre- sumably during his father's lifetime, in order to be accepted as king on the emperor's death. The implication of Herman's account is that in 1053 the princes elected Henry IV as co-ruler with his father, but did not commit themselves to his election as sole king on Henry III's death. Such a conditional election was unprecedented and some historians have therefore distrusted Herman's account, suggesting that, rather than reporting an actual condition imposed by the princes in Tribur, Herman was expressing his own reservations about the Salian regime, inspired by biblical ideas of righteous kingship.[7]

The context of the election of 1053 was one of deteriorating political con- ditions throughout the empire. The peace and prosperity of December 1050 had rapidly given way to military defeat and internal dissension. Henry III's ally, Pope Leo IX was defeated and captured by the papacy's formidable new neighbours, the Normans of southern Italy (18 June 1053), a defeat which threatened imperial prestige as well as the safety of the German papacy. More dangerous was the failure of the imperial campaigns of 1051 and 1052 to subject the kingdom of Hungary to German overlordship, which had serious reper- cussions on the emperor's relations with the duchy of Bavaria. During the second quarter of the eleventh century Bavaria had been the most loyal of the German duchies, but from 1052 it was the source of the fiercest resistance to Henry III. The emperor's main opponent was Duke Conrad of Bavaria, of the Lotharingian Ezzonid family. The account of the emperor's quarrel with Conrad of Bavaria in the chronicle of Niederaltaich traces its origins to a feud inside the duchy between Conrad and Bishop Gebhard of Regensburg. Gebhard, the emperor's uncle, used his considerable influence at the imperial

---

[7] Herman, *Chronicon* 1053, p. 133. See Mitteis (1944) 64; Gericke (1955) 737–41; Scheibelreiter (1973) 3; Haider (1968) 31–3; Reinhardt (1975) 251–2.

court to promote war with Hungary. Conrad, married to a sister of King Andreas I of Hungary, desired peace with his brother-in-law and neighbour. His duchy had suffered badly in the recent frontier skirmishes and was facing acute economic distress: the German famine of 1052–3 was particularly severe in Bavaria. The feud between Conrad and Gebhard was investigated in an assembly of princes in Merseburg (April 1053), which sentenced Conrad to be deposed from his duchy. The emperor conferred the duchy firstly on his elder son, Henry IV (25 December 1053) and soon afterwards (probably on the occasion of Henry's coronation) on the latter's two-year-old brother, Conrad. The sentence of deposition provoked Conrad into an alliance with Andreas of Hungary and open rebellion against the emperor.[8] The deposed duke was not alone in considering his sentence unjust. It is likely that Conrad's deposition revived the criticisms of Henry III's style of government that had been inspired in the early 1040s by his conduct in Lotharingia: that Henry paid too much attention to flattering advisers at court and did not seek the advice of the great men of the region 'to whom the people and the land are well known'.[9] Given this evidence of discontent among the nobility in 1053, the chronicler Herman's account of Henry IV's election in November 1053 must be taken seriously. The political tensions of the past year may have prompted the princes to the unprecedented step of imposing conditions when they elected Henry IV as co-ruler. The young king would not automatically succeed as sole ruler on his father's death but must submit to another election. His succession would depend on whether he had shown himself 'a just ruler' during his years as co-ruler with Henry III. In effect, the conditions imposed by the princes in the election of November 1053 were intended to compel the emperor to alter his style of government. If he did not change his ways, the princes would not accept Henry IV as his successor.

The third stage of the emperor's efforts to secure the throne for his son was the coronation by Archbishop Herman of Cologne in Aachen on 17 July 1054. This ceremony was an important event not only in the life of the Salian dynasty but also in the struggle of the metropolitan churches of the Rhineland for pre-eminence in the German Church. Since the early tenth century the archbishops of Mainz had claimed precedence in the Church and had usually played a leading role in the coronation of the Ottonian kings. After 1024, however, Mainz lost the right of crowning the king to the rival metropolitan see of Cologne. It was the powerful attraction of the Carolingian palace of Aachen

---

[8] Steindorff (1881) 2:181–2, 218–19, 228–31. The Ezzonids and their kinsmen, the Hezelids, owed their prominence to their wealth and kinship with the imperial family: Steinbach (1964) 848–66; Lewald (1979) 120–68.

[9] Herman, *Chronicon* 1053, p. 132. See Steindorff (1881) 2:222–4, 228–9; Störmer (1991) 532–3, 541–2. Earlier criticisms: *Gesta episcoporum Cameracensium* III.60, p. 488.

and the throne of Charlemagne in the second quarter of the eleventh century that boosted the fortunes of the archbishop of Cologne, in whose archdiocese Aachen lay. Archbishop Liutpold of Mainz may have claimed the right to crown Henry IV in 1054, the emperor overruling his claim in favour of Herman of Cologne.[10] Herman owed his eminence in the Church and the imperial counsels to the fact that he was an Ezzonid. Henry III secured the cooperation of this senior member of the powerful clan in perpetuating the Salian monarchy, while continuing to make war on Herman's nephew, Conrad of Bavaria.

An important record of the emperor's efforts to settle the succession is found in the diplomas which he issued between the birth of his son in November 1050 and his death in October 1056. The evidence is found in the clause of the imperial diploma which identifies the 'interveners' (*intervenientes*), the influential persons whose intervention had persuaded the emperor to confer the privilege on the petitioner. In the diplomas of the first two Salian emperors the interveners most frequently cited were members of the imperial family: in Conrad II's diplomas, his wife Gisela and his son Henry; in Henry III's diplomas, his mother and his second wife, Agnes. The 'intervention clauses' in these diplomas illustrate the importance of the dynastic principle, the concentration of political influence in the imperial family, in early Salian government.[11] Characteristic of this dynastic theme in Henry III's diplomas is the appearance of his son as intervener: at first described as 'child' or 'boy'; then after the coronation of July 1054 as 'our most beloved son, King Henry IV'. Of the diplomas of the last six years of Henry III's reign, nearly two-thirds identify Henry IV, always accompanied by Empress Agnes, as intervener, mediating with the emperor on behalf of the petitioner.[12] Given the propagandist motive that was always present in imperial diplomas, it is likely that the inclusion of Henry IV as intervener was not a mere conventional formula but a means of publicising the child's claim to the throne.[13]

Half the diplomas of Henry III recording the intervention of his son were issued in the final year of the emperor's reign. It is tempting to see in these diplomas of 1055–6 an intensification of imperial propaganda in response to the crisis which had overtaken the regime: a wave of rebellions affecting almost every region of the empire. Firstly, the rebellion of the deposed Conrad of Bavaria increasingly attracted support from the south German princes. The south German rebels planned to assassinate the emperor and elect Conrad of

[10] Lampert, *Annales* 1054, p. 66; cf. 1073, p. 168. See Reinhardt (1975) 235–8; Boshof (1978) 36–43.   [11] Schetter (1935) 19–26, 126–7; Gawlik (1970a).

[12] *D H III* 283, 322–3, 328, 331, 335, 337, 340, 344, 346–7, 351–7, 359, 361, 363, 365–81. See Schetter (1935) 19; Gawlik (1970a) 63, 90, 129, 166; Struve (1982) 190–222.

[13] Similarly Henry IV's son Conrad began to appear as intervener in 1079, when he was five; his son Henry V in 1098 when he was twelve. See below pp. 263, 287, 301.

Bavaria to the kingship. Their plot was foiled by the sudden deaths from fever of the two chief conspirators, Conrad and Welf III, duke of Carinthia and margrave of Verona, who on his deathbed sought the emperor's pardon and disclosed the plans of his accomplices.[14] Meanwhile in Lotharingia the regime faced problems which were the result of its own recent success. Henry III's conflict with Godfrey 'the Bearded' of Verdun had damaged ducal authority in Lotharingia without providing an adequate replacement, so endangering the security of the kingdom's western frontier. The principal beneficiary of this development was the count of Flanders. The eleventh-century counts of Flanders were well placed to exploit the difficulties of the German king because of their status as dual vassals: part of their territory ('imperial Flanders') was held from the German king, the rest ('royal Flanders') was a fief held from the French king. During the early 1050s Count Baldwin V's territorial ambitions involved attacks on the possessions of the bishop of Liège in Lower Lotharingia and the annexation of the county of Hainault. The possession of Hainault would allow the counts of Flanders to encroach on the property of imperial bishopric of Cambrai, a vulnerable German outpost. Henry III sought to contain this threat with an expedition against Baldwin V in July 1054, but without success.[15] No less vulnerable was the eastern frontier of the kingdom. In the permanent frontier war against the pagan Slav confederation of the Liutizi, the Saxon nobility suffered their most serious defeat in September 1056, when the emperor's most able commander, Margrave William of the Saxon Nordmark, was killed.[16]

The threat to his authority that provoked the emperor to take the strongest counter-measures was that in the kingdom of Italy. In 1054 Godfrey 'the Bearded' secretly married his kinswoman, Beatrice, widow of Boniface of Canossa, margrave of Tuscany, and assumed the office of margrave. (Beatrice was a descendant of the German king Henry I and Godfrey was descended from a collateral branch of the Ottonian dynasty, so that both were related to the imperial dynasty.) The creation of this powerful new dynasty of Canossa–Lotharingia, together with reports from Italy that Godfrey 'was about to seize the kingdom from him', prompted the emperor's second Italian expedition (March–November 1055). Godfrey was forced to flee, while the emperor took prisoner Beatrice and the children of her first marriage and brought them back to Germany. (Beatrice was guilty of the offence of marrying without the emperor's permission.) To strengthen imperial control over the Italian kingdom, Henry enlisted the help of the new German pope, Victor II, his former adviser, Bishop Gebhard of Eichstätt. The emperor conferred

[14] Steindorff (1881) 2:317–21; Boshof (1979) 281–3.

[15] Mohr (1976) 2:22, 26–7, 31; Boshof (1979) 271–2.   [16] See below p. 63.

on Victor the duchy of Spoleto and the march of Fermo, which were intended to protect papal and imperial interests against the ambitions of both the pretender to the march of Tuscany and the Norman princes who had defeated Victor's predecessor, Leo IX.[17] Among the emperor's measures of 1055 in the Italian kingdom was the marriage which he arranged for his son. During the Christmas celebrations of 1055 in Zürich the five-year-old Henry IV was betrothed to Bertha, daughter of Adelaide, margravine of Turin and her third husband, Count Otto of Savoy. The infant Bertha of Turin seems to have come from Italy in the emperor's entourage to be brought up by Empress Agnes with her own daughters. Both the princess's parents were of Carolingian descent, and her kinsmen were of the first importance in the kingdoms of Italy and Burgundy. The marriage alliance with the dynasty of Savoy–Turin was intended to guarantee their loyalty and that of their kindred in the two kingdoms and above all to provide a counterweight in north-western Italy to the house of Canossa–Lotharingia.[18]

The emperor's last illness in the autumn of 1056 was sudden and his death unexpected. There is no obvious sign of a slowing-down in the royal itinerary in the months following Henry III's return from Italy. At the beginning of September Henry received Pope Victor II in his palace of Goslar, before setting out for the palace of Bodfeld, to spend the autumn hunting in the Harz region. It was in Bodfeld that he became sick and, after a week confined to his bed, he died on 5 October. Not long before his death the emperor had been reconciled with his opponents of the previous year. In an assembly of princes in Worms in July 1056 the emperor pardoned the surviving leaders of the Bavarian rebellion. Godfrey 'the Bearded' and his wife, Beatrice of Tuscany, were also pardoned either in the summer or the early autumn. There is no suggestion in the sources that these reconciliations were inspired by the emperor's failing health and foreboding of premature death. (Henry was indeed only thirty-nine years old at this time.) After the death of Conrad of Bavaria and the betrayal of his plans, his accomplices had lost the will to continue the struggle and after the capture of Beatrice, Godfrey 'the Bearded' realised that he had been outmanoeuvred. They had no alternative, therefore, but to submit to Henry III.[19] The emperor received them back into his favour, his

---

[17] Glaesener (1947) 379–416; E. Goez (1995) 22–5. Beatrice's ancestry: Twellenkamp (1991) 502; E. Goez (1995) 12, 22 n. 110.

[18] Berthold of Reichenau, *Annales* 1056 (first version) p. 731; (second version) p. 269. Cf. Bonizo of Sutri, *Ad amicum* v, p. 590. See Steindorff (1881) 2:324; Meyer von Knonau (1890) 1:9–10; Previté-Orton (1912) 32–7, 66, 207, 231; Kimpen (1955) 72–4.

[19] *Annales Altahenses* 1056, pp. 52–3; *Chronicon Wirziburgense* c. 17, p. 31; Bonizo, *Ad amicum* v, p. 590. See Steindorff (1881) 2:331–3, 341–6, 350, 353–6; Müller (1901) 113–18; Gericke (1955) 744–6.

usual practice with defeated and penitent princes. It made more sense to rehabilitate a defeated rebel and make use of his services than to keep him in a permanent state of disgrace, so alienating his family and allies and risking a damaging feud. When Henry III succumbed to his final illness, therefore, the government had already resolved the conflicts of 1055. The emperor had created a suitable political climate for his final effort, made on his deathbed, to ensure the succession of his son. This may have taken the form of a further election in the emperor's presence in Bodfeld at the beginning of October. The electors were Pope Victor II, Patriarch Gotebald of Aquileia, Bishop Gebhard of Regensburg and numerous other secular and ecclesiastical dignitaries present at the emperor's deathbed. 'Emperor Henry . . . established his son Henry as king by means of the election of the Roman pontiff and the other bishops and princes.'[20] The form of words used by the Würzburg chronicler suggests a repetition of the election which had already taken place in Tribur in 1053.

The unopposed accession of Henry IV to the German throne was perhaps Henry III's most substantial political achievement. The measures which he had taken in 1050–6 had established his son's status as the legitimate successor: not only his heir but also 'the heir to the kingdom', succeeding 'by hereditary right'.[21] When the princes elected Henry IV as co-ruler with his father in November 1053, they seem to have asserted their right to reconsider his election after his father's death. There is no evidence, however, of a new election after the death of Henry III. The transfer of authority in October 1056 was managed efficiently by Pope Victor II, into whose care the dying emperor had committed his son. Immediately after the emperor's death Victor caused 'the magnates of the whole kingdom to swear an oath to [the emperor's] little son . . . confirming him in the kingship'.[22] On an unknown date between 28 October (Henry III's funeral in Speyer) and the beginning of December the pope performed the inaugural ceremony of the reign of Henry IV. 'King Henry was brought by the lord pope to Aachen and placed on the royal throne.'[23] It is likely that the ceremonies of unction and coronation, already performed in July 1054 in Aachen, were repeated on this occasion. The central

---

[20] *Chronicon Wirziburgense* c. 17, p. 31. Cf. Lampert, *Annales* 1056, p. 69. See Berges (1947) 190–3; Gericke (1955) 745.

[21] *Annales Altahenses* 1056, p. 53; Paul of Bernried, *Vita Gregorii VII* c. 60, p. 506. See Jenal (1974) 155–6. Gericke (1955) 746–7 claimed that the purpose of the assemblies in Cologne and Regensburg (December 1056) was to elect the king; but there is no hint in the sources: see Meyer von Knonau (1890) 1:17–20. According to *Annales Altahenses* 1056, p. 53, these assemblies took place after the enthronement in Aachen.

[22] *Chronica monasterii Casinensis* II.91, p. 345.

[23] *Annales Altahenses* 1056, p. 53. See Scheibelreiter (1973) 3–5.

role of Victor II in the opening days of the reign was interpreted by adherents of the reform papacy as an important enhancement of papal authority. Peter Damian, soon to become cardinal bishop of Ostia, wrote to Victor that Christ had 'added monarchies' to the pope's other powers and 'allowed [him] jurisdiction over the whole of the vacant Roman empire'. Victor II's role in 1056 would later attract the attention of Pope Gregory VII and Gregorian historians of the later eleventh century, who claimed that Henry became king 'by the permission of the Roman pontiff Victor'.[24] But Victor II was also Bishop Gebhard of Eichstätt: like his predecessors of Henry III's 'German papacy', he had retained his German bishopric after becoming pope. It was probably as imperial bishop, German prince and former imperial adviser that Victor supervised the succession to the throne. In 1053, when Henry IV had briefly held the office of duke of Bavaria, the emperor had appointed Gebhard of Eichstätt as regent in the duchy. In October 1056 he was again entrusted with the guardianship of the child-king. Early in 1057 he returned to Italy, presumably considering his pupil safely installed. His departure, soon followed by his death (28 July 1057), deprived the new regime of its most reliable supporter.

'The supreme administration of all affairs remained with the empress, who protected the interests of the endangered realm with such skill that, despite the extreme novelty of this situation, there was no rebellion or unrest.'[25] During the first five-and-a-half years of the reign Empress Agnes bore the responsibility for governing the kingdom on her son's behalf. The most important evidence of her role in government is that of the royal diplomas. Every important privilege of the period from December 1056 to March 1062 was issued 'through the intervention of our most beloved mother'.[26] During these years the king's role in the issuing of diplomas must have been a purely formal one, the initiative being taken by the regent, to whom belonged the disposal of royal patronage. There is no direct evidence that the dying Henry III nominated his widow as regent. Shortly before his death, however, he made the empress responsible for the restoration to the original owners of property 'which he had acquired by evil means', which may suggest that he envisaged Agnes administering the affairs of the monarchy in the immediate future.[27] The recent history of the Ottonian empire offered a clear precedent of an

[24] Peter Damian, *Letter* 46: *Briefe* 2, 21. Cf. *Annales Romani* [1056], p. 470; Paul of Bernried, *Vita Gregorii VII* c. 60, p. 506. See Berges (1947) 190–202; Jenal (1974) 158–9; Beumann (1977) 35–6; W. Goez (1980) 11–21. See also below p. 112.

[25] Lampert, *Annales* 1056, p. 69; but see Adam, *Gesta* III.34, p. 176. See Meyer von Knonau (1890) 1:13–15; Bulst-Thiele (1933) 33–4.

[26] Of eighty-five diplomas she appeared in seventy-two (as sole intervener in fifty-eight). See Bulst-Thiele (1933) 34–5; Gawlik (1970a) 125–7; Black-Veldtrup (1995) 22–8, 85–91.

[27] Berthold, *Annales* 1056, p. 270; *Liber concambiorum mon. Eberspergensis* c. 10, p. 45.

empress-widow acting as regent, in the person of Theophanu, mother of Otto III. Whether Agnes received an oath of fidelity from the princes at the beginning of the reign is not apparent from the narrative sources. An oath of a different character is, however, recorded in an unexpected quarter: a letter of Pope Gregory VII of 3 September 1076. The pope reminded the German princes of 'the oath which was sworn to our most beloved daughter, the august empress Agnes, in case her son departed this life before her'. According to this oath, the princes must seek the empress's 'advice . . . concerning the person found to govern the kingdom'. The oath probably belonged to the period immediately following the death of Henry III, when the recent death of the empress's second son, Conrad, before his third birthday, suggested the possibility that the six-year-old Henry IV might also die young. In that case the empress was to play a major role in the election of his successor. The fact that the electors were bound by their oath to seek the empress's 'advice' might mean that Agnes was accorded the right of designating the heir to the throne usually exercised by the reigning monarch. Alternatively the oath may have enabled the empress to approve or confirm the candidate elected by the princes.[28]

It is uncertain whether Agnes had any independent experience of government before she became regent. She is scarcely visible in the sources for Henry III's reign except when at the side of her husband. The evidence of the diplomas suggests that, except during her five confinements and during her husband's military campaigns, Agnes was the emperor's constant companion and an influential adviser.[29] The case of the duchy of Bavaria seems to offer evidence of an independent role in government. In 1052 the emperor placed the duchy nominally in the hands of his elder son, and then two years later in the hands of his second son. Finally in 1055, he gave the duchy to Agnes. It is likely, however, that the empress's tenure of the ducal office was no less nominal than that of her sons. There is no record of her playing an active role in the duchy or visiting Bavaria except in the company of the emperor. The chronicler Lampert of Hersfeld reported that 'the emperor gave the duchy [of Bavaria] to the empress as a private possession'. In Lampert's opinion Agnes held the duchy not as a benefice of the empire but as a source of income: the imperial grant permitted her, like her sons before her, to enjoy the ducal revenues of Bavaria.[30] Much of the empress's conduct as regent seems to confirm the impression of a ruler who did not trust her own administrative and political skills. She tried to follow the policies of her husband and chose as her advisers men of whom he had approved. This continuity was particularly

[28] Gregory VII, *Registrum* IV.3, p. 299. See Berges (1947) 189–96. Cf. the role of Empress Cunigunde in 1024: Wipo, *Gesta Chuonradi* c. 2, p. 19.

[29] Schetter (1935) 20–2; Bulst-Thiele (1933) 19–20; Black-Veldtrup (1995) 12–21, 63–84.

[30] Lampert, *Annales* 1056, p. 70. See Bulst-Thiele (1933) 27–8.

apparent in her dealings with the imperial Church. Like her husband, the empress maintained a firm control over episcopal elections. The new bishops of 1056–62 were all her appointees and all were invested with the symbols of their office, the ring and staff, by the young king, according to the custom of the previous reign. Almost all were closely associated with the late emperor and his court: first Gunther of Bamberg (Henry III's chancellor for the Italian kingdom), Gundechar of Eichstätt (the empress's chaplain), Winither of Merseburg (Henry III's chancellor for the German kingdom) and Gebhard of Salzburg (the emperor's principal chaplain and Henry IV's chancellor for Germany). Three of her appointees were members of her husband's foundation of SS. Simon and Jude in Goslar: Gunther of Bamberg, Werner of Merseburg and Burchard II of Halberstadt. In the case of the metropolitan church of Mainz the regent followed the late Ottonian and early Salian practice of appointing the abbot of St Boniface's foundation of Fulda to the saint's archbishopric of Mainz: her appointee was Siegfried I.[31] The regent's attitude towards the monasteries was as conservative as her episcopal appointments. Later in her life Agnes was to be closely associated with the reforming monasteries of Fruttuaria, St Blasien and St Nikolaus in Passau and with reformers like Peter Damian and John of Fécamp. During her regency, however, her principal concern was the protection of the traditional 'imperial monasticism' of the Ottonian and early Salian period. Unlike earlier empresses and unlike the members of her own illustrious family, Agnes did not found a monastery. Her donations and privileges were in most cases made to religious houses that had also benefited from the generosity of Henry III. There was nothing in the regent's conduct to suggest that her last years would be devoted to monastic reform and to the papal reform movement of Gregory VII.[32]

Agnes's advisers in the years 1056–62 were men whom the late emperor had promoted or who were recommended by the emperor's confidants. This was the case, firstly, among the permanent officials of the chancery. The work of the German chancery continued to be directed by Henry III's long-serving chancellor, Winither, until in 1058 he was succeeded by Gebhard, head of the late emperor's chapel. Gebhard's successor in 1060 was Frederick, provost of Magdeburg, of the house of Wettin, a family entrusted by Henry III with the defence of eastern Saxony.[33] The Italian chancery remained in the hands of the late emperor's chancellor, Gunther, until his promotion to the see of Bamberg

---

[31] Exceptions to this pattern: Otto of Regensburg, Einhard of Speyer and Waltolf of Padua. See Meyer von Knonau (1890) 1:22, 44, 94, 154–5, 165–6, 173, 182–4; Bulst-Thiele (1933) 37–8, 45–8; Zielinski (1984) 126–7, 140–1. Goslar and the episcopate: see below pp. 79, 117.

[32] Bulst-Thiele (1933) 49–51, 87–8, 92, 94–5. But see Struve (1984) 411–24: Agnes's letter to Abbot Hugh, requesting the prayers of Cluny.

[33] Bulst-Thiele (1933) 43–4; Gawlik (1978) xxiv–xxix.

(1057). His successor was probably recommended to the empress either by Gunther himself or by an earlier Italian chancellor, Bishop Henry of Augsburg. This newcomer was Wibert of Parma, of a noble Italian family related to the house of Canossa.[34] Agnes's principal advisers were bishops. Archbishop Liutpold of Mainz, a generally respected figure, was regularly in attendance at court in 1057 and early 1058.[35] During the opening months of the reign the empress also sought the advice of Archbishop Anno of Cologne. In marked contrast to his predecessor, the Ezzonid Herman, Anno was of the minor Swabian family of Steusslingen, a 'new man', the first of his family to hold high office and exercise political influence. Henry III had appointed him first to the provostship of SS. Simon and Jude in Goslar and, in the last year of the reign, to the archsee of Cologne. The promotion of Anno's nephew, Burchard, to the see of Halberstadt (1059) has been seen as evidence of the archbishop's influence on the regent; but Burchard's undoubted abilities and especially the fact that, like his uncle before him, he was provost of SS. Simon and Jude in Goslar are perhaps enough to account for his promotion.[36] A churchman apparently high in favour in the early years of the regency was the new bishop of Bamberg, the cultivated and noble Gunther.[37] In the winter of 1060–1, however, Gunther became involved in a bitter dispute with Agnes. The regent's failure to support his claim to the monastery of Bergen against Bishop Gundechar of Eichstätt provoked Gunther to withdraw in anger from the court. Rumour at court accused him of plotting rebellion against the regent, while his neighbours seized the opportunity of his disgrace to plunder his bishopric. A truce was patched up between Gunther and the empress at the end of 1061, but he was not fully reconciled to the court until the regent's withdrawal from active politics.[38]

The adviser to whom the narrative sources attribute the greatest influence over the empress was Bishop Henry of Augsburg. He had served the late emperor as his Italian chancellor in 1046–7 and probably before that as his chaplain. He was at court in February 1058 and the following Whitsun (7 June) the king and his mother were his guests in Augsburg, where the regent held an assembly 'of the princes of the whole kingdom'. The following year the empress intervened to settle a feud between the bishop and his neighbour, Count Diepold. She was presumably exercising her ducal authority in Bavaria to preserve peace in the

---

[34] Bonizo, *Ad amicum* v, p. 593. See Bulst-Thiele (1933) 44; Gawlik (1978) LXXII; Ziese (1982) 4–19.   [35] *DD H IV* 7, 32. See Bulst-Thiele (1933) 36.

[36] Lück (1970a) 24–59, 83–102; Jenal (1974) 169–74.

[37] *DD H IV* 25–6, 39, 62, 67. The promotion of Otto, canon of Bamberg, to Regensburg also testifies to his influence. See Zielinski (1984) 39.

[38] *Briefsammlungen* pp. 115–16, 117–19: see Erdmann (1938) 25–32. See also Meyer von Knonau (1890) 1:270–4; Bulst-Thiele (1933) 40–3; Black-Veldtrup (1995) 28–33.

duchy.[39] The chronicler Berthold of Reichenau reported in 1058 that 'at this time Bishop Henry of Augsburg had the role of the empress's foremost counsellor, which greatly displeased some of the magnates of the kingdom, who found his insolence unbearable'.[40] He retained this ascendancy at court for the remaining years of the regency, but his influence ceased the moment that Agnes herself lost power in the spring of 1062. The chronicle of Lampert of Hersfeld contains a particularly hostile account of Bishop Henry's career, concluding that he died 'hated by the king, hated by all the bishops, because of the arrogance which he showed in governing the kingdom in the time of the empress'. With his characteristic misogyny, Lampert recorded the suspicion that Bishop Henry's power was based on a sexual relationship with the empress. 'This matter gravely offended the princes, who saw that their authority, which ought to be supreme in the realm, had almost been destroyed because of the private affections of a single person.' It was the hated ascendancy of Henry of Augsburg, according to Lampert, which prompted the conspiracy against the regent in 1062.[41]

Throughout her regency Agnes, warned by her husband's experience in 1055, had been well aware of the danger of a princely conspiracy. She had tried to guard against it by means of alliances with powerful, ambitious and potentially dangerous secular princes. At the beginning of her regency she had continued her husband's policy of seeking reconciliation with the surviving rebels of his reign. At an assembly of princes in Cologne on 5–6 December 1056 Godfrey 'the Bearded' of Verdun and his former allies, Count Baldwin V of Flanders and his son, Baldwin VI, 'were restored to the king's grace and to peace and all the turmoils of war were calmed'.[42] Three weeks later, on Christmas day, at a further assembly in Regensburg the king conferred the duchy of Carinthia on Conrad, a member of the Hezelid family involved in the rebellion of his kinsman, Conrad of Bavaria.[43] The pacification of Lotharingia resulting from the reconciliation of Baldwin V and Godfrey 'the Bearded' proved to be the most enduring political achievement of the regency. In the interests of peace the empress was obliged in December 1056 to recognise Baldwin VI's acquisition of the county of Hainault, so rendering likely the union of Hainault and Flanders.[44] Meanwhile Godfrey 'the Bearded', the

---

[39] *DD H IV* 32, 47; *Annales Augustani* 1058, 1059, p. 127. See Black-Veldtrup (1995) 23–4, 88.

[40] Berthold, *Annales* 1058 (first version) p. 731. His influence was demonstrated by the promotion of two Augsburg canons to bishoprics (1060): Einhard to Speyer and Waltolf to Padua. See Meyer von Knonau (1890) 1:85, 168–9, 270–1, 354–5; Bulst-Thiele (1933) 36–7, 46, 48; Black-Veldtrup (1995) 356–60.   [41] Lampert, *Annales* 1062, 1064, pp. 79, 92.

[42] Sigebert, *Chronica* 1057, p. 360. See Meyer von Knonau (1890) 1:17–19; Jenal (1974) 162–5.

[43] *Annales Altahenses* 1057, p. 53. See Meyer von Knonau (1890) 1:19.

[44] That union was ended by the power struggle in the comital family on Baldwin's death (1070): Mohr (1976) 2:30–1, 41.

foremost rebel of the reign of Henry III, transformed himself into a stalwart, although self-interested, supporter of the young king. After his death (1069) his son, Godfrey III ('the Hunchback') of Lower Lotharingia was to prove Henry IV's most loyal ally among the German princes. What may have been conceded to Godfrey 'the Bearded' in December 1056 is not recorded. If a promise was made about the restoration of Godfrey's ducal office in Lotharingia, it can only have been an indefinite promise, since both the Lotharingian duchies were currently held by princes from powerful native clans: Upper Lotharingia (Godfrey's former duchy) by Gerard of the Châtenois family and Lower Lotharingia (formerly the duchy of Godfrey's father and brother) by Frederick of the Luxemburg family. Only on Frederick's death without a male heir in 1065 did a Lotharingian duchy fall vacant: Henry IV immediately conferred Lower Lotharingia on Godfrey. The assembly of Cologne in December 1056 can be assumed to have recognised Godfrey's recently acquired title of margrave of Tuscany. At the beginning of 1057 Godfrey returned to Tuscany with his wife, Beatrice, and her only surviving child, Matilda, perhaps in the company of Pope Victor II, who had assisted in reconciling Godfrey with the royal government.

Godfrey's restoration to royal favour coincided with the sudden rise to prominence of his brother, Frederick. Formerly archdeacon of Liège, Frederick was one of the Lotharingian churchmen brought to Rome by Pope Leo IX in 1049 to act as his advisers. The emperor's hostility towards the house of Verdun in 1055 had caused Frederick to take refuge in the abbey of Monte Cassino. The year 1057, however, saw a change in his fortunes: in May he was elected abbot of Monte Cassino and in June he was raised by Victor II to the dignity of cardinal priest of S. Grisogono. Finally, five days after Victor's death, Frederick was elected to succeed him as Pope Stephen IX (2 August). No doubt the electors were influenced in their choice by the consideration that the new pope's brother, the most powerful prince in the Italian kingdom, would be able to defend the reform papacy from the hostile Roman aristocracy. Godfrey 'the Bearded' would now afford the protection which in the years 1046–56 had been given by the emperor. On the death of Victor II, Godfrey acquired the duchy of Spoleto and the march of Fermo, the imperial offices which Henry had granted the pope in 1055 to enable him to watch over imperial interests in Italy. It is not clear how Godfrey acquired Spoleto and Fermo, but, given the reconciliation of December 1056 and the importance of Godfrey's support for Agnes's vulnerable regime, it is likely that the margrave obtained Spoleto and Fermo by royal grant.[45] The reconciliation of December

[45] *Annales Altahenses* 1067, p. 72; cf. 1062, pp. 60–1; but see Benzo of Alba, *Ad Heinricum* II.15, p. 238. See Meyer von Knonau (1890) 1:26–33; Mohr (1976) 2:31–2.

1056 and the papal election of 2 August 1057 had placed the government of the Italian kingdom firmly in the hands of the house of Verdun. The possibility that this ascendancy might undermine royal authority in the peninsula evidently occurred to some Italian observers. The chronicler of Monte Cassino claimed that Stephen IX 'planned to join his brother Duke Godfrey in Tuscany for a conference and, so it was said, to confer on him the imperial crown'. The pope's plan was forestalled by his sudden death (in his brother's residence in Florence) on 29 March 1058.[46] If this rumour reached the German court, there is no sign of its causing a rift between the regent and the margrave of Tuscany. Godfrey's intimate relationship with the reform papacy did not end with his brother's death. Stephen IX was succeeded in turn by two Tuscan bishops, Gerard of Florence (Nicholas II) and Anselm I of Lucca (Alexander II), who, since they retained their bishoprics during their pontificates, necessarily maintained close relations with the margrave of Tuscany. During the so-called 'Lotharingian–Burgundian papacy' of 1057–73 Godfrey 'the Bearded' and his wife, Beatrice, were the most important secular allies of the reform papacy.

In the German kingdom Agnes strengthened her regime by an alliance with a powerful south German prince, Rudolf of Rheinfelden, on whom in 1057 she conferred the duchy of Swabia. A number of later but reliable sources call Rudolf 'duke of the Swabians and the Burgundians', indicating that he was also entrusted with the government of the kingdom of Burgundy.[47] Simultaneously the empress permitted the betrothal of the new duke to her eldest daughter, the twelve-year-old Matilda. The wedding took place at Christmastide 1059, when the bride had only just reached marriageable age. According to Lampert of Hersfeld, the regent arranged the betrothal of 1057 'so that through family relationship (*affinitas*) [Rudolf] might be the more completely won over and be all the more faithful to the realm in those dangerous times'.[48] Historians have differed widely in their theories of Rudolf's origins, seeing him variously as a 'new man' of obscure origin, as a kinsman of Empress Agnes, as of royal descent. A recent investigation supports the view

[46] *Chronica monasterii Casinensis* ii.97, p. 355. See Meyer von Knonau (1890) 1:80–3; Mohr (1976) 2:32, 179 n. 228; E. Goez (1995) 153.

[47] *Liber de unitate ecclesiae* ii.16, p. 232; Sigebert of Gembloux, *Chronica* 1077, p. 364; Frutolf of Michelsberg, *Chronica* 1075, p. 84; *Annales Leodienses, Continuatio* 1077, p. 29.

[48] Lampert, *Annales* 1058, p. 73. Frutolf, *Chronica* 1057, p. 74 claimed that the regent was outwitted by the audacity of Rudolf, who abducted and married her daughter: 'for her daughter's sake' Agnes was obliged to confer Swabia on her son-in-law. This anecdote has been dismissed by scholars, except Klewitz (1971) 258–60 and W. Goez (1962) 76–7, who saw it as a plausible account of the Swabian succession problem. Frutolf's uncorroborated story (written 1098/9) was probably Henrician propaganda against Rudolf: Maurer (1978) 21–2; Schmid (1988) 190; Black-Veldtrup (1995) 78, 108–9.

that Rudolf was descended from the Burgundian royal house (the main line of which became extinct in 1032, on the death of Rudolf III, when the kingdom became part of the Salian empire). Rudolf was the great-great-grandson of Rudolf II of Burgundy (912–37) and consequently a kinsman of Emperor Henry III, whose mother, Gisela, was the great-granddaughter of Rudolf II.[49] The new duke of Swabia belonged to the foremost circles of the imperial aristocracy and was eminently qualified for the honour which the empress conferred on him. There were clear Ottonian precedents for such a marriage alliance. (Henry IV was to form a similar alliance with the duke whom he appointed as Rudolf's successor in 1079.) In the event Rudolf's marriage lasted less than a year: Matilda died on 12 May 1060. He soon regained the status of royal brother-in-law, however, by marrying Adelaide of Susa, sister of Henry IV's betrothed, Bertha.[50] Rudolf's principal duty during Henry's minority seems to have been the pacification of the kingdom of Burgundy: not only his Burgundian royal descent but also his possession of extensive allodial lands in the kingdom qualified him for this role. A rare glimpse of Rudolf during the minority shows him in 1063 attacking Burgundian rebels 'with a great force of knights' from Swabia.[51] Rudolf was given a free hand in Burgundy. During Agnes's regency the court visited the kingdom only once, proceeding no further than Basel, on the frontier, in October 1061.

Towards the end of her regency the empress conferred the duchy of Bavaria on the Saxon prince who in the early 1070s became Rudolf of Swabia's principal rival, Count Otto of Northeim. From October 1056 to January 1061 Agnes retained the duchy in her own hands, regularly visiting Bavaria in the company of her son.[52] Her decision to appoint a new duke of Bavaria was evidently provoked by problems with the south-eastern neighbour, the Hungarian kingdom. The damage inflicted on Bavaria and Carinthia in the fierce border wars with Hungary in the 1050s inclined the empress to negotiate a permanent peace and the political problems of King Andreas I of Hungary offered an ideal opportunity. Andreas wished to secure the succession of his young son, Salomon, whom he raised to the kingship in 1057, but his plans were threatened by the ambition of his brother, Duke Bela. Andreas saw in a German alliance the means to thwart Bela's attempts to gain the

---

[49] Meyer von Knonau (1890) 1:652–5; Kimpen (1955) 90–6; Jakobs (1968) 157–235; Hlawitschka (1991) 175–220. Wolf (1991) 104–6 claimed Rudolf as a descendant of Henry I of Germany. Rudolf was related to the Brunones and Udo II of Stade.

[50] Meyer von Knonau (1890) 1:526 n. 61; Jakobs (1968) 159–60, 264.

[51] *Briefsammlungen* p. 212. See Maurer (1978) 151. The disorders in Burgundy are known only from Agnes's letter to Hugh of Cluny: Struve (1984) 423.

[52] *DD H IV* 3, 43, 69, 70; 6, 60. See Black-Veldtrup (1995) 85, 87, 88, 90.

throne. In September 1058 Andreas and Agnes, with the approval of the German princes, negotiated the betrothal of the boy king Salomon and Agnes's second daughter, Judith (known in Hungary as Sophia). Bela's determination to end this alliance provoked the outbreak of civil war in Hungary in 1060, in which the duke was assisted by his nephew, Duke Boleslav II of Poland. The regent sent to Andreas's aid a Bavarian army, together with Saxon contingents and the forces of her ally, Duke Spitignev II of Bohemia, but the Germans failed to combine with their Bohemian allies and were overwhelmed by Bela's superior forces. Andreas died in battle; his queen with the young Salomon and his betrothed fled to the German court.[53] The creation of the new Hungarian regime of King Bela I forced the regent to take urgent measures for the security of south-eastern Germany and it was in this context that she conferred her duchy of Bavaria on Otto of Northeim early in 1061. The disastrous Hungarian campaign of 1060 also underlined the need for a duke capable of commanding the Bavarian army and Otto had already established his military reputation. He was 'a man of the most exalted nobility, whose prudence in military matters very few could equal and who was held in the highest regard by all the princes'.[54] He belonged to a Saxon family which had come to prominence at the beginning of Henry II's reign. The already extensive family lands of the counts of Northeim in eastern Saxony were augmented by Otto's marriage to Richenza, widow of Count Herman of Werl (*c.* 1050), who brought her second husband great estates in Westphalia and northern Saxony. Perhaps it was this marriage which made Otto eligible for promotion to ducal office; for Richenza was an Ezzonid princess, the great-granddaughter of Emperor Otto II. The early Salians and their Ottonian predecessors had regularly conferred the duchy of Bavaria on a kinsman of the imperial family. Since Richenza was the cousin of Duke Conrad of Bavaria, whom Henry III had deposed in 1053, it is possible that Otto's promotion was regarded by the empress as a conciliatory gesture towards the Ezzonids and Conrad's former supporters in Bavaria.[55]

The virtually simultaneous appointment of a new duke of Carinthia was likewise intended to secure the south-eastern frontier against the Hungarians. In the case of Carinthia the need was the more urgent because the regent's first appointee, Duke Conrad (1056–61) had been 'duke in name only', incapable of imposing his authority on the nobility of Carinthia (especially of Count Markward of the Eppenstein family). His successor was the Swabian prince Berthold I 'the Bearded' of Zähringen. He seems, like Otto of Northeim, to

---

[53] Meyer von Knonau (1890) 1:92–3, 95–6, 192–8; Boshof (1986) 185.
[54] Frutolf, *Chronica* 1071, p. 80. Cf. Lampert, *Annales* 1061, p. 79.
[55] Meyer von Knonau (1890) 1:210–11; Lange (1961) 10–14.

have been married to a kinswoman of the imperial family: his wife, Richwara, was perhaps the granddaughter of Empress Gisela and her second husband, Duke Ernest I of Swabia.[56] (Henry IV was the grandson of Gisela and her third husband, Conrad II.) In appointing Berthold of Zähringen, Rudolf of Rheinfelden and Otto of Northeim to the three south German duchies, Agnes chose powerful and ambitious princes whose military and administrative talents would be useful to her regime and whose family connections with the imperial dynasty might be expected to guarantee their loyalty. In the event, however, one at least of these princes joined the conspiracy against the empress which ended her regency in 1062. In the early 1070s the empress's three appointees became Henry IV's most formidable opponents and they devoted the rest of their lives to rebellion against the Salian monarchy.

The defeat of the German army in Hungary in 1060 and the resultant loss of prestige was presumably one of the causes of the conspiracy against the regent. Equally important was the breach between the regency government and the reform papacy in 1061–2. Henry III had been the creator and protector of the reform papacy. He had assumed the principal role in the election of the four German popes Clement II, Damasus II, Leo IX and Victor II by virtue of the office of 'patrician of the Romans', which he had received from the Romans on the day of his imperial coronation (25 December 1046). Henry III's conception of the office of patrician (which was also to play a major part in Henry IV's relations with the papacy) had a complex history. During the Byzantine period of papal history (until the mid-eighth century) the patrician had been the emperor's representative in Rome, a role which Otto III had attempted to restore in 1000. The popes of the later eighth century had conferred the title of patrician on the Frankish kings to emphasise their role as protectors of the papacy. In the later tenth century the title had been usurped by the most powerful Roman aristocratic clan: it symbolised their dominion over the city and the papacy. Henry III's revival of the title in 1046 was intended to deny this dominion to the contending noble families of the Tusculani and Crescentii and ensure the emperor's continuing influence over the papacy. He and his advisers believed that the title conferred on him (in the words of the reformer Peter Damian) 'perpetual control over the election of the pope'.[57] The Romans swore that they would recognise as pope only the emperor's appointee. Henry IV inherited this title: his Italian subjects considered that 'as he was heir to the kingdom, he was also heir to the patriciate'.[58] Nevertheless in the first papal elections of the new reign – those of Stephen

---

[56] Meyer von Knonau (1890) 1:208–10; Kimpen (1955) 82 and n. 233; Klewitz (1971) 260.

[57] Peter Damian, *Letter* 89: *Briefe* 2, 547; *Annales Romani* 1046, p. 469. See Schramm (1929) 58–63, 113, 229–38; Vollrath (1974) 11–44.

[58] Bonizo, *Ad amicum* VI, p. 595. Cf. Henry IV, *Letter* 11, p. 15. See below p. 144.

IX (August 1057), Benedict X (April 1058) and Nicholas II (December 1058) – the royal government did not take the initiative and impose its own appointees. The regency was incapable of intervening directly in Rome in the manner of Henry III, so that the role of protector of the reform papacy devolved on the house of Canossa–Lotharingia: on Godfrey 'the Bearded', margrave of Tuscany and his wife, Beatrice. It was obviously no coincidence that Stephen IX, the first pope to be elected in these altered circumstances, was Godfrey's brother. Frederick of Lotharingia, the protégé of Leo IX, was committed to the papal reform programme. Equally important, however, his election was a means of committing his powerful brother to the defence of the reformers against the Roman aristocracy. Stephen IX's election was held five days after the death of Victor II, the reform party acting quickly before the Roman nobility could install their own candidate. It was evidently too dangerous to wait for the royal government in Germany to provide a pope. Stephen was elected (commented the chronicler of Niederaltaich) 'without the king's knowledge but the king afterwards approved his election'. In December 1057 the new pope sent two legates to secure the regent's confirmation of his election.[59] The Roman reformers still desired royal approval of their actions: there was no question in 1057 of the reform papacy liberating itself from imperial control.

On Stephen IX's death, however, the reform papacy did not act quickly enough to outmanoeuvre its opponents. On 5 April 1058, seven days after Stephen died in Florence, the Tusculani and Crescentii enthroned Cardinal Bishop John II of Velletri as Pope Benedict X. The rival families joined forces to restore the Roman aristocratic domination of the papacy, taking advantage of the absence of the leading reformers who had accompanied the late pope to Tuscany. The reformers' response was the counter-election of Pope Nicholas II, the former Bishop Gerard of Florence, a Burgundian reformer who enjoyed the confidence of Margrave Godfrey of Tuscany. This election took place in Siena, probably on 6 December (St Nicholas's day) 1058. The new pope was enthroned in St Peter's on 24 January 1059, after Godfrey had marched on Rome and defeated the supporters of Benedict X. Six months before the papal election in Siena, however, the reform party had 'sent an envoy to the king in Augsburg, requesting that the bishop of Florence should be promoted to the apostolic see'. At the Whitsun assembly in Augsburg (7 June 1058) 'the king, having deliberated with the princes, designated Bishop Gerard of Florence as pope'. The reformers secured the approval of the German court for their candidate before proceeding to the papal election, unlike their enemies, the

---

[59] *Annales Altahenses* 1057, p. 54. See Meyer von Knonau (1890) 1:30–1, 52–3; H.-G. Krause (1960) 59–62; T. Schmidt (1977) 62–3.

Roman nobles, who had elected Benedict X 'without consulting the king and the princes'. The reformers were also careful to involve the king's new Italian chancellor, Wibert of Parma, in their proceedings. In 1058 the reform party once more respected the principle that the approval of the imperial court was necessary for the election of a pope, on this occasion using that principle to quash the election of Benedict X and to replace him with a reforming candidate, Nicholas II.[60]

The Lateran synod over which the new pope presided in April 1059 issued a decree regulating papal elections. This decree was the first to give a preeminent role in the election to the cardinals and above all to the cardinal bishops, the function of 'the rest of the clergy and people' being limited to giving their consent to the election made by the cardinals.[61] The effect was to place the choice of the pope in the hands of the leaders of the Roman reform party and thus render the papal reform irreversible. Four months later the new procedure for electing the pope became an integral part of the treaty between the papacy and its former enemies, the Norman princes of southern Italy. In August 1059 Robert Guiscard, duke of Apulia, and Richard, prince of Capua became vassals of the pope and, besides promising fealty and service, they swore that in future papal elections they would help the cardinals to carry out the terms of the 1059 decree. They promised that on the death of the pope they would place themselves at the disposal of 'the better cardinals, the Roman clerks and laymen' and 'give assistance so that a pope is elected and ordained to the honour of St Peter'.[62] The Papal Election Decree of 1059 was regarded by scholars of the late nineteenth and early twentieth centuries as playing a central role in the history of the reform papacy, marking 'the first step towards the emancipation of the papacy' from imperial control. This interpretation seems to be confirmed by a report from the year 1062, that shortly before Nicholas II's death (20 July 1061) a German synod condemned the pope and annulled all his proceedings. 'The alliance sealed by Henry III between Germany and the holy see had been broken; the struggle of the priesthood and the empire was beginning.'[63] More recent scholarship, however, has placed the Papal Election Decree firmly in the context of the events of 1058, rather than that of the later struggle of papacy and empire. The decree was intended,

---

[60] *Annales Altahenses* 1058, p. 54. Cf. Lampert, *Annales* 1059, pp. 73–4; Bonizo, *Ad amicum* VI, p. 593. See Meyer von Knonau (1890) 1:85–92, 100–4, 118–22, 674–7; H.-G. Krause (1960) 62–9; T. Schmidt (1977) 72–80; Ziese (1982) 19–20. Wollasch (1968) 205–20 argued that Nicholas II was designated by Stephen IX as his successor; but see Hägermann (1970) 352–61.

[61] Jasper (1986) 98–109.

[62] Deusdedit, *Collectio canonum* III.285, 288, pp. 394, 395. See H.-G. Krause (1960) 127 n. 2.

[63] Fliche (1924) 1:323–4, 325. Cf. Scheffer-Boichorst (1879) 1; Hauck (1954) 686; Haller (1951) 324–5.

firstly, to legitimise the election of Nicholas II. The irregularities of that election, performed by a small group of electors far from Rome during the lifetime of a pope, were now given retrospective justification. Secondly, regarding future papal elections, the intention was 'to take steps so that the evils [of April 1058] do not revive and gain the upper hand'. The secular interference against which the decree was directed was that of the Romans, who had secured the enthronement of Benedict X. As for the role of the imperial court in future elections, the decree included a clause 'saving the due honour and reverence of our beloved son Henry [IV]'. The scholarship of the late nineteenth and early twentieth centuries interpreted this clause as reducing the imperial rights in a papal election to a mere formality: the decree abolished the rights of the patriciate as exercised by Henry III. The more recent literature, however, tends to interpret the 'royal clause' as a confirmation of the existing rights of the emperor, rather than an attempt to diminish them. The decree adopted the procedure followed in 1058, when the reformers obtained the German court's approval for their candidate before electing him pope, as the norm for future elections.[64] This was the interpretation of the 'royal clause' offered in a treatise of 1062 by Peter Damian, cardinal bishop of Ostia, who may have participated in formulating the decree: 'Pope Nicholas granted to my lord the king, and confirmed by the written decree of a synod, this privilege which [Henry IV] had already obtained by hereditary right.' The decree of 1059 'confirmed' the role in papal elections which the young king had inherited from his father.[65]

Like the Papal Election Decree, the papal alliance with the Normans in 1059 has often been interpreted as a measure to free the papacy from imperial control. The Normans were 'enemies of the Roman empire' who, in seizing the duchy of Apulia and the principality of Capua, had invaded territories which were regarded by the German court as fiefs of the empire.[66] During the early eleventh century emperors had invested native princes with the titles of duke of Apulia and prince of Capua, most recently in 1047, during Henry III's first Italian expedition. In 1059, however, the pope assumed the right to invest the Norman adventurers Robert Guiscard and Richard of Aversa with these titles. At first sight this appears to be a deliberate usurpation of imperial rights. Since 1046, however, the pope had often been called on to act as the emperor's representative in southern Italy. In 1050 Leo IX made a progress of southern

[64] Michel (1936); Michel (1939) 291–351; H.-G. Krause (1960); Jakobs (1964) 351–9; Kempf (1964) 73–89; Feine (1965) 541–51; Stürner (1968) 1–56; Hägermann (1970) 157–93; Stürner (1972) 37–52.

[65] Peter Damian, *Letter* 89: *Briefe* 2, 547–8. See H.-G. Krause (1960) 102–3, 259–67; Hägermann (1970) 161; Woody (1970) 33–54.

[66] *Annales Altahenses* 1061, 1063, 1064, pp. 58, 62, 65. See Deér (1972) 43–50.

Italy and 'subjected some of the princes and cities both to himself and to the emperor'; in 1052 he received the government of Benevento allegedly as a 'vicariate' from the emperor.[67] Victor II was responsible for the government of Spoleto 'both on the part of King Henry [IV] and on his own part'.[68] In the light of the authority wielded by these 'German popes' there was nothing unprecedented about Nicholas II's investitures in 1059. Nor is there any evidence that the recruitment of the Normans as papal vassals was intended to counter German influence over the papacy. Firstly, the enemy against whom the Norman alliance was directed was the Roman nobility.[69] Secondly, it is by no means certain that the alliance was initiated by the papacy. If the Norman princes offered themselves as vassals in return for the legitimation of their conquests, Nicholas II's readiness to invest them may have been inspired by the conduct of his predecessors in the reign of Henry III. He may have considered himself justified by the special circumstances of Henry IV's minority, when the imperial government was in no position to intervene in southern Italy. Because of the sparseness of the evidence Nicholas's attitude must remain a matter of speculation. The earliest reference in a papal source to the relative claims of empire and papacy in southern Italy comes from September 1073, when Richard of Capua renewed his oath of fealty to the pope at the beginning of Gregory VII's pontificate. The oath contained the undertaking: 'I shall swear fealty to King Henry [IV] when I am admonished to do so by you or by your successors, nevertheless saving my fealty to the holy Roman church.'[70] Both pope and prince here acknowledged the jurisdiction of the king over Capua. The stipulation that the pope would at some future date 'admonish' his vassal to swear fealty to Henry IV implies that the authority of the pope in the case of Capua was conceived as that of an imperial vicar or co-ruler, rather than an independent suzerain.

The theory that the Papal Election Decree and the Norman alliance were anti-imperial measures was inspired partly by the fact that Nicholas II is known to have been condemned by a German synod in 1061. According to Cardinal Peter Damian, writing in 1062, 'the rulers of the royal court, together with some holy (so to speak) bishops of the German kingdom' assembled a council which 'condemned the pope by synodal sentence and presumed with incredible audacity to annul all his decisions'. Furthermore when the papal legate Stephen, cardinal priest of S. Grisogono, came to present a papal letter to the German court, he was refused admittance and, after waiting for five days outside the closed doors, he returned to Rome with the letter unread. The

---

[67] Herman, *Chronicon* 1050, p. 129; *Chronica mon. Casinensis* II.46, p. 254
[68] Victor II, *JL* 4348: *Italia Sacra* I, 353. See Deér (1972) 88–90.
[69] Bonizo, *Ad amicum* VI, p. 593. See Deér (1972) 87.
[70] Gregory VII, *Registrum* I.21a, p. 36. See Deér (1972) 90.

annulling of Nicholas II's 'decisions' certainly included the Papal Election Decree. For Peter Damian explained that after Nicholas's death the reformers elected a new pope, Alexander II, but on this occasion (unlike in 1058) they did not seek the approval of the German court, since the 'privilege' that required them to do so – that is, the Papal Election Decree – had been annulled by the recent synod. Peter Damian's account makes it clear that the annulment of the decree had not been the intention of the German synod, but an accidental consequence of its actions. The 'incredible audacity' of 'the rulers of the royal court' had rebounded on them, causing them to annul their own 'privilege'.[71] There is no evidence that Nicholas II's condemnation was provoked either by the decree of 1059 or by the Norman alliance (measures taken two years before the condemnation). The breach was caused, according to Peter Damian, by 'the insolence of some man or other'. In the late eleventh century it was believed that Archbishop Anno of Cologne was at the centre of the conflict between Nicholas II and the German court (although in fact Anno was to figure in the years 1062–4 as a champion of the reform papacy).[72] All that can be said for certain is that the context of the dispute of 1061 was one of strained relations between the pope and the German Church. Nicholas had rebuked Bishop Burchard I of Halberstadt for his attempts to exact tithes from the abbey of Hersfeld.[73] The pope had also refused a request to send the pallium to the newly elected Archbishop Siegfried of Mainz, rebuking the 'ignorance' of the regent's advisers who made the request. 'According to the usage of ancient tradition' the archbishop must come to Rome to collect the pallium in person.[74] In fact that 'ancient tradition' had long been neglected and the reform papacy had only just begun to revive it. Nicholas II's pontificate gave the German Church its first experience of the claims of the reform papacy to discipline the universal Church according to the doctrine of the papal primacy. The condemnation of Nicholas in the synod of 1061 was perhaps the response of the German court and episcopate to this novel claim.

It is not surprising that after such a breach the German court determined after Nicholas II's death to influence the election of his successor. Royal intervention was encouraged by two parties anxious to end the reforming regime in Rome: the Roman noble clans and the Lombard bishops. Envoys from the Roman aristocracy brought the insignia of the office of patrician to the young king and 'appealed to him to elect a supreme pontiff'. Remembering how they

---

[71] Peter Damian, *Letter* 89: *Briefe* 2, 559–60. See H.-G. Krause (1960) 128–35; Somerville (1977) 157–66.

[72] Benzo of Alba, *Ad Heinricum* VII.2, pp. 596–8; Deusdedit, *Libellus contra invasores* c. 11, p. 309. See H.-G. Krause (1960) 135–40; Jenal (1974) 166–9.

[73] Lampert, *Annales* 1059, pp. 74–5.

[74] Peter Damian, *Letter* 71: *Briefe* 2, 323–5. See Jenal (1974) 238–9; Zotz (1982) 155–75.

had been outmanoeuvered by the reformers after the election of Benedict X, the Romans revived the institution of the patriciate and invited Henry IV to imitate his father's conduct towards the papacy. The imperial court's response was to summon 'all the bishops of Italy' to a council in Basel (28 October 1061), in which the king put on the insignia brought by the Roman delegation and 'was called patrician of the Romans'.[75] The council elected as Pope Honorius II the Lombard bishop Cadalus of Parma, a member of a prominent family with extensive possessions in the counties of Verona and Vicenza. The Lombard bishops, like their colleagues in Germany, had become alienated from the reform papacy during Nicholas II's pontificate. It was probably they, under the leadership of Denis of Piacenza and Gregory of Vercelli, who promoted the candidature of Cadalus.[76] His connections with the German court, especially with the influential Henry of Augsburg, made him acceptable to the imperial government, but he was essentially the 'Lombard candidate' rather than the 'imperial candidate' for the papacy. The regency did not appoint its own candidate, as in the days of the 'German papacy', but instead backed a candidate whose supporters seemed powerful enough to ensure his peaceful succession. For the German government lacked the resources to install a pope in Rome and it was left to Cadalus himself to secure control of the papacy.[77]

By recognising Cadalus as pope, the regency provoked a papal schism. Four weeks before the council of Basel, on 30 September 1061, the cardinal bishops had elected Pope Alexander II according to the terms of the Papal Election Decree and enthroned him in Rome with the help of the papal vassal, Richard of Capua. The Roman reformers waited for ten weeks after the death of Nicholas II before electing a successor, despite the danger of such a delay. They evidently hoped to install a candidate acceptable to the imperial court, whose election would restore the cordial relationship that had come to an end in the last months of Nicholas II's pontificate. Alexander II, the former Bishop Anselm I of Lucca, seemed an appropriate compromise candidate, a Lombard, a member of the Milanese noble family of Baggio and well known to the imperial court.[78] Rather than electing one of their own number to the papacy, the Roman reformers had chosen a candidate less objectionable to the imperial government. As bishop of Lucca, the favourite residence of Margrave Godfrey of Tuscany, the pope must also have been acceptable to that powerful prince who had figured since 1057 as a protector of the papacy. In the opening months of Alexander II's pontificate, however, it was not Godfrey but his wife,

[75] Berthold, *Annales* 1061, p. 271.   [76] Bonizo *Ad amicum* VI, p. 594.

[77] Meyer von Knonau (1890) 1:216–17, 223–9; Herberhold (1934) 84–104; Herberhold (1947) 477–503; T. Schmidt (1977) 104–14, 125–31: Ziese (1982) 21–3; Black-Veldtrup (1995) 30, 90, 374–5.   [78] Peter Damian, *Letter* 89: *Briefe* 2, 570. See T. Schmidt (1977) 1–4, 30–7, 131.

Beatrice, who defended the interests of the reform papacy. During the winter of 1061–2, when Cadalus of Parma led his first expedition on Rome, Beatrice barred his way through the Apennines.[79]

The papal schism provoked by the council of Basel added to the disaffection caused by the defeat of the German army in Hungary and the ascendancy of Henry of Augsburg at court. In the spring of 1062 a conspiracy was formed against the empress by a group of princes who were alienated not only by the regime's failures but also by their own exclusion from power. According to Lampert of Hersfeld, the princes, realising that 'their authority, which ought to be supreme in the realm, had almost been destroyed', 'held frequent meetings, performed their public duties rather negligently, stirred up the people against the empress and finally sought by all means to seize the boy from his mother and to transfer the administration of the kingdom to themselves'. This conspiracy culminated in the kidnapping of the twelve-year-old Henry IV at Kaiserswerth, probably soon after Easter (31 March) 1062. The most detailed account of this incident is given by Lampert, who must have obtained his information three months after the abduction, when the king and his abductor visited the abbey of Hersfeld (13 July). 'After he had taken counsel with Count Ekbert [I of Brunswick] and Duke Otto of Bavaria, the archbishop of Cologne sailed down the Rhine to the place called St Switbert's island.' The king and his entourage were staying here in the royal palace of Kaiserswerth, after celebrating Easter in Utrecht. When the king was in high spirits after a banquet, Archbishop Anno of Cologne persuaded him to inspect a ship 'which he had fitted out with admirable workmanship, precisely for this purpose'. As soon as Henry stepped on board, 'the oarsmen at once leaned over their oars and propelled the ship into the middle of the river more rapidly than words can express'. The king, fearing an attempt on his life, sprang overboard. He would have drowned, had not Count Ekbert dived into the river and 'snatched him from death with the greatest difficulty'. The conspirators then brought Henry to Cologne.[80] According to the chronicle of Niederaltaich, the conspirators seized not only the king but also the emblems of his authority: 'they took the royal cross and lance from the chapel'.[81] Their purpose was not simply to put pressure on the regent by kidnapping her son, but to usurp for themselves the government of the kingdom.

Anno of Cologne appears as the leader of this conspiracy in every contemporary or near-contemporary account of the abduction. In some of these

[79] E. Goez (1995) 158–9, 206.
[80] Lampert, *Annales* 1062, p. 80. Cf. *D H IV* 88. See Meyer von Knonau (1890) 1:274–9; Jenal (1974) 175–6, 183–5; Böhmer-Struve (1984) 103–4 (no. 252).
[81] *Annales Altahenses* 1062, p. 59.

sources he is assumed to have been the leader of a party of princes, 'the dukes and magnates of the realm'. He acted 'with the support of certain princes of the realm', 'on the advice of the foremost men of the realm who were offended that the kingdom was not governed in a virile manner by Agnes', as the representative of 'some princes guided by envy'. Of these fellow-conspirators only two can be identified with certainty. It is clear from Lampert's account that the king's cousin, Ekbert I of Brunswick (later margrave of Meissen) took part in the abduction and a second Saxon prince, Otto of Northeim, duke of Bavaria, participated at least in planning the abduction.[82] It is difficult to believe that so momentous a coup could have been successfully carried out without the backing of a considerable number of princes. Certainly the comment of the Niederaltaich chronicler, that the king was brought to Cologne 'with resistance from no one', suggests either that Anno had large-scale support or that the empress's regime had so forfeited the sympathy of the princes that they made no effort to hinder the conspiracy.

The narrative sources agree that the conspiracy brought an immediate end to the empress's control of the royal government. Without her son she was powerless and she withdrew from politics to live privately on her own estates. The shock that she had suffered at Kaiserswerth is apparent from the letter which she sent soon afterwards to the abbot and monks of Fruttuaria. She interpreted the abduction of her son as a divine punishment for her sins: 'my conscience terrifies me more than any ghost and any vision'. She sought the prayers of the brethren and begged to be received into their congregation.[83] It has often been assumed that soon after sending this letter, in the winter of 1062–3, the empress went to Italy, first to Fruttuaria, then to Rome to seek forgiveness from Alexander II for her role in the schism of Cadalus. A recent reassessment of the evidence, however, concludes that Agnes did not leave Germany until the summer or autumn of 1065.[84] 'She intended to renounce the world,' wrote Lampert, 'and would have rushed headlong to perform what she had decided, had not her friends calmed her inward tumult with their timely counsels.'[85] It is possible that the empress reappeared at court towards the end of 1062, since she is mentioned in a royal diploma of 26 November. Her name does not appear in the surviving diplomas for 1063, but reappears

[82] *Annales Augustani* 1062, p. 127; Benzo, *Ad Heinricum* II.15, p. 236. See Jenal (1974) 177–81. Meyer von Knonau (1890) 1:274–6; Bauernfeind (1929) 29; Bulst-Thiele, (1933) 80, linked a letter of Gunther of Bamberg (*Briefsammlungen* pp. 501–2) with the conspiracy of 1062. The letter almost certainly relates to a later and lesser intrigue: Erdmann (1938) 283–4; Jenal (1974) 182 n. 32; Böhmer-Struve (1984) 119 (no. 277).   [83] Struve (1984) 424.

[84] Meyer von Knonau (1890) 1:280–4, 320–1; Bulst-Thiele (1933) 81–2, 84–6; W. Goez (1974) 462–94; but see Struve (1985) 1–29; Black-Veldtrup (1995) 27–36, 92–4.

[85] Lampert, *Annales* 1062, p. 81.

in the intervention clauses of four diplomas of 1064, indicating that she was again at court in January and in July 1064. She was continuously at court from the end of March until late May 1065. During the two months following the king's coming of age (29 March 1065) his mother became once more the most frequent intervener in the royal diplomas, as she had been during the five-and-a-half years of her regency.[86] It was at this moment of her restoration to a position of influence at court that the empress seems to have decided to carry out her intention of 1062 and departed for the abbey of Fruttuaria and thereafter for Rome.

The royal diplomas of the period following the conspiracy of 1062 show that the ringleader at Kaiserswerth, Anno of Cologne, immediately replaced the empress as the foremost intervener and retained this dominant position until July 1064. In eight of these diplomas he is distinguished by the special title 'master' (*magister*).[87] According to Lampert of Hersfeld, Anno's intention after the abduction was to share power with his colleagues: 'In order to lessen the resentment caused by his action and lest it appear that he had interfered out of private ambition rather than for the common good, the archbishop decreed that when the king was visiting a particular diocese, the bishop of that diocese should have the duty of ensuring that the commonwealth suffered no harm and should have a special responsibility for the cases which were referred to the king.'[88] Such a project for the reform of the government, involving the whole episcopate in administrative duties and judicial decisions, may have been put forward to secure approval for Anno's coup, but there is no evidence that it was ever put into effect. The intervention clauses of the diplomas of 1062–4 show Anno occasionally in the company of a small group of princes, who were either his colleagues in government or his rivals for power. In the latter part of 1062 this group consisted of the archbishops Adalbert of Bremen and Siegfried I of Mainz and Otto of Northeim, duke of Bavaria. Of these three politicians only Otto is known certainly to have participated in the conspiracy of the previous spring. Archbishop Adalbert belonged to the family of the Thuringian counts of Goseck, counts palatine of Saxony. He had been a trusted adviser of Henry III and his church had benefited greatly from imperial generosity.[89] Siegfried, the empress's appointee to the archbishopric of Mainz, was a member of a noble family related to the counts of Saarbrücken.[90] None of these princes figures as prominently as Anno of Cologne.[91]

In the diplomas of the following year, however, the pattern changes. The

[86] Gawlik (1970a) 127–8; Black-Veldtrup (1995) 93–4.
[87] Gawlik (1970a) 135; Jenal (1974) 218–24.   [88] Lampert, *Annales* 1062, p. 180.
[89] Adam, *Gesta* III.31, pp. 173–4. See Glaeske (1962) 55–97.
[90] G. Schmidt (1917) 54–6; Zielinski (1984) 60.
[91] Gawlik (1970a) 24–7; Jenal (1974) 218, 219, 220, 222.

appearances of Siegfried and Otto diminish, while those of Adalbert increase. The growing importance of Adalbert of Bremen during 1063 is evident from the fact that three of the diplomas of the year record donations to his church, referring to the archbishop as the king's 'protector' (*patronus*), a title which parallels Anno's honorific title of 'master'.[92] The narrative sources also record Adalbert's changing status at court. His biographer, Adam of Bremen, presented him as Anno's equal; 'Archbishops Adalbert and Anno were proclaimed consuls and henceforward the whole government depended on their counsel.'[93] Lampert of Hersfeld wrote that in 1063 Adalbert quickly gained so great an influence over the young king that he was able to oust the other bishops and 'seemed almost to usurp the monarchy'.[94] The evidence of the diplomas, however, suggests that in 1063 Adalbert's influence had not yet eclipsed that of Anno. It also reveals a development which escaped the attention of the chroniclers: the appearance at court of a new adviser, Bishop Burchard II of Halberstadt. He was to distinguish himself in 1063 as a diplomat in the papal schism and in 1068 as a military commander on the Saxon frontier against the Slav confederation of the Liutizi.[95] Burchard's name appears as an intervener in the diplomas of 1063 with the same frequency as that of Adalbert of Bremen and three of the diplomas of this year were privileges for his church of Halberstadt. Since Burchard was the nephew and ally of Anno of Cologne, his presence at court must be attributed to his uncle's influence: perhaps Anno had summoned him to court to consolidate his authority in the face of the challenge from Adalbert. The diplomas of 1064 show that Anno's dominant position at court continued throughout the first half of that year. Adalbert's appearances diminished; Siegfried of Mainz and Burchard of Halberstadt each figured only in a single diploma and Otto of Northeim did not appear at all.[96] After July 1064 the names of both Anno and Adalbert disappear from the royal diplomas, to reappear only after Henry IV's coming of age in March 1065. For these eight months there is no clear guide to the personnel of the Salian court.

The ascendancy of Anno of Cologne was reflected in four preoccupations of the years 1062–4: the enriching of the church of Cologne, the advancement of the archbishop's family, the education of the king and the reversal of the government's attitude towards the papacy. Evidence of Anno's influence at court is found, firstly, in a royal diploma of 14 July 1063 for the church of Cologne, issued 'especially on account of the indefatigable merit and faithful service' of the archbishop. This privilege conferred on the church one-ninth

---

[92] Gawlik (1970a) 27–30; Jenal (1974) 218–22.   [93] Adam, *Gesta* III.34, p. 176.
[94] Lampert, *Annales* 1063, p. 88.   [95] Brüske (1955) 83–4. See below pp. 78, 88, 362.
[96] Gawlik (1970a) 30–2; Jenal (1974) 220–2.

of the imperial income from all sources, to be divided at the discretion of Anno and his successors among the monasteries of the diocese, so as to secure the prayers of the religious as a perpetual memorial for Henry IV and his ancestors. The earlier Salian emperors had been much preoccupied with their *memoria* and the mature Henry IV shared their concern with preserving the memory of himself and his dynasty. It is possible, therefore, that this benefaction was initiated by the young king.[97] It is indicative of Anno's influence, however, that he was able to convert the king's desire for a memorial into a project that gave special prominence to the church of Cologne and bound it closely to the Salian dynasty. Anno used this influence to further the interests not only of his church but also of his family. 'He exalted his kinsmen, his friends and his chaplains, heaping the most important dignities on them all,' wrote one critic, citing in particular the case of Anno's brother, Werner, who in 1063 was appointed archbishop of Magdeburg. The twelfth-century historian of the church of Magdeburg deplored 'the harm inflicted on [his] church' by this appointment 'both because of the violation of free election by the brethren and because of general considerations of usefulness': for Werner, 'a mild man and not sharp-witted', lacked the qualifications for this high office. Anno, probably with the support of Burchard of Halberstadt, caused the king to overrule the election made by the cathedral chapter and appoint Werner, provost of Anno's own foundation of Maria ad Gradus in Cologne. Anno's sole purpose in forcing his brother on the church was to consolidate his influence in the kingdom.[98] He was to repeat this tactic in 1066, when he attempted to secure the appointment of his nephew, Conrad, to the archbishopric of Trier.[99]

Anno's blatant nepotism, his advancement of the obscure family of Steusslingen, was doubtless the principal reason for the negative view of his ascendancy found in many narrative sources. He 'seized King Henry from his mother and set himself over him as his master'.[100] 'With rash daring he did not hesitate to transfer the right of dominion to himself.'[101] Even Lampert of Hersfeld, who had no doubt that Anno was a saint, did not conceal the hostility which his regime aroused: 'very many complained that the royal majesty had been violated and rendered powerless.'[102] The more favourably disposed sources claim that, on the contrary, the purpose of Anno's regime was to restore royal authority, which had been endangered by the mistakes of the regent, and in particular to ensure a suitable education for the boy king.

---

[97] *D H IV* 104. Cf. *Vita Annonis Coloniensis* I.7, p. 470. See Schmid (1984) 674, 700.

[98] Adam, *Gesta* III.35, pp. 177–8. Cf. *Gesta archiepisc. Magdeburgensium* c. 21, p. 400. See Meyer von Knonau (1890) 1:352–4; Lück (1970a) 44–51; Claude (1972) 323–4.

[99] See below p. 116.   [100] *Annales Weissenburgenses* 1062, p. 51.

[101] *Triumphus sancti Remacli* I.2, p. 438.

[102] Lampert, *Annales* 1062, p. 80. Cf. 1075, pp. 242, 248–50.

According to the Niederaltaich chronicle, before the abduction at Kaiserswerth 'those who were in power at court concerned themselves only with their own interests and no one taught the king what was good and just'. After Anno's coup, however, 'since the [arch]bishop then in power at court was zealous for justice, the commonwealth began to flourish'.[103] Henry IV's education had hitherto been the responsibility not only of his mother but also of Cuno, a royal *ministerialis*, that is, an unfree servant of the crown. 'Cuno, servant and educator (*nutritor*) of the king' is identified, firstly, in a passage in the Niederaltaich chronicle, which reveals that in 1069 he was still the king's close confidant.[104] His name appears, secondly, in two royal diplomas granting an estate to 'Cuno, our servant' (28 May 1057) and another to his wife, 'the noblewoman' Matilda, 'on account of the faithful service . . . of Cuno, the servant (*pedissequus*) of our youth' (26 October 1064).[105] In 1062 Cuno must have lost his role of 'educator' to Anno, whose title of *magister* in diplomas of 1063 and 1064 indicates that he was personally responsible for Henry IV's upbringing, as well as being his principal adviser.

Of all the contemporary assessments of Anno's regime the most positive is that of Peter Damian, cardinal bishop of Ostia, in a letter to Anno of 1063. 'You have preserved, venerable father, the boy left in your hands; you have strengthened the kingship; you have restored to your pupil the power that is his by hereditary right.' Peter Damian urgently sought Anno's help for the reform party in Rome: hence his flattering view of the archbishop's regime. It is clear from the letter that he regarded Anno as an ally of the reform papacy and believed that one of his objectives in seizing power was to achieve victory for the reformers' candidate in the papal schism. 'You have laboured to confirm the bishop of the apostolic see on the throne of his dignity.'[106] There is no evidence that Anno participated in the council of Basel (October 1061), which produced the papal schism. The council of Augsburg in late October 1062, which initiated the reversal of the decision of Basel, was doubtless Anno's personal response to the schism. The council of Augsburg decided to send Burchard of Halberstadt to Italy to 'hear the claims of both sides and to pronounce judgement justly on behalf of [Henry IV] and the princes'.[107] Burchard presumably owed this mission to the influence of his uncle, Anno,

---

[103] *Annales Altahenses* 1062, pp. 59–60. Cf. Bruno, *Saxonicum bellum* c. 1, p. 13.

[104] *Annales Altahenses* 1069, p. 76. See below p. 66.

[105] *DD H IV* 21, 137. See Meyer von Knonau (1890) 1:51 n. 52, 389 and n. 46, 611 and n. 7; Bosl (1950) 1:64–70; Keunecke (1978) 30–2; Arnold (1985) 34, 35 n. 63, 70; Zotz (1991) 41–2.

[106] Peter Damian, *Letter* 99, *Briefe* 3, 97–100.

[107] *Annales Altahenses* 1061, pp. 58–9. Cf. Benzo, *Ad Heinricum* III.25(26), pp. 338–40. See Meyer von Knonau (1890) 1:300–1; Zimmermann (1968) 151–3; Jenal (1974) 231–40; T. Schmidt (1977) 119–21.

and the fact that Burchard hastened to recognise Alexander II as the lawful pope can be interpreted as evidence of his uncle's sympathies. Soon afterwards Alexander conferred on Burchard a pallium and other archiepiscopal insignia (13 January 1063) as a reward for his services in restoring 'ecclesiastical peace' and 'for his sincere affection for us and the Roman church'.[108] Burchard's conduct in Italy suggests that Anno was already a committed supporter of the reform papacy and used the council of Augsburg to promote the cause of Alexander II. This is certainly how Anno's role was interpreted by Peter Damian, who urged the archbishop in his letter of 1063 to continue his support: he must organise a general council 'to extinguish the madness of Cadalus'.[109] The following year Anno demonstrated his commitment to Alexander II's cause by his participation in the council of Mantua (31 May 1064), which definitively recognised Alexander as pope and excommunicated the antipope. Anno was both powerful enough to overrule the decision of the council of Basel and sufficiently sympathetic towards the Roman reform party to ensure Alexander II's victory.

The sources for the council of Mantua unanimously claim for Anno the central role in achieving the recognition of Alexander II by the imperial bishops. The council met in the jurisdiction of the margrave of Tuscany, Godfrey 'the Bearded', who escorted Anno to Mantua but played no further part in the proceedings. The sources insist that it was his wife, Beatrice of Tuscany, who was Anno's principal ally in the council and that she, unlike Godfrey, was a stalwart defender of Alexander throughout the schism. The most reliable report is that of the chronicle of Niederaltaich (which may be regarded as an eyewitness account, since Abbot Wenceslas of Niederaltaich was present at the council). The chronicler recorded that, although both popes initially agreed to attend the council at Whitsuntide 1064, only Alexander appeared. Cadalus of Parma informed Anno that he would not attend unless the council recognised him as pope unconditionally, a demand that was rejected as 'unseemly and unjust'. Alexander was consequently invited to preside over the council. On the first day of the council Anno, on the king's behalf, called on Alexander to answer the allegations circulating in Germany that he 'came to the apostolic see by means of simoniacal heresy' and obtained his office through the help of his 'allies and friends, the Normans, the enemies of the Roman empire'. Alexander declared on oath that he was free of simony and that he had been elected to the papacy by those 'who according to the ancient usage of the Romans are known to have the duty and power of electing and consecrating a pope'. As for his relations with the Normans: when

---

[108] Alexander II, *JL* 4498: *Gesta ep. Halberstadensium* pp. 97–8. Cf. Lampert, *Annales* 1063, pp. 81–2.   [109] Peter Damian, *Letter* 99, *Briefe* 3:100. Cf. *Letter* 89, *Briefe* 2, 541–72.

Henry IV came to Rome to receive the imperial crown, he would learn for himself what was the nature of the pope's Norman alliance. Alexander's statement persuaded the assembled prelates and secular princes to confirm his election and to condemn Cadalus as a heretic. On the second day of the council, however, 'the archbishop of Cologne was not present and behold! the supporters of Cadalus burst into the church with a great noise' and threatened Alexander with their swords. The pope stood his ground, although most of the prelates fled, and the prompt arrival of Beatrice of Tuscany and her vassals routed the enemy and restored order.[110]

Anno was determined that the council should vindicate Alexander's title, but this determination sprang not from reforming aspirations but from political considerations. By the beginning of 1064 it was clear that the attempts of Cadalus of Parma to seize the papacy by force had failed. After an initial success against the Norman allies of the reform papacy in May 1063, which gave him temporary control of Rome, the antipope's hold over the city was reduced to the fortress of Castel S. Angelo. Here he remained a virtual prisoner until he bribed his way out of the city with a payment of 300 pounds of silver. His failure caused the dissolution of the coalition of Roman aristocracy and Lombard episcopate which had promoted his election in October 1061. Without their support the German government could not hope to impose Cadalus on the Roman church. The only realistic policy in 1063–4 was that which Anno adopted: to make peace with Cadalus's rival without delay so as to restore normal relations between the German court and the papacy. It is possible that Anno's task was made more urgent by the antipope's attempt to meddle in court politics. There is evidence that Cadalus looked for support to Anno's rival, Adalbert of Bremen.[111] Above all Anno needed to settle the schism to vindicate his claim to manage the affairs of the Italian kingdom and the relations of the German court with the papacy. He based this claim, firstly, on his office of arch-chancellor of the Italian kingdom. The importance which he attached to this office is apparent from his letter to the pope in spring 1066, in which he described the arch-chancellor as the officer 'by whom, before all others, the business of Italy ought to be administered'.[112] Secondly, Anno also held the office of arch-chancellor of the Roman church, which Pope Leo IX had conferred on his predecessor in 1052. For the church of Cologne this honorific office was a valuable weapon in her constant struggle with her neighbour, Trier, for the ecclesiastical primacy in Lotharingia. The papacy had

---

[110] *Annales Altahenses* 1064, pp. 64–6. Cf. Benzo, *Ad Heinricum* III.26(27)-28(29), pp. 342–52. See Meyer von Knonau (1890) 1:378–85; Zimmermann (1968) 155–8; Jenal (1974) 241–74; T. Schmidt (1977) 122, 129, 133, 211; E. Goez (1995) 160–1.

[111] Benzo, *Ad Heinricum* III.2–4, pp. 274–82. See Herberhold (1947) 486–503; Glaeske (1962) 68; T. Schmidt (1977) 104–33.   [112] Von Giesebrecht (1890) 1259.

become the principal guarantor of the 'honour' of the church of Cologne and consequently the archbishop of Cologne had a special interest in avoiding controversy between the papacy and the imperial Church.[113] Anno's conduct during the 'schism of Cadalus' was governed by this special interest rather than by a close sympathy with the ideals of the Roman reform party.

The council of Mantua marked the apogee of Anno's power at the imperial court: within a year he had been replaced as Henry IV's chief adviser by his rival, Adalbert of Bremen. In a letter sent to Alexander II in the summer of 1065 Anno explained that he had been ousted from the conduct even of the affairs of the Italian kingdom, to which he had a special claim.[114] Adalbert's dominant position is confirmed by the royal diplomas of 1065, especially by the five diplomas of this year recording donations to the church of Bremen. The other prelates who had figured as Anno's colleagues at court in the aftermath of the coup of 1062, Burchard of Halberstadt and Siegfried of Mainz, do not appear in these diplomas.[115] Siegfried was absent from the German kingdom when Adalbert replaced Anno as the king's chief adviser. Together with the bishops of Bamberg, Regensburg and Utrecht, he made a pilgrimage to Jerusalem (autumn 1064 – summer 1065) at the head of 'a multitude of counts and princes, rich and poor'.[116] The departure of two such prominent politicians as Siegfried of Mainz and Gunther of Bamberg and also of William of Utrecht, allegedly an ally of Anno of Cologne,[117] has been interpreted as a response to the political changes at court. Adalbert's potential rivals abandoned the field to their more ruthless colleague.[118] There is, however, no evidence of any motives other than the conventional reasons for pilgrimage stated by Siegfried in his letter of 1064 to Alexander II.[119]

'Archbishop Adalbert of Bremen seized the opportunity of [Anno's] absence [in Mantua], as his avarice knew no bounds, to use all his cunning on the courtiers so that the boy king's upbringing and education were committed to him.'[120] This was the interpretation of the late twelfth-century chronicler of Lorsch; but a different chronology is suggested by the royal diplomas. In the diplomas of July 1064, two months after the council of Mantua, there is no sign of Adalbert's having ousted Anno.[121] The most likely date for this development is Eastertide 1065, when Henry IV attained his majority. In a ceremony on

[113] Gregory VII, *Registrum* I.79, p. 113. See Lück (1970b) 1–50.
[114] Von Giesebrecht (1890) 1257–8. [115] Gawlik (1970a) 32–8; Jenal (1974) 294–302.
[116] *Annales Altahenses* 1065, pp. 66–71; Lampert, *Annales* 1064, p. 92; 1065, pp. 93–100. See Meyer von Knonau (1890) 1:390–4, 445–50; Joranson (1928) 3–43.
[117] Adam, *Gesta* III.35, p. 177. [118] Glaeske (1962) 69.
[119] *Codex Udalrici* 28, pp. 54–5. Cf. *Vita Altmanni Pataviensis* c. 3, p. 230.
[120] *Codex Laureshamensis* c. 123c, p. 391. See Meyer von Knonau (1890) 1:387–8; Glaeske (1962) 69. [121] Gawlik (1970a) 32.

Easter Tuesday (29 March) in Worms, the ancestral territory of the Salian dynasty, the fifteen-year-old king was girded with a sword and thereby declared to be of age, according to the Frankish custom inherited by the German kings from their Carolingian predecessors. The fifteenth year marked the transition from boyhood to adolescence. The blessing was pronounced by Archbishop Eberhard of Trier (in the absence of the metropolitan of the diocese of Worms, Siegfried of Mainz) and Godfrey 'the Bearded' of Verdun performed the office of shield-bearer (evidently an honorific office conferred on the foremost vassal of the crown). Lampert of Hersfeld wrote two separate accounts of the king's coming of age, both linking the event with Adalbert's ousting of his rival. According to the earlier account, 'when Henry had reached maturity, he abandoned [Anno] and lived according to his own will . . . Anno renounced the court to the extent of going into retirement. Archbishop Adalbert of Bremen replaced him in his office, although not in his diligence.'[122] In the dramatic account of the Easter celebrations of 1065 in Lampert's chronicle, Adalbert plays a central role. He preached the sermon during mass on Easter day, on which occasion 'he cleansed a man from possession by a demon'. (It was surprising, thought Lampert, 'that a man of such evil repute among the people, who had not led a virtuous life, should perform a miracle'.) Two days later Henry IV was ceremonially girded with the sword 'by the concession of that same archbishop'. Lampert presumably meant that it was Adalbert himself who armed the king during this ceremony. Henry 'would immediately have made his first trial of the arms which he had received against the archbishop of Cologne and would have hastened to pursue him with fire and sword, had not the empress calmed the storm by her most timely counsel. He hated [Anno] in particular because some years before, when the latter wished to seize from the empress the right and the power to govern, he had placed the king himself in the greatest danger.'[123] No other source mentions an attempted assault on Anno on the occasion of Henry's coming of age. Lampert was probably not reporting an actual incident, but dramatising his interpretation of the political transformation at court that enabled Adalbert to replace Anno as the king's principal adviser. He was doubtless right in believing that the king felt hostility towards the ringleader of the conspiracy of 1062, in which he had almost lost his life. The coming of age gave him his first opportunity to express his personal preferences in the matter of advisers.[124]

In the royal diplomas of April and May 1065 the principal intervener was

[122] Lampert, *Libellus de institutione Herveldensis ecclesiae* II, p. 353.
[123] Lampert, *Annales* 1065, p. 93. See Meyer von Knonau (1890) 1:400–2, 404–6; Scheibelreiter (1973) 9–10; Jenal (1974) 275.
[124] Bruno, *Saxonicum bellum* c. 1, 5, pp. 13, 16; cf. c. 42, p. 41.

Empress Agnes. In the two months following the king's coming of age, his mother recovered the influence at court of which she had been violently deprived three years before. On the empress's departure for Italy in summer 1065, Adalbert of Bremen became the king's principal adviser. He bore 'the supreme power and the whole burden of affairs', according to correspondents who sought his help during the summer.[125] Adalbert owed his influence to his close relationship with Henry IV. The hostile Lampert wrote that he 'had usurped a blatantly tyrannical power under the pretext of friendship with the king'.[126] The historian of the church of Bremen reported the archbishop's own estimate of the relationship. He informed his clergy that he felt obliged to absent himself from his archdiocese and devote himself to the court 'because he could not bear to see his lord and king a captive in the hands of kidnappers'. Adalbert 'alone seemed to protect [the king], out of love for the empire and its rights rather than for the sake of his own profit'.[127] The most important factor in confirming Adalbert's friendship with the king was their joint participation in the military campaign against Hungary in September 1063. This successful campaign reversed the consequences of the defeat which the German army had suffered in 1060 and effaced the memory of that disaster. It also gave the young king his first experience of the all-important military functions of the kingship. The victor of 1060, King Bela I of Hungary, had sought to stabilise his regime by making peace with the German kingdom. Henry IV and his advisers, however, remained committed to the restoration to the Hungarian throne of Salomon (the betrothed of Henry's sister, Judith-Sophia). The prestige of the Salian dynasty was at stake. The death of Bela soon after the German invasion and the flight of his son, Geisa, gave Henry's army a bloodless victory. Salomon was restored to the throne of his father, Andreas I, and the wedding of Salomon and Judith-Sophia now took place.[128] The prince who had been most energetic in promoting this expedition was Otto of Northeim, duke of Bavaria. That at least was the opinion of the Hungarian queen-mother Anastasia. 'Since it was on [Otto's] advice and with his support that King [Henry] had restored her son to his father's kingdom', Anastasia conferred on him one of the most precious objects in the Hungarian treasury, the so-called 'sword of Attila'.[129] Otto's enthusiasm for this campaign arose from the need, firstly, to secure the frontier of his newly acquired duchy of Bavaria and, secondly, to establish himself as the leader of the Bavarian

[125] *Briefsammlungen* pp. 232–3.

[126] Lampert, *Annales* 1066, p. 100. Cf. Bruno, *Saxonicum bellum* c. 5, 8, pp. 16, 18.

[127] Adam, *Gesta* III.46, pp. 188–9.

[128] *Annales Altahenses* 1064, pp. 62–4; Adam, *Gesta* III.43, p. 186. See Meyer von Knonau (1890) 1:342–8; Boshof (1986) 185–6.

[129] Lampert, *Annales* 1071, p. 130. See Schramm (1955) 2:485–91 and below p. 66.

nobility by means of a successful and profitable campaign. Archbishop Adalbert's participation in this campaign enabled him to win the young king's confidence and to demonstrate that he was the member of the imperial episcopate with the widest experience of secular affairs.[130]

The first indication of the political transformation at court after Henry IV's coming of age is found in the sphere of Italian and papal affairs. Early in 1065 Cardinal Meinhard of Silva Candida visited the court as the legate of Alexander II to invite the king to Rome, where the pope would confer the imperial crown on him, as he had promised at the council of Mantua. The king accepted this invitation in an assembly of princes in Worms during Eastertide, in which it was decided that the royal expedition would take place the following May.[131] Alexander was anxious to crown Henry IV as emperor, now that he was of age, since he was still threatened by the ambitions of Cadalus of Parma. Henry's imperial coronation would commit the imperial court once for all to Alexander as the lawful pope, hence the consternation among the reformers in Rome when it was learned that the Italian expedition had been deferred. Cardinal Peter Damian wrote to the king, bidding him to 'stop [his] ears against evil counsellors as against the hissing of poisonous snakes' and to fulfil his duty as protector of the Roman church by making war on Cadalus. This reminder of the special function of the emperor elect was accompanied by a threat. 'If [a king] fails in his duty to God and the Church, he will be held in contempt by his subjects.'[132] The postponement of the Italian expedition was an unmistakable sign that Anno of Cologne had been ousted by his rival, as Anno himself made clear in his letter to Alexander II of summer 1065. Anno assured the pope that he was not responsible for deferring the royal expedition to Rome. The archbishop, with the help of Margrave Godfrey of Tuscany, had made all the preparations for the expedition when, five days before the date fixed for departure, a royal messenger arrived to postpone the expedition until autumn. Anno and Godfrey, the principal German experts on Italian affairs, were informed that they were not to accompany the king to Italy. 'It seemed to [the king] and to his faithful servants, I mean those who are now high in his favour, that Italian affairs could be settled satisfactorily without us.'[133] It was doubtless Adalbert of Bremen who caused the expe-

[130] Adam, *Gesta* III.43, p. 186. See May (1937) 60; Glaeske (1962) 60, 62 n. 36.

[131] *Vita Anselmi Lucensis* p. 14. See Schumann (1912) 10–11; Lück (1970b) 21; Hüls (1977) 135. In 1065 Benzo of Alba appeared at the German court to promote a royal expedition to Italy (*Ad Heinricum* III.13–22, pp. 306–30): see Meyer von Knonau (1890) 1:396–402.

[132] Peter Damian, *Letter* 120: *Briefe* 3, 384–92. See Meyer von Knonau (1890) 1:430–4; Fornasari (1979) 117–22.

[133] Von Giesebrecht (1890) 1257–8. See Meyer von Knonau (1890) 1:425–8; Glaeske (1962) 69–70; Jenal (1974) 282–94.

dition to be deferred until the autumn of 1065 and then postponed indefinitely. He must have feared that any involvement with the Italian kingdom and the papacy would make the court dependent on Anno's expertise and he was determined to deny his rival any opportunity of recovering his influence.

Henry IV devoted the summer of 1065 to a circuit of his German kingdom and a visit to his kingdom of Burgundy. It is likely that this was intended to be a 'royal journey' (*iter regis*), the tour of the kingdom that traditionally followed the king's election and coronation, as part of the formal procedures of a royal accession. There is no evidence of such an *iter* at the beginning of Henry's reign: this ceremonial visitation was perhaps delayed until the king came of age. In the case of the kingdom of Burgundy, the evidence of the private diplomas of secular and ecclesiastical princes suggests that Henry's visit to Basel in June 1065 was regarded as the beginning of his reign as king of Burgundy.[134] During his sojourn in Basel Henry may have received the homage of the Burgundian nobility, a ceremonial recognition of the king's authority that was a well-established part of the royal *iter*.[135] On the final stage of his journey the king entered Upper Lotharingia for the first time. A royal diploma issued on this occasion states the purpose of the journey in the conventional language of the eleventh-century *iter*: the king had come 'for the sake of ordering [his] kingdom'.[136] The *iter regis* of 1065 was presumably intended to secure the loyalty of the German and Burgundian kingdoms, especially those regions that seldom saw their king. This, in the opinion of Adalbert of Bremen, was a more important consideration than the Italian *iter* and the imperial coronation desired by Anno of Cologne and the reform papacy. The German *iter* served to consolidate Adalbert's regime, while an Italian expedition might have undermined his influence. This preoccupation with strengthening the government in Germany is also apparent in two appointments made by the king in 1065. Firstly, on the death of Duke Frederick of Lower Lotharingia, the king granted the duchy to Godfrey 'the Bearded' of Verdun (October 1065), who henceforward combined the office of duke with that of margrave of Tuscany.[137] Secondly, the bishopric of Worms was conferred on Adalbero, monk of St Gallen, whom the chronicler Lampert regarded as utterly unsuitable: lame, 'excessively gluttonous and so fat as to inspire horror rather than wonder in those who saw him'. Adalbero, however, possessed one important qualification to which he owed his bishopric: he was

---

[134] Meyer von Knonau (1890) 1:443 n. 96.
[135] *D H IV* 155. See Meyer von Knonau (1890) 1:443–4.
[136] *D H IV* 156. See Meyer von Knonau (1890) 1:444–5; Gawlik (1970a) 36; Scheibelreiter (1973) 9–15. See above p. 8.
[137] Meyer von Knonau (1890) 1:470–3; Mohr (1976) 2:41. See above p. 32.

the brother of Rudolf of Rheinfelden, duke of Swabia.[138] In both cases the appointment was made to obtain the goodwill of a powerful prince for the regime of Adalbert of Bremen. Adalbert (according to his biographer) disdained to use his influence to promote his own kinsmen to high office, like the low-born Anno of Cologne, but he was clearly prepared to influence royal appointments to safeguard his position at court. Since both Godfrey 'the Bearded' and Rudolf of Rheinfelden were regarded as allies by Anno,[139] it is possible that these appointments were intended by Adalbert to isolate his rival.

Further measures taken by Adalbert to neutralise opposition were summarised by the Weissenburg annalist. Adalbert, 'a wicked man', 'among the very many evils which he perpetrated, caused abbacies, provostships and everything that he could extract from the houses of the saints, to be delivered to the supporters of his iniquity through the king's hands. In addition he claimed for himself the two abbeys of Corvey and Lorsch.'[140] Lampert's chronicle gives a more detailed account, according to which Adalbert's only close associate in government was Count Werner, 'a young man inclined to wildness as much by his temperament as by his age' and a confidant of the king. 'These two governed in the place of the king: they sold bishoprics and abbeys, ecclesiastical and secular dignities.'[141] Lampert cited the example of a bishop appointed through Werner's influence: his 'kinsman' (probably his brother-in-law) Werner II of Strasbourg.[142] Adalbert and his ally seized the estates of monasteries and conferred them on their adherents or used them for the king's service. 'Then, as their audacity grew, they began to attack the monasteries themselves and shared them out between them like provinces, the king agreeing to all their demands with childish eagerness.' The imperial abbeys, those abbeys founded by the German kings and emperors, had since Ottonian times enjoyed the royal privilege of 'freedom' (*libertas*): royal protection, conferring immunity from the interference of secular officials and the right to elect their own abbot. They were also regarded, however, as 'proprietary monasteries', at the king's disposal and among the assets of the crown.[143] Adalbert obtained for himself the imperial abbeys of Lorsch and Corvey, declaring 'that this was a reward for his fidelity and devotion to the king'. 'Lest this should arouse the envy of the other princes of the kingdom, he persuaded the king to give the archbishop of Cologne two [abbeys], Malmédy and Cornelimünster, the arch-

[138] Lampert, *Annales* 1065, 1070, pp. 100, 117. See Meyer von Knonau (1890) 1:469–70; Jakobs (1968) 160–1; Zielinski (1984) 43.   [139] Anno, letters: von Giesebrecht (1890) 1257–9.

[140] *Annales Weissenburgenses* 1066, p. 53.

[141] Lampert, *Annales* 1063 (*sic*), pp. 88–90. See Meyer von Knonau (1890) 1:484–5; Tellenbach (1988) 358.

[142] Lampert, *Annales* 1065, p. 93. See Meyer von Knonau (1890) 1:486; Zielinski (1984) 58.

[143] Szabó-Bechstein (1985) 78–101; Seibert (1991) 503–69; and below pp. 354–5.

bishop of Mainz one in Seligenstadt, Duke Otto of Bavaria one in Niederaltaich and Duke Rudolf of Swabia one in Kempten.'[144] Lampert's account is incomplete. A series of royal diplomas of summer and autumn 1065 record similar grants: Polling to Bishop Altwin of Brixen, Benediktbeuren to Bishop Ellenhard of Freising, St Lambert and Limburg an der Haardt (founded by Emperor Conrad II on Salian family land) to Bishop Einhard of Speyer. Two further grants can be reconstructed from other sources: Vilich to Anno of Cologne and Rheinau to Bishop Rumold of Constance.[145] These donations were accompanied by the alienation of many of the crown's richest estates. The king's father and grandfather had also been generous in reward-ing their faithful adherents, such generosity being an indispensable attribute of kingship; but the lands given away by Conrad II and Henry III were in most cases estates newly acquired by the crown, which the king could afford to regrant without impoverishing himself. The royal estates which Henry IV granted in 1065 to the churches of Verdun, Naumburg and Speyer and to Anno of Cologne's new monastic foundation of Siegburg were long-standing possessions of the crown.[146]

In 1065, therefore, the crown's income was depleted in favour of certain secular and ecclesiastical princes. According to Lampert, this was the work of Archbishop Adalbert (who appeared as intervener in most of the relevant royal diplomas) and his intention was to reconcile the princes to the gains of the church of Bremen. These extensive gains[147] were the culmination of a series of acquisitions which began in the first year of the reign and increased in fre-quency as soon as Adalbert established himself at court in 1063. In these years Adalbert acquired all the counties in his archdiocese of Bremen, except the Frisian counties, and a number of counties in the dioceses of Münster, Osnabrück and Verden. The royal donations of 1063, like those of 1065, included jurisdiction over extensive tracts of forest and the right to impose tolls, mint coins and hold markets. Not the least significant of the acquisitions of 1063 was the royal estate of Lesum: with this donation Henry IV surren-dered the last royal property in the archdiocese of Bremen. Behind all these acquisitions the historian Adam of Bremen saw a coherent policy. Firstly, Adalbert planned to restore his church to its 'former freedom', that is, to the conditions of the archiepiscopate of Adaldag (937–88), who had obtained

---

[144] Lampert, *Annales* 1065, pp. 89–90.

[145] *D H IV* 101, 155, 164, 166, 165, 192; *Codex Laureshamensis* c. 123c, p. 392. See Meyer von Knonau (1890) 1:443–4, 462–3, 466–9; Seibert (1991) 537–50.

[146] *DD H IV* 140–1, 144, 162–3. See Stimming (1922) 83–5; Büttner (1952) 438.

[147] *DD H IV* 168–9, 172–3, 175; Adam, *Gesta* III.28, pp. 171–2. See Meyer von Knonau (1890) 1:474–8, 481–4; May (1937) 71–2 (nos. 309–10, 313–14, 316): Glaeske (1962) 71–2, 91; Johanek (1991) 100–3.

from Emperor Otto I the privilege 'that no duke or count or any judicial officer should have any jurisdiction or power in his bishopric'. Adalbert wished to imitate the success of the bishop of Würzburg, who alone among contemporary bishops enjoyed a monopoly of secular as well as spiritual authority in his bishopric, 'since he himself [held] all the counties of his diocese'.[148] This was what Adalbert meant by 'the freedom of the church', using that expression in the sense in which it was understood by the eleventh-century imperial episcopate: the immunity of a particular church from all secular jurisdiction. Secondly, Adalbert aimed to build up the territorial possessions of his church, which had been seriously diminished during the archiepiscopate of Unwan (1013–29) in disputes between the archbishop and the noble clans of the archdiocese. The feud with the greatest of the Saxon families, the Billungs, continued throughout Adalbert's archiepiscopate. Since the beginning of the century the Billungs had striven to extend their authority within the duchy, only to be thwarted by the parallel strivings of Saxon bishops, with imperial support, to free their churches from secular jurisdiction. The Billungs' feud with the archbishop of Bremen was the bitterest of these confrontations and explains Adalbert's constant attendance at court, even when his absence from his archdiocese tempted the Billungs to new acts of aggression. His influence over the king was Adalbert's most effective weapon against the Billungs, enabling him to conduct the feud from the safety of the court. When, for example, Count Herman Billung attacked Bremen in revenge for the archbishop's refusal to grant him a benefice, Adalbert obtained from the king a judgement against the Billungs and Duke Ordulf Billung was obliged to offer fifty hides of land to be reconciled with the archbishop.[149] The king's generosity, expressed in eleven diplomas of the years 1057–65, served to protect Bremen from 'the wicked power of the dukes', 'to restore the church to its former freedom' and (in the diplomas of autumn 1065) to enrich it with royal property outside the archdiocese.[150]

Adalbert 'had now pushed his rivals aside and he alone possessed the citadel of power', wrote Adam of Bremen. 'Our metropolitan, aiming to renew the golden age during his term of government, is said to have planned to remove from the city of God all those who practised iniquity and especially those who had laid hands on the king or were seen to have plundered the churches. Since nearly all the bishops and princes of the kingdom were

---

[148] Adam, *Gesta* III.5, 46, pp. 146–7, 188.

[149] *Ibid.* III.44–5, pp. 186–7; cf. III.5, p. 147. See Meyer von Knonau (1890) 1:421; Glaeske (1962) 86–91; Fenske (1977) 25–6, 64; Althoff (1991) 326–8. See also below p. 69.

[150] *DD H IV* 18, 103, 112–13, 115; Adam, *Gesta* III.5, 46, pp. 146–7, 188–9. See Meyer von Knonau (1890) 1:36–7, 335–6, 356–8, 421–3; May (1937) 59–60, 65–7 (nos. 250, 271, 280–2); Glaeske (1962) 65–7, 89–90; Johanek (1991) 90–7.

conscious of having committed these offences, they conspired against him, united by their hatred.'[151] Adalbert's biographer thus accounted for the conspiracy of princes that expelled the archbishop from the king's counsels at an assembly in Tribur in January 1066, devising an explanation consistent with his idealised interpretation of Adalbert's conduct in government. All the other narrative sources, however, attribute the archbishop's fall to his 'tyranny', his exclusive hold on power and his rapacious attacks on the property of the crown. They mention in particular Adalbert's acquisition of the abbey of Lorsch and his plans to overcome the resistance of the monks of Lorsch during the winter of 1065–6. According to Lampert of Hersfeld, the principal conspirators of January 1066 were Siegfried of Mainz and Anno of Cologne, 'together with others who were concerned for the good of the commonwealth'.[152] These fellow-conspirators probably included Archbishop Gebhard of Salzburg and the dukes Otto of Bavaria, Rudolf of Swabia and Berthold of Carinthia, who are known to have been present in Tribur when the conspirators struck.[153] Lampert's account of Adalbert's fall is the most detailed but is not corroborated by any other author. He claimed that the princes themselves summoned the assembly of Tribur and there confronted the king with the demand 'that he should either abdicate from the kingship or remove the archbishop of Bremen from his counsels and from his share in the government of the kingdom'. Uncertain how to respond to this ultimatum, the king was advised by Adalbert to 'flee the following night secretly, taking with him the royal insignia, and go to Goslar or to some other place where he would be safe from attack, until this storm was over'. That evening Adalbert himself attempted to carry the royal treasure away with him, but his design was somehow betrayed to the king's servants, who maintained an armed watch around the king's residence all night and thwarted Adalbert's plans. 'In the morning everyone was so enraged against the archbishop that they would have laid hands on him, had not the royal majesty with the greatest difficulty restrained them.' Adalbert was ignominiously driven from the court, the king allowing him 'a considerable band of his friends, lest he should be ambushed on the road by his enemies'.[154] According to the short and sober account of the Weissenburg annals, the conspirators 'exhorted the king in Tribur to cancel whatever had been enacted on the advice of the [arch]bishop and to have done with him'. When Henry acquiesced in this demand, Adalbert 'fled by night, no one pursuing him'.[155] When Adalbert realised his total isolation, despite all his attempts to win allies by means of

---

[151] Adam, *Gesta* III.47, pp. 190–1.   [152] Lampert, *Annales* 1066, p. 101.

[153] Anno, letter: von Giesebrecht (1890) 1258.   [154] Lampert, *Annales* 1066, pp. 100–2.

[155] *Annales Weissenburgenses* 1066, p. 53. Cf. *Codex Laureshamensis* c. 124, p. 394. See Meyer von Knonau (1890) 1:487–9; Jenal (1974) 303–6.

royal patronage, he saw that his friendship with the king could no longer assist him and he gave up hope of clinging to power.

Lampert's chronicle is the only source to suggest that Henry IV himself was in danger in January 1066: that the princes called on him to renounce either throne or favourite. This was a threat of great political and constitutional importance, reminiscent of the condition allegedly imposed by the princes at a previous assembly in Tribur, thirteen years before, when they promised to obey the three-year-old Henry as their future king 'if he was a just ruler'.[156] According to Lampert, the princes in 1066 contemplated the removal of the king if, by retaining Adalbert as his adviser, he failed to conform to their notion of a just ruler. There is good reason to believe, however, that Lampert's story was a polemical exaggeration. He composed his chronicle in the mid-1070s, when a faction of princes was indeed planning Henry IV's deposition. An important theme of his chronicle is that Henry deserved to lose his throne because he behaved like a tyrant rather than a just king, preferring evil counsellors to good ones. It suited Lampert's polemical presentation of Henry to introduce this theme into his account of Adalbert's fall.[157] Nevertheless, even if the conspirators did not contemplate the forced abdication of the king in January 1066, they certainly succeeded in compelling him to dismiss his principal adviser. Already in the first year of his majority Henry IV was faced with the demand that the personnel and methods of his government conform to the standards expected by the princes.

Four months after Adalbert's fall the princes in real earnest 'began to confer about the succession to the throne', not because of any conspiracy to depose Henry IV, but because of the king's serious illness. In the middle of May, while he was staying in Fritzlar, Henry fell sick 'so that the physicians gave up all hope of his survival and certain princes had hopes of seizing the royal throne'. By Whitsun (4 June), however, Henry had recovered, disappointing 'the greedy ravens' who coveted his crown.[158] Soon after his recovery Henry was married to the princess to whom he had been betrothed in 1055, Bertha, daughter of Count Otto of Savoy and Margravine Adelaide of Turin.[159] The royal wedding in the summer of 1066 was presumably intended to allay the widespread anxiety caused by the threat of the king's death and the uncertainty of the succession. A royal diploma issued in Tribur on 13 July 1066 introduces the queen as intervener with the words: 'we have lawfully associated Queen

---

[156] See above p. 21.   [157] Meyer von Knonau (1894) 2:810–11; Struve (1970) 33–139.

[158] Lampert, *Annales* 1066, p. 103; *Annales Altahenses* 1066, pp. 71–2. See Meyer von Knonau (1890) 1:522–5.

[159] In Tribur (Lampert, *Annales* 1066, pp. 103–4) or Ingelheim (*Annales Altahenses* 1066, p. 72). See Meyer von Knonau (1890) 1:525–6. Bertha was crowned queen in Würzburg before being married in Tribur.

Bertha with us in the kingship'.[160] The language of the diplomas, like the double ceremony of coronation and marriage, underlines the importance of the queen's constitutional position. She was married to both king and kingdom. In the diplomas of 1066–7 Bertha is described as 'consort of our kingdom and of our marriage-bed' and similar formulas appear in the diplomas of later years. Henry IV's mother had been identified by a similar formula in her husband's diplomas, as had his grandmother, Gisela, and likewise the last two empresses of the Ottonian dynasty, Theophanu and Cunigunde. The '*consors* formula' in Ottonian and Salian diplomas, by associating the monarch's consort with her husband's office and dignity, served to concentrate political authority exclusively in the imperial family. The wife of the present monarch and mother of his successor, as 'consort of the kingdom', was the guarantor of dynastic continuity, participating in government on her husband's behalf or ruling as regent in the event of his premature death, as Empress Agnes had ruled between 1056 and 1062.[161]

The royal marriage underlined the fact that the king was now of age and master in his own house. The banished Adalbert of Bremen was not succeeded by a similar overmighty counsellor. After January 1066 Adalbert was totally preoccupied with his feud with the Billungs, emboldened now by the archbishop's disgrace and determined to avenge the injuries that he had recently inflicted on them.[162] His old rival, Anno of Cologne, who had played a major role in the conspiracy of January 1066, regained a place in the king's counsels, but he was never to recover the dominant role of the two years following the abduction at Kaiserswerth. Henry IV never again allowed a single adviser to secure a monopoly of influence at court. During the later 1060s Henry began the work of restoring the authority and replenishing the wealth of the crown. The encroachment of the princes on the material resources of the crown was a consistent theme of the king's minority, culminating in the distribution of the imperial abbeys in 1065. How the authority of the monarchy had diminished in this same period is apparent from an incident at the royal court in Goslar on the eve of Whitsunday (7 June) 1063: the fight between the adherents of the abbot of Fulda and those of the bishop of Hildesheim in the presence of the king. Widerad of Fulda claimed the right, by virtue of 'a custom observed in the kingdom for many generations', to sit in the place of honour next to the archbishop of Mainz, but his claim was contested by the diocesan, Hezilo of Hildesheim. During the vesper service in the church of SS. Simon and Jude, Goslar, an armed struggle broke out, in which the king's cousin, Count Ekbert I of Brunswick, sided with Hezilo,

---

[160] *D H IV* 181.   [161] Vogelsang (1954) 40–1; Gawlik (1970a) 189–91.
[162] Adam, *Gesta* III.48–9, pp. 191–3. See Meyer von Knonau (1890) 1:513–16 and below p. 69.

and there were many casualties. 'The king, raising his voice and adjuring the people by the royal majesty, seemed to be speaking to the deaf.' He was persuaded by his servants to withdraw to the safety of the palace.[163] This remarkable incident – the violation of a religious service in the king's presence in a church so closely linked to the Salian dynasty; the inability of the king to restore the peace of which he was the principal guardian – illustrates how respect for 'the royal majesty' had declined in the aftermath of the abduction at Kaiserswerth. The first decade of Henry IV's personal rule was to witness the most energetic efforts to build up the authority and the material resources of the monarchy.

[163] Lampert, *Annales* 1063, pp. 81–3. See Meyer von Knonau (1890) 1:328–31, 664–8; Leyser (1979) 97; Franke (1987) 162–4; Struve (1987) 326; Vogtherr (1991) 445–6.

2

Henry IV and Saxony, 1065–1075

From the time of the young king's assumption of personal control of the government until the outbreak of the conflict with the papacy in 1076, Henry IV's main concern was with eastern Saxony. In the later 1060s and early 1070s the king stayed with unprecedented frequency in his palace of Goslar and the royal presence involved an intensification of governmental activity in the region. Grievances against the royal government provoked rebellions by individual princes in 1069 and 1070 and a much more formidable rebellion of the east Saxon and Thuringian nobility in 1073–5. There is evidence of Saxon dissatisfaction with the Salian regime, however, even before Henry IV's accession, although not on the scale of the rebellion of 1073. Henry III had aroused the suspicions of the princes by his frequent visits to Goslar and by his generosity to Saxon bishops. The fear that the emperor intended to undermine the standing of the princes provoked the unsuccessful assassination attempt by Count Thietmar Billung, brother of Duke Bernard II of Saxony, in 1047.[1] On 10 September 1056, a month before the emperor's death, the regime suffered a serious defeat, threatening the security of eastern Saxony. Margrave William of the Saxon Nordmark was killed 'together with an infinite multitude of the Saxon army' in an encounter with the Slav confederation of the Liutizi. This setback, with its resultant loss of prestige and credibility, may have inspired the conspiracy of 1057 reported by the chronicler Lampert of Hersfeld. The Saxon princes 'in frequent secret meetings' debated 'the injuries which had been inflicted on them under the emperor' and plotted to 'seize the kingship from his son, while he was still at an age when such a wrong could be perpetrated; for they believed that the son would follow in his father's footsteps both in his character and in his way of life'. The ringleader was Otto, illegitimate half-brother of William of the Nordmark, who had lived most of his life in exile in Bohemia. Otto returned to Germany to claim the inheritance and office of his half-brother, but was persuaded by the Saxon conspirators to

---

[1] Adam of Bremen, *Gesta* III.8, pp. 148–9. See Freytag (1951) 17–18, 68–9; Fenske (1977) 19–20; Althoff (1991) 309, 319–20.

depose the boy-king and take his place. This crisis was resolved when the conspirators were attacked by Henry IV's kinsmen, the counts Ekbert and Bruno of Brunswick, acting both in the public interest and in pursuit of a personal vendetta. In a bloody skirmish Bruno and Otto inflicted mortal wounds on each other: 'Thus the commonwealth was delivered from the greatest danger and, once deprived of the standardbearer of the rebellion, the Saxons attempted no further hostilities against the king.' [2]

For the rest of Henry IV's minority indeed there is no report of a plot against the crown. The first Saxon rebellion occurred four years after Henry's coming of age. This was the vendetta that Margrave Dedi I of Lower Lusatia and his stepson-in-law Count Adalbert of Ballenstedt waged against the king in 1069 in support of territorial claims in east Saxony. Dedi, a prince of the Saxon house of Wettin, had married the Lotharingian princess Adela of Louvain, widow of Margrave Otto of Meissen, and simultaneously laid claim to the benefices held by Margrave Otto, the last male descendant of the comital family of Weimar-Orlamünde. When the claim proved unsuccessful, Dedi and Adalbert rebelled against the king, whom they regarded as responsible for their failure.[3] Lampert's account of the rising introduces an important theme of the Saxon rebellions: the grievances of the Thuringians. Dedi 'held frequent talks with the Thuringians to draw them into a military alliance. For he hoped that the king had lost their sympathy by the support which he had given to the archbishop [of Mainz] in his demand for tithes.' Dedi tried to broaden the scope of his rebellion by exploiting the contentious issue of Thuringian tithes. During the 1060s Archbishop Siegfried of Mainz sought to reimpose the payment of tithes to his church by the laity of Thuringia. He aimed to bring to an end the 'Thuringian freedom from tithes': the exemption enjoyed since the ninth century by all the nobility and peasantry of Thuringia, except for those holding land directly from the king, the archbishop or the abbeys of Fulda and Hersfeld. Siegfried easily enlisted the support of Pope Alexander II, since the reform papacy was dedicated to restoring the ancient rights of churches and to eradicating such 'evil customs' as the ninth-century tithes exemption. Siegfried's first opportunity to demand his rights had occurred in 1062, when Otto of Meissen succeeded to the office of his brother, Margrave William. Many of the lands of the late margrave were benefices held of the archbishop of Mainz. He could be enfeoffed with these 'only by promising to pay tithes of his possessions in Thuringia and to force the rest of the Thuringians to do the same'. When, on Otto's death in 1067,

---

[2] Lampert of Hersfeld, *Annales* 1057, pp. 71–2. See Meyer von Knonau (1890) 1:39–41; Brüske (1955) 78; Fenske (1977) 23–4; Giese (1979) 149–50.

[3] Lampert, *Annales* 1069, pp. 106–7. See Meyer von Knonau (1890) 1:617–23; Fenske (1977) 23–4.

Dedi of Lower Lusatia married his widow and laid claim to his benefices, he presumably encountered the same response from Siegfried of Mainz. This may have inspired his strategy of making common cause with the Thuringians.[4] According to Lampert (whose abbey of Hersfeld had the keenest interest in Siegfried's proceedings), 'all the Thuringians . . . declared that they preferred to die rather than to lose the rights of their forefathers'. The archbishop therefore secured the support of Henry IV for his claims. The scene was apparently set for a Thuringian rebellion. Instead, however, the Thuringians offered the king their help against Dedi, if in return he would protect their rights. Henry (according to Lampert) promised his protection and so gained a free hand to deal with the rebels. The king led an army into Thuringia and captured Dedi's castles of Beichlingen and Burgscheidungen, leaving the rebels no choice but to submit. Dedi was 'held for some time in prison' and 'deprived of no small part of his possessions and revenues'.[5]

In the following year there occurred a similar rising, involving the most formidable of the Saxon princes, Otto of Northeim. The count of Northeim, who since 1061 had been duke of Bavaria and a prominent figure at the royal court, suddenly fell from power in 1070, for reasons that remain obscure. In the later 1060s Otto had consolidated his hold over Bavaria with the help of the influential Welf family, whose head, Welf IV, married Otto's daughter, Ethelinde. During these years Otto was trusted by the king and cooperated closely with him. In 1068 he negotiated on the king's behalf with the princes of northern Italy; early in 1069 he accompanied Henry on a campaign against the Liutizi. After the successful conclusion of this campaign Otto remained in the royal entourage in Saxony. The following summer the king visited Otto's duchy and stayed in the principal Bavarian city of Regensburg.[6] This cooperation suggests that Henry harboured no suspicions about the duke, which makes all the more puzzling the charge of high treason brought against Otto soon after Whitsun (23 May) 1070. The charge was brought by 'a certain Egeno', whose identity has never been more precisely established. The chronicler Lampert called him 'a nobleman, but infamous for every kind of wickedness', who lived by theft and highway-robbery.[7] In 1070 Egeno accused Otto of Northeim of having suborned him to murder the king. According to the chronicler of Niederaltaich, a royalist sympathiser who believed Otto to be guilty, early in 1069 Otto invited Henry to visit one of his estates in Saxony.

[4] Lampert, *Annales* 1069, p. 107; cf. 1062, p. 79; Alexander II, *JL* 4577: *Mainzer Urkundenbuch* I, 201 (no. 313). See Jäschke (1963–4) 279–82; Fenske (1977) 36.
[5] Lampert, *Annales* 1069, p. 108. See Meyer von Knonau (1890) 1:622–3.
[6] *Annales Altahenses* 1069, pp. 76, 77. See Meyer von Knonau (1894) 1:586, 589–90, 610; Brüske (1955) 84; Lange (1961) 25–31.
[7] Lampert, *Annales* 1070, 1072, 1073, pp. 113–14, 135, 172. See Fenske (1977) 92–4.

His intention was to kill the king: he had given Egeno a sword for this purpose, which the latter produced as evidence. After the king's entourage had retired for the night, the conspirators planned to attack the king's faithful servant, Cuno, who guarded the entrance to the king's bedchamber. The noise would bring the king from his chamber, allowing Egeno to run him through with the sword. In the event, however, Cuno and other royal servants easily overcame the attackers. Otto then conspired with eleven other princes of Saxony and Franconia to rise against the king, but only two of the princes, Dedi of Lower Lusatia and Adalbert of Ballenstedt, had openly rebelled. 'The rest pretended to keep faith with the king.'[8] The chronicler, therefore, linked Otto's alleged treason with the rebellion of 1069. No other source implicates Otto in that rebellion. Indeed Lampert's account supplies a detail that speaks against an alliance between Otto and Dedi in 1069. Otto was the close friend of the margrave's son, Dedi II, who during the rebellion of Dedi I 'attacked his father with a fiercer enmity than anyone else'. Otto gave Dedi II 'as a pledge of his undivided love' the famous 'sword of Attila', which the duke himself had received for his part in restoring Salomon to the throne of Hungary in 1063.[9]

The unusually detailed character of the Niederaltaich chronicler's account of the alleged assassination attempt suggests that he had obtained information about an affray during a royal visit to one of Otto's residences, a brawl during which the king's servant Cuno was attacked by servants of Duke Otto. Such a disturbance in the royal entourage was not an unprecedented event. The representation of this affray as an assassination attempt, however, was probably a later rationalisation by Otto's accuser, Egeno. The accusations against Otto of Northeim are unconvincing. He had indeed been involved in two previous conspiracies: the abduction of the king in 1062 and the expulsion of Adalbert of Bremen from the court in 1066. On both occasions Otto's motive, like that of his fellow-conspirators, had been to end the concentration of power in the hands of a single adviser and to secure for himself an important role in the king's counsels. The evidence for the years 1068–9 shows that he had achieved this object. It is difficult to understand how Otto's interests could have been served by the murder of the king, especially since the sources give no indication of whom Otto expected to succeed to the throne.[10] Otto of Northeim was not the only prominent political figure to be accused of plotting an assas-

[8] *Annales Altahenses* 1069, 1070, pp. 76–7, 79. Cf. Lampert, *Annales* 1070, pp. 113–14; Bruno of Merseburg, *Saxonicum bellum* c. 19, p. 25; *Annales sancti Disibodi* 1075, p. 6. See Meyer von Knonau (1894) 2:9–13; Lange (1961) 28–9.

[9] Lampert, *Annales* 1071, p. 130. See above p. 53.

[10] There is no suggestion that Otto (married to an Ezzonid) intended to exploit his wife's Ottonian descent to secure his own succession.

sination during the early 1070s. In 1072 Duke Rudolf of Swabia was similarly accused of planning to murder the king and in 1073 Henry IV himself was accused of plotting the murder of both Rudolf and Duke Berthold of Carinthia.[11] In both cases the accusation seems to have been a device for discrediting a political enemy and it is likely that the accusation against Otto of Northeim in 1070 was of a similar character.

The two principal historians of the Saxon war, Lampert of Hersfeld and Bruno of Merseburg, had no doubt of the innocence of Otto of Northeim, but offered different explanations of the false accusation. Bruno represented Otto as the victim of Henry IV, who bribed Egeno 'with money and promises' to allege 'that the duke had plotted with him the death of the king'. The king feared that Otto would join his compatriots in resisting the extension of royal control over eastern Saxony and would use his position as duke of Bavaria to negotiate a Bavarian–Saxon alliance against the crown.[12] More probable, in view of the royal confidence that Otto enjoyed until the moment of Egeno's denunciation, is Lampert's interpretation of his downfall. Otto was envied by 'very many worthless men, who resented the fact that his power and immeasurable fame stood in the way of their wickedness'. These enemies 'carefully sought an opportunity to bring him down', employing Egeno for this purpose.[13] Later in his chronicle Lampert supplied the names of three of Otto's enemies. The first was the Swabian knight Liupold of Meersburg, 'very dear to the king, who was accustomed to rely most familiarly on his aid and advice'. Lampert recorded his accidental death in late July 1071, when the royal entourage was travelling from Hersfeld to Mainz. The king and his escort broke into a race, in the course of which Liupold was thrown from his horse and fell on his sword. This was the same 'sword of Attila' that Otto of Northeim had given to his friend, Dedi II, son of the margrave of Lower Lusatia. On Dedi II's death the sword had come into the hands of the king, who had given it to Liupold of Meersburg. 'Very many of Duke Otto's supporters interpreted as a divine judgement the fact that [Liupold] was killed by that sword which had once been Duke Otto's, since he was said to have been mainly responsible for urging the king to persecute [Otto] and drive him from the palace.'[14] Lampert thus identified the royal adviser Liupold as Otto's principal enemy at court. He identified Otto's principal enemies in Saxony as 'Count Giso and Adalbert' (perhaps Count Giso of Gudensberg and Count Adalbert of Schauenburg), 'at whose instigation the accursed [Egeno] invented that tragic story' of Otto's assassination plot. Giso and Adalbert died

[11] See below pp. 92, 93, 125–6, 359–60.
[12] Bruno, *Saxonicum bellum* c. 19, p. 25. Cf. the Saxon polemic preserved in the early twelfth-century *Annales s. Disibodi* 1075, p. 6.   [13] Lampert, *Annales* 1070, p. 113.
[14] *Ibid.* 1071, p. 130. See Schmid (1984a) 247–9; Tellenbach (1988) 357–8. See also below p. 359.

in a vendetta in 1073 and 'God thus declared the innocence of Duke Otto'.[15] It is not clear whether Liupold of Meersburg was a party to the plot of Giso and Adalbert or whether, acting independently of the Saxon conspirators, he seized the opportunity presented by the false accusation of Egeno. Presumably the grievance of Giso and Adabert against Otto related to Saxon local politics, while Liupold's motive was to increase his own influence at court by ousting a rival for royal favour.

The keen interest of Lampert and the Niederaltaich chronicler in the judicial proceedings against Otto of Northeim make this one of the best-documented political trials of the central Middle Ages. Otto was first confronted with Egeno's accusations in an assembly of princes in Mainz in mid-June 1070. A nobleman faced with a charge of treason could clear himself by fighting a judicial duel against his accuser. Otto, therefore, 'was ordered . . . to come to Goslar . . . and purge himself of that charge in single combat in the presence of the king and the princes'. On the appointed day, 1 August 1070, Otto appeared in the neighbourhood of Goslar with an armed following, but kept away from the scene of the trial and began to negotiate with the king through messengers. According to Bruno of Merseburg, 'Otto was warned by his friends among the bishops and other princes that if he came to Goslar, where the duel was to be fought, he would never escape with his life even if he defeated his adversary.' The suspicions of Otto's friends were probably justified. Given the likelihood that the treason charge was a fabrication and the evidence of the hostility of the influential Liupold of Meersburg, it is likely that the judicial duel was a trap from which Otto was not intended to escape. The duke returned to his estates in eastern Saxony, 'thinking it better to take up arms to defend himself as long as he could, than to be basely slaughtered . . . to satisfy the hatred of his enemies'.[16] Otto's departure laid him open to the charge of contumacy, that is, wilful contempt of the king's justice. There was disagreement among the princes attending the trial: some wished to pursue the duke immediately as a criminal, but Otto's friends secured a postponement of the judgement. On 2 August Otto was judged in his absence according to Saxon law. The princes judged Otto guilty of treason and outlawed him: 'they decreed that if he was captured, the death sentence was to be enacted'. He was deprived of his benefices and his duchy of Bavaria, which returned to the crown. The first to exploit Otto's outlawry were 'the king's friends', who 'immediately began to pursue him with fire and sword'.[17] (These

[15] Lampert, *Annales* 1073, p. 172. See Meyer von Knonau (1894) 2:11 n. 23.

[16] *Annales Altahenses* 1070, p. 79; Bruno, *Saxonicum bellum* c. 19, p. 25. Lampert, *Annales* 1070, pp. 113–14, alone claimed that Otto failed to stand trial because the king refused to grant him a safe-conduct. See Meyer von Knonau (1894) 2:14–18; Mitteis (1927) 34–5; Höss (1945) 19; Lange (1961) 33–7.   [17] *Annales Altahenses* 1070, p. 79; Lampert, *Annales* 1070, pp. 114–15.

'king's friends' were presumably the royal advisers who had resented Otto's influence at court, notably Liupold of Meersburg.) Henry IV himself lost no time in gathering an army and spent the rest of August laying waste Otto's east Saxon estates. Otto, the Northeim family and their vassals regarded the king's proceedings not as the execution of a judicial sentence but as unprovoked aggression. In such a case the house of Northeim considered itself justified in pursuing a vendetta against the crown. Otto raised a formidable army with which he attacked the crown lands in Thuringia, distributing the plunder among his knights and the peasants from his estates, who had been reduced to poverty by the recent depredations of the king's army.[18] The Thuringian nobility, led by Count Ruotger of Bilstein,[19] defended their territory against these inroads, but were heavily defeated by Otto's army near Eschwege on 2 September 1070.

Otto's principal confederate in his feud with the king was Magnus Billung, son of Ordulf Billung, duke of Saxony. During the winter of 1070–1 Otto used Magnus's estates as his base. The princes remained close allies until in June 1071 they were finally compelled to submit to the king. The sources offer no explanation of Magnus's involvement in Otto's vendetta. The background to Magnus's rebellion was that alienation of the Billungs from the crown which is intermittently mentioned in the eleventh-century Saxon sources. A major factor in this development was Billung resentment of the favour that the monarchy showed to the imperial Church in Saxony, especially the church of Bremen. Archbishop Adalbert of Bremen used his influence at the court of Henry III and Henry IV to free the patrimony of his church from the control of the local nobility, particularly the Billungs, a strategy which could easily draw the king into the feud between archbishop and princes. Duke Ordulf Billung and his brother, Count Herman Billung, exploited the opportunity presented by the death of Henry III and the minority of Henry IV to force Adalbert to surrender to them benefices of the church of Bremen. In 1063, however, when Adalbert was once more an influential royal adviser, a judgement of the king's court punished the Billungs and compensated the church of Bremen.[20] The Billungs exacted a heavy revenge when, in January 1066, Adalbert fell from power at the Salian court. The archbishop's principal persecutor was the young Magnus Billung, who extorted from the church of Bremen benefices amounting to 1,000 hides in return for a promise to leave Adalbert in peace.[21] It was not long, however, before Adalbert's political fortunes changed again: already in 1069 he seems to have resumed his role of royal

---

[18] Lampert, *Annales* 1070, pp. 115–17; *Annales Altahenses* 1070, pp. 79–80. See Meyer von Knonau (1894) 2:19–22.   [19] Eckhardt (1964) 67, 97; Fenske (1977) 80–1, 254.

[20] Adam, *Gesta* II.48, III.41–5, pp. 108–9, 184–7. See Freytag (1951) 16–21; Glaeske (1962) 42, 86–92; Fenske (1977) 18–20, 64; Althoff (1991) 319–22.   [21] Adam, *Gesta* III.49, pp. 191–2.

adviser.[22] Perhaps it was Adalbert's recovery of influence at court, threatening the gains of the Billungs, that prompted the rebellion of Magnus Billung in 1070. Significantly, while the Billung heir rebelled against the crown, his father Duke Ordulf remained loyal to Henry IV.[23] Magnus rejected his father's conciliatory attitude, presumably believing that conciliation would not avert the threat to Billung influence in Saxony. Pride in his family's greatness may have been the factor that dominated Magnus's political conduct. He was the heir of the oldest ducal family in the kingdom, whose ancestors had been dukes of Saxony since 936. He also had royal blood: his mother was the Norwegian princess Wulfhilde, daughter of King Olaf II and sister of King Magnus of Norway. Magnus Billung himself contracted a royal marriage. During his rebellion of 1070–1 he married Sophia, daughter of the late King Bela I and sister of King Geisa of Hungary, the bitter opponents of the Salian monarchs.[24]

According to Lampert's account of the rebellion, the rebel victory at Eschwege so perturbed the king that he abandoned his campaign and withdrew to Goslar, where he remained throughout the autumn and winter of 1070–1. He feared to leave Goslar 'lest in his absence his enemies reduced that town, so dear and pleasing to him . . . to ashes and cinders'.[25] Meanwhile he took a decisive step to isolate Otto of Northeim and secure his own position. During the Christmas festivities of 1070 he conferred the duchy of Bavaria on Otto's son-in-law, Welf IV. This powerful and ambitious prince, founder of the younger line of the Welf dynasty, was the son of an Italian father, Margrave Adalbert Azzo II of Este, and a German mother, Cuniza (daughter of Count Welf II and sister of Welf III, duke of Carinthia). On the extinction of the older Welf line with the death of Welf III in 1055, the latter's mother, Countess Imiza (widow of Welf II) invited her grandson, Welf IV, to lay claim to his uncle's inheritance in southern Germany. After securing control of the extensive Welf patrimony in Swabia and Bavaria, Welf IV became the ally of the duke of Bavaria, Otto of Northeim, and married his daughter, Ethelinde.[26] When Otto was disgraced in 1070, however, Welf IV rapidly distanced himself from his ally. He sent Ethelinde back to her father and took a new bride, who was not only of illustrious birth but also fabulously wealthy: Judith, daughter of Count Baldwin V of Flanders and widow of Earl Tostig of Northumbria. Since Welf 'did not care how much gold and silver and how much of his rev-

---

[22] See below pp. 85–6.

[23] *Gesta episcoporum Halberstadensium*, p. 96. See Meyer von Knonau (1894) 2:69 n. 59.

[24] Meyer von Knonau (1894) 2:34, 70.   [25] Lampert, *Annales* 1070, p. 117.

[26] *Ibid.* 1071, p. 118; *Annales Altahenses* 1071, p. 80; *Genealogia Welfonum* c. 8, p. 734; *Historia Welfonum Weingartensis* c. 10, 13, pp. 461, 462. See Meyer von Knonau (1894) 2:24–6; Fleckenstein (1957) 71–136; Störmer (1991) 516–17.

enues and possessions he wasted in acquiring [Otto's] duchy' from the king, this marriage served to reimburse him for the acquisition of his expensive dignity. For Henry IV, Welf IV's appointment was not only a profitable transaction but also a shrewd blow against Otto of Northeim, whose hold on Bavaria had been so much strengthened by his alliance with Welf. According to Lampert, it was 'through the intervention of Rudolf, duke of the Swabians' that Welf obtained the duchy.[27] This is the earliest reference to the alliance between Rudolf of Rheinfelden and Welf IV, which was to be of central importance in German politics during the 1070s. Rudolf's involvement in the appointment of the new duke of Bavaria suggests that he was as determined to exclude Otto of Northeim from power as the king himself. Perhaps Rudolf had been one of the enemies who secured Otto's downfall in 1070: certainly he became an influential royal adviser in the aftermath of Otto's disgrace.

Early in 1071 Henry IV planned a journey to Bavaria to install the new duke in his office, but he was detained in Goslar by news of the rebels' approach. Otto entered northern Hesse and garrisoned the fortress of Hasungen, intending that his feud with the king should be decided by a pitched battle. In the event, however, the rebellion ended in a negotiated settlement. The rebels failed to attract the support of other Saxon princes, who instead rallied to the king and defended Goslar, allowing Henry to visit Bavaria. This setback, together with the demoralisation of the rebels by the royal army's war of attrition, predisposed Otto to surrender. His submission was negotiated by the royal adviser Count Eberhard 'the Bearded', who promised Otto a reexamination of his case by the princes. On Whitsunday (12 June) in Halberstadt the king received the submission of Otto and Magnus Billung and placed them in the custody of the princes.[28] During the spring of 1071 Otto had become reconciled with Archbishop Adalbert of Bremen, now fully restored to influence at court. Adalbert forgave Otto his part in the conspiracy against him in January 1066 and agreed to mediate on Otto's behalf. 'During the celebration of mass [Adalbert] did not cease to plead for [Otto] until he had obtained the king's grace for him to possess his allodial lands in full, but he lost the greatest part of the vast benefices that he had held.'[29] Adalbert could afford to be generous, for Magnus Billung's submission enabled him to recover the lands of the church of Bremen that had been extorted from him.

It was Magnus Billung, who had played only a secondary role in the rebellion, who bore the brunt of the royal government's displeasure. While Otto of

---

[27] Lampert, *Annales* 1071, p. 118.

[28] *Ibid.* p. 119; Bruno, *Saxonicum bellum* c. 99, 102, pp. 90, 91–2. See Meyer von Knonau (1894) 2:42–4, 70; Lange (1961) 42.

[29] *Annales Altahenses* 1071, pp. 81–2. Cf. Lampert, *Annales* 1071, p. 127; Adam, *Gesta* III.60, p. 206. See Meyer von Knonau (1894) 2:70.

Northeim was released from prison at Whitsun (27 May) 1072, Magnus continued to be held prisoner in the royal fortress of Harzburg. The loyalty that Ordulf Billung had shown the king won no remission for his son. When Ordulf died on 28 March 1072, the king showed no sign of releasing or recognising Magnus as the heir to his father's title and possessions.[30] The harsh treatment of the Billungs presumably represented Adalbert's revenge for the humiliations of the late 1060s. The chroniclers Lampert and Bruno, however, interpreted it as an attempt by the crown to destroy the Billung lordship in Saxony. They attached particular importance to the secret meeting of Henry IV and Adalbert with King Swein Estrithson of Denmark in Lüneburg, in the heart of Billung territory, during the summer of 1071. The purpose of this meeting is not known: it was perhaps concerned with Swein's plans for the reorganisation of the Danish church or with military and missionary activity among their common neighbours, the Liutizi. Bruno and Lampert, however, believed that Henry IV himself had organised the meeting for his own sinister ends. 'The king of the Danes swore to King Henry that he would bring what help he could by land and sea against [Henry's] enemies, and particularly against the Saxons, and King Henry promised to give him possession of all the regions bordering on his kingdom.'[31] Such a promise threatened the Billung lands in eastern Saxony. The king's refusal to release Magnus seemed to be an attempt to end the Billung hold on the duchy of Saxony. Lampert and Bruno cited as evidence of this intention the king's seizure of the Billung fortress of Lüneburg after Ordulf's death.[32] The polemical purpose of Lampert and Bruno makes them unreliable guides to Henry IV's intentions. What can be deduced from their accounts, however, is that the king's treatment of Magnus Billung in 1071–2 significantly worsened relations between the Saxon princes and the crown, intensifying the princes' suspicions of royal policy in eastern Saxony.

The accumulated anger of the east Saxon nobility assailed the king in summer 1073, when he entered the province intent on organising a campaign against the Poles. His purpose was to punish Duke Boleslav II of Poland for breaking the truce with Bohemia that Henry himself had negotiated in 1071. Henry summoned 'all the princes of the kingdom' to assemble their forces on 22 August 1073 in Saxony. During the Whitsun celebrations (19 May) in Augsburg, he held an assembly of south German princes, in preparation for the Polish campaign, and summoned a similar assembly of Saxon princes to

---

[30] Lampert, *Annales* 1073, pp. 149, 150. See Meyer von Knonau (1894) 2:148.

[31] Bruno, *Saxonicum bellum* c. 20, pp. 25–6. Cf. Lampert, *Annales* 1073, p. 147; Adam, *Gesta* III.60, p. 206. See Meyer von Knonau (1894) 2:73–4; Seegrün (1982) 1–14.

[32] Lampert, *Annales* 1073, pp. 149, 160; Bruno c. 21, p. 26. See Meyer von Knonau (1894) 2:235–7; Freytag (1951) 21; Althoff (1991) 323–5.

meet in Goslar on 29 June. When the Saxons assembled, however, it was to demand that the king abandon the Polish campaign and redress their grievances concerning royal government in eastern Saxony. The king's reply failed to satisfy them and Henry felt obliged to withdraw to the greater safety of the Harzburg.[33] Bruno of Merseburg regarded Henry's refusal to make concessions at Goslar on 29 June as the turning-point in his relations with the Saxon princes. 'This was the day and this the cause that first began the war: this was the beginning of all the evils that followed.'[34]

Immediately after their rebuff on 29 June the princes met in a church in Goslar and 'fixed a day and a place in which they might meet with all the Saxons', namely at Hoetensleben (south of Helmstedt) not long after 29 June. Bruno's account of the assembly of Hoetensleben discloses that the decisive contribution to the debate was made by Otto of Northeim. Otto appealed to his compatriots to repudiate their oath of fealty to the king and to take up arms against him. After a number of princes had stated their personal grievances against the royal government, all those present bound themselves by an oath. The vow of the bishops was 'that, to the best of their ability and saving their order, they would defend the freedom of their churches and of the whole of Saxony with all their might against all men'. The oath of the laity was 'that as long as they lived, they would not give up their freedom nor permit anyone henceforward to attack and plunder their land'.[35] They then marched on the Harzburg, where they pitched camp. Henry IV sent out three members of his entourage – Duke Berthold of Carinthia and perhaps Bishop Frederick of Münster and the royal chaplain Siegfried (later bishop of Augsburg) – to warn the Saxons to lay down their arms, lest they incur the guilt of starting a civil war. The king promised to refer their complaints to an assembly of princes and to abide by the princes' advice. Otto of Northeim, replying to the king's representatives on behalf of the Saxons, demanded the immediate redress of the grievances discussed at Hoetensleben. The Saxons placed guards on all the roads leading from the Harzburg, lest the king escape before conceding their demands. Nevertheless Henry was able to elude them during the night of 9 or 10 August and to flee in the company of Berthold of Carinthia and the trusted

[33] *Annales Altahenses* 1073, p. 85: when the Saxons came to Goslar, they were not admitted to the king's presence. After some days' delay the king sent them away without a satisfactory answer. Cf. Bruno c. 23, pp. 27–8. The different account of Lampert, *Annales* 1073, pp. 151–3 ('around 1 August') suggested to Meyer von Knonau (1894) 2:222–5, 238–40 and Lange (1961) 48 that he was describing a later legation to Goslar. *D H IV* 261 shows that the king had removed to the Harzburg by 26 July.   [34] Bruno c. 23, p. 28.

[35] *Ibid.* c. 23–6, pp. 28–31. The identification of Hoetensleben is a conjecture by Bruno's editor, Lohmann. The sole complete manuscript gives the place-name as Wormsleben: hence the account given by Meyer von Knonau (1894) 2:242–6.

royal advisers, Bishops Eberhard of Naumburg and Benno II of Osnabrück. According to Lampert, the hill on which the Harzburg stood was covered by dense forest 'which extended for many miles to the frontier of Thuringia and therefore no effort on the part of the besiegers could prevent the comings and goings of those who were shut in'. The king's party fled through this forest, with a hunter as their guide, travelling for three days without food, until they reached the royal estate of Eschwege. Finally, on 13 August, Henry arrived in Hersfeld, where contingents of the army for the Polish campaign were gathering. Meanwhile the rebel princes appealed to their neighbours, the Thuringian nobility, to join them in opposing the king. A conference was held in Tretenburg (near Erfurt), where the Thuringians swore an oath to support the Saxon rebels.[36]

This was clearly a rising different in character and in scale from the rebellions of 1069 and 1070–1 in eastern Saxony. That of 1069 was confined to the followers of Dedi I of Lower Lusatia and his stepson-in-law and concerned with Dedi's claims to the benefices of the late margrave of Meissen; that of 1070–1 was confined to the followers of Otto of Northeim and Magnus Billung and concerned principally with Otto's unjust deposition from his duchy. The rebellion of 1073, according to its historians, Bruno of Merseburg and Lampert of Hersfeld, involved 'all the Saxons' and was a general protest movement against the conduct of the royal government in their region. Both chroniclers provided a list of rebel leaders, Bruno giving fifteen and Lampert twenty-five names. These names suggest that the rebellion of 1073 was a movement, not of 'all the Saxons' but predominantly of the east Saxon princes and their followers. The rebel leaders included Archbishop Werner of Magdeburg, his nephew, Bishop Burchard II of Halberstadt and the bishops Werner of Merseburg and Imad of Paderborn. The most frequently mentioned of the secular princes were Otto of Northeim, Count Herman Billung and (after his release from prison in 1073) his nephew, Magnus Billung. The leaders also included two former allies of Adalbert of Bremen: the archbishop's brother, the Saxon count palatine Frederick II of Goseck, and Count Udo II of Stade (whose family had since 1057 held both the office of margrave of the Saxon Nordmark and important benefices of the church of Bremen). Members of the Wettin family were prominent: Dedi I of Lower Lusatia; his ferocious wife, Adela; her son-in-law, Count Adalbert of Ballenstedt and Dedi's nephews, William, Theoderic and Gunther (later bishop of Naumburg), the sons of Count Gero. There is also evidence to suggest that Dedi's brother, Count Thimo (who was married to Ida, daughter of Otto of

---

[36] Bruno c. 27, pp. 31–2; Lampert, *Annales* 1073, pp. 153–6, 158–9. See Meyer von Knonau (1894) 2:250–5, 264–5.

Northeim) was a rebel. Henry IV's kinsman, Margrave Ekbert II of Meissen, also took part in the rebellion, even though in 1073 he was, according to Lampert, 'a boy not yet old enough to be a knight'. Ekbert II's brother-in-law, Count Theoderic II of Katlenburg was likewise a rebel leader. Bruno's account mentions the burgrave of Magdeburg, Meinfried (not a Saxon by birth but of a noble family in Hesse), the loyal supporter of his archbishop. These east Saxon princes, the original conspirators of July 1073, made an alliance the following August with Thuringian noblemen, of whom three can be identified with reasonable certainty: Count Ruotger (ancestor of the counts of Bilstein), Count Sizzo of Schwarzburg-Käfernburg and Count Berengar of Sangerhausen.[37]

Both Bruno and Lampert identified Otto of Northeim as the leading figure in the rebellion and agreed that the reason for Otto's involvement was the same as his reason for rebelling in 1070: to recover the duchy of Bavaria. According to Bruno, in the assembly at Hoetensleben Otto gave as his motive for proposing rebellion, 'that the king unjustly seized from him the duchy of Bavaria . . . although he had not been convicted of any crime'. Otto used the opportunity of the rebellion of 1073 to continue the feud with the king that had begun with the accusation of treason in 1070, with the essential difference that in 1073 his east Saxon compatriots were prepared to make his cause their own. Lampert, recording the negotiations of the rebels with the king's representatives in January 1074, included among the rebels' demands, 'that [the king] should restore the duchy of Bavaria to Duke Otto, whom he had sought to destroy by shamelessly making use of a false charge and of a criminal's wicked invention'. The participation of other east Saxon princes in the rebellion was likewise attributed by the chroniclers to their private grievances against the king. Lampert claimed that the involvement of Count Herman Billung was prompted partly 'by personal hatred, because of Magnus, son of the Saxon duke Ordulf, whom the king had been holding in captivity for two years after receiving his surrender'. According to Bruno, at Hoetensleben Herman cited the king's seizure of the Billung fortress of Lüneburg as his motive for rebellion. At that same assembly Dedi of Lower Lusatia 'complained that he had unlawfully been deprived of estates which belonged to him by right': a reference both to the benefices of the margrave of Meissen that the king had refused to grant to him and to the lands that were confiscated after Dedi's rebellion in 1069. The Saxon count palatine Frederick II of Goseck complained that he had been deprived by the king's command of 'a great benefice that he held from the abbey of Hersfeld'. The nobleman William,

---

[37] Lampert, *Annales* 1073, 1075, pp. 149–50, 238; Bruno c. 26, 39, 46, pp. 30, 40, 45. See Fenske (1977) 61–81.

nicknamed 'the king of Lodersleben', complained that 'the king wished to seize his inheritance'. [38]

The rebellion of 1073, however, amounted to more than the collective revenge of prominent princes for their personal grievances. The leading rebels were in most cases bound together by ties of family and territorial interest, but they also saw themselves as defenders of a political cause in common with the rest of the east Saxon and Thuringian nobility. At Hoetensleben the east Saxons 'swore an oath, one by one . . . that they would not give up their freedom or permit anyone' (meaning specifically the king) 'henceforward to attack and plunder their land'. At Tretenburg the Thuringians bound themselves by oath to their cause. The rebellion was a sworn confederation (*coniuratio*), a movement of political protest against the royal government. For the protesters' objections to the king's methods of governing their region we are again dependent on the information of Bruno and Lampert. There is a difference of emphasis in the two accounts. Bruno, writing in the entourage of the bishop of Merseburg, saw the rebellion as the struggle of 'the Saxons' against tyranny, while Lampert, writing in the abbey of Hersfeld, represented the rebellion as the joint struggle of 'the Saxons and Thuringians'. Henry's objective was 'to reduce all Saxons and Thuringians to slavery and add their estates to the crown lands': hence the appeal of the east Saxons to the Thuringians at Tretenburg 'to take up arms for the sake of their freedom and because of the frequent insults that had been inflicted on them'.[39] Lampert identified one 'insult' in particular: the efforts of Archbishop Siegfried of Mainz to compel the Thuringian nobility to pay tithes to his church. Siegfried's campaign to end the 'Thuringian freedom from tithes' culminated in the synod of Erfurt (10 March 1073), which ruled in his favour. Lampert detected the secret influence of Henry IV behind this decision. 'In order to cloak his impiety with the appearance of devotion' the king had instigated Siegfried's demand for tithes, promising his help in enforcing payment in return for a percentage of Siegfried's gains. Henry then put pressure on the synod of Erfurt to secure a favourable decision. The outbreak of the rebellion, however, prevented the exaction of the tithes. 'The Thuringians rejoiced that they had found an opportunity to defend the rights handed down by their ancestors, while the king grieved for the fact that his greed for tithes had almost lost him his kingdom and his life.' All the other evidence suggests that it was Siegfried of Mainz, not the king, who forced the issue of the Thuringian tithes in 1073. The value of Lampert's account is that it records the suspicions

---

[38] Bruno c. 26, p. 30; cf. c. 16, p. 23; Lampert, *Annales* 1073, p. 149; 1074, p. 178. Cf. *Annales s. Disibodi* 1075, p. 7.

[39] Lampert, *Annales* 1073, pp. 147, 158; cf. 1073, pp. 140–1, 146; 1074, p. 177.

of the Thuringians themselves, whose belief that Henry IV was responsible for the imposition of the tithes influenced their decision to join the rebellion.[40]

The rebels' criticisms of Henry IV's government are summarised in Bruno's report of the assembly of Hoetensleben and presented more fully in Lampert's account of the demands submitted to the king in Goslar and also the demands formulated by the rebels in January 1074. Bruno's account of Hoetensleben concentrates on a single issue: that of the many castles that Henry had recently built in the province and garrisoned with 'considerable numbers of his vassals'. They were built, not on the frontier as a defence against 'the heathen', that is, the Liutizi, 'but in the midst of our land, where no one would ever expect to fight a war'. Already the garrisons had begun to steal the property of those who lived near the castles: if they continued unchecked, the king would use them to disinherit the nobility and to reduce them to slavery.[41] Lampert's account of the meeting in Goslar (June 1073) lists four demands concerning the conduct of government in eastern Saxony. Henry must release the Saxons from service on the forthcoming Polish campaign, since all their forces were needed to defend their frontiers against the Liutizi. He must dismantle the castles 'that he had built on every mountain and hill for the destruction of Saxony' and 'make restitution to the princes of Saxony whose property he had illicitly seized, according to the judgement of their fellow princes'. The king must in future spend far less time in Saxony and must reside in other parts of his kingdom. Finally, he must dismiss from his court 'those most vile counsellors by whose advice he had brought both himself and the kingdom to destruction' and be advised instead by the princes. Lampert subsequently recorded the peace conditions laid down by the rebels in talks with the king's representatives in January 1074. The basic demands of the previous summer were restated: the royal castles in Saxony and Thuringia must be destroyed and restitution made to those who had been wrongly deprived of their patrimonies; the king must reside less frequently in Saxony. In addition the rebels demanded the restoration of the duchy of Bavaria to Otto of Northeim, an amnesty for all the political opponents of the king and justice for churches, widows, orphans and others who had suffered an infringement of their rights.[42]

Lampert believed that of these grievances, it was that of the Polish campaign that sparked off the rebellion, because it marked the final stage of Henry's conspiracy against the Saxons. According to rumour, 'on the pretext of a war

[40] *Ibid.* 1073, pp. 141–2, 172. Holder-Egger (1894) 186–90 and Jäschke (1963–4) 282 n. 479 saw no connection between tithes dispute and rebellion; but see Patze (1962) 180.

[41] Bruno, *Saxonicum bellum* c. 25, pp. 29–30.

[42] Lampert, *Annales* 1073, p. 150; 1074, pp. 177–8.

against the Poles, he wished to lead an army into Saxony so as to destroy the Saxons utterly'. This 'rumour' probably originated in an incident following Henry's escape from the Harzburg in August 1073. At the village of Cappel (now Grebenau) near Hersfeld on 18 August Henry met the princes from central and southern Germany who were gathering for the Polish campaign and appealed for their support against the rebels. Some princes replied that 'since they had come armed and ready for the expedition against the Poles, he should lead the army immediately into Saxony' to suppress the rebellion. Others, however, argued that their forces were insufficient for this purpose and this argument carried the day. It was presumably this proposal of 18 August that prompted Lampert's rumour that Henry's army was intended from the outset for use against the Saxons.[43] The Saxon princes had informed the king in Goslar on 29 June 1073 that they could not join the Polish campaign because they expected an attack from 'their bitterest enemies', the Liutizi. 'If they relaxed their guard even a little, they would see their foes cross their frontiers, bringing with them fire and slaughter.' Lampert and Bruno regarded it as characteristic of Henry's regime that, instead of providing the east Saxons with the protection that a king owed to his subjects, he showed a cynical disregard for the danger presented by the Liutizi. His castles had been built to oppress the Saxons rather than to defend them against their pagan neighbours. In fact during the 1070s the power of the Liutizi was in decline and the threat to eastern Saxony consequently reduced. In the winter of 1073–4 the freezing of the rivers and marshes gave the enemy easy access to the duchy and the Saxon frontier was undefended because the princes were preparing to resist an attack from the king. Nevertheless there was no invasion by 'the heathen'. The military confederation of the Liutizi had begun to disintegrate: for the rest of the century it would be weakened by faction-fighting.[44] It is likely that the decline in the military strength of the Liutizi predated the Saxon rebellion and was caused by the crushing defeats inflicted by German armies in 1068–9: the campaign of Bishop Burchard II of Halberstadt, which destroyed the Liutizi's cult centre, Rethra, in 1068, followed up by the campaign of Henry IV and Otto of Northeim in 1069.[45]

Perhaps the diminution of the Liutizi threat to eastern Saxony after 1069 was one of the reasons for the rebels' demand in 1073–4 that the king should in future spend less time in Saxony. If the power of 'the heathen' was noticeably in decline, there was no justification for his continual residence in the province. Henry 'should sometimes leave Saxony, where he had resided since

[43] *Ibid.* 1073, pp. 147, 157–8. See Meyer von Knonau (1894) 2:256–7.
[44] Bruno c. 16, 32, pp. 23, 34–5; Lampert, *Annales* 1073, pp. 151, 163. See Brüske (1955) 83–6.
[45] Meyer von Knonau (1890) 1:584–5, 609–10; Brüske (1955) 83; Fenske (1977) 103–4. See above pp. 46, 65.

boyhood in sluggish idleness, so that he had become almost completely inactive, and should visit other regions of his kingdom'. 'He should not spend all his life exclusively in Saxony in sloth and indolence but should sometimes leave Goslar and travel round his kingdom, which the efforts of his ancestors had made so extensive.'[46] Lampert's emphasis on the king's inactivity (*otium, ignavia*), makes clear that Henry was no longer regarded as having a useful function in Saxony. Lampert exaggerated in claiming that the king treated Goslar as a permanent residence, but it is true that in the first two decades of his reign Henry spent more time in Saxony than in any other region of his kingdom. An analysis of his itinerary shows three visits to Magdeburg, three to Halberstadt, four to Quedlinburg, five to Allstedt, five to Merseburg, three to Meissen, three to Gerstungen, two to Erfurt and, most important, thirty-two visits to his birthplace, Goslar.[47] Eastern Saxony had held the same attraction for Henry IV's father and grandfather. Conrad II, following the example of his Ottonian predecessors, regularly included Paderborn and Magdeburg in his itinerary; Henry III visited Merseburg and Quedlinburg.[48]

Both Conrad II and Henry III recognised the unique advantages of Goslar as a royal residence. The strategic importance of the location, together with the silver that had begun to be mined in nearby Rammelsberg in the later tenth century, persuaded Henry II to found a royal palace on the site of his hunting lodge of Goslar. Conrad II continued his predecessor's building and added a chapel dedicated to the Virgin Mary to provide a setting of appropriate splendour for the religious services and royal ceremonials on the great festivals of the Christian year. In his son's reign the connection between Goslar and the Salian dynasty became even closer. Henry III visited Goslar more frequently than any other place in his empire (twenty-two visits in his seventeen-year reign). Here Henry founded the religious house dedicated to SS. Simon and Jude, closely linked with the imperial chapel, many of the emperor's chaplains receiving benefices in the Goslar foundation. The church of SS. Simon and Jude had the rank of a minster, equal in dignity to an episcopal church. The canons of the foundation were all appointed by the emperor and many were eventually promoted to bishoprics. Between 1051, the date of the consecration of SS. Simon and Jude, and 1077, when Henry IV finally lost control of Goslar to his enemies, twenty-one canons of the Goslar foundation became bishops (almost one-third of the sixty-eight bishops appointed in the German kingdom during this period). Henry III's foundation played a central role in securing for the monarchy the loyalty of the imperial Church.[49] Goslar also

---

[46] Lampert, *Annales* 1073, p. 151; 1074, p. 178.   [47] Kilian (1886) 4–73, 137–44.

[48] Rieckenberg (1942) 95–101; Brühl (1968) 1:132–41.

[49] Brackmann (1912) 168; Fleckenstein (1966) 251–2, 263–4, 278–85, 294–5; Zielinski (1984) 140–1; Dahlhaus (1991) 373–428.

provided the setting for the most impressive 'crown-wearings', the ceremonial demonstrations of royal authority that were an essential element of the Salian monarch's relationship with his subjects.[50] On these occasions the monarch went in procession from the chapel of the Virgin Mary to the minster of SS. Simon and Jude 'in royal splendour'. In particular Goslar was the scene of the crown-wearing on Christmas day, for during the second and third quarters of the eleventh century Goslar became the king's usual Christmas residence. Between December 1031 and December 1075 fourteen royal Christmases were celebrated in the palace of Goslar: three by Conrad II, four by Henry III and seven by Henry IV. That is what prompted Lampert to describe Goslar as 'the most famous residence of the kingdom', 'the town that the German kings were accustomed to treat as their homeland (*patria*) and their private residence'. Goslar was 'the very wealthy place, always most dear to him', where Henry IV sojourned 'as if in a permanent camp', the place most intimately connected with his kingship.[51]

The family lands inherited by Henry IV in the region of Worms and Speyer could not compare in extent and wealth with the crown lands and the lands of the Liudolfing (Ottonian) family, which the Salian dynasty inherited when Conrad II succeeded the last of the Ottonians in 1024. The greater part of the Liudolfing inheritance was in their homeland of Saxony and it was here also, above all in the east, that the Ottonian crown lands and residences were most thickly concentrated: hence the frequency with which the Salians visited Saxony. The replacement of a Saxon by a Franconian dynasty in 1024 involved no shift in the centre of gravity in the German kingdom from Saxony to the land between the middle Rhine and the Main. Having no property to rival what they inherited from the Liudolfings, the Salians continued to depend on the Saxon lands that had been the basis of their predecessors' power. A south German chronicler commented that the Salians 'dwelled in Saxony so often that the province was known as the emperor's kitchen'.[52] The new dynasty, however, lacked the close personal ties, especially those of kinship, that had bound the Liudolfings to their homeland. Henry IV's closest relatives in the province were the Brunones, the descendants of his grandmother, Empress Gisela, by her first marriage (to Count Bruno of Brunswick): Count Ekbert I of Brunswick, margrave of Meissen and his son, Ekbert II. In the crisis of 1073, however, the Brunones showed that their principal loyalty was not to their royal kinsman but to their compatriots. The youthful Ekbert II participated

[50] Klewitz (1939) 70–5. See below pp. 351–2.

[51] Lampert, *Annales* 1066, 1071, 1075, pp. 100, 117, 119, 225. See Rothe (1940) 21–31; Wilke (1970) 18–24, 30–3.

[52] *Casus monasterii Petrishusensis* II.31, p. 645. See Rieckenberg (1942) pp. 95–6; Jordan (1970) p. 543; Leyser (1981) pp. 734–44; Leyser (1983) p. 434, taking issue with Giese (1979) p. 149.

in the rebellion, as did Theoderic II of Katlenburg, who was married to a princess of the Brunones, and Adalbert of Ballenstedt, the descendant of a half-sister of Empress Gisela.[53] The attitude of the Saxon nobility to the Salian kings was inevitably different from their attitude to the Ottonians. 'Since no close ties of blood bound them to the new ruling house, the Saxons considered themselves to be exploited rather than honoured by the all too frequent sojourns of the emperors.'[54]

Henry IV undoubtedly inherited a dangerous situation in Saxony. The material basis of the Salian kingship was deeply rooted in the province, while the king himself was not. Already in the first year of his reign some of the Saxon princes had plotted the deposition of the boy-king, lest he 'follow in his father's footsteps'. What transformed this situation of potential danger into one of open rebellion was the attempt to add to the crown's resources in eastern Saxony in the early years of Henry IV's personal rule. This was the process to which Lampert of Hersfeld and Bruno of Merseburg referred when they described Henry's castle-building in Saxony and Thuringia and his seizure of the lands of the nobility. Lampert recorded that the king had 'covered all the mountains and the little hills of Saxony and Thuringia with strongly fortified castles and placed in each a garrison'. He permitted the garrisons to extort their provisions from the nearby villages, as if they were conquerors in hostile territory, and to use the forced labour not only of the peasantry but even of 'very many men of noble birth'. Henry's ultimate purpose was 'to exterminate the Saxons and establish in their place the race of the Swabians. For this race was most agreeable to him and he had raised very many of them, men sprung from obscure or almost non-existent ancestry, to the highest honours.'[55] The reality behind this polemical statement can be deduced from two incidental details in Bruno's account of the Saxons' grievances: firstly, that the garrison of one of the controversial fortresses, Lüneburg, consisted of Swabians, 'seventy of his most trusted men', and, secondly, that the king gave Saxon noblewomen in marriage to his household servants and thus 'dishonoured the noblewomen of this country with shameful marriages'.[56]

This information has assumed great significance in modern studies of the administration of the crown lands and the *ministeriales*, the unfree royal servants entrusted with their supervision in Henry IV's reign. On the basis of the evidence of Lampert and Bruno, it has been suggested that the garrisons

---

[53] Schölkopf (1957) 107–8. Henry's only other Saxon kinsmen were the grandsons of Herman of Werl, half-brother of Empress Gisela. See Fenske (1977) 377; Meier (1987) 236 n. 87.
[54] Brühl (1968) 1:132; Fenske (1977) 18; Leyser (1983) 433–4.
[55] Lampert, *Annales* 1073, pp. 140–1, 146, 147–8.
[56] Bruno, *Saxonicum bellum* c. 8, 21, pp. 18, 26–7. Cf. c. 14, p. 21.

placed by Henry in his Saxon and Thuringian castles were composed of Swabian *ministeriales*, who were perceived by the local inhabitants as foreign invaders. The king also placed Swabian *ministeriales* in charge of the lands that he had seized from the Saxon nobility and permitted Swabians from his household to marry Saxon heiresses of superior birth, so as to plant his own adherents in the province.[57] This insistence on identifying the king's Swabian adherents in Saxony exclusively as *ministeriales*, however, goes beyond the evidence. Although Lampert referred to the 'obscure or almost non-existent ancestry' of the king's Swabian agents in Saxony, he also identified among them at least one man of undoubted nobility, the royal kinsman Eberhard, son of Count Eberhard of Nellenburg and brother of Archbishop Udo of Trier. Moreover Bruno's account states that Eberhard's command at Lüneburg included men with 'noble and powerful kinsmen'. It was, therefore, Swabian noblemen that the Saxon rebels were denouncing in 1073, when they demanded that the king dismiss his 'most vile counsellors' and be advised instead by 'the princes of the kingdom'. The king must remove all the Swabians to whom he had given positions of trust in Saxony and replace them by native princes.[58]

According to Lampert and Bruno, the rebels' most important demand was the destruction of the royal castles in Saxony and Thuringia. Henry IV's initial unwillingness to concede this point, his hesitation in carrying out the destruction when he finally conceded it in February 1074 and the rapidity with which he resumed his castle-building after defeating the rebels in June 1075, all indicate that the castles were the vital issue for the king as well as for the rebels. Lampert's annal for 1073 names seven castles built since the beginning of the reign, of which five can be identified with certainty: the Harzburg, Sachsenstein, Spatenburg, Heimburg and Hasenburg. The other two were *Moseburg*, perhaps on the southern border of the Harz, and the hitherto unidentifiable *Wigantestein*. In the case of two of Lampert's 'new' castles, the Hasenburg and Sachsenstein, archaeological evidence suggests that they were built long before Henry IV's reign and that the king merely added to their fortifications. Lampert also named two castles seized by Henry from Saxon princes: Lüneburg from the Billungs and *Vokenroht* from Frederick of Goseck, the Saxon count palatine. Lampert stated that he had listed those castles 'that sprang immediately to [his] mind': the list was not exhaustive. Certainly his list does not support his claim that the king 'covered all the mountains and the little hills' with a dense network of fortresses. Of his nine castles, five of

[57] Stimming (1922) 92–9; Bosl (1950) 1:82–8. Criticisms of Bosl: Fenske (1977) 280–1; Wilke (1970) 33–6. See also Heinrichsen (1954) 24–116. See also below pp. 356–7.
[58] Bruno c. 21, pp. 26–7; Lampert, *Annales* 1073, p. 159; cf. 1073, p. 151. See Fenske (1977) 53–4.

them in Thuringia, some were as much as fifty miles away from their nearest neighbour. There is no doubt, however, that these castles provoked among the east Saxon and Thuringian nobility the fears for their liberty that were recorded not only by the local historians Lampert and Bruno, but also by contemporary south German chroniclers.[59] Were they justified in representing the castles as instruments of royal aggression against the nobility? A glance at conditions in eastern Saxony before Henry IV's castle-building of *circa* 1070 suggests a different interpretation. The lordship of the Saxon nobility was based on their castles and the eleventh century witnessed an intensification of noble castle-building. These castles served as a defence against invasion by the Slavs but could also be used by noble families in their vendettas. In his rebellion of 1069 Dedi I of Lower Lusatia used his castles of Beichlingen and Burgscheidungen as the bases from which he laid waste neighbouring crown lands. In 1070 Otto of Northeim used his castles of Hanstein and Desenberg for the same purpose. These military operations, according to Lampert, revealed to Henry IV the vulnerability of Goslar. During the autumn and winter of 1070–1 the king was reluctant to leave his favourite palace lest his enemies 'reduce that most famous royal residence to ashes'.[60] It was probably the existence of the noble castles, threatening the security of Goslar and other crown-properties, that prompted the royal government to build new castles and strengthen existing ones. Far from having an aggressive purpose, Henry IV's castles may well have originated as a 'counter-system against the threat of the aristocratic castles'.[61]

Despite their defensive purpose, however, the royal castles had two features that convinced the nobility that they were intended to serve as an instrument of tyranny: their novel appearance and their Swabian garrisons. Lampert regarded the castles as 'very strongly fortified'. Bruno described the Harzburg, 'the first and greatest' of the castles, as 'fortified without with a strong wall, towers and gates'. Their opinions are corroborated by archaeological findings. The fortifications of the surviving castle of Sachsenstein, a round tower and gate-towers, were on a scale unprecedented in the region.[62] Even more threatening was the manning of the castles. Instead of fulfilling local expectations by entrusting the castles to vassals chosen from the Saxon nobility, the king kept a firmer grip on them by providing them with garrisons of Swabians, an

[59] Lampert, *Annales* 1073, pp. 159–60 (*Vokenroht* is perhaps Volkenrode, north-east of Mühlhausen, or Vockenrode, west of Eschwege). Cf. *Annales Altahenses* 1073, p. 85; Berthold of Reichenau, *Annales* 1072, p. 275; Bernold of St Blasien, *Chronicon* 1072, p. 429. See Baaken (1961) pp. 81–4; Fenske (1977) pp. 28–32.

[60] Lampert, *Annales* 1069, p. 108; 1070, p. 115; 1071, p. 119; cf. 1070, p. 117.

[61] Spier (1962) 31. Cf. Spier (1967–8) 185–201; Fenske (1977) 29–30.

[62] Lampert, *Annales* 1073, pp. 140–1; Bruno c. 16, p. 22. See Fenske (1977) 30–2.

alien military presence with no respect for local rights or customs. The Swabians, by requisitioning food and exacting labour services, injured the prosperity of the local nobility, whose peasantry they terrorised. A late eleventh-century royalist chronicler underlined the political significance of the Swabian presence. The king placed 'his personal garrisons' in the castles, because he was unwilling to entrust them to 'the powerful men of the kingdom'.[63] The earliest reference to the royal castles and their lawless garrisons is found in a letter of 1074/5 written by Archbishop Werner of Magdeburg in support of the rebels. This is the only passage in the Saxon polemics that explains the connection between the castles and the lands that the king had confiscated from members of the Saxon nobility. Henry sought 'to seize our property from us and grant it to his familiars, not because of any fault on our part but because they possessed little or nothing at home and they saw that our land was fruitful. He therefore fortified the more inaccessible places in our region with very strong castles, in which he placed considerable numbers of armed men who compelled us to serve them like slaves and killed those who wished to defend their liberty.' Having seized the nobles' lands, the king built his castles to prevent the dispossessed from recovering their estates. The Saxon sources represent these confiscations as the arbitrary action of a tyrant. Henry's purpose was to 'add the estates [of the Saxons and Thuringians] to the crown lands'.[64]

The only account of these proceedings written from Henry IV's point of view is an anonymous narrative poem, the *Song of the Saxon War*, of which the central message is: 'I wish to tell of the battles of King Henry IV against the Saxon race, who denied him his rights.' During Henry's minority this 'wild race' escaped from royal control, the rule of law gave way to brute force and the strong plundered the weak. As soon as Henry came of age, however, 'he tightened the reins that had become too loose', enforced the laws and compelled the guilty to surrender their plunder. Infuriated by the king's actions, the Saxon princes sent a delegation to him, which accused him of depriving the Saxons of their rights and permitting outsiders to rob Saxons of their inheritances. Henry denied the accusation: he had simply reimposed order and restored the property of the dispossessed.[65] Modern scholars have found in this apologia for Henry IV the essential clue to his conduct in Saxony before 1073 that is missing from the Saxon polemics. What lay behind the king's confiscation of noble estates and his castle-building was a 'policy of recuperation', a systematic attempt to recover lands and rights in eastern Saxony to compensate for the serious losses of the crown during the decade of Henry's

[63] Frutolf, *Chronica* 1068, p. 78.   [64] Bruno c. 42, pp. 41–3. See Kost (1962) 25–8, 35.
[65] *Carmen de bello Saxonico* I.1,11–65, pp. 1–3. See Schluck (1979) 30–2, 102–4.

minority.[66] Emperor Henry III's energetic exploitation of the crown's resources in Saxony had created such deep resentment that immediately after his death a group of princes plotted to depose his son. The weakness of the regency government of the late 1050s and early 1060s temporarily eased the tension between the crown and the Saxon nobility. The regency government felt too vulnerable to imitate the aggressive style of Henry III and sought to win friends by making concessions. The royal diplomas of Henry IV's minority contain a series of grants of crown lands and royal revenues, counties and other rights of jurisdiction to Saxon petitioners, especially bishops. The diplomas also reveal that this royal generosity ended abruptly in 1069.[67] The obvious inference is that this was the moment at which the policy of conciliation ended and that of recuperation began. It was in this same year that Henry's refusal to grant Margrave Dedi of Lower Lusatia the benefices of the deceased margrave of Meissen provoked the first of the Saxon rebellions against him. The following summer witnessed Otto of Northeim's first rebellion. Already at Eastertide 1070 a violent incident in the king's entourage revealed the growing tensions in eastern Saxony. Henry celebrated Easter (4 April) as the guest of Bishop Hezilo of Hildesheim, whose church had been a major beneficiary of the crown's generosity during the minority. During the celebrations fighting broke out between the king's knights and those of the bishop. Nothing further is known about this breach of the king's peace than that it cost the lives of 'very many' of Hezilo's knights.[68]

The beginning of Henry IV's 'policy of recuperation' coincided with the return of Archbishop Adalbert of Bremen to court as a royal adviser. The chronicler Bruno deduced that Adalbert must therefore be the initiator of this policy: 'When the king came of age, he immediately took Bishop Adalbert of Bremen as his adviser and was persuaded by him to seek out high mountains with natural fortifications in lonely places and to build castles on them.'[69] The narrative sources agree that at the time of his death (17 March 1072) Adalbert had once more become the king's most important adviser: in Lampert's exaggerated phrase, 'almost co-ruler of the kingdom and party to all that was done, both public and private'.[70] On one occasion at least during these years Adalbert took an active role in Saxon politics: in the summer of 1071 he took

---

[66] G. Meyer von Knonau (1894) 2:227–32, 857–69; Stimming (1922) 96–100; Bosl (1950) 1:74–89; Baaken (1961) 80–95; Berges (1963) 154; Wilke (1970) 24–30; Fenske (1977) 22–9; Giese (1979) 154; Leyser (1983) 423–6.

[67] *DD H IV* 22, 83, 132, 206, 218–19 (Hildesheim); 32, 108–10 (Halberstadt); 64 (Verden); 65, 107 (Magdeburg); 131 (Naumburg); 184 (Merseburg); 87 (Ordulf, duke of Saxony, or Otto of Northeim).   [68] Lampert, *Annales* 1070, p. 112. See Meyer von Knonau (1894) 2:7.

[69] Bruno, *Saxonicum bellum* c. 16, p. 22.

[70] Lampert, *Annales* 1072, p. 134. See Meyer von Knonau (1894) 2:71.

part in the secret meeting in Lüneburg between Henry IV and King Swein Estrithson of Denmark.[71] As an expert in Saxon affairs, he must have played a part in formulating the king's plans for eastern Saxony in 1069–72. The principal executive role in the 'policy of recuperation' seems to have belonged to Benno, the royal servant who in 1067 became bishop of Osnabrück. All that is known of Benno's career before his promotion to Osnabrück is that he combined the spiritual offices of provost of the cathedral chapter of Hildesheim, archpriest of Goslar and royal chaplain, with the important administrative duty of *vicedominus* in Goslar, the steward of the palace and the royal estates.[72] During the rebellion of 1073 Benno and his colleague, Bishop Eberhard of Naumburg, were the king's chief advisers.[73] These two Saxon bishops (both driven from their dioceses because of their refusal to join the rebellion) had succeeded to the role of Adalbert of Bremen.

Benno's late eleventh-century biography links him directly to the royal castles in Saxony and Thuringia. Benno was 'an outstanding architect and builder and it was on this account that he was always bound to the king in inseparable friendship'. At Henry's request he reinforced the foundations of the cathedral of Speyer, threatened by the Rhine. Most importantly, 'the king began to fortify the whole of Saxony with new and strong castles, attempting to forestall the rebellion of the traitors by the fortification of the country. He entrusted to the lord Benno the development and careful execution of this enterprise, knowing that he had no servant more faithful nor more zealous in performing this office.'[74] Another passage in the biography shows Benno recovering for his church the property of Iburg, which was being used as common land by the local peasants. He proved his church's ownership of the land using the inquest procedure, the summoning and interrogation under oath of local inhabitants to establish legal title.[75] The importance of this incident is emphasised in the first modern study of the origins of the Saxon rebellion (1886).[76] The inquest procedure used on this occasion by Benno, the principal executor of Henry IV's Saxon policy, was probably the method used by Henry IV's servants to recover crown property in eastern Saxony. It is likely that an inquest or similar legal procedure lay behind the royal confiscations reported by the chroniclers: for example, the fortress of Lüneburg seized from

[71] See above p. 72.
[72] *Vita Bennonis* c. 1, p. 374. See Jäschke (1965–6) 357–74; Zielinski (1984) 25.
[73] Lampert, *Annales* 1073, p. 153.
[74] *Vita Bennonis* c. 6, 9, 21, pp. 382, 388, 420. See Meyer von Knonau (1890) 1:576–82; Stimming (1922) 101–6; Spier (1962) 31–2, 36–7; Berges (1963) 143, 155; Jäschke (1965–6) 280–5.
[75] *Vita Bennonis* c. 14, pp. 398–400.
[76] Ulmann (1886) 119–29. Cf. Meyer von Knonau (1894) 2:864 n. 19; Stimming (1922) 95; Baaken (1961) 90; Leyser (1983) 424–6.

the Billungs and that of *Vokenroht* from Frederick of Goseck and the estates about which Frederick, Bishop Burchard II of Halberstadt and William of Lodersleben complained at Hoetensleben.[77]

The property recovered by Henry IV *circa* 1070 included not only lands given away by the government during his minority but also lands alienated by the crown at a much earlier date, preceding the succession of the Salian dynasty: that is, crown lands or Liudolfing family lands granted by the Ottonian kings to their followers before 1024. A recent study traces the origin of the tension between the Salian kings and the Saxon nobility, and in particular the rebellion of 1073, to the nature of Ottonian grants of land to the nobility. Ottonian land grants could revert to the crown more easily than historians used to suppose. When the king granted an estate from his own hereditary lands to one of his followers, that estate was not automatically absorbed into the follower's patrimony: it was a royal *proprietas* and remained distinct from the grantee's *hereditas*. The purpose of the grant was to ensure the follower's continued loyalty and service and if he failed to make the proper return for the king's generosity, the land would revert to the crown. Furthermore the recipient of the *proprietas* could bequeath it only to a close male blood-relation, son or brother or brother's son. More distant kindred would have no difficulty in inheriting a nobleman's *hereditas*, but could not inherit an estate granted by the king *in proprietatem*, which reverted to the crown. Conrad II and Henry III applied this rule strictly and were greatly enriched by such reversions in eastern Saxony: hence the progressive estrangement of their dynasty from the Saxons.[78] The Saxons experienced some relaxation of royal government during Henry IV's minority, a respite which must have had the effect of making the subsequent enforcement of royal rights seem the more unacceptable. The king's insistence on his rights created many enemies among the kindred of noblemen who died without a direct male heir (like Otto of Weimar–Orlamünde, whose widow, Adela married Dedi I of Lower Lusatia). The unsuccessful rebellions of 1069 and 1070–1 meant a further windfall for the king: the rebels were punished by the reversion to the crown of lands held *in proprietatem*. The king's severity, however, was regarded by many Saxons as a threat to their own tenure, so that they were ready to respond to Otto of Northeim's call at Hoetensleben. 'Awake, if you wish to bequeath to your children the inheritances left to you by your parents: lest through your negligence and lethargy you allow yourselves and your children to become the slaves of foreigners.'[79]

---

[77] Ulmann detected a reference to the inquest procedure in Lampert's statement (*Annales* 1073, pp. 155, 158; 1074, pp. 177–8) that the king seized the nobles' property by force and *per calumniam*.   [78] Leyser (1983) 425–41.   [79] Bruno, *Saxonicum bellum* c. 25, p. 29.

When noblemen were persuaded by such arguments to rebel, they were supported by east Saxon bishops, whose grievances, according to Bruno of Merseburg, were of the same character as those of the secular princes. The chronicler claimed that Archbishop Werner of Magdeburg and his nephew, Bishop Burchard II of Halberstadt, were provoked into rebellion by royal attacks on their property, that is, by Henry IV's 'policy of recuperation'.[80] The role of the two prelates was in fact more complex than this. Although from 1073 until the end of their lives they were among Henry IV's bitterest enemies, they had previously enjoyed close contact with the court and as late as 1072 they were still in the king's confidence. Henry celebrated Whitsun (27 May) 1072 in Magdeburg, his second visit to the city during Werner's archiepiscopate. Werner had been a fairly frequent visitor at court, his last appearance being in March 1072 in Goslar, and his church had benefited from royal generosity.[81] Werner is a shadowy figure, however, compared with his nephew, the astute and energetic politician Burchard, who had enjoyed an unusually active career in the service of the crown. The evidence of the royal diplomas reveals two periods during which Burchard was continuously in the royal entourage: in July 1062 – May 1064 and in May 1068 – April 1070. During the former period Burchard was entrusted with an important mission in the Italian kingdom; during the latter period he commanded the successful expedition of 1068 against the Liutizi.[82] The church of Halberstadt reaped the reward of her bishop's faithful service.[83] On 12 June 1071 the king celebrated Whitsun in Halberstadt and was present at the consecration of Burchard's new cathedral and on 27 April 1072 Burchard appeared at court for the last time before the rebellion.[84]

Werner and Burchard were members of the Steusslingen family, Swabians of the minor nobility, who first came to prominence when Anno of Steusslingen became archbishop of Cologne. Werner was Anno's brother, Burchard his sister's son. Anno's family established itself with particular success in Saxony. During the eighty years following Anno's appointment to Cologne his family produced two archbishops of Magdeburg, two bishops of Halberstadt and a bishop of Münster. Simultaneously some of their lay kinsmen settled in the region.[85] The careers of the Steusslingen family help to explain Lampert's allegation that Henry IV intended to replace the Saxons with Swabian settlers, very many of whom, 'men sprung from obscure or almost non-existent ancestry', he raised 'to the highest honours'.[86] Werner of

---

[80] *Ibid.* c. 26, p. 29.   [81] *DD H IV* 65, 107, 238. See Claude (1972) 326–7.

[82] Gawlik (1970) 132; Fenske (1977) 100–5.   [83] *DD H IV* 32, 108–10.

[84] *Gesta episcoporum Halberstadensium* p. 96; *D H IV* 254.

[85] Heinrichsen (1954) 50–1, 53–4, 71–2; Lück (1970a) 31–6, 42–3; Fenske (1977) 104.

[86] Lampert, *Annales* 1073, 147.

Magdeburg and Burchard of Halberstadt were, therefore, characteristic figures of the Henrician regime in Saxony against which (according to Lampert and Bruno) the rebellion of 1073 was directed; but they themselves were leading rebels. The consequence of their refusal to join the rebellion would probably have been the loss of their sees, which was the fate of three royalist prelates in 1073. 'Archbishop Liemar of Bremen, Bishop Eberhard of Naumburg and Bishop Benno of Osnabrück were driven out of Saxony because they would not concur with the general opinion of their race.'[87] It is unlikely, however, that this was what prompted Burchard of Halberstadt to rebel. He was not a reluctant rebel, forced to participate by the threats of his neighbours, the secular princes. Henry IV allegedly regarded him as 'the leader of the whole Saxon rebellion and the originator and instigator of all the evils which flowed from it'.[88] The crucial factor in Burchard's rebellion was his devotion to ecclesiastical reform. Burchard was one of the first German bishops to play an active part in defending the interests of the reform papacy. His role in ending the papal schism (1062) resulted in a close friendship with Pope Alexander II, who proclaimed him 'the special son' of the Roman church.[89] Like his uncle, Anno of Cologne, Burchard promoted monastic reform in his diocese.[90] The close connection between support for monastic reform and opposition to Henry IV is also apparent in the career of Bishop Werner of Merseburg, the founder of the monastery of St Peter on the Altenburg. Werner, like Burchard, had close contacts with the court during the early years of the reign, while Henry IV (imitating his father's practice) visited Merseburg five times in the years 1057–71.[91] After 1073, however, Werner became the king's enemy. It was in his entourage that Bruno composed his *Saxon War* and to him that the chronicler dedicated the work.[92]

The presence of reform-minded bishops in the Saxon conspiracy of summer 1073 is reflected in Lampert's version of the princes' demands at Goslar on the eve of the rebellion. The complaints against the king's castle-building, confiscations, evil counsellors and frequent visits to eastern Saxony, are accompanied by complaints about Henry's failure to behave like a Christian king. He must dismiss 'the swarm of concubines with whom he slept, contrary to the dictates of the canons', adhere to the queen, whom he had married 'according to the traditions of the Church' and abandon the youthful vices with which 'he had defamed the royal dignity'. The princes had sworn an oath of fealty to him, but it was valid 'only if he wished to be a king

---

[87] *Ibid.* 1073, pp. 148, 150. See Leyser (1983) 416–17.
[88] Lampert, *Annales* 1076, p. 265; cf. 1073, p. 148; 1076, p. 268.
[89] *Urkundenbuch des Hochstifts Halberstadt* 1:60 (no. 83).   [90] Fenske (1977) 118–33; 133–6.
[91] Kilian (1886) 137–42; Gawlik (1970) 144; Fenske (1977) 289–92.
[92] Bruno, *Saxonicum bellum* prologue, pp. 12–13.

who would build the Church of God, not destroy it'. If he failed to preserve the rights of Church and people, the princes would 'fight for the Church of God, the Christian faith and their liberty' and make war against him 'as against a barbarian enemy and oppressor of the name of Christ'.[93] A holy war against 'a barbarian enemy' was a concept which Burchard of Halberstadt knew well, having waged such a war in 1068 against the Liutizi. He destroyed their cult centre of Rethra, seized their sacred horse and used it as his mount when the expedition returned to Saxony.[94] Five years later Burchard was ready to fight a similar holy war against a king whose conduct towards his subjects and towards the Church seemed to him as bad as that of the heathen Liutizi. The attitude of Burchard of Halberstadt, Werner of Merseburg and perhaps the shadowy Werner of Magdeburg anticipates that of the Gregorian bishops who would obey the command of Pope Gregory VII to rebel against the king in 1076. In 1073 in eastern Saxony Henry IV already faced the combination of political and spiritual opposition that was to be characteristic of the late eleventh-century conflict of empire and papacy.

When the rebellion broke out in August 1073, the king was awaiting the arrival of the army for the Polish campaign. He was obliged to postpone the campaign and request the princes to collect a much stronger force, which was to assemble at Breitungen (an estate of the abbey of Hersfeld) on 6 October.[95] This delay allowed the rebels to seize the initiative. Their strategy was to put the royal castles out of action and so deny the king the means of controlling the province. Most of the rebels withdrew from the siege of the Harzburg, which was too strong for them, and instead, under the command of Count Herman Billung, laid siege to Lüneburg, the fortress that Henry had seized from the Billungs. Lüneburg was not provisioned for a siege and the Swabian garrison, commanded by Eberhard, son of Count Eberhard of Nellenburg, was soon forced to surrender. To save the lives of his garrison, the king agreed to Herman Billung's demand to release Magnus Billung from his prison in the Harzburg. Magnus was joyfully acknowledged by the Saxons as their duke, even though the king had not invested him with his father's office, and he immediately joined the leadership of the rebellion.[96] Before the end of the summer an army of Saxons and Thuringians commanded by Count Frederick II of Goseck destroyed the castle of Heimburg. Other rebel forces besieged Hasenburg and the Harzburg. By the end of the year the garrisons were close

---

[93] Lampert, *Annales* 1073, p. 152.
[94] *Annales Augustani* 1068, p. 128; Berthold, *Annales* 1068, p. 429. See Meyer von Knonau (1890) 1:585; Brüske (1955) 83.
[95] Lampert, *Annales* 1073, p. 158. See Meyer von Knonau (1894) 2:256–7.
[96] Bruno c. 21–2, pp. 25–7; Lampert, *Annales* 1073, pp. 160–1. See Meyer von Knonau (1894) 2:259–61; Freytag (1951) 21–2.

to starvation.[97] The king still hoped to lead an army against the rebels, but during the autumn it became clear that the princes of central and southern Germany would not supply him with the necessary forces. According to Lampert, the king was 'terrified by the loss of his castles' and 'asked the archbishops of Mainz and Cologne to meet the Saxons and try to find some remedy for the troubles'. Two such meetings took place, in Corvey on 24 August and in Homburg on 13 September, at which an assembly of princes was arranged for 20 October in Gerstungen to investigate the Saxon complaints. Lampert also reported, however, that 'some believed that [Siegfried of Mainz] and the archbishop of Cologne and very many other Rhineland princes were aware of the conspiracy [of the Saxons] and party to it from the very beginning'.[98] This suggests the possibility that the archbishops negotiated with the Saxons not on the king's, but on their own behalf: Siegfried, to secure the Thuringian tithes; Anno, because of sympathy with his kinsmen Werner of Magdeburg and Burchard of Halberstadt. Perhaps the king was unable to prevent a *rapprochement* between the Saxons and the Rhineland princes on whom he was most dependent.

The proceedings of the assembly of Gerstungen on 20 October are described in the sharply differing accounts of Lampert and the *Song of the Saxon War*. In Lampert's version the Saxon princes negotiated for three days with seven princes 'sent by the king', the archbishops of Mainz and Cologne, the bishops of Metz and Bamberg and the dukes Godfrey III of Lower Lotharingia, Rudolf of Swabia and Berthold of Carinthia. The unanimous decision of all the princes was that Henry IV should be deposed and a new king elected. The princes would have made Rudolf king, had he not refused, on the grounds that such a decision could only be made 'by all the princes in an assembly'. The only decisions that the assembly made public were that the Saxons should make amends for their rebellion and the king should not inflict any punishment on them. The version of the *Song of the Saxon War* is less complicated. The Saxons met the 'bishops and foremost counts and dukes' from the rest of the kingdom and won their support by stating the Saxon grievances against the crown. The other princes promised on oath that they would admonish the king to restore to the Saxons 'the rights of their fathers' and let them go unpunished, otherwise the princes would refuse him their military service. Henry, however, refused to be bound by the princes' decision and determined to settle the Saxon question by military means.[99] Lampert's story

---

[97] *Carmen de bello Saxonico* 1.87–138, pp. 3–5. Cf. *Annales Altahenses* 1073, p. 86; Lampert, *Annales* 1073, p. 161. See Meyer von Knonau (1894) 2:266–8, 297–8.

[98] Lampert, *Annales* 1073, pp. 161–3; cf. p. 159. Cf. Frutolf, *Chronica* 1072, p. 82. See Meyer von Knonau (1894) 2:270–2; Jenal (1975) pp. 374–80.

[99] Lampert, *Annales* 1073, pp. 164–6; *Carmen de bello Saxonico* 11.26–50, pp. 8–9. See Meyer von Knonau (1894) 2:287–8.

of the decision to depose Henry has been dismissed by scholars on the grounds that no other source shows any knowledge of it. Lampert claimed that initially the decision was a secret, known only to the conspirators at Gerstungen, but that subsequently the Saxons urged the Rhineland princes 'by means of frequent legations' to elect a new king. Archbishop Siegfried summoned an assembly to Mainz to carry out their wishes, but Henry IV responded with a lavish distribution of 'gifts and promises', which averted the threat of his deposition.[100] By December, therefore, according to Lampert, the deposition plot was public knowledge. It is hard to imagine why such a sensational story went unreported by every other chronicler. All that can be assumed about the proceedings at Gerstungen (here Lampert's chronicle and the *Song of the Saxon War* are in agreement) is that the Saxons succeeded in convincing the southern and Rhineland princes of the justice of their cause. The negotiations in October resulted, therefore, in the political isolation of the king and destroyed his hopes of leading an army against the rebels.

The readiness of the other princes to sympathise with the Saxons is explained by the political developments of 1072, which are reported most strikingly in the Niederaltaich chronicle. 'The king had begun long ago to despise the magnates and to bestow riches and power on lesser men and to govern according to their advice', with the result that 'the bishops, dukes and other princes of the kingdom withdrew from royal affairs'. In particular the withdrawal from court of dukes Rudolf of Swabia and Berthold of Carinthia gave rise to the suspicion that they were plotting rebellion. The dukes averted a punitive expedition by sending the king guarantees of their good behaviour.[101] According to this south German chronicler, therefore, it was not only the Saxons who resented the king's low-born advisers: all the princes were alienated by the favour shown to 'lesser men'. Lampert also reported conflict between the king and the south German dukes in 1072. Rudolf of Swabia 'was accused before the king of plotting evil against the king and the commonwealth'. To escape the fate of Otto of Northeim in 1070, Rudolf requested Empress Agnes to make peace between him and her son. This she achieved in an assembly of princes in Worms on 25 July, supported by the archbishops of Cologne and Mainz and 'a very great number of abbots and monks', including Abbot Hugh of Cluny. At the end of the year Henry was involved in conflict with Berthold of Carinthia, while simultaneously hectic diplomacy was necessary to avert a war between the king and Rudolf. The dukes were finally reconciled with the king on Palm Sunday (24 March) 1073.[102] The fol-

---

[100] Lampert, *Annales* 1073, pp. 168–9. See Meyer von Knonau (1894) 2:820–3; Jakobs (1968) 266; Thomas (1970) 394–5; Jenal (1975) 381–6.   [101] *Annales Altahenses* 1072, p. 84.

[102] Lampert, *Annales* 1072, pp. 137–8. See Meyer von Knonau (1894) 2:153–6, 159–62; Jakobs (1968) 269–71; Vogel (1984) 1–30. See also below pp. 125–7.

lowing November, however, Rudolf and Berthold were warned by one of the king's most trusted servants, Regenger, that Henry was planning their murder. The accuser undertook to prove the king's guilt in a judicial duel, which was arranged for January 1074. A few days before the duel Regenger 'was seized by a terrible demon and died a horrifying death'.[103] The mutual suspicions of the king and the south German dukes throughout 1072–3 explain why Lampert thought it likely that the princes were plotting Henry IV's deposition during the autumn of 1073.

The Saxon rebellion broke out at a time of discontent with the royal government throughout the kingdom. When the king celebrated Easter (8 April) in Utrecht in 1072, 'the people shouted at him, complaining about the injuries and misfortunes with which the innocent were oppressed everywhere in the kingdom' and their complaints were corroborated by 'all the princes of the kingdom'. Henry's response was to reinstate Archbishop Anno of Cologne as his adviser, his task being to reconcile the king with his opponents. His work was far from complete, however, when after less than a year advanced age and growing weakness forced Anno to retire from the court.[104] The king's critics in the Rhineland and southern Germany saw in the Saxons' grievances an extreme version of their own complaints and in the Saxon rebellion a possible model for their own future conduct. Their sympathy encouraged the rebels to intensify the siege of the Harzburg and Hasenburg. The royal garrisons faced starvation but the king was powerless to help them. Since early December he had been confined to his bed in Ladenburg (an estate of the church of Worms). His illness was so severe that his enemies had high hopes that the political crisis would be resolved by his death.[105] Henry disappointed them by recovering sufficiently to proceed to the city of Worms, where he discovered his most enthusiastic supporters. Bishop Adalbert of Worms, an opponent of the king, wished to close the city gates against him, but the citizens rebelled against their bishop, defeated his knights and would have thrown him into prison, had he not fled. The citizens received Henry 'with great pomp', offered him military service and took an oath to contribute to the costs of his wars. 'Thus the king obtained a strongly fortified city,' wrote Lampert, 'and henceforward this was to be his military headquarters, the citadel of the kingdom and a most secure refuge, whatever might befall.'[106]

The evidence of Henry IV's itinerary shows that during the Saxon rebellion Worms replaced Goslar as the place where he most frequently resided.

---

[103] Lampert, *Annales* 1073, pp. 140, 144–5, 166–8; 1074, p. 174. Cf. Berthold, *Annales* 1073, p. 276. See Meyer von Knonau (1894) 2:174, 195, 291–3, 297, 307–8. See also below pp. 359–60.

[104] Lampert, *Annales* 1072, pp. 134–5; 1073, p. 140. See Jenal (1975) 357–69.

[105] Lampert, *Annales* 1073, p. 169. See Meyer von Knonau (1894) 2:294–6.

[106] Lampert, *Annales* 1073, p. 169; 1074, p. 173.

Between 1073 and 1075 he stayed there on at least twelve occasions.[107] Lampert claimed that in Worms the king 'lived far less well than befitted royal magnificence'.[108] The rebellion had cut him off from the rich estates in eastern Saxony and the opposition of many churchmen denied him their hospitality and services. For the moment he was dependent on the generosity of the citizens of Worms. He expressed his gratitude in a privilege of 18 January 1074, which freed the inhabitants of Worms from the payment of customs duties to the crown. This diploma praises the spontaneous and unexpected loyalty of the citizens. 'We call [their fidelity] outstanding because when all the princes of the kingdom abandoned the faith that they owed and raged against us, [the citizens of Worms] alone . . . adhered to us against the will of all.'[109] The city of Worms had a special connection with the Salians: their ancestors in the ninth and early tenth centuries had been counts in the Wormgau and were buried in the cathedral of Worms. It was probably not ancient loyalties, however, but modern considerations that prompted the citizens' fidelity. The economic development of the Rhineland cities in the later eleventh century evidently encouraged ideas of political independence. The citizens of Worms wished to free themselves from the jurisdiction of their lord, Bishop Adalbert, and saw their opportunity in his conflict with the king. Lampert deplored the effect of their 'most evil example' on other cities, notably Cologne, where the citizens rebelled against Archbishop Anno in April 1074, only to suffer a disastrous defeat.[110] In the case of Worms Henry IV was the principal beneficiary of this economic and political development, but there is no evidence that he actively promoted it. Later centuries would witness an alliance between German kings and cities, but Henry IV was not the architect of this alliance. In accepting the help of the citizens of Worms, he was seizing a political opportunity rather than inaugurating a political programme.[111]

The Christmas festivities of 1073 in Worms, according to Lampert, were attended only by reluctant princes, anxious to avoid the appearance of 'open defection'. They arrived without 'the customary entourage of servants and their following of knights and clerks, but with only a few followers and with little of the ceremonial apparel of their office'. Nevertheless the king would not permit them to leave the court, calculating that, although they were of no practical help to him, their presence at the court would conceal his powerlessness.[112] The more impartial evidence of the royal diplomas for January 1074 shows that the king was attended by a group of prelates – the archbishops of

[107] Kilian (1886) 143–4; Meyer von Knonau (1894) 2:294–6, 307–9, 310–14; Brühl (1968) 1:178–9, 210–11; Kottje (1978) 134–8, 157.   [108] Lampert, *Annales* 1074, p. 173.
[109] *D H IV* 267: Gawlik (1970a) 52–3. See C. Schneider (1972) 72–3; Büttner (1973) 355.
[110] Lampert, *Annales* 1074, pp. 185–93. See Strait (1974) 25–30; W. Goez (1983) 122–31.
[111] Schwineköper (1977) 144; Kottje (1978) 131–57.   [112] Lampert, *Annales* 1074, p. 173.

Bremen and Trier and the bishops of Naumburg, Verdun, Bamberg, Basel, Eichstätt, Metz, Freising and Augsburg – most of whom served him faithfully in the following years.[113] With the help of his episcopal supporters and the men of Worms, Henry assembled an army for an expedition against the rebels. At the beginning of the year the news from Saxony continued to be bad. The rebels had burned Hasenburg, before laying siege to the nearby castle of Spatenberg, while the Thuringians had begun the siege of *Vokenroht.* The king clearly regarded *Vokenroht* as particularly secure, since before the onset of winter he had placed his consort, Bertha, in the fortress to await the birth of her child. When *Vokenroht* came under siege, Henry ordered Abbot Hartwig of Hersfeld to bring her to the safety of his abbey, which he did with the consent of the besieging Thuringians. On 12 February the queen gave birth to a son in Hersfeld, who was named after his great-grandfather, Conrad.[114]

Ten days before the birth of the heir to the throne Henry reached a settlement with the rebels. His original plan had been a surprise attack on the Saxons in January, long before the beginning of the campaigning season, but when he reached Hersfeld, he realised that his force could not match the rebels in battle.[115] On 27 January the royal army was dangerously close to the rebels, encamped on the opposite bank of the Werra, the river dividing Thuringia from Hesse, now frozen hard enough to guarantee an easy crossing. Henry began at once to negotiate with the enemy, at first through the mediation of Abbot Hartwig of Hersfeld and subsequently through four bishops from his entourage. The rebels' demands were those which the king had rejected at Goslar on 29 June 1073. The central issue was still that of the royal castles. According to Lampert, Henry was so loath to surrender them that he was ready even now to break off the negotiations and to do battle, but he was foiled by his followers' refusal to fight. On 2 February 1074, therefore, in Gerstungen the king's representatives, 'fifteen bishops and such princes as were in his camp', made peace on the Saxons' terms.

In Bruno's version of the peace settlement, the royal castles were to be destroyed; the king was to make no more 'depredations' in the province; Saxon affairs must be regulated according to the advice of the Saxons and 'no man of a foreign race' was to be admitted to the government of the province. Lampert's version represents the settlement as a complete reversal of Henry IV's 'policy of recuperation'. Not only were the castles to be razed, but 'the patrimonies seized by force or by legal claim' must be restored and henceforward the king must spend far less time in Saxony. In return the Saxon and

---

[113] *DD H IV* 267–9. See Gawlik (1970a) 52–3.
[114] Lampert, *Annales* 1074, p. 174. See Meyer von Knonau (1894) 2:309–10, 327; E. Goez (1996) 2–3. [115] Bruno, *Saxonicum bellum* c. 31, p. 33; Lampert, *Annales* 1074, p. 176.

Thuringian nobles pledged themselves to dismantle the castles that they had built during Henry's reign. The duchy of Bavaria was to be restored to Otto of Northeim. Finally, Siegfried of Mainz, Anno of Cologne, Rudolf of Swabia and other princes were not to be punished for their sympathy with the rebellion.[116] The curious account of the events of 27 January – 2 February in the *Song of the Saxon War* represents the peace of Gerstungen as a great victory for the king. An army of 60,000 rebels was terrified into surrender by a royal army of one-tenth that size, without attempting resistance, 'a triumph, the like of which has not happened since the time of Charles [the Great]'. After receiving the Saxons' submission, 'the invincible king travelled through their homeland, righting wrongs, re-establishing their laws and rights, restoring the property of those who had been plundered'. The author concealed the fact that Henry was forced to surrender the gains that his government had made in eastern Saxony since *circa* 1070.[117]

There was one sense, however, in which the peace of Gerstungen could be represented as a political success for the king. By making peace with the Saxons, Henry broke up the coalition between the rebels and the princes of central and southern Germany that had developed during 1073. This was the aspect of the peace that attracted the attention of the chronicler Berthold of Reichenau. 'The king feigned a reconciliation with the Saxons in the absence of the dukes [of Swabia, Carinthia and Bavaria] and of the other magnates of the kingdom'. It was for this reason that Bruno of Merseburg considered that the Saxons had made a serious mistake in concluding peace. They had neglected the interests of the south Germans who had refused to serve in the king's army because of their sympathy with the Saxon cause. The peace of Gerstungen transformed the allies 'from faithful friends into the bitterest enemies'.[118] The dangerously divisive issue was the king's undertaking to restore the duchy of Bavaria to Otto of Northeim.[119] This promise gravely injured the interests of Welf IV of Bavaria and also of his closest allies, Rudolf of Swabia and Berthold of Carinthia. The king's relations with Rudolf and Berthold had seriously deteriorated in 1072–3 and the court suspected the dukes of plotting rebellion. According to Berthold of Reichenau, in 1073 all three south German dukes 'departed from the king because other counsellors had been introduced and they saw that their counsel no longer weighed with the king'.[120] It was presumably the threat presented by the south German princes that caused Henry to contemplate the restoration of Otto of Northeim to the duchy of Bavaria and the place in the king's counsels that

[116] Bruno c. 31, pp. 33–4; Lampert, *Annales* 1074, pp. 175–80. See Meyer von Knonau (1894) 2:315–25; Giese (1979) 158–9.   [117] *Carmen de bello Saxonico* II.183–4, 207–9, p. 13.

[118] Berthold, *Annales* 1074, p. 276; Bruno c. 31, p. 34; Lampert, *Annales* 1074, pp. 178, 183.

[119] Lange (1961) 53–4.   [120] Berthold, *Annales* 1073, p. 276.

he had held before June 1070. The peace of Gerstungen, therefore, reversed the consequences of the coup of 1070, when Otto's enemies at court ousted him from the king's favour. If (as there is reason to suspect) Rudolf of Swabia was involved in that coup, Otto's agreement with the king effectively turned the tables on the duke and his allies. Otto accomplished in 1073–4 what he had failed to do in 1070–1: to use rebellion as a means of forcing himself back into royal favour. Otto had become the leader of the rebellion: 'all their plans depended on him'.[121] Not even the ducal house of Billung challenged his ascendancy. Otto could make the restoration of his duchy one of the objectives of the rebellion and bring the rebellion to a halt when his objectives were attained. His political success depended, however, on his continued ability to command his compatriots and soon after the settlement of 2 February it became clear that he no longer controlled a significant part of the Saxon army.

The peace caused a serious division in the Saxon ranks. 'All the lesser folk (*plebs*) raged against the princes', wishing to inflict a crushing defeat on the king, now that they had him at a disadvantage. 'They loudly insisted that Duke Otto should rule over them as king and lead them in the coming struggle.'[122] Bruno's account of the peace settlement of 2 February distinguishes between the Saxon leadership, who were satisfied with the king's concessions, and the rank-and-file, who were not. 'Duke Otto and the others to whom great promises had been made, persuaded the rest to accept' Henry as king and to make peace. Far from accepting the settlement, the rank-and-file broke the peace as soon as Henry withdrew from Saxony and travelled back to Worms at the end of March. 'The common people (*vulgus*) of Saxony and especially those who lived in the villages near the castle of Harzburg' were too impatient to wait for the king's servants to dismantle the fortifications, according to the terms of the peace. Instead they attacked the Harzburg, 'the source of all the misfortunes that they had suffered', and reduced it to rubble. Both Lampert and Bruno emphasised that the peasantry acted 'without the knowledge and counsel of the princes'.[123] With the destruction of the Harzburg in 1074 'the common people' assume the central role in the narratives of the Saxon resistance to the government of Henry IV. It is clear from the accounts of both Lampert and Bruno that the *plebs* or *vulgus* (Lampert's terms) or *rustici* (Bruno's term) had served in the rebel army in 1073. According to Bruno, they were present in the Saxon army in such numbers that Henry could describe the rebels as 'rustic men unskilled in war'. Lampert wrote that the Saxon army

---

[121] Bruno, *Saxonicum bellum* c. 30, p. 33.

[122] Lampert, *Annales* 1074, p. 179. Cf. Bruno c. 30, 31, pp. 33, 34.

[123] Lampert, *Annales* 1074, pp. 183–4. Bruno c. 33, p. 35; cf. c. 42, p. 42. See Meyer von Knonau (1894) 2:331–3.

was dismissed by its opponents as 'an absurd crowd of commoners, more used to farming than fighting, who had come to war because of fear of the princes rather than military valour'.[124] The details given by the chroniclers suggest that the rebellious 'common people' were the peasantry living in the neighbourhood of the royal castles. They had undoubtedly suffered most from the depredations of the king's Swabian garrisons and desired a more thorough revenge than that contained in the peace terms of February 1074.[125]

The aspect of the revenge of the Saxon *vulgus* that most shocked contemporaries was the sacrilege involved in the destruction of the Harzburg. They burned and plundered the church that Henry had built inside the castle and broke up its altars. 'Finally, so that the king would have no reason for restoring the castle, they exhumed his son and his brother, whom he had caused to be buried there to make the place more acceptable to the people.'[126] The graves of these Salian princes who had died in infancy – Conrad, Henry IV's younger brother, who had died in 1055, and Henry, his first-born son, who died in 1071 – were intended (to judge from Lampert's account) to be objects of reverence to the local population. Evidently royal graves were regarded as possessing some of that sacral character that distinguished the living monarch.[127] The desecration of the royal graves in the Harzburg was the turning point in the Saxon rebellion of 1073–5. Lampert wrote that the peasants' action 'struck the princes of Saxony with the greatest dread, lest the king . . . hold them guilty of having violated the treaty, seize upon this as a just occasion for renewing the war and arouse the entire strength of the kingdom against them'.[128] The anger provoked by the sacrilege, together with alarm at the spectacle of the peasantry acting 'without the knowledge and counsel of the princes', created widespread sympathy for the king among the nobility and ended his political isolation. At Easter (20 April) 1074 the royal court at Bamberg was attended by the suspected rebel of the previous year, Berthold of Carinthia, by Siegfried of Mainz and 'very many others who had fallen away from [the king] during the Saxon war'.[129] The rallying of the south German dukes to the king was complete when, in November, Henry came to Regensburg and the court was attended by Welf IV of Bavaria, the intended victim of the peace of Gerstungen.[130] It is fair to assume that this readiness of the south German dukes for reconciliation was not solely the result of outrage at the desecration of the royal graves. Threatened by the prospect of Otto of Northeim's return

[124] Bruno c. 16, 31, pp. 23, 34; Lampert, *Annales* 1075, p. 216; cf. 1074, p. 179.

[125] On the identity of these peasants: Baaken (1961) 80–95; but see also the criticisms of Fenske (1977) 293–325.   [126] Lampert, *Annales* 1074, p. 184; Bruno c. 33, pp. 35–6.

[127] Leyser (1979) 93.   [128] Lampert, *Annales* 1074, p. 184.

[129] *Ibid.*, p. 185. Cf. Berthold, *Annales* 1074, p. 276.

[130] *D H IV* 276. See Meyer von Knonau (1894) 2:405, 407.

to royal favour, the dukes must have welcomed the breach of the peace of Gerstungen, since it would end the king's *rapprochement* with their Saxon rival. Henry indeed held the Saxon princes responsible for the fate of the Harzburg, despite their attempts at exculpation and offers to make whatever reparation he demanded. Henry rejected their envoys' explanations and made it clear that he considered the peace of Gerstungen to have been violated.[131]

The king could not immediately renew the Saxon war, since the summer had to be devoted to a campaign in Hungary. In mid-June 1074 Henry received an appeal from his brother-in-law, King Salomon of Hungary, who had been deposed by his cousin, Duke Geisa. Salomon offered Henry 'six of the strongest fortified cities in Hungary' in return for an expedition to restore him to the throne. Henry responded by invading the Hungarian kingdom in August with an army of 'common soldiers and his own knights'. He succeeded in establishing Salomon's lordship only over the western borderlands of Hungary.[132] It was only at Easter (5 April) 1075 that an expedition against the Saxons was ordered: the royal army would assemble in Breitungen on 8 June. Some of the Saxon princes sent envoys to the court in Worms during Eastertide to plead their cause, but were denied a hearing. According to Lampert, they attempted to make an alliance with the dukes of Swabia, Carinthia and Lower Lotharingia, only to find themselves outmanoeuvred by 'the foresight of the king, which was far beyond his years'. 'He had taken an oath from all his princes that they would receive no legations from [the Saxons] without consulting him, that they would support them neither openly with their arms nor secretly with their counsel and that they would not intercede on their behalf. . . '[133] Evidence of the Saxon efforts to avert the royal expedition is found in a letter of Werner of Magdeburg to Siegfried of Mainz. He proclaimed the princes' innocence of the crime of desecrating the graves in the Harzburg, which was the work of 'the peasants with the characteristic ignorance of the peasantry'. The princes had responded to the outrage by submitting themselves 'like humble slaves' to the judgement of the king and their fellow princes, but had met only with rebuffs. Werner therefore begged Siegfried 'to mitigate the anger of our lord the king' and 'persuade him to think of us as human beings, lest he wish to destroy us, innocent as we are, and so imperil his soul'.[134] According to Bruno, the king offered reconciliation to Werner and the majority of the Saxon princes, if they would surrender to him Burchard of Halberstadt, Otto of Northeim, Frederick of Goseck and the other chief conspirators of 1073. This the Saxons refused to do without

---

[131] Lampert, *Annales* 1074, pp. 184–5; Bruno, *Saxonicum bellum* c. 34, p. 36. See Meyer von Knonau (1894) 2:336–9.

[132] Lampert, *Annales* 1074, pp. 197–8. See Meyer von Knonau (1894) 2:402–4; Boshof (1986) 186.   [133] Lampert, *Annales* 1075, pp. 201, 210, 213.   [134] Bruno c. 42, pp. 41–3.

the guarantee of a trial by all the German princes. Significantly, Bruno claimed that the king's intransigence was reinforced by Rudolf of Swabia. Rudolf had 'not forgotten the treaty that the Saxons suddenly made with the king' in February 1074. He urged Henry to avenge the attack on the Harzburg, an 'injury both to God and to [the king] and his princes' and 'promised to make himself and all his armed might available' to the king.[135] Henry could safely ignore pleas for moderation in Saxony and contemplate a military conquest that would enable him to resume his 'policy of recuperation'. The military strength that had been lacking in 1073 would be provided by Rudolf of Swabia and like-minded princes, determined to overturn the settlement of Gerstungen and prevent the return of Otto of Northeim to power.

When the royal army assembled at Breitungen (8 June 1075), it seemed to Lampert, observing from nearby Hersfeld, that 'never in human memory had so great, so strong, so well-equipped an army been led by any king in the German kingdom'. So determined was the king on a full attendance of the princes that he refused to exempt the crippled Abbot Widerad of Fulda, for whom the waggon-journey to Breitungen proved fatal. The king accepted, however, the excuse of the sick and aged Anno of Cologne, whose kinship with the rebels Burchard of Halberstadt and Werner of Magdeburg made his loyalty suspect. The foremost of Henry's commanders was Rudolf of Swabia. The chroniclers emphasised 'the special privilege of the Swabians, a right given to them in ancient times, that in every expedition of the German king they must lead the army and join battle first'.[136] The *Song of the Saxon War* emphasises the importance of the contingents of Welf IV of Bavaria and the two Lotharingian dukes, Godfrey III and Theoderic; Lampert's account, that of Duke Vratislav II of Bohemia, who was 'accompanied by so great a force that (deluded by a vain hope) he thought himself powerful enough to win the Saxon war solely with his own resources'. Meanwhile the ranks of the opposing Saxon and Thuringian army had been seriously diminished by desertions: 'all the Westphalians and all those living in the region around Meissen', who were 'corrupted by the king's gold', and all the Saxon bishops except for Werner of Magdeburg, Burchard of Halberstadt, Werner of Merseburg and Imad of Paderborn. Bruno's harshest strictures were reserved for William of Lodersleben and Frederick *de Monte*, who 'fled by night to the king, the enemy of the fatherland', despite the fact that the statement of their grievances at the assembly of Hoetensleben in 1073 had been 'the principal cause of the war'. The desertion of the nobility meant that 'common foot-

---

[135] *Ibid.* c. 44–5, pp. 43–4. See Meyer von Knonau (1894) 2:487–93.
[136] Lampert, *Annales* 1075, pp. 215–16; Berthold, *Annales* 1075, p. 278; *Carmen de bello Saxonico* III.57–90, pp. 16–17. See Meyer von Knonau (1894) 2:496–7.

soldiers' constituted a large proportion of the forces commanded by Otto of Northeim.[137]

The royal army added the advantage of surprise to that of numbers, catching the enemy unawares at Homburg on the River Unstrut on 9 June. The Saxons had not expected so large an army to march so rapidly from Breitungen. The battle lasted from midday until the hour of nones (3 p.m.), ending with the rout of the Saxon army. The decisive royal victory enabled the king to lay waste to enemy territory as far afield as Halberstadt. Bruno characterised it as 'a very fierce battle, finished in a very short time' and fought in a dust-cloud, 'so that it was hardly possible to distinguish between friend and foe'. Lampert's account emphasises the courage of Otto of Northeim and the young knights of his household. The *Song of the Saxon War* equally characteristically concentrates on the deeds of the king, depicted with epic exaggeration.[138] Rudolf of Swabia had a narrow escape when the nose-guard of his helmet saved him from a mortal thrust from the sword of Count Udo II of Stade, margrave of the Saxon Nordmark.[139] Both armies suffered severe losses, although they are impossible to calculate. The names only of the princely casualties were recorded. On the royal side these were Margrave Ernest of the Bavarian Ostmark, Count Engelbert and the sons of the royal kinsman Count Eberhard of Nellenburg, Henry and Eberhard, together with 'very many Bavarian and Swabian noblemen'; on the Saxon side, Count Gebhard of Supplinburg (father of the future Emperor Lothar III) and Folcmar and Suidger 'of the middling nobility'. Noble casualties were few on the Saxon side because 'their knowledge of the ground, the darkness of the air [caused by the dust-cloud] and the swiftness of their horses' assisted the nobles' flight. The 'common foot soldiers' could not escape so easily and many were slaughtered.[140] The fate of the foot soldiers at the battle of Homburg aggravated the tension among the rebels which had first become evident early in 1074. During the summer of 1075, wrote Lampert, 'the Saxons and Thuringians held frequent assemblies in which the common people (*plebs*) raged against the princes and the princes against the commoners'. The nobles were denounced for abandoning the *plebs* to be slaughtered like cattle. Not surprisingly, after 9 June the commoners declined to serve as foot soldiers in the rebel army: a refusal that explains the military collapse of the Saxons the following autumn.

[137] Bruno c. 39, 45, pp. 39–40, 44; Lampert, *Annales* 1075, pp. 216, 221. See Meyer von Knonau (1894) 2:493–4.   [138] *Carmen de bello Saxonico* III.170–1, p. 19.

[139] Lampert, *Annales* 1075, p. 219; Bruno c. 46, p. 45. Udo was Rudolf's first cousin: Jakobs (1968) 185.

[140] Lampert, *Annales* 1075, pp. 219–21; Bruno c. 46, p. 45; Berthold, *Annales* 1075, p. 279 ('almost 8,000' Saxon dead and 'more than 1,500' of Henry's army); *Carmen* III.197–202, p. 20. See Meyer von Knonau (1894) 2:874–84; Giese (1979) 159–61.

The princes' fear that the *plebs* might decide to hand them over to the king to secure pardon for themselves contributed to their growing demoralisation.[141]

The king planned a further Saxon expedition in autumn 1075 and the royal army was commanded to reassemble in Gerstungen on 22 October. The south German dukes, who had played so important a role at Homburg, this time ignored the king's command. Lampert and Bruno believed that the dukes 'repented of their error in shedding so much blood during the previous expedition'.[142] They may well have repented their imprudence in allowing the king to win an overwhelming victory in Saxony. Despite their absence, however, the contingents of the other princes, especially the Lotharingian contingent of the loyal Duke Godfrey III, amounted to an army formidable enough to persuade the Saxon princes to submit to the king. Henry permitted the negotiations to be conducted by those members of his entourage whom the Saxons requested: the archbishops of Mainz and Salzburg, the bishops of Augsburg and Würzburg and Duke Godfrey of Lower Lotharingia.[143] Finally on 26 or 27 October the rebels surrendered to the king at Spier. Their submission provided the author of the *Song of the Saxon War* with a striking final scene for his epic in which 'the Saxon magnates . . . laid down their arms and bent their proud necks'. The *Song* concludes with an appeal to 'the unconquered king' to show mercy to the defeated.[144] Henry was disinclined to heed such an appeal. The hostile chroniclers claimed that, although the rebels were induced to surrender by a promise of lenient treatment, the king broke his promise as soon as the rebels were in his power.[145] At Spier the rebels were placed in the custody of loyal princes and despatched to prisons in the Rhineland, southern Germany, Burgundy and Italy, while the king distributed their benefices to those vassals who had served him best during the Saxon war. Two confiscations are recorded in detail. Firstly, Henry gave the benefices of his kinsman, Margrave Ekbert II of Meissen, to his trusted adviser, Udalric of Godesheim. Secondly, on the death of Margrave Dedi I of Lower Lusatia, the king ignored the claims of Dedi's son (who was currently his hostage) and gave his march to Duke Vratislav II of Bohemia. The submission at Spier enabled the king to rebuild his regime in eastern Saxony. 'He commended the castles . . . to his followers and ordered them to implement tyranny throughout the region.'[146]

---

[141] Lampert, *Annales* 1075, p. 228. See Fenske (1977) 55–6.

[142] Lampert, *Annales* 1075, p. 235; Bruno c. 54, p. 51.

[143] Lampert, *Annales* 1075, p. 235; Bruno c. 48–9, pp. 46–8. See Meyer von Knonau (1894) 2:520–5.   [144] *Carmen de bello Saxonico* II.284–6, 289–90, p. 23.

[145] Lampert, *Annales* 1075, p. 238; Bruno c. 54, p. 51; Berthold, *Annales* 1075, p. 279. See Meyer von Knonau (1894) 2:528–38.

[146] Lampert, *Annales* 1075, p. 239; Bruno c. 55–6, pp. 51–2. See Meyer von Knonau (1894) 2:525–6, 538–40.

One Saxon prince, however, escaped the penalties of rebellion and was soon in the king's confidence. Otto of Northeim was 'the most energetic author of [the Saxons'] surrender' in October.[147] Perhaps he had already begun to reach an understanding with the king. At Spier he was placed, together with Burchard of Halberstadt, in the custody of Bishop Rupert of Bamberg, but his imprisonment was shortlived. During the Christmas celebrations of 1075 at Goslar the king released Otto, on condition of taking two of his sons as hostages. It is likely that at Christmastide 1075 the king restored to Otto the benefices which he had lost in 1070 and also conferred on him a county confiscated from Count Ruotger of Bilstein.[148] Otto's admirers, the chroniclers Bruno and Lampert, recorded that Otto was transformed from 'the bitterest enemy' into 'the most faithful counsellor' of the king. He was received 'not only into the king's grace but into so great a familiarity that henceforward he gave [the king] his counsel in all matters, both private and public, on more intimate terms than other courtiers'.[149] Neither Lampert nor Bruno attempted to account for this transformation. The explanation is probably to be found, as in the exactly analogous case of Henry's rapprochement with Otto in February 1074, in the king's deteriorating relationship with the south German dukes. In October 1075 they had refused to serve in the royal army in Saxony: Henry's reaction was to seek reconciliation with their rival, Otto of Northeim. Lampert emphasised the king's complete confidence in the rehabilitated Otto. 'The former duke of Bavaria, Otto, resided alone in the castle of Harzburg. The king had delegated to him his authority and the administration of public affairs throughout Saxony, giving him the additional duty of rebuilding the Harzburg with all its former strength and of building another castle on the hill known as the Steinberg, which towers over Goslar.' The leader of the rebellion against the 'royal policy of recuperation' in eastern Saxony had now been entrusted with the implementation of that policy. Lampert's report makes clear that the Billungs 'and very many other princes' regarded Otto as a traitor. He had persuaded his fellow rebels to surrender in October 1075, with the result that they had been consigned to prison, while he 'received from the king the government of all Saxony as the reward for his treachery'.[150] His critics were keenly aware that while the rebellion had ended in the defeat of the cause for which he had fought, the outcome was nevertheless a personal victory for Otto of Northeim.

The outcome was a victory also for Henry IV and he exploited it in the interests of dynastic continuity. During the Christmas celebrations of 1075 in

[147] Lampert, *Annales* 1076, p. 261.   [148] Lange (1961) 57–61.

[149] Lampert, *Annales* 1076, p. 251; Bruno c. 57, pp. 52–3. See Meyer von Knonau (1894) 2:584–6, 645.   [150] Lampert, *Annales* 1076, p. 261. See Meyer von Knonau (1894) 2:679.

Goslar the king 'demanded and received from those [princes] who had come there, an oath that they would elect as their king after him none other than his son, who was still a child'. Henry imitated the example of his father on 25 December 1050 by securing from the princes a promise to elect his heir, Conrad, who was not yet two years old. The occasion seems to have been less impressive than the king had intended. He had summoned 'all the princes of the kingdom' but 'very few came except the duke of Bohemia'.[151] The south German dukes, whose military support had been crucial six months before, remained aloof. The defeated Saxons would not easily forget the humiliation of Spier and the king now depended principally on Otto of Northeim to contain their resentment. At Christmastide 1075, therefore, Henry IV was both victorious and vulnerable. He owed his current success to the mutual hostility of the greatest princes rather than to their loyalty to the crown. Even as he celebrated his triumph, a new storm was already brewing, more dangerous than the crisis of 1073. Henry would soon face a conspiracy of princes bent on deposing him and electing Rudolf of Swabia as king, the most powerful member of the conspiracy being Rudolf's old enemy, Otto of Northeim. In the middle of 1076 the Saxon war broke out afresh. It raged for thirteen years, during which Saxony served as the power base of Henry's enemies and Goslar as the residence of the anti-kings who aimed at Henry's throne. In 1088 Henry suffered his last defeat in Saxony and withdrew, never to return. It was in eastern Saxony, therefore, that the king encountered his most implacable enemies. No less important, it was here that he first acquired that reputation for tyranny that he could never afterwards shake off.

[151] Lampert, *Annales* 1076, pp. 250–1. Cf. Bernold, *Chronicon* 1076, p. 431. See Meyer von Knonau (1894) 2:584; E. Goez (1996) 4.

The conflict with Pope Gregory VII

3

Henry IV, the imperial Church and the reform papacy, 1065–1075

'The royal and the priestly dignity . . . are bound together in the Christian people by a reciprocal treaty. Each must make use of the other . . . For the king is girded with the sword so that he may be armed to resist the enemies of the Church and the priest devotes himself to prayers and vigils so as to make God well-disposed towards king and people.' So Cardinal Peter Damian of Ostia described the mutual dependence of the ecclesiastical and the secular power in his letter of 1065 to Henry IV, exhorting the king to defend the Roman church against the attacks of the antipope.[1] He had stressed the same theme three years earlier, when exhorting the German court to recognise Alexander II as lawful pope.[2] This theory derived from the teaching of Pope Gelasius I (492–6) concerning 'the sacred authority of bishops and the royal power'. 'Christ . . . separated the offices of both powers according to their proper activities and their special dignities . . . so that Christian emperors would have need of bishops in order to attain eternal life and bishops would have recourse to imperial direction in the conduct of imperial affairs.'[3] This Gelasian idea remained the basis of the papacy's political thought at the beginning of the pontificate of Gregory VII. A papal letter of August 1073 underlines the equal importance of the two powers and their need for cooperation by likening them to a pair of eyes. 'Priesthood and empire are joined in the unity of harmony. For just as by means of two eyes the human body is ruled by temporal light, so by means of these two dignities, agreeing in pure religion, the body of the Church proves to be ruled and illuminated by spiritual light.'[4]

This was written at a period of tension in the relations of the papacy and the German court, when the 'reciprocal treaty' envisaged by Peter Damian in 1065 had not materialised. The royal expedition to defend Alexander II against the antipope, planned for May 1065, was deferred: a postponement that suggested to reformers in Rome that Henry IV preferred to listen to 'evil

---

[1] Peter Damian, *Letter* 120: *Briefe* 3, 389. [2] *Ibid.* 89: *Briefe* 2, 572.
[3] Gelasius I, *Letter* 12: *Epistolae Rom. pont. genuinae* 1, 350; Gelasius I, *Tractatus* IV.11, *Epistolae* 1, 567. See Ryan (1956) 82–3, 90–2, 105–6. [4] Gregory VII, *Registrum* 1.19, p. 31.

counsellors' rather than perform his duty to the Roman church.[5] A second opportunity to defend the papacy in 1067 similarly came to nothing. Late in 1066 Prince Richard of Capua, the pope's Norman vassal, invaded the Patrimony of St Peter and laid waste the Campagna.[6] Once more the Roman church appealed for Henry IV's assistance. The journey that Empress Agnes undertook at the most unseasonable time of the year from her retirement in Rome to her son's court was probably intended to lend weight to the papal appeal.[7] The king commanded an army to muster in Augsburg (the usual assembly point for Italian expeditions) before the end of January 1067. When Henry reached Augsburg, however, he discovered that Godfrey 'the Bearded', duke of Lower Lotharingia and margrave of Tuscany, had already crossed the Alps into Italy. The absence of the margrave of Tuscany, whose participation was indispensable for any Italian expedition, caused the king to abandon his plans. It was subsequently learned that Godfrey was preparing to campaign against Richard of Capua. Godfrey's expedition, accompanied by Alexander II and his cardinals, eventually secured the withdrawal of the Normans from papal territory in June 1067. It is not clear why Godfrey 'the Bearded' took this initiative. The historian of the Roman reform party, Bonizo of Sutri, believed that 'the magnificent Duke Godfrey' had reverted to the role of protector of the reform papacy, which he had played intermittently since the pontificate of his brother, Stephen IX.[8] It is possible, however, that Godfrey was mainly preoccupied with his interests as margrave of Tuscany, which he regarded as being threatened by the king's recent marriage to Bertha of Turin. One of the motives that had inspired the royal marriage alliance with the house of Savoy–Turin a decade earlier was that of providing a safeguard against the ambitions of the house of Canossa-Lotharingia. The solemnisation of this marriage and the plans for an Italian expedition which followed soon after may have suggested to Godfrey a plot to curtail his power in Tuscany and prompted him to forestall the royal expedition.[9]

The abortive royal expedition was followed in 1068 by the sending of a distinguished legation to the Italian kingdom: Archbishop Anno of Cologne (whose office of arch-chancellor for Italy and whose previous experience of the kingdom especially qualified him for such an embassy), Otto of Northeim, duke of Bavaria (who had been on two previous legations to Italy) and the Italian bishop Henry of Trent. The purpose of the mission is not mentioned

[5] See above p. 54.   [6] Meyer von Knonau (1890) 1:542–56.
[7] Peter Damian, *Letter* 144, 149: *Briefe* 3, 525–7, 546–54. See Bulst-Thiele (1933) 92; Struve (1985) 27; Black-Veldtrup (1995) 45, 95.
[8] Bonizo of Sutri, *Ad amicum* VI, p. 599. Cf. *Annales Altahenses* 1067, 1068, pp. 72–4; Amatus of Monte Cassino, *Historia Normannorum* VI.9–10, pp. 270–2.
[9] Meyer von Knonau (1890) 1:551–2; Mohr (1976) 2:43–6.

in the sources, but the eminence of the envoys and the timing of their legation (apparently in February, unusually early in the year for a journey to Italy)
suggest that the most important matters of state were involved. The intention
was perhaps to prepare for the royal 'journey' (*iter*) through the Italian
kingdom and the imperial coronation. According to the Niederaltaich chronicler, 'when they arrived in Ravenna, they conversed and dined with the
bishop of that place, nor did they avoid the company of the bishop of Parma,
whom they met elsewhere, despite the fact that Pope Alexander had bound
them both with the bond of anathema'. Because of their contact with the antipope Cadalus of Parma and his adherent, Archbishop Henry of Ravenna, the
envoys were obliged to perform public penance before Alexander II would
receive them.[10] The envoys' controversial meeting with the antipope cannot
have been a chance encounter: their commission was perhaps to persuade
Cadalus to renounce his claim to the papacy, unless the German court had
begun to reconsider Cadalus as a papal candidate. Either interpretation fits the
picture of an attempted pacification of the Italian kingdom in preparation for
the royal *iter*. This is also the context in which we should place the information that in 1068 Godfrey 'the Bearded' was also in contact with Cadalus.
Alexander II imposed on him the penance of living apart from his wife until
he had founded a monastery.[11] Whatever the motive of Anno's legation and
Godfrey's action, however, the meeting with the antipope can only have
inspired the reform papacy with a deep distrust of the German court.

The following year witnessed papal involvement in the kingdom and the
personal life of the king of a type unprecedented in the Salian period. The
occasion was Henry IV's unsuccessful attempt to obtain a divorce from Queen
Bertha. In an assembly of princes in Worms in June 1069 the king announced
that, although he could not accuse the queen of any offence that would justify
a divorce, he wished to be freed 'from such an ill-omened bond', since it was
impossible for him to consummate the marriage.[12] The rumours of estrangement in the narrative sources are corroborated by the evidence of the royal
diplomas. For two years after the royal wedding in the summer of 1066 the
'intervention' clauses of Henry's diplomas regularly indicate the presence of
Bertha, 'consort of our kingdom and of our marriage-bed', as an influential
personage at court. After 5 August 1068 her name disappears from the diplomas for more than a year, until after the defeat of the king's plans for divorce.[13]

[10] *Annales Altahenses* 1068, p. 74. Cf. *Triumphus s. Remacli* 1.22, p. 448. See Meyer von Knonau
   (1890) 1:585–91; Lange (1961) 25–6; Jenal (1974) 317–28.
[11] Peter Damian, *Letter* 154: *Briefe* 4, 68–71; *Chronicon s. Huberti Andaginensis* c. 23, p. 581. See
   Meyer von Knonau (1890) 1:602–3 and n. 51; E. Goez (1995) 161–3.
[12] Lampert, *Annales* 1069, pp. 105–6; *Annales Altahenses* 1069, p. 78. See Meyer von Knonau
   (1890) 1:612–15.   [13] *DD H IV* 187–8, 191, 193, 197–202 (1067); 205–6 (1068).

The reason for this estrangement can only be guessed. It is possible that the king had always resented the dynastic marriage planned for him when he was only five.[14] It was possibly no coincidence that in this same year of 1069 the king's brother-in-law, Duke Rudolf of Swabia, sought a divorce from his second wife, Adelaide, sister of Queen Bertha. The duke 'falsely accused [Adelaide] of not preserving her chastity', but was subsequently reconciled to her when she cleared herself of the accusation in the presence of Pope Alexander II.[15] This episode seems to have done nothing to diminish the high esteem in which Rudolf was held in ecclesiastical reforming circles, whereas the king's attempt to obtain a divorce resulted in censure from the Church.

The question of the royal divorce was referred by the assembly of Worms to a synod in Frankfurt early in October 1069. The inconclusive proceedings in Worms are recorded in a letter of Archbishop Siegfried of Mainz to Pope Alexander II in the summer of 1069. Siegfried wrote that he had opposed the king's request 'and declared that, unless [the king] gave a convincing reason for the divorce . . . [he] would separate him from the bosom and communion of the Church'. Siegfried referred the king's request to papal judgement since 'the more important business of the Church and the settlement of the more difficult cases should be referred to [the Roman church] as to the head'. This matter 'neither could nor should be settled by our efforts except by [the pope's] authority'.[16] This letter is one of six which Siegfried sent to Rome during Alexander II's pontificate, all expressing the same reverence for the office of pope, 'who is especially charged with the care of all the churches'. Siegfried was indeed one of the first correspondents to Rome to use the special language of the Roman primacy that the reform papacy had adopted since the pontificate of Pope Leo IX.[17] The issue that prompted Siegfried to 'show special reverence [to Alexander II] as a son to a father' was probably the Thuringian tithes dispute. During the 1060s Siegfried strove to enforce the payment of tithes to his church by the laity of Thuringia and sought the help of Alexander II and Archdeacon Hildebrand (the future Pope Gregory VII), in his struggle with 'the rebellious Thuringians'.[18] The hostile chronicler Lampert claimed that Siegfried of Mainz supported the king's demand for a

[14] Bruno of Merseburg, *Saxonicum bellum* c. 6, pp. 16–17 Cf. Berthold, *Annales* 1068, p. 274.

[15] *Annales Weissenburgenses* 1069, 1071, p. 55. See Meyer von Knonau (1890) 1:614–15; (1894) 2:27–8; Jakobs (1968) 160.

[16] *Codex Udalrici* 34, p. 65. *Annales Altahenses* 1069, p. 78 and Lampert, *Annales* 1069, pp. 105–6 claimed that Siegfried supported the king. This contradiction prompted the attack on Lampert's veracity by von Ranke (1888) 125–49. See also Meyer von Knonau (1890) 1:612–17, 662; Schmeidler (1920) 141–9.   [17] Robinson (1990) 179–81, 183, 186–7.

[18] *Codex Udalrici* 28, 31, 34, 36, 38, 40, 42, 45, pp. 54–6, 58–9, 64–6, 68–9, 77–81, 84–7, 88–91, 97–100. See G. Schmidt (1917) 58–60.

divorce in return for royal support in the Thuringian tithes dispute.[19] Siegfried's letter to Alexander II, however, suggests that the archbishop referred the case to the pope, firstly, to avoid giving a negative decision that would offend the king and, secondly, to win favour in Rome by a conspicuous demonstration of respect for the papal primacy.

Siegfried asked for envoys from Rome with a papal letter authorising him to decide the question at the forthcoming synod. Instead Alexander II sent a papal legate to settle the case: Peter Damian, cardinal bishop of Ostia. The choice of this most distinguished reformer indicates the significance that the papacy attached to the royal divorce: it was a matter too important to be left to the discretion of the metropolitan. The legate announced to the synod of Frankfurt the pope's opposition to a divorce: he was prepared to use 'the power of the Church to prevent [the king's] offence by means of canon law'. 'One who had betrayed the Christian faith by setting so pestilential an example would never be consecrated emperor by [the pope's] hands.' All the princes urged the king to obey the pope, reminding him of the wealth and military resources of Bertha's family in the kingdoms of Italy and Burgundy, which might be used to avenge the insult of the divorce. The king 'should not give the queen's kindred a cause for rebellion and a just reason for disturbing the commonwealth'.[20] The dynastic considerations that prompted Henry III to betrothe his son to a princess of the family of Savoy–Turin in 1055 were now cited to urge Henry IV to adhere to that alliance. Not only was that family strong 'in arms and wealth': the queen's mother, Margravine Adelaide of Turin, was highly regarded by the reformers in Rome.[21] Approval of the house of Savoy–Turin as allies in the work of reform may have intensified the papacy's opposition to the divorce. The combined pressure of the legate and the princes in the synod of Frankfurt compelled Henry IV's surrender.[22] The name of 'Queen Bertha, beloved consort of our kingdom and of our marriage-bed' accordingly reappears in royal diplomas from 26 October 1069.[23] Lampert reported that the king, smarting from his defeat, 'decided to share with [the queen] only the royal title and to treat her thereafter as if she was not his wife'. This report is contradicted by the evidence that Bertha bore the king two children in rapid succession in 1070 and 1071, the short-lived Adelaide and Henry.[24]

The defeat of the king's project in 1069 by the papacy and the princes is a

---

[19] Lampert of Hersfeld, *Annales* 1069, pp. 105–6.

[20] *Ibid.*, p. 110. See Meyer von Knonau (1890) 1:624–7, 631–4.

[21] *Annales Altahenses* 1069, p. 78; Peter Damian, *Letter* 114: *Briefe* 3, 302.

[22] Lampert, *Annales* 1069, p. 110.

[23] *DD H IV* 224, 227–9. On *D H IV* 218 see Gawlik (1970a) 45.

[24] Meyer von Knonau (1894) 2:85 n. 82.

striking anticipation of the pattern of the politics of the last three decades of the reign. For the first time the reform papacy imposed its will on the German king. Four years after he wrote to Henry IV about the 'reciprocal treaty' that bound together kingship and priesthood, Peter Damian declared that the king would destroy that alliance if he persisted in defying canon law by seeking a divorce. The cardinal's letter of 1065 had contained a prophetic warning. 'A king must be revered while he obeys the Creator, but when a king opposes the divine commands he is rightly held in contempt by his subjects.'[25] In 1069 Peter Damian actually threatened Henry with 'the power of the Church' if he continued to demand a divorce. According to Lampert, Alexander II achieved Henry's submission by using the sanction of withholding imperial coronation, the same sanction that Gregory VII seems to have used six years later. The pope felt compelled to intervene directly in Henry's affairs 'lest the poison of so wicked an example, beginning with the king, should stain the whole Christian people and he who ought to be the punisher of crimes should himself become the author and standardbearer of wickedness'.[26] The king's central role in Christian society made him a potentially dangerous source of contamination. The responsibility of the pope to monitor the king's conduct is the theme of a letter sent to Alexander II by Siegfried of Mainz (1066/7). Siegfried requested the pope's goodwill for the young king 'because the crown of the kingdom and the diadem of the Roman empire are in your hand by the hand of St Peter . . . As from the earliest moment of your accession to the holy see you have fostered and cherished the boy-king by your counsel and aid, so may you continue with him in the constancy of apostolic vigour until he attains the crown of the empire.'[27] Siegfried's letter combined the ninth-century tradition that St Peter alone could confer the imperial crown[28] with the fact that Henry III had committed his son to the care of Pope Victor II.[29] In Roman reforming circles this event of 1056 was reinterpreted as a precedent for papal supervision of the affairs of the German kingdom. Peter Damian wrote that Christ had 'added monarchies' to Victor II's spiritual authority and 'granted [him] jurisdiction over the whole Roman empire during the vacancy'. Two decades later Gregory VII cited the fact that Henry III had 'commended his son to the Roman church' as a reason for papal vigilance concerning the conduct of Henry IV.[30]

Perhaps the most important aspect of the divorce proceedings of 1069 was their long-term effect on the king's reputation. The polemics of his enemies

[25] Peter Damian, *Letter* 120: *Briefe* 3, 391.   [26] Lampert, *Annales* 1069, pp. 109–10.
[27] *Codex Udalrici* 32, p. 61.   [28] Ullmann (1970) 97–102, 143–66, 225–8.
[29] Peter Damian, *Letter* 46: *Briefe* 2, 41.
[30] Gregory VII, *Registrum* 1.19, 20, pp. 31–2, 33–4. See Berges (1947) 189–209 and below p. 155.

in the 1070s and 1080s revealed that his fame had been permanently scarred by the rumours that circulated as a consequence of the attempted divorce. Two distinct polemical accounts of Henry IV's sexual depravity are apparent: one associated with the Saxon rebellion of 1073 and a more elaborate account connected with the polemical activity in the imperial territories following the death of Gregory VII in 1085. The demands of the Saxon rebels in 1073 included the requirement that the king should abandon his concubines and live with his wife.[31] The charges in the polemical literature of *circa* 1085 are that Henry fathered illegitimate children and was guilty of incest and pederasty.[32] These allegations of sexual misconduct were intended to support the argument of the Saxon rebels and, a decade later, of the pro-papal polemicists, that Henry deserved to be deposed because he was a tyrant. The definition of tyranny which Henry's enemies knew best, that of the seventh-century encyclopaedist, Isidore of Seville, described tyrants as 'very wicked and *shameless kings*'.[33] Henry IV's alleged sexual misconduct consequently provided his opponents with a useful polemical weapon. The importance of the allegations of misconduct was that they undoubtedly influenced the attitude towards Henry IV both of the papacy and of reforming circles in the empire. According to the anonymous *Life of Emperor Henry IV* Henry's political opponents used the rumours of the king's evil life to poison the pope's mind against Henry and to gain the papacy as an ally. Similarly the polemicist Wido of Ferrara wrote that the allegations of sexual misconduct 'were disclosed by letters and testimony of many men and reached the ears of Hildebrand', who admonished the king 'by means of frequent legations, commands and letters to change his life for the better'.[34] Gregory VII himself attested that he had received 'an evil and most shameful report of the king's behaviour', prompting him to admonish the king 'by letters and envoys to cease from his wickedness'.[35] Allegations of sexual misconduct were particularly lethal to the reputation of a king because of his central role in Christian society, as defender of the Church, of the faith and of the laws. 'How is he to be a punisher of crime, an avenger of sin, when he himself is in the toils of the same errors? Under what covenant will he preserve the law for others, when he has destroyed the rule of justice in himself?'[36] An important factor in the conflict

---

[31] Lampert, *Annales* 1073, pp. 151–2, 162; Bruno, *Saxonicum bellum* c. 6–14, pp. 16–22.

[32] Manegold of Lautenbach, *Ad Gebehardum* c. 29, pp. 362–3; Wido of Ferrara, *De scismate* I.3, p. 536. The rhetorical methods of late eleventh-century polemic: Manegold, *Contra Wolfelmum* c. 24, p. 107. See Robinson (1976) 209–38.

[33] Isidore of Seville, *Etymologiae* IX.19.

[34] *Vita Heinrici IV* c. 3, pp. 15–16; Wido of Ferrara, *De scismate* I.3, p. 536.

[35] Gregory VII, *Registrum* IV.1, p. 290: Gregory VII, *Epistolae Vagantes* 14, pp. 34, 38. Cf. *Registrum* III.10a, pp. 270–1.   [36] Wido of Ferrara, *De scismate* I.3, p. 536.

between Gregory VII and Henry IV in the years 1076–85 was the pope's belief that the king, despite his warnings, had failed 'to order his conduct as befitted a king and (if God granted it) a future emperor'.[37]

Gregory gave three reasons for his decision to excommunicate Henry in 1076: he failed to do penance 'for the guilty acts of his life'; he had associated with simoniacs; he had caused schism in the Church. Gregory's most serious charge was that, on the advice of his familiars, 'he had polluted bishoprics and many monasteries with the simoniac heresy by introducing, for a price, wolves instead of shepherds'.[38] It was to this offence that Henry himself referred in the penitential letter of September 1073 through which he sought reconciliation with the new pope. 'Not only have we laid hold of ecclesiastical property, but we have even sold the churches themselves to unworthy men, embittered by the gall of simony.'[39] Simony, trafficking in holy things and in particular receiving money from candidates for ecclesiastical office, was the offence most detested by the eleventh-century reform movement. The reformers regarded 'simoniacal heresy' as the earliest and most destructive of the heresies of the Christian Church. Henry IV's alleged simony contrasted sharply with the conduct of his father, whose reforming sympathies were celebrated in the writings of the most distinguished reformers of the mid-eleventh century.[40]

Henry IV wielded the same authority over the churches in his kingdom that had characterised his father's regime, the traditional authority of the Ottonian and Salian rulers over the 'imperial Church'. He regarded the bishops of the empire as 'joined to us like most sweet members': they were the limbs, he the head of Christian society.[41] Consequently he controlled their appointment and demanded the traditional service that they owed the crown. On the death of a bishop the cathedral chapter sent a deputation to deliver his pastoral staff to the king. There were then three ways in which Henry, following the practice of his predecessors, could determine the choice of successor: by nominating a candidate of his own choice, approving a candidate suggested by his advisers, or accepting the candidate of the chapter. In all cases the final decision belonged to the king. Episcopal appointments were made in the royal presence (as also the appointments of abbots of 'imperial abbeys') and the central act in the making of a prelate was the ceremony of investiture. The king conferred on the candidate the symbols of his office, the episcopal staff and ring (in the case of an abbot, the abbatial staff), with the words 'receive

---

[37] Gregory VII, *Epistolae Vagantes* 14, p. 34.   [38] *Ibid.* 14, p. 34.

[39] Henry IV, *Letter* 5, p. 9.

[40] Peter Damian, *Letter* 40: *Briefe* 1, 501; Humbert of Silva Candida, *Adversus simoniacos* III.7, p. 206. The succeeding generation of reformers saw Henry IV as 'the chief of heretics': Deusdedit, *Libellus contra invasores* II.11, pp. 328–9; Paschal II, *JL* 5889: *MGH Libelli* 2, 451–2.

[41] Henry IV, *Letter* 11, p. 14.

the church'. The new prelate then performed the act of homage and swore an oath of fealty to the king.[42] While Henry III could control episcopal appointments in this way without criticism from reformers, soon after his death the practice of investiture came under attack. In 1057/8 Humbert of Silva Candida composed the first denunciation of the royal investiture of bishops in his polemic *Against the simoniacs*. He recalled seeing 'men invested by secular princes with bishoprics and abbacies by means of staffs and rings and although their metropolitans and primates were present, the latter were not consulted and did not dare to speak out against it'. The practice of investiture had turned upside-down the prescriptions of canon law, which required that 'the choice of the clergy be confirmed by the judgement of the metropolitan'. In assuming the foremost role in electing and confirming the candidate, the secular prince had usurped the functions of clergy and metropolitan.[43]

The previous absence of criticism of royal control of episcopal appointments is presumably attributable to the widespread belief in the sacral character of the king's authority. Humbert, however, discarded this justification by denying this sacral character: the king was merely a layman. The most preposterous aspect of the practice of investiture was that 'lay *women*, who are permitted neither to speak in church (1 Corinthians 14.34) nor to rule over men (1 Timothy 2.12), . . . invest clerks with bishoprics and abbacies by means of pastoral staffs and rings'.[44] The succession of Empress Agnes, as regent, to her late husband's authority over episcopal appointments was, for Humbert, the *reductio ad absurdum* of 'the imperial Church system'. It was for this reason that the practice of investiture came under attack as soon as Henry III was dead. Humbert's attack on lay investiture seems, however, to have had no immediate impact on reforming opinion. Only in the pontificate of Gregory VII did papal synods begin to formulate decrees embodying the objections of the treatise *Against the simoniacs*.[45] The critical references to investiture in the reforming literature of the intervening years did not challenge the legality of the practice but merely censured secular rulers for investing unsuitable candidates with bishoprics.[46] Critics of lay investiture in the 1060s and early 1070s were concerned not with the legality of the practice but with the qualifications of the candidates. By *circa* 1070 reformers believed that the episcopal appointments of Henry IV's government were not characterised by the reforming conscience apparent in Henry III's reign. Henry III's diplomas had proclaimed

---

[42] Fleckenstein (1966) 288–9; Minninger (1978) 54–6; Schieffer (1981) 10–13.

[43] Humbert, *Adversus simoniacos* III.6–9, 11, pp. 205–8, 211. See Schieffer (1981) 36–47; Laudage (1984) 169–84; Szabó-Bechstein (1985) 130–7.

[44] Humbert III.12, p. 212. See Schieffer (1981) 13 n. 22.   [45] Schieffer (1981) 41–2, 44–7.

[46] Peter Damian, *Letter 69: Briefe* 2, 305. Cf. 140–1, 147:3, 478–502, 543–4. See Dressler (1954) 139; Schieffer (1981) 45.

the imperial obligation 'to care for all the churches of the Roman empire', which was reflected in his careful selection of candidates of spiritual and intellectual distinction.[47] His successor, however (according to his penitent letter of 1073), led astray by his youth, 'by the freedom of tyrannical power' and 'by the seductive deception' of evil counsellors, 'sold the churches to unworthy men'.[48]

Critics detected a deterioration in the episcopal appointments of the first two decades of Henry IV's reign: a deterioration that had begun before Henry assumed the personal direction of the government. During the regency of Agnes there was no apparent change in the nature of appointments (despite Cardinal Humbert's grave apprehensions about female governance of the Church).[49] Soon after the empress was driven from power in 1062, however, episcopal appointments began to fall below the high standard of Henry III's reign. The first appointments to provoke criticism were in fact those of the regime of Anno of Cologne, ally of the reform papacy during the schism of Cadalus and patron of monastic reform. Two of the appointments for which he was responsible in 1063–4, to the archbishopric of Magdeburg and the bishopric of Münster, were clearly dictated not by reforming but by political considerations.[50] According to the hostile Adam of Bremen, Anno, 'notorious for his avarice', 'raised up his kinsmen, friends and chaplains, heaping the foremost dignities and honours upon them'.[51] Lampert of Hersfeld, a fervent admirer of Anno, remained silent about his conduct towards the imperial Church, but accused his rival, Adalbert of Bremen, of selling bishoprics and abbeys.[52] Three controversial appointments were made during Adalbert's ascendancy in 1065: Werner II of Strasbourg, Adalbero of Worms and Herman I of Bamberg.[53] The last and most disastrous of the appointments of the first decade of the reign was made after the fall of Adalbert of Bremen and the restoration of Anno of Cologne to court. In May 1066 Anno secured the investiture to the vacant archbishopric of Trier of a kinsman, his nephew Conrad of Pfullingen, provost of the cathedral chapter in Cologne, against the will of the clergy and people of Trier. It was a bold attempt both to consolidate Anno's

---

[47] *DD H III* 225, 230, 235, 306. See Fleckenstein (1966) 287–97.

[48] Henry IV, *Letter* 5, p. 9.   [49] See above p. 29.

[50] *Gesta archiepiscoporum Magdeburgensium* c. 21, p. 400. See Meyer von Knonau (1890) 1:352–3; Fleckenstein (1968) 225–6; Claude (1972) 323; Fleckenstein (1973) 123. See also above p. 47.

[51] Adam of Bremen, *Gesta* III.35, pp. 177–8. See Meyer von Knonau (1890) 1:337–8, 354.

[52] Lampert, *Annales* 1063, p. 89.

[53] *Ibid.*, 1065, pp. 93, 100; 1070, p. 117; Gregory VII, *Registrum* 1.77, pp. 109–10. See Meyer von Knonau (1890) 1:469–70, 486; Fleckenstein (1968) 226–7 and above pp. 55–6. Herman I of Bamberg: see below pp. 119, 132.

authority and to settle the long struggle for precedence between the great Lotharingian churches of Cologne and Trier, which ended, however, in disaster for the candidate. Conrad was abducted by Theoderic, advocate of Trier and burgrave of the city, who subsequently ordered four of his vassals to murder the new archbishop. Neither Anno nor the king was able to punish the perpetrators of this murder, nor could they prevent the clergy and people of Trier from electing a canon of their cathedral, Udo of Nellenburg, as archbishop. Anno denounced Udo to the pope as an intruder, but his appeal was unavailing. Anno's attempt to exploit the royal right of investiture had resulted in a victory for the principle of the free election of a prelate by clergy and people.[54]

In the decade following Henry IV's assumption of power in 1066, episcopal appointments began once more to conform to the pattern of the previous reign. In a sharp reaction against the trend of 1063–6 the candidates invested in the late 1060s and 1070s were drawn from the same institutions as Henry III's bishops: the imperial chapel, Henry III's foundation of SS. Simon and Jude in Goslar and cathedral chapters with close links with the imperial chapel, Liège, Bamberg and Speyer. Of the sixteen bishops invested in the years 1066–76, eight or nine were members of the imperial chapel and ten belonged to SS. Simon and Jude.[55] The response of the new regime to the controversial appointments of 1063–6 was to accentuate loyal service and proximity to the king as the essential qualifications for episcopal office. There was one important lesson, however, that the royal government had failed to learn from the experience of 1063–6: the necessity of appointing bishops who were acceptable to their clergy and people. Resistance to the royal appointee is recorded in the cases of Speyer, Constance, Worms, Toul, Bamberg and Cologne. Henry of Speyer, canon of SS. Simon and Jude in Goslar, was under the canonical age when he was appointed in 1067, which together with his conduct as bishop eventually provoked a complaint to Rome.[56] In Worms the unsatisfactory Adalbero was succeeded by Adalbert, whom the citizens expelled in 1073.[57] The king's candidate for the bishopric of Toul, his former chaplain and chancellor, Pibo (1069), was denounced to the pope in 1074 as guilty of simony and unchastity by a clerk of Toul.[58] In Bamberg the investiture of the royal confidant Rupert, provost of SS. Simon and Jude in Goslar (1075), was deeply resented.[59] In the case of Cologne in 1076, the chronicles

---

[54] Von Giesebrecht (1890) 1245. Cf. Theoderic of Tholey, *Vita Conradi archiepiscopi* pp. 214–19. See Meyer von Knonau (1890) 1:499–513; Gladel (1932) 10.

[55] Fleckenstein (1966) pp. 276–87; Fleckenstein (1973) pp. 125–8.

[56] Lampert, *Annales* 1067, p. 104. Cf. Gregory VII, *Registrum* II.29, p. 162.

[57] Lampert, *Annales* 1073, p. 169; 1074, pp. 185–6: see above p. 93. See Meyer von Knonau (1894) 2:34 and n. 55.   [58] Schieffer (1972) 41–6. See below pp. 119–20, 134.

[59] Lampert, *Annales* 1075, p. 240.

record the extreme reluctance of the clergy and people to accept the king's candidate, Hildolf, chaplain and canon of SS. Simon and Jude. When the delegation from Cologne, in the king's presence for the election of their archbishop, rejected the royal candidate, Henry dismissed them, saying 'that as long as he lived, they should have either him or no one for their bishop'.[60]

The best-documented case of resistance to a royal episcopal appointment is that of Constance (1070–1). The clergy and people of Constance wished to elect Siegfried, a canon of their cathedral, trusting that his being an imperial chaplain would recommend him to the king. Henry, however, invested Charles, canon of Magdeburg and provost of the church in the Harzburg, 'because of the very many services which he had very frequently and most opportunely rendered, particularly in personal matters'. Opposition from the clergy soon took the form of accusations of simony and theft of ecclesiastical property that so perturbed the metropolitan, Siegfried of Mainz, that he refused to consecrate Charles. Both parties appealed to Rome, the cathedral clergy desiring the deposition of the 'simoniac', the king and his bishop requesting a papal investigation and exoneration of Charles. Alexander II referred the case to the decision of Archbishop Siegfried, who summoned the rival parties to a synod in Mainz (15–18 August 1071). The Constance clergy repeated their accusations; the king denied involvement in simoniacal transactions, although he did not exclude the possibility that his 'servants and familiars' had received money from Charles without his knowledge. On 18 August Charles brought the proceedings to an end by resigning his episcopal ring and staff into the king's hands.[61] He declared that his election had violated the canon law principle expressed in the decretal of Pope Celestine I: 'no bishop is to be given to unwilling [subjects]'.[62] Charles's resignation on these grounds prevented his being found guilty of simony, which would have been damaging for the king.

The synod of Mainz revealed how much the harmonious relationship of monarch and episcopate, characteristic of the regime of Henry III, had been injured by Henry IV's episcopal appointments. Although the participants included some of the king's closest collaborators among the bishops (Henry of Speyer, Werner of Strasbourg, Herman of Bamberg and Benno of Osnabrück), the synod compelled the resignation of Henry's candidate for Constance. The king was forced to take account of the reforming principle of the suitability of a bishop for his office, which he had sacrificed in the inter-

[60] *Ibid.* 1076, p. 251. See Meyer von Knonau (1894) 2:646–7 and n. 42.

[61] *Codex Udalrici* 36–8, pp. 68–81; Lampert, *Annales* 1069, 1071, pp. 111, 129; Berthold of Reichenau, *Annales* 1070, pp. 274–5. See Meyer von Knonau (1894) 2:1–6, 78–85; Fleckenstein (1968) 228–30; Schieffer (1972) 46–50.

[62] Celestine I, *JK* 369, disseminated in Burchard of Worms, *Decretum* 1.7, 551CD.

ests of creating a loyal and compliant episcopate. The synod did not challenge the king's right to choose bishops. Charles's resignation was followed by the investiture of a successor who was also the king's personal choice, but who differed from his predecessor in being acceptable to his clergy and people: Otto, canon of SS. Simon and Jude in Goslar. Nevertheless, although royal investiture had not been questioned, Charles's opponents had found a way to veto a royal appointment and, most importantly, had involved the papacy in their strategy. While the opponents of Conrad of Trier in 1066 had achieved their objective by the murder of the royal appointee, Charles of Constance's opponents found an equally effective instrument in the appeal to Rome. The canonical principle asserted by the supporters of the reform papacy – 'the Roman church has the right of judging every church . . . appeals are to be made to her from any part of the world'[63] – provided a means of solving disputes like that of 1071 without resorting to violence. The king himself adopted this principle, hoping to use papal authority to stifle the opposition of Constance to his candidate, while Siegfried of Mainz used appeal to Rome (just as he had during the divorce proceedings of 1069) to avoid a personal collision with the king.

A second dispute in the same diocese, this concerning the abbey of Reichenau, also involved the reform papacy in the affairs of the imperial Church. A few months before the synod of Mainz, Meinward of Reichenau resigned his abbatial staff to the king. Henry had imposed him on the abbey without consulting the monks, who, accusing their new abbot of simony, resisted his authority for a year until Meinward felt compelled to resign. The successor appointed by the king, Rupert, encountered an even more hostile reaction. The monks' appeal to Rome resulted in the deposition of Rupert on a charge of simony by papal synod (1072). Henry was obliged to dismiss him and permit the monks to elect one of themselves, Ekkehard, as his successor.[64] In the cases of Constance and Reichenau the canonical electors joined forces with the papacy to compel the king to observe reforming standards when appointing prelates. The effectiveness of an appeal to Rome as a weapon against an unpopular bishop was soon appreciated by German churchmen. The cathedral chapter of Bamberg, whose hostility towards Bishop Herman was mainly inspired by his enthusiasm for the monastic at the expense of the canonical life, denounced him to the pope as a simoniac and secured his deposition in 1075. In the diocese of Toul an opponent of Bishop Pibo among his clergy pursued his vendetta against the bishop by accusing him in Rome of

---

[63] *Collectio in LXXIV titulos* 10, p. 24. See Maccarrone (1974) 21–122.
[64] Gregory VII, *Registrum* 1.82, pp. 116–18. See Meyer von Knonau (1894) 2:2–3, 33, 165–6, 407–9; Feierabend (1913) 37–40; Schieffer (1972) 46–7.

simony and unchastity in 1074, but his conspiracy was foiled by the staunch support shown for Pibo by his metropolitan and fellow-bishops.[65]

To his Roman synod in February 1073 Alexander II summoned 'many [German bishops] polluted not only with carnal vice but also with the shame of simony'.[66] It was at this moment, two months before the accession of Gregory VII, that Rome took the initiative in investigating the condition of the German episcopate, rather than waiting for local churches to appeal for papal intervention. This initiative was no doubt a consequence of the cases of 1071–2, which, despite efforts to shield the king, had tainted Henry IV's regime with simony. During the synod of Mainz Henry had admitted the possibility that his 'servants and familiars' were guilty of simony. In his letter of September 1073 to Gregory VII Henry confessed that, misled by evil counsellors, he had 'sold the churches to unworthy men, embittered by the gall of simony'. The question of Henry IV's simony, which dominated his relations with the papacy for the rest of his reign, is complicated by the fact that the term 'simony' expanded its meaning in the later eleventh century, as reformers intensified their campaign to free the Church from every kind of secular influence. It had long been customary in the empire, as elsewhere in western Christendom, for a clerk, on being appointed to a church, to offer a gift to the lay or ecclesiastical proprietor of that church, in recognition of his lordship. A new prelate would bring a gift to the king who invested him with his office and the king would usually reciprocate with more valuable gifts and privileges. Such customs began to be denounced by the reform papacy in the 1050s as 'the madness of simoniacal transactions'. According to Cardinal Humbert, kings used the spurious excuse of 'custom' 'to claim for themselves the ecclesiastical property which they were assigned [by God] to protect'. Humbert refused to recognise the rights of the king as proprietor of the churches, seeking to limit his role to that of defender of the Church.[67]

The cases of 'simony' in the German Church in 1071–2 demonstrated not only that Henry IV regarded himself as the proprietor of the bishoprics and imperial abbeys but also that he was determined to extend his proprietorial rights. It has been suggested that during this phase of his reign Henry pursued a 'consistent policy' of drawing on the material resources of particular churches to cover the expenses of his government (a policy that paralleled his

[65] Schieffer (1972) 22–46; Schieffer (1975) 55–76.
[66] Gregory VII, *Registrum* 1.77, p. 109. The earlier intervention claimed by Lampert, *Annales* 1070, pp. 111–12: Schieffer (1971) 152–74.
[67] The king's letter to Gregory VII: Henry IV, *Letter* 5, p. 9. Humbert, *Adversus simoniacos* III.7, p. 206; cf. III.5, p. 204. See Szabó-Bechstein (1985) 131–7. The term *simoniaca haeresis*: Gilchrist (1965) 214; Lynch (1976) 65–8; Tellenbach (1988) 77, 136, 140–5.

attempts to recover royal rights in Saxony).[68] An anecdote in the chronicle of Niederaltaich illustrates this interpretation of Henry's conduct towards the churches. The royal favourite Liupold of Meersburg, a knight of the king's household, came to Reichenau and demanded, in the king's name, to be given one of the abbey's estates as a benefice. Abbot Meinward's response was to surrender his staff to Henry with the words: 'I am prepared to give up the abbacy entirely rather than offend God and St Mary in order to find favour with you.'[69] A similar attempt by the king to use ecclesiastical estates as benefices for his knights perhaps lies behind the charges brought against Charles of Constance in 1071, referring to 'ecclesiastical benefices given and promised to the king and his counsellors'.[70] It was such transactions that inspired the judgement of the chronicler Bernold of St Blasien, a devoted adherent of Gregory VII, in 1076: 'King Henry did not cease to pollute holy Church by investing with bishoprics and abbeys for payment.'[71]

Nevertheless not all the evidence from the decade 1066–76 portrays the king as an exploiter of the Church. The account of Henry's ecclesiastical appointments given by the hostile Lampert of Hersfeld is ambivalent. After reporting that the king imposed on the church of Bamberg 'a man of very bad repute among the people' on 30 November 1075, he described how on the following day Henry appointed an abbot of Fulda (the wealthiest abbey in the kingdom). The rival candidates competed for the abbacy: 'one promised mountains of gold, another huge benefices from the Fulda estates, another heavier services to the commonwealth than were customary'. None of these competitors was elected, however: 'driven, it was believed, by the divine spirit', Henry appointed a monk of Hersfeld who had made no unseemly promises. Similarly in the case of Lorsch, Henry refrained from appointing the provost of the monastery who had previously striven to recommend himself by 'many services'.[72] A few royal documents offer insights into Henry's alleged exploitation of the churches in the earlier 1070s. Two diplomas of 27 October 1073 show Henry, at the request of numerous illustrious interveners, reducing the *servitia* owed to the crown by the convents of Obermünster and Niedermünster in Regensburg.[73] In a letter of 1075 to Abbot Theoderic of St Maximin, Trier, the king rejoiced that his 'servant H.' had decided to 'restore to [St Maximin] the benefice which he holds from [the abbey], so as to cancel out the damage to the property' of the abbey.[74] Throughout his reign Henry

---

[68] Schieffer (1972) 19–60.
[69] *Annales Altahenses* 1071, pp. 82–4. Cf. Lampert, *Annales* 1071, p. 127. See above p. 84 and below p. 355.   [70] Berthold of Reichenau, *Annales* 1069, p. 274.
[71] Bernold of St Blasien, *Chronicon* 1076, p. 431.   [72] Lampert, *Annales* 1075, pp. 240–1.
[73] *DD H IV* 264–5. See Meyer von Knonau (1894) 2:290; Gawlik (1970a) 51–2; Boshof (1991) 131; Kolmer (1991) 197.   [74] Henry IV, *Letter* 6, p. 10.

can be found responding to such appeals from churches to protect their interests. He was not prepared, however, to relinquish his rights as the proprietor of the churches. Henry's attitude seemed to reformers to contravene the principle that ecclesiastical possessions were offerings to God and were sacrosanct, not subject to secular burdens. In the opinion of the papacy Henry's claims and the royalist bishops' acquiescence in them amounted to simony. When Henry IV confessed to 'simony' in 1073, he subscribed to this radical definition of simony, adopting the terminology of the reform papacy in the interests of reaching an understanding with Rome.

The problem that dominated the king's relations with the papacy in 1073 was that of Milan, the foremost city of northern Italy in economic and political terms and the metropolitan see of the eighteen dioceses of Lombardy. The royal government and the papacy were involved on opposing sides in the conflict between the reforming party of the Pataria and the Milanese establishment in the shape of the senior clergy and the 'captains' (the greater aristocracy), hostile alike to ecclesiastical reform and political change. When the original leaders of the Pataria, the deacon Ariald and the priest Landulf, campaigned against simony and clerical marriage (circa 1057–1066), the Milanese populace seems to have supported them. Similarly, when in 1071 the Pataria opposed Archbishop Godfrey, whom the king had invested with his office without consulting the Milanese, the populace again joined the reformers in barring Godfrey from their city. Some later eleventh-century chronicles present the Milanese disturbances as a conflict between archbishop and nobility on the one hand and Pataria and *populus* on the other, virtually equating the Pataria and the common people. The reality in the years 1057–75 was that two small factions, that of the archbishop, the senior clergy and their allies and that of the Pataria, competed with each other for the support of the populace and for control of the city.[75] Beneath the apparent alliance of the Patarini and the Milanese *populus* there were fundamentally different attitudes and objectives. The Milanese resistance to Archbishop Godfrey in 1071 signified a wish to be consulted in the matter of an archiepiscopal election, not a criticism of the practice of royal investiture of bishops. The Patarini in 1071 were pursuing the totally different objective of replacing an archbishop invested by the king with a candidate who would be obedient to the pope.

Like other local reform movements, the Pataria during the 1060s increasingly felt the centripetal attraction of the reform papacy and sought the help of the Roman church in the campaign against simony and clerical marriage. The devout lay nobleman Herlembald Cotta, who assumed the leadership of

[75] Miccoli (1966) 101–67; Cowdrey (1968a) 25–48; Violante (1968) 597–687; Keller (1970) 34–64; Keller (1973) 321–50.

the Pataria in 1066, became the confidant of the Roman archdeacon Hildebrand, principal adviser of Alexander II. This friendship transformed the papacy into the uncritical ally of the Pataria, regarding Herlembald as the leader in a holy war to reform the Milanese church and appoint an archbishop obedient to the holy see.[76] The fundamental weakness in the position of the Patarini was their willingness to sacrifice the ecclesiastical independence of Milan to the principle of the papal primacy. Their critics accused them of injuring 'the honour of St Ambrose', the patron saint of Milan. The expression, 'the honour' or 'the integrity of St Ambrose', summed up the Milanese sense of the city's ancient independence. It served as a rallying cry against the Patarini when they attempted to enforce conformity with Rome, notably by replacing the traditional Ambrosian liturgy with that of the Roman church.[77] Herlembald and his knights gained a precarious ascendancy over the city in the early 1070s, thanks to the absence of the archbishop and the disarray of the clerical faction, but he was ultimately defeated by the slogan 'the honour of St Ambrose'. In 1075 Herlembald used the Easter festivities to stage a demonstration of Patarine determination to subordinate Milan to the papal primacy. This provocation enabled his enemies to persuade 'a great part of the common people' to swear an oath to uphold 'justice and the honour of St Ambrose and to accept a bishop given by the king'. This sudden shift of the *populus* to the support of the anti-Patarine faction deprived Herlembald of control of the city. His opponents were able to kill him as a public enemy and disturber of the peace (5 April) and to expel his adherents from the city, a defeat from which the Pataria never recovered.[78] The Patarine attempts to exploit Milanese political divisions in the interests of the papacy failed because they underestimated the unifying character of the cult of St Ambrose.

The growing strength of the Pataria had driven the anti-Patarine party to seek the help of the imperial court. It was characteristic of the Milanese (and Lombard) attitude towards their overlord that they turned to him in moments of danger, while in normal circumstances regarding themselves as independent of external control. This attitude was possible because the king was rarely able to intervene in his Italian kingdom. Henry IV's father and grandfather each made only two expeditions to Italy: the first to obtain recognition of their rights as king of Italy and to be crowned emperor in Rome;

---

[76] Arnulf of Milan, *Liber gestorum* III.17, p. 192; cf. IV.10, p. 215; Landulf Senior, *Historia Mediolanensis* III.15, pp. 83–4; cf. III.30, p. 97; Andreas of Strumi, *Vita Arialdi* c. 15, p. 1059. See Erdmann (1935) 129, 167–8; Miccoli (1956) 57–72; Miccoli (1966) 161–7.

[77] Peter Damian, *Letter* 65: *Briefe* 2, 231; Bonizo of Sutri, *Ad amicum* VII, p. 604. See Peyer (1955) 25–45.

[78] Arnulf, *Liber gestorum* IV.9–10, pp. 214–16; Landulf Senior, *Historia* III.30, pp. 96–7. See Meyer von Knonau (1894) 2:473–6.

the second to deal with a dangerous challenge to their power in the kingdom. The pattern of government that developed in the reigns of Conrad II and Henry III allowed much of the royal authority to be delegated to bishops, especially to the Lombard metropolitan.[79] It was the importance of the arch-bishop's role in government that prompted Henry III's insistence (greatly resented by the Milanese) on appointing Archbishop Wido (1045).[80] Soon after the emperor's death Wido began to face violent opposition in Milan. During the last four years of his life he lost control of the city and even of his own revenues to the Pataria. By 1070 Wido was aware that the Pataria planned that the election of his successor should be conducted according to canon law and subject to papal approval. He therefore secretly resigned his office to the king, who then invested Wido's preferred successor, Godfrey. He was a Milanese subdeacon of noble family, who 'had already gained the king's goodwill through his great services' (1071).[81] The Patarini claimed that Godfrey had bought his office and the current reputation of the German court was such that this accusation was believed in Rome. Alexander II excommunicated Godfrey as a simoniac and intruder. The Milanese popu-lace allied with the Pataria to prevent Godfrey from entering the city, but differed from the Pataria on the question of a successor to Wido. Herlembald organised the election of a Patarine candidate, the Milanese clerk Atto, in the presence of a papal legate (6 January 1072). The populace, however, immedi-ately intervened, forcing Atto to take an oath renouncing the see forever.[82] Although they had rejected the royal candidate, Godfrey, the Milanese were still willing to recognise the king's rights as overlord, provided that he did not ignore their own carefully guarded rights. Patarine propaganda and violence failed to persuade the Milanese to abandon the traditional protection of the king in favour of a closer relationship with the papacy. During the years 1072–5 the adherents of Godfrey and Atto continued to press the claims of their candidates, but since neither could establish himself in Milan, there was effectively a vacancy in the archsee. A papal synod in 1072 ruled that Atto was the lawfully elected archbishop, but he seems to have made no further attempt to claim the archsee. Alexander II wrote to Henry IV, admonishing him to 'permit the church of the Milanese to have a bishop according to God'.[83] Henry's response was to send his trusted envoy, the Bavarian Count

---

[79] Kehr (1930) 592–5; Violante (1952) 157–76, 293–314; Cowdrey (1966) 1–15.

[80] Steindorff (1874) 1:246–8.

[81] Arnulf, *Liber gestorum* III.20, pp. 196–7. See Meyer von Knonau (1890) 1:58–70, 672; (1894) 2:99–103.

[82] Arnulf III.23, pp. 204–5. See Meyer von Knonau (1894) 2:175–7; Keller (1973) 344–5; Schieffer (1981) 105–6.

[83] Alexander II, *JL* 4701: Bonizo, *Ad amicum* VI, pp. 599–600. See Hüls (1977) 185.

Rapoto of Cham, to order the consecration of Godfrey as archbishop, which took place in Novara.[84]

The final stage of Henry IV's relations with Alexander II was recorded only by the pro-papal polemicist Bonizo of Sutri, writing in 1085. In the papal synod of Lent 1073 'the pope publicly excommunicated certain advisers of the king who wished to separate him from the unity of the Church'. Bonizo's narrative subsequently reveals that five advisers were excommunicated, one of them being 'Count Eberhard'.[85] A passage from the chronicle of Lampert of Hersfeld refers indirectly to the same incident. Lampert identified among the king's advisers in 1076 'Udalric of Godesheim, Eberhard, Hartmann and the other excommunicates on whose aid and counsel he used to depend most willingly'.[86] Alexander II's excommunication has usually been linked by historians to Henry IV's support of Godfrey of Milan, since the king's penitent letter of September 1073 to Gregory VII is concerned 'first and foremost' with 'the church of Milan, which is in error through our fault'.[87] When in the papal synod of Lent 1075, however, Gregory VII threatened to excommunicate 'five members of the household of the king of the Germans', presumably the same five as before, it was because 'churches [were] sold on their advice'.[88] It is possible, therefore, that Alexander's disciplinary measure of 1073 was inspired not only by the case of Milan but also by the other irregularities that had come to light in the imperial Church. Henry's admission that his 'servants and familiars' may have practised simony perhaps suggested to the pope that the reform of the imperial Church could most readily be achieved by a purge of royal advisers.

According to Bonizo, the pope excommunicated the royal advisers in 1073 'at the instigation of the empress'. Empress Agnes had been living in Rome since autumn 1065, placing herself under the spiritual guidance of Peter Damian and, after his death (1072), of Abbot John of Fécamp.[89] If Bonizo's claim is accurate, it is possible that the condemnation of the royal advisers in the Lenten synod was linked with an incident of the previous year in the German kingdom in which Agnes was also involved. In 1072 Duke Rudolf of Swabia was accused by his enemies of planning 'an attack on the king and the commonwealth'. Fearing condemnation on a false charge, he appealed to Empress Agnes 'to check the calamity of civil war' by coming to Germany to

---

[84] Arnulf IV.3, pp. 207–8; Bonizo VII, p. 606. See Meyer von Knonau (1894) 2:178–9, 196–7.

[85] Bonizo VI, p. 600; VII, pp. 601, 605. See Meyer von Knonau (1894) 2:198–9; Schieffer (1981) 109–10. Hils (1967) p. 75 refuted the identification of 'Count Eberhard' with Eberhard of Nellenburg (founder of the monastery of Schaffhausen) or his son of the same name.

[86] Lampert, *Annales* 1076, pp. 282–3 (see also below p. 360). Cf. Berthold, *Annales* 1074, p. 277.

[87] Henry IV, *Letter* 5, p. 9.   [88] Gregory VII, *Registrum* II.52a, p. 196 (see below p. 135).

[89] Bulst-Thiele (1933) 97–8; Struve (1985) 1–29; Black-Veldtrup (1995) 37–48, 94–7.

intercede for him. He believed himself to be 'most dear to the empress', having served her faithfully during her regency and having formerly been her son-in-law. Agnes came to his aid, escorted by 'a very large number of abbots and monks', including Abbot Hugh of Cluny, her son's godfather. She succeeded, with the help of the archbishops of Cologne and Mainz, in exonerating Rudolf at an assembly of princes in Worms (25 July 1072).[90] There is evidence that Agnes's journey in 1072 was not only concerned with the reconciliation of her son and the duke of Swabia but also involved cooperation with Rudolf in the reform of the Swabian monastery of St Blasien. St Blasien commemorated Rudolf as a 'founder' of the abbey and remembered Agnes as 'the bringer of the regular discipline of our monastery' because of her role in introducing the monastic customs of the north Italian abbey of Fruttuaria, the model for the reform of St Blasien (Agnes was a benefactress of Fruttuaria and had stayed there on first withdrawing from the world in 1065). The fact that the empress arrived in Germany in 1072 'attended by a very large number of abbots and monks' suggests that it was on this occasion that Agnes assisted in the transmission of the customs of Fruttuaria to St Blasien, perhaps at the request of Rudolf, their patron. Fruttuaria was in the privileged position of enjoying royal protection without being an 'imperial abbey', subject to the duties of the 'imperial Church system'. The proliferation of this monastic liberty in Germany would have serious implications for the authority of the crown at a time when Henry was asserting his proprietorial rights over imperial abbeys. It is possible, therefore, that the king objected to Rudolf's plans for St Blasien and that the reform eventually adopted in that abbey – the monastic customs of Fruttuaria without her 'liberty' – was a compromise negotiated by the king and the duke, with the mediation of the empress, at the assembly of Worms.[91]

The new wave of monastic reform in Germany is reported in Lampert's annal for 1071 (the year in which Rudolf made his first benefaction to St Blasien). As a result of recent scandals in the monasteries, caused by the ambition and simony of 'pseudo-monks' (Lampert was thinking in particular of Reichenau) 'the princes of the kingdom summoned monks from beyond the Alps to create a school of divine service' in Germany.[92] It was hardly a coincidence that all the prominent figures associated with Rudolf in the crisis of 1072 – not only the empress but also the archbishops of Cologne and Mainz and the duke of Carinthia (like Rudolf, suspected of treachery by the king) – were also associated with monastic reform. Anno of Cologne founded his

[90] Lampert, *Annales* 1072, pp. 137–8. Cf. *Annales Altahenses* 1072, p. 84. See Meyer von Knonau (1894) 2:159–62; Jakobs (1968) 269–71; Vogel (1984) 1–30.

[91] Meyer von Knonau (1894) 2:167; Jakobs (1968) 39–42, 160, 266–90; Jakobs (1973) 106–12; Vogel (1984) 1–5, 24–30; Tellenbach (1988) 183 n. 30; Black-Veldtrup (1995) 48–9.

[92] Lampert, *Annales* 1071, p. 133.

monastery of Siegburg in 1070 and reformed the Cologne monastery of St Pantaleon with the help of monks from Fruttuaria.[93] Siegfried of Mainz, who cooperated with Anno in the foundation of the Thuringian monastery of Saalfeld (1071) attempted unsuccessfully to resign his archbishopric and become a monk of Cluny.[94] As for Rudolf's ally, Duke Berthold of Carinthia: one of his sons, Margrave Herman I of Baden, renounced the world to become a monk of Cluny and another, Gebhard, entered the abbey of Hirsau, the most influential centre of monastic reform in south-western Germany.[95] The plans of Rudolf of Rheinfelden for St Blasien were part of an important monastic reform movement, beginning in the early 1070s, with parallels in the reform of Hirsau (under the patronage of Count Adalbert of Calw), Schaffhausen (Count Eberhard of Nellenburg) and Muri (Count Werner of Habsburg).[96] Dissatisfaction with the conduct of the king and his advisers in ecclesiastical affairs doubtless contributed to this movement to reform monastic life outside the framework of the imperial Church. It was no coincidence (as Lampert pointed out) that the reform of St Blasien and Anno of Cologne's foundations took place against a background of accusations of simony against the king's familiars, culminating in the case of Abbot Rupert of Reichenau. By the time of the assembly of Worms in 1072 a clear difference of attitude had emerged between the king and his advisers and the princes and prelates who patronised monastic reform. It is possible, given the presence of the empress, that the subject of ecclesiastical reform was debated in the assembly of Worms. In the course of that assembly Agnes reconciled her son with her ally, Rudolf, but the latter left Worms 'by no means certain that the king had forgotten his hostility'.

Early in 1073 'Duke Rudolf of Swabia, Duke Berthold of Carinthia and Duke Welf of Bavaria deserted the king because new advisers had appeared and [the dukes] perceived that their advice had no effect on the king'.[97] Soon afterwards the pope excommunicated five of the king's advisers 'at the instigation of the empress'. The next papal intervention in German affairs, made by the new pope, Gregory VII, was an invitation to Rudolf (1 September 1073) to come to Rome to discuss 'the harmony of the priesthood and the empire' with the pope and Empress Agnes. This was a response to a letter from Rudolf, congratulating Gregory on his accession.[98] Seen in the context of the relations

---

[93] Semmler (1959) 35–50, 60–3, 118–20; Schieffer (1971) 154–6; Vogel (1984) 7.
[94] Meyer von Knonau (1894) 2:168–70; Büttner (1949) 40–64; Schieffer (1971) 164–7; Vogel (1984) 8.   [95] Jakobs (1968) 231–2; Wollasch (1987) 27–53.
[96] Bernold, *Chronicon* 1083, p. 439. See Schmid (1973) 295–319.
[97] Berthold, *Annales* 1073, p. 275. Cf. Lampert, *Annales* 1073, pp. 140, 144–5; *Annales Altahenses* 1073, p. 85. See Meyer von Knonau (1894) 2:195–6.
[98] Gregory VII, *Registrum* I.19, pp. 31–2.

of king, princes and pope in the period July 1072 – September 1073, the excommunication of the royal advisers looks like a second attempt by the friends of reform to curb the king's heavy-handed treatment of the Church, this time by forcing Henry to dismiss the advisers most distrusted by his mother and his brother-in-law.

Archdeacon Hildebrand, who succeeded to the papacy on 22 April 1073, had doubtless participated in the decision to discipline the royal advisers. Perhaps it was he, as principal papal adviser, rather than the dying Alexander II, who decided on confrontation. In 1076 he would recall that before his accession he had 'frequently admonished [the king] by letters and envoys to desist from his wickedness and, remembering his most illustrious family and his office, to order his life as befitted a king and, if God grants it, a future emperor'.[99] Since Hildebrand was an outspoken critic of the king before 1073, it is not surprising to learn of opposition to his election in the imperial territories. A correspondent warned the new pope of a conspiracy against him, led by Bishop Gregory of Vercelli, the imperial chancellor for Italy.[100] Lampert of Hersfeld recorded that the German bishops feared that Hildebrand's 'ardent temperament and passionate faith in God' would prove an embarrassment to them and urged the king, perhaps at the Whitsun assembly in Augsburg (19 May), to declare the papal election invalid.[101] These reports suggest a situation similar to that in October 1061, when the chancellor for Italy (Wibert of Parma) and the Lombard and German episcopate participated in the election of an antipope, in opposition to the candidate of the Roman reforming party. The connecting link between the schism of 1061 and the conspiracy of 1073 was Gregory of Vercelli, the ringleader on both occasions. By October 1073, however, the new pope could claim that the bishop of Vercelli 'promises to obey our command to the uttermost'.[102] There is no evidence that Henry IV supported the initiative of his Italian chancellor. He must soon have realised that there was no chance of running an alternative candidate: too many prominent princes and prelates had hastened to acknowledge Gregory VII.[103]

Henry IV was to challenge the legality of the papal election only in the third year of Gregory's pontificate, when in the synod of Worms (24 January 1076) he called on the pope to abdicate. This synod claimed that the election violated the terms of the Papal Election Decree of 1059, specifically the 'royal clause' of the decree, stating that the electors must respect 'the due honour and

---

[99] Gregory VII, *Epistolae Vagantes* 14, p. 34. See Borino (1948) 463–516; T. Schmidt (1977) 195–216.

[100] Walo of St Arnulf in Metz: *Vetera Analecta* I, 248–9. See Borino (1959) 28–33.

[101] Lampert, *Annales* 1073, p. 145.   [102] Gregory VII, *Registrum* 1.26, pp. 43–4.

[103] *Codex Udalrici* 40, p. 84: see Borino (1959–61a) 265–75. Cf. Gregory VII, *Registrum* 1.9, 19, 20, 24, 53, pp. 14, 31, 41, 80. See C. Schneider (1972) 41 n. 105.

reverence of our beloved son Henry [IV]'. The papal council of 1059, in which Hildebrand had participated, had decreed that a pope could be elected only 'with the consent and authority of the king', but Hildebrand did not receive this consent in 1073.[104] Almost all the narrative sources agree that Gregory VII was elected 'without the king's consent', the exceptions being the accounts of Lampert of Hersfeld and Bonizo of Sutri, neither of which is credible. Both authors were writing after the synod of Worms of 1076; both were critics of Henry IV whose purpose was to represent Henry as a treacherous king, faithlessly repudiating a pope whose election he had originally approved.[105] The evidence that effectively refutes the claims of Lampert and Bonizo is found in two letters of Gregory VII to Anselm, bishop-elect of Lucca (1 September 1073) and to Empress Agnes (15 June 1074). The letter to the bishop elect warned him not to receive investiture of his bishopric from the king 'until he satisfies God concerning his communion with excommunicates and . . . can have peace with us'.[106] This letter did not call into question the king's right of investiture in normal circumstances, but insisted that the circumstances in 1073 were not normal. As long as Henry broke the Church's law by failing to dismiss the five advisers whom Alexander II had excommunicated, he could not lawfully exercise his traditional authority over the imperial Church. Gregory's letter to the empress, written after she had helped to restore good relations between king and pope, emphasised that during 1073 Henry had been outside the communion of the Church. 'While he was outside the communion, the fear of divine punishment prohibited us from coming to an agreement with him.'[107] In 1073 Henry was 'outside the communion' and therefore incapable of exercising his rights in ecclesiastical matters. It follows that he was not entitled to 'the due honour and reverence' specified in the Papal Election Decree. Henry's failure to dismiss his excommunicated advisers prevented Gregory from seeking royal approval for his election.

While Gregory refused to compromise on the issue of the royal advisers, he nevertheless assured correspondents during the summer of 1073 that he bore the king no ill will and desired only 'that priesthood and empire be joined in the unity of harmony'. Already he was looking forward to the imperial coronation. In a letter to the empress's adviser, Bishop Rainald of Como, Gregory

---

[104] Henry IV: *Die Briefe Heinrichs IV.* p. 68. Cf. Henry IV, *Letter* 11, p. 14. See H.-G. Krause (1960) 171–6; C. Schneider (1972) 151.

[105] Lampert's story (*Annales* 1073, pp. 145–6) is chronologically impossible: Meyer von Knonau (1894) 2:209–10; Borino (1956a) 313–43; H.-G. Krause (1960) 164–9. The details in Bonizo, *Ad amicum* VII, p. 601 are drawn from John the Deacon's description of the election of Pope Gregory I (590): Robinson (1978a) 31–9.

[106] Gregory VII, *Registrum* I.21, p. 35. See Borino (1956b) 361–74; Violante (1961) 399–407.

[107] *Registrum* I.85, p. 121. See C. Schneider (1972) 85–6.

(using the language of the 'royal clause' of the Papal Election Decree) described Henry as 'the head of the laity . . . king and, if God wills, future emperor in Rome'. There was no objection to crowning Henry as emperor, provided that he was willing to discharge the imperial duties – 'to love religion', 'to increase and defend the property of the churches' – and provided that 'he avoids the counsels of wicked men like poison'. The pope planned a meeting in September to discuss 'the concord of the Roman church and the king' with Rainald, the empress, Rudolf of Swabia and Beatrice, margravine of Tuscany, the principal papal ally in northern Italy.[108] This plan was overtaken by the news of the king's submission. This had been achieved by Rudolf, who now reappeared at the German court, and Beatrice, Henry's kinswoman. The return of Rudolf, together with the dukes of Carinthia and Bavaria, to the king's presence and the king's willingness to listen to the advice of the papal ally Beatrice of Tuscany signalled precisely the change at court for which the papacy and the empress had been hoping. In late September Gregory received from the king a letter 'full of sweetness and obedience . . . such as we recall neither he nor his predecessors have sent to Roman pontiffs'. This was the 'suppliant letter' in which Henry confessed that, led astray by his advisers, he had 'sold the churches to unworthy men, embittered by the gall of simony'. He begged the pope to correct whatever was amiss, especially the situation of the Milanese church, 'which through our fault is in error'.[109] The letter reflects the theme of the papal correspondence of the previous summer: unity ('the kingship and the priesthood . . . always need each other's help') and the imperial coronation. The title in the opening protocol, 'Henry by God's grace king of the Romans', deviates from the conventions of the royal chancery to emphasise the king's status as 'future emperor'.[110] The 'deeply submissive' tone of the letter, dramatising Henry's penitence in the language of the parable of the prodigal son (Luke 15.21), has been attributed by historians to the influence of Rudolf of Swabia. Either Rudolf extorted the letter from the reluctant but vulnerable king, or Henry sent the letter to forestall Rudolf's meeting with the pope, fearing the effect of such a meeting on his own authority.[111] An alternative suggestion is that the letter was a response to 'the remonstrances of some of the bishops'.[112]

---

[108] *Registrum* I.20, pp. 33–4. See Stürner (1968) 42–3. Cf. *Registrum* I.11, 19, 24–5, pp. 19, 31–2, 41–2. See C. Schneider (1972) 41–7; W. Goez (1974) 488–9; Bertolini (1965) 359; E. Goez (1995) 165–6.   [109] Henry IV, *Letter* 5, pp. 8–9. Cf. *Registrum* I.25, p. 42.

[110] Erdmann (1939) 251; Buchner (1963) 335–6; but see also C. Schneider (1972) 60 n. 184.

[111] Meyer von Knonau (1894) 2:270 n. 142; Caspar in Gregory VII, *Registrum* 47 n. 4; Erdmann (1938) 231 n. 2.

[112] Borino (1956a) 331. The involvement of Siegfried of Mainz: G. Schmidt (1917) 62, 92; Schmeidler (1927) 274–9; C. Schneider (1972) 66–8.

Gregory VII correctly identified the motive for the king's submission when, three years later, he ceased to believe in the sincerity of Henry's repentance. 'When the grievances of the Saxons against the king began to increase and he saw that the strength and the military resources of the kingdom would largely abandon him, again he sent us a suppliant letter full of humility.'[113] The outbreak of the Saxon rebellion in August left the king with no room for manoeuvre. The rebels were clearly ready to exploit the issues that divided the king from the papacy: they demanded the expulsion of evil counsellors from the court and spoke of the danger of contact with 'a man who had betrayed the Christian faith by crimes worthy of death'.[114] Moreover among the rebels were bishops with close links with the papacy, Hezilo of Hildesheim and especially Burchard of Halberstadt.[115] The likelihood that they would exploit their links with Rome in the rebels' interests left the king with little choice but submission to the pope. Siegfried of Mainz and Berthold of Carinthia, both of whom had interceded for Rudolf of Swabia during the crisis of July 1072, were commissioned, together with Rudolf himself and Anno of Cologne, to negotiate with the rebels in October 1073. The outbreak of the Saxon rebellion prompted Henry to turn for help to that powerful group of princes whose enthusiasm for reform had been demonstrated at the assembly of Worms in July 1072. Their advice was, predictably, that he should make his peace with the pope.[116] Gregory's welcome response to the king's appeal for 'counsel and help' was a letter to the Saxons, exhorting them to suspend their hostilities against 'King Henry, [their] lord' and announcing the arrival of papal legates to negotiate peace (20 December 1073). This papal intervention probably contributed to the making of the peace of Gerstungen on 2 February 1074 (which was completed, however, before the legates' arrival).[117] The 'suppliant letter', the first of Henry IV's demonstrations of penitence, achieved its purpose. Whether it was sincere has often been doubted.[118] Evidence of a genuine change of heart has, however, been detected in a series of six royal diplomas issued between May 1073 and January 1074. Here the king is unprecedentedly described as 'most humble'.[119] It is worth recalling an earlier submission of Henry IV to the Church: his reluctant abandonment of divorce proceedings

---

[113] Gregory VII, *Epistolae Vagantes* 14, p.36. See C. Schneider (1972) 68, 70; Cowdrey in *Epistolae Vagantes* 36 n. 1; Struve (1991) 31.

[114] Lampert, *Annales* 1073, pp. 151–2. See above p. 77.

[115] Kost (1962) 68–72; Erdmann (1938) 119–53; see also above pp. 89–90.

[116] Lampert, *Annales* 1073, pp. 153, 157, 162–3, 164–5. Cf. *D H IV* 264. See Meyer von Knonau (1894) 2:248, 253, 270–2, 287–91.

[117] Gregory VII, *Registrum* 1.39, pp. 61–2. See above p. 95.

[118] Martens (1894) 1:80; Meyer von Knonau (1894) 2:268–70.

[119] *DD H IV* 258–60, 264–5, 267. See C. Schneider (1972) 87–8. Cf. Mikoletzky (1960) 60.

after being threatened with excommunication in 1069.[120] The fear of exclusion from communion apparent in 1069 did not immediately recur when the pope excommunicated his advisers in 1073, but it may have been reawakened by the outbreak of the Saxon rebellion. The rebellion may have seemed to be a divine punishment for his neglect of papal warnings, just as Henry subsequently interpreted his victory over the Saxons in 1075 as divine approval for his kingship and an invitation to reassert his rights over the imperial Church.

Henry's request to the pope to correct whatever was amiss in the imperial Church invited the resumption of the reforming initiatives of Alexander II's last years. Seizing this opportunity to resume the campaign against simony in the imperial Church, Gregory VII emphasised the king's own role in the work of reform. He must 'restore to the Church her freedom and . . . learn that you rightfully hold the royal power if you incline your high authority to Christ, the King of kings, for the purposes of the restoration and defence of His churches'.[121] This statement provides an interesting contrast with the well-known negative Gregorian assessments of royal authority in the later years of conflict. In 1074 Gregory's conception of Henry's kingship had much in common with the traditional Ottonian–Salian ideas of the imperial court. The royal power was the instrument by means of which 'the King of kings' achieved the reform of the Church. As he contemplated a reforming partnership with Henry IV, Gregory remembered the model of Henry III's close cooperation with Victor II.[122]

Given the central role which Henry IV was expected to play in the reform of the imperial Church, his restoration to communion was a matter of urgency. This was the first task of the legates, the cardinal bishops of Ostia and Palestrina, whom Gregory sent to Germany after the papal synod of Lent 1074. Their second task was to hold a reforming synod, the most pressing business being the case of Bishop Herman of Bamberg, the royal confidant accused of simony by his clergy. The legates, accompanied by Empress Agnes and the bishops Rainald of Como and Henry of Chur, were honourably received by the king in Pforzen. Negotiations about the excommunicated advisers and the king's promise to support reform were at once satisfactorily concluded, the empress playing a major role. The only difficulty was the legatine synod. The king proposed that it be held in Bamberg, hoping to settle the dispute between the bishop and his chapter. The legates, convinced, like the pope himself, of Herman's guilt, insisted on a different location and it was therefore in Nuremberg that the king was absolved from the guilt of contact with excommunicates and reconciled to the Church on 27 April. After a public act of

---

[120] See above p. 111.   [121] Gregory VII, *Registrum* II.30, p. 164. See C. Schneider (1972) 87–8.
[122] *Registrum* I.19, p. 32.

penance Henry confirmed the promises of his 'suppliant letter' by an oath sworn 'by the sacred stoles which [the legates] wore around their necks' and was restored to communion. His five advisers were perhaps also absolved on this occasion.[123] The legates' plan of presiding over a council of the whole German Church was foiled by the opposition of the bishops assembled in Nuremberg. Archbishops Siegfried of Mainz and Liemar of Bremen, when requested to compel their brethren to obey the legates' command, refused to comply, on the grounds that the whole episcopate had the right to be consulted on such a matter. Identifying Liemar as their particular opponent, the legates cited him to Rome to answer for his disobedience. The pope suspended him from his office. Gregory also summoned Siegfried of Mainz and six suffragans to the next Lenten synod.[124] What had been left unfinished in Nuremberg must be completed in Rome.

The pope did not blame Henry IV for the failure of the council. He praised him for his 'goodwill and mildness' towards the legates, at whose behest he had 'corrected certain ecclesiastical matters in a praiseworthy manner.' Underlining Henry's central role in the reform of the Church, he requested that, if any bishops evaded the papal summons to Rome, 'they be compelled to come by the force of [his] royal power'.[125] Gregory VII believed that he had found in Henry a suitable agent for curbing the proud independence of the German bishops in the interests of reform. The two papal letters to Henry IV of 7 December 1074 mark the culmination of the period of cooperation inaugurated by the king's 'suppliant letter'. The first letter dealt with the practical details of the reform of the imperial Church: the summoning of eight German bishops to Rome and the problem of Milan. Henry had not yet fulfilled his promise to settle the affairs of the Milanese church in a manner acceptable to the pope. He should now send his advisers, 'religious and prudent men', to the pope to discuss the problem of the Milanese schism. Gregory had concluded from the events of 1072–3 that the reform of the imperial Church depended primarily on the quality of the royal advisers. Henry 'should consult such advisers as love you, not your possessions, and care for your salvation, not their own gain'.[126] The exhortation is repeated in the second letter of 7 December.

---

[123] Gregory VII, *Epistolae Vagantes* 14, p. 36; *Registrum* 1.85, p. 121; Berthold, *Annales* 1074, p. 277; Bonizo, *Ad amicum* VII, p. 601. See Meyer von Knonau (1894) 2:377–8; Erdmann (1938) 238; Schumann (1912) 23–8; C. Schneider (1972) 73–83.

[124] *Registrum* II.28, 29, pp. 160–3.

[125] *Ibid.* II.30, pp. 163–5, suggesting to Erdmann (1938) 238–55 an 'alliance of curia and king against the episcopate'. This account of Henry's strategy involves dating his *Letter* 15, pp. 21–2 immediately after the synod in Nuremberg; but a more plausible date is October 1076. See Borino (1959–61b) 297–310; Schneider (1972) 83 n. 265.

[126] *Registrum* II.30, pp. 163–5

The letter is addressed to 'the glorious King Henry' and assures the king four times of the pope's love for him. The traditional language of divine ordination is used to evoke Henry's role as future emperor: 'God has placed [him] at the supreme summit of the world.' The relationship of the secular power and the papacy is described in Gelasian terms, insisting on the need for cooperation between 'the imperial majesty and the gentle power of the apostolic see'. Gregory used the Gelasian language of mutual dependence to teach the king his role in his new project: an expedition to Jerusalem to defend the Christians of the Near East from Moslem persecution. The distinguished participants were to include Count Amadeus II of Savoy (son of Adelaide of Turin and Henry IV's brother-in-law), Margrave Azzo II of Este, Duke Godfrey III of Lower Lotharingia and his wife, Matilda (daughter of Beatrice of Tuscany) and Empress Agnes. From Henry the pope requested 'counsel and, if you please, help, because if with God's favour I go thither, I leave the Roman church to you, after God, to protect her as a holy mother'. The defence of the Roman church was of course one of the principal duties of the emperor.[127]

Gregory clearly believed that Henry would soon be emperor. He assured Henry on 7 December that he had 'greater hopes of [him] than most men think'. While his relations with the king had remained cordial, however, his relationship with the imperial episcopate continued to deteriorate. Siegfried of Mainz, for example, had received a papal rebuke for his conduct in the case of his suffragans in the Bohemian bishoprics of Prague and Olmütz.[128] Theoderic of Verdun was censured for his failure to obey the instructions of the Roman see concerning his dispute with the monastery of S. Mihiel.[129] Gregory's handling of the accusations of simony and unchastity against Pibo of Toul provoked a protest from the metropolitan, Udo of Trier. Udo and his colleagues were shocked by the pope's presumption of Pibo's guilt: the archbishop's investigation showed him to be innocent.[130] Another protest appears in Liemar of Bremen's letter to Hezilo of Hildesheim (January 1075), complaining of his treatment by the pope. 'This dangerous man wishes to order the bishops about according to his will, as if they were stewards on his estates; and if they fail to do all his bidding, they must come to Rome or are suspended without trial.'[131]

Papal intervention in the imperial Church culminated in the proceedings of the Roman synod of 24–8 February 1075. The synod punished the non-

[127] *Ibid.* II.31, pp. 165–8. The expedition never materialised: Cowdrey (1982) 27–40. The Gelasian ideal: Knabe (1936) 154.
[128] *Registrum* I.60, pp. 87–9 (a reply to *Codex Udalrici* 40, p. 85).
[129] *Registrum* I.81, pp. 115–16.
[130] *Ibid.* II.10, pp. 140–2. Cf. Udo of Trier, *Briefsammlungen* pp. 39–41.
[131] *Briefsammlungen* pp. 33–5. See Erdmann (1938) 245–8, 252–3.

attendance of the bishops summoned in December 1074 and Henry IV's failure to send 'religious and prudent' advisers to Rome to settle the Milanese question. Five prelates were suspended and Denis of Piacenza, the inveterate opponent of the reform papacy, was deposed. Henry's broken promise provoked the pope to resort to the device used two years before. He 'separated from the threshold of holy Church five members of the household of the king of the Germans, on whose advice churches are sold'. They were given until 1 June to escape excommunication by giving a satisfactory account of themselves in Rome.[132] Once more the papacy returned to the theme of Henry's advisers, which had preoccupied reformers in Rome and Germany since the beginning of the decade. This demonstration of papal authority brought both Siegfried of Mainz and Liemar of Bremen to Rome, seeking reconciliation not only on their own account but also on behalf of the whole imperial episcopate and of the king. It was through their efforts that peace with the papacy was restored in the summer of 1075. Siegfried's negotiations with the pope concentrated on the case of Herman of Bamberg, whom the German episcopate had come to regard as a serious embarrassment. Herman's deposition by the pope (12 April) was the price that Siegfried, and doubtless also Henry IV, was prepared to pay to rid the German Church of its reputation for simony and to end Gregory's campaign against the episcopate. Siegfried's reward was to be entrusted by the pope with the holding of a reforming council in Germany.[133] His colleague, Liemar of Bremen, arrived in Rome in the company of three learned clerks, Meinhard of Bamberg, Wezilo of Halberstadt and Widukind of Cologne. It is likely that Liemar, one of the king's most trusted advisers, came to negotiate on Henry's behalf and that his companions were the 'religious and prudent men' whose help Gregory had requested in December 1074 to resolve the Milanese problem.[134] The pope was satisfied with their discussions and congratulated the king on having 'begun to commit our cause, or rather that of the whole Church, to religious men'.[135]

Central to modern discussions of the Roman synod of 1075 is the question of the synodal decree prohibiting lay investiture, which some historians have identified as the principal cause of the conflict between king and pope in 1076. According to the chronicler Arnulf of Milan, in the synod of 1075 'the pope openly forbade the king thenceforward to have any right to confer bishoprics

---

[132] *Registrum* II.52a, pp. 196–7. Cf. Berthold, *Annales* 1075, p. 278. See Meyer von Knonau (1894) 2:451–5.

[133] *Codex Udalrici* 45, pp. 97–100; Lampert, *Annales* 1075, pp. 208–9. See Erdmann (1938) 257–60.

[134] Bonizo, *Ad amicum* IX, p. 616. See Erdmann (1938) 266–70; C. Schneider (1972) 124–8.

[135] Gregory VII, *Registrum* III.7. p. 257.

and removed all lay persons from the investiture of churches'.[136] No other chronicler mentioned this decree and, more significantly, there is no reference to it in the summary of the synodal decrees of 1075 in the papal register.[137] Nor is the prohibition of lay investiture mentioned in any of Gregory VII's letters of 1075, although the pope was clearly anxious to publicise other synodal decrees on the familiar themes of simony and clerical marriage. In his letters to Henry IV of July and September 1075 there is mention only of the decree that punished the five royal advisers. The king was urged to follow only 'the advice of religious men'.[138] A passage in the papal letter of 8 December 1075 to Henry IV has often been supposed to refer to an investiture decree: 'this decree, which certain persons, preferring human to divine honours, call an unbearable grievance and an enormous burden, we call by its proper name, the truth and the light necessary for obtaining salvation'.[139] The pope was here defending a decree, presumably but not necessarily of the Lenten synod of 1075, the content of which is not specified. The decree in question may have concerned investiture, but it may equally have concerned the problem of simony in general (which had dominated papal–royal relations since *circa* 1070) or the related matter of the five royal advisers. As for the impact of the alleged investiture decree on the events of 1076, none of the sources for the conflict of 1076 identifies the papal prohibition of investiture as one of the issues dividing king and pope. Henry IV's manifestos of 1076 never accuse the pope of diminishing the rights of the crown by forbidding the investiture of bishops, nor do the documents relating to the negotiations at Tribur and Oppenheim (October 1076) and the settlement at Canossa (January 1077) mention investiture.

The resolution of this contradiction between the statement of Arnulf of Milan and the silence of Gregory VII in 1075 and of his opponents in 1076 has long taxed the ingenuity of historians. The most influential theory is that the synod of 1075 formulated a decree against lay investiture but did not promulgate it. Gregory had no intention of putting the decree into immediate execution: it was a programme of future action, the details of which had yet to be negotiated.[140] The strongest evidence for the alternative view, that the synod actually promulgated a general prohibition of lay investiture,[141] is

---

[136] Arnulf, *Liber gestorum* IV.7, pp. 211–12. There is no reference to the decree by Berthold, *Annales* 1075, p. 277, who was perhaps present at the synod: Tangl (1967) 516.

[137] Gregory VII, *Registrum* II.52a, pp. 196–7.   [138] *Ibid.* III.3, 7, 10, pp. 246–7, 256–9, 263–7.

[139] *Ibid.* III.10, p. 266

[140] Von Giesebrecht (1866) 129–33; Scharnagl (1908) 32; Brooke (1939) 227. Cf. Erdmann (1938) 270: the synod merely issued a 'threat' against Henry IV, which Arnulf mistakenly interpreted as a decree forbidding investiture.

[141] Borino (1959–61c) 329–48; C. Schneider (1972) 108–10.

found in the fact that on three occasions during the period 1077–9 Gregory VII rebuked bishops for having received investiture of their bishoprics contrary to papal decree. All three of these bishops – Gerard II of Cambrai, Huzman of Speyer, Henry of Aquileia – had been invested with their offices by Henry IV in the period 1075–7.[142] Each of these investitures predated the prohibition of lay investiture by the papal synod of November 1078, the earliest surviving investiture decree. The decree which the three prelates had infringed was obviously an earlier decree, already in existence in April/May 1075 (the date of the investiture of Huzman of Speyer); presumably, therefore, the decree mentioned by Arnulf of Milan. These three cases, however, only add to the problems raised by 'the investiture decree of 1075'. The fact that the defence offered by the bishops of Cambrai and Speyer and the patriarch of Aquileia was ignorance of the decree and, more importantly, the fact that the pope accepted this defence, throws into relief Gregory's failure to publicise this decree during 1075. Equally puzzling is the case of the succession to the bishopric of Bamberg. On 20 July 1075 Gregory wrote to Henry IV, reporting the deposition of Herman of Bamberg and bidding him organise the appointment of a successor. This surely was the appropriate moment for the pope to explain to Henry the precise meaning of the decree prohibiting investiture. Instead Gregory wrote: 'we exhort your Highness . . . that, on the advice of religious men, that church should be so ordered according to God that you may deserve to obtain the protection of St Peter.' In early September Gregory wrote again to 'command that such a pastor be ordained in the aforesaid church according to God, who may bring to life what [Herman] destroyed'.[143] The wording of these letters cannot be construed as forbidding the king to exercise his traditional rights in the case of an episcopal vacancy. The new bishop, Rupert, was invested by the king with his office (30 November), but – in sharp contrast to Huzman of Speyer, who had been invested with his bishopric in the same manner six months before – he was never rebuked by the pope for receiving staff and ring from the hands of the king.

The difficulty that historians have experienced in reconstructing the decree of 1075 arises largely from the inconsistency with which Gregory VII himself interpreted the decree. The most likely explanation is that, whatever the original purpose of the decree, the conflict of 1076 so magnified the decree's importance in Gregory's eyes that by 1077 he had come to think of it as a general prohibition of lay investiture. A persuasive recent interpretation sees the 'investiture decree of 1075' as merely a by-product of the proceedings of the papal synod against the five royal advisers. As long as the king failed to dismiss them

[142] Gregory VII, *Registrum* IV.22, V.18, pp. 330–1, 381; Berthold, *Annales* 1079, pp. 317–18.
[143] *Registrum* III.3, 7, pp. 246–7, 256–9. Cf. *ibid.* III.1–2, pp. 242–5.

from his court, he rendered himself liable to be excommunicated himself and therefore unfit to exercise his authority in ecclesiastical affairs (as in 1073). The presence of the advisers at court constituted a *de facto* prohibition of investiture. By May 1077, when a 'decree concerning the prohibition of this kind of acceptance' was first mentioned in a papal letter, Gregory's ideas of freeing the imperial Church from royal control had matured and the *de facto* ban of 1075 had assumed a new importance in his reforming programme.[144]

Gregory's cordial letters to Henry IV of 20 July and early September 1075 demonstrate the success of the conciliatory efforts of the archbishops of Mainz and Bremen and subsequent royal envoys. The September letter congratulated the king on having defeated 'the Saxons who were unjustly resisting [him]': the royal victory at Homburg (9 June) was a 'divine judgement'. As in his letters of 7 December 1074, the pope's thoughts turned to the imperial coronation in Rome. Referring to the 'religious men' whom Henry had now adopted as his advisers, Gregory wrote: 'on their advice, I am prepared . . . to open the bosom of the holy Roman church to you and to receive you as lord, brother and son.'[145] Before the conclusion of the Saxon rebellion, Henry was still preoccupied with the threat of an alliance between princes and papacy that had haunted him since 1072, and he warned the pope: 'I perceive that almost all the princes of my kingdom rejoice more at our discord than at our mutual peace.' He therefore proposed that his future negotiations with the pope should be kept secret from all except the empress and Henry's kinswomen, Beatrice of Tuscany and her daughter, Matilda.[146] Henry's victory in Saxony, however, inspired a change of strategy. By 11 September Gregory had learned from the Tuscan princesses that 'what he had decided to do secretly [the king now] wished to do openly'. Henry was taking into his confidence the princes whom he had recently described as untrustworthy, in particular, Duke Godfrey III of Lower Lotharingia (Matilda's estranged husband), whom the pope distrusted. Gregory concluded from this that Henry did not take his negotiations with Rome seriously.[147]

The Saxon victory, freeing Henry from dependence on papal goodwill, coincided with the changed political situation in the Italian kingdom. The defeat of the pope's allies in Milan offered Henry the opportunity of dealing with the vacancy in the archbishopric according to his own wishes. On the eve of the battle of Homburg he had thought it prudent to send Rabbodi and Adelpreth, the 'noble and religious men' approved by Gregory, to negotiate

[144] Schieffer (1981) 132–52. See also Kempf (1982) 409–15.
[145] *Registrum* III.7, pp. 256–9. See Meyer von Knonau (1894) 2:565 n. 154.
[146] Henry IV, *Letter 7*, pp. 10–11 (surviving as a quotation in *Registrum* III.5, p. 251).
[147] *Registrum* III.5, p. 251.

the Milanese problem and the forthcoming Italian expedition along the lines dictated by the pope. Soon after his victory Henry sent an envoy of whom Gregory did not approve to make preparations for the Italian expedition that must have confirmed Gregory's suspicion that the king no longer desired peace with the papacy. The envoy was Count Eberhard 'the Bearded', one of the five advisers excommunicated in 1073 and threatened with excommunication at the Lenten synod of 1075. The envoy held an assembly of Lombard magnates in Roncaglia at which he declared the Patarini to be public enemies, the first open denunciation of the pope's Milanese allies by the royal government.[148] The full scope of the king's Italian schemes was revealed when Eberhard travelled south in the company of the Italian chancellor, Gregory of Vercelli, to negotiate with the papal vassal Robert Guiscard, duke of Apulia and Calabria. Henry IV's envoys called on the duke to hold his territories as a benefice from the king. Robert Guiscard replied that it was with the help of God and through the intervention of SS. Peter and Paul that he had conquered Apulia and Calabria and theirs was the only lordship that he was prepared to acknowledge. If Henry wished to enfeoff him with imperial lands, he would of course acknowledge himself as the king's vassal in respect of those lands.[149] These negotiations were probably not directed primarily against the pope, but reflected the traditional concern of the imperial government to assert jurisdiction over southern Italy. (The polemicist Bishop Benzo of Alba reminded Henry *circa* 1080 that his predecessors had ruled southern Italy and that it was therefore his right to drive out the Normans and regain possession of his own lands.)[150] The attempt of the royal envoys in 1075 to reassert the king's rights in the case of Apulia was unsuccessful, but seven years later Prince Jordan of Capua would acknowledge himself to be the vassal of Henry IV.[151]

Henry completed the pacification of Lombardy by ending the long vacancy in the Milanese church, although in a controversial manner that offended both conservatives and reformers. The chronicler Arnulf, champion of the privileges of the Milanese clergy, presented the investiture of a new archbishop as an irregular proceeding, offensive to the tradition of Milanese independence. 'Tedald, a subdeacon of the Milanese church, served in the royal chapel and it was to him that the king, after lengthy reflection finally indulging his own will, gave the Ambrosian archbishopric.' This new appointment ignored

---

[148] Bonizo, *Ad amicum* VII, p. 605. See Meyer von Knonau (1894) 2:571.

[149] Amatus, *Historia Normannorum* VII.27, pp. 320–1. Cf. the interpolation in a Würzburg manuscript of Lorenzo Valla, *De falso credita et ementita Constantini donatione* p. 26 n. 58; Arnulf, *Liber gestorum* IV.7, p. 211. See Meyer von Knonau (1894) 2:572–3; Deér (1972) 117–19.

[150] Benzo of Alba, *Ad Heinricum* I.15; III.15–17, 19, 24; VII.8, pp. 144, 314–18, 324, 334, 654. See Deér (1972) 87–90.   [151] See below p. 218.

the claim not only of the papal candidate, Atto, but also of Henry's own former candidate, Godfrey, whom the king's supporters in Lombardy had hitherto acknowledged as their metropolitan.[152] The investiture of Tedald was a characteristic royal appointment of the decade 1066–76: that of a noble Milanese clerk whose service in the royal chapel was the guarantee of his future cooperation.[153] Henry had inherited from his father an Italian episcopate of exemplary loyalty, especially in Lombardy, where opposition to the reform papacy had intensified the bishops' adherence to the crown. The investiture of Tedald, like that of the bishops of Fermo and Spoleto in the late summer or autumn,[154] was intended to perpetuate this loyalty. Henry assumed that the solution of the Milanese problem was to appoint an archbishop unconnected with the conflicts of the previous two decades, but his action was an affront to those who, in obedience to the crown, had supported the claims of Godfrey.

Henry's intervention in Italian ecclesiastical affairs was interpreted by Gregory VII as a breach of the 'peace' of empire and papacy. It provoked the papal ultimatum of 8 December 1075, which in turn precipitated the conflict of 1076. The king cannot have foreseen that Count Eberhard's mission and the investiture of the three Italian prelates would be interpreted in Rome as breaking off the dialogue that had continued since September 1073. Henry's envoys, Rabbodi and Adelpreth, had been in Rome since the summer and had recently been joined by a third envoy, Udalschalk, as an earnest of the king's desire to continue negotiations. Tedald notified Rome that he desired the pope's 'friendship', assuming, like Henry, that he would be acceptable as a replacement for the controversial Godfrey. Gregory VII's reaction to the new situation is found in three letters of 8 December, addressed to Tedald, to the suffragans of Milan and to the king. The letter to the suffragans admonished them not to consecrate Tedald, 'whom the king has placed in the Milanese church contrary to what he promised us in his letters and in the words of his envoys', until the pope had investigated this appointment.[155] Tedald himself was admonished to attend the next Lenten synod in Rome to give an account of his promotion: if the synod found in his favour, the pope would not oppose him.[156] The ultimatum to the king conveys even in its salutation the pope's frustration and sense of betrayal: 'to King Henry, greetings and apostolic blessing – if he obeys the apostolic see as befits a Christian king'.[157] The first grie-

---

[152] Arnulf, *Liber gestorum* v.5, pp. 222–4. Cf. Bonizo, *Ad amicum* vII, pp. 605–6. See Meyer von Knonau (1894) 2:573–4; Cowdrey (1968) 39–40.

[153] Landulf Senior, *Historia Mediolanensis* III.32, p. 100.   [154] Schwartz (1913) 234, 240.

[155] Gregory VII, *Registrum* III.9, pp. 261–3.

[156] *Ibid.* III.8, pp. 259–61. See A. Hauck (1952) p. 789 n. 5.

[157] *Registrum* III.10, pp. 263–7. See Meyer von Knonau (1894) 2:576–80; C. Schneider (1972) 137–45; Schieffer (1981) 134–41.

vance was that which had dominated the papal correspondence with the king since 1073: the royal advisers. Henry was said to be consulting the five advisers excommunicated at the synod of 1075: he must do penance and seek absolution from 'any religious bishop'. (It was this grievance of contact with excommunicates that Gregory mentioned first when in 1076 he listed the reasons for Henry's excommunication.)[158] Secondly, the pope rebuked Henry for his recent investiture of three Italian prelates. In the case of Milan the king was reproved for breaking the promises made to his mother and the papal legates at Eastertide 1074, but a stronger reproof was reserved for his conduct in the cases of Fermo and Spoleto. 'Contrary to the statutes of the apostolic see' Henry had conferred these churches – 'if indeed a church can be conferred or given by a man' – on 'persons unknown to us', whose qualifications for office had not been established.[159] The letter concluded with an exhortation to obedience, especially with reference to an unspecified decree of the recent Lenten synod, which, as we have seen, has usually been assumed to be an 'investiture decree of 1075'.

The papal sanctions to enforce the king's obedience – the threats to which Henry would respond so violently in January 1076 – were to be conveyed by the bearers of the letter, the royal envoys Rabbodi, Adelpreth and Udalschalk. The first was a refusal to continue negotiations on the subject which Henry now regarded as most urgent: Gregory would 'remain silent about what is in [the king's] letters' until the royal envoys returned to Rome with a satisfactory response to the papal complaints. The unspoken subject of these negotiations was almost certainly the imperial coronation, to which Gregory had referred in positive terms in his letter of early September. The 'ultimatum letter' contained unmistakably imperial language. Henry was advised that, since he was 'superior to other men in glory, honour and valour', he 'should excel also in devotion to Christ'. He must 'recognise the empire of Christ above [him]'. He should lend his aid to God and St Peter so that his 'glory may deserve to be increased' and remember that 'every kingdom and empire' is in God's hand. The obvious implication was that the pope would refuse to crown Henry emperor unless he embraced the papal reforming measures. The second sanction threatened in the 'ultimatum letter' appeared in the form of the biblical analogy of King Saul (1 Samuel 15.1–35). Saul had won a great military victory, like Henry IV at Homburg, but because he subsequently failed to obey God's commands, he was rejected by God and by His prophet, Samuel. Gregory VII, the new Samuel, warned Henry that if he failed to obey the pope, he would

---

[158] Gregory VII, *Epistolae Vagantes* 14, p. 38.
[159] *Registrum* III.10, p. 264. This rebuke has been supposed to refer to the 'investiture decree of 1075', but is probably a reference to the pope's authority as metropolitan in central Italy with the right of confirmation of episcopal candidates.

suffer a similar rejection: that is, excommunication and deposition. The pope instructed the bearers of the letter to repeat this warning to their master in the clearest terms. In the summer of 1076 he recalled that he had 'secretly admonished' Henry through these envoys 'to do penance for his offences'. If he failed to do so – particularly, if he continued to associate with the excommunicated advisers – 'not only must he be excommunicated until he had made due satisfaction, but he must also be deprived of all the honour of the kingship without hope of recovery'.[160] In the polemics which he issued a month after receiving the pope's warning, Henry declared that the message relayed to him by the envoys was that Gregory 'would take from [the king] both soul and kingdom' or die in the attempt.[161] Throughout the ensuing conflict with Gregory VII royalist propaganda would identify this papal claim to excommunicate and depose the king as the most dangerous of Gregory's innovations and the most compelling reason for deposing him.

---

[160] *Epistolae Vagantes* 14, p. 38. Cf. Bernold, *Chronicon* 1076, p. 432; Lampert, *Annales* 1076, pp. 251–2.   [161] Henry IV, *Letter* 11, p. 14; cf. *Letter* 13, p. 19.

4

Worms, Canossa, Forchheim, 1076–1077

The papal ultimatum was delivered to Henry on 1 January 1076 in Goslar. There the king had held an assembly concerned with the fate of the defeated Saxons and the succession of his son Conrad. At the moment when the pope threatened to deprive him of 'both soul and kingdom', Henry seemed more powerful than at any time since his accession. For the first time since the reform papacy began to interest itself in his advisers and his conduct towards the Church, Henry was freed from the need to dissemble his response. The king's reaction to the pope's message was to turn to the excommunicated advisers.[1] It was on their advice that the king summoned a council to meet in Worms on 24 January 1076. The council had the character both of an assembly of princes and of a synod. Henry himself described it as 'a general assembly of all the princes of the kingdom'.[2] It was attended by the archbishops of Mainz and Trier, twenty-four of the thirty-eight German bishops and one Burgundian and one Italian bishop, together with numerous abbots. Of the secular princes the sources identify by name only Duke Godfrey III of Lower Lotharingia, believed by the south German chroniclers to be 'the author of the conspiracy' of Worms.[3] Godfrey certainly enjoyed the king's trust, alone among the secular princes. 'His outstanding service in war' in Saxony had enabled him recently to obtain the vacant bishopric of Liège for his kinsman Henry.[4] In September 1075 he had become involved, much to the pope's alarm, in the king's negotiations with the papacy. It is possible, therefore, that Godfrey played an influential part in the council of Worms. Gregory VII was to attribute the leading role in the council to Siegfried of Mainz.[5] It is indeed likely that Siegfried assumed the leadership

---

[1] Berthold of Reichenau, *Annales* 1075, 1076, pp. 281, 282; Bernold of St Blasien, *De damnatione schismaticorum* III.7, p. 49; Lampert of Hersfeld, *Annales* 1076, p. 253.

[2] Henry IV, *Letter* 11, p. 14. .

[3] Berthold, *Annales* 1076, p. 283; Bernold, *Chronicon* 1076, p. 433. See Meyer von Knonau (1894) 2:615; Mohr (1976) 2:60–2.

[4] Lampert, *Annales* 1075, p. 225. See Meyer von Knonau (1894) 2:515–17.

[5] Gregory VII, *Registrum* III.10a, p. 268. See Böhmer and Will (1877) 207 (no. 125); G. Schmidt (1917) 64–5.

of the imperial Church traditionally claimed by his archsee. Certainly Anno of Cologne's death (4 December 1075) left Siegfried as the most experienced politician of the German episcopate. Bishop William of Utrecht was identified by Lampert of Hersfeld as the ringleader at the council: 'he was at that time especially dear to the king, who had delegated to him the management of all private and public business.' William was the ally of the royal confidant Godfrey III of Lower Lotharingia (they were currently resisting the efforts of Count Theoderic of Holland to exercise lordship over Utrecht), and this association would account for William's prominence at the council of Worms.[6]

According to Lampert, the purpose of the council was to achieve 'the deposition of the Roman pontiff by whatever means or for whatever reason they could find'. The actual outcome, however, was the bishops' letter 'in which the pope was informed that he should abdicate from the papal office which he had usurped contrary to the laws of the Church'.[7] A comparison with the documents arising from the council – the letter of the bishops withdrawing their obedience from the pope, the two versions of Henry's letter to the pope and his letter to the Romans[8] – shows that Lampert's formulation of the council's decisions was correct. In neither version of his letter to the pope did Henry announce the pope's deposition: instead he demanded Gregory's abdication. In the shorter version, the letter actually sent to the pope (a copy also being sent to the Romans), he commanded, by virtue of his authority as patrician of the Romans, that 'Hildebrand' should 'step down from the see of the city' of Rome. In the longer version (not sent to the pope, but disseminated in Germany as royal propaganda)[9] he wrote: 'I, Henry, king by the grace of God, together with all our bishops, say to you, "come down, come down!"' The letter to the Roman clergy and people commanded them to 'force [the monk Hildebrand] to step down'. The records of the council of Worms (unlike the decree of the council of Brixen four years later) make no reference to the *deposition* of the pope.

The council's approach to the problem of Gregory VII may have been influenced by the sixth-century canonical principle that the pope must be judged by no one. The bishops at Worms simply deemed Gregory never to have been pope, so that there was no need for judgement or deposition. The grounds for this assumption were, firstly, that his election was invalid and, secondly, that his conduct since his election demonstrated his unfitness for the papal office.[10] The information about his 'usurpation' of the holy see and 'the

---

[6] Lampert, *Annales* 1076, p. 254.   [7] *Ibid.*, pp. 252, 254.

[8] Henry IV: *Die Briefe Heinrichs IV.* pp. 65–9; Henry IV, *Letters* 10–12, pp. 12–17; Lampert, *Annales* 1076, pp. 253–4. See Meyer von Knonau (1894) 2:613–28; W. Goez (1968) 117–44; C. Schneider (1972) 146–53.   [9] Erdmann (1936) 491–512; Erdmann (1939) 219–20.

[10] Zimmermann (1970) 121–31: Henry planned the pope's deposition (as Lampert claimed) but could not obtain a judgement of deposition from the council.

incredible crimes' of his pontificate was supplied to the council by Hugh Candidus, cardinal priest of S. Clemente, who had recently been deposed for his opposition to the pope.[11] The conciliar records concentrate on two of Gregory's 'crimes': his attacks on the authority of the episcopate and on the rights of the crown. The principal complaint in the letter of the bishops is that 'brother Hildebrand' robbed the bishops of their spiritual power and 'granted the control of ecclesiastical affairs to the ravening frenzy of the mob'. Henry's letters repeat this accusation: 'you have unlawfully conferred [the bishops'] authority over priests on laymen'. The accusation referred to Gregory's support of the Milanese Pataria and perhaps also to his letter of January 1075 to the south German dukes, instructing them to usurp the reforming role of the king and the episcopate. They were to boycott the masses of simoniac and unchaste priests, 'whatever bishops may say or not say about it', and remove such priests from their altars 'by force, if necessary'.[12]

Henry IV presented himself at Worms as the champion of an episcopate victimised by the pope. At the time of the papal interventions in the imperial Church of 1074–5 the king gave no support to the bishops (not even his confidant, Herman of Bamberg) for fear of jeopardising good relations with the pope. Now he denounced Gregory for daring 'to lay hands on the most reverend bishops, who are joined to us as our dearest limbs'. The prominence given to the bishops' grievances in the conciliar documents has prompted the suggestion that the German episcopate 'was to a great extent the prime mover in the conflict with the curia'.[13] Henry's complaint that Hildebrand had 'trodden [the bishops] under [his] feet like slaves' reflected the shock and resentment of an imperial episcopate, largely drawn from the greater aristocracy, that only a decade before had made and unmade popes during the 'schism of Cadalus', just as their predecessors had done in the reign of Henry III. Nevertheless the episcopate in January 1076 did not constitute a united front, capable of forcing an anti-papal policy on the king. Thirteen bishops, a third of the episcopate, did not attend the council. Some of these absentees undoubtedly intended to distance themselves from the royal policy: for example, Gebhard of Salzburg and Altmann of Passau, soon to be leaders of the papal party in Germany, and Adalbert of Worms, driven from his diocese by the king's supporters.[14] Two participating bishops, Adalbero of Würzburg and Herman of Metz, declared the council's proceedings to be contrary to canon law, invoking the principle that the pope must not be accused by his inferiors. They were silenced by William of Utrecht, with the argument that

---

[11] Lampert, *Annales* 1076, pp. 253–4.

[12] Gregory VII, *Registrum* II.45, pp. 182–5. See Robinson (1978c) pp. 114–16.

[13] Jordan (1964) 257.   [14] The absence of Liemar of Bremen: Glaeske (1962) 107–8.

bishops were bound by their oath of fealty to the king to follow royal policy.[15] Hezilo of Hildesheim and Burchard of Halberstadt subscribed the bishops' letter unwillingly.[16] That the king did not trust the bishops to adhere to their declaration is apparent from the written statement that he demanded from them. 'I, N., bishop of the city of N., from this hour and henceforward renounce subjection and obedience to Hildebrand and I shall neither regard him as, nor call him pope hereafter.'[17] Gregory VII claimed in a letter of summer 1076 that at the council of Worms the king 'compelled [the bishops] to deny their due obedience to St Peter and the apostolic see', a version of events which he must have learned from penitent bishops.[18] The rapidity with which many bishops deserted the king after the council suggests that it was the king and his advisers, rather than the bishops, who were responsible for the policy decided in Worms. The council was indeed as much a royal exercise in reasserting control over the German episcopate as an attempt to solve the problem of the papacy.

The attempt to force Gregory VII's abdication in January and the dogged pursuit of this purpose throughout spring and summer have usually been regarded by historians as rash and not fully thought-out. The king was provoked into an unrealistic course of action in attempting to remove the pope without intervening personally in Rome. There were two reasons, however, why Henry and his advisers might have regarded their plans as realistic. The first was Hugh Candidus's evidence concerning Hildebrand's election and conduct as pope. To the German court it must have appeared that these allegations needed only to be publicised to undermine the pope's authority irreparably. There is a parallel with the conduct of Henry III towards Pope Gregory VI in 1046, whom he initially acknowledged as pope. When it became known that Gregory was a simoniac, Henry III pressed forward with his deposition at the synod of Sutri, motivated partly by the political consideration that the pope who crowned him emperor must be beyond reproach, lest his imperial title be suspect.[19] The allegations of Hugh Candidus may have awakened a similar concern in Henry IV, now that he was actively contemplating his imperial coronation, and prompted him to adopt his father's remedy. A second factor influencing royal policy at Worms may have been news from Rome suggesting that Gregory's situation in the city was so vulnerable that it

---

[15] Lampert, *Annales* 1076, p. 254.
[16] *Chronicon episcoporum Hildesheimensium* c. 17, p. 854. See Meyer von Knonau (1894) 2:614, 621.   [17] Bruno of Merseburg, *Saxonicum bellum* c. 65, p. 57.
[18] Gregory VII, *Epistolae Vagantes* 14, p. 38. Cf. Berthold, *Annales* 1076, p. 282; Bernold, *Chronicon* 1076, p. 433; Bruno c. 65, p. 57. See Meyer von Knonau (1894) 2:617 n. 10; A. Hauck (1954) 790–4; Fleckenstein (1968) 232–4.
[19] Steindorff (1874) 1:307–14; Kehr (1930) 49–51; Violante (1952) 157–76, 293–314.

was possible to end his pontificate without mounting an Italian expedition. When the council of Worms met, Henry may already have learned that the pope had been abducted on 25 December 1075 and imprisoned for a short time by his enemy Cencius Stephani.[20] This would naturally suggest the royal strategy of appealing to the Romans to 'rise up against [Hildebrand]'. 'We do not say that you are to shed his blood . . . but that, if he refuses to step down, you are to force him to do so and you are to receive another, elected to the apostolic see by the advice of all the bishops and of us.'[21] When Cencius Stephani was expelled from Rome by papal supporters and fled to the German court, it was in his interests to encourage the king to persist in this strategy, since he had no hope of returning to Rome while Gregory was pope. Henry IV could have obtained more reliable information about the situation in Rome from the royal envoys who had spent the summer there, Rabbodi, Adelpreth and Udalschalk, but he no longer trusted them, presumably because they had won the pope's approval. It was on the misleading reports of Hugh Candidus and Cencius that Henry and his advisers chose to base their flawed strategy in the first half of 1076.

Immediately after the council the letters of the bishops and the king to the pope were brought into Italy by the bishops of Speyer and Basel and by Count Eberhard, still one of the most active and influential of royal advisers. In Piacenza a well-attended assembly of north Italian princes and bishops (including the whole Lombard episcopate) called on the pope to abdicate.[22] Committing themselves further than their colleagues in Worms, the bishops in Piacenza bound themselves by an oath never to obey Gregory as pope in the future.[23] The delivery of the letters informing the pope of the conciliar decisions was entrusted to Roland, a canon of Parma.[24] Count Eberhard sought to gain the support of the Italian princes for the crown 'with large gifts and larger promises',[25] but there was no evidence of a royal expedition to Italy. Henry relied on the Romans and the united imperial episcopate to execute his plans: both parties would disappoint him.

It was two months later, when Henry was in Utrecht, that he learned the outcome of his legation to Rome. News of a serious political reversal had brought him to Utrecht: the murder of his valuable ally Godfrey III of Lower Lotharingia (22 February). It was urgently necessary to resolve the problems

---

[20] Meyer von Knonau (1894) 2:586–90; Borino (1952) 373–440.
[21] Henry IV, *Letter* 10, p. 13.
[22] Berthold, *Annales* 1076, p. 284; Bonizo, *Ad amicum* VII, p. 606. The large attendance was prompted by the consecration of Tedald (5 February): Meyer von Knonau (1894) 2:629–30; Zey (1996) 496–509.   [23] Empress Agnes, letter: Hugh of Flavigny, *Chronicon* II, p. 435.
[24] Gregory VII, *Registrum* v.14a, p. 369. See Schwartz (1913) 61.
[25] Bruno, *Saxonicum bellum* c. 65, p. 57. Cf. *Vita Anselmi Lucensis* c. 14, p. 17.

of his inheritance. The duke died childless; his male heirs were Count Albert III of Namur (husband of his elder sister), and Godfrey of Bouillon (son of his younger sister). Resorting to a measure formerly used by his father in southern Germany, Henry conferred the duchy of Lower Lotharingia on his own son, the two-year-old Conrad. To hostile observers this action seemed to be an attack on the hereditary rights of Godfrey of Bouillon, whom Duke Godfrey III had acknowledged as his heir.[26] Modern commentators have suggested that Henry, buoyed up by his success in Saxony, seized the opportunity of Godfrey's death to increase the crown's authority in Lotharingia. His initiative alarmed the princes and contributed to the development of a conspiracy against the king in 1076.[27] The royal measures are more likely, however, to have been a compromise than an act of royal aggrandisement. It would have been injudicious to invest Godfrey of Bouillon with the duchy immediately, since he was too much of an unknown quantity: a mere youth and the son of Count Eustace of Boulogne, a vassal of the French crown. Nevertheless Henry did not wish to exclude Godfrey from the succession to the duchy by conferring it on a candidate from outside the Verdun dynasty: hence Albert of Namur was appointed not duke but deputy (*vice-dux*) of the king's son. Meanwhile Godfrey received the late duke's march of Antwerp, perhaps as an earnest of future generosity.[28]

As Henry prepared to celebrate Easter (27 March) in Utrecht, an envoy brought him news of developments in Rome (a striking example of how slowly even the most important news could travel in the eleventh-century empire).[29] The envoy Roland of Parma had carried out his mission in all the publicity of the papal synod. Empress Agnes was present and reported to her confidant Bishop Altmann of Passau. 'The envoys of my son the king came into the synod and, in the presence of all, they told the pope, on my son's behalf, that he should rise and renounce the apostolic see, which he had acquired not canonically but by robbery. They were at once seized by the Romans.' Gregory's response, according to the empress, was to 'deprive of office and communion all those who consented willingly [to the bishops' declaration at the council of Worms] and [give] a respite until the feast of St Peter [in chains, 1 August] to those who gave their consent under compulsion. He deprived my son the king of the royal dignity and struck him down with the sword of anathema, because of [the proceedings in Worms] and because he communicates with excommunicates and because he refuses to do penance for his crimes, and he absolved all men from the oaths that they had sworn to

---

[26] Berthold, *Annales* 1076, pp. 283–4; Lampert, *Annales* 1076, pp. 255–6.
[27] Meyer von Knonau (1894) 2:650–3, 658–9; Mohr (1976) 2:62–6.
[28] See below p. 263.   [29] Elze (1980) 6.

him.'[30] The empress's account of the reasons for Henry's deposition and excommunication agrees with that given by the pope himself in the sentence pronounced in the synod (in the form of a prayer to St Peter)[31] and in the letter to the German faithful, justifying the sentence: 'firstly, because he refused to withdraw from the society of those who were excommunicated for the sacrilege and crime of simoniacal heresy; then because he would not so much as promise, let alone perform penance for the guilty actions of his own life . . . and because he was not afraid to rend . . . the unity of holy Church.'[32] The papal sentence of February 1076 was the culmination of three years of papal efforts to compel the king to dismiss his five advisers. In this process the empress had proved herself an active ally of the papacy in 1072 and 1074 and she evidently supported the pope's action in the synod of 1076. 'I see the greatest danger threaten the Church,' she wrote to Altmann, 'because my son places too much faith in the words of fools.'

On receiving the news of his condemnation, Henry assembled a synod in Utrecht, which met on 26 March (the eve of Easter day) and decided 'that on the next day during mass the pope was to be publicly excommunicated because he had dared to excommunicate the king, his lord'. The bishop assigned the task of pronouncing this sentence, Pibo of Toul, evaded this duty by secretly leaving the city that night, together with other prelates. Although loyal adherents of the king, they feared to violate canon law by excommunicating the pope. On Easter day only William of Utrecht was willing to do the king's bidding. His sermon announced the fact that the pope had excommunicated the king (the first public announcement of this event in the kingdom), denounced the pope as a criminal and pronounced his excommunication.[33] The Easter mass in Utrecht was intended as a 'liturgical counter-demonstration' to the papal anathema and the principal role was played by Henry himself.[34] The king staged a 'crown-wearing', one of the rituals of power that, like the coronation, were designed to dramatise the Ottonian–Salian idea of the monarch as 'the vicar of God'. On a great Church festival the king appeared crowned and enthroned in one of the cathedrals of his empire, to the accompaniment of the royal *laudes*, hymns celebrating the majesty of Christ and of the king, who exercised His authority on earth.[35]

[30] Hugh of Flavigny, *Chronicon* II, p. 435. See Meyer von Knonau (1894) 2:632–45; Bulst-Thiele (1933) 101–2; C. Schneider (1972) 154–7; Black-Veldtrup (1995) 54, 98.

[31] Gregory VII, *Registrum* III.10a, p. 270.   [32] Gregory VII, *Epistolae Vagantes* 14, pp. 38–40.

[33] Hugh, p. 458. Following Lampert, *Annales* 1076, p. 258; Berthold, *Annales* 1076, p. 283; Bruno, *Saxonicum bellum* c. 74, p. 76, van de Kieft (1955) 70–9 argued that Gregory was not excommunicated. But see Henry IV, *Letter* 12, p. 17.

[34] Paul of Bernried, *Vita Gregorii VII* c. 80, pp. 521–2. See Meyer von Knonau (1894) 2:661.

[35] Klewitz (1939) 93–6; C. Schneider (1972) 166.

It was in Utrecht that Henry issued the first royal polemics intended to influence 'public opinion' (that is, of the bishops and higher clergy and perhaps also of the secular princes) in the German kingdom. These royal polemics were provoked by Gregory VII's first attempt to promote the rebellion against the king which he had authorised in the Lenten synod. Gregory's letter of February 1076 addressed 'to all who desire to be counted among the sheep which Christ committed to St Peter', citing in full the papal sentence of deposition and excommunication, denounced Henry and his supporters as schismatics and heretics.[36] The king sought to refute papal claims in two letters composed in Utrecht: a new version of the letter to 'Hildebrand' reporting the decisions of the council of Worms (never sent to the pope) and a letter summoning the bishops to a council in Worms at Whitsun (15 May) to take further measures against Hildebrand.[37] These two letters were composed by the royal chaplain Gottschalk (later provost of St Mary in Aachen and monk of Klingenmünster). He became Henry's mouthpiece in the conflict with Gregory VII, clothing the ideas of the king – who may have played an active role in the composition of the polemics – with biblical and theological arguments that had a lasting influence on the controversial literature of the late eleventh century.[38] The first letter is addressed to 'Hildebrand, no longer pope but a false monk' and ends with the command, 'come down, come down!' It contrasts the legitimacy of the divinely ordained king with the lawlessness of the pope. Henry is described as 'king not by usurpation but by the pious ordination of God': an allusion to the central text of Ottonian–Salian political thought, Romans 13:2, 'the powers that be are ordained by God' (which figured prominently in the coronation service). Gottschalk's principal argument was that according to 'the tradition of the holy Fathers' the king could be judged only by God and could be deposed only for heresy. Hildebrand had deviated from the doctrine of 'the true pope, St Peter', who wrote, 'fear God, honour the king' (1 Peter 2:17). In the second royal letter Gottschalk used the language of Pope Gelasius I to evoke the ideal of the harmonious cooperation of the secular and spiritual powers, now disrupted by 'Hildebrandine madness'. Far from performing his duty of preaching obedience to the king, as God's vicar on earth, Hildebrand had 'usurped the royal power' which God conferred on Henry.[39]

The Easter crown-wearing in Utrecht and the letters rebuking the pope

---

[36] Gregory VII, *Registrum* III.6, pp. 254–5.   [37] Henry IV, *Letters* 12, 13, pp. 15–20.

[38] Erdmann and von Gladiss (1939) 115–74. Henry's participation in the composition of the political letters issued in his name: Erdmann (1939) 246–53. Cf. Erdmann (1936a) 491–512; C. Schneider (1972) pp. 157–71; Koch (1972) 31–6, 64–5 and above p. 11.

[39] Henry IV, *Letter* 13, p. 19. Gottschalk's original interpretation of Luke 22:38 (the 'two swords'): Robinson (1978a) 135–7.

were intended to demonstrate that Henry retained the authority of the kingship despite the sentence of deposition and excommunication. Almost immediately, however, two accidents occurred which seemed to negate the effects of the royal demonstration. On Easter day (27 March) the cathedral of St Peter in Utrecht, the scene of the crown-wearing, recently rebuilt at great expense by Bishop William, was struck by lightning and reduced to ashes. Moreover, one month after he pronounced the pope's excommunication William himself suffered a sudden and painful death (27 April). The king's critics regarded these events as a divine judgement on the king's most diligent supporter and on the king himself.[40] The disquiet that these accidents aroused in Henry and his entourage is apparent in two royal diplomas drawn up by Gottschalk of Aachen. The first records a royal gift to the church of St Mary in Aachen, founded by Charlemagne (21 April), an attempt to secure for Henry's regime the patronage of the Virgin and the great emperor.[41] The second diploma, recording a donation to the cathedral of St Peter in Utrecht (23 May), was an attempt to regain the saint's protection after Peter had manifested his anger against the cathedral and its bishop. The diploma contains an admission of guilt: 'we grieve that [the church of Utrecht] was consumed by fire, ascribing this to our sins.' [42]

Henry accepted that the destruction of the cathedral was a punishment for his sins, but he was not prepared to give up his plan to dethrone Hildebrand, whom he still regarded as a usurper. After Easter a council of Lombard bishops and abbots in Pavia, organised by Archbishop Wibert of Ravenna, is alleged to have excommunicated the pope.[43] The Whitsuntide council in Worms (15 May), although well attended, did not attempt a similar demonstration.[44] Further proceedings were postponed to 29 June (the feast of SS. Peter and Paul) in Mainz. The council of Mainz declared the pope excommunicate and the sentence of the Lenten synod invalid, as the king intended, but the episcopate was no longer as united as it had appeared to be in Worms in January. Dissension was introduced by Archbishop Udo of Trier, returning from Rome where he had received absolution from the pope. He scrupulously avoided his excommunicated colleagues and spoke only to the king, having obtained

---

[40] Berthold, *Annales* 1076, p. 283; Lampert, *Annales* 1076, pp. 258–9. See Meyer von Knonau (1894) 2:661–2, 669–70; C. Schneider (1972) 170–1.

[41] *D H IV* 283 (probably issued on the occasion of a memorial service at Charlemagne's tomb): Meyer von Knonau (1894) 2:667–8; C. Schneider (1972) 169.

[42] *D H IV* 284. See Meyer von Knonau (1894) 2:678 n. 94; C. Schneider (1972) 170–1.

[43] Bonizo of Sutri, *Ad amicum* VIII, p. 609; Arnulf of Milan, *Liber gestorum* V.7, pp. 226–7. See Meyer von Knonau (1894) 2:676. But see also Ziese (1982) 45.

[44] Berthold, *Annales* 1076, p. 284; Lampert, *Annales* 1076, p. 263. See Meyer von Knonau (1894) 2:671, 676–7; C. Schneider (1972) 166, 170, 172.

papal permission for an interview with him. Udo's conduct inspired some of the bishops loyal to the king to desert him.[45]

The narrative sources are full of rumours of conspiracies against the king in spring and summer 1076. The dukes of Swabia, Bavaria and Carinthia had ignored the summons to the recent councils of Worms and Mainz. Lampert of Hersfeld reported a meeting which they held with 'very many other princes' during Eastertide to discuss 'the great disasters that plagued the commonwealth', which they attributed to the king's 'shallowness, cruelty and intimate friendship with very wicked men'.[46] Bishop Herman of Metz's reaction to the news of the king's excommunication was to release the prisoners entrusted to his care after the defeat of the Saxons in 1075.[47] The return of the prisoners-of-war to Saxony rekindled the spirit of resistance stifled by Henry's victory. The Saxons were especially heartened by the escape of Burchard of Halberstadt in June. Burchard, regarded by the king as 'the leader of the whole Saxon rebellion', was kept in close captivity in the royal household until an opportunity occurred to send him into a secure exile. A distinguished visitor, the king's sister, Queen Judith-Sophia of Hungary, returning to her husband's kingdom, agreed to take the prisoner with her. During the journey down the Danube Burchard jumped ship and returned to his diocese.[48] Henry sought to check the growing unrest in Saxony by freeing Archbishop Werner of Magdeburg and Bishop Werner of Merseburg and sending them to assure the Saxons of the king's goodwill and love of justice. Their mission did nothing to calm the duchy.[49]

The opening hostilities in this new phase of the Saxon rebellion were the work of the Wettin princes Theoderic and William, sons of Count Gero of Brehna. They had fled to the Slav lands beyond the Elbe to avoid surrendering in 1075 and now returned to make war on the king's adherents in Saxony.[50] Henry's principal representative in the province was Otto of Northeim, who since his submission at Christmastide 1075 had exercised 'the government of the whole of Saxony' from his headquarters in the Harzburg. As resistance to

[45] Lampert, Annales 1076, pp. 263–4; Berthold, Annales 1076, p. 284. See Meyer von Knonau (1894) 2:681–2; C. Schneider (1972) 170–1.

[46] Lampert, Annales 1076, p. 257, identified the fellow conspirators as the bishops of Würzburg and Metz; Berthold, Annales 1076, p. 283, as the patriarch of Aquileia, archbishop of Salzburg, bishops of Würzburg, Passau, Worms 'and almost all the Saxons'.

[47] Lampert, Annales 1076, p. 258; Bruno, Saxonicum bellum c. 84, p. 80. See Meyer von Knonau (1894) 2:675–6 and n. 89.

[48] Lampert, Annales 1076, pp. 265–8; Bruno c. 83, pp. 78–9. See Meyer von Knonau (1894) 2:680–1.

[49] Bruno c. 86, p. 81; Lampert, Annales 1076, pp. 268–9. See Meyer von Knonau (1894) 2:682–3.

[50] Lampert, Annales 1076, pp. 260, 269, 272. See Meyer von Knonau (1894) 2:713–14, 717; Fenske (1977) 53–4, 73.

the crown began to revive, Otto was pressed by his compatriots to expiate his recent treachery by embracing the cause of Saxon liberty again. The consequence was that 'henceforward he lived in friendship and alliance with the Saxons'. Initially he adopted the role of mediator between Henry and his Saxon opponents, communicating the Saxons' demands that Henry release the remaining prisoners and dismantle the controversial royal castles. Otto privately promised the Saxon princes that he would join their rebellion if the king refused these demands. His opposition to the crown became overt when, in August, Henry decided, against Otto's advice, to lead an expedition into Saxony to check the incursions of the rebel Wettins. The king entered the march of Meissen with his ally, Duke Vratislav II of Bohemia. Otto then declared that 'since [the king] had more faith in foolish flatterers than in [Otto] and placed more hope and trust in the Bohemian contingent than in the German army', he considered himself absolved from his oath to serve Henry. The king's arrival provoked 'many thousands' of Saxons to take up arms against him, and his small army might have been cut to pieces had not the flooding of the River Mulde hindered the Saxon advance and allowed Henry to retreat to Bohemia.[51] As a reward for his loyal service, the king conferred the march of Meissen on Duke Vratislav, having already granted him the march of Lower Lusatia in 1075. Henry hoped to secure control of the Thuringian marcher territories by using the power of his Bohemian ally, his own resources having proved inadequate. In so doing he disinherited his own kinsman, Ekbert II of Brunswick, 'a boy still far below the age of knighthood'. Ekbert's youth would have disqualified him, in the opinion of most contemporaries, from holding such a responsible office as the march of Meissen: nevertheless the king's action confirmed the Saxon view of Henry as a lawless tyrant. The Saxon rebels expelled Vratislav's garrisons from the fortresses of his march and replaced them with knights loyal to Ekbert II.[52]

The failure of Henry's Saxon expedition emboldened his enemies elsewhere. In late August or early September a number of conspirators met in Ulm: the dukes Rudolf, Welf and Berthold and the bishops Adalbero of Würzburg, Adalbert of Worms and Altmann of Passau. They decided to summon all the German princes to an assembly in Tribur on 16 October 'to bring to an end the various misfortunes that for many years had disturbed the peace of the Church'.[53] Bishop Altmann came to the assembly in Tribur as the legate of Gregory VII (who trusted him not least because he was the

---

[51] Lampert, *Annales* 1076, pp. 261–2, 269–73. See Meyer von Knonau (1894) 2:714–17; Lange (1961) 58–63.

[52] Lampert, *Annales* 1076, pp. 270, 273. See Meyer von Knonau (1894) 2:715–19; Schramm (1968) 350; Fenske (1977) 74–5 and above p. 102.

[53] Lampert, *Annales* 1076, pp. 273–4. See Meyer von Knonau (1894) 2:725–7.

former chaplain and confidant of Empress Agnes).[54] He and his fellow-conspirators in Ulm had to take account of the attitude of the pope, as indicated in the letters sent to Germany during the months April–September 1076.[55] In the letters of April–July the emphasis was on the pope's desire for peace with the king: 'if he comes to his senses . . . he will find us ready to receive him into holy communion'.[56] The letter of 29 August, however, warned that 'we have learned from the faithful of holy Church that the king is trying his best to divide us from each other and to deceive us, sometimes through spiritual and sometimes through secular persons'. Nothing further is known about this royal tactic of sowing dissension among opponents. Gregory's response was to forbid anyone to absolve Henry from excommunication 'until the news of his satisfaction and penance is announced to [the pope] by suitable messengers of [the princes]'.[57]

The letter of 3 September began by instructing the princes that, for the sake of his parents, 'whose equals in governing the empire cannot be found in our age', they must 'treat [Henry] kindly', provided he removed 'the evil counsellors' and rejected 'customs contrary to the freedom of holy Church'. If Henry failed to repent, however, 'someone should be found . . . to govern the kingdom' who would promise to do 'whatever seems necessary for the Christian religion and for the safety of the whole empire'. For the first time in his correspondence with Henry's opponents Gregory broached the election of a new king. He assumed that such an election would be the work of three parties: the German princes, Empress Agnes and the pope. The princes, to whom tradition gave the right to elect a king, were to seek the advice of the empress, according to the terms of 'the oath that was sworn to our most beloved daughter Agnes . . . in case her son departed this life before her'.[58] This oath, presumably sworn at the time of Henry IV's accession in 1056, now came into effect because of the *spiritual* death of the excommunicate king.[59] The princes were to inform the pope about 'the person and morals' of their candidate, 'so that we may confirm your election (if it is really necessary) by apostolic authority, as ought to be done, and strengthen the new order in our times, as we know was done by our holy Fathers'. This claim that papal approval was necessary for the installation of a new king was a characteristic

[54] Bernold of St Blasien, *Pro Gebhardo* p. 110.

[55] Gregory VII, *Registrum* III.12, 14, 15, IV.1–3, pp. 273–4, 275–7, 289–300; *Epistolae Vagantes* 14, 15, pp. 32–40, 42. Only in the letter to Herman of Metz (IV.2) did the papal chancery respond to the Eastertide letters of Gottschalk of Aachen. See Meyer von Knonau (1894) 2:672, 694–703, 719–23; C. Schneider (1972) 187–98.

[56] Gregory VII, *Epistolae Vagantes* 14, p. 40.   [57] *Ibid.* 15, p. 42.

[58] Gregory VII, *Registrum* IV.3, pp. 298–9.

[59] Berges (1947) 189–209. See also above p. 28.

Gregorian 'creative misinterpretation' of the conduct of two predecessors ('our holy Fathers'): Pope Zacharias's recommendation that the Carolingian Pippin III should replace the 'useless' Childeric III as king of the Franks (750)[60] and Victor II's role as guardian of the young Henry IV (1056–7).[61]

Gregory's letters of April–September continued the papal strategy, first apparent in Alexander II's pontificate, of forcing reforming ideas upon the king with the help of a pressure-group of princes. This strategy achieved success in the assembly of princes in Tribur, during which Henry was compelled to negotiate with the pope's legates and promised to submit to the pope to avoid being deposed by the princes. The papal representatives who played so notable a part in the assembly did not share a common political outlook: Patriarch Sigehard of Aquileia (a former chancellor for the German kingdom) was treated by Henry with the greatest favour; Altmann of Passau had since Easter been associated with the king's enemies. Altmann was charged by the pope with the duty of absolving the penitent, who included Siegfried of Mainz, many bishops and abbots 'and no small crowd of greater and lesser men'. A small group of prelates – the archbishop of Cologne and the bishops of Bamberg, Strasbourg, Basel, Speyer, Lausanne, Naumburg and Osnabrück – remained with the king in Oppenheim, on the opposite bank of the Rhine, throughout the negotiations, together with his most trusted secular advisers, Count Eberhard, Udalric of Godesheim and Hartmann, three of the five advisers excommunicated in 1073. According to Berthold of Reichenau, the absolution of the bishops preceded all the other business of the assembly.[62] The bishops' submission was perhaps an important factor in persuading the king to abandon the stand taken in January.

'From the outset only one party of princes sought a new election; the others certainly wished to humble Henry, but also to keep him as king.'[63] The single eyewitness account of the Tribur assembly, a letter by an unknown bishop, is written from this moderate viewpoint. 'It was judged to be just that the royal dignity should show due reverence to priestly excellence, in that the excommunicate should be reconciled to the Church in the presence of the excommunicator either by proving his innocence or by making appropriate satisfaction for his fault.'[64] The aims of the small 'deposition faction' who had summoned the assembly of Tribur – the conspirators of Ulm (the south

---

[60] *Registrum* IV.2, p. 294. See Affeldt (1969) 313–46.

[61] See above pp. 26–7, 112.

[62] Berthold, *Annales* 1076, p. 286. See Meyer von Knonau (1894) 2:729–35, 885–93; C. Schneider (1972) 171–87; Beumann (1973) 33–44; Hlawitschka (1974) 25–45.

[63] Erdmann (1937) 376.

[64] Holder-Egger (1905) 188–9, identifying the author as Siegfried of Mainz. Erdmann (1937) 386 n. 78 suggested Otto of Constance. See also Tellenbach (1940) 230–4.

German dukes and the bishops of Würzburg and Worms), together with the leaders of the Saxon rebels – are found in the account of Lampert of Hersfeld. They 'firmly resolved to remove King Henry from the government of the kingdom and to create another, elected by common consent'.[65] Berthold of Reichenau, however, reflecting the attitude of the majority in the assembly and of the papal legates, wrote that the princes hoped 'that they might be permitted to serve their lord and king, once he had been admonished, converted to penitence and reconciled'.[66] The legates were obliged to follow the instructions in the papal letter of 3 September 1076: the election of a new king was a last resort, to be adopted only 'if [the king] was not wholeheartedly converted to God'.[67] It was the strategy of reconciliation, rather than that of the 'deposition faction', that prevailed in Tribur. The assembly chose Udo of Trier, who had probably emerged as the leader of the 'moderates', as the envoy who was to carry to Rome the details of the king's concessions.

The assembly of Tribur lasted from 16 October to 1 November and consisted of seven days of debate among the princes, followed by ten days of negotiation between the princes and the king, encamped in Oppenheim.[68] The length of these proceedings must be attributed to the difference in aims between the 'deposition faction' and the 'moderates'. Crossing and recrossing the Rhine, the royal envoys eventually negotiated a settlement with the papal legates and the princes. The king was to restore to Bishop Adalbert the city of Worms, which had served as his principal residence since autumn 1073. He was to free the remaining Saxon hostages, disband his army and withdraw to Speyer. Most importantly, he promised to dismiss his excommunicated advisers and repudiate the measures taken against the pope by the council of Worms. These were the concessions specified in Gregory VII's letter of 3 September and demanded by the papal legates during the Tribur negotiations. The king's written promise 'to preserve due obedience in all things' to the pope, the so-called 'Promise of Oppenheim', was to be brought to Rome by Udo of Trier. Simultaneously Henry issued a manifesto addressed to the bishops, princes 'and every office-holder': 'it has pleased us, following sounder counsel, to change our former judgement and in the manner of our predecessors and ancestors to preserve due obedience in all things to the holy see and ... to the lord Pope Gregory.' He urged his subjects likewise 'to show solemn obedience to St Peter and his vicar'.[69]

Before the assembly dispersed, the princes gained a further concession from

[65] Lampert, *Annales* 1076, pp. 276–83. Cf. Bruno, *Saxonicum bellum* c. 88. pp. 82–3.
[66] Berthold, *Annales* 1076, p. 286.   [67] Gregory VII, *Registrum* IV.3, p. 299.
[68] Berthold, *Annales* 1076, p. 286; Bruno c. 88, p. 82; Lampert, *Annales* 1076, p. 278.
[69] Henry IV, *Letter* 14, pp. 20–1. His letter to Agnes, *Letter* 15, pp. 21–2, may refer to Tribur–Oppenheim; but see above p. 133 n. 125.

the king. Henry agreed to the proposal of the princes to refer their grievances against him to the pope's judgement at an assembly in Augsburg on 2 February 1077. Lampert, reporting the view of the 'deposition faction', wrote that at this assembly the pope 'would sentence the accused [king] or absolve him, according to his judgement. If, however, [Henry] was not absolved, through his own fault, before the anniversary of his excommunication, his case would at once be lost forever and he could not thereafter lawfully claim the kingship.'[70] The anonymous eyewitness account of the Tribur assembly presents the view of the 'moderate' princes. The purpose of the pope's coming to Augsburg was not that he should 'sentence the accused or absolve him', but that Henry 'should be reconciled to the Church ... either by proving his innocence or by making appropriate satisfaction for his fault'. Even if the pope judged the king to be guilty as charged, Henry would still be absolved from his excommunication, after a suitable penance, and restored to the kingship.[71] The contradiction between these accounts provides an insight into the manoeuverings of the last ten days of the assembly. Henry's decision 'to change [his] former judgement' and offer the concessions demanded in the papal letter of 3 September, was a bid for the support of the 'moderates' and the papal legates. The 'Promise of Oppenheim' was intended to exploit the differences between the 'moderates' and the 'deposition faction'. The king's timely display of penitence foiled his enemies' plan of transforming the meeting in Tribur into an assembly for electing a new king. The 'deposition faction', however, responded with the new ploy of inviting the pope to the assembly of Augsburg, confident that they could convince Gregory VII of Henry's unsuitability for the office of king. Their decision to regard Henry as definitively deposed if he failed to obtain absolution was the final attempt of these relentless enemies to prevent Henry's rehabilitation.

The 'Promise of Oppenheim' contained the king's promise 'to preserve due obedience in all things to the apostolic see and to you, Pope Gregory' and 'to amend and faithfully to make reparation for any injury to that see or to your honour which seems to have been occasioned by us'. The 'Promise' recorded

---

[70] Lampert, *Annales* 1076, p. 281. Berthold, *Annales* 1076, pp. 286–7 and Bruno c. 88, p. 83 make it clear that this condition was a last-minute addition, made after the 'Promise of Oppenheim' and the invitation to the pope had been sent to Rome.

[71] The letter of the anonymous eyewitness makes Epiphany (6 January) the date of the Augsburg assembly: Holder-Egger (1905) 189. Hence Beumann (1973) 42, 45 suggested that the princes originally wished to hold the assembly on 6 January, but their envoys in Rome were induced to accept a postponement to 2 February. This delay enabled Henry to intercept the pope at Canossa. But Hlawitschka (1974) 44 argued that *epiphania* in the eyewitness's letter was a scribal error for *hypante*, the Greek term for the Feast of the Purification (2 February).

the concessions in terms similar to the letter of the anonymous eyewitness. Henry promised to 'clear away . . . with a plea of innocence' or perform penance for the 'serious accusations' being made about his intentions towards the Roman church and Gregory VII.[72] The debate about the 'Promise of Oppenheim' – whether it was a 'peace-treaty' advantageous to the king or 'unconditional surrender' on his part[73] – has concentrated on the last sentence of the 'Promise'. 'It is fitting that your holiness should not overlook those [accusations] that have been published about you, bringing scandal to the Church, but that this difficulty should be removed from the public conscience and the universal tranquillity of both Church and kingdom consolidated by your wisdom.' This apparent reference to the accusations made at the council of Worms certainly does not suggest unconditional surrender: it amounts in fact to a remarkable concession by the legates and the princes. The last sentence of the 'Promise of Oppenheim' has been ingeniously defended against the charge of forgery.[74] Nevertheless it is unlikely that the papal legates could have admitted into the 'peace-treaty' of Oppenheim the demand that the pope clear himself of the accusations made in Worms. A useful analogy has been drawn with the two versions of Henry IV's letter to the pope of 1076, the longer version being a justification of the king's action, intended solely for a German audience. The extant version of the 'Promise' may be a longer 'German version' of the document negotiated at Tribur-Oppenheim with a face-saving addition made by the royal chancery after the original version had been sent to Rome.[75] The royal 'Promise' approved by the legates and princes and sealed in their presence probably amounted, therefore, not to a 'peace-treaty' but to 'unconditional surrender'. In the dangerous situation of October 1076 an honourable surrender was the best that the king and his advisers could achieve. It was not a negligible achievement, since it prevented the 'deposition faction' from persuading the more numerous 'moderates' in the assembly of Tribur to endorse their plans to replace the king.

From Oppenheim the king withdrew, as he had promised, to Speyer, where he lived as a penitent preparing for absolution. The excommunicated advisers had been dismissed; of the bishops, only Theoderic of Verdun remained in his company. He received one notable guest in Speyer during the autumn: Abbot Hugh I of Cluny visited his godson in Germany before visiting Gregory VII

---

[72] *Die Briefe Heinrichs IV.* p. 69.

[73] Haller (1939) 264–5, 270 ('unconditional surrender'); cf. Haller (1906) 102–47. Brackmann (1927) 410 ('peace-treaty'); cf. Brackmann (1939) 3–37.

[74] Against its authenticity: A. Hauck (1954) 806 n. 1; Schmeidler (1927) 309; Haller (1939) 268–9; Baethgen (1941) 408–11. In favour: Brackmann (1927) 406–10; Erdmann (1937) 365–70; Beumann (1973) 35–45.   [75] C. Schneider (1972) 172–86.

in Rome in late December.[76] Hugh's objective was his godson's reconciliation to the Roman church, an objective for which he was still working at Canossa in January 1077. Meanwhile Henry awaited the pope's reaction to his submission. Gregory referred in a letter of December 1076 to the princes to 'the many and great debates that we have had with the envoys of the king and the arguments with which we have resisted his words', indicating that far more was at issue than the 'Promise of Oppenheim' brought to Rome by Udo of Trier.[77] According to Berthold of Reichenau, 'the king obstinately requested permission to come to the pope in Rome to be reconciled. The pope, however, would not consent, but commanded by apostolic authority that [Henry] should meet him in Augsburg to be heard and reconciled in the presence of the princes of the kingdom.'[78] Gregory was determined to adhere to the plan of the 'deposition faction', whose envoys followed Udo of Trier to Rome with the invitation to the assembly of Augsburg. The invitation to arbitrate between king and princes was irresistible, since it offered Gregory the opportunity of demonstrating that papal supremacy in secular affairs which he had claimed in his letters to the faithful during the summer of 1076.

'The king was well aware that his safety depended entirely on his being absolved from excommunication before the end of the year. He considered, however, that it was not in his own interests to await the arrival of the Roman pontiff in Germany and to allow his case to be investigated by so hostile a judge and by such inflexible accusers. He judged that his best course was to enter Italy and meet the Roman pontiff while he was still on his way to Germany and seek to obtain absolution from the anathema by whatever means he could.'[79] Lampert's version of Henry's reflections in the last days of 1076 rings true. When Henry learned of the failure of his envoys in Rome, he recalled his advisers, who counselled him to intercept the pope in Italy. Shortly before Christmas he set out for the kingdom of Burgundy with Queen Bertha and their son Conrad, not yet three years old. The royal family celebrated the festival in Besançon as the guests of their kinsman, Count William of Burgundy (cousin of Empress Agnes), but almost immediately they continued their journey, crossing the Rhône at Geneva.[80] German kings usually travelled to their Italian kingdom by way of the Brenner, the Augsburg–Verona route being the shortest and easiest. In December 1076, however, all the Alpine passes in southern Germany were in enemy hands, the south German

---

[76] Berthold, *Annales* 1077, p. 289: Hugh had to receive absolution from the pope because of his contact with the excommunicate king. See Cowdrey (1970a) 160.

[77] Gregory VII, *Epistolae Vagantes* 17, p. 48; cf. *Registrum* IV.12, p. 312.

[78] Berthold, *Annales* 1076, p. 287; Paul of Bernried, *Vita Gregorii VII* c. 87, p. 526. See Meyer von Knonau (1894) 2:737–40.   [79] Lampert, *Annales* 1076, p. 283.

[80] *Ibid.* 1077, pp. 285: see Meyer von Knonau (1894) 2:741–2.

dukes having set guards on the passes in their territories. The friendship of Count William of Burgundy gave Henry access to the Burgundian pass of Mont Cenis. In the neighbourhood of Geneva, perhaps in Gex, the king met other kindred: his mother-in-law, Adelaide of Turin, and her son, Count Amadeus II of Savoy, through whose lands Henry intended to travel. Adelaide and Amadeus stood high in Gregory VII's favour and may therefore have been out of sympathy with the king. Lampert represented them as determined to profit from Henry's predicament: their assistance was eventually purchased with 'a very wealthy province of Burgundy'.[81]

The winter of 1076–7 was unusually severe.[82] Snow and ice made the Mont Cenis (2,084 metres above sea-level) extremely dangerous but the king would allow no delay and hired native guides to clear a track. The men of the royal party made the treacherous descent to the Italian side of the pass crawling on hands and knees or clinging to the shoulders of guides; the queen and her ladies were drawn on sledges of ox-skin. The descent brought them into the region of Turin, whence they travelled by way of Vercelli and Pavia to the fortress of Canossa. The journey of 816 kilometres from Besançon to Canossa took approximately four weeks.[83] When the party reached Pavia, 'all the bishops and counts of Italy' were ready to welcome the king on his first visit to the kingdom. The Lombard bishops, who had been excommunicated by the pope and some of whom had suffered violence from the pope's Patarine allies, were ready to assist Henry in deposing Gregory VII.[84] Such a measure would, however, have only increased Henry's problems in Germany: the breach of the 'Promise of Oppenheim' would have united the 'moderate' princes behind the plans of the 'deposition faction'. Henry assured the Italian princes that his purpose was reconciliation with the pope. Gregory VII had advised the German princes of his intention of being in Mantua on 8 January 1077, where he would await the escort whom they would send to bring him safely to Augsburg.[85] After crossing the Apennines, he learned both that the king was in Italy and that the princes were unable to provide the promised escort. Since it was rumoured that Henry intended to take him prisoner, Gregory turned back to Canossa, the fortress of his most trusted ally, Matilda, margravine of Tuscany, on the northern edge of the Apennines. The pope was first approached by German bishops and laymen who had travelled to Italy

---

[81] Lampert, *Annales* 1077, pp. 285–6. See Meyer von Knonau (1894) 2:748–9. Previté-Orton (1912) 237–8: the province was North Bugey or Tarentaise or a 'grant of immunity for the Savoyard possessions scattered outside their own *comitatus*'.

[82] Meyer von Knonau (1894) 2:750 n. 7.

[83] Lampert, *Annales* 1077, pp. 286–7. Cf. Berthold, *Annales* 1077, p. 288. See Meyer von Knonau (1894) 2:747; Schrod (1931) 16–17; Zimmermann (1975) 154; Elze (1980) 6–7.

[84] Lampert, *Annales* 1077, p. 287.   [85] Gregory VII, *Epistolae Vagantes* 17, p. 48.

independently of the king, seeking absolution from the papal excommunication.[86] Their petitions were succeeded by those of the mediators acting on behalf of the king, now in Reggio, twenty miles north-east of Canossa. These mediators were Henry's kinswoman, Matilda of Tuscany,[87] his mother-in-law, Adelaide of Turin and her son, Abbot Hugh of Cluny (who had accompanied the pope since he set out from Rome), the royal adherent Margrave Adalbert Azzo II of Este and 'other foremost princes of Italy'.[88]

At first the mediators were unable to gain a hearing for the king and Henry had received no sign from the pope when he demonstrated his penitence for three days before the gates of Canossa. In the company of other penitent excommunicates Henry was admitted within the second of the three walls of the fortress.[89] 'He remained for three days before the castle-gate, having cast aside all the splendour of a king': so the pope described the penitent, 'in a wretched condition, barefoot and clad in wool, he did not cease to weep and to beg for the aid and consolation of apostolic compassion.'[90] Only on 28 January, after the third day of penance, did the pope state the conditions on which Henry could be reconciled to the Church. In the ensuing negotiations the pope was represented by the cardinal bishops of Ostia and Palestrina (whom the king had met during their legation of 1074). The king was represented by Liemar of Bremen, Gregory of Vercelli (the Italian chancellor), Benno II of Osnabrück and Hugh of Cluny. The conditions for the absolution were formulated as an oath of security, taken not by the king himself but by a number of distinguished oath-helpers: the bishops of Vercelli and Naumburg, the margravines Matilda and Adelaide and Margrave Adalbert Azzo swore an oath on holy relics. Hugh of Cluny also acted as a guarantor on behalf of his godson, but his monastic vows forbade him to take the oath. After these preliminaries the pope allowed the penitents to enter the castle. Absolving them from excommunication, Gregory conducted them to the chapel where, after bestowing the kiss of peace, he celebrated mass. Henry then dined with the pope, who bade him keep his oath and avoid contact with excommunicates.

In the account of these proceedings that he sent to the German princes (28 January 1077) Gregory emphasised the reluctance with which he had conceded absolution: 'some exclaimed that we were showing not the gravity

---

[86] Lampert, *Annales* 1077, pp. 289–90.
[87] See the miniature in the earliest manuscript of Donizo of Canossa, *Vita Mathildis* (Vat.lat. 4922, reproduced: *MGH SS* 12, plate vii at p. 381). Cf. Donizo, *Vita* ii.97, p. 381.
[88] Lampert, *Annales* 1077, p. 290.   [89] *Ibid.* p. 292. See Tondelli (1952) 365–71.
[90] Gregory VII, *Registrum* iv.12, p. 313. Cf. Lampert, *Annales* 1077, pp. 289–96; Berthold, *Annales* 1077, pp. 288–90. See Meyer von Knonau (1894) 2:755–62, 894–903; Struve (1995) 44–5.

appropriate to apostolic severity but rather the cruelty of tyrannical ferocity'. The pope assured the princes that he had had no choice but to absolve the king and that he had not betrayed their interests at Canossa. He assured his allies that, although this delay meant that he would not now reach Augsburg by 2 February, he was still determined that the assembly should take place. 'As you can perceive in the copy of the guarantees' – that is, the copy of the king's oath that was included in this letter – 'the whole conduct of this business has so far been suspended, so that our coming [to Germany] and your unanimous advice seem to be extremely necessary.'[91] This claim is confirmed by the text of 'the oath of Henry, king of the Germans', which is concerned principally with the strategy agreed by the pope and the princes at the end of the assembly of Tribur. The oath begins with a promise to 'do justice according to [Gregory's] judgement or make an agreement according to his counsel' in respect of the princes' grievances. Secondly, the king guaranteed the pope's safety if he crossed the Alps or travelled elsewhere in the imperial territories. Henry also guaranteed the safety of the papal entourage and envoys and promised to assist the pope in the case of 'any impediment that may be against his honour'.[92] The oath envisages the pope as arbiter of German politics: the role that the princes conferred on Gregory in the autumn of 1076 and that he could continue to play only with their active cooperation. 'Strive to remain in that faith in which you have begun', he exhorted the princes, 'knowing that we are not bound to the king otherwise than in what we have said, in our accustomed straightforward manner, that he can hope from us.' Henry's oath suggests that the main preoccupation of the pope at Canossa was to keep faith with the princes whose invitation he had accepted after the assembly of Tribur.

Historians have long debated whether the negotiations at Canossa involved the restoration of Henry to his royal functions.[93] That question is prompted by an apparent conflict between the text of the oath and papal letter of 28 January 1077 and the version of events given by Gregory three years later. In the Roman synod of March 1080 the pope claimed: 'I restored to [Henry] communion alone, but I did not install him in the kingship, from which I had deposed him in a Roman synod.'[94] Doubtless this distinction was also in Gregory's mind three years earlier at Canossa, but the language of the documents of 28 January 1077 is more ambiguous. The papal letter accords Henry the title of king; the oath describes him as 'king of the Germans'. Given that

[91] *Registrum* IV.12, pp. 313–14.
[92] *Ibid.* IV.12a, pp. 314–15. See H. Krause (1965) 433; C. Schneider (1972) 203–9; Beumann (1973) 48–55.
[93] Fliche (1947) 373–86; Arquillière (1950) 157–64; Arquillière (1952) 1–25; Morrison (1962) 121–48; Miccoli (1966) 203–23; Beumann (1973) 49–55.
[94] Gregory VII, *Registrum* VII.14a, p. 484. See below pp. 195–6.

Gregory's letters since February 1076 had called Henry the 'so-called king', the reappearance of the royal title on 28 January 1077 suggests that Henry was once more qualified to exercise his office. The assumption behind the guarantees of the pope's security in Henry's oath is that he would henceforward perform the functions of the kingship. The guarantee that the pope would suffer no injury from 'those whom I can control' implies that Henry was once more a lord of vassals and that, therefore, the pope must have withdrawn his sentence of February 1076, absolving the king's vassals from their fealty to him. To Gregory it seemed that the question of Henry's restoration to the kingship could only be settled by pope and princes in a council in Germany. 'We absolved him from the bond of anathema and received him into the grace of communion,' Gregory wrote to the princes a month after the event, 'but we made no other arrangements with him, except what we thought would be for the safety and honour of you all.'[95] It did not occur to the pope that in making the practical arrangements of 'the oath of Henry, king of the Germans', he might appear to be settling the question of the kingship out of hand. That is how his conduct eventually appeared to some disappointed supporters in Germany. The Saxons complained (probably in 1078) that, although the pope claimed not to have recognised Henry as king, in enlisting his aid in the holding of the German council, by demanding an escort from him, he was actually treating Henry as the master of the kingdom.[96] There is no doubt that Henry IV believed himself restored to the kingship by the absolution of 28 January 1077. What brought him to Italy was the ultimatum of the 'deposition faction' at Tribur: 'if he was not absolved . . . before the anniversary of his excommunication, his case would at once be lost forever and he could not thereafter lawfully claim the kingship.' The successful journey to Canossa fulfilled this demand, just as the 'Promise of Oppenheim' had satisfied the earlier demands of the assembly of Tribur. The purpose of both measures was to avert deposition by the princes.

The anti-Henrician chroniclers emphasised the 'unheard-of humiliation' of Henry's penance. After Canossa, if Henry continued to be king, it would be on condition that 'he was subject to the Roman pontiff and always obedient to his word'.[97] Henry's anonymous biographer in the early twelfth century, however, interpreted Canossa as a tactical victory for the king. 'With one deed he achieved two purposes: namely, he obtained absolution from the ban and by his personal intervention he prevented a conference of the pope with his opponents, which would have endangered him.'[98] These two opposite viewpoints tend to recur in the modern historiography of Canossa. The

[95] Gregory VII, *Epistolae Vagantes* 19, p. 52.
[96] Bruno, *Saxonicum bellum* c. 108, p. 98; cf. c. 110, pp. 100–1.
[97] Lampert, *Annales* 1077, p. 294; cf. 1076, p. 281. Cf. Bernold, *Chronicon* 1077, p. 289.
[98] *Vita Heinrici IV* c. 3, p. 16.

submission was 'a symbol of the capitulation of secular power before ecclesiastical claims to dominion'.[99] It was the means by which Henry 'regained his freedom of action'[100] and 'showed himself vis-à-vis the princes as the superior politician. He did after all save the crown.'[101] By intercepting the pope before he met the 'deposition faction', Henry foiled the princes' plan to have the absolution take place (if at all) only in the assembly of Augsburg and ensured that that assembly, at which he anticipated many injurious allegations against his regime, would be postponed.

It has been argued that Henry's tactical victory was won at the expense of his royal authority. Submission to the pope was 'seriously damaging for the idea of the sacral ruler. Henry had accepted in principle the claim of the pope . . . to be able to excommunicate the king and remove him from his office – the same king who only a few months before had proclaimed that his authority came directly from God.'[102] To papal supporters the absolution doubtless seemed to vindicate Gregory's claim to be supreme judge in secular matters; but there is no evidence that Henry saw Canossa in this light. Henry's kingship was not an issue in the negotiations at Canossa.[103] He sought only absolution: he did not ask for the reversal of the papal deposition and the withdrawal of the fealty of his vassals. Henry's letter of Eastertide 1076 refused to recognise the papal claim to depose the king.[104] There is no reason to suppose that Henry's attitude had changed a year later. Acceptance of the validity of the papal deposition was certainly not one of the concessions demanded in Oppenheim or in Canossa. Henry probably regarded the penance at Canossa as no more damaging to his authority than the penance at Nuremberg in April 1074.[105] On both occasions the purpose of the penance was to forestall a rapprochement between the pope and rebel princes. It was as the ally of the princes that the pope appeared dangerous to Henry in 1076–7, as in 1074. What brought the king to Canossa was the fear that papal authority was about to be used to legitimise the schemes of the 'deposition faction'. The most important effect of the absolution on Henry's situation was that it restored normal relations with the German episcopate, except for the few bishops in the 'deposition faction'. Far from being 'seriously damaging for the idea of the sacral ruler', the absolution at Canossa allowed Henry to function once more as a sacral ruler in the eyes of most of his bishops. As far as Gregory VII was concerned, however, the absolution threatened that relationship with the princes without which he could not intervene in German politics, so that it is possible to conclude that at Canossa Henry 'inflicted a serious political defeat on the pope'.[106]

[99] Hampe (1912) 63 (English translation: 86). See F. Schneider (1926) 163–75.
[100] Schmeidler (1927) 375.   [101] Erdmann (1937) 385.   [102] Jordan (1964) 260.
[103] Mikoletzky (1960) 261; C. Schneider (1972) 206; Beumann (1973) 49–50; Vogel (1983) 6.
[104] Henry IV, *Letter* 12, p. 16.   [105] See above pp. 132–3.   [106] Dempf (1929) 186.

It is possible that Henry's negotiations with the pope continued into early February. Gregory VII remained in northern Italy until early September, delayed by the hope of crossing the Alps and settling the conflict between Henry and his enemies.[107] Henry remained in his Italian kingdom only until April. A single late source claims that the king and the pope met on 3 February, together with Matilda, in her fortress of Bianello and discussed the holding of a 'general conference' in Mantua.[108] Henry's main preoccupation in February–April 1077, however, was to assert his authority over his Italian kingdom, continuing the process begun by his envoy, Count Eberhard, during the summer of 1075. Henry 'travelled through Italy in order to do justice, according to royal custom, to those who had suffered oppression or injustice'.[109] He visited Piacenza, Verona and Pavia, where he issued diplomas in favour of prominent subjects, including Bishop Denis of Piacenza (the excommunicated leader of Lombard opposition to the pope) and the sons of Margrave Adalbert Azzo II of Este. In the twenty-first year of his reign Henry exercised the functions of kingship in Italy for the first time.[110] Two anti-Henrician accounts claim that Henry planned to legitimate his authority in Italy by means of a coronation in Pavia, but that his plan was blocked by the pope.[111] No Henrician document contains any reference to a failed plan for a coronation, but an indirect reference to the Italian kingship may be detected in a royal diploma of 4 March. Here (uniquely among the diplomas of the reign) Henry is called 'king of the Franks and of the Lombards', a title that may suggest that the idea of a coronation in Pavia, the ancient Lombard capital, was under consideration at this date.[112] The cancellation of such a plan is likely to have been caused not by papal intervention, but by the news that Henry's enemies in Germany had elected a rival king.

The conspirators 'set up Duke Rudolf of Swabia over them and . . . fortified the Alpine passes against Henry'.[113] Henry must return immediately across

---

[107] Gregory VII, *Registrum* IV.13–28, V.1–2, pp. 316–50. Cf. IV.23–4, pp. 334–8. See Meyer von Knonau (1900) 3:78–81.

[108] Donizo, *Vita Mathildis* II.125–47, p. 382: the conference never took place because Matilda was warned of Henry's secret plan to imprison the pope. The Bianello meeting was discounted by Köhncke (1888) 32; Meyer von Knonau (1894) 2:765 n. 31; but accepted by Beumann (1973) 59; Zimmermann (1975) 40, 159; Vogel (1983) 23, 25; Struve (1995) 45. Gregory's itinerary: Santifaller (1957) 1:129.   [109] Lampert, *Annales* 1077, pp. 299, 301.

[110] *DD H IV* 286–91. At least six judicial hearings (*placita*) were held between 17 February and 1 April: *I Placiti del 'Regnum Italiae'* 3: nos. 438–43. See Meyer von Knonau (1894) 2:765–8; (1900) 3:12–13; Vogel (1983) 25–9.

[111] Berthold, *Annales* 1077, p. 290; Paul, *Vita Gregorii VII* c. 86, pp. 525–6. See Meyer von Knonau (1894) 2:769–71; Vogel (1983) 29–32.

[112] *D H IV* 290 (modelled on a lost diploma of Henry II): see Vogel (1983) 30–1.

[113] Marianus Scottus, *Chronicon* 1078, p. 561.

the Alps, but the south German passes were still in enemy hands. Since the Burgundian route which he had recently used would have involved too great a delay, he concentrated on securing the eastern Alpine route into Germany, which necessitated an understanding with the princes who controlled it, the duke of Carinthia and the patriarch of Aquileia. During his visit to Pavia the king appointed a new duke of Carinthia. The rebel Berthold I of Zähringen, ally of Rudolf of Swabia, was deposed and Liutold of Eppenstein was invested with the duchy of Carinthia and the march of Verona.[114] The new duke was a royal kinsman, whose family was already firmly entrenched in the duchy.[115] He first appeared with the ducal title as intervener in a royal diploma for Patriarch Sigehard of Aquileia, recording that the county of Friuli had been detached from Carinthia and conferred on the patriarch, as a reward for his 'faithful service'.[116] The diploma is evidence of Henry's success in promoting an accord between these princes in the interests of securing a safe route into Germany. Sigehard of Aquileia had appeared at the assembly of Tribur as a papal legate: henceforward he was the loyal adherent of the king. Henry celebrated Easter (16 April) in Aquileia and, escorted by Sigehard and Liutold, travelled through Carinthia into Bavaria. His three-year-old son Conrad was left behind as his father's representative in the Italian kingdom, in the care of Archbishop Tedald of Milan and Bishop Denis of Piacenza, two royal adherents who were also the excommunicated opponents of Gregory VII.[117]

The 'deposition faction' of German princes learned of the king's absolution from the papal letter of 28 January, which perhaps reached them in the second week of February. At a meeting in Ulm they decided to hold an assembly of princes 'to discuss the needs of the commonwealth' in Forchheim on 13 March.[118] The princes wrote to Gregory VII that 'since he was prevented by the king's cunning from coming to Augsburg', he should attend the Forchheim assembly. Assuring the princes of his wish 'to travel to [them] for the common good', Gregory replied that his envoys were negotiating with the king for an escort across the Alps.[119] Nothing came of these negotiations and it was not the pope but his legates, Cardinal deacon Bernard and Abbot Bernard of St Victor in Marseilles, who came to Forchheim. The most prominent member of the 'deposition faction', Rudolf of Swabia, wrote to king and

---

[114] Klaar (1966) 108–9. Berthold had proved unable to establish himself in the duchy.
[115] Henry and Liutold had a common great-grandfather, Duke Herman II of Swabia: Meyer von Knonau (1900) 3:21 n. 26.
[116] *D H IV* 293. See Meyer von Knonau (1900) 3:20–1; Schmidinger (1954) 63, 162; Vogel (1983) 33–4.
[117] Berthold, *Annales* 1077, p. 291. See Meyer von Knonau (1900) 3:20; E. Goez (1996) 7–8.
[118] Lampert, *Annales* 1077, p. 301; Paul, *Vita Gregorii VII* c. 88, p. 526. See Meyer von Knonau (1894) 2:775–85; Vogel (1983) 40–6.   [119] Gregory VII, *Epistolae Vagantes* 19, pp. 50–4.

pope on his own account. His envoy first requested Henry not to return to Germany until either the pope or Empress Agnes had preceded him there, then pressed the pope to come in person to Forchheim.[120] There is some evidence that the conspirators in Ulm intended the assembly in Forchheim to be 'a conference for the election of a new king'.[121] Certainly Rudolf must have seen the assembly in this light and regarded himself as the principal candidate in the election.[122]

Although the anti-Henrician narratives claim that Rudolf's election as antiking involved 'the greater part of the princes of the realm', there is reason to believe that the election was solely the work of the 'deposition faction'. The only participants who can be identified with certainty were the king's avowed enemies: the three south German dukes, the staunch Gregorian bishops and the Saxon rebels.[123] Archbishop Siegfried of Mainz also played a prominent role in the election, appearing for the first time as the king's enemy. It is not clear why Henry's faithful lieutenant at the council of Worms in January 1076 became the principal elector of Rudolf fourteen months later. Perhaps the way in which he was singled out in the papal sentences of February 1076 made Siegfried fear that he would be the scapegoat whose dismissal would facilitate Henry's reconciliation with the pope. Certainly the plans of the 'deposition faction' offered Siegfried an opportunity that fidelity to Henry would never have brought him: 'To [the archbishop of Mainz] was principally granted the authority of electing and consecrating the king, on account of the primacy of the see of Mainz.' So Lampert of Hersfeld described the right intermittently claimed for Mainz since the later tenth century. In practice, however, the archbishop of Mainz had last been able to exercise the right in 1024, the privilege of crowning the king having subsequently been lost to the archbishop of Cologne. By assuming a preeminent role in the election of Rudolf and by crowning him in Mainz on 26 March 1077, Siegfried was able to vindicate a long neglected right of his church.[124]

The first day of the assembly (13 March) was devoted to complaints about Henry's conduct in secular and ecclesiastical affairs, perhaps culminating in

---

[120] Berthold, *Annales* 1077, p. 291.   [121] Paul of Bernried, *Vita Gregorii VII* c. 88, p. 526.

[122] *Chronicon Ebersheimense* c. 26, p. 444: he secretly caused a crown to be made in the abbey of Ebersheimmünster (where Abbot Adelgaud was his kinsman). See Jakobs (1968) 161; Schlesinger (1973) 63, 71.

[123] Berthold, *Annales* 1077, pp. 291–2. Cf. Bernold, *Chronicon* 1077, p. 433; Paul, *Vita* c. 93, p. 529. The identifiable electors: archbishops of Mainz, Magdeburg and Salzburg, bishops of Passau, Halberstadt, Worms and Würzburg, Rudolf, Welf IV, Berthold, Otto of Northeim and perhaps Magnus Billung and Udo of Stade. See Robinson (1979) 721 n. 1.

[124] Lampert, *Annales* 1073, p. 168. See G. Schmidt (1917) 72–7; Thomas (1970) 368–99. See also above pp. 22–3.

the formal deposition of the king. On the next day the assembly heard urgent appeals for the immediate election of a new king. The papal legates, mindful of their instructions, attempted to delay the election until the pope's arrival. Finally, however, since the princes were 'uncertain whether the pope could come, but most certain that the greatest discord and danger would occur if they failed to act' and given that the pope had forbidden them (in February 1076) to recognise Henry as king, the assembly, under the guidance of the archbishop of Mainz, proceeded to elect a new king.[125] According to Bruno of Merseburg, Rudolf of Rheinfelden was chosen 'at length . . . from the many whose probity made them worthy of election', despite an unexpected hitch that occurred when the electors were called on individually to confirm his election. 'Certain of them wished to introduce particular conditions so that they would raise him over them as king on these terms: that he promised specific redress for their grievances.' In particular Otto of Northeim would not accept him 'unless he promised to restore the honour [the duchy of Bavaria] unjustly taken from him'. The papal legates intervened, however, to forbid such a promise, on the grounds 'that if [Rudolf] were to be elected in that manner in which they had begun, having made promises to individuals, the election would not appear authentic, but instead polluted by the poison of simoniacal heresy.'[126] By applying the conventions of an episcopal election to the election of a king, the legates rescued Rudolf from severe political embarrassment. Otto of Northeim had come to Forchheim in pursuit of the same objective that inspired his rebellions in 1070 and 1073: his support for Rudolf's candidature was conditional on the promise of the restoration of the duchy of Bavaria. Rudolf, however, was in no position to make this promise, since the duchy was currently in the hands of his closest ally, Welf IV. The legates' intervention saved Rudolf from having to choose between the claim of his most powerful supporter among the south German princes and that of his old rival, who could guarantee him the support of the Saxons. The legates' role in the proceedings in Forchheim was to ease the tensions within the 'deposition faction' caused by the old enmity between Otto and the south German dukes.[127]

The close alliance between Rudolf and the reform papacy, dating from the crisis of 1072, culminated in the papal recognition of Rudolf as king of the

---

[125] Berthold, *Annales* 1077, pp. 291–2; Bruno, *Saxonicum bellum* c. 91, pp. 85–6; Paul, *Vita* c. 93–6, pp. 529–31. See Meyer von Knonau (1900) 3:3–8, 627–38; Böhme (1970) 65–75; Schlesinger (1973) 61–85; Giese (1979) 37–49.

[126] Bruno c. 91, p. 85. Paul, *Vita* c. 93–6, pp. 529–31, the only account that states that the assembly lasted for more than one day, was perhaps derived from a lost official document (a letter of the legates or Rudolf to the pope). See Giese (1979) 44.

[127] Schumann (1912) 36–44; Lange (1961) 67–70.

Germans in 1080. Royalist accounts of Forchheim invariably declare that
Rudolf was elected 'at the command of Pope Gregory'. 'Hildebrand and his
bishops . . . set up another king, Rudolf, against the ordinance of God.'[128]
Gregory VII always denied having played any role in the election: 'God is our
witness that Rudolf, who was made king by those beyond the mountains, did
not then accept the kingship on our orders or with our advice.'[129] There is no
reason to doubt that Gregory was taken by surprise by the election. The proceedings in Forchheim had not shown that respect for the rights of the apostolic see in 'the business of the kingship' that Gregory tried to inculcate in his
letters to the princes, especially the pope's right to vet 'the person and the
morals' of the princes' candidate before confirming their election. His legates
in Forchheim had departed from their instructions, under pressure from the
princes.

It is likely that the legates made common cause with the 'deposition faction'
not only because they learned from the princes 'how sacrilegious a man
[Henry] was',[130] but also because of Rudolf's qualifications for the kingship.
He was 'a man of outstanding humility, suitable for the honour of the kingship in his age and his morals'.[131] Gregory VII's letter to the princes of 3
September 1076 declared that, if a royal election became necessary, they
should elect the candidate best qualified to safeguard the Christian religion
and the empire and who enjoyed the approval of the pope and Empress Agnes.
The 'deposition faction' chose a patron of reformed monasticism and an ally
of Empress Agnes (in the crisis of 1072) and the reform papacy, so as to overcome any papal reluctance to approve their election. Rudolf's election was
intended to halt Henry's rehabilitation, begun at Canossa, and to draw the
pope back into the role that the 'deposition faction' had devised for him, that
of legitimating Henry's deposition and replacement.

The bid for papal support is apparent also in the promises made by Rudolf
on his accession. Firstly, he conceded the reforming principle of episcopal elections free from secular interference: 'he should not confer bishoprics for
payment or for the sake of friendship, but should permit each church to elect
its own [bishop], as the canons command'. Secondly, he conceded 'that the

[128] *Liber de unitate ecclesiae* II.9, p. 220. Sigebert, *Chronica* 1077, pp. 363–4: Rudolf received 'a
     crown sent by the pope'; cf. Landulf Senior, *Historia* III.31, p. 98; *Chronica monasterii
     Casinensis* III.49, p. 429; Helmold of Bosau, *Cronica Slavorum* I.28, p. 56; Otto of Freising,
     Gesta Friderici I.7, p. 23.
[129] Gregory VII, *Registrum* VII.14a, c. 7, IX.29, pp. 484–5, 613. Cf. Wido of Ferrara, *De scismate*
     I, p. 540. See Robinson (1979) 724–31; Vogel (1983) 47–52.
[130] Berthold, *Annales* 1077, p. 292.
[131] Paul, *Vita Gregorii VII* c. 95, p. 530 The Gregorian term 'suitable' (*idoneus*): see Robinson
     (1990) 312–18.

royal power should belong to no one by heredity, as was formerly the custom, but that the son of the king, even if he was extremely worthy, should succeed as king rather by spontaneous election than by the line of succession. But if the king's son was not worthy or if the people refused to accept him, the people should have it in their power to make king whomsoever they wished.'[132] The election of Rudolf was the occasion for the repudiation of the idea of heredi-tary claims to the kingship and an assertion of the princes' right to determine the succession to the throne. Bruno of Merseburg's account juxtaposes Rudolf's promise that bishops will be elected canonically with his promise of the free election of future kings. Both episcopal and royal elections were made subject to canon law: both must be free of 'simoniacal heresy'.[133] The elec-toral promises reveal the 'deposition faction' using the canon law of the reform papacy to legitimate Rudolf's election The reforming language of the Forchheim election reveals the influence not only of the papal legates but also of the three distinguished scholars in the 'deposition faction': Gebhard of Salzburg, Altmann of Passau and Adalbero of Würzburg. These three 'most learned men' had studied together in their youth (perhaps in the school of Paderborn) and served as imperial chaplains during the reign of Henry III. Survivors from an age of papal-imperial cooperation in the reform of the Church, they ended their episcopal careers as rebels against the emperor and partisans of the reform papacy.[134]

---

[132] Bruno, *Saxonicum bellum* c. 81, p. 95. Cf. Paul, *Vita* c. 95, p. 530. The Gregorian concept of kingship: Manegold of Lautenbach, *Ad Gebehardum* c. 30, p. 365: '"king" is not the name of a natural quality but the title of an office' (c. 1085). See Fuhrmann (1975) 21–42; Robinson (1978b) 124–31.

[133] Kern (1939) 31–2 (analogy with the reformers' concern with 'excluding nepotism at an epis-copal election'). The 1077 concessions and later 'electoral capitulations': Rörig (1948) 28; Mitteis (1950) 83; Schlesinger (1973) 74–82; Keller (1983) 130–2, 145–50; U. Schmidt (1987) 27–33.

[134] *Vita Altmanni Pataviensis* c. 2, p. 231; *Vita Adalberonis Wirziburgensis* p. 129; *Annales Patherbrunnenses* p. 69. See Fleckenstein (1973) 122 n. 22; Zielinski (1984) 144 n. 446, 147 n. 478, 156 n. 549.

5

Civil war in Germany, 1077–1081

The reign of the anti-king began inauspiciously. After his coronation in Mainz (26 March) Rudolf planned to make a 'royal journey' through the kingdom, but it soon became clear that he had overestimated his support in the Rhineland and southern Germany, including his own duchy of Swabia. The coronation provoked riots in Mainz; the citizens of Worms refused him admission to their city; in Augsburg the bishop refused to acknowledge him as king.[1] Once Henry returned from Italy in April, Rudolf was forced to withdraw to Saxony. His splendid reception in Merseburg (29 June), where 'the greater and middling men from all parts of Saxony' did homage to him, was the apogee of his reign as anti-king.[2] He proved incapable of establishing his authority outside the province. From June 1077 until his death in October 1080 he resided there permanently, leaving Saxony only to campaign against Henry. By the end of his reign Rudolf was being described as 'king of the Saxons' by contemporaries who considered that the Forchheim election had caused a 'division of the kingdom', producing 'a German and a Saxon kingdom'.[3]

Immediately after the election the rival kings had sought papal support. Rudolf sent an envoy, informing Gregory VII that 'he had been compelled to assume the government of the kingdom' and 'was ready to obey [the pope] in every way'. 'Meanwhile', the pope recalled, 'Henry began to entreat me to help him against Rudolf. I replied that I would gladly do so, when I had heard the arguments on both sides and learned whom justice most favoured.'[4] Gregory devoted three years to examining the rival arguments before reaching a decision in March 1080. Far from committing himself unreservedly to the candidate of the 'deposition faction', the pope pursued a policy of strict neutrality towards the two kings. He first formulated this policy in letters of 31 May 1077 to his legates and to the princes, in which he

---

[1] Berthold of Reichenau, *Annales* 1077, pp. 292–4, 298; Sigebert of Gembloux, *Chronica* 1077, p. 364; *Annales Augustani* 1077, p. 129; *Vita Heinrici IV* c. 4, p. 17. See Meyer von Knonau (1900) 3:8–12, 23–34; Scheibelreiter (1973) 15–21; Vogel (1983) 53–68.
[2] Bruno of Merseburg, *Saxonicum bellum* c. 93, p. 87. [3] See below p. 206.
[4] Gregory VII, *Registrum* VII.14a, c. 7, pp. 484–5.

announced his continued determination to come to Germany to settle the dispute between Henry and his opponents. He made no direct reference to the Forchheim election, but instructed the legates to 'urge both kings, Henry and Rudolf, to open up a safe passage for us into [Germany] and to provide aid and an escort'. This was to be the test of their suitability for royal office. 'If either of them, puffed up by pride, should hinder us from coming to you', he was to be excommunicated and denied the office of king, while he who obeyed the apostolic see was to be accepted as king.[5]

Gregory emphasised that the 'business of the kingship' must be settled by the pope in a council; the 'deposition faction' considered that the business had already been settled in Forchheim. Bruno of Merseburg recorded the Saxon reaction to the letter of 31 May. 'When our countrymen received this letter, they lost the great hopes that they had placed on the apostolic rock, although previously they would have believed that the heavens would stand still or that the earth could move like the heavens, rather than that the see of Peter would lose the constancy of Peter.'[6] The papal legates were equally committed to Rudolf's kingship, even after Gregory sent them his letter insisting on neutrality. The legate Abbot Bernard of St Victor in Marseilles denounced Henry as 'an open enemy of the Church and a limb of Antichrist'. In summer 1078 he was present in the rebel army with his fellow legate, Cardinal deacon Bernard, who had remained in the anti-king's entourage throughout 1077. On 12 November 1077 he held a council in Goslar, where he excommunicated Henry, 'since he had shown himself disobedient to the supreme pontiff by usurping . . . the kingship of which a just sentence in a Roman synod had deprived him'. Bernard 'confirmed Rudolf in the kingship by apostolic authority and most firmly commanded all the magnates of the kingdom to give the king their support'.[7] Gregory VII did not confirm his legate's action, remaining wedded to the idea of a council as a means of resolving the 'business of the kingship'

Meanwhile the 'moderate' princes rallied to Henry when he returned from Italy, 'bringing back the great glory of his absolution'.[8] This positive response enabled the king to reassert his authority in May and June 1077, holding court with impressive ceremony in Regensburg, Ulm and Nuremberg. In Regensburg the princes of Bavaria, Carinthia and Bohemia assembled to hear Henry's complaints against the rebels and to promise nearly 12,000 knights for his war against the anti-king.[9] Henry's army, with a formidable Bohemian contingent, then marched into Swabia, disrupting Rudolf's 'royal journey'

[5] Ibid. IV.23–4, pp. 334–8. See Vogel (1983) 47–52.   [6] Bruno c. 104, 107, pp. 93, 96.
[7] Briefsammlungen pp. 69–72; Berthold, Annales 1077, pp. 302–3. See Schumann (1912) 38, 41, 43.   [8] Holder-Egger (1905) 189.
[9] Berthold, Annales 1077, p. 294. See Meyer von Knonau (1900) 3:22–3.

and forcing his withdrawal to Saxony. The king was able to celebrate Whitsun (4 June) in Ulm, where he sat in judgement on his enemies. Rudolf, Welf IV, Berthold of Zähringen and their Swabian supporters were deprived of all their offices and benefices and sentenced to death in their absence. The south German dukes, all previously counts in Swabia, were tried in Swabia 'according to Swabian law', the unwritten customary law of the duchy.[10] Rudolf's offences were described as 'many impious attacks on [the king] and the kingdom', contrary to 'all divine and human law'. He was an 'oath-breaker and a traitor'.[11]

Of the three south German duchies, Carinthia had already been conferred on Liutold of Eppenstein.[12] Henry retained Swabia in his own hands until 1079, when he conferred it on his supporter, Frederick of Büren.[13] Bavaria remained in the king's hands until 1096, when it was finally restored to Welf IV. During these two decades the effectiveness of the Henrician regime depended in no small degree on the material support that the duchy provided. There was nothing novel in the direct royal administration of Bavaria. For more than half of the eleventh century the duchy was effectively a 'crown province', ruled either by the king himself or by a member of the imperial family.[14] The resultant close ties between the duchy and the crown explain the readiness of the Bavarian nobility in the years 1077–96 to acknowledge Henry IV both as rightful king and as lawful ruler of their duchy. Henry enjoyed the military support of the nobility and the financial support especially of the citizens of Regensburg, the principal city of the duchy. After his minority Henry visited Regensburg on at least thirty occasions.[15] Not even his tax on the cities in 1084 – the 'very large sum of money' that Henry 'took from the men of Regensburg and from almost all the inhabitants of the cities in the kingdom' – created a lasting breach between Regensburg and the king.[16] Of the great noble families of Bavaria only that of Formbach fought for the anti-king. Judicious royal patronage secured the support of the other princes, notably the Viehbach-Eppensteiner, the Weilheimer, the Lechsgemünd-Graisbacher and their kinsmen, the Aribones, whose ambitions had been held in check by

---

[10] Berthold, *Annales* 1077, p. 295. See Meyer von Knonau (1900) 3:36–7; Vogel (1983) 72–86.
[11] *D H IV* 311 (March[?] 1079). Cf. Brixen decree, *Die Briefe Heinrichs IV.* p. 71. See Mitteis (1927) 33, 36; Maurer (1978) 91. Evidence of Henrician propaganda against Rudolf in *Annales Augustani* 1077, p. 129, and *Casus monasterii Petrishusensis* II.33, p. 646: 'Pilate, the crucifier of the Lord, is said to have originated in [Forchheim] . . . Hence the people sang of Rudolf in their songs that a second Pilate had arisen.' See K. Hauck (1959) 171–92: propaganda was cast in the form of songs to ensure wide and rapid transmission.   [12] See above p. 166.
[13] See below p. 189.   [14] Störmer (1991) 506–7, 537–9, 542–3, 545–7.
[15] Kraus (1972) 60; Kottje (1978) 145–7; Kolmer (1991) 198–200, 210, 213.
[16] *Annalium Ratisbonensium fragmentum* p. 88. See also below p. 239.

Henry's father and grandfather.[17] The Bavarian episcopate showed similar loyalty, with the exceptions of Archbishop Gebhard of Salzburg and Bishop Altmann of Passau, irreconcilable enemies of the king, who were expelled from their dioceses by his supporters. Henry was able to rely on the loyalty of Rupert of Bamberg, his trusted adviser, of Otto of Regensburg and his successor, Gebhard IV, of Udalric of Eichstätt and Altwin of Brixen. Ellenhard of Freising was a staunch Henrician, as was his successor, Meginward, until in 1086 pressure from Welf IV drove him into the enemy camp. It was characteristic of Henry's reliance on the imperial episcopate in southern Germany that bishops were the principal beneficiaries of the deposition of Welf IV. Benefices confiscated from the rebel duke were conferred on the bishops of Brixen and Augsburg, whose loyalty strengthened Henry's hold over the Alpine region.[18]

The Whitsun assembly in Ulm which saw the punishment of the south German rebels also witnessed a demonstration of the sacred nature of royal authority: the first 'crown-wearing' since the absolution in Canossa. The hostile chronicler Bernold of St Blasien represented Henry's crown-wearing as an infringement of the conditions imposed on him by the pope at Canossa: he 'usurped the kingship that he had been forbidden to assume'.[19] The ceremony in Ulm was intended to publicise Henry's own view of what he had achieved in Canossa. The Whitsun crown-wearing demonstrated to Henry's subjects that he was no longer excommunicate and therefore he had the right to function and be obeyed again as a king.[20] The principal theme of the royal diplomas of summer and autumn 1077 was the restoration of 'the stability of the kingdom'. Three diplomas issued in Nuremberg (where Henry celebrated the festival of the Trinity on 11 June) rewarded the patriarch of Aquileia and the bishop of Brixen for their faithful service, the effect being to strengthen Henry's hold over the central and eastern Alpine region.[21] The diplomas declared that the king endowed the churches to obtain an eternal reward and achieve 'the stability of our kingdom'. This theme is restated in a diploma for Bishop Werner of Strasbourg, in which the Virgin Mary, patron of the church of Strasbourg, is invoked as 'the founder of the stability of the kingdom and of our honour'. In this case 'stability' was promoted by conferring on the loyal Werner the county in the Breisgau confiscated from the rebel Berthold of Zähringen.[22]

---

[17] Bosl (1971) 1121–46.   [18] *DD H IV* 304, 306.

[19] Bernold of St Blasien, *Chronicon* 1077, p. 434. See Klewitz (1939) 52; Schlesinger (1967) 28; Vogel (1983) 77–82.

[20] Berthold, *Annales* 1077, p. 296; Bernold, *Chronicon* 1077, p. 434: Bishop Embrico of Augsburg publicly defended Henry's kingship in Ulm. See Meyer von Knonau (1900) 3:37, 62 and n. 97; Zoepfl (1952) 308–9.

[21] *DD H IV* 295–7. Cf. Berthold, *Annales* 1077, p. 299.

[22] *D H IV* 298: see Vogel (1983) 83–7.

A similar transfer of power occurred in Worms on 30 October 1077. The Saxon rebel Ekbert II of Brunswick, Henry's kinsman, was deprived of the Frisian county of Stavoren, which was conferred on Bishop Conrad of Utrecht because of his proven fidelity. The diploma recording this transaction, the work of Gottschalk of Aachen, contains an unusually elaborate discussion of the crime of rebellion and its punishment. According to 'the law of the nations', 'the enemies of the king . . . since through the infamy of their perjury they are outlaws, should be disinherited of all their possessions'. Ekbert, 'who strove to deprive us of the whole kingdom, shall have no part in the kingdom'.[23] The presence of twenty bishops and ten abbots in Worms on 30 October 1077 to see a 'just judgement' pronounced on Ekbert bore witness to the speed with which Henry had resumed the royal functions of protector and benefactor of the imperial Church after Canossa.

Equally striking is the ease with which he filled three vacancies in the imperial Church in September 1077. At the request of the monks of St Gallen, who had expelled an abbot imposed by the anti-king Rudolf, Henry conferred the office of abbot on Udalric of Eppenstein, his kinsman and brother of the new duke of Carinthia. In the churches of Augsburg and Aquileia the clergy and people had elected members of the local clergy. When, however, Henry IV came to Augsburg in early September, he set aside these elections and invested his own candidates, two former royal chaplains.[24] The chronicler Berthold accused Henry of acting in the interests not of the churches but of his struggle against the anti-king. Siegfried II of Augsburg was appointed 'not that he might rule the church but that he might with his wealth assist [Henry] to make war'. Since, however, the king had recently enriched the church of Augsburg and enhanced the political importance of Aquileia, he must ensure that they remained in safe hands. He made a similar appointment the following May, when he provided a successor for his trusted adviser, Werner of Strasbourg: another royal chaplain, Thiebald, provost of Constance, enthroned 'against the will of the canons'.[25] In ignoring the wishes of clergy and people and appointing royal chaplains in preference to local candidates, Henry was following the practice of the years 1066–76, which had provoked criticism from reformers and contributed to the conflict with the papacy. The king's response to the threat presented by the anti-king was to exploit to the full the traditional royal rights over the Church. Significantly, neither he nor the majority of his clerical subjects regarded these rights as diminished by the events of 1076 or the capitulation at Canossa.

---

[23] *D H IV* 301: see Meyer von Knonau (1900) 3:68–9 with n. 106; Köbler (1971) 71–2; Vogel (1983) 94–5.

[24] Berthold, *Annales* 1077, pp. 293, 301; Gregory VII, *Registrum* v.5–6, pp. 352–5. See Meyer von Knonau (1900) 3:62–6, 132; Fleckenstein (1973) 129; Schieffer (1981) 157; Vogel (1983) 88–9.   [25] Berthold, *Annales* 1078, p. 311.

These assertions of authority in summer 1077 were accompanied by preparations for an expedition to Saxony, the only region of the kingdom that refused to acknowledge him as king. Henry's recruiting of troops brought him in late June 'into his own Franconia',[26] the province in which he could expect the most enthusiastic support for his war-effort. Henry held court in July and August in Mainz, recently the scene of Rudolf's coronation. The rioting of the citizens during the coronation caused Archbishop Siegfried to flee from his city in the anti-king's entourage, never to return. The devotion of the citizens to his cause enabled the king to visit Mainz more frequently than anywhere else in his kingdom.[27] During his war against the anti-king Rudolf the city had an importance for the Henrician regime similar to that of Worms during the Saxon rebellion of 1073–5 and the crisis of 1076. Mainz's importance was both strategic and economic. From Mainz the king could rapidly move an army down the ancient highway along the River Main to attack either the anti-king in Saxony or his supporters Welf IV and Berthold of Zähringen in Swabia. As a major commercial centre, Mainz possessed a citizenry that was prosperous and ready to provide men and money for the king's wars. Hence the chronicler Bruno of Merseburg remarked contemptuously of Henry's army of 1077 that 'it was composed for the most part of merchants'.[28]

While Henry gathered an army in Mainz, the anti-king made the first move, laying siege to Würzburg in August with a large Saxon army. He intended to punish the citizens for rebelling against his ally, Bishop Adalbero, but failed to capture the city. Hearing that a force of 5,000 men led by Welf IV and Berthold of Zähringen was coming from Swabia to Rudolf's support, Henry was tempted to intercept them. After coming within two miles of the enemy, however, he avoided battle and withdrew to Worms, considering his forces inadequate. Encouraged by Henry's unwillingness to fight, Rudolf abandoned the siege of Würzburg and advanced on the army of his rival, determined to force a battle. He found Henry awaiting his Bavarian and Bohemian reinforcements and unprepared for battle, but encamped securely between the Rhine and the Neckar, with the fords so closely guarded and the river-banks so steep, as to be unassailable. Rudolf was anxious to give battle before the enemy's reinforcements arrived, while Henry refused to be drawn into the open until the arrival of the Bavarians and Bohemians.[29] This stale-

---

[26] *Ibid.* 1077, p. 299.

[27] Eight visits between July 1077 and August 1080: Meyer von Knonau (1900) 3:43–4, 49; Büttner (1973) 357; Kottje (1978) 138–41.

[28] Bruno, *Saxonicum bellum* c. 95, p. 88.

[29] Berthold, *Annales* 1077, p. 300: Rudolf proposed to end the stalemate by an appeal to divine judgement; Henry refused to answer his challenge. This is a familiar motif of Ottonian–Salian historiography, 'the challenge on the river': Cram (1955) 68–70.

mate was resolved by the decision of the princes in Henry's army, acting independently of the king, to approach Welf IV and Berthold of Zähringen to discuss a truce. The parties agreed that all the princes should meet on the Rhine on 1 November, in the presence of the papal legates but without Henry and Rudolf, to negotiate a permanent peace. Both parties swore to compel their respective kings to accept this peace.[30] Once more, as in the assembly of Tribur ten months earlier, the princes assumed the responsibility for settling the 'business of the kingship'. There was no word of complying with the request in Gregory VII's letter of 31 May, to provide an escort so that he might preside over their deliberations. The princes were determined to pacify the kingdom on their own terms.

Rudolf returned to Saxony without resuming the siege of Würzburg. Henry placed the city and diocese in the care of his trusted adviser, Eberhard of Naumburg, who had been driven from his own diocese by the Saxon rebels. The king remained in his camp on the Neckar, where he was joined, almost immediately after his rival's withdrawal, by the long awaited troops from Bavaria and Bohemia. Disregarding the truce that his representatives had negotiated, the king used his greatly enlarged army on an expedition, the second that year, to punish the anti-king's adherents in Swabia.[31] The meeting of the princes on 1 November never took place. The chronicle of Berthold of Reichenau alone offers an explanation, characteristically blaming Henry for the failure of the meeting. The princes were beginning to assemble when Henry's army appeared, contrary to the terms of the truce. 'Like a wild beast, thinking nothing of the treaty of peace, he ingeniously obstructed [the princes] on all sides so that they could not meet.'[32] As for the truth of this account, Henry was certainly in the right place to play the role attributed to him by Berthold.[33] He had not participated in the negotiation of the truce on the Neckar: the princes of his party had seized the initiative without consulting him. There is no reason to suppose that he approved of the princes' method of settling the 'business of the kingship'. He was no more willing to have his cause judged by the proposed assembly of princes than he was to submit his cause to the council envisaged by Gregory VII. Henry's purpose in the years 1077–80 was to suppress a rebellion rather than to participate in a debate about the kingship. It is likely, therefore, that he used his army on 1 November to intimidate his enemies and perhaps also to discipline some of his own supporters. More

---

[30] Berthold, *Annales* 1077, pp. 300–1; Bruno c. 95, p. 88. See Meyer von Knonau (1900) 3:46–54, 58–9.
[31] Berthold, *Annales* 1077, pp. 301–2; Bernold, *Chronicon* 1077, p. 434. See Meyer von Knonau (1900) 3:60–1.
[32] Berthold, *Annales* 1077, p. 301. See Meyer von Knonau (1900) 3:68–73.
[33] In Worms on 30 October: *D H IV* 301.

powerful now than he had been in October 1076, Henry was able to prevent the assembly of princes from becoming another Tribur. His determination to punish his enemies was not at all diminished by the early onset of winter. From November until early March 1078 he campaigned in Bavaria against Rudolf's principal adherent in the duchy, Count Ekbert of Formbach, and finally compelled him to flee with his household to the Hungarian court.[34]

Henry was determined to prevent the pope or his legates from holding a council in Germany to settle the question of the kingship. Nevertheless he was well aware that the pope could assist him against his enemies by excommunicating Rudolf and recognising Henry as sole king. Henry, therefore, sent two distinguished and reliable envoys, Bishops Benno II of Osnabrück and Theoderic of Verdun, to represent his interests in the papal synod of 27 February – 3 March 1078 in Rome. A favourable papal pronouncement at this synod would neutralise the sentence of excommunication pronounced by the papal legate (12 November 1077). There is no doubt that Gregory was disappointed in Henry in the months following Canossa.[35] Nevertheless his assessment of the German situation differed entirely from that of his legates. The principal function of a king, in Gregory's view, was to assist the pope in the reform of the Church; but only a strong king could perform this function. At the end of 1077 it seemed unlikely that Rudolf, for all his reforming credentials, would ever prove a useful papal agent. By September 1077 Gregory had decided that his best chance of influencing events in Germany was through Archbishop Udo of Trier, the royal adviser most trusted in Rome. He informed Udo fully about papal objectives in Germany and urged him to ensure that Henry kept the oath sworn at Canossa.[36] Gregory seems to have made no further attempt to communicate with his legates. At the end of the Lenten synod of 1078 he wrote to Udo of Trier, asking him to obtain from Henry a safe conduct for the two legates to return to Rome.[37] Udo had now become indispensable for the implementation of the pope's plans. For at the end of 1077 Gregory lost both the cardinal with most experience of German affairs, Gerald of Ostia,[38] and the one member of his circle capable of exerting direct influence over the king, Empress Agnes.[39] Meanwhile the murder of the Roman prefect Cencius Johannis, his most important adherent among the Roman nobility, threatened Gregory's security in Rome, while the restless ambition of his vassal Robert Guiscard, duke of Apulia and Calabria, seemed likely to endanger the Patrimony of St Peter. As for northern Italy, Gregory's

---

[34] Berthold, *Annales* 1077, p. 302. See Meyer von Knonau (1900) 3:96–7.
[35] Gregory VII, *Registrum* v.7, p. 357.   [36] *Ibid.*, pp. 356–8.   [37] *Ibid.* v.16, p. 378.
[38] Hüls (1977) 100–1.
[39] Meyer von Knonau (1900) 3:93–5; Bulst-Thiele (1933) 110–11; Black-Veldtrup (1995) 58–61, 100, 342.

recent visit had revealed to him that the bishops were irreconcilably opposed to his reform programme.[40] Only an effective king could protect the papacy and impose reform on a recalcitrant episcopate.

These considerations inevitably influenced the handling of the question of the kingship in the Lenten synod of 1078. Rudolf's supporters would later complain that Henry's envoys were given preferential treatment.[41] The anti-king's envoys (whose identity is unknown) were heard by the pope only in private, while Benno of Osnabrück and Theoderic of Verdun were permitted to put their case before the whole synod. They represented Rudolf as a false vassal, 'a perjurer and traitor', who had seized the kingship for himself. These arguments made so strong an impression that some members of the synod called for Rudolf's immediate excommunication. The synod eventually decided that 'unless the archbishops and bishops who made him king could lawfully defend their action, they should depose them from their offices and depose Rudolf from the kingship'.[42] Gregory had not given up the idea of settling the 'business of the kingship' in a council, although he no longer spoke of coming to Germany to preside over it. His legate, together with Udo of Trier, 'who favours Henry', and 'a bishop of Rudolf's party', was to settle the time and place of the council. Udo and the 'bishop of Rudolf's party' were to travel to Rome to inform the pope of the two kings' responses to the papal instructions. They were then to return to Germany in the company of the new papal legates who would preside over the council.[43] That Udo of Trier was to play the principal role in these negotiations is clear from the pope's letter advising him that if Rudolf's party could not provide a fellow mediator, he was competent to carry out the pope's instructions alone.[44]

Henry's envoys had failed to obtain Rudolf's excommunication: nevertheless they had greatly advanced their lord's cause in Rome. They returned to Germany in the company of the unnamed legate commissioned by the pope to organise the council in Germany. The legate's participation in Henry's Easter celebrations in Cologne (8 April) proclaimed to the king's enemies that the pope had discounted the excommunication pronounced by Cardinal deacon Bernard in November 1077.[45] Henry's response to the papal synod was to initiate talks with the Saxons 'for the sake of making peace'. He issued a summons to the Saxon princes to attend a meeting in Fritzlar in Hesse, citing the authority of the Roman synod. The negotiations in Fritzlar resulted in a

---

[40] Meyer von Knonau (1900) 3:81–7, 101–3; Vogel (1983) 100–4.
[41] Bruno, *Saxonicum bellum* c. 108, p. 98.
[42] Gregory VII, *Registrum* IX.29, p. 613. Cf. Berthold, *Annales* 1078, pp. 306–7.
[43] *Registrum* v.14a, c. 6; v.15, pp. 370–1, 374–86. See Meyer von Knonau (1900) 3:103–15; Schumann (1912) 44–5; Vogel (1983) 104–9. [44] *Registrum* v.16, pp. 376–8.
[45] Meyer von Knonau (1900) 3:122.

truce. The Saxons appointed an envoy to return to the Rhineland with Henry's representatives to continue negotiations with the king himself. At this stage, however, the negotiations broke down over the Saxon demand for the exchange of hostages. The Saxon envoy was sent home with the message that the king was not prepared to enter into further negotiations but that, 'for love of the lord pope', he was willing to receive into his grace any rebel who repented and submitted to the king. According to Berthold of Reichenau (the sole source for the Fritzlar negotiations) Henry's purpose, under the pretext of cooperating with the pope's plan for a council, was to negotiate the submission of the Saxons and so deprive the anti-king of his powerbase.[46] This interpretation of Henry's strategy is consistent with his conduct towards the 'deposition faction' since his return to Germany. He treated them as rebels and oath-breakers, not as adherents of a rival for his throne, whose claim required adjudication by a papal council. The Saxon adherents of the anti-king were no more willing to submit their case to the council than was Henry: 'it seems to us extraordinary . . . that a closed matter should be reopened and questions raised about a case that was settled beyond doubt.'[47] They regarded the pope's proposal as a betrayal of their alliance. Gregory could rely, therefore, on neither of the parties in pursuing his cherished scheme.

An immediate consequence of the failure of the Fritzlar negotiations was the defection from Henry's party of Bishop Herman of Metz. Herman and 'very many Lotharingians' appeared at court and attempted to persuade the king to accept papal guidance. Finding that this intervention had aroused the king's anger, Herman withdrew to his diocese. Henry construed his conduct as rebellion and in May a royal army captured Metz, placed a garrison in the city and expelled the bishop.[48] Fearing that Herman's example would inspire disaffection elsewhere in Lotharingia, Henry acted decisively to forestall such a development and his measures proved successful: the province remained loyal and peaceful. Henry celebrated Whitsun (27 May) in Regensburg with the papal legate, who afterwards departed for Rome to report on the failure of that spring's negotiations. It is evident both that the legate had been instructed to work closely with the king and that they had cooperated without acrimony.[49] Gregory VII's response to the news of the Fritzlar negotiations was to threaten with excommunication 'the sons of the devil among [the Germans who] . . . contrive to bring the council to nothing'.[50] Gregory did not accuse

---

[46] Berthold, *Annales* 1078, pp. 310–11. See Meyer von Knonau (1900) 3:123–6; Giese (1979) 169–70; Vogel (1983) 113–14.

[47] Bruno, *Saxonicum bellum* c. 108, pp. 97–9. See Kost (1962) 106.

[48] Berthold, *Annales* 1078, p. 311. See Meyer von Knonau (1900) 3:131; Salloch (1931) 38–9.

[49] Berthold, *Annales* 1078, p. 311. See Schumann (1912) 45.

[50] Gregory VII, *Registrum* VI.I, pp. 389–91. See Vogel (1983) 122.

Henry of sabotaging the council: his legate must have reported positively about the king's cooperation in the negotiations.

Even as the pope sent this command to renew the negotiations, the two parties were preparing to settle their dispute by force of arms. The initiative was again taken by the party of the anti-king. While Rudolf planned an expedition with the Saxons and Thuringians, his south German allies struck savage blows against the king's supporters in Swabia and Franconia. Berthold II of Zähringen (son of the deposed duke of Carinthia) routed a royalist army led by the bishops of Basel and Strasbourg; Berthold I of Zähringen and Welf IV plundered and burned in eastern Franconia. Leaving Saxony, the anti-king proposed to his allies a joint Saxon and Swabian attack on Henry at the beginning of August.[51] Henry moved at once to hinder this dangerous manoeuvre. He stationed on the Neckar an army of 12,000 Franconian peasants to bar the advance of Welf and Berthold, cutting them off so effectively from the Saxon army that they could not even communicate by messenger. Henry then marched towards Rudolf's army, encountering the enemy on the River Streu at Mellrichstadt.

The battle of Mellrichstadt on 7 August was a fiercely fought engagement in which the fortunes of the rival armies were constantly changing. Early in the battle four eminent churchmen of the anti-king's party, the archbishops of Mainz and Magdeburg and the bishops of Merseburg and Worms, together with Cardinal deacon Bernard (who remained in the anti-king's entourage, although his legation was over), fled from the field. Their flight caused panic in Rudolf's army, and so many others followed their example that the anti-king believed that his army was disintegrating. Failing to halt the retreat, Rudolf himself joined the flight, not pausing until he had crossed the frontier of Thuringia. Unknown to the anti-king, the fortunes of the Saxon army had been redeemed by his allies Otto of Northeim and the young Count Frederick I of Sommerschenburg (nephew of the late Archbishop Adalbert of Bremen). Unaffected by the flight of their comrades, Otto and Frederick drove Henry's army from the field and pursued the fugitives for some distance along the River Main. Henry's retreating army, however, met the forces of Duke Vratislav of Bohemia coming to his support. With these reinforcements he turned back to the River Streu, only to find that the Saxon army had withdrawn beyond his reach.[52]

The battle brought no tactical advantage to either side: both armies had

---

[51] Berthold, *Annales* 1078, p. 311. See Meyer von Knonau (1900) 3:132–3.

[52] Bruno, *Saxonicum bellum* c. 96–102, pp. 88–92. Cf. Berthold, *Annales* 1078, p. 312; Bernold, *Chronicon* 1078, p. 435; Frutolf of Michelsberg, *Chronica* 1078, p. 90; *Casus monasterii Petrishusensis* II.34, p. 646. See Meyer von Knonau (1900) 3:135–46; Cram (1955) 140–3; Vogel (1983) 123.

fallen apart and both kings had fled. Henry had achieved his objective of preventing the rebel armies from joining forces, but had proved unable to defeat either army. Each army had suffered serious losses. On the Saxon side Werner of Magdeburg was killed as he fled; Adalbert of Worms and Count Herman Billung (uncle of Duke Magnus of Saxony) were taken prisoner. The most serious loss among the more numerous princely casualties on Henry's side was Count Eberhard, who for the past decade had been one of his foremost advisers.[53] Moreover on the same day as Mellrichstadt, the king suffered heavy losses in another battle. The peasant army that he had placed on the Neckar was cut to pieces by the forces of Welf IV and Berthold I of Zähringen.[54] It was a warning that the king could not safely campaign in Saxony until he had overcome his enemies in the south. When Henry returned to Bavaria in October to prepare a new expedition, it was rumoured that he intended to invade Saxony; but his November campaign was to be devoted instead to crushing resistance in Swabia.[55] During the autumn of 1078 the Henrician party strove to promote Mellrichstadt as a royal victory, both in an assembly of princes in Regensburg in October[56] and in letters to the pope, the Romans and the Lombards.[57] In fact the importance of Mellrichstadt was not, as royal propaganda pretended, that Henry had defeated the rebellion but rather that the anti-king had failed to break out of his isolation in Saxony. Rudolf's premature retreat effectively signalled the end of his claim to govern the whole kingdom. During autumn 1078 he gathered an army of unprecedented size, but his object was not an expedition against Henry, but the defence of Saxony against the expected invasion. In October Rudolf fell victim to a serious illness lasting more than two months and his followers despaired of his recovery.[58] While he lay sick, he lost his close ally, Berthold I ('the Bearded') of Zähringen, the deposed duke of Carinthia, who died on 5 or 6 November.[59] His death and Rudolf's failing health seriously weakened the anti-king's party at the moment when, on 19 November, a papal synod once more investigated the 'business of the kingship'.

The autumn synod of 1078 was intended to lead the parties back to the

[53] Bruno c. 102, pp. 91–2.

[54] Berthold, *Annales* 1078, p. 312; Bernold, *Chronicon* 1078, p. 435. See Meyer von Knonau (1900) 3:146.

[55] Bruno c. 103, pp. 92–3; Berthold, *Annales* 1078, p. 313. See Meyer von Knonau (1900) 3:147–50.   [56] Bruno c. 103, p. 92.

[57] Berthold, *Annales* 1078, p. 313. Influence of royal propaganda: *Annales Augustani* 1078, p. 129; *Liber de unitate ecclesiae* II.16, p. 231. See Vogel (1983) 123–4.

[58] Berthold, *Annales* 1078, p. 313; 1079, p. 316; Bruno c. 103, pp. 92–3. See Meyer von Knonau (1900) 3:154.

[59] Berthold, *Annales* 1078, p. 313; Frutolf, *Chronica* 1077, p. 88; *Genealogia Zaringorum* p. 735. See Meyer von Knonau (1900) 3:152–3.

peaceful procedures laid down by the Lenten synod, but the negotiator who was to have played the central role in these procedures died a week before the synod met. Udo of Trier died suddenly while accompanying the king on his Swabian campaign (11 November).[60] Udo was irreplaceable: no other German prelate was trusted both in Rome and in Henry's court. The pope made no attempt to appoint a new mediator. His immediate concern was to receive an oath from the envoys of the rival kings that their respective lords had not 'deceitfully hindered the holding of the conference of the legates of the apostolic see in the German kingdom' and to excommunicate 'those men' (unidentified) 'through whose fault the conference did not take place'. Further discussion of the kingship was deferred to the next Lenten synod.

The purpose of the November synod, according to the record in the papal register, was 'the restoration of holy Church'. The synodal decrees gave precise legislative expression to the programme of 'freedom of the Church' (*libertas ecclesiae*) developed in Rome over the past three decades.[61] The urgent concern was to check the abuses of the 'proprietary church system', the custom of laymen possessing churches, their buildings, lands and revenues, which had become widespread in the west.[62] The measures of November 1078 were particularly aimed at 'the German adversaries'. An immediate consequence of the German civil war was that the rival parties, desperately seeking some means of financing their military expeditions, placed the churches under contribution. Gregory's synodal legislation attempted to protect the German Church from the effects of the war. The synodal decree that has most preoccupied scholars concerns the aspect of secular control of the Church most important to the Salian regime. 'Since we have learned that in many regions investitures of churches are made by lay persons contrary to the statutes of the holy Fathers . . . we have decreed that no clerk is to receive the investiture of a bishopric or an abbacy or a church from the hand of an emperor or king or any lay person, man or woman.' This is the earliest extant papal decree against lay investiture.[63] The issue of investiture had arisen in the Lenten synod of 1075, probably in the form of a warning to Henry IV that he should not invest churchmen with their offices as long as he remained in contact with his five excommunicated advisers. The events of 1076–7 increased the importance of the issue of investiture in Gregory's eyes. In the light of the conflict with Henry, it became a matter of urgency to free episcopal elections from royal control at all times, not merely when the king was excommunicate or in

---

[60] Bruno c. 103, p. 93. See Meyer von Knonau (1900) 3:151–2.

[61] Gregory VII, *Registrum* VI.5b, pp. 400–6. See Meyer von Knonau (1900) 3:163–8; Schieffer (1981) 171–3; Vogel (1983) 126–35.

[62] *Registrum* VI.5b, c. 1, pp. 402–3. Cf. VI.5, pp. 398–9: see Salloch (1931) 39. Cf. V.19, pp. 430–1.

[63] *Ibid.* VI.5b, c. 3, p. 403. See above pp. 135–8.

danger of becoming so.[64] Gregory desired an episcopate more susceptible to reforming influence and more amenable to papal control. Since the absolution in Canossa the majority of the imperial episcopate had rallied to the king and distanced themselves from the papacy. It was this solidarity between the king and the bishops whom he had invested – a solidarity inhibiting the reform of the German Church – that the investiture decree was intended to combat.

The decree sought to unravel the traditional relationships of the 'imperial Church system' and was potentially a serious threat to Henry's authority over his kingdoms. Nevertheless, compared to later papal versions of investiture legislation, the decree of November 1078 was expressed in conciliatory terms. The decree of the papal synod of March 1080 would pronounce excommunication on 'emperors, kings, dukes, margraves, counts or any secular powers or persons' who conferred the investiture of an ecclesiastical office.[65] The decree of November 1078, excommunicated only the recipient, not the donor of lay investiture. Gregory was attempting to attack the 'imperial Church system', while avoiding direct confrontation with the king. Whether or not he accepted the Henrician claim that the battle of Mellrichstadt was the definitive victory of the civil war, Gregory evidently assumed that Henry would eventually overcome his enemies. It was therefore necessary for the pope to remain on amicable terms with the king, while restricting his power to damage the imperial Church. Gregory's assessment of the German situation appears in his letter of 30 December 1078 to the anti-king's party. The pope exhorted the princes not to criticise his 'policy of neutrality'. The 'business of the kingship' must be judged 'according to the equity of the papal office, not according to the personal inclination' of the pope's supporters. The princes must 'trust in justice and rely on the help of St Peter'. At a moment when Gregory seemed to regard the restoration of Henry's authority as inevitable, he pronounced a blessing on Henry's enemies: 'May Almighty God . . . absolve you and all your allies who love justice and love St Peter's see from all your sins and lead you to eternal life.'[66] Gregory firmly believed that Welf IV and his colleagues were the loyal adherents of St Peter ('St Peter!' had indeed been the battlecry of the anti-king's army at Mellrichstadt)[67] and he was determined to retain them as allies, whatever the outcome of the German civil war.

---

[64] In *Registrum* IV.13, pp. 316–17 (to the archbishop of Tours, March 1077) investiture is identified for the first time as equivalent to simony. In *Registrum* IV.22, pp. 333–4 (to his legate in France, May 1077) he formulated legislation, the result of which was the decree against investiture in the legatine synod of Poitiers (January 1078): Beulertz (1991) 5–6. See Schieffer (1981) 159–67.   [65] *Registrum* VII.14a, c. 2, pp. 480–1.

[66] *Ibid.* VI.14, pp. 418–19. Cf. Gregory VII, *Epistolae Vagantes* 25, pp. 64–6. See Vogel (1983) 136–7.   [67] Bruno, *Saxonicum bellum* c. 97, p. 90.

It was in this spirit that Gregory returned to the question of the kingship in the Lenten synod of 11 February 1079. The anti-king's party was represented in the synod by Bishops Altmann of Passau and Herman of Metz, both exiled from their dioceses, whose allegations against Henry made a great impression on the synod, as did an account given by Rudolf's envoy of the atrocities committed in Swabia by Henry's army.[68] An unidentified envoy of Henry denied the charges against his lord. His prepared statement announced the imminent arrival of 'very many men from the nobility of the kingdom to make peace between kingship and priesthood'. The rest of the envoy's statement seems to have been his own spontaneous response to the accusations made by Rudolf's representatives and to calls for Henry's excommunication from 'very many' members of the synod. 'Since the subject of the false charges is absent, since those who bring the charges are known to be his enemies and since the lord king himself wishes to be obedient in everything, I appeal to your dignity, reverend father; I appeal to the discretion of the Roman and apostolic see, not to pronounce judgement on the lord king.'[69] Gregory seized on the assurance that Henry wished 'to be obedient in everything' – surely a desperate improvisation by the envoy rather than part of Henry's original message – to impose an oath on the royal envoy. He swore that the promised envoys would be in Rome by Ascension day (2 May) and would escort the papal legates to Germany and back; that the king would obey the legates 'in all things according to justice and judgement'.[70] The oath committed the king, therefore, to the papal plan of settling the question of the kingship in a legatine council in Germany. Henry's message to the synod had ignored this papal plan. He would send envoys whose instructions confined them to making peace 'between [Henry's] kingship and [Gregory's] priesthood'. This was a revival of the programme of the 'Promise of Oppenheim', ignoring all that had happened since October 1076: there was to be no question of allowing a German council to pronounce on the 'business of the kingship'. The favourable impression made on the synod by Rudolf's supporters took Henry's envoy by surprise and enabled Gregory to commit his lord to the papal plan. Gregory's plan was impossible to execute without the king's active cooperation, since Henry's measures in 1077 had secured control of the routes between the German and Italian kingdoms. While, therefore, the synod demanded that Henry provide safe conduct for the papal legates who were to settle the German conflict, a less important role was envisaged for the anti-king. The

---

[68] *Registrum* VI.17a, pp. 425–9. Cf. Berthold, *Annales* 1079, pp. 316–18; Bernold, *Chronicon* 1079, pp. 435–6. Bernold was present at the synod: Weisweiler (1937) 91. See Meyer von Knonau (1900) 3:171–81; Vogel (1983) 137–42.

[69] *MGH Constitutiones* I, 552, no. 338. See Erdmann (1936b) 30–40.

[70] *Registrum* VI.17a, c. 2, p. 428.

oath required of Rudolf's envoys stated that the anti-king or his representatives would be present at the conference and would abide by the legates' judgement.[71]

In the event Gregory did not wait for the arrival of Henry's envoys, but despatched his legates less than a month after the end of the synod. These legates were Cardinal bishop Peter of Albano, one of the most eminent personages of the papal curia and a hero of the reform movement, and Bishop Udalric of Padua, whose reputation for loyalty towards the king would ensure a favourable reception for the legation at the royal court.[72] The legates' instructions were to reach agreement with the king about the time and place of the proposed conference, so that the pope could send 'wise and suitable legates' to reach a final settlement.[73] The papal legates were accompanied on their two-month journey into southern Germany by Patriarch Henry of Aquileia, in fulfilment of his oath in the Lenten synod to be 'faithful and obedient to St Peter and Pope Gregory'. It was for this reason that the legates did not need to await the arrival of the escort requested from the king. The patriarch would conduct them across the Alps through his own territories, avoiding the fiercely royalist province of Lombardy.[74] Although willing to fulfil his oath to the pope, Henry of Aquileia remained 'one of the intimate friends of King Henry'. Before the legates entered Germany, he sent messengers to his lord, warning him of the pope's change of plan. The king responded by sending Bishop Benno of Osnabrück to Rome, where he was able to conciliate the pope and perpetuate the papal 'policy of neutrality' despite the recent allegations by Rudolf's supporters.[75]

Gregory's legates in Germany were forbidden to take any initiative on the question of the kingship and 'to pass judgement . . . concerning all those who have received investiture from lay hands'. This would be the work of the 'wise and suitable legates' who would follow them. Now that the synod of November 1078 had formulated its investiture decree, the king's conduct on the occasion of episcopal vacancies would be closely scrutinised for evidence of that obedience to the pope that his envoy had promised. No record survives of Henry's reaction to the investiture decree of November 1078. During Christmastide 1078, however, the king filled the vacant archsees of Cologne

---

[71] *Ibid.*, c. 3, p. 428.

[72] Berthold, *Annales* 1079, pp. 318–19, 322; Bonizo of Sutri, *Ad amicum* VIII, pp. 611–12. See Schumann (1912) 46–52; Borino (1958) 63–79; Miccoli (1960) 47, 147; Hüls (1977) 90–1.

[73] Gregory VII, *Epistolae Vagantes* 31, pp. 80–4; *Registrum* VII.3, p. 463. See Meyer von Knonau (1900) 3:182–3; Vogel (1983) 142–4.

[74] *Registrum* VI.17a c. 4, pp. 428–9. See Gottlob (1936) 45; Vogel (1983) 144–8.

[75] Berthold, *Annales* 1079, pp. 319, 320. See Meyer von Knonau (1900) 3:209 and n. 62; Jäschke (1965–6) 335.

and Trier by means of investiture. By contrast anti-Henrician authors praised the canonical propriety of the episcopal elections carried out under the aegis of the anti-king and his adherents.[76] Egilbert of Trier, denounced by his critics as an intruder in the archbishopric, described himself as having been 'elected with the consent of both the clergy and the people'.[77] This is doubtless how the king himself viewed his appointment: a correct, canonical election, including the procedure of royal investiture, which no papal decree could render unlawful.

There was no question of abandoning a right enjoyed by his predecessors and essential to the security of the regime. Nevertheless a change in Henry's handling of episcopal appointments is discernible just at the time at which lay investiture became a major preoccupation of the papacy. Unlike the episcopal appointees of the first decade of Henry's personal rule, the bishops of the period 1078–84, although staunch adherents of the king, were not drawn from the imperial chapel or the college of SS. Simon and Jude in Goslar, the two principal institutions through which Henry III and the young Henry IV had influenced the imperial Church. 'An old tradition is suddenly interrupted.'[78] SS. Simon and Jude, which had produced fifteen bishops in the first two decades of Henry's reign, produced only one in this period: Hartwig, elected archbishop of Magdeburg under the auspices of the anti-king Rudolf and at the behest of the pope. Goslar was now in the hands of the anti-king and the Saxon rebels. Two of Henry IV's appointments of 1078–9 resembled the practice of Henry III's reign, rather than that of 1066–77. The new bishop of Freising, Meginward, was a former canon of Freising; Archbishop Sigewin of Cologne had been the dean of Cologne cathedral. In both these cases the king seems to have consulted the wishes of the cathedral clergy in the manner of his father.[79] In the case of Trier, Henry imposed his candidate, Egilbert, after a failed attempt at cooperation between the king and the chapter.[80] In the case of Chur the will of the chapter was subordinated to strategic considerations (Chur commanded a number of important Alpine passes).[81]

After filling the vacancies in the two Lotharingian archbishoprics, Henry remained in the Rhineland until mid-Lent 1079, while his envoys again

---

[76] Berthold, *Annales* 1078, p. 314; 1079, p. 315; *Gesta Treverorum, Continuatio* I.11, pp. 184–5. See Meyer von Knonau (1900) 3:155, 187–9; Gladel (1932) 33; Vogel (1983) 150–1; 153–4; Schieffer (1991) 17. Rudolf's bishops (Wigold of Augsburg, Hartwig of Magdeburg, Gunther of Naumburg, Udo of Hildesheim): Meyer von Knonau (1900) 3:122–3, 229–32; Schieffer (1981) 170–1; Vogel (1983) 133–4, 177–9.   [77] *Codex Udalrici* 61, p. 129.

[78] Fleckenstein (1973) 129–31.

[79] Berthold, *Annales* 1079, p. 323; *Annales sancti Stephani Frisingensis* p. 52. See Meyer von Knonau (1900) 3:120.   [80] *Gesta Treverorum, Continuatio* I.11, pp. 184–5.

[81] Berthold, *Annales* 1079, p. 323. See Meyer von Knonau (1900) 3:233.

attempted to reach an agreement with the Saxons. The Fritzlar negotiations of late February 1079, like those of the previous year, were fruitless. The king's purpose, as in the negotiations of 1078, was to win back the allegiance of the Saxons.[82] If Rudolf lost his supporters in Saxony, his claim to the kingship would go by default and there would be no need for a council to settle the contest under papal auspices. The negotiations in Fritzlar failed to achieve the Saxons' submission, but they revealed considerable support for Henry in the western part of the province. The nobility of Westphalia and Hesse had never been as hostile towards Henry as their eastern neighbours and western Saxony contained a number of points of resistance to the anti-king, notably Benno of Osnabrück's castle of Iburg.[83] In February 1079 Rudolf, at the head of an army for the first time since his dangerous illness, forced the Westphalians to pay tribute and in Hesse he burned Fritzlar and its famous monastery in his efforts to regain control.[84]

Elsewhere a second enclave of support for the anti-king had been constructed in the southern region of Swabia, between the River Reuss and Lake Constance, by the efforts of Welf IV, Berthold II of Zähringen (son of the late duke of Carinthia) and their allies.[85] Henry IV's most energetic supporter in this region was his kinsman Udalric of Eppenstein, abbot of St Gallen, who, 'always in armour, waged war on King Rudolf most skilfully and unlike a monk'. Early in 1079 the king attempted to consolidate the power of this valuable adherent by conferring on him the anti-Henrician abbey of Reichenau. The bitterest contest of the civil war in southern Swabia was that between these two great imperial abbeys and their respective allies during the long abbatiate of Udalric III of St Gallen (1077–1121).[86] In March 1079 Henry took decisive measures to extend royal control in Swabia. Two faithful adherents, Bishop Burchard of Lausanne and the Swabian count Frederick of Büren, became his most important agents in the duchy. Burchard assumed the office of chancellor for the Italian kingdom (1079–87).[87] As a reward for his faithful service, the church of Lausanne received estates formerly in the possession of Rudolf of Rheinfelden, both crown lands with which he had been invested on his accession as duke and allodial lands of the Rheinfelden family.[88] The

---

[82] Berthold, *Annales* 1079, pp. 315, 316. See Meyer von Knonau (1900) 3:190–3; Vogel (1983) 151–2.   [83] *Vita Bennonis Osnabrugensis* c. 15, p. 402.

[84] *Annales Patherbrunnenses* 1079, p. 97. See Meyer von Knonau (1900) 3:192–3.

[85] Berthold, *Annales* 1077, pp. 297, 301. See Peyer (1972) 150; Vogel (1983) 153.

[86] Berthold, *Annales* 1079, p. 319. See Meyer von Knonau (1900) 3:196–8; (1903) 4:118–21; Feierabend (1913) 46–62; Beyerle (1925) 125–6; Vogel (1983) 158.

[87] Gawlik (1978) LXXV–LXXVI.

[88] *D H IV* 311. See Meyer von Knonau (1900) 3:189–90; von Gladiss in *MGH DD* 6/2, 409; H.-E. Mayer (1959) 482; Vogel (1983) 155–7.

confiscations following Rudolf's deposition in 1077 had involved only benefices formerly bestowed by the crown. The seizure of Rheinfelden family lands for the benefit of the church of Lausanne signalled an intensification of Henry's campaign against the rebels.

Swabia must be secured so that Henry would be free to strike the decisive blow against the anti-king in Saxony. During the Easter celebrations (24 March) in Regensburg, therefore, Henry conferred the office of duke of Swabia on Frederick of Büren.[89] According to the historian Otto of Freising (grandson of Henry IV), it was on this same occasion that the king arranged the betrothal of his seven-year-old daughter Agnes to Frederick.[90] The measures taken to secure control of Swabia in 1079 recall those of Empress Agnes in 1057, when she betrothed her daughter to Rudolf of Rheinfelden on installing him in the ducal office. Marriage into the imperial dynasty was intended both to ensure the appointee's future loyalty and to provide the 'proximity to the crown' that should make the new duke's authority universally respected in his duchy. Frederick's ancestors were Swabian counts palatine and counts in the Riesgau; his patrimony was in central Swabia, concentrated in the neighbourhood of Lorch, Göppingen and the fortress of Staufen (which was to give its name to his dynasty), to which was added the dowry of his mother (of the comital family of Mousson-Montbéliard) in Alsace. Modern discussions of Frederick's appointment have focussed on the strategic significance of his allodial property for a king anxious to consolidate his influence in central Swabia and Alsace. The Staufen lordship in Swabia could be used to control important roads running through Swabia (notably that between Speyer and Ulm) and to protect the neighbouring royal estates in the Remstal. Above all, the new duke's property could serve as 'a safety-bolt which isolated the anti-king, operating in Saxony, from his south German partisans'.[91]

The king's Swabian opponents moved quickly to undermine the new duke's authority. Soon after Easter Welf IV brought Berthold of Rheinfelden, son of the anti-king, to Ulm, where the princes 'did homage to [Berthold] according to custom and . . . confirmed him as their lord and duke'. There is no evidence of Rudolf's participation in his son's appointment, which seems to have been entirely the work of Welf IV and possibly of Berthold II of Zähringen. The latter married Rudolf's daughter soon after Easter 1079 and proved himself a zealous adherent of his brother-in-law, the anti-duke (whose heir he eventually became).[92] This independent action of Rudolf's Swabian partisans suggests

---

[89] Berthold, *Annales* 1079, pp. 319–20. See Meyer von Knonau (1900) 3:194–6.
[90] Otto of Freising, *Gesta Friderici* I.8, p. 24.
[91] Schreiner (1977) 7–8. Cf. Heyck (1891) 118; Vogel (1983) 157–60.
[92] Berthold, *Annales* 1079, p. 320. See Meyer von Knonau (1900) 3:198–200; Maurer (1978) 129–34.

that difficulty of communication had prompted Rudolf to give his allies a free hand in managing Swabian affairs. Needing urgently to demonstrate his authority, Frederick of Büren tried to seize Ulm, the 'secular centre of Swabia', the scene of the recent elevation of Berthold of Rheinfelden and of numerous meetings of the 'deposition faction' of princes since 1076. Frederick intended to celebrate Whitsun (12 May) in Ulm, but was able to spend only one night there, withdrawing at the approach of Welf.[93] This initial setback revealed how difficult Frederick would find it to exercise ducal authority outside his own region in Swabia. During his twenty-six years as duke, Frederick proved unable to extend his power south of the Danube. The principal obstacle was the power of the Zähringen, whose lands in Breisgau and Ortenau effectively divided the Staufen property in central Swabia from that in Alsace. While the Rheinfelden–Zähringen–Welf coalition held firm, there was little chance that the king's agent in Swabia would be recognised as duke outside the northern and central regions of the duchy.

Meanwhile Frederick's lord had better fortune elsewhere in southern Germany. Between Easter and Whitsun Henry campaigned in eastern Bavaria against Margrave Leopold II of Austria, who had rebelled in May 1078 and was in league with King Ladislaus I of Hungary. Henry compelled the submission of the margrave of Austria and secured the south-eastern frontier of his kingdom.[94] After this vigorous campaign Henry celebrated Whitsun (12 May) in Regensburg where he received the papal legates and their escort, Patriarch Henry of Aquileia. The arrival of Cardinal bishop Peter of Albano and Bishop Udalric of Padua opened a new phase of negotiations between the parties in the civil war. The legates eventually secured the agreement of the king to the holding of a conference in Fritzlar. At last Henry was persuaded to abandon his own strategy of separate negotiations in favour of the papal plan of a conference of both parties under the presidency of papal legates. The participants in the conference in June were the anti-king, Siegfried of Mainz, numerous Saxon princes and, on the other side, the patriarch of Aquileia 'and other familiars of the king' who escorted the papal legates to this meeting. The negotiations ran into difficulties on the question of hostages. The Saxons declared that an exchange of hostages was the only way to ensure the peace; the king's representatives vigorously resisted this condition but yielded at last to the joint pressure of their opponents and the legates.[95] Having agreed on this issue, the parties deferred their further negotiations to an assembly in

[93] Berthold, *Annales* 1079, pp. 319–20. See Meyer von Knonau (1900) 3:207–8.
[94] Berthold, *Annales* 1079, p. 319; *Annales Augustani* 1079, p. 129. See Meyer von Knonau (1900) 3:207.
[95] Berthold, *Annales* 1079, pp. 320–1. See Meyer von Knonau (1900) 3:208, 210–11; Schumann (1912) 46; Borino (1958) 73; Miccoli (1960) 98–101; Vogel (1983) 160–2.

Würzburg in August. Würzburg was a city notoriously loyal to the king[96] and this choice of meeting place was an attempt to conciliate the Henrician party after its defeat on the hostage question. Henry's representatives knew that their lord would oppose the Saxon demand. An exchange of hostages meant treating the anti-king's party as equals, but Henry regarded them as no more than rebels. He had informed the two previous meetings in Fritzlar that he would make peace with the Saxons only if they first submitted to his authority.

After the incomplete negotiations in Fritzlar the legates returned with the king's representatives to the court in Regensburg. Peter of Albano and Udalric of Padua remained in Henry's entourage, since their instructions required them to reach an agreement with Henry 'about holding a conference, making a permanent peace in the kingdom and restoring bishops to their sees'. To the party of the anti-king, however, it seemed that the legates had fallen under Henry's influence. Gregory VII, who had heard rumours of bribes and threats, wrote to his legates: 'there are many men (although we give them no credence) who begin to complain of your conduct as legates . . . and allege that one of you will act too innocently and the other will not act innocently enough'.[97] The subject of the rumours of bribery was Udalric of Padua. The only evidence of a special understanding between this legate and the king is the royal diploma of 23 July 1079, confirming the rights and privileges of his church, a conventional mark of favour towards an imperial church, inappropriate only in its timing.[98] Their experience of the legates of 1077 led Rudolf's party to assume that the pope's representatives would act as the open enemies of the king. The unexpected phenomenon of legates who obeyed the pope's instructions prompted the sending of hostile propaganda to Rome. So convinced were Rudolf's supporters that the legates had been 'entirely seduced to favour [the king]' that none of them attended the council in Würzburg in mid-August. Distrust of the legates combined with fear of Henry's motives: he came to Würzburg accompanied by numerous bishops of his party and also by a great army. Rudolf's absence offered the king an advantage which he quickly exploited, opening the council by demanding the excommunication of his opponents on the grounds of disobedience towards the holy see. This was a measure, however, that the legates were not permitted to take: they must 'pass no judgement in the case of the kings or of the kingship'.[99]

---

[96] Bruno, *Saxonicum bellum* c. 112, pp. 104–5. See Kottje (1978) 142–3.

[97] Gregory VII, *Epistolae Vagantes* 31, pp. 80–4. Cf. Berthold, *Annales* 1079, pp. 320–1.

[98] *D H IV* 312. See Meyer von Knonau (1900) 3:213–15; Schumann (1912) 50–1; Borino (1958) 74–5; Miccoli (1960) 104–5; Vogel (1983) 161–6.

[99] Berthold, *Annales* 1079, pp. 321–2; *Annales Augustani* 1079, pp. 129–30. See Meyer von Knonau (1900) 3:215–17.

After this meeting, which failed to achieve the purposes either of the pope or of the king, Henry 'rashly set his army into motion . . . to attack the Saxons'. This expedition was not, as the chronicler Berthold represented it, a spontaneous response to the failure of the Würzburg council. His rival's failure to attend the council merely gave Henry a pretext for the military action against Saxony that he had already planned. A glimpse of his planning appears in a diploma of 16 August issued en route for the council, recording timely financial aid for the king from the abbey of Niederaltaich.[100] Rudolf's response to the royal expedition was to send envoys to the princes in Henry's army, declaring his willingness to participate in a conference, according to the pope's command. Neither the king nor his bishops wished to be deflected from the campaign, but they were eventually overruled by the secular princes of their party. Through the mediation of the papal legates a truce was negotiated between the two parties.[101] By October Henry was back in Regensburg, but his agents were still active on his behalf in Saxony. 'By promising much he divided the Saxons one from another.'[102] He freed Count Herman Billung (a prisoner since the battle of Mellrichstadt) after he and his nephew Magnus had given an oath of security for their future good conduct. Count Wiprecht I of Groitzsch and the Wettin prince Theoderic, son of Count Gero of Brehna, were also among the deserters. The royal kinsman Ekbert II of Brunswick waited on events, poised to abandon the anti-king's party at the first sign of danger.

Henry determined to exploit this, his first major breakthrough in Saxony since the beginning of the civil war, by a winter campaign against the anti-king. He had always hoped to solve the problem of the kingship either by the military defeat or by the political isolation of his rival. He was deflected from his purpose by the Lenten synod of 1079, which obliged him to cooperate with the pope and his legates; but cooperation gained him nothing. Now at the end of the year he was free to pursue his own objectives and well placed to achieve them. He gathered forces from Burgundy, Franconia, Swabia, Bavaria and Bohemia. Royal diplomas from the last three months of the year show the king making his military preparations in Bavaria and in the Rhineland.[103] His episcopal supporters proved an indispensable source of men and money. Perhaps the bishops were more committed than the secular princes to the idea of an

[100] D H IV 31. See Meyer von Knonau (1900) 3:212; Stadtmüller and Pfister (1971) 127, 133; Vogel (1983) 164–5.

[101] Berthold, *Annales* 1079, p. 321; *Annales Augustani* 1079, p. 130. See Meyer von Knonau (1900) 3:216–17.

[102] Bruno, *Saxonicum bellum* c. 117, p. 109. Cf. Berthold, *Annales* 1079, p. 323; 1080, pp. 325–6. See Meyer von Knonau (1900) 3:218–19, 235–6; Fenske (1977) 65–6, 73.

[103] DD H IV 317–19 (grants of land to *ministeriales*). See Vogel (1983) 184–5.

outright victory over the anti-king.[104] In mid-January 1080 the royal army left Mainz for Saxony. At its approach the Saxon princes with whom he had been in secret communication deserted Rudolf, some choosing neutrality, some joining Henry's army. It was unusual to campaign at this season: Bruno of Merseburg concluded that Henry expected to surprise an unprepared enemy.[105] Rudolf, however, was not taken by surprise. He moved his 'huge army' into Thuringia to meet the royal forces, then fell back before them until he reached the neighbourhood of the village of Flarchheim (in north-western Thuringia). On 27 January the anti-king drew up his forces on the steep bank of one of the many streams running into the River Unstrut.

The battle of Flarchheim began with a skilful royal manoeuvre which came close to giving Henry a complete victory. The royal army carried out an encircling movement, suddenly appearing on the right flank and at the rear of the enemy. This manoeuvre was possible because of the weather conditions: a blizzard blew up and so darkened the sky that the warriors could hardly see who was standing next to them. For a time there was confusion in the Saxon ranks, but once order was restored, it became clear that theirs was the stronger army. 'The fighting was fierce on both sides, but it was soon over.'[106] The Bohemians were in the vanguard of Henry's army and suffered the worst casualties.[107] The Bavarian and Franconian forces fled from the field, as also, according to the anti-Henrician chronicles, did the king himself.[108] The royal army regrouped near the fortress of the Wartburg, but while they were resting there, they were attacked by the garrison of the fortress and forced again to flee, leaving an immense booty in their attackers' hands. The loss of his supplies, together with the extreme cold, compelled Henry to abandon the campaign, dismiss his army and return through eastern Franconia to Regensburg. Rudolf was left in possession of the field, which, according to the eleventh-century convention, signified that he was the victor;[109] but he derived no strategic advantage from Flarchheim. He did not pursue his retreating enemy, but instead withdrew to Goslar. Nor did he gain any political advantage: the Saxon princes who had deserted him on the eve of the battle were not persuaded to return to his allegiance. Henrician propaganda, as in the case of Mellrichstadt, claimed a victory for the king.[110] In fact Henry had once more failed to implement his military

---

[104] Berthold, *Annales* 1079, p. 323. Prelates in the royal entourage, late 1079: Gawlik (1970a) 63–4.   [105] Bruno, *Saxonicum bellum* c. 117, p. 109.

[106] *Ibid.* c. 117, pp. 109–11; Berthold, *Annales* 1080, pp. 324–5. See Meyer von Knonau (1900) 3:238–41, 639–43; Vogel (1983) 185–6.

[107] Frutolf, *Chronica* 1079, p. 90. See Wegener (1959) 118–19; Schramm (1968) 351.

[108] Bruno c. 117, p. 111. Cf. Berthold, *Annales* 1080, p. 325.

[109] Berthold, *Annales* 1080, p. 325. See Cram (1955) 143–5, 214.

[110] *Annales Augustani* 1080, p. 130. Cf. Frutolf, *Chronica* 1079, p. 90.

solution to the problem of the kingship and again he turned to his alternative strategy of persuading the pope to excommunicate the anti-king.

Meanwhile Gregory VII pressed ahead with his own solution to the problem. While still unaware of the inconclusive outcome of his legation, he wrote to assure the anti-king's partisans of his impartiality despite the great pressure on him: 'All the Italians, save for a very small number, approve of and defend the cause of Henry and accuse me of excessive harshness and undutifulness towards him.' As for his legates, he had heard that, 'compelled by violence and ensnared by deceit', they had not acted according to instructions.[111] The legates did not return to Rome together, suggesting disagreement between them. Udalric of Padua, arriving first, sought to persuade the pope of the justice of Henry's cause, but his version of events was contradicted by the anti-king's envoy. From Peter of Albano Gregory learned that, although his legates had obeyed their instructions as best they could, the legation had proved a failure.[112] Modern scholarship has generally accepted that it was at this moment, late in 1079, that the pope decided to pronounce the second excommunication of Henry IV.[113] A number of factors beside the failure of the pope's scheme for a German council have been detected behind the decision. Berthold of Reichenau's version of events has inspired the idea that Henry's bribing of Udalric of Padua was the factor that turned the pope against him.[114] Gregory's abandonment of neutrality has been interpreted as motivated by a political calculation. The outcome of the battle of Flarchheim may have suggested to him that Rudolf, his preferred candidate, might after all become master of the German kingdom.[115] Alternatively Gregory may have been impelled to act against Henry by fear of losing the loyalty of the anti-king's party, without whom he had no hope of influencing events in Germany.[116]

Less attention has been paid to the idea that Gregory's abandonment of neutrality was prompted not by his political strategy but by his reforming aims. It was now clear that Henry would not surrender royal power over the Church: 'Despite the prohibition of investiture he continued to fill bishoprics in the traditional manner.'[117] This interpretation of the second conflict of pope and king as an 'investiture contest' is supported by the evidence of the legislation of the Lenten synod of 7 March 1080. The more conciliatory investiture decree of November 1078 was now superseded by a decree that excommunicated not only the clerical recipient but also the lay person who conferred

---

[111] Gregory VII, *Registrum* VII.3, pp. 462–3.

[112] Berthold, *Annales* 1079, pp. 322–3; Bernold, *Chronicon* 1080, pp. 436–7. See Meyer von Knonau (1900) 3:223–5; Schumann (1912) 49; Vogel (1983) 168–70.

[113] Meyer von Knonau (1900) 3:246–58.   [114] Berthold, *Annales* 1079, 1080, pp. 322, 326.

[115] Haller (1950) 296.   [116] Jordan (1964) 262.   [117] A. Hauck (1952) 821–3.

investiture, whether 'emperors, kings, dukes, margraves, counts or any secular powers whatsoever'.[118] The decree 'concerning the election of bishops' envisaged an ideal future in which the laity were entirely excluded from episcopal appointments. When a vacancy occurred, 'at the instance of the bishop who is sent as visitor by the apostolic or the metropolitan see, the clergy and people, setting aside all worldly ambition, fear or favour, shall, with the consent of the apostolic see or their metropolitan, elect for themselves a pastor according to God'.[119] After the abolition of lay investiture the archbishop or the pope himself would play that role in episcopal elections previously usurped by the secular power. The synod that announced Henry IV's renewed excommunication and deposition also formulated the definitive version of the Gregorian programme of 'freedom of the Church', cancelling those royal rights to which Henry clung too tenaciously to be a satisfactory partner for Gregory VII.

The most recent examination of the pope's decision to excommunicate Henry argues that it was taken, not late in 1079, but in the Lenten synod of 7 March 1080 as a consequence of the message delivered to the synod by Henry's envoys.[120] This interpretation is based on the account of a possible eyewitness, Gregory's biographer, Bonizo of Sutri. 'King Henry took counsel and sent to Rome envoys, namely Archbishop Liemar of Bremen . . . and the bishop of Bamberg and very many others, bearing a proud and unheard-of message: that if the pope would excommunicate Rudolf without a trial, [Henry] would show him due obedience; if not, he would acquire for himself a pope who would do his will.' It was this threat that provoked his excommunication and deposition.[121] Of this alleged message the first half rings true: Henry had been requesting the anti-king's excommunication since March 1077. The rest of Bonizo's account must be read in the light of his polemical purpose of proving that Henry was the aggressor in the conflict of pope and king. Henry's dealings with Rome in 1077–9 had been directed towards the diplomatic isolation of the anti-king, an objective impossible to achieve without the pope's goodwill. After his failure to defeat Rudolf in January 1080 Henry is far more likely to have continued this strategy of conciliating the pope and isolating the anti-king, than to have reverted (as Bonizo claimed) to the policy of January 1076, of which he had so soon repented.

According to Gregory VII, the judgement against Henry was the direct consequence of the excommunication pronounced in the Lenten synod of the previous year against anyone hindering the holding of a conference between the rival parties. 'Henry, together with his supporters . . . by preventing the

---

[118] Gregory VII, *Registrum* VII.14a, c. 1, 2, 6, pp. 480–1, 482. See Schieffer (1981) 173–5; Vogel (1983) 196–7.   [119] *Registrum* VII.14a, c. 6, p. 482.   [120] Vogel (1983) 186–95.
[121] Bonizo, *Ad amicum* IX, p. 612. Cf. Berthold, *Annales* 1080, p. 326.

conference, incurred excommunication and bound himself with the bond of anathema and caused a great multitude of Christians to be delivered up to death and gave over almost all the kingdom of the Germans to desolation.'[122] The synod accepted the version of events given by the anti-king's envoys, which was presumably corroborated by the legate, Peter of Albano. Henry's conduct had been marked by 'pride, disobedience and falsehood', Rudolf's by 'humility, obedience and truth'.[123] Gregory accepted the claims of Rudolf's envoys, distorted though they were,[124] because he had long been committed to the success of their cause. They were 'the vassals of St Peter' (Gregory's favourite term for the adherents of the papacy), who strove 'to defend the truth of the Church, to defend the freedom of [their] noble status'.[125] Hitherto the pope had trusted in the efficacy of his plan for a German council. Rudolf's envoys now convinced him that such a council would never take place, 'since Henry believed that he could defeat [Rudolf] by his own might'. If the 'business of the kingship' was to be settled by the authority of St Peter, it must be settled quickly, before Henry obtained his victory and rendered the pope's role superfluous. As for the limitations of Rudolf's actual power, of which Gregory had formerly been acutely aware: the pope was now certain that God and St Peter would provide. Depriving Henry of his kingdoms of Germany and Italy and of the fealty of his vassals, the pope prayed to St Peter: 'may Henry, with his supporters, not prevail in any battle and may he never obtain a victory during his lifetime'. Gregory was still in this prophetic vein when, on Easter Monday (13 April), he repeated the sentence of excommunication in the basilica of St Peter, declaring that, unless the excommunicate king repented by 1 August (the feast of St Peter in chains), 'he would die or be deposed'.[126] More confident than ever of his unique status as the earthly representative of St Peter, 'his vicar who lives in the flesh',[127] Gregory committed all the authority of his office to the task of destroying Henry IV.

Henry's response to the synodal judgement is not known. A number of loyal bishops celebrating Easter (12 April) in Bamberg chose during the mass to denounce the pope and withdraw their obedience from him, but there is no evidence that Henry was present or that he instigated this demonstration

[122] *Registrum* VII.14a, pp. 479–87.
[123] *MGH Constitutiones* I, 554–5, no. 390 (=Paul of Bernried, *Vita Gregorii VII* c. 106, p. 538).
[124] A. Hauck (1952) 823.
[125] Gregory VII, *Epistolae Vagantes* 26, pp. 66–8; *Registrum* VII.3, pp. 462–3.
[126] Bonizo, *Ad amicum* IX, p. 616. Cf. Beno, *Gesta Romanae ecclesiae* I.7, pp. 371–2; Sigebert, *Chronica* 1080, p. 364. See Meyer von Knonau (1900) 3:257–8; Vogel (1983) 195–6.
[127] *Registrum* IX.3, p. 576. See Fliche (1925) 194; Erdmann (1935) 185–211; Ullmann (1959–61) 229–64.

against the pope.[128] The inspiration may have come from the returning royal envoy, Bishop Rupert of Bamberg. He and his fellow envoy, Liemar of Bremen hastily returned to Germany after the debacle of the Lenten synod, although they still found time to promote their lord's interests in Tuscany and Lombardy. They 'attempted to release the province from subjection to the most excellent Countess Matilda', the pope's ally, and their efforts were continued after their departure by two Italian princes loyal to the king, Margrave Adalbert and Count Boso. Entering Lombardy, the envoys 'divided kingship and priesthood' by summoning 'all the princes of the Lombards' to a conference.[129] The earliest product of the propaganda war that now broke out in the Italian kingdom was the treatise *The Defence of King Henry*, attributed to Petrus Crassus and written soon after the Lenten synod of 1080. *The Defence* sets out to prove Henry's hereditary right to his kingdoms, using the Roman law of private property. *The Defence* is unique among the many polemics of Henry IV's reign in this use of Roman Law, an important witness to the study of the *Corpus Iuris Civilis* in late eleventh-century Italy.[130]

Henry's first recorded response to his condemnation was the council of Mainz on Whitsunday (31 May), attended by nineteen bishops and unidentified 'princes of the kingdom'. They resolved that 'Hildebrand . . . should be utterly rejected and another, worthier than he, should be elected to the apostolic see'.[131] His deposition and the election of a new pope was to be the work of a future assembly. The proceedings of the council were publicised in the letters of three of the participants: the bishops Huzman of Speyer and Theoderic of Verdun, and Egilbert, archbishop elect of Trier. The letters represent Henry as the victim of the aggression of Hildebrand, 'the accursed disturber of divine and human laws', the 'fountain of all dissension and the head of all schism', who 'arms some men against the king and spurs others to the war that he is waging against everybody'. Theoderic of Verdun and Huzman of Speyer assured the bishops and princes of the Italian kingdom of the support of the German episcopate in removing and replacing the pope. There would be no repetition of 1076, when after Henry's excommunication most German bishops distanced themselves from the king, while most Italian bishops remained loyal. These letters emphasise that after the excommunication of

---

[128] Gebhard of Salzburg, *Epistola* c. 15, p. 270. See Meyer von Knonau (1900) 3:275–6; Vogel (1983) 198–9. *Annales sancti Iacobi Leodiensis* p. 639 and Rupert of Deutz, *Chronicon sancti Laurentii Leodiensis* p. 277: Henry celebrated Easter in Liège. See Kilian (1886) 86; Meyer von Knonau (1900) 3:275 n. 81. Fraeys de Veubecke (1976) 125, 128.

[129] Bonizo, *Ad amicum* IX, p. 612. See Meyer von Knonau (1900) 3:261.

[130] Petrus Crassus, *Defensio Heinrici IV* c. 6, pp. 443–6. See Koch (1972) 37–9; Robinson (1978a) 75–83; Anton (1988) 149–67.

[131] Meyer von Knonau (1900) 3:277–81; Vogel (1983) 200–9.

March 1080 the German episcopate, except for the members of the anti-king's party, regarded Gregory VII as the aggressor and Henry as the protector of the imperial episcopate against the pope's 'innovations'.[132]

After the council of Mainz Henry immediately went to meet the Italian bishops in Brixen on 25 June. The most southerly bishopric of the German kingdom, after Chur, Brixen was easily accessible for the Italians. Twenty-nine prelates attended the council of Brixen: one Burgundian, seven Germans and nineteen Italians, including the three metropolitans, Tedald of Milan, Wibert of Ravenna and Henry of Aquileia. The principal record of the proceedings of 25 June 1080 is the synodal decree of Brixen, stating the allegations against the pope and the sentence pronounced on him. 'A meeting of thirty bishops and of secular princes not only of Italy but also of Germany was assembled by royal command and with a single voice they all uttered dreadful complaints against the wild insanity of a certain false monk Hildebrand, known as Pope Gregory VII.' The legal basis of the council's actions was the 'royal command' that assembled bishops and princes in Brixen, demonstrating the king's traditional right in an emergency to convoke a synod to regulate the affairs of the Church (just as Henry III had done in 1046). The decree emphasised Henry's scrupulous regard for correct judicial procedure. 'It seemed just to the most glorious king and his princes that the judgement of the bishops, as the sentence of divine censure, should precede the drawing of the secular sword against Hildebrand.'

The dominant theme of the decree is the harmonious cooperation of king and bishops and their mutual respect for their respective spheres of jurisdiction. This was how the Brixen decree differed most markedly from the documents of the council of Worms in 1076. Instead of the separate letters of the king calling on the pope to abdicate and the episcopate renouncing their obedience to 'Hildebrand', in 1080 bishops and king issued a single document, in the form of a synodal decree subscribed by them all. 'Henry, by the grace of God, king' appears at the end of the list of episcopal subscriptions.[133] At the head of the list appeared Hugh Candidus, cardinal priest of S. Clemente, who subscribed 'on behalf of all the Roman cardinals'. His role in Brixen was doubtless the same as that in the council of Worms in 1076: he furnished details of Hildebrand's crimes. The Brixen decree gives a more detailed account of these offences than the letters of January 1076: the pope was guilty of simony, ambition, violent intrusion into the apostolic see contrary to the Papal Election Decree of 1059, heresy, necromancy and poisoning four of his predecessors. This dossier, dismissed by modern scholarship as 'the most

---

[132] *Codex Udalrici* 60–2, pp. 126–30.

[133] *Die Briefe Heinrichs IV.* pp. 69–73. See Meyer von Knonau (1900) 3:284–96; Vogel (1983) 209–19.

absurd old wives' tales',[134] ensured that the polemical literature of the 1080s would be dominated by analysis of Gregory VII's personality and career. Because of these offences the synod judged that the pope 'should be canonically deposed and expelled and condemned in perpetuity, if, having heard this [decree], he does not step down from that see'. The bishops did not depose the pope, but decreed that he should be deposed if he refused to abdicate. A forced abdication was still the favoured solution of Gregory's enemies, since this would enable them to avoid transgressing the ancient canon law principle that the pope can be judged by no one.

Although the Brixen decree claims that the synod condemned Gregory 'with a single voice', there are signs of uneasiness among royal supporters at the radicalism of the synodal measures. The dilemma of Bishop Benno of Osnabrück is recorded in a well-known passage of his biography. Benno wished 'to be always faithful to the king and never disobedient to the pope'. He was present at the synod, 'albeit unwillingly', but his name is missing from the subscriptions in the synodal decree, since during the proceedings he hid inside an altar in the church where the synod met. He thus avoided involvement in the condemnation of the pope and the election of a successor, while obeying the royal command to attend the council.[135] Benno's reservations were shared by the royalist author of the *Annals of Augsburg*, who wrote that the council's treatment of Gregory VII was 'presumptuous' and the election of a new pope was the work of the 'less wise' members of the council.[136] No such dissentient voices are heard among the king's Italian supporters. Benzo of Alba expressed the hopes of the Lombard episcopate, when he wrote on the eve of the council: 'Let [Hildebrand] be expelled in disgrace from the City; let an orthodox [pope] be placed on Peter's throne . . . Such a man must crown Henry emperor: one who is learned in all the laws, both ancient and modern.'[137] The impetus behind the radical measures of the Brixen synod came from the Lombard enemies of Gregory VII. Determined to destroy any hope of reconciliation with Gregory, they pressed for the election of Wibert of Ravenna as pope in his stead. It was their veteran leader Denis of Piacenza who persuaded Henry to take a solemn oath to accept the imperial crown from no one except the newly elected Wibert.[138] The Lombard bishops had joined in the rebellion against Gregory VII in 1076, only to see themselves deserted by their German brethren; they had rallied to Henry on his arrival in Italy in January 1077, only to see him submit at Canossa. Henry's oath was the guarantee that they would not be abandoned a second time.

---

[134] W. Goez (1968) 123. [135] *Vita Bennonis Osnabrugensis* c. 18, pp. 410–12.
[136] *Annales Augustani* 1080, p. 130. Cf. *Vita Heinrici IV* c. 6, p. 22.
[137] Benzo of Alba, *Ad Heinricum* v.1, p. 446. [138] Bonizo, *Ad amicum* IX, p. 613.

Pressure to choose a new pope came from the Lombard episcopate, but the king played the principal role in the appointment of Wibert of Ravenna. Some of the German narrative sources speak of his 'designating' or 'nominating' the new pope. The synodal decree of Brixen emphasised the king's right to participate in the election of a pope, as defined by the Papal Election Decree of 1059: 'Whoever presumes to become pope without the consent of the Roman prince, should be regarded by all not as a pope but as an apostate.'[139] Henry IV was 'the Roman prince' by virtue of the office of patrician of the Romans, which he had inherited from his father.[140] In assuming the functions of 'the Roman prince', Henry was evoking his father's regime in Rome, just as the papal name chosen by Wibert of Ravenna, 'Clement III', evoked the events of December 1046 and Henry III's reforming councils of Sutri and Rome. Clement II had been the first of the popes appointed after Henry III's intervention to reform the Roman church: it was he who had crowned Henry emperor. The papal name of Wibert of Ravenna was a declaration that he would follow the example, not of the last four popes, who had increasingly distanced the papacy from the imperial court, but of the four German popes of 1046–57, who had cooperated harmoniously with the empire.[141]

The antipope Wibert of Ravenna was represented by the polemicists of the Gregorian party as heresiarch, apostate, advocate of simony.[142] In fact Wibert was a sincere opponent of clerical marriage and simony and an energetic reformer of the clergy in his own archdiocese. A member of a comital family in the region of Parma and Reggio in Emilia and a kinsman of the house of Canossa, he served as Italian chancellor during the regency of Empress Agnes. It was the empress who in 1072 recommended Wibert to her son as the new archbishop of Ravenna. She had been commissioned by Pope Alexander II to secure the succession of an archbishop who would be able to reconcile the northern Italian episcopate with Rome. At the beginning of his archiepiscopate Wibert was acceptable to the reformers in Rome; by 1078, however, Gregory VII had decided that Wibert was no longer his ally. The Lenten synod of that year excommunicated and suspended him from his office, interpreting his independent stance in Ravenna as 'unheard-of heresy and pride'.[143] The designation of the archbishop of Ravenna as pope was a highly sensitive devel-

---

[139] The text of the Election Decree used in Brixen was probably the falsified version composed, according to Jasper (1986) 69–88, in 1076. This version involved the king in the preliminary selection of a candidate. See H.-G. Krause (1960) 181–3, 234–8.

[140] See above pp. 36, 41–2, 144.

[141] Meyer von Knonau (1900) 3:293–6; Ziese (1982) 55–64; Cowdrey (1983) 140–1, 235–6.

[142] Bernold, *Chronicon* 1080, 1081, 1082, pp. 436, 437; Bonizo, *Ad amicum* IX, p. 613; Deusdedit, *Libellus contra invasores* II.11, p. 329.

[143] Ziese (1982) 4–54; Heidrich (1984) 40–4.

opment in the context of the ecclesiastical politics of northern Italy, especially since Wibert as pope was simultaneously to retain his archbishopric. His appointment threatened the delicate balance of the three metropolitan churches of Ravenna, Milan and Aquileia, whose rivalry for preeminence in Italy had continued for five hundred years. Two royal diplomas issued a year after the council of Brixen show the king labouring to redress the balance in the northern Italian Church by compensating the patriarchate of Aquileia.[144]

Wibert assured correspondents that he had tried 'by many means to escape from the see, or rather the ruin, which (as God is our witness) we received unwillingly'.[145] Wibert's declarations of unwillingness may have been more than a conventional topos. He may have come under strong pressure to accept designation as pope from the king and the Italian opposition to Gregory VII. Wibert's personal distinction and reforming credentials, even more than his record of loyalty to the crown, made him indispensable to the plans of the Brixen council. The new pope must be able to win recognition outside the ranks of the king's adherents. Wibert was clad in the papal insignia on 25 June 1080,[146] but, returning to Ravenna after the council, he made no claim either to the insignia or to the title of pope for the next four years. Royal documents called him 'the pope elect of the supreme see' or 'our pope elect'.[147] Wibert himself, however, took the title only of archbishop of Ravenna until, in March 1084, he was enthroned as pope in Rome. Whatever Henry may have thought, Wibert did not regard himself as pope elect after Brixen: the synod had designated, not elected him. Nevertheless it was he who must bear the brunt of the conflict with Gregory VII and his allies until the king was free to lead an army into Italy. Gregory called on the Ravennese to free themselves from Wibert's 'tyranny' and elect a new archbishop.[148] By the end of 1080 Wibert was confronted by a rebellion of his vassals, the comital family of Imola. It was only when the king began to campaign in Italy, using Ravenna as his base, in 1081–2, that Wibert was at last able to go on the offensive against his rival.[149]

The council of Brixen ended with a confident declaration by the king that he would be present at Wibert's consecration in St Peter's, Rome, on Whitsunday 1081.[150] He remained in Brixen only long enough to celebrate the feast of SS. Peter and Paul (29 June) with Wibert,[151] before returning across

---

[144] *DD H IV* 338–9. See Schmidinger (1954) 15.
[145] Liebermann (1901) 330. Cf. Clement III, letter, in Anselm of Lucca, *Liber contra Wibertum* p. 527; *Chronica monasterii Casinensis* III.50, p. 433. See Cowdrey (1983) 161–2.
[146] Bonizo, *Ad amicum* IX, p. 613. See Gussone (1978) 245.
[147] *D H IV* 322; Henry IV, *Letter* 18, p. 28.
[148] Gregory VII, *Registrum* VIII.7, 12–13, pp. 524–5, 531–2.
[149] Ziese (1982) 64–73; Heidrich (1984) 159–60.
[150] Benzo, *Ad Heinricum* VI, preface, p. 502.   [151] Bonizo, *Ad amicum* IX, p. 613.

the Alps to resume the war against the anti-king. In August he was back in Mainz, where he secured the confirmation of Wibert's 'election' by an assembly of bishops.[152] He must also have begun his preparations for an expedition to Saxony, once more seeking help from the bishops. He was to be accompanied on this expedition by perhaps as many as sixteen prelates.[153] During the past summer Henry's faithful ally Duke Vratislav of Bohemia had been campaigning in Saxony, in his capacity of margrave of Lower Lusatia and of Meissen. Intercepted by Rudolf's army, Vratislav was saved from defeat by the arrival of the forces of Count Wiprecht I of Groitzsch, who put the Saxons to flight.[154] Rudolf now devoted himself to recruiting 'a huge multitude' to defend Saxony against Henry's expected autumn campaign.

Henry's campaign, culminating in the battle of Hohenmölsen (also known as 'the battle on the Grune' or 'the battle on the Elster') on 15 October 1080, was recorded by Bruno of Merseburg, who was evidently an eyewitness. Setting out at the beginning of October, Henry followed the route taken by the royal army on the expedition of June 1075. As in January, the royal army had to devise a strategy to offset the enemy's numerical superiority. Henry's ruse was to move most of his army eastwards towards Erfurt, while sending his 'swiftest horsemen' northwards towards Goslar with instructions to burn a few villages. The Saxons, seeing the smoke, hastened to protect Goslar from the imagined assault by the king, allowing Henry's army to burn and plunder Erfurt. Henry planned similar treatment for Naumburg to punish the church for accepting a new bishop who was an adherent of the anti-king. By now, however, the Saxons were aware of the king's intentions and they succeeded in reaching Naumburg before him. Henry, therefore, turned towards the march of Meissen, urging the Bohemians to join in a combined operation. The Saxons feared that his revised plan was to turn his enlarged army against Merseburg and Magdeburg, to lay waste the whole of Saxony and 'subject it forever to his lordship'. But Henry's eastward progress was blocked by the swollen River Elster. Since the water was too deep for his army to cross, he pitched camp on the western bank to await the pursuing Saxon army.[155]

On the eve of the battle (14 October) in his camp by the Elster, Henry issued a diploma which has attracted attention from students of the king's personal piety and his special relationship with the church of Speyer. The diploma records a gesture of unusual generosity, the donation of two notable royal properties in Swabia to the church and cathedral chapter of Speyer. The

---

[152] Bernold, *Chronicon* 1080, p. 436. See Meyer von Knonau (1900) 3:325–6.
[153] *D H IV* 325; Bruno, *Saxonicum bellum* c. 122, pp. 116–17.
[154] *Annales Pegavienses* 1080, p. 241; *Casus monasterii Petrishusensis* II.38, p. 647. See Meyer von Knonau (1900) 3:331–3; Fenske (1977) 255–8.
[155] Bruno c. 121, p. 114. See Meyer von Knonau (1900) 3:333–6.

diploma states that this donation was made for the sake of the salvation of the king, his parents and grandparents, and requests the aid of the saints in the impending battle. 'We must seek the protection especially of Mary, ever virgin . . . Our fathers found refuge in her mercy and we also, under her protection, seek succour in the church of Speyer, which is especially called by her name.'[156] Henry made twenty-one donations to the church of St Mary in Speyer during his maturity, almost all at moments of political or military crisis,[157] beginning on the eve of the battle of Homburg (1075) with a diploma identifying the Virgin Mary as the king's 'protectress'.[158] The twenty-one diplomas for Speyer emphasise the close relationship between Henry's dynasty and the church where his grandparents and father were buried, and express Henry's devotion to the Virgin Mary as the patron of himself and of his dynasty. The diploma of 14 October 1080 was probably a 'votive diploma', recording a promise made in return for the saint's help in the battle. The visit which Henry paid to Speyer the following December was presumably a pilgrimage in fulfilment of his vow on the eve of battle.[159]

At daybreak on 15 October Henry drew up his army west of the Elster, along a stream called the Grune, where the marshy ground would impede the enemy's approach. His forces included the vassals of the sixteen prelates who accompanied him, Swabians under the command of their duke, Bavarians under the command of Count Rapoto IV of Cham and Lotharingians commanded by Count Henry of Laach (future count palatine in Lotharingia). There were no Bohemians in the royal army: Henry had failed to make contact with Vratislav's forces. When the Saxons arrived on the opposite bank of the Grune, they were exhausted by their rapid march and were without most of their foot soldiers, who could not keep up. As they approached the royal lines, the bishops in the Saxon army ordered the clergy to sing Psalm 82, traditionally regarded as a prayer against the enemies of God's Church. The two armies picked their way through the marshes on opposite banks of the Grune until they reached a safe crossing, whereupon they immediately engaged in close combat. The royal army fought so fiercely that some Saxon knights fled and the rumour that the whole Saxon army was in retreat was so far believed that the clergy in the royal camp began to sing the *Te Deum*. They were interrupted

---

[156] *D H IV* 325, conferring the estate of Waiblingen, on the significance of which: Otto of Freising, *Gesta Friderici* II.2, p. 103. See Meyer von Knonau (1900) 3:335–6; Stenzel (1936) 34; Gawlik (1970a) 9, 65; Maurer (1978) 87; Vogel (1983) 238, 244; Schmid (1984a) 704, 705.

[157] *DD H IV* 165–7, 277, 325, 379–84, 391, 396–7, 426, 464, 466, 474–5, 480, 489. See Heidrich (1988) 268–72; Heidrich (1991) 191–9, 204–11; Weinfurter (1991) 88–9.

[158] *D H IV* 277 (1075). See Perst (1956) 76–97.

[159] Vogel (1983) 249–50: the rebuilding of Speyer cathedral perhaps began between December 1080 and March 1081.

by the arrival of men bearing the body of Rapoto of Cham and urging those in the camp to save themselves by flight. This sudden reversal was the work of the resourceful Otto of Northeim. When the Saxon knights fled and royal forces pursued them, Otto rallied the foot soldiers and forced back the pursuers. Returning to the battlefield, Otto found the royal contingents commanded by Henry of Laach beginning triumphantly to chant the *Kyrie eleison*. Once more the premature celebrations of the royal army were cut short, as the foot-soldiers of Otto of Northeim sent the enemy fleeing across the Elster. The Saxons were free to seize the immense wealth in the royal camp.

Bruno declared that this victory compensated the Saxons twofold for their defeat at Homburg.[160] It was an empty boast, since Hohenmölsen cost the Saxons their king. When Otto's forces returned to their camp, they found Rudolf mortally wounded, his right hand cut off. He died of his wounds either on the evening of the battle or on the following day, 16 October.[161] The death of the anti-king cancelled out any political advantage the Saxons might have gained from their victory.[162] The Saxons' view of Rudolf's death is conveyed by the bronze memorial plate that they placed over his grave in the cathedral of Merseburg. This famous memorial shows Rudolf's portrait in low relief, one of the earliest funerary monuments in Germany to bear a life-sized representation of the deceased, with an inscription detailing his attributes and achievements. The portrait presents Rudolf as a living man invested with all the insignia of royalty. It is essentially a 'political demonstration', asserting the legitimacy of Rudolf's kingship and the lawfulness of the conduct of his electors and subjects. The inscription celebrates his kingship and his death. Rudolf would have been the equal of Charlemagne 'if he [had] reigned in a time of peace'; instead he fell in battle, 'the sacred victim of war'. 'For him, death was life: he died for the Church.'[163] The memorial declared that Rudolf's death was not (as his enemies claimed) the just punishment of a treacherous rebel, but the glorious martyrdom of a lawful king who died defending the Church.[164]

The manner of Rudolf's death provided the Henrician party with a propaganda coup. 'Rudolf, who was not afraid to violate the fealty that he had sworn to his lord, the king, lost his right hand, as a demonstration of the most just

---

[160] Bruno, *Saxonicum bellum* c. 121–4, pp. 114–18. Cf. Frutolf, *Chronica* 1080, p. 94; Bernold, *Chronicon* 1080, p. 436; Bonizo, *Ad amicum* IX, p. 613. See Meyer von Knonau (1900) 3:337–41, 644–52; Cram (1955) 145–8, 214.   [161] Meyer von Knonau (1900) 3:650.

[162] The chronicles composed after the 1080s report a royal victory: Meyer von Knonau (1900) 3:644–52.

[163] Schramm and Mütherich (1962) 176; Bücking (1968) pp. 393–5. See also Panofsky (1924) 1:82–3; 2: no. 13; Bornscheuer (1968) 213; Bauch (1976) 11–13, 305; Vogel (1983) 239–43.

[164] Bernold, *Chronicon* 1080, p. 436.

punishment for oath-breaking.' The anonymous biographer of Henry IV reminded readers that the anti-king's death was the result of the loss of that hand with which he had sworn fealty to his lord. Who could doubt that he had been punished by heaven for failing to keep his oath? Rudolf's death was 'a great lesson to the world that no-one may rebel against his lord'.[165] Rudolf's electors were implicated in the divine judgement on their king,[166] as was the pope who had acknowledged Rudolf as king in 1080. The anti-king 'was called son of St Peter, friend of the pope, victorious prince', wrote the polemicist Wenrich of Trier. Hildebrand conferred his blessings and his friendship not on lawful kings but on 'men who seized kingdoms by tyrannical violence, whose paths to the throne lay through blood, who set a gory diadem upon their heads'.[167] Henry IV's letter of 1082 to the Romans cited as proof that God had ordained him to the kingship the fact that 'He has protected us from the snares of Hildebrand and his supporters'. 'The Lord has destroyed our vassal, the oath-breaker whom [Hildebrand] set up as king over us.'[168] Other polemicists mocked Gregory VII's prophecy foretelling Henry's imminent death or deposition. The Lotharingian monk Sigebert of Gembloux wrote: 'Pope Hildebrand foretold, as though it had been revealed to him by heaven, that in this year the false king would die. Indeed what he foretold was true, but he was mistaken in his interpretation of the prophecy, since he wished King Henry to be regarded as the false king. For King Henry encountered the Saxons in a fierce battle and in the encounter the false king Rudolf perished, together with many of the princes of Saxony.'[169]

In the months following Rudolf's death there were signs that Henry was recovering some of his influence in western Saxony. The royal adviser Benno of Osnabrück, returning to his diocese, 'was received by all honourably and most kindly'.[170] In December 1080 Henry was able to appoint a new bishop to Minden, Folcmar, who succeeded in establishing himself in the see.[171] In this changing situation the king gathered an army for a winter campaign in Saxony. The Saxon princes, assembling in December 'to discuss the state of their kingdom', learned that Henry intended to celebrate Christmas in Goslar. They rapidly gathered 'a great army' to bar his way and compelled him to negotiate. Bruno of Merseburg provided the only account of these negotiations. The king 'sent envoys to the Saxons, requesting them, since they did not wish to be without a king, to make his son their king and swearing to them

[165] *Vita Heinrici IV* c. 4, p. 19.   [166] Frutolf, *Chronica* 1080, p. 94.
[167] Wenrich of Trier, *Epistola* c. 6, p. 294.   [168] Henry IV, *Letter* 17, p. 25.
[169] Sigebert, *Chronica* 1080, p. 364. Cf. Wenrich, *Epistola* c. 2, p. 287; Benzo, *Ad Heinricum* VI.5, p. 554.   [170] *Vita Bennonis Osnabrugensis* c. 19, p. 414.
[171] *Annales Patherbrunnenses* 1080, p. 98; *Liber de unitate ecclesiae* II.24, pp. 241, 244. See Meyer von Knonau (1900) 3:342–3; Löffler (1903) 41, 58–9; Ortmanns (1972) 53.

that he himself would never enter the land of Saxony'. Their answer was given by Otto of Northeim, 'who was accustomed to cover up great and serious matters with a playful jest': 'I have often seen a bad calf begotten by a bad ox, so I desire neither the son nor the father.' Henry allegedly offered the Saxons his son Conrad, not yet seven years old, presumably to avert the election of a new anti-king.[172] Bruno's version of Henry's offer suggests that the king now contemplated a separate kingdom of Saxony, to be ruled by King Conrad. Bruno himself used the term 'kingdom of Saxony' twice in his chronicle[173] and also quoted two letters of Gregory VII, in which the pope referred to Saxony as a 'kingdom'. Gregory believed that 'the great emperor [Charlemagne] offered Saxony to St Peter, with whose help he conquered it' and caused Saxony to pay an annual tribute to Rome. There is no evidence, however, that Gregory used this claim to press for a formal 'division of the kingdoms'. When in 1078 he referred to 'the German and Saxon kingdoms', he was describing the current political situation, rather than putting forward a plan of partition.[174] According to Bruno, in December 1080 Henry proposed such a partition. Bruno's polemical purpose here, almost at the end of his narrative, is clear: he implied that, after seven years of warfare in Saxony, Henry had given up all hope of restoring his authority over the Saxons. This polemical intention is likely to have distorted Bruno's account of Henry's proposal of December 1080. The most plausible reconstruction of the offer of 1080 is that Henry, on the eve of his Italian expedition, proposed the election of his son as king of the Germans (not as king of an independent Saxony), to be the nominal ruler of the kingdom in his father's absence.[175] Conrad's election might have dissuaded Henry's opponents from proceeding to their own election. The plan, however, foundered on the fierce resistance of the Saxons, to whom it was first broached.

Despite this setback, negotiations were resumed early in February 1081. The pressure to reach an agreement came from the royal party. In the context of Henry's imminent Italian expedition, his advisers 'thought it unsafe to leave their territories open to invasion by the Saxons'.[176] The meeting between representatives of the two parties in the forest of Kaufungen is recorded in Bruno's narrative and in a letter written soon after the meeting by the principal speaker on the Saxon side, Archbishop Gebhard of Salzburg. Each party was represented by five prelates and their discussions were held in the presence

---

[172] Bruno, *Saxonicum bellum* c. 125, p. 118.

[173] Bruno c. 30, 121, pp. 32, 114. See Müller-Mertens (1970) 212–25.

[174] Gregory VII, *Epistolae Vagantes* 25, 26, pp. 64, 66. Cf. *Registrum* VIII.23, p. 567. See Müller-Mertens (1970) 179, 221; Vogel (1983) 136, 175–7; Leyser (1991) 231–8.

[175] Meyer von Knonau (1900) 3:343. Cf. Lange (1961) 72; E. Goez (1996) 11. Giese (1979) 56, 171 considered Bruno's story authentic.   [176] Bruno c. 126, pp. 118–19.

of 'almost all the greater men of Saxony and Thuringia'. Gebhard of Salzburg spoke first, revealing a more moderate attitude than that of the Saxon princes in December 1080. He called on his opponents to prove that Henry could be obeyed as king 'without damage to the holy faith'. (It is clear from Gebhard's account that his main anxiety was the papal excommunication rather than the Saxon grievances against Henry.) The king's representatives replied that, since a decision on the king's rights properly 'belonged to the king and all the subjects in his kingdom', the question should be referred to a future assembly of princes. Meanwhile the two parties should agree on a truce from the beginning of February until the middle of June. When the Saxons' five representatives promised to observe such a truce, Otto of Northeim exclaimed: 'Do you think that we are so stupid that we do not understand your cunning purpose? You ask us for peace for your territories so that you can dishonour the apostolic dignity.' The royal party desired the four-and-a-half-month truce so that they would be free to enter Italy to enforce the abdication of the pope. The consequence of this intervention, claimed Bruno, was that the Saxons would agree only to a truce of seven days.[177] Bruno's subsequent narrative, however, belies this claim by revealing that in the event the Saxons waited until June before mounting another expedition.[178] It is likely, therefore, that the meeting in the Kaufungen forest agreed on the truce suggested by the king's representatives.

Immediately after Henry had entered Italy, in March 1081, 'the princes of Saxony sent envoys to all the German-speaking peoples, enemies as well as friends, requesting that, setting aside Henry and his son, they elect some other ruler and promise to serve him faithfully, whoever he was; so that all the members of the kingdom might be joined together under a single king, as in former times'.[179] This initiative seems to have met with no response from the rest of the kingdom. Meanwhile Gregory VII sought to delay the election. He wrote in March to his legate in Germany, Altmann of Passau: 'We think it better that there should be some delay in providing, God willing, a suitable king for the honour of holy Church, than that, through too much haste, an unworthy man should be chosen as king.' This letter contains the definitive version of the Gregorian ideal of a Christian king: 'obedient, humbly devoted and useful to holy Church, just as a Christian king ought to be and as we hoped of Rudolf'. The new king must take an oath of fealty and serve the pope

---

[177] Henry's representatives: archbishops of Cologne and Trier, bishops of Bamberg, Speyer and Utrecht; their opponents: archbishops of Magdeburg, Mainz and Salzburg, bishops of Hildesheim and Paderborn. See Bruno c. 126–8, pp. 118–22; Gebhard of Salzburg, letter to Herman of Metz c. 1, 2, p. 264. See Meyer von Knonau (1900) 3:346–9; Lange (1961) 72–3; Steinböck (1972) 124–31; Giese (1979) 57–8, 171–2; Vogel (1983) 251–3.

[178] Bruno c. 130, pp. 122–3.   [179] *Ibid.*, p. 122. See Meyer von Knonau (1900) 3:415–16.

as his feudal lord.[180] This letter echoed the themes of Gregory's letter of 15 March 1081 to Herman of Metz, defending the second excommunication of the king. Gregory cited the historical example on which the Gregorian political idea of 'suitability' (*idoneitas*) was based: the deposition of the last of the Merovingian kings, Childeric III in 751. A pope 'deposed a king of the Franks from the kingship, not so much because of his iniquities as because he was not useful enough to hold such great power.' It was for the pope to judge whether a king was iniquitous or useless: Henry IV was clearly both. The letter contains Gregory's startling repudiation of the idea of 'sacral kingship'. 'Who does not know that kings and dukes are descended from those who, in disregard of God, through arrogance, plunder, treachery, murder, finally through almost all crimes, prompted by the prince of this world, the devil, strove to dominate their equals, that is, [their fellow] men, in blind greed and intolerable presumption.'[181] Gregory's conflict with Henry had led him, on the eve of the king's arrival in Italy, to reject the traditional 'royal theology' of divinely ordained kingship.

The Saxon initiative to elect a new anti-king was resumed during the summer. In June the Kaufungen truce expired and the Saxons made war on their Franconian enemies, campaigning as far afield as Bamberg. 'There, meeting their old friends, the Swabians, they took counsel together on the common business of appointing a king and after many discussions they all unanimously agreed to elect Herman as king.'[182] The new anti-king, elected at the beginning of August in Ochsenfurt was Herman, count of Salm (in the Ardennes). He was a member of the dynasty of the counts of Luxemburg, one of the foremost families of Lotharingia, son of Giselbert, count of Luxemburg and Salm and the younger brother of Count Conrad I of Luxemburg.[183] Herman had hitherto played no identifiable role in the politics of the kingdom: he is not named in any source before the election in Ochsenfurt. The anti-Henrician sources praise him in Gregorian language ('a nobleman, seemly, energetic and suitable') but say nothing of his previous achievements.[184] The factor that carried most weight in the election in Ochsenfurt

---

[180] Gregory VII, *Registrum* IX.3, pp. 573–7. See Meyer von Knonau (1900) 3:364–8; Robinson (1979) 740–1; Szabó-Bechstein (1985) 148, 172–4; Robinson (1990) 312, 410–11.

[181] *Registrum* VIII.21, p. 554. See Meyer von Knonau (1900) 3:368–73; Arquillière (1952b) 231–42; Szabó-Bechstein (1985) 139–40, 143–4, 149, 169; Robinson (1990) 312, 399, 410. Precedent of 751: Affeldt (1969) 313–46.

[182] Bruno c. 130–1, pp. 122–3. See Meyer von Knonau (1900) 3:415–18, 423–6; Lange (1961) 73–6.

[183] Renn (1941a) 114–15, 137–9; Klebel (1955) 234–5; Twellenkamp (1991) 492–6. Cf. Wolf (1991) 106–7: Herman descended from King Henry I of Germany; his mother perhaps an Ezzonid.

[184] *Casus monasterii Petrishusensis* II.39, p. 647. Cf. Bernold, *Chronicon* 1081, p. 437. Henrician version: Frutolf, *Chronica* 1082, pp. 94, 96. The twelfth-century tradition that Herman was

was probably Herman's connection with the Welf family. His aunt Imiza had married Count Welf II and was the grandmother of Welf IV of Bavaria. The death of Rudolf of Rheinfelden left Welf IV as the most powerful member of the non-Saxon element in the 'deposition faction'. Significantly, Welf is the only prince who can with certainty be identified among the electors in Ochsenfurt.[185] It has been suggested that, given the close links between the house of Luxemburg and the bishopric of Metz, Herman of Metz may have played an important role in Ochsenfurt, promoting the candidature of the Luxemburg prince.[186] There is, however, no proof of Herman of Metz's presence in Ochsenfurt or his later cooperation with the anti-king. Nor is there any evidence that Herman of Salm was associated with ecclesiastical reform like his predecessor or that he enjoyed Gregory VII's confidence as Rudolf had done. The pope is not known to have confirmed Herman's election as king: his name is never mentioned in any letter of Gregory VII. Welf IV (and perhaps Herman of Metz) supported Herman in Ochsenfurt not because he was the 'reforming candidate' (as Rudolf had been in Forchheim) but because of close ties with the Luxemburg family.

The narrative sources identify the electors variously as 'the Swabians and Saxons', the 'Swabians' alone[187] and 'the Saxons' alone.[188] There is every reason to suppose that the election was carried out by a very small number of princes and that few, if any, Saxons participated.[189] Bruno's account implies that the Saxons left Franconia after the protracted negotiations with the Swabians in June and July, but before the actual election in August.[190] His account also reveals that Otto of Northeim waited for four months after the Ochsenfurt election before acknowledging Herman as king. Henry IV's supporters 'greatly feared the king elect and sought by every means to prevent the process of the election from being completed'. Otto of Northeim responded positively to their 'many promises': 'his unsteadiness disturbed almost all Saxony'. By November he was 'totally inclined to the party of our enemies', when a fall from his horse incapacitated him for a month. Interpreting this accident as a divine punishment for his 'unsteadiness', Otto sent envoys to the Saxon princes to declare his support for Herman. His conversion enabled the anti-king to enter Saxony. Herman was received in Goslar by the Saxon

---

nicknamed 'garlic': Helmold, *Cronica* 1.30, p. 58; *Annales Palidenses* 1082, p. 70. See Twellenkamp (1991) 496 n. 142.   [185] *Annales Augustani* 1081, p. 130.

[186] Sigebert, *Chronica* 1082, p. 364: the anti-king was 'the vassal of Bishop Herman'. See Meyer von Knonau (1900) 3:418; Salloch (1931) 45.

[187] *Annales Augustani* 1081, p. 130; Marianus, *Chronicon* 1103 (=1081), p. 562.

[188] *Vita Heinrici IV* c. 4, p. 19.   [189] Bernold, *Chronicon* 1081, p. 437.

[190] *Annales Palidenses* 1082, p. 70: Herman was elected in Eisleben. The alleged second election in Saxony: Giese (1979) 58.

princes 'with great applause' and crowned by Siegfried of Mainz on 26 December.[191]

Bruno's account of Otto's hesitation and eventual rallying to Herman is difficult to interpret. It is hard to believe that Otto was persuaded by the royalists' 'promises', given his irreconcilable hostility towards Henry in the negotiations of December 1080 and the Kaufungen talks of February 1081. The likeliest explanation is that Bruno invented Otto's vacillations in order to conceal the failure of his hero's attempt to be elected anti-king. The Saxons' premature departure from the negotiations about the election; the subsequent refusal of 'almost all Saxony' to recognise Herman until Otto relented: these developments suggest that the Saxons promoted Otto as their candidate for the kingship but their efforts were blocked by the rest of the 'deposition faction'. Otto was the most powerful member of the 'deposition faction' (as he had been at the time of the Forchheim election), his status enhanced by his marriage to an Ezzonid princess, great-granddaughter of Emperor Otto II.[192] He also had the longest record of opposition to Henry IV. His claim to the kingship must have seemed to the Saxons a very strong one.[193] Otto's hopes of the kingship must have been dashed by the opposition of Welf IV, who had been his enemy ever since he profited from Otto's deposition from the duchy of Bavaria in 1070.[194] Otto's candidature must also have been opposed by the pope's adherents in the 'deposition faction', since Gregory VII's preferred candidate was Welf.[195] Welf's candidature would, however, have been resisted by Otto and the Saxons. The two most powerful princes of the 'deposition faction' cancelled out each other's candidature. Herman of Salm was the compromise candidate, proposed by Welf IV and the 'papalists' and reluctantly accepted by the Saxons after they had given up hope of electing Otto to the kingship.

---

[191] Bruno, *Saxonicum bellum* c. 131, p. 123.   [192] See above p. 35.

[193] The foundation of the abbey of St Blasien in Northeim (*c.* 1080) as Otto's attempt to gain the support of the Gregorian party: Naumann (1967) 400–4; Jakobs (1973) 113.

[194] See above p. 70.   [195] Gregory VII, *Registrum* IX.3, p. 57.

6

⊱⊰

The second Italian expedition, 1081–1084

The conviction that the 'deposition faction' was divided by the enmity of Welf IV and Otto of Northeim doubtless persuaded Henry IV that it was safe to proceed with his Italian expedition. As the spring of 1081 approached, his preparations for departure concentrated on the securing of the south-eastern frontier of the German kingdom. On the eve of the king's Italian expedition Margrave Leopold II of Austria rebelled again at the instigation of the papal legate, Altmann of Passau. Henry's response was to confer the march of Austria on Duke Vratislav II of Bohemia. This indispensable ally was now entrusted with the defence of the whole eastern frontier: to his responsibility for the Saxon marches of Meissen and Lower Lusatia was added that for the eastern frontier of Bavaria.[1] Vratislav's son, Borivoi, was to accompany Henry on the Italian expedition of 1081 (and also on those of 1082–4).[2] Since many knights remained behind to secure the German kingdom, Henry's army consisted 'partly of his own forces, partly of mercenaries or common soldiers'.[3]

Entering Italy by the Brenner Pass in March, the army moved rapidly, reaching Verona by Easter (4 April). Ten days later Henry was in Milan; early in May he reached Ravenna. Turning aside from the direct route to Rome, he sought advice and military assistance from Wibert of Ravenna.[4] Gregory VII was informed in May that the king had only 'a small force of Germans and Lombards' and intended 'to recruit an army from those who dwell in the

---

[1] *Vita Altmanni Pataviensis* c. 25, p. 236; *Annales Mellicenses* 1081, p. 500. See Meyer von Knonau (1900) 3:350–1; Wegener (1959) 119; Lechner (1976) 111–12.

[2] *Annales Pegavienses* pp. 237–8. See Wegener (1959) 119; Fenske (1977) 259.

[3] Deusdedit, *Libellus contra invasores* II.11, p. 329. See Meyer von Knonau (1900) 3:353.

[4] Bernold, *Chronicon* 1081, p. 437; *DD H IV* 330–1. See Meyer von Knonau (1900) 3:377–80; Ziese (1982) 74–5; Cowdrey (1983) 146. There is a tradition that in April 1081 in Pavia Henry was exhorted to abandon his plans by Bernard of Menthon, archdeacon of Aosta (renowned for restoring two hostels for pilgrims on the Alpine pass which bears his name, the Great St Bernard). This tradition perhaps arose from a thirteenth-century reworking of an incident involving Henry II in 1004. The saint probably died in 1008, not 1081, as Meyer von Knonau (1900) 3:379 n. 57, concluded. See Pidoux de la Maduère (1935) 690–6; Volpini (1967) 259–63.

neighbourhood of Ravenna and in the march [of Fermo]'. Henry's intention was 'to come to Rome in Whitsuntide'. Gregory felt confident that the king would never reach Rome because he would be unable to requisition supplies in the Italian kingdom: 'he cannot have *fodrum* from those through whose lands he passes'.[5] (The term *fodrum* is defined in an early eleventh-century Italian legal document as 'public service, that is, bread and wine, meat and grain'.)[6] In the event, however, Henry successfully demanded the *fodrum* owed to the crown[7] and the royal army appeared before Rome on 21 May and pitched camp in the 'field of Nero' on the north bank of the Tiber. The efficiency of the operation undoubtedly owed much to Wibert of Ravenna, to whose organising skills Henry would be indebted in the war against Gregory VII's supporters during the next three years.[8]

The pope had relied on his most important ally, Margravine Matilda of Tuscany, to bar the way of any royal expedition to Rome. She had recently linked her fortunes inextricably with those of the papacy by surrendering to St Peter all the allodial lands of the house of Canossa in Tuscany and the estates which she had inherited from her mother in Lotharingia. She had received these properties back from the pope as a benefice, with the duty of defending the cause of St Peter and his vicar, the pope.[9] At the time of Henry's Italian expedition, however, Matilda's power had been seriously damaged. In October 1080, a few days after the battle of Hohenmölsen, her vassals had been defeated at the battle of Volta, south of Lake Garda, 'by an army from almost all of Lombardy'.[10] This army had presumably been recruited by the Lombard bishops who had pressed for decisive action at the council of Brixen. Their continued enthusiasm for the cause of Henry and his antipope was demonstrated by the king's sudden appearance before Rome, made possible only by their cooperation. Henry's Lombard supporters expected him to complete the process begun in Brixen, the enforcing of Gregory VII's abdication and the enthronement of his successor. Gregory, however, believed that Henry had come to negotiate a second Canossa and was prepared to make unprecedented concessions to the pope in return for the lifting of the excommunication and the conferring of the imperial crown, neither of which Gregory was prepared to permit.[11] There is no trace of any such offer on Henry's part in any royal document.[12]

---

[5] Gregory VII, *Registrum* IX.II, p. 588.   [6] Brühl (1968) 1:541.   [7] *DD H IV* 334, 336.

[8] Meyer von Knonau (1900) 3:388; Ziese (1982) 74–6.

[9] *MGH Constitutiones* I, 654–5. See Overmann (1895) 143–4, 239–40; Meyer von Knonau (1900) 3:259; Zema (1944) 160–1; Struve (1995) 46.

[10] Bernold, *Chronicon* 1081, p. 436; Bonizo of Sutri, *Ad amicum* IX, p. 613. See Overmann (1895) 147; Meyer von Knonau (1900) 3:316–17; Struve (1995) 47–8.

[11] Gregory VII, *Registrum* IX.II, pp. 588–9. Cf. IX.4, pp. 577–9. See Meyer von Knonau (1900) 3:376, 380 n. 59; Cowdrey (1983) 146–7.

[12] The only Henrician source that attributes a conciliatory purpose to the expedition is the

The only direct evidence for Henry's intentions in spring 1081 is the manifesto to 'the Roman clergy and people, the greater and the lesser', announcing his imminent arrival. Henry congratulated the Romans on their 'fidelity and goodwill' towards his father. He himself could not visit them previously, because of 'the powerlessness of youth' and subsequently because of 'the fury of tyrannical treachery' (that is, rebellion in Germany). Now he had come to receive his 'due and hereditary dignity', the office of emperor, 'by the common consent and favour of you all'. His tone was conciliatory. He strongly denied his enemies' accusation that he wished to 'overturn the commonwealth' of the Romans. His only criticism was of the Romans' failure to provide the traditional welcoming ceremonies for an emperor elect. 'We wonder that . . . you sent no legation to meet us with customary solemnity.' The manifesto repeated none of the charges made against Gregory VII in Brixen. For the measures agreed in Brixen the manifesto substituted a vague reference to further consultations with the Romans and 'our other faithful men' to remove 'the long discord of kingship and priesthood'.[13] Henry's promise not to 'diminish the honour of St Peter, the prince of the apostles', suggested that Henry was ready to abandon his antipope, if that was the price of the Romans' acquiescence in his imperial coronation.[14] Henry's primary concern, according to the manifesto of 1081, was to be crowned emperor. The resolution of his dispute with the papacy was a secondary matter.

The success of the king's plans depended on the cooperation of the Romans. 'We found you far different from what we hoped,' he wrote to them the following year, 'for those whom we thought to be friends, we found to be enemies.'[15] Henry had reached Rome, apparently without siege machinery, too late in the year to undertake any major operation before the beginning of the summer heat, which would endanger his army. The Romans' refusal to open their gates to him doomed his hopes of being crowned emperor in 1081. His army remained before Rome until the last week of June; then, after laying waste to the surrounding villages, he returned to the north.[16] Gregory VII had been right to boast that 'the Romans and those who are around us are ready faithfully and promptly to serve God and us in all things'. Gregory seems to have purchased the loyalty of the Romans by means of regular gifts.[17] When

anonymous Hersfeld polemic, *Liber de unitate ecclesiae* 1.17, p. 232; cf. 1.7, p. 218. See Zafarana (1966a) 617–700; Robinson (1978a) 91–2, 94–5, 138–9, 140–2, 171–3, 174–5.

[13] Henry IV, *Letter* 16, p. 23. See Meyer von Knonau (1900) 3:387–8; Cowdrey (1983) 148–9.

[14] Wibert was in the royal entourage: Bernold, *Chronicon* 1081, p. 437; Bonizo, *Ad amicum* IX, p. 613. See Meyer von Knonau (1900) 3:385–6; Fliche (1912) 417–22; Williams (1948–9) 820.

[15] Henry IV, *Letter* 17, p. 25.

[16] Bonizo IX, p. 613; Frutolf of Michelsberg, *Chronica* 1081, p. 94. See Meyer von Knonau (1900) 3:387–93; Partner (1972) 131–2.

[17] Gregory VII, *Registrum* IX.11, p. 589. Cf. Lupus Protospatarius, *Annales* 1083, p. 61; Henrician satire of 1084, *MGH Libelli* I, 434.

the king finally won over the majority of the Roman nobility in March 1084, his success was attributed by his enemies to 'money and terror'.[18] The Norman princes of southern Italy, especially Robert Guiscard, played an equally important role in the calculations of pope and king. Gregory VII had been reconciled with his troublesome vassals Prince Jordan I of Capua and Duke Robert of Apulia, a reconciliation forced on the pope by the imminent confrontation with Henry IV. When the king arrived in Italy, however, the Norman princes did not provide the requested military support. Robert Guiscard was preoccupied with plans of conquest in the Byzantine empire, determined to strike before the new emperor, Alexius I Comnenus, could consolidate his power.[19] In May 1081 Gregory received the alarming news that 'the king is to make an agreement with Duke Robert that the king's son will marry the duke's daughter and the king will confer the march [of Fermo] on the duke'.[20]

The king had negotiated with Robert Guiscard once before, in 1075, when his envoys called on the duke to do homage for his lands of Apulia and Calabria. Refusing to hold his duchy as a royal benefice, the duke replied that if Henry were to enfeoff him with imperial lands, he would do homage for them. Six years later, Henry seems to have taken up the duke's suggestion with the offer of the march of Fermo, lying to the north of Guiscard's territories. The negotiations with the duke in 1081 proved fruitless and no more was heard of Guiscard's enfeoffment with Fermo or of the marriage of the king's son with the duke's daughter.[21] The possibility of a rapprochement between king and duke soon disappeared as a consequence of a Byzantine approach to Henry. The beleaguered emperor sought to distract Guiscard from his Byzantine campaign by raising up enemies against him in Italy. The biography of Alexius composed by his daughter, Anna Comnena, cites a letter from Alexius to Henry, written perhaps in 1083, referring to Henry's willingness 'to share the labour of war against this iniquitous man' Guiscard and to the emperor's lavish promises of treasure in return for Henry's cooperation.[22] This letter had clearly been preceded by lengthy negotiations, conducted by two royal envoys, 'your most noble and trustworthy Count Burchard' and 'your most faithful Albert'. These envoys negotiated with the emperor in Constantinople and Burchard had long been detained there so that he might see Alexius's favourite nephew and chosen successor and give a report of him to the king.[23] The timescale

[18] Bonizo IX, p. 614.
[19] Cowdrey (1983) 138–40, 142–6; Vogel (1983) 220–37; Loud (1985) 83, 96.
[20] Gregory VII, *Registrum* IX.II, p. 598.
[21] William of Apulia, *Gesta Roberti* IV.169–84, pp. 212–14. See Meyer von Knonau (1900) 3:376–7; Cowdrey (1983) 147–8; E. Goez (1996) 13–14.
[22] Anna Comnena Porphyrogenita, *Alexias* III.10, pp. 120–3.
[23] Meyer von Knonau (1900) 3:447–8; Cowdrey (1983) 149–50. The envoys cannot be identified from Henrician sources; but see Chalandon (1907) 267.

implied by Alexius's letter suggests that the negotiations with Henry began as early as the summer of 1081.

Henry spent the summer and autumn of 1081 in central and northern Italy, systematically undermining the authority of his enemies, Matilda of Tuscany and Bishop Anselm II of Lucca, and building up the power of his own supporters. A notable beneficiary was Patriarch Henry of Aquileia, whose 'most devoted service' was rewarded with the grant of the two bishoprics of Parenzo and Trieste, including the right to elect and invest bishops in these sees.[24] Henry also invested a new margrave of Fermo and duke of Spoleto: an action which directly challenged Gregory VII's conception of the territorial rights of the papacy. The march and the duchy were regarded by Gregory VII as the property of the Roman church, 'the land of St Peter'.[25] The king, however, regarded the march and the duchy as imperial offices that could be held only by his own appointees. The plan to enfeoff Robert Guiscard with the march of Fermo was soon succeeded by that of conferring the march and the duchy on Rainer II, son of Hugo-Ugiccio I, duke of Spoleto, of the Tuscan house of the Widones.[26] It was an appointment doubly offensive to Gregory VII, not only violating the supposed proprietary rights of St Peter, but also promoting a man who had fallen under papal censure for alleged fratricide.

A series of royal diplomas of June and July showed favour to the opponents of Matilda of Tuscany. The citizens of Lucca[27] and Pisa were freed from the regime imposed by the house of Canossa. The king promised the Pisans that he would not 'send any margrave into Tuscany without the approval of twelve men elected in an assembly summoned together by ringing the bells'. The diploma for Pisa provides an insight into the citizens' political aspirations and reveals that the king was ready to further these aspirations.[28] The rights guaranteed to the Pisans served in the short term to win their support against Matilda and in the long term to provide a salutary check on the authority of any future margrave of Tuscany. In mentioning the king's intention to 'send a margrave into Tuscany' at some unspecified date, the diploma for Pisa corroborates the report of the historian Rangerius of Lucca that during his visit to Lucca (19–20 July) Henry 'deprived Matilda of her former office'.[29] The sentence of the royal court, besides deposing Matilda from the margraviate of Tuscany, deprived her of her benefices and allodial possessions both in

---

[24] *DD H IV* 338–9. See Schmidinger (1954) 15, 69.

[25] Gregory VII, *Registrum* II.47–8, V.14a, c. 7, pp. 186–8, 371.

[26] *DD H IV* 338–9, 345, 356, 359. See Meyer von Knonau (1900) 3:393–4.

[27] *D H IV* 334.

[28] *D H IV* 336. See Meyer von Knonau (1900) 3:394–5, 398–400; Waley (1969) 8, 25; Hyde (1973) 49–50; Struve (1995) 51, 53.

[29] Rangerius of Lucca, *Vita Anselmi* III.2, p. 1257. See Overmann (1895) 232–8; Meyer von Knonau (1900) 3:397; Struve (1995) 52–3.

Tuscany and in Lotharingia. The earliest direct reference to Matilda's deposition in a royal document occurs in a diploma of 1 June 1085, recording the disposal of 'estates which belonged to Countess Matilda and came by law and judicial process into our power'.[30] Henry was welcomed to Lucca in 1081 by the enemies of Bishop Anselm II who had expelled him from the city after Matilda's defeat at Volta the previous October. Anselm's principal opponent, Count Ugiccio, placed his troops at the king's disposal for an expedition against Rome.[31] The king's arrival was equally welcome to the canons of the cathedral who had rebelled against Anselm's attempts to reform the chapter and who now wished to elect the Lucchese subdeacon Peter as bishop in Anselm's place. The king obliged them by investing the anti-bishop and Wibert of Ravenna consecrated Peter on the occasion of the royal visit to Lucca.[32] Almost the whole diocese, with the exception of the fortress of Moriana, fell under the control of the anti-bishop.

After an autumn spent harrying Matilda's forces in Tuscany, the king withdrew north of the Apennines.[33] By the end of February 1082 he was once more encamped before Rome.[34] He was clearly determined to avoid the frustrations of the previous year, when he had arrived too late to attempt a serious military operation. Nevertheless the royal manifesto to the Romans, announcing his imminent arrival in 1082, reveals that Henry still hoped to enter Rome peacefully. He continued to address the Romans in conciliatory language, despite their opposition to him the previous summer. He knew them to be 'friends of justice' who would never have resisted him when he came to Rome in 1081 'purely for the sake of justice', had they not been misled by 'the tricks of Hildebrand'. The king's manifesto revived the themes of the Henrician letters of 1076: the divinely ordained kingship of Henry IV, his hereditary rights in Italy, the crimes of Hildebrand against Church and king. 'God has ordained [us], although unworthy, from our very cradle and daily shows that it was He who ordained us' by frustrating 'the plots of Hildebrand and his supporters'. 'We are still king, even though [Hildebrand] opposes us.' Henry's survival and the death of the anti-king whom the pope had approved, demonstrated the justice of the royal cause. The Romans should, therefore, admit him to their city to be crowned emperor, as they had promised to do in the reign of Emperor Henry III. 'We ask you . . . not to deny us our ancestral honour, which you transmitted to us by the hand of our father.' Henry was

---

[30] *D H IV* 373 (falsified). See Struve (1995) 53–4. Cf. *DD H IV* 379, 385.
[31] W. Goez (1973) 205–39.
[32] Rangerius, *Vita Anselmi* III.2, p. 1257. See Meyer von Knonau (1900) 3:381–2, 400; Struve (1995) 50–1. Anselm II of Lucca resided with Matilda as her most influential counsellor. See Kittel (1931) 220–35; Violante (1961) 399–407.   [33] *DD H IV* 340–1.
[34] Bonizo, *Ad amicum* IX, p. 613. See Meyer von Knonau (1900) 3:432–3; Ziese (1982) 74.

ready to pardon the Romans for their conduct of the previous summer because they had always kept faith with his ancestors and indeed with him, until the accession of Hildebrand, who had deceived them.[35]

While the manifesto of 1081 had been reticent about Hildebrand's misdemeanours, that of 1082 contained a lengthy attack on the pope, whose conduct was 'more cruel than the persecution of Decius'.[36] The 1082 manifesto did not, however, revive the accusations about the pope's life and election made in the Henrician letters of 1076 and the Brixen decree of 1080, concentrating instead on the charge in the polemics inspired by the council of Mainz of 31 May 1080, that Hildebrand was a warmonger and a schismatic.[37] The manifesto of 1081 had said nothing of removing Hildebrand from the papacy: that of 1082 called repeatedly for him to be judged by the king and the Roman clergy and people. For the first time Henrician polemic dealt directly with the principal Gregorian canon law weapon: the claim that the pope cannot be judged. Henry's earlier attacks on Gregory VII had evaded this claim: at the council of Worms (1076) by calling for the pope's abdication; at the council of Brixen (1080) by declaring him an intruder and a heretic and therefore no pope. The 1082 manifesto, however, took issue with Hildebrand's statement 'that he must be judged by no one'. 'This is as much as to say, "he may do whatever he pleases". But this is not Christ's rule, which says: "whoever would be great among you, must be your servant" (Matthew 20:26).'[38] Hildebrand must be judged by a council to be held either in northern Italy in the royal entourage or in Rome on the king's arrival. 'If he can and ought to be pope, we shall obey him; but if not, let another man, suited to the needs of the Church, be provided for the Church by your decision and ours.' As in the 1081 manifesto, there was no word of the claims of Wibert of Ravenna. Nothing better illustrates the flexibility that had governed Henry's conduct since the debacle of 1076 than his treatment of Wibert's candidature for the papacy. He had acquiesced in the nomination of Wibert in Brixen in order to appease the Lombard opponents of Gregory VII: he now ignored Wibert's existence in order to appease the Romans.

Since the manifesto of 1082 had no more effect on the Romans than its predecessor, the royal army spent the whole of Lent (9 March – 23 April) besieging the city. A breach in the Leonine wall almost enabled the royal troops to

---

[35] Henry IV, *Letter* 17, pp. 24–6 (composed by Gottschalk of Aachen). See Meyer von Knonau (1900) 3:433–6; Erdmann (1939) 221–2; Cowdrey (1983) 150–2, suggesting (150 n. 156, 237–8) that the extant version of the 'Promise of Oppenheim' (see above pp. 157–8) was 'a companion-piece' to the 1082 manifesto. [36] Henry IV, *Letter* 17, p. 25. Cf. *Letter* 13, p. 20.

[37] *Letter* 17, p. 25. See above p. 197.

[38] *Ibid.* p. 26. Cf. Gregory VII, *Dictatus papae* 19: *Registrum* II.55a, p. 206, based on the spurious *Constitutum Silvestri* c. 20 and *Decretales Pseudoisidorianae* p. 449.

seize the Leonine city, but they were foiled by the resolute action of the pope and his Roman allies.[39] Having failed to break into the city from the north, the royal army took a circuitous route around the city to renew the siege from the south. This manoeuvre proved equally unsuccessful, despite a fierce attack on the city on the night of Palm Sunday (17 April), which cost many lives.[40] While his army was repositioning, Henry visited the great Sabine abbey of St Mary of Farfa (17 March). The abbey had enjoyed imperial protection since Carolingian times and remained throughout the Ottonian and Salian period a centre of imperialist sympathies.[41] Henry 'was received by all the brethren most nobly, very honourably and lovingly, for previously his coming had been greatly longed for by all'. He fulfilled the expectations of the community by expelling their enemy, Rusticus Crescentii from the fortress of Farfa, which the king restored to the abbey.[42] A series of four royal diplomas from the years 1083–4 reveal how the community of Farfa benefited from Henry's presence in their vicinity, obtaining the confirmation of their possessions and privileges, gifts of former royal property and the restoration of churches and estates misappropriated by enemies.[43]

In spring 1082 the Romans remained loyal to their bishop, but the king won over an important papal ally south of Rome, Jordan I, prince of Capua. 'Terrified by the news of Henry's arrival, Prince Jordan . . . made treaties of permanent peace and submitted to him; he surrendered his son as a hostage and, together with the child, gave many gifts of cash. He did this so as not to be deprived of the government of his patrimony.'[44] Jordan celebrated Easter (24 April) with the king in Albano, where he performed homage and paid a heavy tribute. In return Henry 'confirmed, by means of a privilege sealed with a golden bull, everything appertaining to the principality of Capua but retained for himself and the empire the monastery of Monte Cassino with all its possessions'.[45] Henry imitated here the conduct of his grandfather and father, who in 1038 and 1047 had enfeoffed southern Italian princes with their principalities.[46] Jordan's father, Richard I of Capua had drawn attention to the

---

[39] Bonizo, *Ad amicum* IX, pp. 613–14; Benzo of Alba, *Ad Heinricum* VI, preface, p. 514; Bernold of St Blasien, *Chronicon* 1082, p. 437; Paul of Bernried, *Vita Gregorii VII* c. 8, p. 477.

[40] Benzo claimed to have organised it (*Ad Heinricum* VI, preface, pp. 516–20). Cf. Marianus, *Chronicon* 1104 (=1082), p. 562. See Meyer von Knonau (1900) 3:437–41; Partner (1972) 132–3.

[41] *Orthodoxa defensio imperialis* c. 11, p. 542. See Heinzelmann (1904) 113.

[42] Gregory of Catino, *Historiae Farfenses* c. 8, p. 561. See Toubert (1973) 2:1103–26.

[43] *DD H IV* 350, 355, 358, 361. See Meyer von Knonau (1900) 3:440; Vehse (1929–30) 157.

[44] William of Apulia, *Gesta Roberti* V.110–17, p. 242. Cf. *Chronica monasterii Casinensis* III.50, pp. 430, 431–2. See Meyer von Knonau (1900) 3:442–6; Deér (1972) 35, 138–9, 142–3; Cowdrey (1983) 154–5, 158; Loud (1985) 60–3.

[45] *D H IV* *502 (*Chronica monasterii Casinensis* III.50, p. 432). See Cowdrey (1983) 245–6.

[46] Deér (1972) 7–8, 24, 28, 44, 46–7, 75, 112.

claims of the king of Italy in his oath of 1073 to Gregory VII. 'I shall swear fealty to King Henry when I am admonished by you or by your successors to do so, nevertheless saving my fealty to the holy Roman church.'[47] Henry's presence in Italy prompted Jordan to swear fealty without waiting for papal admonition. Jordan's fealty to the king incurred not only papal excommunication but also an attack on Capua (1083) by his uncle, Duke Robert Guiscard.[48] Nevertheless the prince of Capua remained the loyal vassal of Henry IV until his death in 1090.

Jordan was accompanied to the royal entourage in Albano by his illustrious neighbour, Desiderius, abbot of Monte Cassino. The great abbey of Monte Cassino, like Farfa, had long enjoyed imperial protection and generosity: 'three Ottos, five Henries and Conrad . . . all loved the church of Monte Cassino and adorned her with great gifts'.[49] Meanwhile, however, the abbey had developed close ties with the papacy. Desiderius's predecessor, Frederick, had become, as Pope Stephen IX, the first of the three Cassinese monks who acceded to the papacy during the reform period. (Desiderius himself was to be elected the second Cassinese pope in 1086.) Monte Cassino became 'the spiritual armoury of the reform papacy and its strategic base for the recovery of the southern Italian Church, accomplished through the alliance with the Normans'.[50] When, therefore, early in 1082 the excommunicate Henry IV was in the vicinity of Monte Cassino, Desiderius, pulled by conflicting loyalties, showed none of the alacrity of Berard of Farfa in welcoming his abbey's protector. When the abbot failed to obey a royal summons, Henry threatened that unless Desiderius met him immediately in Farfa, he would 'grievously repent' his conduct. Desiderius replied that he could not join Henry 'because of the Normans' (evidently meaning Robert Guiscard, the pope's ally) 'but if [the king] perhaps wished to make peace with the Roman pontiff, he would find some opportunity of coming to him'. Angered by his prevarication, Henry instructed Jordan of Capua to compel Desiderius's attendance and commanded the abbot to celebrate Easter with him. After writing in vain to Gregory VII for advice, Desiderius obeyed the royal command so as to protect his monks from the revenge of the king or Jordan. Throughout his week's sojourn in Albano, however, he observed the Gregorian prohibitions on contact with excommunicates: 'he did not give the kiss [of peace] to anyone; he did not pray or eat or drink with any [members of the entourage]', even though many of them were his friends.[51]

Henry commanded Desiderius 'to perform fealty to him and become his

---

[47] Gregory VII, *Registrum* I.21a, p. 36.   [48] *Ibid.* IX.27, p. 610.
[49] *Chronica monasterii Casinensis* IV.109, p. 576; cf. III.31, IV.112, pp. 403, 576. See Bloch (1986) 2:632–43, 758–70.   [50] Klewitz (1957) 103.
[51] *Chronica monasterii Casinensis* III.50, pp. 431–4.

vassal by [giving him] his hands and receive the abbey from [the king's] hands'. There are sporadic references in early eleventh-century narrative sources to bishops performing homage to kings, but this incident of 1082 is the earliest recorded case of a specific royal demand for homage from a reluctant prelate.[52] Henry spoke in his manifesto of 1082 of his readiness 'to preserve all honour to St Peter', but these promises did not involve the sacrifice of royal rights over the churches, in accordance with Gregory VII's recent investiture legislation. Desiderius refused the demand of the excommunicate king and only the intercession of Jordan of Capua saved his abbey from severe reprisals. Jordan induced the abbot at last to enter the king's presence and to promise his friendship and his help 'in acquiring the imperial crown'. When he was asked to receive investiture of his abbatial staff from the king's hands, Desiderius managed to defer the matter until 'he had seen [Henry] in possession of the crown of the Roman empire'. Finally, when he departed for Monte Cassino, Henry conferred on him 'a privilege sealed with a golden bull', confirming the abbey's possessions.[53] Behind Henry's insistence on this meeting there presumably lay an attempt to negotiate his imperial coronation at the hands of Gregory VII, using Desiderius as an intermediary acceptable to the pope.[54] As his manifestos of 1081 and 1082 revealed, Henry's principal concern was to secure the imperial crown and he was prepared to jettison his antipope if this was the price of Roman acquiescence.

After Easter Henry returned to the siege of Rome, but the onset of warmer weather persuaded him to withdraw to the north. His subsequent campaign in Tuscany may have involved troops provided by Jordan of Capua.[55] The conduct of the siege of Rome and the small-scale war of attrition against the Romans was left to Wibert of Ravenna, who made his headquarters in Tivoli.[56] The siege was now causing enough hardship to provoke the formation of a peace party in Rome, who by the beginning of 1083 were opening negotiations with the king. Perhaps the Henrician propaganda which portrayed Gregory VII as a warlord who 'stained the Church with the blood of her sons' was not without influence in Rome. On 4 May 1082 an assembly of the Roman clergy unanimously rejected the proposition that 'the property

[52] Minninger (1978) 35–7.
[53] D H IV*503 (Chronica monasterii Casinensis III.50, p. 433). See Meyer von Knonau (1900) 3:441–6; Cowdrey (1983) 154–65.
[54] Desiderius's alleged excommunication as a result of this meeting: Hugh of Flavigny, Chronicon II, pp. 466–8. See Meyer von Knonau (1903) 4:177–81; Leccisotti (1947) 307–19; Loud (1979) 316–21; Cowdrey (1983) 156–65, 245–6.
[55] Rangerius, Vita Anselmi III.2, p. 1259. See Meyer von Knonau (1900) 3:456.
[56] Bonizo, Ad amicum IX, pp. 613–14; Bernold, Chronicon 1082, p. 437. See Meyer von Knonau (1900) 3:446–7; Ziese (1982) 75–6.

of the churches could be mortgaged to raise money to resist Archbishop Wibert of Ravenna, when he tried to seize the Roman see'. Gregory VII's attempt to pay for the defence of Rome was countered with the canonical principle that ecclesiastical property could never be used 'for secular warfare'.[57] The pope was compelled to seek the help of his ally, Matilda of Tuscany, who, together with the papal legate Anselm of Lucca, requisitioned the plate of the monastery of S. Apollonio di Canossa 'to be sent to the pope for the defence of the Roman church'.[58]

The king's summer campaign of 1082 deprived his outlawed vassal Matilda of Tuscany of 'fortresses, estates and monasteries', while the margravine remained pinned in her stronghold of Canossa, 'wringing her hands for the loss of Tuscany'. Henry's autumn campaigning was directed against a new opponent, Margrave Wido II of Sezze, of the Aledramid dynasty, formerly an ally of the king's mother-in-law, Adelaide of Turin. 'The king punished Wido by destroying [his fortress of] Sezze', a punitive operation which forced the margrave's surrender. According to Benzo of Alba, Henry's main business in the north-west was to hold talks with his mother-in-law. 'The lady Adelaide sought out her son, the king: she was willing to be the mediator between the king and Matilda.'[59] A negotiated settlement with his principal enemy in northern Italy would have cut off the pope's most important source of emergency supplies and freed Henry's hands to deal with the Romans. Nothing is known of Adelaide's mediation except Benzo's optimistic account of her meeting with the king. All that is certain is that Matilda remained Henry's enemy for the rest of his life.[60]

Towards the end of 1082 Henry may have anticipated an attack on his Italian kingdom from the north. According to a rumour reported in southern Germany, 'King Herman, grieving for the sufferings of the apostolic see and wishing to deliver her from the hands of Henry, prepared an expedition to Italy.'[61] In November Henry was in Verona, where he met Liutold of Eppenstein, duke of Carinthia and margrave of Verona.[62] The king's talks with Liutold presumably included the matter of closing the Alpine passes to

---

[57] Zafarana (1966b) 399–403. See Meyer von Knonau (1900) 3:452–4; Hüls (1978) 119, 171, 185, 191; Cowdrey (1983) 152–3.

[58] *De thesauro Canusinae ecclesiae, MGH SS* 12, 385 n. 14. See Struve (1995) 60–1.

[59] Benzo, *Ad Heinricum* VI.4, p. 544. See Meyer von Knonau (1900) 3:456–8; Struve (1995) 59–60.

[60] Sigebert of Gembloux, *Leodiensium epistola* c. 13, p. 464: Matilda was commanded by Hildebrand 'to make war on [Henry] for the remission of her sins'. See Erdmann (1935) 244–5; Bischoff (1948) 25–6; Robinson (1973) 184–91; Struve (1995) 61–2.

[61] Bernold, *Chronicon* 1082, p. 437. See Meyer von Knonau (1900) 3:461, 470.

[62] *D H IV* 348. See Meyer von Knonau (1900) 3:459, 461.

prevent the anti-king's expedition. Herman of Salm's proposed expedition was intended to cement his alliance with the pope's adherents in Germany.[63] A successful Italian expedition would establish Herman's qualifications for the kingship, guarantee him the loyalty of the papal party in Germany and offset the failures of the first year of his reign. Neither in Saxony nor in southern Germany had the anti-king made headway against Henry's supporters. His attempts to force Bishop Benno of Osnabrück to commit himself to the anti-Henrician party were rendered ineffective by Benno's diplomacy, exploiting his friendship with powerful members of the rebel party. In south-eastern Germany, meanwhile, the struggle for control of the march of Austria between Henry's ally Duke Vratislav II of Bohemia and the deposed Margrave Leopold II had brought disaster for the rebels. At the battle of Mailberg, on the Austrian-Moravian frontier (12 May 1082) Leopold's forces were annihilated by the army of Vratislav.[64] The final setback that prevented Herman's Italian expedition was the death of Otto of Northeim (11 January 1083), his most powerful ally in Saxony. Herman 'was forced to hasten back to Saxony' because 'he had no doubt that [Otto's] death would result in a very great schism'.[65] This was an accurate prognostication: the anti-Henrician party in Saxony immediately began to fragment, leaving the anti-king without the means of consolidating his hold over Saxony or mounting a serious challenge to Henry IV.

Soon after his meeting with Liutold of Carinthia Henry turned south on his third expedition to Rome. When he arrived before Rome at the end of the year, his army had been reinforced by one thousand picked knights, provided by Archbishop Tedald of Milan and his suffragans.[66] Henry's cause was now prospering. It was perhaps at this time that his negotiations with Byzantium bore fruit and that he received the gifts and the letter from Emperor Alexius I Comnenus that sealed their alliance. The imperial envoy Constantine, 'catepan of dignities' delivered a preliminary payment of silver coins to the value of 144,000 gold pieces and one hundred silken garments. In his letter Alexius addressed Henry as his 'most noble and truly Christian brother'. Using the ancient language of the 'brotherhood of kings' with which the Roman emperors had formerly saluted their neighbours, the oriental monarchs, Alexius nevertheless made clear the respective status of German king and Byzantine emperor by demanding an oath from his ally. Henry must swear to

---

[63] There is no evidence of contact between Herman and the pope, but he received a letter from the prominent Gregorian William of Hirsau, *Briefsammlungen* pp. 41–3. See Erdmann (1938) 166–7.   [64] Meyer von Knonau (1900) 3:462–7.

[65] Bernold, *Chronicon* 1083, p. 437. See Meyer von Knonau (1900) 3:501–5; Lange (1961) 76–7.

[66] Benzo, *Ad Heinricum* 1.20, p. 158; Landulf Senior, *Historia Mediolanensis* III.32, p. 99. See Meyer von Knonau (1900) 3:461.

participate in the expedition against 'the murderous and sinful enemy of God and of Christians', Robert Guiscard, that his envoys in Constantinople had agreed on his behalf. Once he had taken the oath, Henry would receive an additional payment of 216,000 gold pieces and the salaries of twenty court offices. As for their future relations, Alexius's letter referred to the possibility of a marriage alliance.[67] He was thinking of his nephew and heir John: his prospective bride was not identified. (Henry's only daughter, Agnes, had been betrothed to Duke Frederick of Swabia in 1079, although the marriage had probably not yet taken place.) As an earnest of his goodwill, Alexius sent personal gifts of great value, which greatly impressed the Henrician chroniclers.[68]

Henry's improving fortunes, together with the hardships created by Wibert of Ravenna's blockade of the city, were now eroding the loyalty of the Romans towards their bishop.[69] Some members of the nobility and clergy without the pope's knowledge had sent envoys to the king even before his return to Rome at the end of 1082.[70] There now existed in the city a peace party prepared to assist Henry in what had been his primary objective since his first appearance before Rome: the acquisition of the imperial crown with the consent of the Romans. The question of who was to possess the apostolic see had always been subordinate to that of the coronation: it was to be settled with due regard to the sensibilities of the Roman clergy and people. Henry had made no attempt to press Wibert's claims and expressed his readiness to accept Gregory VII as pope, if a council declared in his favour. As late as 1083 Henry was prepared to negotiate directly with Gregory. Bishop Benno II Osnabrück was given the task of 'establishing peace and harmony' between Henry and Gregory: 'almost every day he hastened between king and pope as intermediary.'[71] His previous experience of negotiating in Rome and the fact that Gregory regarded him as a possible recruit to his party,[72] explain why Benno was selected for this role. His efforts, however, achieved nothing: 'such inflexibility could never be softened'. Abbot Hugh I of Cluny seems to have undertaken a similar mission in 1083. He met his royal godson in Sutri but could not reconcile pope and king as he had done at Canossa.[73]

During these negotiations Henry achieved the first military success of the siege of Rome. He renewed his attack on the Leonine city during Lent 1083,

[67] Anna Comnena, *Alexias* III.10, pp. 120–3. See Meyer von Knonau (1900) 3:481–3.

[68] Benzo, *Ad Heinricum* VI.4, p. 548; cf. *ibid.* 1.17, p. 152; Frutolf, *Chronica* 1083, p. 96; *Vita Heinrici IV* c. 1, p. 12.   [69] Gregory VII, *Registrum* IX.35a, p. 628.

[70] Lupus Protospatarius, *Annales* 1083, p. 61.

[71] *Vita Bennonis Osnabrugensis* c. 22, pp. 422–4. See Meyer von Knonau (1900) 3:471; Cowdrey (1983) 166.   [72] Gregory VII, *Registrum* IX.10, p. 587.

[73] Rainald of Vézelay, *Vita Hugonis* IV.26, 903D–904A; Cowdrey (1978) 29 n. 42. See Diener (1959) 368, 387; Cowdrey (1983) 167 n. 195.

three times disrupting the pope's attempt to hold a Lenten synod. After unsuccessful attacks on the Leonine wall and the fortress next to the monastery of
S. Paolo fuori le Mura he returned to the siege in May, this time with better
fortune. On 3 June the Leonine city, including the basilica of St Peter, at last
fell into his hands. The old city on the eastern bank of the Tiber remained in
the hands of the pope's supporters. Gregory VII now established himself in
the Castel S. Angelo, the great fortress on the west bank controlling the Ponte
S. Angelo, which linked the Leonine city with the old city. The account in
the papal register presents the king's success as the result 'not so much of the
courage of his men as of the negligence of the citizens'. The vigilance of the
guards on the Leonine wall had been undermined by famine and dwindling
numbers.[74] The resultant victory is reflected in two royal diplomas issued
during the subsequent three weeks, the work of Gottschalk of Aachen. That
of 15 June for the abbey of Farfa contains a prayer of thanksgiving to the Virgin
Mary.[75] Gottschalk composed the diploma of 22 June for the church of
Bremen as a triumphant piece of royal propaganda with a dating clause which
exaggerates the recent success: 'enacted in Rome after the capture of the city'.
Liemar of Bremen, now Henry's most important German adviser, 'the foremost lover of our name and very greatly deserving of our favour', is portrayed
as the ideal vassal. 'In the Saxon war he stood by [the king] in the greatest
danger in two very fierce battles; he once acted as [Henry's] envoy at the apostolic see, opposing Hildebrand, the disturber of the world, amidst great
difficulties and anxieties; three times he came with [the king] to attack and
capture the city of Rome.'[76]

   These diplomas were issued in Henry's new headquarters, the imperial
palace beside St Peter's.[77] The king now received the submission of the majority of the Roman nobles. The treasure that Henry had recently received from
the Byzantine emperor doubtless played a part in this submission.[78] Most of
the Romans agreed with Henry that the pope should be required to summon
a synod in mid-November to resolve the dispute between king and pope.
Unknown to the pope, however, a secret treaty had been concluded between
the Romans and the king before his departure for northern Italy at the beginning of July. The Romans had sworn to bring about the imperial coronation
within fifteen days of Henry's return to Rome in the autumn. Gregory VII was
to perform the coronation. If he failed to do so, according to the Romans'
oath, 'we shall elect a pope on [Henry's] advice according to the canons and

---

[74] Gregory VII, *Registrum* IX.35a, p. 628; *Vita Heinrici IV* c. 6, p. 23; Landulf Senior, *Historia*
    III.32, pp. 99–100; *Annales Pegavienses* p. 238. See Meyer von Knonau (1900) 3:472–8.
[75] *D H IV* 350.   [76] *Ibid.* 351.
[77] The palace was built for Charlemagne and served later emperors (except Otto III) as their
    residence: see Brühl (1954) 1–30.   [78] Bernold, *Chronicon* 1083, p. 438.

we shall take pains in good faith both that this pope crowns [Henry] and that the Romans do fealty to him'.[79] Both the agreement to hold a synod and the terms of the Romans' oath correspond to the programme of the royal manifesto of 1082. In the measures of 1083, as in the manifesto of 1082, the principal consideration was that Henry should be crowned emperor as soon as possible.

On his departure from the city (1 or 2 July) Henry took hostages from the Roman nobility to ensure the performance of their promises.[80] His most important measure to safeguard the gains of the previous spring was the building of a fortress on the hill known as the Palatiolus, east of St Peter's. Henry left here a garrison of three hundred knights under the command of Udalric of Godesheim, one of the five advisers excommunicated by Alexander II and subsequently by Gregory VII.[81] Dismissing his Italian contingents (29 June), he took only German troops to Tuscany, where he spent the late summer and autumn. His only recorded military operation was the siege of Matilda's castle of Carpi, north of Modena.[82] Meanwhile Gregory VII issued invitations to the November synod in Rome, announcing that the synod's purpose was to bring to a 'fitting end' 'the quarrels and discord that have long disturbed the relations of the apostolic see and the royal power'. Papal representatives had received from 'the more important men who are now at the court of Henry, the so-called king' a sworn guarantee of safe passage for those attending the synod.[83] The letter of invitation to the Germans declared that the pope was prepared to prove in the synod his innocence of the charges brought against him by the king, but with the precondition that 'the property of which the holy Roman church is known to have been despoiled, should be restored'.[84] Gregory here invoked the *exceptio spolii*, the canon law principle that no churchman could stand trial as long as he was deprived of any of his possessions.[85] While part of his city was in royal hands, the pope was not obliged to answer to the synod. Gregory was ready to negotiate a peace settlement at the November synod, but not at the expense of the rights of the apostolic see.

The fall of the Leonine city enabled the Roman peace party to compel the pope to take part in the November synod. The events of late summer, however, weakened the position of the peace party and encouraged the pope to resume

[79] Cowdrey (1983) 248 (text). Cf. Bernold, *Chronicon* 1083, p. 438. See Meyer von Knonau (1900) 3:486–7.

[80] Frutolf, *Chronica* 1083, p. 96; Lupus Protospatarius, *Annales* 1083, p. 61.

[81] Bernold, *Chronicon* 1083, p. 483. See Meyer von Knonau (1900) 3:479, 489–91. See above p. 125 and below p. 360.   [82] Overmann (1895) 150; Meyer von Knonau (1900) 3:491.

[83] Gregory VII, *Epistolae Vagantes* 51, pp. 122–4.

[84] Gregory VII, *Registrum* IX.29, pp. 612–13. See Fliche (1926) 27 n. 1, 418 n. 4; Cowdrey (1983) 174 n. 227.   [85] See below p. 243.

his uncompromising attitude. The unaccustomed heat of the Roman summer proved fatal for Henry's garrison on the Palatiolus. The surviving members of the garrison were unable to prevent the fortress from falling into the hands of the Romans, who razed it to the ground. Henry's immediate response was to take prisoner a number of the pope's leading supporters in violation of his oath guaranteeing the safety of all who wished to attend the November synod. Cardinal bishop Odo of Ostia, who came to Henry's court as a papal legate, found himself detained there. The envoys of the German rebels were captured by the king on 11 November at S. Maria di Forcassi, north-west of Sutri, as he returned to Rome from Tuscany. This breach of his oath of safe conduct lost Henry the sympathy of many churchmen, including his godfather, the abbot of Cluny.[86] The king must have calculated that, having lost his most important foothold in Rome, his principal hope of influencing the November synod lay in preventing the attendance of the pope's staunchest supporters.[87] The synod, however, had nothing of the character agreed on five months before by the king and the Romans: Henry's case was not presented.[88]

Henry's hopes of being crowned emperor on his return to Rome in November were disappointed. According to Bonizo of Sutri, 'to win the favour of the people [the king] said that he was willing to receive the imperial crown from the venerable Gregory'. This concession prompted the Romans to press the pope to perform the coronation so as to save the city from further warfare. Gregory 'utterly refused to do so unless [Henry] first made public satisfaction for his excommunication'. 'For many days' the Romans continued their petitions; the pope remained obdurate and 'the king gradually began to acquire the favour of the mob'.[89] This account helps to explain the loosening of the pope's hold over Rome at the beginning of 1084. The flexibility which Bonizo attributed to Henry in these negotiations is consistent with his conduct since his first appearance before Rome. He must have hoped that the November synod would result in the repudiation of Gregory and the election of his own candidate. When these hopes proved vain, he adhered to his agreement with the Romans and was ready to accept the imperial crown from Gregory. Henry was willing to make concessions to the Romans but would make none to the pope: there would be no repetition of the proceedings at Canossa.

Henry celebrated Christmas 1083 in St Peter's. Despite the loss of his fortress on the Palatiolus, he experienced little difficulty in regaining control of

[86] Bernold, *Chronicon* 1083, p. 438. Becker (1964) 60–1 accepted the suggestion of Sander (1893) 137–8, 143, 208, that Odo's mission was to negotiate the restoration of the papal property demanded in Gregory VII, *Registrum* IX.29, p. 613.   [87] Bernold, *Chronicon* 1083, p. 438.
[88] *Registrum* IX.35a, pp. 627–8.
[89] Bonizo, *Ad amicum* IX, p. 614; Bernold, *Chronicon* 1083, p. 438. See Meyer von Knonau (1900) 3:498–500.

the Leonine city.[90] The new year brought envoys from Constantinople with more money and a letter from Alexius Comnenus, bidding Henry invade the lands of their common enemy, Robert Guiscard, according to their treaty. It was a favourable moment to invade Guiscard's territories, the duke having recently failed to defeat the rebellion of his nephew Herman of Cannae and to compel Jordan of Capua to abandon his fealty to the king.[91] Henry's invasion may have been intended to encourage further resistance to the duke and hinder him from aiding Gregory. The king did not remain long in the south: he left Rome 'around 1 February' 1084 and returned by the third week of March. For 'he was requested by the envoys of the Romans to return in peace. He returned to Rome and, pitching camp at the Porta S. Giovanni, he received the surrender of all [the Romans].'[92] On 21 March with great ceremony Henry entered the old city, in the company of Wibert of Ravenna, and took up residence in the Lateran palace.[93] During his absence in southern Italy Gregory's position in Rome suddenly deteriorated. Papalist authors attributed the collapse of his authority to the king's use of Byzantine gold.[94] Equally importantly, however, Gregory's conduct had finally created a united opposition: the war-weary, infuriated by his refusal to make peace with the king, and those who resented his autocratic style of government.[95] Early in 1084 twelve cardinals defected to the camp of the king and the antipope. Their spokesman, Beno, cardinal priest of SS. Martino e Silvestro, accused the pope of 'the most serious and intolerable errors', including that of having 'removed the cardinals from the counsels of the holy see'. Since many members of the papal administration and the lesser clergy followed the example of the defecting cardinals, Gregory was left without a papal government, a prisoner in the Castel S. Angelo.[96]

Henry was finally able to install in Rome the pope elected in Brixen three years before. Hitherto the claims of Wibert of Ravenna had not been mentioned in the king's negotiations with the Romans. After the basilica of St Peter fell into Henry's hands in June 1083, it was possible for him to complete the

---

[90] Frutolf, *Chronica* 1084, p. 96.

[91] Anna Comnena, *Alexias* v.3, pp. 160–3; Frutolf, *Chronica* 1084, pp. 96–8. But see Bernold, *Chronicon* 1084, p. 440. See Meyer von Knonau (1900) 3:484–5, 521–3.

[92] Frutolf, *Chronica* 1084, p. 98. Cf. Bernold, *Chronicon* 1084, p. 440.

[93] *D H IV* 356. See Meyer von Knonau (1900) 3:526–8.

[94] *Vita Anselmi Lucensis* c. 22, p. 20; Bonizo, *Ad amicum* IX, p. 614; Wido of Ferrara, *De scismate* I.20, p. 549.

[95] An alleged attempt to obtain a divine judgement in S. Maria in Pallara, Rome, which demonstrated the justice of Henry's cause: *Iudicium de regno et sacerdotio*, ed. Cowdrey (1983) 247–8. See Ziese (1982) 83; Cowdrey (1983) 168–9.

[96] Beno, *Gesta Romanae ecclesiae* I.2, p. 370. See Klewitz (1957) 68–9, 77–9; Hüls (1977) 90, 100–2, 110; Robinson (1990) 37, 100.

process begun in Brixen by enthroning Wibert as pope, but he was unwilling to proceed without the approval of a substantial number of the Roman nobility and clergy.[97] Wibert left Rome for Ravenna in July 1083 and remained there for six months. Since Henry's secret treaty with the Romans envisaged a synod in November 1083 preceding the imperial coronation, Wibert's absence at this crucial time might suggest that Henry no longer expected to be crowned by the antipope of Brixen, who had become an embarrassment to him.[98] Wibert returned to Rome in January 1084 and presumably resumed command of the siege, so that it was with him that the Romans began negotiating their surrender to the king. The sudden improvement in Henry's fortunes in March 1084 perhaps originated in talks between Wibert and the rebel cardinals, who then acted as mediators between the royal government and the Roman nobles.[99] The issue that protracted these negotiations must have been the governmental rights that Henry expected to enjoy in Rome: an issue to which the king himself had given prominence by his constant emphasis on his office of patrician of the Romans. Wibert's assurances on this subject evidently overcame the apprehensions of the nobility, while he made so good an impression on the rebel cardinals as to gain their support for his elevation to the papacy. The speed with which he was subsequently installed as pope reveals how much support Wibert enjoyed among the clergy and people.

Soon after the solemn entry of Henry and Wibert to the city, a council was held in St Peter's to resolve the question of the papacy. The earliest reference to the proceedings is in a letter of Henry to Germany in mid-June. 'Know that Hildebrand has been deposed by the lawful judgement of all the cardinals and by the whole Roman people and that our pope elect Clement has been raised to the apostolic see by the acclamation of all the Romans.'[100] The letter makes clear that Wibert's elevation in this council was not a true election. In Henry's eyes Wibert was already his 'pope elect' before the council met, his election having been accomplished in Brixen. Henry's letter expresses a commitment to Wibert that he had prudently concealed from the Romans. The Roman 'election' of March 1084 was a concession to Roman opinion and notably to that of the rebel cardinals.[101] What Henry required of the council

---

[97] *Annales Augustani* 1083, p. 130; Bernold, *Chronicon* 1083, p. 438 suggested that Wibert marked the royal victory by celebrating mass in St Peter's, 28 June 1083; but see Ziese (1982) 84.

[98] On learning of the stalemate in Rome, Wibert may however have thought that he could better serve the king by collecting reinforcements in Ravenna than by returning to Rome in autumn 1083.   [99] Kehr (1921) 986. Cf. Ziese (1982) 88.

[100] Henry IV, *Letter* 18, p. 28.

[101] Benzo, *Ad Heinricum* VI.6, VII, prologue, pp. 564, 578; *Liber de unitate ecclesiae* II.6, p. 217; cf. II.7, 21, pp. 218, 238; *Vita Heinrici IV* c. 6, p. 24. See Meyer von Knonau (1900) 3:528–9. These accounts were perhaps influenced by the falsified version of the Papal Election Decree: Jasper (1986) 103.

of March 1084 was the definitive deposition of Gregory VII, the enemy who had resisted all attempts at reconciliation. Gregory himself was invited to participate in the council; when he did not appear, the council proceeded without him.[102] Only the Lotharingian chronicler Sigebert of Gembloux identified the specific charge on which Gregory was condemned to excommunication and deposition. 'Hildebrand was justly deposed as one guilty of high treason, for he appointed another king against the emperor [Henry IV] and assumed the shameless demeanour of a rebel.'[103] Gregory's support for the anti-king made him guilty of high treason (*maiestas*) towards Henry and it was for this offence that he was condemned. Gregory had indeed been rebuked before in Henrician propaganda for acknowledging Rudolf's title, but on these occasions he was not charged with the offence of *maiestas*,[104] nor had that Roman Law term hitherto been used in royal documents to describe the offence of Rudolf's German supporters.[105] The only earlier reference to the offence of Rudolf's supporters as *maiestas* occurs in *The Defence of King Henry* of Petrus Crassus in 1080, unusual among pro-Henrician polemical writings in supporting its arguments with quotations from Roman Law.[106] The author revised *The Defence* after the king's arrival in Italy precisely 'so that it might be useful to the council' in which Gregory VII was condemned.[107] *The Defence of King Henry* may, therefore, have influenced the conciliar proceedings of March 1084 and inspired a charge of high treason against the pope.

Wibert's enthronement as Pope Clement III on 24 March (Palm Sunday) could not conform to the traditional usages because of the absence of the churchmen who normally officiated at the enthronement of a pope: the cardinal bishops of Ostia and Albano were staunch Gregorians. Instead Wibert was consecrated by diocesans of the archdiocese of Ravenna.[108] The papal diplomas of Clement III date his pontificate from 24 March 1084.[109] His first duty as pope was to perform the imperial coronation of Henry and his consort, Bertha, on 31 March. The earliest reference to this ceremony was that of Henry's letter of June 1084: 'know . . . that on the holy day of Easter we

---

[102] Benzo, *Ad Heinricum* VII, prologue, p. 578.   [103] Sigebert, *Chronica* 1084, pp. 364–5.

[104] *Die Briefe Heinrichs IV* p. 71; Henry IV, *Letter* 17, p. 25.

[105] *D H IV* 301: 'perjury'; *D H IV* 307: 'treachery', 'the most wicked heresy' of conspiring 'to depose a king appointed by God'.

[106] Petrus Crassus, *Defensio* c. 8, p. 452. See Koch (1972) 122–5.

[107] Petrus Crassus, *Defensio* p. 453.

[108] Gebhard of Salzburg, *Letter.* Hugh of Flavigny, *Chronicon* II, pp. 459–60; Bernold, *Chronicon* 1084, p. 440: the bishops of Arezzo and Modena. Bonizo, *Ad amicum* IX. p. 614: the bishops of Bologna, Cervia and Modena. See Meyer von Knonau (1900) 3:529–30.

[109] Köhncke (1888) 55–6.

were, with the consent of all the Romans, ordained and consecrated emperor by Pope Clement, to the joy of the whole Roman people.'[110]

The coronation of an emperor has been described as 'the most magnificent spectacle that medieval Christendom could offer. It made visible the political hierarchy of the west in its spiritual–secular duality and in its indissoluble entwining in the city of the emperors, which was at the same time the city of Peter.'[111] The most elaborate description of an imperial coronation of the central Middle Ages appears at the beginning of the panegyric that Benzo of Alba addressed to the new emperor in 1085.[112] This description draws heavily on the so-called 'Salian imperial *ordo*', which has something of the character of an order of service for the coronation, composed between 1046 and 1085, probably in northern Italy.[113] To the information provided by the *ordo* Benzo added a few details concerning the imperial procession and the hymns sung during the ceremonies, which were perhaps derived from observations made during Henry IV's coronation. Any attempt to reconstruct the ceremonies of Easter 1084 must be based on Benzo's description and the 'Salian imperial *ordo*'. According to these texts, the ceremonies of emperor-making lasted for four days, during which the emperor visited five churches: St Peter's (on the first and second day), St John Lateran (on the second day), S. Paolo fuori le Mura (on the third day), S. Maria Maggiore and S. Croce in Gerusalemme (on the fourth day). The two central rituals of consecration and coronation took place on consecutive days in St Peter's: Henry was consecrated on 31 March and crowned on 1 April.[114] The emperor wore 'a linen tunic embroidered with gold and precious jewels', 'a mantle of cloth of frieze, the imperial garment', golden spurs and a sword; on his hands he wore linen gloves and 'the episcopal ring', on his head 'the imperial diadem'. He went in procession to St Peter's, 'carrying in his left hand the golden apple [orb], which signifies the government of kingdoms, but in his right hand the sceptre of the empire, in the manner of Julius, Octavian and Tiberius'.[115] He was preceded by one of the empire's greatest treasures: the double relic of the 'holy lance' of the leader of the Theban legion, the martyr, St Maurice, which had been refashioned so as to contain a nail from Christ's cross.[116] This double relic was fol-

---

[110] Henry IV, *Letter* 18, p. 28. See Meyer von Knonau (1900) 3:534; Ziese (1982) 105–7.

[111] Schramm (1937) 389.   [112] Benzo, *Ad Heinricum* 1.9–12, pp. 124–34.

[113] Erdmann (1934) 16 n. 5; Schramm (1937) 394–5; Eichmann (1938) 1–26. Cf. *Die Ordines für die Weihe und Krönung des Kaisers* pp. 34–5, no. XIII.

[114] Both the *ordo* and Benzo's account distinguish between the 'diadem' worn for the consecration on the first day and the 'Roman crown' received on the second day.

[115] Benzo's information derived from a Roman treatise of *c.* 1030, the *Graphia-Libellus*: Schramm (1929) 193–217, 264–71.

[116] Henry showed his veneration for the 'holy lance' and the nail by giving them the silver casing in which they still appear: Schramm (1954) 512–13.

lowed by 'the venerable order of bishops, abbots and priests and innumerable clergy', after whom came the emperor himself, supported on the right by the pope and on the left by the archbishop of Milan. They were followed by 'the dukes, margraves and counts and the orders of the various princes'. The clergy sang the traditional hymn in honour of SS. Peter and Paul, *Iam bone pastor*, the emperor's German followers responded with the imperial *laudes*, the hymn glorifying both the emperor and the celestial powers that sustained him. The coronation was followed by a triumphal progress from St Peter's to St John Lateran, with the emperor on horseback 'together with Roman, German and Lombard knights'.

The earliest diplomas bearing Henry's new title were issued on 23 May in Sutri. The intitulations read, 'Henry, by the favour of divine mercy, august emperor of the Romans' and the concluding protocols describe him as 'Henry III emperor of the Romans'.[117] Similar versions of Henry's imperial title are found in the diplomas produced both by the German and by the Italian chancery during the remaining twenty-two years of the reign. The letter of mid-June composed for Henry by Gottschalk of Aachen used the curious title, 'King Henry, by God's grace august emperor of the Romans'. All the subsequent letters of the years 1084–1106 omit the royal title, following the model of the diplomas: 'august emperor of the Romans' (with three exceptions, which use only the form 'august emperor').[118]

During the seven weeks following his coronation Henry resided in the Lateran palace with his antipope.[119] Previous emperors had chosen to live in one of the imperial palaces: that next to St Peter's (where Henry stayed after seizing the Leonine city) or, in the case of Otto III, his residence on the Aventine, replaced by a new palace on the Palatine. For the emperor to establish his residence and government in Rome was contrary to the *Donation of Constantine*, the later eighth-century forgery, highly regarded by the Roman reform party.[120] It is uncertain whether Henry was consciously defying the prohibition in the *Donation*. The most likely explanation of his joint residence with Clement III is that it symbolised the new era of cooperation between empire and papacy that succeeded the conflict of Gregory VII's pontificate. Henrician propagandists enthusiastically embraced the idea of a new era. Henry and Wibert were 'a new Constantine' and 'another Silvester', who would inaugurate an age of reform in ecclesiastical and secular affairs, just as Emperor Constantine I and Pope Silvester I had presided over the conversion

---

[117] *DD H IV* 359–60. Henry was described as 'Henry III' because Henry I, the first king of the Saxon dynasty (911–36), did not receive the imperial title.

[118] Henry IV, *Letter* 18, p. 28. Exceptions: *Letters* 23, 28, 30, pp. 33, 37, 38.

[119] Bernold, *Chronicon* 1084, p. 440. See Brühl (1954) 15–16; Ziese (1982) 107.

[120] *Constitutum Constantini* c. 18, pp. 94–5.

of the Roman empire to Christianity.[121] Henry's letter to Germany in mid-June represented the events of March 1084 as miraculous. 'If our predecessors had achieved with ten thousand men what the Lord has performed for us in Rome with, so to speak, only ten men, it would have been regarded as a miracle . . . We may truthfully say that all Rome is in our hands, except for that fortress in which Hildebrand has shut himself up.'[122]

This was not, however, an accurate account of the situation in Rome. After Henry had been admitted to the city on 21 March, a number of strongholds still offered resistance, most importantly the Castel S. Angelo, where Gregory VII withstood a siege during April and early May. A pro-papal chronicle records an attack on the Castel S. Angelo in Easter week, in which the imperial army suffered numerous casualties.[123] An anti-papal polemic reports an unsuccessful attempt on the emperor's life in April or May 1084. An assassin attempted to drop a rock on Henry's head while he was praying, according to his custom, in the church of St Mary's-on-the-Aventine. The plot miscarried when the assassin fell from the beam on which the rock was poised. (The polemicist's purpose was to implicate Gregory VII: learning from his spies of the emperor's habit of praying in St Mary's, the pope bribed a criminal to kill him.)[124] More plausible are the accounts of the emperor's attempts to reduce two Gregorian strongholds in the old city. He destroyed the fortified residence of the Corsi family on the Capitol.[125] Henry was less successful in his assault on the fortress in the Septizonium, the colonnade at the south-eastern corner of the Palatine, which was in the hands of Rusticus, nephew of Gregory VII. Henry's siege machines destroyed many of the columns of the ancient façade (built for Emperor Septimius Severus) but failed to force the surrender of the garrison.[126] In April and May Henry seized various castles in the region of Tivoli, Porto and northern Rome, subsequently entrusting them to Cardinal bishop John II of Porto. One of the twelve cardinals who had defected to Henry and Wibert at the beginning of 1084, John of Porto immediately became the trusted agent of the emperor and the antipope.[127]

The military threat that prompted Henry's withdrawal from Rome came, not from Gregory VII's supporters in the city, but from his powerful vassal, Robert Guiscard, duke of Apulia and Calabria, who at last obeyed his lord's

---

[121] Benzo, *Ad Heinricum* VI.6, p. 566; cf. p. 572. Cf. *Liber de unitate* II.7, p. 218.

[122] Henry IV, *Letter* 18, pp. 27, 28.

[123] Bernold, *Chronicon* 1084, p. 440. See Meyer von Knonau (1900) 3:540–5; Krautheimer (1980) 149.

[124] Beno, *Gesta Romanae ecclesiae* I.5, p. 371. This story appears in *Vita Heinrici IV* c. 7, pp. 24–5.   [125] *Il Regesto di Farfa* 5, 92 (no. 1097).

[126] *Chronica monasterii Casinensis* III.53, p. 434.

[127] *D H IV* †453: Gawlik (1975) 400–9. See Hüls (1977) 118–20.

summons. Henry's incursion into southern Italy at the beginning of the year must have brought home to Robert the danger of allowing the emperor to become entrenched in Rome. Abbot Desiderius of Monte Cassino 'immediately sent an envoy to Rome who announced to the pope his liberation and informed the emperor of the duke's coming'.[128] (Perhaps Desiderius was acting as the intermediary of the duke, who hoped to rescue Gregory without a battle. The mission also enabled the abbot to fulfil his promise of 'friendship' to Henry, made two years before.) Henry could not risk an encounter with a Norman army much larger than his own. He and the antipope withdrew from the city on 21 May, three days before the arrival of the Normans. While Clement III remained in the vicinity of Rome, Henry moved north. Hostile propaganda represented Henry in headlong flight from the Normans,[129] but the imperial diplomas of May and June reveal a steady journey northwards, attended by numerous princes. The journey from Rome to Pisa took him a fortnight; that from Pisa to Verona (with a delay in Lucca), a further eleven days. The diplomas give the impression of an imperial progress (*iter*), in which the newly crowned emperor was acknowledged by his faithful princes, especially the bishops of northern Italy.[130] From Verona Henry sent his letter to Theoderic of Verdun recording his triumphs in Rome. He announced his intention of being in Regensburg on the feast of SS. Peter and Paul (29 June) and requested the bishop to join him in Augsburg immediately afterwards.[131] Henry left his son, the eleven-year-old Conrad, in the care of the Italian princes 'to watch over the province for him'.[132]

During his last two months in his Italian kingdom Henry attempted no military operations.[133] Before returning to Germany, however, he ordered his adherents in Lombardy to complete the conquest of the lands of Matilda of Tuscany. The Henrician and Matildine armies met on 2 July (after the emperor's departure from Italy) at Sorbaria, north-east of Modena and not far from Canossa. Matilda's forces won a great victory against a superior force, seizing an immense booty and taking many prisoners, including Bishop Eberhard of Parma and six other leading Henricians.[134] Meanwhile the papal vassal Robert Guiscard vigorously defended the Gregorian cause in Rome. He

---

[128] *Chronica monasterii Casinensis* III.53, p. 435. Cf. Wido of Ferrara, *De scismate* I.20, p. 549; Hugh, *Chronicon* II, p. 462. See Meyer von Knonau (1900) 3:545–9; Cowdrey (1983) 171.

[129] Matilda of Tuscany, letter: Hugh II, p. 463; Rangerius, *Vita Anselmi Lucensis* IV.2, p. 1290.

[130] *DD H IV* 359–61, 363–4.   [131] Henry IV, *Letter* 18, pp. 27–9.

[132] *Annales Brunwilarenses* 1080 (*sic*), p. 725. Cf. *Annales Patherbrunnenses* 1084, p. 99. See Meyer von Knonau (1900) 3:570; E. Goez (1996) 15.

[133] Rangerius, *Vita Anselmi* IV.2, p. 1290. See Meyer von Knonau (1900) 3:568.

[134] *Vita Anselmi Lucensis* c. 23–4, pp. 20–1; Bernold, *Chronicon* 1084, p. 441. See Overmann (1895) 151; Meyer von Knonau (1900) 3:565; Struve (1995) 65.

forced his way into the city from the east on 28 May, four days after his arrival before Rome; he rescued Gregory VII from the Castel S. Angelo and brought him back to the Lateran palace. The Norman response to continued Roman resistance was to destroy a considerable part of the city between the churches of S. Silvestro in Capite and S. Lorenzo in Lucina in the north, and between the Colosseum and the Lateran in the south-east.[135] The duke and the pope then campaigned together in the vicinity of Rome, with such success that Matilda of Tuscany informed her German allies that Gregory had 'recovered Sutri and Nepe'.[136]

The pope returned to Rome for the feast of SS. Peter and Paul (29 June), only to find that the city was no longer safe for him to reside in. 'The Roman people were incensed by the [Normans'] violence and conceived an implacable hatred against Hildebrand and transferred all their affections to King Henry.'[137] The Norman atrocities completed what Gregory had begun by his obstinate refusal to negotiate with Henry in 1082–3. Ruined by his vassal's success in conquering Rome, Gregory was obliged to leave the city in Robert Guiscard's entourage when the duke withdrew to the south. Guiscard was anxious that the new cathedral that he had built in Salerno in honour of St Matthew should be consecrated by the pope, who readily performed this ceremony.[138] It is by no means clear that Gregory himself had admitted defeat in the summer of 1084. There was, after all, evidence that the Gregorian cause was beginning to prosper: firstly, Matilda's victory at Sorbaria and secondly, the reconciliation of Robert Guiscard and his nephew, Jordan of Capua, during the papal consecration of St Matthew's cathedral in Salerno. Guiscard had demonstrated that he was devoted to the pope's service: he might yet succeed in enabling his lord to return to Rome.[139]

A papal synod held in Salerno late in 1084 reiterated the excommunication of 'Wibert the heresiarch and Henry and all their supporters'.[140] The news of this sentence was carried to the rest of Christendom by papal legates bearing a papal letter seeking the help of 'all the faithful in Christ who truly love the apostolic see'. The theme of Gregory's last letter is the persecution of the Roman church and the pope. 'The time of Antichrist' was approaching and

---

[135] William of Apulia, *Gesta Roberti* IV.527–66, V.122–4, 255–67 pp. 232–4, 242, 250; Bernold, *Chronicon* 1084, pp. 440–1; Bonizo, *Ad amicum* IX, p. 615. See Meyer von Knonau (1900) 3:551–7, 559–60; Krautheimer (1980) 149–50.

[136] Hugh of Flavigny, *Chronicon* II, p. 463.

[137] Wido of Ferrara, *De scismate* I.20, p. 549. Cf. Frutolf, *Chronica* 1083 (*sic*), p. 96; Sigebert, *Chronica* 1083 (*sic*), p. 364.

[138] Alfanus of Salerno, *I carmi di Alfano* 53. See Cowdrey (1983) 173.

[139] Wido of Ferrara, *De scismate* I.20, p. 549.

[140] Bernold, *Chronica* 1084, p. 441. See Meyer von Knonau (1900) 3:560–1; Vogel (1982) 341–9.

the devil had unleashed against the apostolic see a persecution like those of the pagan Roman emperors.[141] This theme of persecution lies behind the words attributed to Gregory on his deathbed (25 May 1085): 'I have loved righteousness and hated iniquity (Psalm 44:8; Hebrews 1:9) – therefore I die in exile.' With these words the pope claimed that his expulsion from Rome and 'exile' in Salerno had earned him the reward of those 'who are persecuted for righteousness' sake' (Matthew 5:10). The Gregorian partisans who circulated this account of the pope's last words were determined that the world should regard him as a martyr, not as one whose cause had been judged by God and found wanting.[142] The defence of Gregory VII involved the repudiation of the conventional eleventh-century assumption that success, especially military success, was proof of divine approval and failure, evidence of God's rejection. Hence the central argument of Bonizo of Sutri's biography of Gregory VII was that in the circumstances of the 1080s failure was more meritorious than success: 'the sons of obedience and peace lie prostrate but the sons of Belial rejoice with their king'.[143] The polemicists of the imperial party had the easier task and seemed to have the best of the argument. Even the distinguished reformer Lanfranc of Canterbury concluded that Henry IV's success in Rome was evidence of divine favour. 'I believe that the glorious emperor' (so he described the prince excommunicated and deposed by Gregory VII) 'did not attempt so great an enterprise without a good reason and that he could not have gained so great a victory without great assistance from God.'[144]

---

[141] Gregory VII, *Epistolae Vagantes* 54, pp. 128–34.
[142] *Briefsammlungen* pp. 75–6. See Meyer von Knonau (1903) 4:59–62; Hübinger (1973); Cowdrey (1983) 174, 181–5. The Henrician version, Cowdrey (1983) 250, subverts the claim to martyrdom. Cf. Sigebert, *Chronica* 1085, p. 365; Brussels and Hanover codices of Beno, *Gesta Romanae ecclesiae* p. 422.   [143] Bonizo, *Ad amicum* I, p. 571.
[144] *Letters of Archbishop Lanfranc* 52, pp. 164–5. See Cowdrey (1972) 109–11; Ziese (1982) 136–7.

Emperor Henry IV, 1084–1106

7

The pacification of Germany, 1084–1089

'Which of the Charleses or Louis gained such glory; which of the Ottos obtained so special a blessing?' This was the praise with which the returning emperor was greeted by an anonymous south German poet. The emperor had a divinely ordained mission to reform the Church and bring peace to his troubled kingdom.[1] As he approached Germany in June 1084, Henry had written to Bishop Theoderic of Verdun of the possibility of ending the civil war. 'Concerning the Saxons, the archbishop of Salzburg, Count Adalbert and the others who wish to return to us, our reply to you is that we readily acquiesce in your advice, so that there may be true peace in our times, assuming that they remain faithful when they return to us.'[2] These princes had presumably been in communication with Theoderic of Verdun with a view to negotiating with the emperor. By January 1085 their initiative had so far succeeded that Henry's representatives were holding talks with the Saxon rebels and their ally, Gebhard of Salzburg, who was in exile in Saxony.[3]

The anti-Henrician party in south-western Germany, however, had not abandoned the armed struggle. At the beginning of 1084 Augsburg was captured by Welf IV, the deposed duke of Bavaria. The Henrician Bishop Siegfried II of Augsburg was expelled and his rival, Wigold, installed in his place.[4] The emperor's letter to Theoderic of Verdun indicated that he planned to liberate the city immediately on his return: Theoderic was instructed 'to come to us in Augsburg after the feast of the apostles Peter and Paul (29 June)'. Henry went first to Regensburg, the principal city of Bavaria and one of the most important props of his regime.[5] With the supplies and reinforcements furnished by Regensburg, Henry began a fourteen-day siege of Augsburg, which ended with the capture of the city on the night of 6–7 August.[6] Henry

---

[1] Anonymous poem, 1084: Meyer (1882) 253–300. See Meyer von Knonau (1900) 3:572; Vogel (1982) 161–2.   [2] Henry IV, *Letter* 18, p. 28. (Perhaps Adalbert II of Calw is meant.)
[3] See below pp. 242–4.   [4] See above p. 175.
[5] *Annalium Ratisbonensium fragmentum* 1084, p. 88. See above p. 173.
[6] *Annales Augustani* 1084, pp. 130–1. See Meyer von Knonau (1900) 3:574–5; Zoepfl (1952) 312–13; Bosl (1972) 1139–40; Kottje (1978) 149–50; Volkert and Zoepfl (1974) no. 350.

could count on the loyalty not only of the bishop but also of the citizens of Augsburg. They would suffer for their loyalty when, in April 1088, Welf IV attacked Augsburg again, punishing the citizens with the devastation of their city and Bishop Siegfried with long imprisonment.[7] The emperor himself is not known to have visited Augsburg again after August 1084, but his authority was sufficiently respected there for him to be able to appoint a successor to Siegfried in 1096.[8]

In autumn 1084 Henry visited Mainz,[9] where he made his first intervention in the affairs of the imperial Church since the imperial coronation. On 4 October he invested Wezilo with the archbishopric of Mainz.[10] Wezilo was a distinguished scholar and supporter of monastic reform, who had proved his usefulness to the king as an envoy to the Roman synod of Lent 1080.[11] The emperor was careful to select an unexceptionable candidate for the foremost church of the German kingdom. The manner of Wezilo's promotion was also less controversial than the appointments of 1066–77: the new archbishop was elected with the agreement of the clergy and people of Mainz. As previously in 1078–9, perhaps in deference to reforming opinion, Henry imitated the conduct of his father, combining an insistence on the royal right of investiture with respect for the rights of the canonical electors. The long-delayed consecration of Egilbert as archbishop of Trier was also performed in October 1084, during the emperor's visit to Mainz. Egilbert had been appointed in January 1079, two months after the papal promulgation of the decree against lay investiture. None of Egilbert's suffragans was willing to consecrate him, except Theoderic of Verdun, who, however, met resistance to his participation in his own diocese. Now Theoderic received a peremptory order: 'Pope Clement and Emperor Henry command you, as you love us, with all speed to consecrate the archbishop of Trier.' Since his fellow-suffragans still refused to assist, he was obliged to perform the consecration with the help of the suffragans of Mainz.[12]

Three further appointments in 1084 showed Henry asserting his authority over the imperial Church. The Saxon bishopric of Paderborn was conferred

---

[7] Meyer von Knonau (1903) 4:204–5.

[8] *Ibid.*, pp. 479–80; Volkert and Zoepfl (1974) nos. 356, 366.

[9] In *D H IV* 369 (Mainz, 4 October) the title of arch-chancellor reappeared after seven years: Gawlik (1978) xxiii. Archbishop Siegfried died on 17 February 1084: Bernold, *Chronicon* 1084, p. 439. See Meyer von Knonau (1900) 3:577; G. Schmidt (1917) 79.

[10] Meyer von Knonau (1900)3:576, 578.

[11] Bonizo, *Ad amicum* ix, p. 616. See Böhmer and Will (1877) 217, 219; Büttner (1949) 52; Methuen (1966–7) 21–2; Fleckenstein (1973) 135–6.

[12] Henry IV, *Letter* 18, p. 29; *Gesta Treverorum, Continuatio* 1.14, pp. 186–7. See Gladel (1932) 33.

on Henry of Werl, together with the task of ousting the Gregorian candidate for the bishopric.[13] Secondly, the patriarchate of Aquileia was bestowed on Svatabor-Frederick, nephew of Duke Vratislav II of Bohemia and of Frederick of Wettin, bishop of Münster.[14] This appointment ensured that Aquileia remained in loyal hands and strengthened the emperor's ties with Vratislav and the Wettin family. Thirdly, when Münster became vacant on the death of the Henrician adherent Frederick, the emperor secured the succession of the equally loyal Erpo.[15] The appointments of the bishops of Paderborn and Münster marked an important stage in the emperor's growing influence in Saxony.[16] These appointments demonstrated Henry's determination that lay investiture should remain a fact of life of the imperial Church. The earliest defence of his right of investiture against the papal decree of 1078 had appeared in 1081 in a letter issued in the name of Theoderic of Verdun.[17] During Lent 1086 Bishop Wido of Ferrara, writing in the antipope's entourage in Ravenna, produced the first attempt to defend lay investiture, not by reference to 'custom' but by a detailed examination of canonical 'authorities'.[18] It is not surprising that this defence should have been undertaken in the entourage of Clement III, since the antipope's appointment was part of Henry IV's attempt to restore the *status quo* of his father's reign and to reclaim the imperial rights which had come under attack from 'Hildebrandine madness'.[19]

Immediately after the investiture of the new archbishop of Mainz Henry compelled the submission of the bishop and citizens of Metz. Herman of Metz had been a member of the anti-Henrician party since 1078. Expelled from his diocese by the king, he played a leading part in the election of the anti-king in 1081.[20] Herman seized the opportunity of Henry's absence in Italy to return

---

[13] Meier (1987) 64–79.   [14] Schmidinger (1952) 345–6.   [15] Leidinger (1969) 297–8.

[16] Henry of Werl and Erpo were the first canons of Goslar to be invested with bishoprics by Henry since the crisis of 1076–7. Henry invested two more canons of Goslar: Eppo of Worms (1090) and Mazo of Verden (1097).

[17] Wenrich of Trier, *Epistola* 8, pp. 297–8. See Minninger (1978) 106; Schieffer (1981) 185–6.

[18] Wido of Ferrara, *De scismate* II, pp. 564–5, made the crucial distinction between the 'two jurisdictions' granted to bishops, 'one . . . spiritual and divine, the other secular', which remained the principal theme of imperialist polemics defending lay investiture for the next three decades. See Minninger (1978) 107–9, 116; Robinson (1978a) 46–7.

[19] Hence scholarship has frequently ascribed a Ravennese origin and date of *c.* 1084 to the 'forged investiture privileges', supposedly conferred by Pope Hadrian I on Charlemagne and Pope Leo VIII on Otto I: Märtl, *Die falschen Investiturprivilegien*. (It was only in the reign of Henry V that they were mentioned by the imperial government in negotiations with the papacy.) See Jordan (1938a) 426–48; Jordan (1938b) 85–128; Heidrich (1984) 125.

[20] Herman was encouraged by letters from the Gregorian party: Gregory VII, *Registrum* IV.2, VIII.21, pp. 293–7, 544–63; Gebhard of Salzburg, *Epistola* pp. 261–79; also in Hugh of Flavigny, *Chronicon* II, pp. 459–60; Anselm of Lucca: *Briefsammlungen* pp. 50–2.

to his see, where he had continued to express defiance by his refusal to consecrate Egilbert as archbishop of Trier. Neither he nor the citizens of Metz,
however, offered any resistance to Henry when he appeared before their city
in October 1084.[21] From Metz Henry proceeded to Cologne, where he celebrated his first Christmas as emperor. 'Very many people flocked to his court
because they were enthusiastic about his new authority.'[22] The Saxon sources
recording this enthusiasm imply that Henry's former Saxon opponents were
among those attracted to the Christmas celebrations by his new imperial
dignity. Henry presumably seized the opportunity of staging a 'crown-
wearing' of unusual splendour to underline the 'new authority' that the imperial coronation had given him. During these festivities the emperor discussed
with the princes how to end resistance to his authority, especially in Saxony.
The result of their deliberations was a conference between the Henrician
bishops and their opponents 'to debate whether the emperor was guiltless and
worthy to rule the kingdom or whether he ought justly to be deposed because
of capital offences'.[23] An imperialist commentator attributed this measure to
war-weariness, especially among the secular nobility. 'It was agreed by the
bishops on both sides that this long conflict, which could not be finished with
swords, should be ended by means of books, to the great joy of the laity, whose
blood had been shed in so many battles.' The representatives of each party
were to defend their cause 'from the evidence of the holy scriptures', which
were to be 'read and expounded in the hearing of all who were present'.[24]

The conference met on 20 January 1085 in Thuringia. Some sources identify the meeting-place as Gerstungen; others name the nearby village of Berka,
on the opposite bank of the River Werra. Presumably the rival parties were
encamped in these two separate places. On the Gregorian–Saxon side was the
papal legate, Cardinal bishop Odo of Ostia, who had arrived in the German
kingdom at the end of 1084. His letter to the faithful, written immediately
after the conference, is the earliest extant record of the proceedings.[25] He was
accompanied by Gebhard of Salzburg (in the eighth year of exile from his

---

[21] *D H IV* 370; *Annales Augustani* 1084, p. 131. See Meyer von Knonau (1900) 3:580–1.

[22] *Annales Magdeburgenses* 1085, p. 176; *Annalista Saxo* 1085, p. 721. See Meyer von Knonau
(1900) 3:605; Klewitz (1939) 51; Kottje (1978) 144.

[23] *Annalium Ratisbonensium fragmentum* 1085, p. 88. Cf. the 'Saxon report' (*Annales
Magdeburgenses* 1085, p. 176; *Annalista Saxo* 1085, p. 721); Bernold, *Chronicon* 1085, p. 442.
See Giese (1979) 174.   [24] *Liber de unitate ecclesiae* II.18, p. 234.

[25] *Briefsammlungen* pp. 375–80. The 'Saxon report' (*Annales Magdeburgenses* 1085, pp. 176–7;
Annalista Saxo 1085, pp. 721–2) was attributed to Bernard, master of the cathedral school of
Hildesheim by Erdmann (1938) 204 and n. 7. Cf. *Liber de unitate* II.18, pp. 234–5; Bernold,
Chronicon 1085, p. 442; *Annalium Ratisbonensium fragmentum* 1085, p. 88. See Meyer von
Knonau (1903) 4:2–12; Becker (1964) 66–70; Zafarana (1966a) 638–40; Steinböck (1972)
140–1; Robinson (1978a) 105–9; Giese (1979) 174–6; Vogel (1982) 171–6.

archbishopric) and Hartwig of Magdeburg, by the emperor's bitter enemies, the bishops of Halberstadt, Merseburg, Meissen and Naumburg, by Udo of Hildesheim and the newly elected bishop of Verden. The imperial party consisted of Liemar of Bremen and the three Rhenish archbishops, Wezilo of Mainz, Sigewin of Cologne and Egilbert of Trier, together with many of their suffragans. The proceedings were opened by Gebhard of Salzburg, the spokesman of the Gregorian–Saxon party, who produced Gregory VII's letters announcing Henry's excommunication and defended the pope's sentence with canon law texts forbidding contact with excommunicates. When the two parties had last met to negotiate peace, in Kaufungen (February 1081), Gebhard had similarly been the spokesman of the anti-Henrician party and had called on his adversaries to prove that it was possible to obey Henry 'without damage to the holy faith'. His attitude had been conciliatory: the real opposition to the Henrician proposals had come from Otto of Northeim and the Saxon princes.[26] At the conference of Gerstungen-Berka Gebhard was in no doubt about the impossibility of recognising Henry's authority. Perhaps the presence of the papal legate stiffened his resolve.

On behalf of the imperial party Conrad of Utrecht replied that Henry was not excommunicate, 'since the pope dealt unjustly with him, excommunicating someone whom he ought not to have excommunicated'. Wezilo of Mainz then read to the assembly 'a certain chapter from the decrees of the Roman pontiffs', declaring 'that anyone who had been deprived of his property or expelled by violence or terror from his own seat, cannot be accused, summoned, judged or condemned before everything that was taken away from him has been restored in full and he has been reinstated with all his rights and privileges'. Gregory VII could not, therefore, legally excommunicate Henry IV, because the rebellion of 'the Saxons and some of the Swabians' had robbed him of substantial parts of his kingdom. The imperial party countered the Gregorian argument with the canonical doctrine of *exceptio spolii*, quoted from the preface of the Pseudo-Isidorean Decretals: the principle that no bishop should face judicial proceedings if he was not in full possession of his see and all his property.[27] It was the same defence that Gregory VII had used when hardpressed by his enemies in the summer of 1083: he was prepared to answer charges in the forthcoming synod, but only if 'the property of which the holy Roman church is known to have been despoiled, should be restored'.[28] According to the imperial party, their use of this defence at Gerstungen-Berka took their enemies completely by surprise. 'All the bishops of the opposition party were so confounded and so subdued that they could

---

[26] See above pp. 206–7.   [27] *Decretales Pseudoisidorianae* p.18. See Fuhrmann (1982) 52–69.
[28] See above p. 225.

not answer this' and the conference broke up with the Gregorians and Saxons in confusion.[29] Henrician propaganda portrayed Gerstungen-Berka as a victory for the imperial cause.[30] It was to counter this propaganda that the papal legate issued his letter. Having played a secondary role at Gerstungen-Berka, Odo now assumed the leadership of the Gregorian party in Germany, restating the canonical prohibition of association with excommunicates and discrediting the 'authority' produced by the imperial party. The central argument of his refutation of the *exceptio spolii* defence was that the king, as a layman, could not be permitted to enjoy the special status that canon law conferred on bishops.[31] The legate echoed that repudiation of the idea of 'sacral kingship' which had originated in Humbert of Silva Candida's statement that a king was a mere 'lay person' and culminated in Gregory VII's contrast between the episcopal and the royal dignity, the former having a divine, the latter a diabolic origin.[32]

On 21 January 'the Saxons and Thuringians' met 'to find out who among them would continue resistance to the death and who would desert them'. Evidently the previous day's debate had revealed that some former rebels were open to the persuasions of the Henrician party, perhaps impressed by Henry's acquisition of the imperial crown. 'Bishop Udo of Hildesheim, his brother Conrad [of Reinhausen] and Count Theoderic [II of Katlenburg] were accused of having met Henry, their most dangerous enemy and having promised to betray the fatherland to him.' The accused did not deny having been in communication with the emperor, but they protested that they had no intention of submitting to his authority. They refused a demand that they provide their countrymen with hostages as a guarantee of future loyalty, since this was inappropriate to their status as 'princes and defenders of the fatherland'. In the ensuing quarrel Theoderic of Katlenburg was murdered. Bishop Udo, his brother and their associates, narrowly escaping the same fate, fled to Fritzlar and there submitted to the emperor.[33] The murdered Theoderic of Katlenburg was one of the most distinguished and influential of the Saxon princes, married to an imperial kinswoman, sister of Ekbert II of Brunswick, and a leading rebel since 1073.[34] That so prominent a figure should have opened negotiations with the emperor and subsequently met a violent death at the hands of his fellow rebels reveals the tensions that now afflicted the Saxon opposition party.

Odo of Ostia attempted to limit the damage to the anti-Henrician cause by

[29] *Liber de unitate ecclesiae* II.18, p. 235.   [30] *Briefsammlungen* p. 376.   [31] *Ibid.* p. 378.
[32] See above pp. 115, 208.
[33] 'Saxon report' (*Annales Magdeburgenses* 1085, p. 177; *Annalista Saxo* 1085, p. 722). Cf. *Liber de unitate ecclesiae* II.18, p. 235. See Meyer von Knonau (1903) 4:8–9; Fenske (1977) 108–9, 328–9; Vogel (1983) 176–7.   [34] Fenske (1977) 79.

holding a legatine synod in Quedlinburg on Easter day (20 April).[35] The purpose of the synod was to rally the Gregorian–Saxon opposition after the unsatisfactory outcome of the conference of Gerstungen-Berka and to prevent further defections. The synod was attended by Gebhard of Salzburg, Hartwig of Magdeburg and his suffragans and the Saxon suffragans of the archsee of Mainz. The anti-king Herman came to Quedlinburg at the head of an army, to protect the synod.[36] The decrees of the synod of Quedlinburg reaffirmed the principle that papal judgements could not be disputed. The synod excommunicated the 'heresiarch' Wibert of Ravenna, the rebel cardinals and the archbishops of Mainz and Bremen and their 'associates' and emphasised the necessity of avoiding excommunicates, echoing Gebhard of Salzburg's speech at Gerstungen-Berka.[37] The synod also confirmed the acts of Odo of Ostia's legatine synod in Constance (21 December 1084). That synod's most controversial act was the election of a new bishop of Constance in place of the Henrician Otto, deposed by Gregory VII and expelled from his church earlier in the year. The Gregorian candidate was Gebhard of Zähringen, monk of Hirsau and son of the late Duke Berthold of Carinthia, who was soon to become the acknowledged leader of the Gregorian party in Germany.[38]

The confirmation of his election was one of several attacks directed by the synod of Quedlinburg against his metropolitan, Wezilo of Mainz. Wezilo's skilful performance at Gerstungen-Berka had demonstrated that the foremost church of the kingdom was now in the hands of a formidable defender of the Salian cause, an invaluable supporter of Henry IV's efforts to restore his authority over the imperial Church: hence the preoccupation of the synod of Quedlinburg with discrediting 'the intruder of Mainz'.[39] The synod also excommunicated Udo of Hildesheim, who had failed to respond to the appeal of the papal legate to return to the Gregorian fold.[40] After his submission to the emperor in Fritzlar Udo was assigned the task of winning over more

---

[35] *Briefsammlungen* pp. 25–7: the legate intended to hold a synod in Goslar in Lent. Goslar had since 1077 served as a residence of the anti-kings: Rothe (1940) 28–31. See Meyer von Knonau (1903) 4:12–13; Becker (1964) 70–1; Fenske (1977) 109–10; Vogel (1982) 177.

[36] Herman was accused of marrying within the prohibited degrees (*MGH Constitutiones* I, 653; Bernold of St Blasien, *Chronicon* 1085, p. 443) but the synod did not proceed against him. See Meyer von Knonau (1903) 4:17; Klebel (1962) 232–4; Erkens (1987) 15.

[37] *MGH Constitutiones* I, 652–3. Cf. Bernold, *Chronicon* 1085, pp. 442–3; *Liber de unitate ecclesiae* II.22, p. 239. See Sdralek (1890) 178–81; Meyer von Knonau (1903) 4:14–21; Becker (1964) 71–4; Vogel (1982) 179–84.

[38] Bernold, *Chronicon* 1084, p. 441. See Ladewig and Müller (1895) 67–8 (no. 520); Meyer von Knonau (1900) 3:605–9; Hofmann (1931) 218–19; Becker (1964) 64–5.

[39] The synod excommunicated 'the sect of Wezilo and his allies, which declares that laymen who have been despoiled of their goods are not to be judged. . .'.

[40] *Briefsammlungen* pp. 25–7.

princes to the imperial cause. Henry IV allegedly promised Udo on oath that 'if the Saxons returned to him and permitted him to exercise the kingship in the same way as his father, he would never infringe the rights that they had most properly and creditably enjoyed since the time of their conqueror, Charles [the Great]'. The 'princes and bishops' of the Henrician party likewise swore that 'if Henry ever neglected this decision, they would never aid him against Saxony'. Armed with these promises, Udo persuaded 'many of his compatriots' to go over to the imperial party.[41] The Gregorian party attributed their 'apostasy' to war-weariness.[42]

Before the beginning of Lent the emperor had summoned a 'general synod' to meet in Mainz a fortnight after Easter. The Saxon bishops were included in this summons and threatened with deposition if they failed to attend. None of the bishops attending the Quedlinburg synod was present when the imperial synod assembled in the monastery of St Alban, Mainz at the end of April. The synod was nevertheless well attended: three or four archbishops and fifteen bishops were present, together with the representatives of three other bishops.[43] The largest assembly of bishops in the German kingdom since the council of Worms (24 January 1076), the synod of Mainz demonstrated that Henry could once more command the obedience of a majority of the German episcopate. The secular princes present in Mainz were Duke Vratislav II of Bohemia and his brother, Margrave Conrad of Moravia, the dukes Frederick of Swabia and Liutold of Carinthia and the Bavarian count palatine Rapoto of Cham, one of the emperor's most valuable adherents in southern Germany. Information about the proceedings of the synod derives mainly from the German polemical literature of the decade after 1085, notably the polemic of the anonymous monk of Hersfeld, *The Preservation of the Unity of the Church*. The polemicist presented the synod as a triumphant demonstration of imperial power. The emperor was 'first and foremost the author of this synod; for nothing can be secure and permanent in such matters, unless the royal authority defends and approves it by virtue of the supreme power of the empire'.[44]

The main purpose of the synod was 'to restore the peace of Church and commonwealth', which in turn involved the excommunication and deposition of the enemies of peace. The synod condemned the anti-king Herman as

---

[41] 'Saxon report' (*Annales Magdeburgenses* 1085, p. 177; *Annalista Saxo* 1085, p. 722).

[42] Bernold, *Chronicon* 1085, p. 444. See Meyer von Knonau (1903) 4:46–7; Giese (1979) 176–8.

[43] *Liber de unitate ecclesiae* II.19, p. 236; *D H IV* 390: see Gawlik (1970a) 73–4; Gawlik (1978) XLII n. 115.

[44] *Liber de unitate* II.22, p. 239. Cf. *Annalium Ratisbonensium fragmentum* 1085, p. 89. The Gregorian polemicists: Bernard of Hildesheim, *Liber canonum* c. 34, pp. 503–4; Bernold, *Chronicon* 1085, p. 443. See Meyer von Knonau (1903) 4:21–5, 547–50; Zafarana (1966a) 642–3; Vogel (1982) 184–9.

'one guilty of treason and an enemy of the peace of the Church'. The same sentence was imposed on those bishops who failed to attend the synod. They were guilty of 'cherishing and defending the party of their Gregory rather than the whole community of the catholic Church' and seeking 'to destroy the kingship conferred by God on King Henry'. After waiting for three days for the bishops of the Gregorian–Saxon party to appear, the synod condemned the two archbishops and thirteen bishops of that party. Of the eight Saxon prelates now deposed, three – the bishops of Halberstadt, Merseburg and Meissen, all appointed in the first decade of the reign – had been bitter opponents of Henry IV since the outbreak of the Saxon rebellion in 1073. Three of the other Saxon prelates condemned in Mainz were the appointees of the Saxon opposition, installed in their sees with the assistance of the anti-king: Archbishop Hartwig of Magdeburg and the bishops of Naumburg and Verden. In addition the synod deposed four members of the 'deposition faction' of 1076, who had remained loyal supporters of Gregory VII: Gebhard of Salzburg and the bishops of Würzburg, Worms and Passau. The only Lotharingian bishop to be deposed, Herman of Metz, had submitted to the emperor six months before. He was condemned for his failure to obey the imperial summons to the synod. The other four casualties of the synod were anti-bishops, intruders in the sees of loyal Henricians.[45]

'The emperor . . . excommunicated the bishops who were opposed to him and entrusted their bishoprics to his faithful clerks.'[46] Appointments were made to nine of the sees that had been declared vacant: all, that is, except Naumburg and Verden, for which no appointment is recorded. While Gregorian polemicists, echoing the criticisms of 1066–76, denounced the new bishops as 'simoniacs' and 'intruders'[47] the Hersfeld polemicist saw them as men of distinction, canonically elected to their sees. The new archbishop of Magdeburg was his superior, Abbot Hartwig of Hersfeld, who now faced the task of defending the archbishopric against a Gregorian rival, also named Hartwig. 'Exceedingly learned both in moral disciplines and in holy scriptures', Hartwig of Hersfeld owed his archbishopric to 'the election of the clergy and people of the church' of Magdeburg.[48] As in the case of Wezilo of

---

[45] *Liber de unitate* II.19–20, pp. 236–7; cf. II.18, 28–9, 31–2, pp. 234–5, 250, 253, 257–8.

[46] *Annalium Ratisponensium fragmentum* p. 89. Cf. *Annales Augustani* 1085, p. 131. Vogel (1982) 187 suggested that the 'forged investiture privileges' (Hadrian I and Leo VIII: above p. 241 n. 19) were used at the synod to prove the emperor's right to invest bishops: see Anselm of Lucca, *Contra Wibertum* p. 522. Cf. A. Hauck (1954) 845. There is no evidence that the forgeries were in existence in 1085. See also Schieffer (1981) 21; Märtl in: *Die falschen Investiturprivilegien* pp. 54–7.

[47] Bernard, *Liber canonum* c. 34, p. 503; Anselm, *Contra Wibertum* p. 522.

[48] *Liber de unitate ecclesiae* II.28, p. 250.

Mainz, the emperor seems to have imitated his father's conduct. Hartwig was one of three abbots invested with bishoprics during the synod of Mainz: Walo of St Arnulf in Metz was appointed to the bishopric of Metz; Winither of Lorsch to Worms. All three were conscientious supporters of monastic reform who eventually withdrew from their bishoprics and returned to the monastic life.[49] Their appointments reveal that Henry IV was anxious to enlist monastic support for his ecclesiastical regime. Two of the new bishops, Meinhard II of Würzburg and Hamezo of Halberstadt, were former canons and so conformed to the usual pattern of Henry IV's appointments. The promotion of Hamezo had the appearance of canonical propriety: a canon of the cathedral of Halberstadt appointed bishop of that city.[50] Meinhard was a candidate of the greatest distinction: master of the cathedral school of Bamberg and one of the most distinguished scholars of his day, his name coupled with that of Wezilo of Mainz as 'the philosophers of the kingdom'.[51]

At least five of the episcopal candidates of 1085 belonged to influential princely families. One of the new bishops, Herman of Passau, was a kinsman of the imperial family: an Eppenstein, brother of Duke Liutold of Carinthia and Abbot Udalric of St Gallen.[52] Felix of Meissen was somehow connected to Duke Vratislav II of Bohemia.[53] Berthold, imperial anti-archbishop of Salzburg, belonged to the Bavarian comital family of Moosburg.[54] Hamezo of Halberstadt was the uncle of the Thuringian count Ludwig 'the Leaper'.[55] Such appointments rewarded loyal families for their support or enlisted the cooperation of neutral or hostile families in the task of gaining control of dioceses. The case of Winither of Worms illustrates the importance which family connections could assume in the emperor's choice of a bishop. Winither was the son of Count Sigebert I of Saarbrücken. The Gregorian bishop of Worms, Adalbert, whom he was intended to replace, was Sigebert's brother-in-law. It was evidently necessary for the emperor to retain the friendship of this important Lotharingian family, even while ridding himself of his old enemy, their kinsman, Adalbert.[56] A similar consideration inhibited Henry from investing a new bishop of Naumburg after the synod of Mainz deposed Gunther. Gunther was one of the Wettins, some of whom now supported the emperor. The desire not to offend this powerful Saxon family seems to have prompted

---

[49] Zielinski (1984) 128–30: such appointments were exceptional in the Salian period. Henry appointed two more monk-bishops: Udalric of Aquileia (1086) and Arnold of Constance (1092), both from St Gallen.   [50] *Annalista Saxo* 1085, p. 723.

[51] Erdmann (1932) 332–431; Erdmann (1938) 16–24; Märtl (1991) 331–40.

[52] Zielinski (1984) 34, 250.   [53] *Briefsammlungen* p. 392.

[54] Steinböck (1972) 143–9; Zielinski (1984) 57 n. 247.

[55] Fenske (1977) 111–12. In the late 1080s Ludwig became a formidable enemy of Henry.

[56] Zielinski (1984) 60, 65–6.

the emperor to conciliate rather than replace Gunther, a strategy which proved successful in 1088.[57]

The synod of Mainz was an attempt by the imperial party to restore the imperial Church to its former unity and obedience by a single act of policy, the expulsion of the Gregorian party. Simultaneously the synod aimed 'to restore the peace of the Church and the commonwealth'.[58] According to the chronicler, Frutolf of Michelsberg, 'by general advice and agreement, the peace of God was established' in Mainz.[59] The 'peace of God' (*pax Dei*) originated in southern France in the late tenth century as an initiative by bishops, through the medium of peace councils, to limit the destruction wrought in their dioceses by the private warfare of the aristocracy. The related institution of the 'truce of God' (*treuga Dei*) called for the suspension of hostilities at particular periods of the ecclesiastical year.[60] The first appearance in the German kingdom of an episcopal peace movement on the French model was in 1082, the peace negotiated by Bishop Henry of Liège. Earlier in the century, however, the German kingdom had experienced a peace movement of a different character. In the period 1043–7 peace councils were held on the initiative not of the bishops but of the monarch, Henry III, and influenced by his conception of royal authority. The pacification of the kingdom was the responsibility of the king; the disputes of the aristocracy must be settled by royal justice not by resorting to arms.[61] There is evidence that on two occasions in the second decade of his reign the young Henry IV imitated his father's example. In 1068 'at Christmastide in Goslar peace and reconciliation among the people were confirmed under oath by royal edict'.[62] The second instance occurred immediately after the treaty of Gerstungen of 2 February 1074, in which the Saxon rebels successfully imposed their terms on the king. Afterwards in Goslar Henry 'commanded that there should be peace and tranquillity throughout the whole fatherland. He settled lawsuits with just and equitable judgement.'[63]

After this second royal proclamation of peace in Goslar in 1074 there is no evidence of a peace council for almost a decade until Henry's second Italian expedition. During the king's absence the French model of the 'truce of God' was introduced into the Lower Lotharingian archdiocese of Cologne: the peace organised by Henry of Liège (before Easter 1082) and that of Sigewin of Cologne (20 April 1083). These peace initiatives prohibited warfare during Advent and Christmastide, from Septuagesima until the week after Whitsun

---

[57] Fenske (1977) 70–3.   [58] *Liber de unitate ecclesiae* II.19, p. 236.

[59] Frutolf, *Chronica* 1085, p. 98. See Meyer von Knonau (1903) 4:23–4; Gernhuber (1952) 44; Wadle (1973) 147–8.   [60] Hoffmann (1964) 11–89; Cowdrey (1970b) 42–67.

[61] Schnith (1962) 22–57.

[62] Berthold, *Annales* 1069, p. 274; Bernold, *Chronicon* 1069, p. 429.

[63] *Carmen de bello Saxonico* II.212–13, p. 14. See above pp. 95–6.

and on certain other days. To the ecclesiastical sanction of excommunication was added the secular punishments of the loss of inheritance and benefices and exile from the diocese.[64] The next reference to the 'peace of God' in Germany concerned the anti-Henrician party in Saxony at Eastertide 1084: 'most solemn truces were made among the faithful men of the lord pope'.[65] These local instances of the 'peace of God' in the years 1082–4 provided the inspiration for the proclamation of the peace in the synod of Mainz in 1085. No details of the Mainz peace are extant: indeed nothing survives except the statement of Frutolf of Michelsberg that 'the peace of God was established'. There exists a detailed document regulating the 'peace of God' which was identified by its first editor as the text issued by the synod of 1085. The second editor of the text, however, identified it as the peace instituted in his diocese by Rupert of Bamberg, perhaps before the meeting of the synod of Mainz. The text closely resembles that of the peace organised by Sigewin of Cologne, except that it does not restrict the operation of the peace to a single diocese.[66] This suggests the possibility that the 'Bamberg peace' was part of a programme devised in the synod of Mainz, extending the peace to all the dioceses of the kingdom. In that case it is likely that the Mainz peace was an episcopal rather than an imperial initiative. (The Bamberg text says nothing of the emperor's participation in the institution of the peace.) The Henrician bishops proclaimed a peace, the details of which were drawn from the precedents of Liège and Cologne, perhaps in response to the peace recently instituted by the Saxons.[67] The Mainz peace of 1085 was not, therefore, an attempt by Henry IV to imitate the peace councils held by his father between 1043 and 1047. Eighteen years passed before the emperor instituted the 'peace of God' on this model, in the council of Mainz of 1103.[68]

The synod of 1085 was concerned with 'the peace of the Church and the commonwealth' not only in Germany but also in Bohemia. Duke Vratislav II was present, together with his brothers, Margrave Conrad of Moravia and Bishop Gebhard (Jaromir) of Prague (until recently chancellor of the German kingdom). The synod witnessed, firstly, the settlement of the boundaries of the diocese of Prague and, secondly, the promotion of Vratislav to the dignity of the

---

[64] The Liège peace is known only from the thirteenth-century chronicle of Gilles of Orval, *Gesta episcoporum Leodiensium* III.13, pp. 89–90 and *Gesta abbreviata* p. 131. See Meyer von Knonau (1900) 3:467–9; Joris (1961–2) 503–45; but see Hoffmann (1964) 220 n. 20. The Cologne peace: *MGH Constitutiones* I, 603–5. See Meyer von Knonau (1900) 3:506–8.

[65] Bernold, *Chronicon* 1084, p. 440: see Meyer von Knonau (1900) 3:583. The 'Pax Dei incerta', *MGH Constitutiones* I, 608–9, has been identified as the text of this peace: Gernhuber (1952) 42, 98; Wadle (1973) 145–6.

[66] *MGH Leges* 2, 55–8; *MGH Constitutiones* I, 606–8. See Gernhuber (1952) 43; Wadle (1973) 147–8.   [67] Bernold, *Chronicon* 1084, p. 440.   [68] See below p. 319.

kingship, both matters closely linked with the conflict of the empire and the Gregorian papacy. The imperial diploma for Prague of 29 April 1086 records that Gebhard had complained to the emperor 'that the bishopric of Prague had been divided and diminished' by the creation of the diocese of Olmütz. The synod of Mainz resolved this complaint by incorporating Olmütz in the diocese of Prague.[69] This marked the successful culmination of Gebhard's long struggle with Bishop John I of Olmütz, which began in 1068 as a property dispute and eventually involved the duke, the metropolitan (the archbishop of Mainz) and the pope. The diploma recording victory for Gebhard has often been dismissed as a forgery made after the death of John of Olmütz (25 November 1086). Particularly suspicious is the diploma's claim that Vratislav II consented to Gebhard's request at the synod of Mainz, since the duke had previously blocked his brother's ambitions. Vratislav imitated the attempts of his predecessors to secure for the duke the right to invest bishops in the Bohemian bishoprics and simultaneously to establish Prague as an archbishopric, independent of Mainz and the ecclesiastical structure of the German kingdom, seeking the friendship of the reform papacy to this end.[70] Friendship with Gregory VII did not, however, bring Vratislav the desired Bohemian archbishopric. Meanwhile the duke became more closely allied with Henry IV and increasingly benefited from royal patronage, receiving the marches of Lower Lusatia, Meissen and Austria: generosity which culminated in the conferring of the royal title in the synod of Mainz. In this context it is possible to defend the authenticity of the diploma of 29 April 1086 on the supposition that Vratislav made a truce with Gebhard, acquiescing in his project for the aggrandisement of Prague.[71]

According to the chronicle of Cosmas of Prague, the emperor raised Vratislav to the kingship in the synod of Mainz 'with the approval of all the princes of his realm'. 'Placing a royal circlet on [Vratislav's] head with his own hand, he commanded Archbishop Egilbert of Trier to anoint him as king in his principal city of Prague and to place the diadem on his head.' It was accordingly Egilbert who anointed and crowned Vratislav on 15 June 1086.[72] Two aspects of the coronation arrangements are puzzling: firstly, the delay of over

---

[69] *D H IV* 390. Cf. Cosmas of Prague, *Chronica Boemiorum* II.21, 27, 30, 41, III.33, pp. 113, 121, 125, 145–6, 204. See Meyer von Knonau (1903) 4:25, 549–50; Beumann and Schlesinger (1955) 236–50; Wegener (1959) 105–6, 210–13, 216–19, 226; Gawlik (1978) XLII n. 115, 739–40.

[70] Deusdedit, *Collectio canonum* III.279, p. 385; Gregory VII, *Registrum* 1.38, II.7, pp. 60, 135–6. See Schramm (1954) 74–7.

[71] In 1088 Vratislav restored Olmütz by appointing Bishop Andreas-Wezel (his former chaplain). The emperor invested Andreas with Olmütz in 1092, so cancelling *D H IV* 390.

[72] Cosmas, *Chronica Boemiorum* II.37, 38, pp. 135, 140. See Spangenberg (1899) 382–96; Meyer von Knonau (1903) 4:25, 49 (dating the coronation in 1085); Schmeidler (1927) 180–4; Gladel (1932) 54–5; Wegener (1959) 99–102, 225–8; Patze (1963) 1–62.

a year between the decision of the Mainz synod and the ceremony in Prague; secondly, the fact that the coronation was performed by Egilbert of Trier rather than by the metropolitan of the Bohemian Church, Wezilo of Mainz. The explanation may lie in the antipope's opposition to Vratislav's coronation. A letter of Wezilo of Mainz to Clement III (1085/6) suggests that the archbishop (presumably on behalf of the synod of Mainz) sought papal approval of the coronation, but met with a rebuff.[73] The coronation was consequently delayed and had to be performed by the archbishop of Trier, since Wezilo would not risk offending the antipope by crowning Vratislav without his permission. Clement III's opposition to the coronation seems to be explained by a letter which he sent to Vratislav between 1088 and 1092, voicing a long-standing grievance: Vratislav's failure to pay the tribute promised to the Roman church by his predecessor.[74] Whether Vratislav ever paid the tribute and Clement confirmed his royal title is unknown. The case of the Bohemian coronation provides an unexpected glimpse of the relations of Henry IV and his antipope. In his determination to vindicate papal claims, Clement III was ready to pursue a line independent of that of his protector. Henry IV was eager to have his pope's sanction for the creation of a Bohemian king. While he was prepared to delay the project in the light of Clement's reservations, however, he was not prepared to abandon it: Vratislav was too important an ally.

The coronation in Prague marked a further stage in the process of integrating Bohemia in the empire, which began in the early tenth century when the Ottonian kings extorted tribute from the Bohemians. It was accelerated in the reign of Henry III, who received an oath of fealty from Duke Bretislav I (1041) and invested his successor Spitignev II with his duchy (1055). Now in 1085 Henry IV rewarded the distinguished services of Vratislav II in a manner which accentuated the superiority of his own office. Vratislav's royal title was not, however, inherited by his heirs: his sons Bretislav II and Borivoi II bore the title of duke. The next Bohemian ruler to bear the royal title was Vratislav's grandson, Vladislav II, raised to the kingship by Emperor Frederick I (1158). At the synod of Mainz 'Henry IV created a new form of kingship', unprecedented in Europe: kingship *ad personam*, a personal dignity conferred on a particular individual and incapable of being inherited by his successors. The synod of Mainz did not transform the Przemyslids into a royal dynasty, but held out to Vratislav's successors the possibility that if they served the emperor with equal distinction, they might receive the same reward. Henry shrewdly retained the power of conferring or withholding the royal title.[75]

After the synod of Mainz Henry's immediate concern was to enforce the

[73] *Briefsammlungen* pp. 389–91.   [74] *Ibid.* pp. 387–9. See Ziese (1982) 114–18.
[75] Schramm (1968) 346–56.

decisions concerning the deposition and replacement of bishops. He went first to Metz to ensure that Bishop Herman was removed and Walo installed. Herman fled the city before the emperor's arrival and eventually took refuge with Matilda, margravine of Tuscany.[76] The emperor used this visit in June to mediate in a conflict further north, in the duchy of Lower Lotharingia.[77] A decade earlier, on the death of Duke Godfrey III, Henry had conferred the duchy on his two-year-old son Conrad, appointing as his deputy Count Albert III of Namur (the husband of Godfrey III's elder sister) and ignoring the will of the late duke, who wished to be succeeded by Godfrey of Bouillon (the son of his younger sister). Of Godfrey III's territories his nephew received only the march of Antwerp.[78] During the ensuing decade Lower Lotharingian politics came to be dominated by the younger Godfrey's attempts to gain a larger share of his inheritance. His principal success was to capture from Albert the fortress of Bouillon (near the southern frontier of the duchy), one of the most important Verdun family possessions.[79] Godfrey could rely on the support of Bishop Henry of Liège, a kinsman of the house of Verdun who had owed his promotion as bishop to the influence of Duke Godfrey III. The bishop of Liège had been Godfrey III's closest associate in the government of the duchy.[80] Bishop Henry wished to restore this close cooperation and enhance the influence of his church by promoting Godfrey of Bouillon's claim to the ducal office. Albert of Namur was supported by the counts of Chiny and Limburg and most importantly by Bishop Theoderic of Verdun. The consequence of this internal strife in Lower Lotharingia was a notable decline in ducal authority. The Salian prince Conrad was an absentee duke: he spent most of the period 1076–85 in the Italian kingdom, representing or accompanying his father.[81] The clearest indication of the diminishing significance of the duke's authority was the appearance of the 'peace of God', beginning in 1082 in the diocese of Liège.[82] Bishop Henry organised the peace with the cooperation of the princes of his diocese, including Margrave Godfrey IV of Antwerp, and enhanced his own prestige and influence in the duchy, while neutralising hostility within his diocese towards Godfrey's ambitions.

Bishop Henry's ambitions were opposed by his Upper Lotharingian neighbour, Bishop Theoderic of Verdun, who had spent much of his long episcopal career disputing control of the county of Verdun with the Verdun family. After

---

[76] Herman, kinsman of the house of Verdun, was related by marriage to Matilda: *Briefsammlungen* pp. 50–2; Hugh, *Chronicon* II, p. 471. See Salloch (1931) 51.

[77] *D H IV* 373; Hugh II, p. 471. See Meyer von Knonau (1903) 4:35–9.

[78] See above p. 148.   [79] Mohr (1976) 2:63–9; Werner (1991) 444–5, 450–2, 464–5.

[80] Meyer von Knonau (1894) 2:65–8.

[81] E. Goez (1996) 6–15. Henry had made only three brief visits since investing Conrad with the duchy: Kilian (1886) 145–6, 148.   [82] See above p. 249.

Godfrey III's death he had therefore readily acquiesced in the transference of the county to Albert of Namur, a candidate far more acceptable to him than the nephew of the late duke. As the ally both of Albert, the 'vice-duke' appointed by the king, and of Matilda of Tuscany, the close confidante of the pope, Theoderic wished to avoid taking sides in the conflict of Gregory VII and Henry IV. Initially his strategy was to mediate between the opponents, working in concert with Matilda.[83] Henry's second Italian expedition and condemnation of Matilda in 1081 finally compelled Theoderic to take sides. On his triumphant return from Italy in 1084 the emperor wrote to Theoderic as to one enjoying his special trust. Theoderic at last obeyed his command to consecrate Egilbert of Trier and also consecrated the new bishop whom Henry invested in place of Herman of Metz. Theoderic was at last fully committed to the imperial party and Henry IV was careful to consult his interests in the settlement which he now devised for Lotharingia. The emperor was anxious both to end a conflict between such valued supporters of the regime as Theoderic of Verdun and Henry of Liège and to enlist the support of Godfrey of Bouillon for the imperial cause. His solution was to confer the county of Verdun on Godfrey and compensate Theoderic by granting to his church estates confiscated from Matilda of Tuscany. These were family possessions of Duke Godfrey III to which both his widow and his nephew laid claim.[84] The emperor's settlement failed, however, to satisfy Godfrey's ambitions. He continued to extend his control over Lower Lotharingia and now had new grounds for quarrelling with the church of Verdun, in the shape of the confiscated estates. Henry IV was obliged to reconsider the question of the government of Lower Lotharingia in 1087, this time imposing a more radical solution.[85]

Meanwhile in the early summer of 1085 conditions in Saxony encouraged the emperor to mount the expedition postponed from the previous Lent. 'The face of Saxony [was] irrevocably altered' as, deaf to the arguments of their bishops, the Saxon princes competed with each other to win the emperor's favour, 'now that he was about to become master of Saxony and of the whole German kingdom'. An embittered Saxon observer attributed this disintegration of the successful Saxon alliance of 1073–85 to the inconstancy and incompetence of the younger generation of Saxon princes: 'the Saxon principalities had fallen into the hands of vacillating boys'.[86] The case of Theoderic of

[83] Theoderic and Albert were jointly entrusted by Matilda with the management of her inheritance in Lotharingia: *Chronicon sancti Huberti Andaginensis* c. 44, p. 591; Laurence, *Gesta episcoporum Virdunensium* c. 8, p. 495. See Overmann (1895) 207–8.

[84] *D H IV* 373: estates of Stenay and Mouzay. See Overmann (1895) 152; Meyer von Knonau (1903) 4:39; Mohr (1976) 2:67–8.   [85] See below p. 263.

[86] 'Saxon report' (*Annales Magdeburgenses* 1085, p. 177; *Annalista Saxo* 1085, p. 723). Cf. *Liber de unitate ecclesiae* II.28, p. 250.

Katlenburg, murdered by compatriots on 21 January, shows that the disintegration of the Saxon opposition was a violent process. A similar case was the murder on 5 February 1085 of Frederick of Putelendorf, son of the Saxon count palatine Frederick II of Goseck (a rebel leader in 1073), allegedly by the Thuringian count Ludwig 'the Leaper'.[87] At the beginning of July the emperor entered Saxony 'with a great army' and, meeting with no resistance, made for Magdeburg, where 'he was received according to royal custom'. The news of his approach prompted his foes Archbishop Hartwig of Magdeburg and the bishops of Halberstadt, Merseburg and Minden, together with the anti-king Herman, to take refuge among the Danes. The east Saxon bishops, a Gregorian faction within the Saxon opposition, alone refused to submit to Henry. The secular princes, 'who had previously declared that they would resist Henry solely in defence of the apostolic see', now demonstrated that the Gregorian cause was not their primary motive for rebellion.[88] The princes' submission was achieved by the emperor's guarantee reported by Udo of Hildesheim, that 'he would never infringe the rights that [the Saxons] had most properly and creditably enjoyed since the time of their conqueror Charles [the Great]'. The emperor's promises convinced the princes 'that they no longer had any reason to disinherit Henry of the kingdom of his ancestors, since he had experienced the might of Saxons and been corrected and wished to assure them that the laws of their ancestors would never be broken'.[89] This was the cause for which the Saxon rebels had been fighting since 1073 and, although they had been allied since 1076 with the German supporters of Gregory VII, they still fought principally for 'the laws of their ancestors' rather than for the 'defence of the apostolic see'. In the summer of 1085 they believed themselves victorious: Henry IV had conceded their essential demand.

On 13 July in Magdeburg the emperor began the process of installing his appointees in the Saxon bishoprics declared vacant by the synod of Mainz. Abbot Hartwig of Hersfeld was consecrated archbishop of Magdeburg in the presence of the emperor, the archbishops of Mainz and Cologne and 'very many other bishops'.[90] It is possible that during Henry's sojourn in Magdeburg the Saxon princes carried out the formal deposition of his rival, the anti-king, in an assembly that was 'a Forchheim in reverse'.[91] It was

---

[87] *Cronica Reinhardsbrunnensis* 1062, p. 522. Cf. *Annalista Saxo* 1056, p. 690. See Meyer von Knonau (1903) 4:48; Patze (1962) 177; Fenske (1977) 243, 247, 251, 255.

[88] 'Saxon report', pp. 177, 723. Cf. *Liber de unitate* II.22, p. 239.

[89] 'Saxon report', pp. 177, 723.   [90] *Liber de unitate* II.28, p. 250.

[91] *Annales Wirziburgenses* 1086, p. 245; Frutolf, *Chronica* 1087, p. 102; *Annales Augustani* 1088, p. 133. 'Deposition' in 1085: Bernold, *Chronicon* 1085, p. 444; 'Saxon report', pp. 177, 723; *Annalium Ratisbonensium fragmentum* 1085, p. 89; *Gesta archiepiscoporum Magdeburgensium* p. 40. See Giese (1979) 177–8.

perhaps on the same occasion that the princes renewed their oaths of fealty to Henry. The restoration of Henry IV's authority in Saxony was shortlived. After he disbanded his army in July, 'the Saxons and Thuringians reverted to their customary disloyalty and after barely two months, oblivious of the fealty and peace that they had promised on oath, made war on the emperor and forced him to depart from Saxony'.[92] The Saxons' grievances are reported by two Henrician chronicles, giving different but equally plausible reasons for their revolt. According to a Lotharingian account, many princes submitted to the emperor 'on condition that their property was to be restored to all those who had been outlawed for their part in the rebellion. Since this was not performed, they rebelled once more.' The Regensburg chronicler recorded that Henry 'wished to make changes in certain governmental offices without [the Saxons'] consent, which he lived to regret. Previously, when he took away the bishoprics of the bishops in Saxony who opposed him and gave them to clerks who were his subjects, they had been in agreement; but when he wished to change the secular powers in the same fashion, he perceived that almost all the Saxon princes were conspiring against him.' The emperor seems to have attempted to depose some of the Saxon counts and confer their counties on his own appointees.[93]

The emperor misjudged the situation, supposing himself to be the master of the province, with the power to purge the administration of unreliable elements and withhold the confiscated benefices of former rebels. He misinterpreted the secular princes' acquiescence in the deposition and replacement of their former allies, the Gregorian bishops. The princes were ready to sacrifice the bishops, the irreconcilable core of the Saxon opposition, for the sake of peace. They respected the monarch's right to control episcopal appointments and were evidently unconvinced by the Gregorian view of investiture. Henry's attempt 'to change the secular powers' was, however, instantly recognisable as an attack on 'the laws of their ancestors'. According to the Henrician chroniclers, 'the instigator [of the rebellion] was Count Ekbert, the emperor's kinsman': Ekbert II of Brunswick, kinsman of both emperor and empress.[94] Ekbert may have been one of the rebels disappointed in their hopes of the restoration of confiscated property: in his case, the march of Meissen, confiscated after his second rebellion in 1076.[95] Perhaps, however, he had larger ambitions,

---

[92] *Liber de unitate* II.28, p. 250.

[93] Sigebert of Gembloux, *Chronica* 1085, p. 365; *Ann. Ratisbonens. fragmentum* 1085, pp. 89–90. See Meyer von Knonau (1903) 4:49–55; Fenske (1977) 111–12; Giese (1979) 176–9; Giese (1991) 299–300.

[94] Sigebert, *Chronica* 1085, p. 365. Cf. Frutolf, *Chronica* 1085, p. 98; *DD H IV* 386, 388, 402.

[95] See above p. 153. Meyer von Knonau (1900) 3:350–1: Ekbert was reconciled to the king in 1081 and recovered Meissen. But see Fenske (1977) 76–7.

intending to exploit Saxon discontents in order to achieve the leadership in the region once enjoyed by Otto of Northeim. It is possible that he already entertained the ambition, ascribed to him two years later, of becoming the Saxons' third anti-king.[96]

Henry IV 'was compelled to retreat secretly and ingloriously to Franconia with his men', enabling the Gregorian refugees to return to their sees and Herman of Salm to celebrate Christmas in Saxony.[97] Henry was 'anxious to return with all speed with an army to lay waste the province of the Saxons', but was obliged instead to visit Bavaria in November. He must settle the conflict which followed the recent investiture of the anti-archbishop of Salzburg. Archbishop Berthold used the authority of his new office to pursue his family's vendetta against Count Engelbert of Spanheim, advocate of the church of Salzburg, laying waste the count's estates in Carinthia. Engelbert responded by excluding the archbishop from his city. This struggle, like that which had brought the emperor to Lotharingia in June, was unrelated to the conflict between the Henrician party and the adherents of the anti-king. It was damaging to the emperor, because, like the Lotharingian disorders, it divided his allies or potential allies. He was bound to support his appointee, Archbishop Berthold; but Engelbert had given useful military support in the past and Henry urgently needed his assistance in the forthcoming Saxon campaign. When the two opponents refused to suspend hostilities at the behest of his envoys, Henry himself came to Bavaria and his arrival imposed a temporary peace.[98] He conferred new benefices on Engelbert and secured his participation and that of other Bavarian princes in an expedition to Saxony after the second week of January 1086.[99]

Henry celebrated Christmas 1085 in Worms with his faithful supporters, the archbishops of Mainz, Trier and Bremen, the bishops of Bamberg, Utrecht and Würzburg and Duke Frederick of Swabia, who had doubtless been summoned to provide their contingents for the forthcoming expedition. These celebrations were the occasion for a striking demonstration of imperial generosity. The services of Liemar of Bremen and the new adherent, Udo of Hildesheim, were richly rewarded.[100] Seven diplomas for the church of Speyer were issued during a brief visit to Speyer (11–12 January 1086) and on the emperor's return to Worms (14 January), the most extensive of the series of

---

[96] See below p. 265.
[97] *Annalium Ratisbonensium fragmentum* 1085, p. 90; Bernold 1085, p. 444. See Meyer von Knonau (1903) 4:54.
[98] *D H IV* 376. See Bishop Meginward of Freising's letter to Berthold: Meyer (1882) 259–60, 263. See Meyer von Knonau (1903) 4:56–7; Steinböck (1972) 150.
[99] *Ann. Ratisbonens. fragmentum* 1085, pp. 90–1.
[100] *D H IV* 377–8. See Meyer von Knonau (1903) 4:58.

donations made to the church during the episcopate of Bishop Huzman (1075–90). The donations were made 'for the relief of [the emperor's] soul' and in memory of his parents and grandparents.[101] The context of these diplomas is reminiscent of that of the 1075 diploma conferred on Speyer before the battle of Homburg and the 'votive diploma' issued on the eve of the battle of Hohenmölsen. Perhaps like these earlier diplomas issued at moments of crisis in Henry IV's relations with the Saxons, the donations of 1086 were made to secure the aid of the Virgin Mary, the patron of the church of Speyer and the Salian dynasty, in the forthcoming Saxon campaign. Three of the diplomas of 1086, conferring property in Saxony and Hesse, have an obvious connection with the emperor's plans for Saxony. Henry's generosity implicated the church of Speyer directly in the defence of imperial interests in the province.[102]

The emperor returned to Saxony immediately after the expiration of the Christmastide truce prescribed by the peace legislation of the synod of Mainz. He was on the move by 27 January with a large army recruited 'from every one of the provinces subject to him'.[103] By 7 February he was in Wechmar in Thuringia, presiding over the trial of Ekbert II of Brunswick. Ekbert was condemned in his absence for his part in the recent rebellion. The sentence is recorded in three diplomas conferring the rebel's confiscated benefices on the church of Utrecht. '[Ekbert's] countrymen, both Saxons and Thuringians, together with all our other princes in our presence, passing sentence according to the law of nations, judged that he should be punished as a manifest enemy of the kingdom and of the Roman empire. They assigned his estates and the benefices that he held of us to our imperial dominion and power.'[104] The emphasis on the participation of Ekbert's Saxon and Thuringian compatriots was intended to underline the legality of the condemnation. On the occasion of Ekbert's previous trial as a rebel (30 October 1077) he was found guilty of 'perjury', the breach of his oath of fealty to the king (the offence for which Rudolf of Rheinfelden and his allies were also condemned in 1077).[105] In 1086 he was condemned as 'a manifest enemy of the kingdom and of the Roman empire', the closest approach in any German document of Henry IV's reign to the formulation of a concept of 'high treason'.[106]

Henry's army penetrated Saxony as far north as the River Bode without encountering the enemy. The rebels continually retreated, not risking an engagement with so powerful a force. Finally in mid-February Henry aban-

---

[101] DD H IV 379–85. See Meyer von Knonau (1903) 4:111–13; Heidrich (1988) 269, 271, 280; Heidrich (1991) 191–2. See also above pp. 202–3.   [102] Heidrich (1991) 196.
[103] Ann. Ratisbonens. fragmentum 1085, 1086, p. 91.
[104] DD H IV 386, 388, 402. See Meyer von Knonau (1903) 4:113–14.   [105] See above p. 173.
[106] See above p. 229.

doned the expedition and withdrew from the province. According to the Augsburg chronicler, the Saxon expedition failed because of a conspiracy within the imperial army. 'While his enemies retreated in various directions, [the emperor] laid waste part of the province. He would have forced those who resisted him to come to terms, had not the secret deceit of certain of his followers prevented this.'[107] The fragmentary report of the Regensburg chronicler seems to identify Count Engelbert of Spanheim as the traitor, the timing of his conspiracy being influenced by his brother, the Gregorian Archbishop Hartwig of Magdeburg, who was with the rebel army.[108] The underlying cause of his treachery was his vendetta against the Henrician anti-archbishop of Salzburg, which the emperor's mediation had failed to settle. Engelbert must already have resolved on the restoration of his brother Hartwig's ally, Gebhard of Salzburg, which he was to accomplish in 1086.[109]

Henry 'returned to Bavaria and established his court in Regensburg, where he celebrated Easter' (5 April).[110] The filling of the vacancy in the patriarchate of Aquileia at this time gave him an opportunity to review the security of the south-eastern frontier. He appointed an imperial kinsman, Udalric of Eppenstein, abbot of St Gallen since 1077. Udalric had proved himself the most active member of the Henrician party in southern Swabia in the bitter struggle against Berthold II of Zähringen and his brother, Gebhard, the Gregorian bishop of Constance and diocesan of the abbey of St Gallen. From 1086 until his death in 1121 he combined the office of abbot with that of patriarch of Aquileia.[111] The new appointment intensified his family's connection with the church of Aquileia, of which the Eppensteins were already advocates, and consolidated the hold of this family of imperial cousins over Carinthia and the neighbouring territory. Three of his brothers were already great officeholders in the region: Liutold, duke of Carinthia and margrave of Verona; Henry, margrave of Istria and Carniola; Herman, anti-bishop of Passau. The emperor had placed the defence of the south-eastern frontier of the German kingdom firmly in the hands of his Eppenstein kindred.

While Henry was celebrating Easter in Regensburg, his enemies in Bavaria struck a shrewd blow at his authority in the duchy by winning over Bishop Meginward of Freising. 'They then summoned Duke Welf [IV] and the

---

[107] *Annales Augustani* 1086, p. 131. But see *Liber de unitate ecclesiae* II.28, p. 250. Cf. Bernold 1086, p. 444. See Meyer von Knonau (1903) 4:114–15.
[108] *Ann. Ratisbonens. fragmentum* 1086, p. 91.
[109] Meyer von Knonau (1903) 4:123; Steinböck (1972) 152.
[110] *Annales Augustani* 1086, p. 131; *DD H IV* 388–90. See Meyer von Knonau (1903) 4:115.
[111] *Annales Augustani* 1085 (*sic*), p. 131; *Casus monasterii Petrishusensis* III.29, p. 656; *Casuum Sancti Galli Continuatio* II.7, p. 159. See Meyer von Knonau (1903) 4:118–20: Feierabend (1913) 54–8; Klaar (1966) 109. See above p. 188.

Swabians and ravaged almost all the province.'[112] Those 'Swabians' were probably the princes who joined Welf IV at the synod held by Bishop Gebhard in Constance on 1 April: Berthold II of Zähringen, his brother-in-law Berthold of Rheinfelden (whom the anti-Henrician party recognised as duke of Swabia) and the counts of Nellenburg, Wülflingen and Veringen.[113] The joint forces of the rebels laid siege to Regensburg and trapped Henry there 'for a long time', but then withdrew from the city, the chroniclers giving no reason for their action.[114] The likeliest explanation is that the siege was raised by the army of Duke Frederick of Swabia and Count Rapoto of Cham and Vohburg, who were campaigning in Bavaria. These imperial supporters are known to have recaptured Freising and placed a garrison there, but this was a shortlived triumph.[115] The rebel army forced the garrison's surrender and obliged Bishop Meginward to bind himself by oath to the anti-Henrician party. Soon afterwards Meginward joined Bishop Altmann of Passau and Count Engelbert of Spanheim in conducting Gebhard of Salzburg back to his archbishopric after his nine years' exile.[116]

During the summer the rebels revived the strategy of 1077–80, a joint Saxon and Swabian challenge to Henry's power at the heart of the German kingdom. The initiative came from Burchard of Halberstadt, Hartwig of Magdeburg and Ekbert II of Brunswick. The Saxons and south Germans were to confer together 'after the feast of the apostles' (29 June) near Würzburg.[117] Just as in 1077 the anti-king saw this Franconian bishopric as holding the key to the kingdom, so in 1086 the anti-Henrician party regarded the capture of Würzburg as the most dangerous blow that they could strike against the emperor. Their objective was to expel the imperial anti-bishop Meinhard and restore their ally, Adalbero. Once Würzburg was in his hands, the lines of communication between the Saxon and south German rebels would be secured. The emperor, however, anticipated their plan. Coming to Würzburg in June, he entrusted the defence of the city to Frederick of Swabia and Bishop Meinhard and set out to recruit an army of sufficient strength to encounter the rebel forces. Early in July the rebel armies began a five-week siege of Würzburg. At the news of the approach of the emperor with 'an army well supplied both with foot soldiers and with cavalry', the besiegers marched out to intercept him at Pleichfeld, north-east of the city.[118]

---

[112] *Annales Augustani* 1086, pp. 131–2. Cf. Bernold, *Chronicon* 1086, p. 444. See Meyer von Knonau (1903) 4:122.

[113] *Notitiae fundationis sancti Georgii* c. 19–21, p. 1011. See Wollasch (1964) 14–15, 97–8; Maurer (1991) 179–80.   [114] *Annales Augustani* 1086, p. 132.

[115] *Ibid.* 1086, p. 132, with the correction of von Giesebrecht (1895) 1180.

[116] *Vita Gebehardi archiepiscopi* c. 4, p. 26. See Meyer von Knonau (1903) 4:123; Steinböck (1972) 151–2.   [117] *Liber de unitate ecclesiae* II.28, pp. 250–1.

[118] *Ibid.* II.28, p. 251. See Meyer von Knonau (1903) 4:125.

The eyewitness account of the battle of Pleichfeld (11 August) by Bernold of St Blasien identifies three distinct elements in the rebel army: 'Duke Welf with his contingent', 'the Magdeburg contingent' and 'the vassals of St Peter', his term for the Swabians responsible for the siege of Würzburg. These 'vassals of St Peter' declared themselves to be participants in a holy war by bringing to the field of battle 'a very tall cross set up in a wagon and decorated with a red banner'. They won an overwhelming victory. Bernold counted 'nine huge piles of corpses' of the enemy, while claiming only thirty dead and wounded on his own side.[119] The imperial defeat was the consequence of treachery or perhaps merely of panic, originating probably among the vassals of the churches of Cologne and Utrecht. Their conduct infected the rest of the army, provoking the flight of most of the mounted warriors and paralysing the resistance of the foot soldiers.[120] If the latter were raw levies of peasants and citizens such as Henry had recruited in his campaigns against the anti-king Rudolf, that would explain the huge numbers of casualties on the imperial side.

The victorious rebels resumed the siege of Würzburg, which now surrendered without bloodshed. Bishop Adalbero was solemnly restored to his cathedral in a ceremony conducted by Hartwig of Magdeburg, Gebhard of Constance and Herman of Metz. Adalbero's restoration was, however, of short duration. When the rebels departed, leaving a garrison in the city, the emperor reappeared with fresh forces, recaptured Würzburg and reinstated Bishop Meinhard. Adalbero refused to submit to Henry, but the emperor allowed him and his garrison to go free, treating him with a leniency which surprised the chroniclers. This leniency was not, however, out of character with the emperor's recent conduct towards Adalbero. Henry genuinely desired a reconciliation.[121] The status and influence that he enjoyed as the longest-serving member of the German episcopate would have made Adalbero's reconciliation at the least a considerable propaganda coup for the regime. The ephemeral nature of Adalbero's triumph highlights the failure of the rebels to exploit the victory of Pleichfeld. The most plausible explanation is that the anti-Henrician opposition was paralysed by internal divisions: the divisions between Swabians and Saxons which had previously surfaced at the time of the elections of the anti-kings in 1077 and 1081; the divisions between the ecclesiastical and secular princes of Saxony which had made possible Henry's temporary restoration in 1085. Only the Gregorian bishops, led by Hartwig of Magdeburg, seem to have

---

[119] Bernold, *Chronicon* 1086, pp. 444–5. See Robinson (1989) 186–7.
[120] *Annales Augustani* 1086, p. 132; *Liber de unitate* II.16, 28, 29, pp. 231, 250–1, 253–6; *Mariani Chronici Continuatio II* 1108(=1086), pp. 563–4; *Vita Heinrici IV* c. 4, pp. 18–19; *Annales Hildesheimenses* 1086, p. 49. See Meyer von Knonau (1903) 4:125–31; Cram (1955) 148–9, 215.
[121] *Liber de unitate* II.29, p. 254.

been resolute for war.[122] The unpredictable ambitions of Ekbert of Brunswick must have compelled the other rebels to exercise caution.

It is evident that the victory of Pleichfeld did nothing to revive the fortunes of Herman of Salm. No contemporary author mentioned Herman's participation in the battle, although there is no reason to doubt that he was present, probably in the Swabian contingent (Bernold's 'vassals of St Peter').[123] During his subsequent sojourn in Swabia, Herman 'had no royal income such as would enable him to live as befitted the royal dignity because none of the bishops was willing to be his subject', so that he was obliged to return to Saxony.[124] He had presumably hoped for assistance in reversing the deposition recently decreed by the Saxons, but the Swabians were not interested in his restoration. The divisions in the anti-Henrician party were revealed by an incident of December 1086. Henry, campaigning in Bavaria, was besieging a fortress, when the arrival of Welf IV and Berthold of Rheinfelden on 24 December forced him to abandon the siege. Before the imperial army withdrew, however, the princes on both sides agreed to hold a conference in Oppenheim in February 1087.[125] This incident reveals that the south German rebel leaders negotiated with the imperial party without consulting either Herman of Salm or, more importantly, their Saxon allies. There is no sign of any Saxon involvement in the Oppenheim conference, which is doubtless why it failed to secure peace. 'The council arranged in Oppenheim broke up without accomplishing anything'.[126] The emperor's enemies blamed the failure of the conference on his refusal to attend. Six months later, however, he was to meet his enemies in a 'general conference' in Speyer. This conference in August involved the Saxons, whose participation Henry regarded as essential to the peace process.[127]

By the time of the council of Speyer the emperor had strengthened the hold of his dynasty over the kingdom by securing the coronation of his thirteen-year-old son. Conrad was consecrated by Archbishop Sigewin of Cologne in Aachen on 30 May 1087. The ceremony was attended by an impressive gathering of bishops and secular princes, including Godfrey of Bouillon, margrave of Antwerp, Count Albert III of Namur and Duke Magnus Billung of Saxony, apparently now a loyal adherent of the emperor.[128] (This same imperial

---

[122] *Ibid.* II.28, p. 251.

[123] *Annales sancti Disibodi* 1086, p. 9. See Meyer von Knonau (1903) 4:132.

[124] *Casus monasterii Petrishusensis* c. 44, p. 648.   [125] Bernold, *Chronicon* 1086, p. 445.

[126] *Annales Augustani* 1087, p. 132; Bernold, *Chronicon* 1087, p. 446. See Meyer von Knonau (1903) 4:133–4, 158.   [127] *Annales Patherbrunnenses* 1087, p. 100.

[128] *Annales Weissenburgenses* 1087, p. 57; *Annales Patherbrunnenses* 1087, p. 100. Cf. *DD H IV* 394–5. See Meyer von Knonau (1903) 4:159–61; E. Goez (1996) 16. Magnus Billung: Freytag (1951) 22–3; Fenske (1977) 66; Althoff (1991) 328.

Carolingian setting of Aachen had been chosen by Henry III for the coronation of the young Henry IV, who came here again in 1056 for the ceremony
that marked the beginning of his reign.)[129] Conrad had already served for two
lengthy periods as his father's representative in the Italian kingdom and he was
soon to resume that duty, with his authority enhanced by the royal title. By
January 1088 he was once more in Italy, in the company of the new Italian
chancellor, Bishop Ogerius of Ivrea, whom the emperor had probably
appointed as the young king's special adviser.[130] Conrad's elevation to the
kingship created a vacancy in the office of duke of Lower Lotharingia.[131]
Henry seems to have used this opportunity to complete the process of restoring the duchy to the house of Verdun, in the person of Godfrey of Bouillon,
nephew and heir of the late Duke Godfrey III.[132] Given that Godfrey had been
invested in 1085 with the county of Verdun and that he was already master of
Bouillon, it would have been impossible for the emperor to withhold the
duchy for long.[133]

Two months after his son's coronation the emperor was in Speyer for the
conference of the two rival parties in the kingdom, which assembled on 1
August. According to the Augsburg chronicler, 'the council of Speyer began
badly and ended worse'.[134] There seems to have been a debate like that of
Gerstungen-Berka in 1085. The princes 'faithfully promised to help [Henry]
to gain control of the kingdom, if he would free himself of his excommunication'. On Henry's refusing to acknowledge himself lawfully excommunicate,
the opposition faction 'decided to have no peace and no agreement with
him'.[135] The resolution of the anti-Henrician party was strengthened by two
messages received during the conference: a promise of support from King
Ladislaus I of Hungary[136] and a letter from the pope. The newly consecrated
Victor III 'announced his promotion to the princes of the kingdom'.[137]
Elected on 24 May 1086, the former Abbot Desiderius of Monte Cassino, cardinal priest of S. Cecilia, was persuaded to accept the papal insignia only in
early March 1087. His reluctance was the consequence of ill-health, the opposition of the extreme wing of the Gregorian party and the internal quarrels of

---

[129] See above pp. 22, 26.
[130] *D Konrad* I (*DD H IV*, appendix); Gawlik (1970b) 215–16; E. Goez (1996) 18–20.
[131] Conrad's last appearance as duke: *DD H IV* 394–5.
[132] *Annales sancti Jacobi Leodiensis* 1087, p. 639. Sigebert, *Chronica* 1089, p. 366 is contradicted
      by a St Trond charter of 1088: Despy (1958) 1281. See also Meyer von Knonau (1903)
      4:249–50; Mohr (1976) 2:68–9; Werner (1991) 402, 465.
[133] Laurence, *Gesta episcoporum Virdunensium* p. 494.
[134] *Annales Augustani* 1087, p. 132. Cf. *Annales Patherbrunnenses* 1087, p. 100.
[135] Bernold, *Chronicon* 1087, p. 446. See Meyer von Knonau (1903) 4:162–3.
[136] Bernold, *Chronicon* 1087, p. 446.   [137] *Ibid.*

his allies, the Normans of southern Italy.[138] The Gregorian Bernold of St Blasien was the only chronicler to claim that Victor 'confirmed the judgement of his predecessor of pious memory Pope Gregory on Henry and all his supporters'. His claim is at odds with the account of Victor's synod of Benevento (August 1087) in the Monte Cassino chronicle. This account mentions the excommunication and deposition of 'the heresiarch Wibert', but says nothing of a similar condemnation of Henry IV.[139] Modern scholarship represents Victor III, in contrast to his predecessor, as conciliatory in his attitude towards the emperor.[140]

After his opponents declared at the Speyer conference that they would 'have no peace and no agreement' with him, Henry planned to lead an expedition against them in the first week of October 1087. This expedition was, however, delayed by the illness that overtook the emperor during the autumn.[141] He was still not fully recovered when his troops eventually marched into Saxony with their Bohemian allies. King Vratislav's forces had already been active in the march of Meissen, where they had won 'a bloody victory' against Ekbert II of Brunswick (2 July).[142] The emperor's expedition was cut short by a Saxon initiative: they would make peace 'according to the honour of the emperor and the advice of his princes', if Henry 'would desist from killing and devastation and withdraw from the province'. In the opinion of the Augsburg chronicler, the emperor's war of attrition in Thuringia and Saxony had forced the rebels' submission.[143] Henry agreed to the Saxon terms and withdrew to the abbey of Hersfeld, where he set up his headquarters. The Saxon commander, Ekbert of Brunswick, 'appeared there as a suppliant to the emperor, promised him fealty on oath [and] received his march and his counties from the emperor'.[144] An imperial diploma records that after Ekbert's submission Henry committed to him 'the care of all our affairs in Saxony and in Thuringia so that we might enter and leave [the province] in complete security'. The diploma also records the emperor's motives in pardoning this kinsman who had been condemned three times for rebellion. Ekbert promised 'that we should never find him unfaithful towards us and that through him we should bring the scattered princes of the kingdom together in unity'.[145] The restoration of Ekbert seemed

[138] Meyer von Knonau (1903) 4:185–7; Cowdrey (1983) 185–206.

[139] *Chronica monasterii Casinensis* III.72, pp. 453–5.

[140] Becker (1964) 83–5; Deér (1972) 137, 140–1; Ziese (1982) 96–8: Victor as the 'candidate of the Italian Normans'. But see Cowdrey (1983) 207–13; Loud (1985) 84–5, 97.

[141] Bernold, *Chronicon* 1087, pp. 446, 447. See Meyer von Knonau (1903) 4:169.

[142] Cosmas, *Chronica Boemorum* II.39, pp. 141–2. See Meyer von Knonau (1903) 4:170; Wegener (1959) 119.   [143] *Annales Augustani* 1087, p. 133.

[144] *Liber de unitate ecclesiae* II.33, pp. 259–60. Cf. Bernold, *Chronicon* 1087, p. 447; *Annales Augustani* 1087, p. 133; *Annales Patherbrunnenses* 1087, p. 101. See Meyer von Knonau (1903) 4:171–3; Fenske (1977) 114–16; Althoff (1989) 284–6.   [145] *D H IV* 402.

to offer the chance of a general reconciliation. It was a risky venture, not least because it would offend those imperial adherents who had profited from Ekbert's deposition, above all King Vratislav of Bohemia, on whom Henry had conferred his march of Meissen. Ekbert's restoration must have contributed to the cooling of relations between Vratislav and the emperor which is discernible at this time.[146]

This costly attempt at reconciliation proved vain. According to the Hersfeld polemicist, on the day after the reconciliation Ekbert sent envoys to inform the emperor that he considered himself bound by his previous oath to his Saxon compatriots and would not perform what he had promised. 'The emperor had already dismissed his army and so he could not punish the great impiety and disloyalty of this man.' Ekbert's mind was changed by the intervention of 'those false bishops' Hartwig of Magdeburg and Burchard of Halberstadt, who 'promised him that he would be their king'.[147] There is no reason to doubt the claim of the Hersfeld polemicist that Hartwig and Burchard were responsible for the scheme of setting up Ekbert as the third of the anti-kings supported by the Saxon rebels. As the commander of the rebel forces, the most powerful of the Saxon princes, successor to the position of Otto of Northeim, with a record of rebellion against the crown dating back to 1073, Ekbert was indispensable to the continuance of the rebellion. His reconciliation with the emperor must signal the break-up of the opposition movement in Saxony. As in 1085, the Gregorian prelates faced political isolation: they had no choice but to bind Ekbert to their cause by outbidding the emperor with the offer of the crown. The quickest way for Henry IV to regain his lordship over Saxony was to win over the most influential Saxon prince and delegate to him the government of the province. It was the strategy that he had used in 1075, when he granted 'his authority and the administration of public affairs throughout Saxony' to the rebel leader, Otto of Northeim.[148] Ekbert was to have played a similar role (analogous to that currently played by another imperial kinsman, Liutold of Eppenstein, in south-eastern Germany). The restoration of Margrave Ekbert would enable the emperor to demonstrate his magnanimity and his respect for 'the laws of the Saxons'. (Henry doubtless recalled that one reason for the failure of the pacification of Saxony in 1085 was his refusal to restore the property of 'all those who had been outlawed for their part in the rebellion'.)[149] The emperor's hopes were thwarted by the volatile personality and boundless ambition of his kinsman. Lacking an adequate force to pursue the traitor, the emperor was obliged to

---

[146] Wezilo of Mainz, letter to Vratislav: *Briefsammlungen* pp. 399–400. See Meyer von Knonau (1903) 4:173.

[147] *Liber de unitate* II.33, p. 260. Cf. *Annales Augustani* 1087, p. 133; Bernold, *Chronicon* 1087, p. 447.   [148] See above p. 103.   [149] See above p. 256.

withdraw from Hersfeld and make for Bavaria, where he celebrated Christmas.[150]

It was during this season that his empress died in the twenty-second year of their marriage (27 December 1087).[151] Bertha of Turin was perhaps thirty-six (a year younger than her husband) at the time of her death. She was buried in the cathedral of Speyer, the mausoleum of the Salian dynasty, beside her husband's grandmother, Empress Gisela. Bertha was to be commemorated in eleven imperial donations for the repose of her soul, in 1091, 1097, 1101, 1102 and 1103, appearing as part of a family group including Conrad II, Gisela and Henry III.[152] She had given birth to five children, two of whom (Adelaide and Henry) died in infancy. Agnes (born in 1072 or 1073), Conrad (born in 1074) and Henry V (born in 1086) survived their mother. The narrative sources contain little information about the queen and empress: Bertha is known to historians mainly from the royal and imperial diplomas in which she appears as intervener. The formula 'consort of the kingdom' used in the eleventh century to convey the unique status of the woman married both to the monarch and to the monarchy, a symbol of the continuity of his dynasty, was regularly applied to Bertha. Like her predecessors Agnes and Gisela, she was described as 'most beloved consort of our kingdom and our marriage-bed' and (after the imperial coronation) 'august empress, the associate of kingdom and marriage-bed'.[153] If the interventions of Bertha in her husband's diplomas are compared with those of Agnes during the years of her marriage to Henry III,[154] it is evident that Bertha was a far less visible personage in the royal entourage, far less consistently involved in the workings of royal government than Agnes had been in the years 1043–56. Nevertheless no other intervener appears in the diplomas of 1066–87 as frequently as Bertha.[155] In terms of their appearance in diplomas, there is a strong contrast between Bertha and Henry IV's second wife, Eupraxia-Adelaide, whose name appears in only one extant diploma.[156]

The emperor's betrothal to Eupraxia-Adelaide took place before the end of 1088 in Saxony. By the time of this visit the province had undergone a political transformation, originating in the disappointment of the hopes of Ekbert II of Meissen at the beginning of the year. He 'made public his desire for the

---

[150] Meyer von Knonau (1903) 4:173 n. 23, correcting Kilian (1886) 110–11.

[151] *Annales Augustani* 1088, p. 133; Frutolf, *Chronica* 1088, p. 102. See Meyer von Knonau (1903) 4:174.   [152] *DD H IV* 424, 426, 454, 468, 470a, 471, 473–5, 477, 479. Cf. *D Konrad* 5.

[153] Gawlik (1970a) 189–91. See also above p. 61.

[154] Agnes appeared in 119 of 135 diplomas containing intervention clauses: Schetter (1935) 20–5; Black-Veldtrup (1995) 63–84.

[155] In 135 diplomas she appeared 58 times as intervener (nine times as sole intervener), once as witness: Gawlik (1970a) 128–9.   [156] *D H IV* 407.

kingship but it was in vain, for the princes of the kingdom refused to give their approval'.[157] The Hersfeld polemicist claimed that Hartwig of Magdeburg and Burchard of Halberstadt 'duped [Ekbert] and did not confer on him the kingship, as they promised': their promise had been a ploy to prevent his reconciliation with the emperor. It is more likely that the Gregorians genuinely wished to strengthen their party by replacing Herman of Salm with a more effective anti-king. Their candidate, however, was unacceptable to the secular princes of Saxony, who had experienced Ekbert's unreliability, and to the south Germans, who had consistently foiled the election of a Saxon anti-king. The consequence was that Ekbert 'withdrew from his alliance with [the Gregorian] party and again confirmed a treaty of peace and fealty with the emperor, giving hostages and swearing oaths'.[158] Ekbert now launched a vendetta against Burchard of Halberstadt, laying waste his diocese. While Burchard was in Goslar, conferring with his allies, Hartwig of Magdeburg and Count Cuno of Beichlingen (son of Otto of Northeim), he was killed in a fight between the citizens of Goslar and the vassals and *ministeriales* of Halberstadt (7 April). Ekbert was widely regarded as responsible for his death.[159] The immediate sequel of Burchard's death suggested that the Hersfeld polemicist was correct in identifying him as the backbone of the anti-Henrician opposition.[160] The loss of Burchard and the hostility of Ekbert caused the Saxon opposition to disintegrate. 'Immediately the great majority of the Saxons surrendered to the emperor.'[161]

Hartwig of Magdeburg was the first to submit, promising to bring about the surrender of all Henry's enemies.[162] During the summer the bishops of Merseburg and Naumburg joined Hartwig in the imperial entourage, together with Count Siegfried III of Boyneburg (second son of Otto of Northeim) and the Wettin prince Henry I of Eilenburg.[163] Hartwig was immediately restored to the archbishopric of Magdeburg, despite the sentence pronounced against him at the synod of Mainz in 1085 and without reference to the antipope, by whose authority he had been deposed.[164] The emperor was obviously anxious that the process of reconciliation in Saxony should not lose momentum. He

---

[157] Bernold, *Chronicon* 1088, p. 447.

[158] *Liber de unitate* II.35, p. 261. See Meyer von Knonau (1903) 4:206–9; Giese (1979) 180.

[159] *Annalista Saxo* 1088, pp. 724–6 (Herrand of Ilsenburg's account). Cf. *Liber de unitate* II.31, 35, pp. 257, 261; Bernold, *Chronicon* 1088, p. 447. See Meyer von Knonau (1903) 4:209–13; Fenske (1977) 116–18, 201.

[160] *Liber de unitate* II.31, p. 257. Cf. *Annales Augustani* 1088, p. 133.

[161] *Annales Brunwilarenses* 1083 (*sic*), p. 725.

[162] *Liber de unitate* II.25, 35, pp. 246, 261–2. See Meyer von Knonau (1903) 4:213–14; Claude (1972) 360–4, 375–6, 378–9; Fenske (1977) 201–4.   [163] *D H IV* 402.

[164] *Liber de unitate* II.25, p. 246; cf. II.35, pp. 261–2. See Zafarana (1966a) 637–8.

conferred on Hartwig the role of his representative in Saxony and Thuringia, the same role that he had intended for Ekbert after his submission in 1087. An imperial letter of 1088/9 illustrates Henry's reliance on the archbishop. 'We have a special trust in you before all others and shortly before we departed from you, we entrusted all our affairs to you . . . We regard you as a most intimate friend . . . As proof of this trust we once more commit ourselves and all our affairs to you.'[165] Hartwig's conduct in office demonstrated that the emperor's strategy was a wise one, which gained him the trust of the Saxons. From his submission in 1088 until his death in 1102 Hartwig remained loyal to the emperor without, however, losing his attachment to the principles of the Gregorian reform movement.[166] The apparent contradictions in Hartwig's situation are explained in an obituary identifying Hartwig's two main preoccupations: he was 'zealous in increasing the income of the church over which he presided' and he was 'a tireless mediator between the two parties in the work of ending the schism'.[167] The 1070s and 1080s were a period of material decline in the history of the church of Magdeburg, in which the church's property was used to purchase secular support for the struggle against Henry IV. As a prudent steward, Hartwig realised that the decline could only be reversed by making peace with the emperor; as a Gregorian, he believed that permanent peace in the kingdom depended on the settlement of the conflict of empire and papacy.

Soon after the murder of Burchard of Halberstadt and the resultant dissolution of his faction in Saxony, the German Gregorian party suffered another serious loss with the death of Archbishop Gebhard of Salzburg (15/16 June 1088), for so long the spokesman and coordinator of the Saxon and south German enemies of Henry IV. In the opinion of the Augsburg chronicler, Gebhard and Burchard of Halberstadt were the two 'instigators' of the civil war, whose deaths made possible the pacification of the kingdom.[168] Gebhard's death coincided with the departure of the former anti-king Herman of Salm from Saxony. Without adequate resources to sustain the royal title and dependent throughout his reign on the generosity of the Gregorian leaders, Herman was compelled by their desertion to abandon his royal ambitions.[169] 'With the permission of the emperor'[170] he returned to his native land of Lotharingia, where he died on 28 September 1088. Contemporary chroni-

---

[165] Henry IV, *Letter* 22, p. 32.
[166] Urban II, *JL* 5784: *Monumenta Historica Ducatus Carinthiae* 3, 204–5 (no. 508). See Claude (1972) 369.   [167] Ekkehard of Aura, *Chronica* I, p. 180.
[168] *Annales Augustani* 1088, p. 133. Cf. Bernold, *Chronicon* 1088, p. 448. See Meyer von Knonau (1903) 4:214–17; Steinböck (1972) 157.   [169] *Liber de unitate* II.16, p. 231.
[170] Frutolf, *Chronica* 1087, p. 102. Cf. *Gesta episcoporum Halberstadensium* p. 100. See Meyer von Knonau (1903) 4:221.

clers believed that Herman met his death while besieging a fortress.[171] It is likely that he spent the last months of his life pursuing claims to land and office in Lotharingia and that the siege in which he died was connected with these claims. Herman's opponent is likely to have been Henry of Laach, who was probably his first cousin, a loyal Henrician on whom the emperor had conferred the office of Lotharingian count palatine in 1085.[172] The luckless Herman, acknowledged as king only in the chronicle of Bernold of St Blasien, 'was honourably buried in his homeland of Metz'.[173]

Herman's departure completed the transformation of the Saxon political landscape. The emperor returned to the province in summer 1088 to receive the submission of the Gregorian bishops and their associates and perhaps also to negotiate his betrothal. His second wife was the Russian princess Eupraxia, known in Germany by the name Adelaide, daughter of Vsevolod, grand prince of Kiev, and perhaps twenty years old at the time of her betrothal to the emperor. She was the widow of Count Henry III of Stade, margrave of the Saxon Nordmark (son of one of the rebel leaders of 1073), who had died in 1087.[174] The emperor's motive in seeking the hand of this young widow is probably to be sought in her Saxon, rather than her Russian, connections. It was part of a campaign to win friends in Saxony in the aftermath of the disintegration of the Gregorian faction.[175] It was appropriate that after the wedding in the summer of 1089, Eupraxia was crowned in Cologne by Hartwig of Magdeburg.[176] The emperor was able to accord this signal honour to Hartwig probably because the new archbishop of Cologne, Herman (a kinsman of Hartwig) had not yet received consecration and could not perform the ceremony.

While the other Saxon princes sought peace in summer 1088, Ekbert of Meissen, who had 'confirmed a treaty of peace and fealty with the emperor' at the beginning of the year, now resumed his rebellion.[177] Ekbert's motives have been variously interpreted: he was angered by the emperor's concessions to Vratislav of Bohemia in the march of Meissen; he resented the imperial favour shown to his brother-in-law, Henry I of Eilenburg, margrave of Lower

---

[171] Bernold, *Chronicon* 1088, p. 448; *Annales Augustani* 1088, p. 133; *Annales Patherbrunnenses* 1088, p. 101; *Annales Palidenses* 1087 (*sic*), p. 71; *Vita Heinrici IV* c. 4, p. 20. See Meyer von Knonau (1903) 4:226–9; Twellenkamp (1991) 496.

[172] Meyer von Knonau (1903) 4:229; Renn (1941) 109–13, 135.

[173] Bernold, *Chronicon* 1088, p. 448.

[174] *Annalista Saxo* 1082, p. 721; *Annales Augustani* 1089, p. 133; *Liber de unitate* II.35, p. 262. (Some chroniclers gave Eupraxia the name 'Praxedis'.) Vsevolod was the son of grand prince Yaroslav 'the Wise', ally of Emperor Conrad II: Bresslau (1879) 331.

[175] Von Giesebrecht (1890) 628.

[176] *Liber de unitate* II.26, p. 248. Cf. Frutolf, *Chronica* 1089, p. 104. See Meyer von Knonau (1903) 4:217, 251–2.   [177] *Liber de unitate* II.35, p. 262.

Lusatia, on his recent submission; his hopes of the crown were reawakened by Herman of Salm's departure from Saxony.[178] The most obvious explanation is that Ekbert renewed his fealty to the emperor in the expectation of receiving 'the care of all affairs in Saxony and in Thuringia', only to see this office conferred on his enemy, Hartwig of Magdeburg. The emperor's response to the rebellion was to hold an assembly of princes in Quedlinburg, in which Ekbert was judged by his compatriots and condemned in his absence. It was an impressive gathering, uniting the leaders of the opposing Saxon parties: the Henricians Liemar of Bremen and the bishops of Münster, Minden, Halberstadt and Hildesheim and the Gregorians Hartwig of Magdeburg and the bishops of Naumburg and Merseburg, together with the secular princes Siegfried III of Boyneburg and Henry of Eilenburg. Their display of unity was an index of the alarm generated in the province by the unstable ambitions of Ekbert of Meissen. The imperial record emphasised that the proceedings against Ekbert (like those in Wechmar in 1086) were initiated by his fellow princes. 'Siegfried, the son of Otto [of Northeim] the former duke, judged that Ekbert should be prosecuted as a public enemy of the kingdom and as the enemy of his lord, the emperor. Margrave Henry and his peers judged that the same Ekbert must be deprived of his march and of his other property and they assigned what had been taken from him to [the emperor's] power.'[179] The march of Meissen was conferred on Henry I of Eilenburg, margrave of Lower Lusatia, the investiture perhaps taking place at this assembly.

On 14 August 1088 the imperial army laid siege to Ekbert's castle of Gleichen in Thuringia (south-west of Erfurt).[180] Gleichen was so well defended that the siege continued until the end of the year. Ekbert had sufficient resources to stage a counter-offensive intended to draw off part of the besieging army. He attacked the abbey of Quedlinburg, of which the emperor's sister Adelaide was abbess and where the emperor's betrothed, Eupraxia, was residing under the abbess's protection.[181] When Henry despatched a force under Hartwig's command to the defence of Quedlinburg, Ekbert and his followers doubled back towards Gleichen to mount a surprise attack on the depleted besieging army. His manoeuvre was a complete success. The attack took place on Christmas eve towards nightfall, when the imperial army was totally unprepared. The look-outs had barely time to give a warning of the approach of the margrave's 'great multitude'. The battle of Gleichen continued far into the night until at last the imperial army was forced to

---

[178] *Vita Heinrici IV* c. 5, p. 20. See Meyer von Knonau (1903) 4:218–19; Giese (1979) 181–2.
[179] *D H IV* 402. See Mitteis (1926–7) 36.   [180] *D H IV* 402; *Ann. s. Disibodi* 1089, p. 9.
[181] *Liber de unitate* II.35, p. 262. See Meyer von Knonau (1903) 4:222.

flee.[182] The imperial army suffered heavy losses, the most serious being that of Henry's loyal servant, Bishop Burchard of Lausanne, the Italian chancellor.[183] The invaluable imperial adviser Archbishop Liemar of Bremen was taken prisoner.[184] The scale of Ekbert's success indicates that he must have retained some allies among the Saxon nobility, even though their identity is uncertain. The margrave could not have surprised the emperor at Gleichen with 'a great multitude' and could not have sustained his resistance (which continued until his death in July 1090) without the support of other princes.[185]

After his defeat at Gleichen the emperor withdrew from Thuringia with the remnants of his army. On 1 February 1089 he held an assembly in Regensburg, which confirmed the sentence pronounced in Quedlinburg. The archbishops of Bremen and Magdeburg, six Saxon bishops, the bishop of Bamberg and 'vassals of various dignities' heard a recital of the offences committed by Ekbert since 1081. After his condemnation in Quedlinburg Ekbert, aggravating his offences, had 'even slain a bishop and other members of the clergy, for which he deserved to be deprived not only of his property but also of his life'. His property was confiscated without hope of restoration.[186] There was no attempt to mount an expedition against the rebel, however, until the autumn of 1089. The emperor spent the spring and early summer in Lotharingia: he was in Cologne for his wedding and the coronation of the new empress.[187] Hartwig of Magdeburg, who performed the coronation, was at his side throughout the year.[188]

Meanwhile Ekbert made war on the emperor's adherents in eastern Saxony. His particular targets were the brothers Udo of Hildesheim and Count Conrad of Reinhausen, whose desertion of the rebels in 1085 had heralded the disintegration of the anti-Henrician opposition in Saxony. Conrad fell in battle against Ekbert; Udo was held prisoner 'until he promised to surrender Hildesheim'.[189] It was presumably to secure Hildesheim against further attack that Henry came to Saxony in the autumn. There was, however, no military engagement and the

[182] *Annales sancti Disibodi* 1089, p. 9; *Liber de unitate* II.35, p. 262; *Annales Augustani* 1088, p. 133; Frutolf, *Chronica* 1089, p. 104; *Annales Hildesheimenses* 1089, p. 49; *Annales Stadenses* 1089, p. 316; Bernold, *Chronicon* 1088, 1089, p. 448. See Meyer von Knonau (1913) 4:222–6.

[183] Frutolf, *Chronica* 1089, p. 104.   [184] *Annalista Saxo* 1089, p. 726.

[185] Albert, *Annales Stadenses* 1089, p. 316: Liemar's captor was Lothar of Supplinburg, the future Emperor Lothar III: see Reincke (1971) 86. But see Hucke (1956) 87, 143: the captor was Udo III of the Saxon Nordmark.

[186] *D H IV* 402. See Meyer von Knonau (1913) 4:246–7; Giese (1979) 182.

[187] Sigebert, *Chronica* 1089, p. 366: it was during this visit that Henry conferred the duchy of Lower Lotharingia on Godfrey of Bouillon; hence Meyer von Knonau (1913) 4:249–50. But see above p. 263.

[188] *D H IV* 407; *Liber de unitate* II.25, p. 247. See Meyer von Knonau (1913) 4:257, 261.

[189] *Liber de unitate* II.18, p. 235; *Chronicon episcoporum Hildesheimensium* c. 18, p. 854. See Meyer von Knonau (1903) 4:258.

rebel did not submit.[190] In the event no further imperial expedition against Ekbert was necessary, since his career came to a violent end six months after the emperor's withdrawal from Saxony. Early in 1090 Ekbert launched an attack on his brother-in-law Henry I of Eilenburg, whom the emperor had invested with the confiscated march of Meissen. Ekbert's defeat at the hands of Henry of Eilenburg finally unleashed against him the fury of the Saxon princes, including those who had recently supported his rebellion: 'The hands of all the princes of Saxony were against him and his hand was against every man.'[191] On 3 July the fugitive was resting in a mill on the bank of the River Selke, when his hiding place was betrayed to his pursuers, vassals of Abbess Adelaide of Quedlinburg. They burst into the mill and killed him.[192] The male line of his family being extinct, the bulk of the inheritance of the Brunones now passed to Ekbert's sister, Gertrude and so into the hands of her husband, Count Henry 'the Fat' of Northeim, eldest son of Otto of Northeim.[193] This inheritance made Henry 'the Fat' incontestably the most powerful prince in Saxony. He dominated the politics of the province until his murder in 1101.

According to the chroniclers' reckoning, the uneventful campaign of autumn 1089 was 'the fifteenth expedition of the emperor into Saxony'. It was also the last: Henry IV never again set foot in the province. He was to plan another expedition at the end of 1104, but it proceeded no further than Fritzlar. The seventeen years of 'the Saxon war' were now succeeded by fifteen years, if not of harmonious cooperation, at least of peaceful coexistence. It appeared to the Lotharingian Sigebert of Gembloux in 1092 that 'the inciters of the Saxon war had almost all been destroyed and the Saxons, wearied by misfortunes, made peace among themselves and refrained from all warfare'.[194] There is no evidence, for example, of a notable Saxon contribution to the campaigning in Italy that preoccupied the emperor between 1090 and 1097. In fact the military activity of the Saxon princes was directed against the Slavs.[195] The emperor's absence from Saxony for the remainder of his reign meant in practical terms abandoning the royal property in eastern Saxony, to the consolidation of which his servants had formerly devoted so much energy. It was a great

---

[190] Bernold, *Chronicon* 1089, p. 449; *Annales Ottenburani* 1089, p. 8. See Meyer von Knonau (1903) 4:259.   [191] *Liber de unitate* II.35, p. 263. See Fenske (1977) 376.

[192] *Liber de unitate* II.35, pp. 262–3; *Annales Pegavienses* 1090, p. 243; Bernold, *Chronicon* 1090, p. 450; *Annales Ottenburani* 1090, p. 8; Frutolf, *Chronica* 1090, p. 104; *Vita Heinrici IV* c. 5, p. 21. See Meyer von Knonau (1903) 4:291–4.

[193] Lange (1961) 82–8; Faußner (1973) 417–18; Fenske (1977) 148.

[194] Sigebert, *Chronica* 1092, p. 366.

[195] *Annales Hildesheimenses* 1093, p. 49; Helmold, *Cronica Slavorum* I.34, p. 68 (Magnus Billung). *Annales Hildesheimenses* 1100, p. 50; *Annalista Saxo* 1101, p. 734; *Annales Palidenses* 1100, p. 72 (Udo III of Stade). See Meyer von Knonau (1903) 4:416; (1904) 5:101.

sacrifice, but the cost of an interminable Saxon war was greater still. Royal authority in the province devolved on Count Henry 'the Fat' of Northeim, who, 'second only to the king, governed the whole of Saxony'.[196] The count of Northeim in the 1090s enjoyed the viceregal role that had briefly belonged to his father in 1076.[197] The emperor's dependence on Henry 'the Fat' for the maintenance of peace in Saxony is apparent from the documents of the 1090s. Firstly a letter of Bishop Rupert of Bamberg (1093) reported to the emperor the findings of two imperial envoys, sent to Saxony to discover whether there was any danger of rebellion in the province. They had approached Henry 'the Fat', who had assured the emperor of his loyalty 'if only he obtains his estate of Greding, as he was promised'. Rupert advised the emperor to grant him the estate, so as to enjoy the support of Henry and his brothers and so fear no unrest in Saxony.[198] Six years later Henry 'the Fat' secured from the emperor the Frisian county confiscated from Ekbert and conferred on the church of Utrecht in 1089. After the murder of Bishop Conrad of Utrecht in 1099 the emperor chose at last to recognise the claim of Gertrude, Ekbert's sister, to that county and conferred it on her husband.[199] At the end of his life Henry 'the Fat' appears in the chronicles as 'margrave of the Frisians'.[200]

Perhaps the emperor's absence from the province and the conferring of vice-regal status on the most powerful of the Saxon princes was the price that the Saxons demanded for the peaceful coexistence of 1089–1104. They would elect no more anti-kings if the emperor would recognise one of their number as 'second only to the king'. The viceregal office was the guarantee of their right to enjoy their own 'laws' and the symbol of their freedom from the interference of an innovating monarchy. The Saxons had deeply resented the practice of the young Henry IV, in common with his predecessor, of residing for long periods in eastern Saxony. The rebels of 1073–4 had demanded that Henry 'should not spend all his life exclusively in Saxony'. The abortive peace settlement of 1085 had revealed how easily the emperor's presence in the province could trigger the same apprehensions that had provoked the uprising of twelve years earlier. In absenting himself permanently from the province, Henry IV conceded the central demand of the Saxons.[201]

---

[196] Ekkehard, *Chronica* I, 1103, p. 184.

[197] Henry V, letter to Henry IV: *Codex Udalrici* 94, pp. 182–3 (1099 or 1100), concerning his projected visit to Saalfeld in Thuringia. See below p. 307.

[198] *Codex Udalrici* 87, pp. 170–2. Greding was an estate confiscated from Ekbert of Meissen and conferred on the church of Eichstätt (*D H IV* 418). Count Henry claimed it as part of his wife's inheritance. See Meyer von Knonau (1903) 4:411–13; Giese (1979) 183–4; Giese (1991) 301–2.   [199] *Annalista Saxo* 1101, p. 734. See Fenske (1977) 148.

[200] Ekkehard, *Chronica* I, 1103, p. 184. See Meyer von Knonau (1904) 5:120–1; Lange (1961) 87.

[201] See above p. 79.

The pacification of Saxony removed the most serious military threat and freed the emperor's hands to deal with his enemies elsewhere in the kingdom. The immediate response of these enemies, Welf IV of Bavaria, Berthold of Rheinfelden and Berthold of Zähringen, was to initiate peace negotiations. 'There were peace talks with the emperor in various councils.'[202] According to the Gregorian chronicler, Bernold of St Blasien, the south German princes 'promised their counsel and aid in holding the kingdom, if he would repudiate the heresiarch Wibert and return to the communion of the Church through the catholic pastor'. Henry was willing to accept this condition, but he was overruled by his bishops, 'who had no doubt that they would be deposed together with Wibert'.[203] The Henrician bishops were indeed aware that their legitimacy was inextricably involved with that of Clement III. The emperor, however, had his own motive, independent of their persuasions, for rejecting the condition of the south German princes. Henry contemplated abandoning his antipope in 1083, when there was a chance of reconciliation with Gregory VII, but in 1084 Clement III performed his imperial coronation. The emperor could not now abandon his antipope without casting doubt on his own imperial title.

---

[202] *Liber de unitate* II.25, p. 247. Cf. *Annales Augustani* 1089, p. 133. See Meyer von Knonau (1903) 4:259–61.
[203] Bernold, *Chronicon* 1089, p. 450. See Ziese (1982) 182–3.

8

Henry IV, the imperial Church and the
papacy: the third Italian expedition,
1090–1097

By 1089 the Gregorian party in the German episcopate had greatly diminished. The chronicler Bernold of St Blasien recorded that only the bishops of
Würzburg, Passau, Worms, Constance and Metz 'remained steadfast in the
catholic communion'.[1] Of these only Gebhard III of Constance resided in his
own diocese: his Gregorian colleagues had seen their bishoprics usurped by
imperial anti-bishops. Gebhard, whom the new pope Urban II named as his
permanent legate in Germany (18 April 1089), proved an energetic leader of
the Gregorian party and an uncompromising opponent of the emperor for the
remaining years of the reign.[2] Elsewhere in the kingdom the episcopate solidly
supported the emperor. Henry's episcopal appointments were intended to perpetuate this loyalty. The best documented of the new appointments of 1089 is
that of Archbishop Herman III ('the Rich') of Cologne (invested on 25 July).
A member of the family of the counts of Hochstaden, he was the kinsman of
two of his colleagues, Hartwig of Magdeburg and John I of Speyer. He had
served since 1085 as the chancellor of the German kingdom. Like his predecessor, Sigewin, he had been educated in the household of Anno of Cologne
and like Sigewin's predecessor, Hildolf, he was a canon of Cologne cathedral,
his close connection with the church of Cologne making him acceptable to
the chapter.[3]

The same elements – membership of a noble family whose allegiance was
important to the emperor, service to the crown, membership of a cathedral
chapter, acceptability to the canonical electors – had determined the episcopal
appointments of 1085 and recur during the rest of the reign. Information about
the appointees of the later years of the reign is relatively sparse but the importance of noble birth is unmistakable. Five candidates were kinsmen of the impe-

---

[1] Bernold, *Chronicon* 1089, p. 449. Herman of Metz submitted in 1089: Meyer von Knonau
(1903) 4:248.
[2] Urban II, *JL* 5393: 297B–299A. See Meyer von Knonau (1903) 4:252–6; Schumann (1912) 67;
Becker (1964) 148–51; Wollasch (1987) 27–53.
[3] *Chronica regia Coloniensis* 1089, p. 39. See Meyer von Knonau (1903) 4:251; Zielinski (1984)
60.

rial family: John I of Speyer (1090), Adalbero IV of Metz (1090), Henry of Freising (1098), Eberhard of Eichstätt (1099) and Bruno of Trier (1101).[4] A further five appointees belonged to prominent families: Arnold of Constance (1092), Herman of Augsburg (1096), Burchard of Utrecht (1100), Frederick of Cologne (1100) and Otto I of Bamberg (1102).[5] Three of the appointees of these later years had served the emperor in the office of German chancellor: Humbert of Bremen (1101), Erlung of Würzburg (1105) and Otto of Bamberg (1102). Otto was one of the most important royal servants of Henry IV's last years, entrusted with keeping the imperial treasure, with escorting the emperor's sister Judith to Poland on the occasion of her second marriage (to Duke Vladislav-Herman) and, above all, with rebuilding the cathedral of Speyer.[6]

Thirteen candidates were former canons, including seven who were appointed to preside over churches which they had previously served as canons: Herman III of Cologne (1089), Emehard of Würzburg (1089), Otbert of Liège (1091), Walcher of Cambrai (1093), Wido of Osnabrück (1093), John of Osnabrück (1101) and Bruno of Trier (1101).[7] These seven promotions are perhaps reminiscent of the ecclesiastical regime of Henry III, who tried to harmonise the rights of the canonical electors with the interests of the emperor. From 1078 onwards, in marked contrast to the first decade of his personal rule, Henry IV had sometimes made appointments similar to those of his father. The evidence suggests that such appointments became more frequent from the time of the synod of Mainz (1085) until the end of the reign. The reason for this development was presumably the conflict with the reforming popes, who legislated against the monarch's customary rights in the appointment of prelates. The attack on his rights seems to have inclined Henry to act in concert with the cathedral chapter in the election of a bishop. It also prompted him to appoint candidates whose personal distinction was acknowledged even by their enemies, especially candidates distinguished for their scholarship, like Sigewin of Cologne, Wezilo of Mainz, Meinhard II of Würzburg and Walo of Metz. Similar cases from the later years of the reign were Wenrich of Piacenza (the polemicist and master of the cathedral school of Trier), Bruno of Trier, Herman III and Frederick I of Cologne, Erlung of Würzburg, the former cathedral schoolmaster Albuin of Merseburg and the polemicists Wido of Osnabrück and Walram of Naumburg. The most famous example was the

---

[4] *Annales Spirenses* 1090, p. 82; *Vita Theogeri Mettensis* II.1, p. 466. See Meyer von Knonau (1903) 4:291, 286; (1904) 5:37, 69, 132; Zielinski (1984) 33, 43, 45, 48.

[5] Meyer von Knonau (1903) 4:374–5, 479–80; (1904) 5:68, 97–8, 163–5; Zielinski (1984) 43, 58, 63.   [6] Gawlik (1978) XLI–LI.

[7] Zielinski (1984) 144, 147, 151, 153, 154. Two exceptional cases were the monk-bishops Markward of Osnabrück (1088) and Arnold of Constance (1092): *ibid.* 126, 127. See Feierabend (1913) 150–3: Leidinger (1969) 308–9.

learned and saintly Otto I of Bamberg, the great missionary bishop, 'apostle of the Pomeranians'.[8]

Nevertheless there were at least four instances in which the emperor ignored the choice of the local electors. When the clergy and people of Metz elected Poppo, canon of Trier (1090), 'setting him over the church by election alone, without a grant from the king', the emperor responded by imposing Adalbero IV. In Halberstadt in 1090 the emperor supported Frederick against the candidate of 'the sounder part' (the Gregorian faction) of the electors. In Naumburg (also in 1090) Henry set aside the election made by the clergy and invested Walram with the bishopric.[9] In 1091 he filled the bishopric of Liège 'without a canonical election of clergy and people', conferring the church on his chaplain Otbert. The appointment of Otbert was one of four during the later years of the reign which the emperor's enemies declared to be tainted by simony. Henry was alleged to have received 300 marks on the occasion of Otbert's investiture.[10] In 1089 Henry was alleged to have 'sold [Gebhard IV] Regensburg . . . in return for military service'.[11] Richer of Verdun was obliged to wait four years to be consecrated because of suspicions of simony.[12] Finally, Herman of Augsburg was alleged to have received investiture of his church after his brother, Count Udalric of Passau, paid the emperor 500 pounds of silver.[13] These hostile accounts show that in Gregorian circles Henry was still regarded as a simoniac. The reality behind this polemical language was that the emperor continued to defy Gregorian legislation against lay investiture.

The two most detailed non-polemical accounts of episcopal appointments in the later years of the reign contain no hint of simony, but they reveal Henry's insistence on his right of investiture. Firstly, on the death of Bishop Gunther of Naumburg (1090) the clergy unanimously elected the candidate whom they had long foreseen as his successor, Abbot Frederick of Goseck (son of the Saxon count palatine and nephew of Archbishop Adalbert of Bremen). The bishop elect hastened to present himself to the emperor and receive investiture from him. Henry, however, accused the electors of having violated 'the decrees of [his] imperial predecessors' and 'offended both the kingdom and

---

[8] Meyer von Knonau (1903) 4:251; (1904) 5:3, 98, 132, 163–5; Schwartz (1913) 193–4.
[9] Hugh of Flavigny, *Chronicon* II, p. 473; *Vita Theogeri* II.1, p. 466: see Meyer von Knonau (1903) 4:286. *Gesta episcoporum Halberstadensium* p. 101: see Meyer von Knonau (1903) 4:294–5, 297; Fenske (1977) 137–8.
[10] *Chronicon sancti Huberti Andaginensis* c. 90, pp. 623–4; Rupert of Deutz, *Chronicon sancti Laurentii Leodiensis* c. 45, p. 277. Cf. Urban II, *JL* 5538, 395B–397D.
[11] Herrand of Halberstadt, *Epistola* p. 289. See Meyer von Knonau (1903) 4:262.
[12] Laurence, *Gesta episcoporum Virdunensium* c. 10, p. 497. See Meyer von Knonau (1903) 4:250.
[13] Udalschalk of Augsburg, *De Eginone et Herimanno* c. 12, pp. 436–7. See Meyer von Knonau (1903) 4:479–80.

[his] own person'. He refused to invest Frederick, lest their premature action stand as a precedent. In vain the Naumburg delegation continued to argue their cause before the emperor from 30 November until Christmas. On Christmas day envoys arrived from Hersfeld, bringing the abbatial staff of the deceased Abbot Hartwig. Frederick was eventually persuaded by the emperor and princes to accept Hersfeld, while Walram, canon of Bamberg received investiture of the bishopric of Naumburg.[14] Secondly, in 1101 the chancellor Otto was offered and refused the church of Bremen. Otto's biographer explained for the benefit of his audience of *circa* 1155 the practice of Henry IV. 'Whenever any bishop went the way of all flesh, immediately the chief persons of that city would send the pastoral ring and staff to the palace and thus the authority of the king, after taking counsel with courtiers, would confer a suitable prelate on the bereaved people.'[15]

During the last two decades of the reign the reform papacy restated and extended Gregory VII's legislation against lay investiture, but this issue was rarely at the forefront of papal preoccupations. In his first papal synod, in Melfi (September 1089), Urban II issued a short decree, but there was no reference to investiture in his subsequent synods of Benevento (March 1091), Troia (March 1093) and Piacenza (March 1095).[16] There was likewise no mention of investiture in the legatine synod of Constance held in April 1094 by Urban's permanent legate in Germany, Bishop Gebhard III of Constance.[17] Confronted early in his pontificate with the cases of prelates who had received investiture and who subsequently submitted themselves to his judgement, Urban restored them to their offices 'for the sake of the utility of the Church'.[18] Urban II did not place the same emphasis on the prohibition of investiture that Gregory VII had done after 1078. He was more concerned with ending the schism in the Church, defeating the challenge of the antipope Clement III and reconstructing the obedience of the reform papacy. He could not afford to be distracted by the issue of investiture.

Urban II (like Gregory VII) probably regarded investiture as a problem that could only be resolved in cooperation with the secular ruler. Since the excommunicate Henry IV was not in papal eyes a legitimate ruler, a solution of the investiture problem must be postponed. The issue eventually re-emerged in Urban's council of Clermont in November 1095, by which time there was a

---

[14] *Chronicon Gozecense* I.22–5, p. 149. See Meyer von Knonau (1903) 4:295–7; Fenske (1977) 161.   [15] Ebo of Michelsberg, *Vita Ottonis* I.7, p. 827. See Meyer von Knonau (1904) 5:125.

[16] Beulertz (1991) 9–16, 106–21; Minninger (1978) 84–103.

[17] Bernold, *Chronicon* 1094, p. 458. See Meyer von Knonau (1903) 4:428–9; Schumann (1912) 70; Robinson (1989) 186.

[18] Archbishop Anselm III of Milan (see below p. 281); Henry of Soissons, Fulco of Beauvais and Ivo of Chartres. See Beulertz (1991) 113–18.

new papal anti-king with whom Urban was able to negotiate.[19] The canons of the council of Clermont (the most wide-ranging legislation in the history of the papal reform movement) included a prohibition not only of investiture but also of the performance of homage to the secular ruler by bishops and abbots.[20] Urban II's double prohibition of investiture and homage made explicit (unlike Gregory VII's decrees) the feudal implications of these ceremonies and the danger that they represented to 'the freedom of the Church'. Lay investiture and homage, firstly, transformed a clerk or a monk into a feudal vassal, contaminating him with the sins of the secular world and, secondly, declared that the church and its property with which he was invested constituted a feudal benefice, held entirely at the pleasure of the secular ruler. Pope Paschal II restated his predecessor's double prohibition of investiture and homage in his Lateran synod of March 1102.[21] After this synod, however, the prohibition of homage never reappeared in the legislation of the reform papacy. All subsequent decrees were concerned solely with the ceremony of investiture. By the end of Henry IV's reign the investiture debate had come to focus on the distinction between the spiritual functions of the bishop's office and the material possessions of his church.[22]

Although Urban II was keenly aware of the threat presented by homage to the purity of the priesthood and the freedom of the Church, the campaign against investiture was never his foremost concern. He regarded his struggle against Henry IV not as an 'Investiture Contest' but as a defensive war against a schismatic emperor and his antipope. For their part, the emperor and his advisers seem to have been equally unaware of being participants in an 'Investiture Contest'. The subject is not known to have arisen in any negotiations between the imperial party and their opponents during the pontificate of Urban II. No Henrician polemic on the subject of investiture has survived from the period between 1086 and 1103.[23] The object of the war which Henry waged in Italy against Urban II and his supporters between 1090 and 1097 was to strengthen the authority of Clement III and to compel the submission of the Gregorian rebels.

The most formidable of these rebels in the years 1090–7 (as during Henry's second Italian expedition of 1081–4) was Matilda, margravine of Tuscany. On

---

[19] See below p. 291.   [20] Beulertz (1991) 11; Minninger (1978) 84–6, 99–100.

[21] Beulertz (1991) 16. Cf. Ekkehard, *Chronica* I, 1102, p. 180. See Meyer von Knonau (1904) 5:170–1; Minninger (1978) 90.

[22] Wido of Ferrara, *De scismate* II, pp. 564–5. On the influential treatise of Ivo of Chartres, *Epistola ad Hugonem* pp. 640–7: Hoffmann (1959) 393–440.

[23] Wido's defence of investiture was composed in 1086: above p. 241. In 1103 Sigebert of Gembloux issued his *Leodicensium epistola* pp. 457–8. See Minninger (1978) 39–10, 111, 114, 194–5.

the eve of the third imperial expedition, between early September and early November 1089, Matilda contracted a second marriage, intended to bind together the leaders of the Gregorian parties in northern Italy and southern Germany. According to the Gregorian version of events, 'the most noble princess Matilda ... was joined in marriage to Duke Welf [V], son of Duke Welf [IV]. This she did as the consequence not of unchastity but of obedience to the Roman pontiff, so that she might the more vigorously aid the holy Roman church against the excommunicates. ... Henry the so-called king was much grieved by this marriage.'[24] Matilda was probably forty-three years old and her second husband no more than eighteen. The initiative in negotiating this marriage is usually assumed to have come from the Welfs, eager (as their subsequent conduct revealed) to secure control of the bride's extensive territories,[25] Urban II's role being to overcome Matilda's reluctance to remarry.[26] In the context of this Welf conspiracy, the emperor's Italian expedition of 1090 appears to have been a panic response to the marriage alliance of 1089. An alternative explanation is that the marriage alliance was the result of a papal initiative. Urban II negotiated the marriage so as to disrupt the peace talks of 1089 between the emperor and the south German princes.[27] Urban's principal objective was to disrupt the emperor's plans for an Italian expedition, calculating that Henry would not dare to leave Germany if he had not concluded a permanent peace with his enemies in Swabia and Bavaria. The marriage was the papal response to the threat of an Italian expedition. This version of events sees the third Italian expedition as the result of long-term planning rather than a reaction to sudden political danger. The evidence is, firstly, a letter of Clement III sent either late in 1089 or early in 1090, announcing the imminent arrival in Italy of 'his son, the emperor of Germany', and, secondly, a Ravennese tradition that at this period the antipope enfeoffed 'many men' with benefices of the church of Ravenna.[28] Perhaps, therefore, Clement III was recruiting a large contingent of knights for an imperial expedition at a time when the emperor was just learning of the marriage of Matilda and Welf V.

That marriage, by causing the withdrawal of the Welfs and their allies from peace negotiations with the emperor, ensured their failure. Henry neverthe-

---

[24] Bernold, *Chronicon* 1089, p. 449 Cf. *Annales Rosenveldenses* 1089, p. 101. See Overmann (1895) 155; Meyer von Knonau (1903) 4:273–4; Simeoni (1947) 362; Becker (1964) 120–1; Struve (1995) 67.

[25] Cosmas of Prague, *Chronica Boemorum* 11.32, pp. 127–9: concern about the succession to Tuscany.

[26] Perhaps Urban gave the couple a dispensation to marry within the prohibited degrees since both were descended from the early ninth-century Boniface, count of Lucca and margrave of Tuscany: Forni (1964) 278–80.   [27] Ziese (1982) 182–3.

[28] W. Holtzmann (1924–5) 182–5. See Ziese (1982) 183–5.

less departed for his Italian kingdom in March 1090, even though this meant leaving unreconciled rebels in southern Germany. In Italy he was 'courteously received by the princes of the territory', who had not yet fallen under the influence of the coalition of the dynasties of Canossa and Welf.[29] The emperor found that Urban II had hitherto made little progress in drawing the Lombard bishops into his obedience, despite the initial success of the submission of Archbishop Anselm III of Milan (1088).[30] The Milanese suffragans remained loyal to the emperor and the antipope at least until 1095, Urban II's year of triumph. In Wibert's own archdiocese of Ravenna Gregorian anti-bishops were more numerous: only his birthplace of Parma unequivocally recognised his claim to be pope.[31] Matilda strove to ensure that the bishoprics of the march of Tuscany were faithful to the cause of Urban II, in particular that of Pisa, which became one of his most important power-bases.[32] The secular powers in north-eastern Italy, Henry of Eppenstein, duke of Carinthia, Margrave Burchard of Istria and the duchy of Venice, remained obedient to the emperor and his antipope.[33]

The successful first two years of Henry IV's third Italian expedition (1090–1) were spent campaigning against Matilda of Tuscany and Welf V in the northern part of the march of Tuscany. As on the second Italian expedition, the antipope played a major role in recruiting and organising supplies for the imperial army.[34] Little is known about the German contribution to this expedition. Of the secular princes only Duke Frederick I of Swabia (the emperor's son-in-law) and his brother Conrad of Staufen are known to have participated.[35] Soon after Easter (21 April) Henry launched an attack on Mantua, the most northerly of the margravine's Tuscan strongholds. The siege of Mantua lasted eleven months, forcing Matilda to seek refuge in the mountains.[36] By 26 June the emperor had captured the fortress of Rivalta, standing

---

[29] *Annales Augustani* 1090, p. 133; Donizo of Canossa, *Vita Mathildis* II.4, pp. 388–9. See Meyer von Knonau (1903) 4:278; Struve (1995) 67.

[30] *Liber pontificalis* 2, 293. This submission was facilitated by the development in Milan of reform movements less radical than the Pataria and by the ancient rivalry of Milan and Ravenna, exacerbated when Wibert combined his office of archbishop of Ravenna with that of pope. See Schwartz (1913) 83–4; Becker (1964) 124; Cowdrey (1968a) 43–8; Cowdrey (1968b) 285–8; Cowdrey (1970a) 251–2.

[31] Archdiocese of Milan: Schwartz (1913) 112–14, 148; Becker (1964) 122–5. Archdiocese of Ravenna: Schwartz (1913) 164–5, 178–9, 183–4, 192–3, 197–8; Berschin (1972) 11–13; Ziese (1982) 180; Heidrich (1984) 160.

[32] Schwartz (1913) 54–5, 206, 210, 213–14, 216, 217–18, 220, 224; Becker (1964) 122–3.

[33] Meyer von Knonau (1903) 4:285; Gawlik (1970a) 81.   [34] Ziese (1982) 190.

[35] *DD H IV* 424, 426. See below p. 286.

[36] Donizo, *Vita Mathildis* II.4, p. 389; Bernold, *Chronicon* 1091, p. 451. See Meyer von Knonau (1903) 4:279–80, 282–3; Struve (1995) 68. The importance of Mantua: Overmann (1895) 15–19.

on the River Mincio above the city.[37] Before the end of the year he had inflicted a more serious defeat by taking the fortress of Governolo, which barred the way to the principal possessions of the house of Canossa, lying south of the Po.[38] Towards the end of November the emperor left the siege to celebrate Christmas in Verona, returning to Mantua early in 1091.[39] The city finally surrendered on the night of 10 April, enabling Henry to celebrate Easter (13 April) in Mantua.[40] The fact that Bishop Ubald had fled to Matilda's court enabled Henry to appoint an imperial anti-bishop in Mantua.[41] For the rest of the year the emperor remained in the region of Tuscany north of the Po, systematically capturing Matilda's fortresses. By the end of 1091 he 'held almost all the lands beyond the Po except for Piadena and Nogara', fortresses situated in the counties of Brescia and Verona respectively.[42] The imperial diplomas of this summer reveal Henry's entourage travelling through the counties of Mantua, Brescia and Verona, continually attended by numerous Italian and German princes.[43]

In August 'the emperor held a conference in Verona with the princes of the kingdom about making peace'.[44] The peace talks broken off in Speyer in February 1090 were resumed in Verona but again without success: the emperor rejected the demands of Welf IV of Bavaria. The first demand, as in the negotiations of 1089–90, was that the emperor should repudiate Clement III. The second was that Welf should recover the duchy of Bavaria, from which he had been deposed in 1077, and his allies regain the lands that they had lost since the outbreak of the civil war.[45] The readiness of Welf IV to resume peace negotiations reveals how little he had gained from the marriage alliance with Matilda of Tuscany and how great was the impression that Henry IV's successes of 1090–1 had made on his enemies.[46] The German Gregorian party had been seriously weakened by the loss of five leaders in 1090–1: Herman of Metz, Adalbero of Würzburg, the anti-duke of Swabia, Berthold of Rheinfelden, Abbot William of Hirsau and Altmann of Passau.[47] The death of Ekbert II of

[37] D H IV 414.

[38] Overmann (1895) 16–17; Meyer von Knonau (1903) 4:280; Struve (1995) 71.

[39] Chronicon Gozecense 1.23, p. 149: see above pp. 277–8.

[40] Donizo, Vita II.4, p. 389: see Meyer von Knonau (1903) 4:333–4; Struve (1995) 68–9.

[41] Cono: Donizo, Vita II.6 p. 390. See Schwartz (1913) 55.

[42] Donizo, Vita II.6, pp. 390–1. See Overmann (1895) 157; Meyer von Knonau (1903) 4:334–5; Struve (1995) 70–1.

[43] DD H IV 418–19, 423–4. See Meyer von Knonau (1903) 4:335–6; Gawlik (1970a) 79–80.

[44] Annales Augustani 1091, p. 133.

[45] Bernold of St Blasien, Chronicon 1091, p. 452. See Meyer von Knonau (1903) 4:338–9; Ziese (1982) 191.   [46] Bernold, Chronicon 1091, p. 452.

[47] Ibid. 1090, 1091, pp. 450, 451, 452. See Meyer von Knonau (1903) 4:284, 285–6, 287–8, 348–65.

Meissen brought peace to Saxony and diminished hope of an alliance between the Saxons and the south German rebels.[48] While the south German opposition showed signs of disintegration, Henry IV was in a strong enough position to reject Welf's demands. The restitution of Bavaria would have meant a significant loss of income and political influence for the imperial government, which had directly administered the duchy for fourteen years. Even if the emperor had been favourably disposed towards Welf, he would have met resistance in the assembly of Verona from his own faithful supporters, Bishop Altwin of Brixen and the Bavarian count palatine Rapoto, who had benefited from Welf's disgrace.[49]

Welf's demand that the emperor abandon his antipope came at a moment when Clement III, once more demonstrating his usefulness to his lord in the practical business of the Italian expedition, was at the height of his influence. Early in 1091 the Castel S. Angelo fell into the hands of Clement's forces and made possible the longest residence in Rome of his pontificate (February 1091 – February 1092). Clement celebrated a papal synod, which condemned the 'novel' and 'impious dogmas' of the Gregorian party from which stemmed the current turmoil in the empire. The synod deplored in particular the Gregorian 'error' of freeing vassals from their oath of fealty to an excommunicated lord, which Clement regarded as 'the root and origin' of all the evils that had befallen the empire since Gregory VII excommunicated Henry IV.[50] Clement's penetrating attack on his opponents may well have won over some waverers to his party, while Henry's victories in Italy and his refusal to repudiate the antipope in the peace negotiations of August 1091 strengthened Clement's authority.

1091 ended with another victory: a surprise attack at Tricontai, inflicting an overwhelming defeat on the forces of Matilda of Tuscany.[51] The victorious emperor proceeded to Mantua, where he celebrated Christmas 1091. The splendour of his court, with its large assembly of secular and ecclesiastical princes, was witnessed by the historian Cosmas of Prague, who arrived in Mantua on 1 January 1092 in the entourage of the bishop elect of Prague, also named Cosmas. King Vratislav of Bohemia had sent the bishops elect both of Prague and of Olmütz to the emperor's presence, escorted by the Bavarian

---

[48] See above p. 272.   [49] *D H IV* 424 (for Brixen).

[50] Wibert of Ravenna, *Decretum Wiberti vel Clementis* pp. 621–6, dated 1089 by Dümmler, but 1091 by Ziese (1982) 191–202. Cf. Wido of Ferrara, *De scismate* 1.7, pp. 539–40. The synod also condemned the Gregorian doctrine that the sacraments 'celebrated by those who do not communicate with their faction are not sacraments at all'. See Saltet (1907) 205–54; Schebler (1936) 229–81; Gilchrist (1965) 209–35; Miccoli (1966) 169–201.

[51] Donizo, *Vita Mathildis* II.6, p. 391. See Overmann (1895) 157–8; Meyer von Knonau (1903) 4:346; Struve (1995) 71.

count palatine Rapoto, so that Henry might confirm their elections. Henry's decision to invest Vratislav's candidates signalled that after the tensions of recent years he desired a reconciliation with this former ally. The gesture of reconciliation, however, was almost immediately followed by the death of King Vratislav.[52] The emperor remained in Mantua to celebrate Easter (28 March). During Eastertide he was persuaded by his kinsman Patriarch Udalric I of Aquileia to challenge the authority of Bishop Gebhard III of Constance, leader of the Gregorian party in Swabia, by appointing an imperial candidate in his diocese. Henry invested Arnold of Heiligenberg, a monk of Udalric's abbey of St Gallen. Towards the end of 1092 Udalric sought to force a way into the city of Constance for his protégé. Only after a twelve-year struggle, however, did the imperial party succeed in expelling Gebhard and enthroning Arnold.[53]

The emperor resumed his campaign against Matilda of Tuscany and Welf V in June 1092, turning his attention to the Matildine fortresses south of the Po, in the counties of Modena and Reggio. He took the fortress of Montemorello and Montalfredo, but met his first check before the stronghold of Monteveglio, where he 'wasted the whole summer' with a siege. After lengthy talks with the antipope, the siege was intensified.[54] Meanwhile Matilda came under increasing pressure from her vassals to make peace with the emperor. In September she gave way to this pressure and authorised negotiations with the imperial party in the fortress of Carpineta, south of Canossa. The negotiations at Carpineta were protracted, recognition of the imperial antipope being the most contentious issue. A peace settlement seemed close until the Tuscan vassals, having initially desired peace at almost any price, were persuaded by Matilda at a late stage in the negotiations to support the continuance of the war.[55] Henry returned his attention to the siege of Monteveglio, only to abandon operations soon after the failure of the negotiations at Carpineta.[56]

---

[52] Cosmas, *Chronica Boemorum* II.49, pp. 155–6. See Meyer von Knonau (1903) 4:370–3: Wegener (1959) 119. See above p. 265.

[53] *Casuum sancti Galli Continuatio* II.7, p. 160; *Casus monasterii Petrishusensis* III.29, p. 656; Bernold, *Chronicon* 1092, p. 455. See Meyer von Knonau (1903) 4:374–5, 386–7; (1904) 5:181–2; Diebolder (1916) 189–91, 196; Schmid (1989) 197–8; Maurer (1991) 176, 181–2.

[54] Donizo, *Vita* II.7, pp. 391–4. See Overmann (1895) 158; Meyer von Knonau (1903) 4:375–6; Struve (1995) 72–3.

[55] Donizo, *Vita* II.7, p. 392. The mood of the vassals was changed by 'the hermit John', who promised victory if Matilda continued the struggle. See Overmann (1895) 159; Meyer von Konau (1903) 4:376–7; Ziese (1982) 210–11; Struve (1995) 73–4. It is usually assumed that 'the hermit John' was Donizo's abbot, John of S. Apollonio di Canossa; but Bischoff (1948) 27 saw a connection with the themes of the Canticle commentary addressed by John of Mantua to Matilda *c*. 1082: John of Mantua, *In Cantica Canticorum Tractatus* pp. 51–2, 107.

[56] Donizo, *Vita* II.7, p. 392: Henry withdrew from Monteveglio because he was griefstricken

The decision taken by the Matildine party at Carpineta to reject the emperor's terms proved to be the turning-point in the war. The series of imperial victories of 1090–2 was succeeded from the autumn of 1092 only by reverses. After abandoning the siege of Monteveglio, the emperor 'feigned to be making for Parma', but doubled back and set up camp at Caviliano, immediately to the north of Canossa. Perceiving the threat to her most powerful stronghold, Matilda left Canossa, taking most of the garrison. She entered the neighbouring fortress of Bianello, while Henry laid siege to Canossa. One day in October the garrison seized the opportunity of a thick fog to organise a sortie. The besieging army was taken by surprise; the royal banner was seized from the standard-bearer, the son of Margrave Otbert, and this loss provoked panic in the Henrician army. The emperor ordered a retreat to Baiano. He then hastened to cross the Po and moved his remaining forces northwards.[57] For the second time in his reign Canossa was the scene of a decisive change in the fortunes of Henry IV. The rout before Canossa and his rapid retreat encouraged the fortresses south and north of the Po which had submitted to the emperor to abandon him. Before the end of 1092 the northern fortresses of Governolo and Rivalta, the former containing imperial supplies and equipment, were again in the margravine's hands.[58] The emperor seems to have spent the winter of 1092–3 in Pavia, in the company of the antipope.[59] Henry's state of mind is indicated in a diploma of 12 May 1093, restoring the march of Carniola to the church of Aquileia. This restoration was intended 'to reconcile to us St Mary, the mother of God', the patron saint of the church of Aquileia.[60] The language of this privilege resembles that of the 'votive diplomas' that Henry IV had issued during the crises of the early years of the German civil war.[61] The diploma for Aquileia reveals the reaction of the emperor and his advisers to the deteriorating military situation, which the saint might be induced to remedy.

The services of the faithful Patriarch Udalric of Aquileia were urgently needed, not only in northern Italy but also in Swabia, where for the past fifteen

by the death of his son during the siege. He 'sent his body to Verona and a beautiful tomb was built for him.' The son has never been identified, but Meyer von Knonau (1900) 3:296 n. 112, 316 and n. 145; (1903) 4:377, linked Donizo's account with the reference to Henry's son at the battle of Volta, 15 October 1080 (Bonizo of Sutri, *Ad amicum* IX, p. 613). Dümmler (*ibid.* p. 613 n. 2) identified him as an illegitimate son born before Henry's marriage in 1066: cf. Stenzel (1827) 463 n. 16, 471 n. 34, 547 n. 21; Meyer von Knonau (1890) 1:613 n. 14; (1894) 2:296 n. 112, 316 and n. 145; Struve (1995) 74.

[57] Donizo, *Vita* II.7, p. 393. See Overmann (1895) 159; Meyer von Knonau (1903) 4:377–9; Becker (1964) 131; Struve (1995) 74.

[58] Donizo, *Vita* II.7, pp. 393–4. See Overmann (1895) 159; Meyer von Knonau (1903) 4:379; Struve (1995) 75.   [59] Bernold, *Chronicon* 1093, p. 455. Cf. *DD H IV* 430–2.

[60] *D H IV* 432.   [61] See above pp. 202–3, 258.

years he had fought for the imperial cause. In 1092 the anti-Henrician faction among the Swabian princes elected as 'duke of all Swabia' Berthold II of Zähringen, brother-in-law of the late Berthold of Rheinfelden. Berthold II's brother, Bishop Gebhard of Constance, played a central role in this election. Perhaps on the same day as the election Gebhard, acting as papal legate, received his brother as 'vassal of St Peter'. The following year Welf IV similarly did homage to the legate and became a 'vassal of St Peter'.[62] Gebhard of Constance used his legatine authority to rebuild the Gregorian party after its recent losses. His consecration of the Gregorian Udalric as bishop of Passau was followed by an attempt to impose a Gregorian anti-bishop on Augsburg.[63] Meanwhile, after the fruitless negotiations in Verona in August 1091 Welf IV urged on the Swabians the election of a new anti-king. 'A general conference with the Saxons' was planned for summer 1092, but a severe famine in Saxony prevented their meeting.[64] The south German rebels were attempting, despite their setbacks, to revive the opposition strategy of the late 1070s and early 1080s. They were rallied by Gebhard of Constance, fired by enthusiasm for the Gregorian cause, and by Welf IV, driven by resentment at the emperor's refusal to restore his duchy of Bavaria. This dangerous development may have forced Henry IV to send his German forces back over the Alps. Duke Frederick I of Swabia and his brother, who had been at the emperor's side in September 1091, were absent from the imperial entourage for the rest of the Italian expedition. Henry tried to augment his fighting strength in Italy by making an alliance with King Ladislaus I of Hungary. He planned a 'conference' with Ladislaus during the Christmastide either of 1091 or of 1092, but Welf IV was able to prevent the meeting from taking place, presumably by blocking Ladislaus's route into Italy.[65]

Before any reinforcements could come to his aid, Henry IV was overwhelmed by a series of events that left him isolated and powerless in the northeastern corner of his Italian kingdom. In 1093 the anti-Henrician coalition attracted new allies, most importantly the emperor's elder son. King Conrad 'forsook his father and, together with his vassals, aided Duke Welf [V] and the other vassals of St Peter against his father'. Almost immediately Conrad 'was

---

[62] Bernold, *Chronicon* 1092, p. 454; cf. 1093, p. 457. See Meyer von Knonau (1903) 4:383, 402–3; Maurer (1970) 53–6; Wadle (1973) 148–52; Maurer (1978) 160–1; Wollasch (1987) 36–7.

[63] Bernold, *Chronicon* 1092, p. 454; *Annales Augustani* 1093, 1094, p. 134. See Meyer von Knonau (1903) 4:384, 400–1.

[64] Bernold, *Chronicon* 1091, 1092, pp. 452, 454. See Meyer von Knonau (1903) 4:368–9.

[65] Henry IV, *Letter* 23, p. 23; Bernold, *Chronicon* 1092, p. 453. See Meyer von Knonau (1903) 4:379–80; Ziese (1982) 214–15; Boshof (1986) 188. Ladislaus's negotiations with Clement III about subjecting northern Croatia to the metropolitan authority of Gran: Deér (1936) 27–8; Ziese (1982) 161–3.

captured by his father in Lombardy by means of a ruse', but he was able to escape to Milan. 'He was crowned king by the archbishop of Milan and other vassals of St Peter, with the support of Welf, duke of Italy and Matilda, his most beloved wife.'[66] During this same period between mid-March and late July the Welf–Matildine alliance was augmented by a league of Lombard cities. The formation of this league by Milan, Cremona, Lodi and Piacenza constituted a greater danger to the emperor than the defection of the young king, since they provided the hostile coalition with the means of cutting Henry off from all possible sources of help.[67]

Since his coronation in 1087 the twenty-year-old Conrad had served as his father's representative in the Italian kingdom. In 1091 Henry's 'most beloved son' was in his father's entourage.[68] Early in 1092 the emperor entrusted him with the task of securing control of the march of Turin after the death of Adelaide, margravine of Turin and countess of Savoy (19 December 1091). The margravine had recognised as her heir, her ten-year-old great-grandson, Peter, son of Frederick, count of Montbéliard (in Alsace). The emperor, however, judged that the rightful heir was Conrad, son of Empress Bertha and grandson of Adelaide of Turin.[69] The acquisition of the march would give the emperor control of the roads from Turin, Susa and Ivrea over the Alpine passes and the road from Asti to Genoa. (It was the strategic importance of her territories that had caused Adelaide of Turin to play so important a role in her son-in-law's calculations.)[70] During 1092 the young king campaigned in the march with the army which his father had placed at his disposal.[71] In spring or summer 1093 Conrad and his army joined the rebellion of Matilda of Tuscany and her husband. His treachery involved the abandonment of one of the fundamental principles of Salian government in Italy during the past four decades. An important motive for the matrimonial alliance with the house of

[66] Bernold, *Chronicon* 1093, p. 456; Landulf Junior de Sancto Paulo, *Historia Mediolanensis* c. 3, p. 21; *Annales Augustani* 1093, p. 134. See Haase (1901) 35–6; Meyer von Knonau (1903) 4:391–6; Becker (1964) 131–2; Struve (1995) 76–7; E. Goez (1996) 24–5.

[67] Bernold, *Chronicon* 1093, p. 456. See Ziese (1982) 213–14.

[68] *DD H IV* 420–1, 426–7 See E. Goez (1996) 22–3.

[69] Bernold, *Chronicon* 1092, p. 454. Since 1080 Adelaide had shared power with Frederick, husband of her granddaughter and designated heir of Turin (cousin of Matilda of Tuscany), who died on 29 June 1091. A rival claim was advanced by Adelaide's nephew, Margrave Boniface I of Vasto, who by the end of the decade had seized the southern counties of the march. See Meyer von Knonau (1903) 4:347–8; Previté-Orton (1912) 249–51, 255–8; Struve (1995) 72; E. Goez (1996) 23.

[70] *DD H IV* 427, 430, 436 for the church of Asti. Bishop elect Oddo received the county of Asti, two fortresses and other properties, as an incentive to support the emperor. See Schwartz (1913) 97–8; E. Goez (1996) 23

[71] Bernold, *Chronicon* 1092, p. 454. See Meyer von Knonau (1903) 4:373–4; E. Goez (1996) 24.

Turin in 1055 had been to protect the Salian dynasty from the ambitions of the house of Canossa. In 1093 King Conrad chose to aim at his father's crown by making common cause with the heiress of Canossa and her allies.

The chronicler Ekkehard, abbot of Aura recorded that the young king acted in 1093 solely on the advice of 'one of his father's *ministeriales*, who was likewise named Conrad'.[72] The anonymous biographer of Henry IV represented the young king as the dupe of his kinswoman, Matilda of Tuscany.[73] The most favourable accounts of the young king are found in pro-papal works of the earlier twelfth century, which represent him as a convert to Gregorian views. According to Ekkehard of Aura, 'he was a thoroughly catholic man, most devoted to the apostolic see, inclining to religion rather than to government or war. Although he was well enough furnished with courage and boldness, he preferred to occupy his time with reading rather than with sports'.[74] This testimony has prompted the conclusion that Conrad's quarrel with his father stemmed from differences about papal authority and the freedom of the Church.[75] Conrad's attitude towards the reform papacy may, however, have been inspired by political calculation rather than religious conversion. Perhaps he saw reconciliation with the legitimate papacy as the only means of escaping from the otherwise insoluble problem of the schism.[76] A similar motive has been suggested for the rebellion of Conrad's younger brother, Henry V, a decade later. This seems a likely explanation in the case of both rebellions. Conrad's decision to rebel was probably inspired by the military setbacks experienced by the emperor late in 1092 and perhaps also by the threatening developments in southern Germany.

The chronicler Bernold of St Blasien represented Henry IV in the months following Conrad's rebellion as utterly defeated, solitary and desperate. 'He was so afflicted by grief that, so they say, he would have killed himself, had not his followers prevented him from achieving his object.'[77] No other source mentions this rumour of attempted suicide and it is likely that Bernold's story was a fiction derived from an Old Testament parallel. The wicked King Saul, rejected by God and defeated in battle, took his own life (1 Samuel 31:4). (The career of Saul had provided Gregory VII with his favourite historical parallel with Henry IV, a monarch similarly doomed because of his failure to obey

---

[72] Ekkehard, *Chronica* I, 1099, p. 128. Perhaps he was the envoy of the same name whom Conrad sent to Roger I of Sicily: Geoffrey Malaterra, *De rebus gestis Rogerii* IV.23, p. 101 ('Count Conrad'). See W. Holtzmann (1963) 161.

[73] *Vita Heinrici IV* c. 7, p. 26. Cf. *Annales Augustani* 1093, p. 134. See E. Goez (1996) 26–7.

[74] Ekkehard of Aura, *Chronica* I, 1099, pp. 128–30. Cf. *Annales sancti Disibodi* 1093, p. 14; *Casus monasterii Petrishusensis* II.45, p. 648.   [75] Meyer von Knonau (1903) 4:391–2.

[76] Boshof (1979) 105; Boshof (1987) 256; E. Goez (1996) 27–8.

[77] Bernold, *Chronicon* 1093, p. 456. See Robinson (1989) 187.

divine commands.)[78] There is no doubt that the emperor was deserted by a number of his former allies.[79] He had retreated to Pavia after the reverses of autumn 1092 and remained there until May 1093. Soon afterwards he was compelled by the league of Lombard cities to withdraw from Lombardy. By the end of the year he had moved north to the march of Verona, which belonged to the jurisdiction of his kinsman, Henry of Eppenstein, duke of Carinthia and margrave of Verona.[80] It was on Duke Henry and his brother Patriarch Udalric of Aquileia that the emperor principally depended for support during the three years in which the rebellion of King Conrad and the Welf–Canossa coalition continued to prosper. During these years the emperor's movements would be confined to the march of Verona and the neighbouring duchy of Venice. It was in Verona that the emperor celebrated Christmas 1093 with Clement III. The antipope, who never returned to Rome after February 1092, seems to have resided almost permanently in the imperial entourage for the remaining years of Henry's residence in Italy. During the winter of 1093–4 Clement 'pretended that he would gladly surrender the papacy if there was no other way by which peace could be restored'.[81] This was his response to Conrad's rebellion. If the reason for Conrad's quarrel with his father was Henry's refusal to acknowledge the legitimacy of the Gregorian papacy, the loyal Clement would stand aside to enable his master to negotiate a settlement with the rebel. The antipope's offer, probably addressed to Conrad and public opinion in northern Italy, produced no peace negotiations, but may have made a favourable impression on the north Italian episcopate.[82]

The year 1094 is the only year of the reign in which the actions and even the precise whereabouts of Henry IV are unrecorded. It is likely that he remained in the march of Verona, waiting on events. Early in 1094 a second betrayal inside the imperial family gave the anti-Henrician coalition a spectacular propaganda coup. Empress Eupraxia-Adelaide, to whom Henry had been married for four-and-a-half years, joined the rebellion against her husband. Information about this desertion derives from numerous pro-papal authors who eagerly disseminated the accusations which Eupraxia made against the emperor. At the time of her decision to desert her husband, the empress was in Verona, allegedly treated as a prisoner in the imperial entourage.[83] Henry

---

[78] See above p. 287 and below p. 292.
[79] Sigebert, *Chronica* 1093, p. 366. See Meyer von Knonau (1903) 4:396.
[80] *DD H IV* 430–2, 435. See Kilian (1886) 118–21.
[81] Bernold, *Chronicon* 1094, p. 457. Cf. the contemporary polemic *Altercatio inter Urbanum et Clementem* pp. 170–2, suggesting that the rival popes' claims be judged by a council.
[82] Ziese (1982) 223.
[83] Donizo, *Vita Mathildis* ii.8, p. 394. Cf. Bernold, *Chronicon* 1094, p. 457; *Annales Augustani* 1094, p. 134. See Meyer von Knonau (1903) 4:422–3; Becker (1964) 133; Struve (1995) 77–8.

perhaps had reason to doubt his wife's loyalty: it is likely indeed that the young king's treachery had made the emperor suspicious of all those around him. It is clear from the evidence of the few imperial diplomas from the period of their married life that Eupraxia was a far less important figure in the regime than her predecessor had been.[84] Her almost total invisibility suggests that she soon lost or perhaps never gained the emperor's confidence, which may have been one of the considerations that prompted her flight. On receiving her plea for help, Matilda of Tuscany 'secretly sent a small force to Verona', which liberated the empress without encountering serious resistance and brought her to the Tuscan court.[85] The account that Eupraxia gave to her protectors of her inhuman treatment at the emperor's hands rapidly spread among reforming circles in Italy and Germany. Her story was repeated, presumably in the form of a written deposition sent by Welf V, to the legatine synod held in Constance by Bishop Gebhard (April 1094). The empress appeared in person at Urban II's council of Piacenza in mid-Lent (1–8 March) 1095 to denounce her husband before the whole assembly.[86]

According to the earliest account, that of Bernold's chronicle, Eupraxia 'complained that she had suffered so many and such unheard-of filthy acts of fornication with so many men as would cause even her enemies to excuse her flight [from her husband] and move all catholics to compassion for her great injuries'. The wrongs of Eupraxia continued to be recalled in Gregorian polemics for half a century.[87] Her public statements at the synod of Constance and the council of Piacenza have never been taken seriously by modern scholarship,[88] not because scholars could accurately judge the empress's mentality or the emperor's conduct, but because of their knowledge of the nature of eleventh-century propaganda. Polemicists were accustomed to 'pay no heed to what was done or not done' but to use fictions in order to convince their audience. The story of Eupraxia's wrongs became public after she had taken refuge at the court of Matilda of Tuscany, a court which for more than a decade had been one of the most important centres of papal polemic.[89] Eupraxia's public statements were formulated in the feverishly anti-Henrician atmosphere of

[84] 'Our wife, Queen Adelaide' appeared only in *D H IV* 407 (14 August 1089). See above p. 266 n. 155.   [85] Donizo, *Vita* II.8, p. 394.

[86] Bernold, *Chronicon* 1094, 1095, pp. 458, 462. See Meyer von Knonau (1903) 4:428–9, 444; E. Goez (1996) 31–2.

[87] Herrand, *Epistola* p. 288; Deusdedit, *Libellus contra invasores* II.12, p. 330; Laurence of Liège, *Gesta episcoporum Virdunensium* c. 9, p. 495; *Annales sancti Disibodi* 1093, p. 14. See Meyer von Knonau (1903) 4:423 n. 12.

[88] Meyer von Knonau (1903) 4:423 n. 12; Nitschke (1971) 58; Boshof (1979) 105–6; Boshof (1987) 257–8.

[89] Bischoff (1948) 23–6; Robinson (1978a) 100–3. The use of 'fictions' by eleventh-century polemicists: above p. 113.

this court, perhaps drafted by one of the learned Gregorians who acted as Matilda's advisers. Whatever had driven the empress to leave her husband's court, she had now committed herself to the Welf–Canossa coalition and in return for the protection of these allies, she must support their propaganda war against the emperor. Eupraxia's usefulness to the emperor's enemies ceased with the acrimonious ending of the marriage of Matilda and Welf V in 1095. After the council of Piacenza the empress's name disappears from the contemporary German and Italian sources. Russian sources record that she became a nun in Kiev in December 1106, four months after the death of her second husband, and died on 10 July 1109.[90]

The council of Piacenza (March 1095) marked the beginning of a year of triumph for Urban II. His council, attended by 'countless multitudes', was intended to demonstrate the strength of support for the Gregorian papacy and to dismantle the obedience of Clement III. Piacenza was situated in the archdiocese of Ravenna, so that the excommunication of 'the heresiarch Wibert, intruder in the apostolic see' was pronounced inside his own metropolitan jurisdiction. The conciliar legislation of Piacenza offered reconciliation to all the clergy of the antipope's party, except the leaders themselves.[91] One month after the council King Conrad strikingly demonstrated his support for the reform papacy. An official memorandum intended for the papal register records that 'King Conrad . . . went to meet the lord Pope Urban as he arrived in Cremona on 10 April and performed for him the office of a groom'.[92] The young king held the bridle of the pope's horse, a ceremonial duty allegedly first performed by Emperor Constantine I. The 'office of a groom' had not been performed since the ninth century.[93] Urban II and his advisers must have revived the ceremony for the occasion of his encounter with Conrad. At a second meeting in Cremona on 15 April the king swore an oath to the pope 'concerning life, limbs and the Roman papacy'. This was the 'oath of security' which the German king swore to the pope before the imperial coronation, guaranteeing the safety of the pope's person and protection for the papacy and the property of the Roman church.[94]

During this meeting Urban promised to crown Conrad emperor. In return Conrad was expected to support the programme of the reform papacy. Eight

[90] Meyer von Knonau (1903) 4:444 and n. 10.

[91] *MGH Constitutiones* 1, 561–3. Cf. Bernold, *Chronicon* 1095, pp. 461–3. See Meyer von Knonau (1903) 4:441–7; Ziese (1982) 223–6.

[92] *MGH Constitutiones* 1, 564; Bernold, *Chronicon* 1095, p. 463. See Meyer von Knonau (1903) 4:449; Becker (1964) 133–6; E. Goez (1996) 32–3.

[93] *Constitutum Constantini* c. 16, p. 92. See Eichmann (1942) 290.

[94] Bernold, *Chronicon* 1095, p. 463 referred to it as an oath of 'fealty', but see Robinson (1990) 417.

years after his coronation in Aachen as heir to the Salian kingship, he transformed his status to that of papal anti-king, on the model of Rudolf of
Rheinfelden, dependent on the pope's 'advice and aid' and the cooperation of
the pope's allies. Urban II, who had hitherto shown no interest in the creation
of an anti-king, seemed now to have been offered the means to end the schism:
once Conrad had been placed on his father's throne, he would depose the antipope and restore unity to the Church. This prospect prompted the reappearance of the issue of lay investiture on the papal reforming agenda after an
absence of six years.[95] The young king must first be provided with the means
to acquire 'the kingship and the crown of the empire' and Urban proposed to
do this by negotiating a suitable marriage. Undaunted by the breakdown of
the previous matrimonial project between Matilda of Tuscany and Welf V,
which occurred at this moment, the pope, together with the margravine,
urged Conrad to seek the hand of Maximilla, daughter of Count Roger I of
Sicily. His proposal was accepted and the marriage was celebrated in Pisa with
the greatest splendour.[96] The advantage of this match for Urban was that it
would bind together the papal anti-king and one of the pope's powerful
Norman vassals. The advantage for Conrad was Maximilla's dowry.[97]

During the summer of 1095 Urban II travelled to France, where his authority was widely respected and where he held three reforming councils:
Clermont, Tours and Nîmes. His conduct at Clermont, the most important
of these councils, especially his preaching of the crusade, did much to raise his
own prestige and that of the Gregorian papacy throughout Christendom.[98]
Urban's successes and the emperor's plight in the Italian kingdom prompted
the desertion of two Henrician bishops, Emehard of Würzburg and Otto of
Strasbourg (brother of the emperor's son-in-law, Duke Frederick I of
Swabia).[99] Urban's most important success in detaching the antipope's
German adherents from his obedience was in Upper Lotharingia, where he
secured the support of all three of the suffragans of Archbishop Egilbert of
Trier.[100] Elsewhere the Gregorian party made no such spectacular encroach-
ments on the German obedience of the antipope. In south Germany Gebhard

---

[95] See above p. 278.

[96] Geoffrey Malaterra, *De rebus gestis Rogerii* IV.23, p. 101; Bernold, *Chronicon* 1095, p. 463. See
Meyer von Knonau (1903) 4:449–50; W. Holtzmann (1963) 161–2; Becker (1964) 136–7:
E. Goez (1996) 35.

[97] Geoffrey Malaterra, *De rebus* IV.23, p. 101. Cf. Bernold, *Chronicon* 1095, p. 463.

[98] Becker (1964) 187–93; Somerville (1970) 56–65.

[99] Bernold, *Chronicon* 1096, p. 464. See Meyer von Knonau (1903) 4:470; Becker (1964) 161;
Ziese (1982) 219–20.

[100] Bernold, *Chronicon* 1093, p. 456; *Codex Udalrici* 86, p. 169. See Meyer von Knonau (1903)
4:404–6; Becker (1964) 152–4; Ziese (1982) 218–19.

of Constance secured the succession of a Gregorian bishop in Passau but failed to gain control of Augsburg.[101] Urban II's greatest disappointment was his failure to draw the Saxon churches into his obedience. He pinned his hopes on the Gregorian candidate for the see of Halberstadt, Herrand (nephew of Bishop Burchard II), whom he himself had consecrated in Rome (29 January 1094).[102] Neither the triumphs of Urban II at Piacenza and Clermont, nor the defeats of Henry IV in Italy, enabled Herrand of Halberstadt to regain Saxony for the Gregorian papacy, and this was also the experience of his colleagues in most regions of the German kingdom.

The historian Donizo of Canossa contrasted the different situations of Urban II and Henry IV in 1095: while the pope was free to 'travel through the regions of France', the emperor 'still remained fixed in Lombardy, since fortune forbade him to wear the crown any more'.[103] Early in 1095 Henry attempted, with forces supplied by the city of Verona, to capture Nogara, a fortress of Matilda in the county of Verona. He was soon compelled to abandon the siege, however, by the army which Matilda sent to the relief of her garrison.[104] The Gregorian chronicler Bernold recorded that Henry 'lingered in Lombardy, deprived of almost all the dignity of a king'.[105] The eight imperial diplomas surviving from 1095 reveal, however, that Henry's royal authority continued to be exercised in the north-eastern corner of the Italian kingdom. They show the emperor visiting Treviso, Padua, Mestre (in the jurisdiction of the duchy of Venice), Verona, Mantua and Garda. In this narrow area he continued to perform the traditional functions of monarchy, sitting in judgement on property disputes, conferring his protection on religious houses, bestowing imperial largesse on favoured subjects, commanding the attendance of local princes at his court: the bishops of Verona, Feltre and Piacenza, the margraves Burchard of Istria and Werner of Ancona and Count Manfred of Padua.[106]

The emperor's main concern in summer 1095 was to strengthen his ties with Venice. This duchy, formerly a province of the Byzantine empire, subsequently a tributary of the Ottonian emperors, was now an independent commercial and maritime power, determined to avoid absorption in the kingdom of Italy or subjection to Constantinople. Venice had been the ally of Byzantium in the war against Robert Guiscard of Apulia and been richly

---

[101] Becker (1964) 156; Ziese (1982) 218.
[102] Urban II, *JL* 5505: 375C–376C. See Fenske (1977) 138–42; Ziese (1982) 215–17.
[103] Donizo, *Vita Mathildis* II.II, p. 396.
[104] *Ibid.* II.9, pp. 394–5. See Overmann (1895) 161; Meyer von Knonau (1903) 4:448–9.
[105] Bernold, *Chronicon* 1095, p. 461.
[106] *DD H IV* 442–8, 450. See Meyer von Knonau (1903) 4:453–4. These diplomas also reveal the breakdown of the Italian chancery: Gawlik (1970b) 217–18.

rewarded by Emperor Alexius I Comnenus. It was characteristic of the Venetians' diplomatic balancing act that, after being rewarded by the Byzantine emperor as his 'true and faithful servants', they sought to renew their treaty with the western emperor. Henry agreed to the renewal of the treaty regulating trade between the duchy of Venice and the kingdom of Italy, first negotiated with the Venetians by Emperor Otto I (967) and confirmed by his successors, including Henry III. Henry IV's diploma confirming the treaty describes the doge as 'the wise and discreet ruler of the Venetian kingdom' and as 'the friend' (*amicus*) of the western empire.[107] The term 'friendship' (*amicitia*) denoted, in the political language of the late eleventh century, collaboration and alliance between two independent powers.[108] During June 1095 Henry visited Venice 'for the purpose of prayer'.[109] Venice was an important pilgrimage centre at this moment because of the recent translation of the relics of St Mark (8 October 1094) in the newly rebuilt church of St Mark. In his straitened circumstances the emperor may well have made a pilgrimage to seek the assistance of the illustrious patron of the Venetians. No doubt Henry IV also hoped for material assistance from the prince whom he had recently designated 'the friend' of his empire, but Venice gave him no more than the annual tribute of fifty pounds of Venetian pence, fixed in the time of Otto III.

A few months later, still confined to the north-eastern corner of the Italian kingdom, the emperor was seeking the help of the new Hungarian king, Coloman. He wrote to the latter's brother, Duke Almus, commending him for his 'firm friendship' for the emperor. Henry expressed his wish to continue the alliance negotiated with King Ladislaus I and urged the duke to 'persuade [his] brother by all possible means to pursue [Welf], who is no duke, but has been deposed by due process of law, and oppose him in all things as [the emperor's] most dangerous enemy'.[110] At the time of this appeal in 1096 Coloman's attention was engrossed by the disorderly progress through his kingdom of the participants in the First Crusade. There was no hope, therefore, of a positive response to the emperor's letter.[111] It was not through the

---

[107] *D H IV* 442. Henry also agreed to become the godfather of the daughter of Doge Vitalis Falieri: Meyer von Knonau (1903) 4:454. See also Nicol (1988) 55–65.

[108] Cowdrey (1972) 93–4.

[109] *D H IV* 445. Cf Andrea Dandolo, *Chronicon Venetum* IX.9, pp. 251–2. See Meyer von Knonau (1903) 4:454. Otto III, the last emperor to visit Venice (1001), had prayed in St Mark's church and become the godfather of the doge's daughter: R. Holtzmann (1941) 376; Giese (1993) 219–43.

[110] Henry IV, *Letter* 23, pp. 33–4. See Meyer von Knonau (1903) 4:475–6; Boshof (1986) 188.

[111] Coloman later figured as a champion of the reform papacy (Urban II, *JL* 5662: 480D–482B). He faced rebellion by Almus, who sought the aid of Henry IV and his successor to seize the Hungarian throne: Becker (1964) 167; Servatius (1979) 167–8.

intervention of the Hungarians that the emperor escaped from his impasse, but through a rapprochement with the prince whom he described in his letter of 1096 as his 'most dangerous enemy', Welf IV. The turning-point in the fortunes of Henry IV and Conrad was the failure of the marriage of Matilda of Tuscany and Welf V, which brought Welf IV 'in great wrath' to Lombardy in a vain attempt to reconcile them in 1095.[112] Welf V had evidently been disappointed in his expectation that the marriage would give him control of the march of Tuscany and the margravine's property.[113] Returning to Germany, the Welfs 'held lengthy negotiations with the princes of the kingdom about the restoration of Henry to the kingship'.[114] These negotiations of 1095 achieved nothing because the emperor's supporters did not trust Welf IV, while the Gregorians feared excommunication if they agreed to Henry's restoration. Early in 1096, however, Welf finally achieved a reconciliation with Henry IV.

'Welf, formerly duke of Bavaria . . . came back into the emperor's favour and obtained the duchy.'[115] The politicians who were present when this reconciliation was negotiated are identified in the witness lists of two imperial diplomas. They included the Bavarian count palatine Rapoto, the prince who stood to lose most by the restoration of Welf IV, and noblemen from Bavaria and Carinthia who had escorted Welf to the imperial court. Liemar of Bremen, the longest serving of the German archbishops and for many years a most valued adviser, was in the emperor's entourage at the time of the negotiations. Also present was the centenarian head of the Otbertine clan, Margrave Adalbert Azzo II of Este, the father of Welf IV, who is likely to have played the leading role in the reconciliation. Clement III rejoined the imperial entourage during the negotiations.[116] During the two previous attempts to make peace (winter 1089–90 and August 1091), Welf had insisted on the renunciation of 'the heresiarch Wibert'. The reconciliation of 1096 was achieved without any such condition. Welf was content with the restitution of the duchy of Bavaria, for which he had been fighting for the past nineteen years.[117] This must have seemed to the emperor a small price to pay to escape at last from north-eastern Italy and return to his German kingdom.

---

[112] Bernold, *Chronicon* 1095, p. 461. Cf. *Historia Welfonum Weingartensis* c. 14, p. 462. See Overmann (1895) 161; Meyer von Knonau (1903) 4:447–8; Simeoni (1947) 367; Becker (1964) 133; Struve (1995) 80.   [113] Bernold, *Chronicon* 1095, p. 461.

[114] *Ibid.*, p. 463. See Meyer von Knonau (1903) 4:460–1.

[115] Frutolf, *Chronica* 1096, p. 106. See Meyer von Knonau (1903) 4:477–9.

[116] *D H IV* 451–2. See Jakobs (1968) 122–4; Gawlik (1970a) 87–8; Ziese (1982) 230–4; Struve (1995) 80.

[117] Bernold, *Chronicon* 1095, p. 461: He sought Henry's help 'to force [Matilda] to yield up her property to his son'.

9

The restoration of royal authority in
Germany, 1097–1103

The reconciliation with Welf IV meant that the Alpine passes were once more open for Henry IV to return to Germany. The journey took place in the spring of 1097, probably through the Brenner Pass, since the first record of Henry on German soil is in Nußdorf on the River Inn (15 May). He was attended by Welf IV, who must have accompanied him over the Alps.[1] The emperor celebrated Whitsun (24 May) in Regensburg. He depended as much as ever on the material support of Regensburg (making five visits during the next nine years) and the bishop and citizens remained loyal to him to the end of his reign.[2] His court was attended by princes from southern and northern Germany, including Duke Frederick I of Swabia and four Saxon princes: Cuno of Beichlingen (son of Otto of Northeim), Frederick I of Sommerschenburg, the Saxon count palatine, Count Wiprecht I of Groitzsch and Henry I of Eilenburg, margrave of Meissen and of Lower Lusatia (a notable participant in the pacification of Saxony in 1088–9).[3] From Regensburg the imperial entourage moved north to Nuremberg, where 'very many of the greater men of the kingdom' had come, the Merseburg chronicler explained, 'to be reconciled to the king'.[4] The imperial visit to Nuremberg witnessed the formal submission of a number of former rebels, continuing the process of pacification begun in Verona in 1096. A similar assembly was held at the end of the year: 'a conference with the princes in Mainz around 1 December concerning peace.'[5]

---

[1] *D H IV* 454: see Schmid (1984a) 714; Schmid (1984b) 262. Cf. Udalschalk of Augsburg, *De Eginone et Herimanno* c. 12, pp. 436–7. See Meyer von Knonau (1903) 4:479–80.

[2] Meyer von Knonau (1904) 5:2; Kraus (1972) 59; Kottje (1978) 145–7.

[3] *DD H IV* 485, 455. See Gawlik (1970a) 104–5.

[4] *Chronicon episcoporum Merseburgensium* c. 12, p. 186. See Meyer von Knonau (1904) 5:3–4.

[5] Frutolf of Michelsberg, *Chronica* 1097, p. 110; *Chronicon sancti Huberti* c. 89, p. 620. See Meyer von Knonau (1904) 5:4. Erdmann (1939) 208–9 suggested that Henry IV, *Letter* 20, p. 30 referred to the 1097 meeting (although the letter mentions the emperor's plan to celebrate Christmas in Cologne, when he actually celebrated the festival in Strasbourg: Frutolf, *Chronica* 1097, p. 110). See Meyer von Knonau (1900) 3:579–80, dating the letter in 1084.

A letter of Henry IV to Bishop Rupert of Bamberg in 1098 contains a summons to a council in Worms to 'discuss the business of Duke W[elf] and his sons'.[6] Welf V and Henry 'the Black', the sons of Welf IV, had imprisoned Anzo, whom the emperor had recently appointed bishop of Brixen.[7] Their conduct threatened to undermine the peace which their father had concluded with the emperor in 1096. Welf IV, however, could ill afford a renewal of his conflict with the emperor. Immediately after the death of his father, Margrave Adalbert Azzo II of Este (1097), he had become embroiled in a dispute over his Italian inheritance with his half-brothers, the margraves Hugh and Fulco of Este, the allies of King Conrad. Welf IV enlisted the support of Duke Henry III of Carinthia and his brother, Patriarch Udalric of Aquileia, with whose help he eventually gained possession of the greater part of the inheritance.[8] Were he now to quarrel with the emperor, he would lose these valuable allies, who were Henry IV's kinsmen and loyal adherents. Welf IV succeeded in salvaging the peace at the assembly of Worms by persuading or compelling his sons to submit to the emperor. He found Henry IV equally eager to preserve the peace and ready to reward his efforts with an unprecedented imperial concession.

The duke 'secured the succession of one of his sons to the duchy after his death'.[9] In the years 1077–96 Bavaria had been a 'crown province' ruled directly by the emperor and during this period he had received extensive material support from the duchy for his wars and built up close ties with the Bavarian nobility. Now in 1098 he 'abandoned all the Salian principles concerning the duchy by conceding its hereditary character'.[10] It is possible that the emperor risked this concession precisely because of the closeness of his links with Bavaria. For two decades all the Bavarian princely families, with the exception of that of Formbach, had fought for Henry IV against Welf. The greater part of the Bavarian episcopate had defied the Gregorian papacy and their loyalty had been richly rewarded by the emperor. Although he was the first eleventh-century duke of Bavaria actually to have territorial interests in the duchy before his accession, Welf IV seems always to have been regarded with suspicion by the Bavarians.[11] The limited success of Welf IV and his successors in consolidating their power in Bavaria suggests that fifty-four years of

---

The authenticity of Henry's letters to Rupert of Bamberg: Schmale (1957) 434–74; Classen (1964) 115–29.   [6] Henry IV, *Letter* 29, p. 38. See Erdmann (1939) 209–10.
[7] *Annales Augustani* 1097, p. 135. Cf. Frutolf, *Chronica* 1098, p. 110. See Meyer von Knonau (1904) 5:22–3.
[8] Bernold, *Chronicon* 1097, p. 465. Cf. *D Konrad* 2. See Meyer von Knonau (1904) 5:10–11; E. Goez (1996) 42.   [9] Frutolf, *Chronica* 1098, p. 110.
[10] Störmer (1991) 517; cf. 534, 542–3, 547; Goetz (1991) 266.
[11] Otto of Freising, *Chronica* VII.7, p. 316.

direct imperial control during the eleventh century had caused the erosion of ducal authority. The Bavarian nobility gave little support to the dynastic ambitions even of a family with an acknowledged hereditary right to the duchy. Welf IV's restless energy never again threatened the emperor. Four years after his restoration to the duchy he enlisted in the crusade of 1101 and died on the return journey.[12]

The resolution of 'the business of Duke Welf and his sons' was followed, perhaps in the same assembly of 1098, by the settlement of the struggle for the office of duke of Swabia, in which the Welfs were also involved. According to the historian Otto of Freising, writing half a century later, 'Frederick [I], duke of the Swabians and the king's son-in-law . . . at last compelled Berthold [II of Zähringen] to seek peace.' This Swabian settlement was presumably part of the general pacification of southern Germany initiated in 1096. It is likely that Welf IV, rather than Frederick, played the leading role in the settlement with Berthold of Zähringen, the Gregorian anti-duke. 'A condition of the peace was that Berthold should renounce the duchy, but should retain Zürich, the most noble city of Swabia, to be held from the hand of the emperor.' Zürich was part of an extensive tract of imperial estates, serving as one of the administrative centres of the duchy of Swabia. The former dukes' practice of residing there had symbolised the viceregal character of their office. This territory was now extracted from the ducal jurisdiction and converted into a benefice held by Berthold in return for renouncing the office of duke of Swabia.[13] Berthold was permitted, however, to retain the title of 'duke'. Otto of Freising regarded this as an absurd anomaly. 'All [Berthold's descendants] up to the present day [1157] have been called dukes, although they have held no duchy, possessing only the title without the thing itself.'[14] Modern scholarship, following Otto of Freising's assessment, has often designated Berthold II as a new kind of duke, a 'titular duke', bearing only an honorific title to which no governmental rights and functions were attached. In fact Berthold exercised lordship over a considerable part of southern Swabia. The crown lands of Zürich served as a vital connecting link between the Zähringen family lands in the Breisgau and southern Rhineland and the lands inherited from the Rheinfelden in the region of the Aare and the Jura. Zürich became the centre of the lordship constructed by Berthold, where he held assemblies of his adherents in southern

[12] Ekkehard of Aura, *Chronica* I, 1101, pp. 164–6, 170. See Meyer von Knonau (1904) 5:135–42.

[13] Otto, *Gesta Friderici* I.8, pp. 24–5. See Meyer von Knonau (1904) 5:23–4. See Schreiner (1977) 9; Maurer (1978) 213–14, 218–22; Althoff (1986) 43–58.

[14] Otto, *Gesta* I.9, pp. 25–6. In Henry V's diplomas Berthold II was called simply 'duke', as were his sons and successors. In his own diplomas he styled himself 'duke of Zähringen', a title that first appeared in an imperial diploma in the reign of Lothar III. See Kienast (1965) 576–7; Kienast (1968) 340; Maurer (1978) 221; Ott (1986) 11–15.

Swabia, the political connection created during the civil war. In his adherents' eyes Berthold was truly a duke, in the traditional sense of the leader of the nobility in the region. Henry IV legitimised this political ascendancy when he exempted Berthold's territories from the jurisdiction of Duke Frederick in the Swabian settlement of 1098.

The twelfth-century Petershausen chronicler wrote that there were three 'dukes of the Swabians' at the end of the eleventh century: Frederick of Staufen, the appointee of the emperor; Berthold of Zähringen, elected by the Swabians; and the latter's ally, Welf IV.[15] The chronicler was referring to the fact that the most important Welf family possessions were situated in southern Swabia, including the castle of Ravensburg, the principal seat of the dynasty. Here Welf IV's power was concentrated during the years in which he was deprived of the duchy of Bavaria and the title 'duke of Ravensburg' was ascribed to subsequent members of the dynasty. As in the case of the 'duke of Zähringen', these Welfs were given a ducal title attached to territory inside the duchy of Swabia. By the mid-twelfth century the Welf 'duchy of Ravensburg' enjoyed the same exemption from ducal authority as the 'duchy of Zähringen'. It has been suggested that this exemption dated from the settlement of 1098. If so, Henry IV's settlement must have partitioned Swabia into the three spheres of influence that the Staufen, the Zähringen and the Welfs had created during the civil war.[16] The emperor judged that the nobility of southern Swabia could not be coerced into withdrawing their fidelity to their Zähringen and Welf lords. Frederick I's ducal authority was consequently restricted to the northern part of the duchy. The principal advantage that he derived from the peace of 1098 was the recovery of access to Ulm, the imperial property to which the duke of Swabia traditionally summoned assemblies of the nobility of the duchy.

The Petershausen chronicler considered that the peace of 1098 signalled the complete restoration of Henry IV's authority over the German kingdom after two decades of civil war. 'Henry finally gained sole possession of the monarchy; almost all the princes were reconciled with him; they acknowledged that he was the lawful emperor. He had always been allied with all the cities by the River Rhine and with other great and powerful cities and very many bishops were so closely bound to him that they could by no means be torn asunder.' The consequence of this restoration was the total isolation of Bishop Gebhard III of Constance, papal legate and leader of the Gregorian party.[17] Gebhard was confirmed in his legatine office in 1099 by Urban II's successor, Paschal II,

---

[15] *Casus monasterii Petrishusensis* II.32, p. 646.
[16] Maurer (1978) 221. Cf. Tellenbach (1943) 59 n. 153; Werle (1956) 264–71.
[17] *Casus monasterii Petrishusensis* II.46, p. 648; III.30, p. 656.

who expected his legate to continue the struggle against the emperor.[18] The disintegration of his party, however, forced Gebhard virtually to withdraw from political activity and to devote himself to the reorganisation of his diocese and to the promotion of monastic reform.[19]

The completion of the pacification of southern Germany in 1098 was followed by the reordering of the succession to the throne. This grave measure had probably already been discussed in the emperor's conferences with the princes since his return to Germany. The rebel Conrad was formally deposed and his younger brother Henry elected to the kingship in an assembly held while the emperor was in Mainz in May 1098.[20] By the time of his deposition Conrad had ceased to be a threat to his father's authority.[21] After the breakup of the Welf–Canossa alliance and Welf IV's reconciliation with the emperor, Conrad came to depend entirely on the support of his kinswoman, Matilda of Tuscany.[22] Urban II, who had 'faithfully promised his advice and aid in obtaining the kingship and the crown of the empire', seems to have had no further contact with the young king after his return from France. The great enterprise of the crusade now absorbed his attention. His successor Paschal II is not known to have communicated with the young king. Nor did Conrad receive from the family of his Sicilian bride any assistance beyond the 'many gifts of treasure' produced at his wedding. Forgotten by most of his former allies, Conrad died suddenly in his twenty-eighth year (27 July 1101) in Florence, where he was buried.[23]

Conrad's place as heir apparent was taken by his twelve-year-old brother, Henry V. A letter issued by the emperor eight years later declared that he had 'raised [his] son to the throne of the kingdom against the will of many men'.[24]

---

[18] Paschal II, *JL* 5817: *Acta pont. Rom. inedita* 2, 169. See Meyer von Knonau (1904) 5:84–5, 99; Schumann (1912) 71; Servatius (1979) 147–9.

[19] Diebolder (1916) 195–9. Gebhard's sole triumph was the submission of the Henrician Herman of Augsburg (1099): Paschal II, *JL* 5825: *Regesta pont. Rom.* 1, 705. See Meyer von Knonau (1904) 5:99–100, 169; Zoepfl (1952) 319–20; Servatius (1979) 149–50.

[20] *D H IV* 460. Cf. *Vita Heinrici IV* c. 7, p. 27. See Meyer von Knonau (1904) 5:26.

[21] Landulf Junior de Sancto Paulo, *Historia Mediolanensis* c. 3, pp. 21–2. Cf. *DD Konrad* 2–5. See Meyer von Knonau (1904) 5:13; E. Goez (1996) 44–5.

[22] Donizo of Canossa, *Vita Mathildis* II.13, p. 397. See Meyer von Knonau (1904) 5:147; Becker (1964) 137–8.

[23] Landulf Junior, *Historia* c. 3, p. 22; Ekkehard, *Chronica* I, 1101, pp. 162–4 (death by poison). See Meyer von Knonau (1904) 5:147; E. Goez (1996) 48–9. Ekkehard recorded *post mortem* evidence of his sanctity: 'the sign of the cross . . . on the arm', the miraculous sign that appeared on the bodies of many crusaders: Hagenmeyer (1877) 117 n. 31; Riley-Smith (1986) 34, 81–2, 114. This suggests that members of the Gregorian party attempted to develop the cult of King Conrad.

[24] Henry IV, *Letter* 37, p. 47. Cf. *Conquestio Heinrici IV* 30–1, p. 25. See Meyer von Knonau (1904) 5:26–7.

The anonymous *Life of Emperor Henry IV* attributed this opposition to 'fear that there would be a civil war between the two brothers and that a great disaster would befall the kingdom'.[25] The emperor's own anxiety on this occasion is indicated by the oath of security which he demanded from Henry V. 'On the occasion of his election in Mainz,' the emperor declared in 1106, 'he guaranteed us our life and the safety of our person on oath and swore that he would never interfere during our lifetime and against our will and our command in matters concerning our kingship, our honour and all our present and future possessions.'[26] This oath was demanded, explained the anonymous biographer, 'lest [Henry] go the same way as his brother'.[27] Henry V was required to repeat this oath at his coronation in Aachen on 6 January 1099. This time the oath was taken on the most sacred relics of the German kingdom and the most precious objects in the imperial treasury.[28] (As in 1087, the emperor chose for the coronation of his heir the same place in which he himself had received the crown.) A third ceremony completed the process by which Henry V assumed the role of his deposed elder brother. On Easter day (21 April) 1101 he was girded with the sword in Liège, indicating that he had now come of age. He was in his fifteenth year, the same age as Henry IV when he received his sword in 1065.[29] In an imperial diploma issued in Aachen on 10 February 1099 'our beloved son King Henry' appeared for the first time as an intervener. Five more such interventions are found in the diplomas of 1101–3.[30] Four imperial privileges of 1099–1103 were granted to gain spiritual benefits for the young king.[31] As for the practical involvement of Henry V in the government of the kingdom during these years, there were at least two occasions on which he performed royal functions on behalf of his father. He settled a dispute between the abbey of Prüm and its advocate.[32] In 1103 he intervened successfully in the vendetta of the counts of Gleiberg against Count Siegfried of Ballenstedt.[33] Clearly Henry V's oath of 1098 and 1099 not to 'interfere in matters concerning [his father's] kingship' was not intended to prevent his playing a role in imperial affairs at least as active as that of Conrad in the years 1087–93.

The assembly of Mainz of 1098 which settled the succession seems also to

---

[25] *Vita Heinrici IV* c. 7, p. 27.   [26] Henry IV, *Letter* 37, p. 47. Cf. *Letter* 39, p. 53.

[27] *Vita Heinrici IV* c. 7, p. 27.

[28] Henry IV, *Letter* 37, p. 47. Cf. *Conquestio* 29, 33–4, p. 25. See Meyer von Knonau (1904) 5:55.

[29] *Würzburger Chronik* 1101, p. 57. See Meyer von Knonau (1904) 5:114; Haider (1968) 45–7; Scheibelreiter (1973) 25–6. Henry V's date of birth: Gaettens (1962) 52–71; Hlawitschka (1990) 471–5.   [30] *DD H IV* 458, 469, 471–2, 476, 479.

[31] *DD H IV* 463, 465, 468, 477.

[32] *D H IV* 476 (1102?). See Meyer von Knonau (1904) 5:60.

[33] *Annales Patherbrunnenses* 1103, p. 108. See Meyer von Knonau (1904) 5:183.

have witnessed the beginning of a conflict between the emperor and Archbishop Ruothard of Mainz which lasted for the rest of the reign.[34] The context of this dispute was the treatment of the Jewish community in Mainz at the beginning of the First Crusade in 1096. Almost all the crusading armies had inaugurated the expedition of 1096 with pogroms against the Jewish communities in French and German cities. In Mainz the entire Jewish community was massacred between 25 and 29 May by the army of Count Emicho of Leiningen, the most savage enemy of the Rhineland Jewry, and other crusading bands, including that led by the Swabian Count Hartman II of Dillingen and Kyburg.[35] According to the mid-twelfth-century Jewish account, on the eve of the pogrom the Jewish community sent envoys to Italy to inform the emperor of their danger. Henry IV responded with a letter to all the princes, counts and bishops, bidding them protect the Jews. A number of imperial documents reveal the importance that Henry IV attached to the defence of the Jews. The 'peace of God' which he decreed at the council of Mainz in January 1103 was characterised by the novelty of adding the Jews to the vulnerable groups who were traditionally protected by the 'peace' (clergy, monks, merchants, women). Already in 1090 he had issued privileges for the Jewish communities of Speyer and Worms, confirming their rights and ensuring their protection.[36] In the case of Speyer the guarantee of protection for the Jewish community was conceded when the emperor was urgently in need of funds and it is likely that the issuing of the privilege was accompanied by the payment of considerable sums of cash to the emperor. Such payments were perhaps the reason for Henry IV's preoccupation with the protection of the Jews.[37]

During the pogroms of 1096 Bishop John I of Speyer was alone in providing effective protection for the Jewish community. In Mainz the Jews sought refuge in the palace of Archbishop Ruothard, but when the army of Emicho of Leiningen surrounded the palace, the archbishop and his vassals abandoned the Jews to their fate. A group of fifty-four survivors succeeded in fighting their way out of the palace and Ruothard secured their escape down the Rhine to Rüdesheim. There he suddenly demanded that the refugees accept baptism and, when they refused, he allowed them to fall into the hands of the pursuing crusaders and the local villagers.[38] Henry IV's response to the pogroms was

---

[34] Ruothard was invested with Mainz on 25 July 1089: *Chronicon Lippoldesbergense* c. 4, p. 548. See Meyer von Knonau (1904) 4:257; Fenske (1977) 142–6; Zielinski (1984) 130.

[35] Meyer von Knonau (1903) 4:487–94; Riley-Smith (1984) 51–72.

[36] *MGH Constitutiones* I, 125; *DD H IV* 411–12: Gawlik (1970a) 78. See Straus (1937) 234–9; Dasberg (1965) 66–72; Heidrich (1988) 274–7; Heidrich (1991) 205–6; Stehkämper (1991) 105–6.   [37] Schiffmann (1931) 44–55.

[38] Meyer von Knonau (1904) 5:500–3; Schiffmann (1931) 241–3.

recorded by the chronicler Frutolf of Michelsberg. Firstly, on the emperor's return to Germany in 1097 'he granted to the Jews who had been compelled to receive baptism the use of their own laws'. The survivors hastened to take advantage of imperial permission to return to their own religion.[39] The emperor's concession was sharply criticised by his own antipope. Clement III commanded the bishops to 'correct' the apostasy of the baptised Jews.[40] There is no evidence either that the German bishops obeyed this command or that their opposite views led to any conflict between the emperor and the antipope. Secondly, Frutolf recorded that on his visit to Mainz in 1098, 'the emperor held a judicial investigation concerning the property of murdered Jews and certain of the archbishop's kinsmen were among those who were accused of seizing their property'. Witnesses claimed that Ruothard himself 'had received a great portion of the stolen money'. Ruothard fled with his kinsmen to the Thuringian estates of the church of Mainz, where he plotted vengeance against the emperor.[41] He quickly attached himself to the survivors of the anti-Henrician party in Thuringia and eastern Saxony, most importantly Herrand, the Gregorian candidate for the bishopric of Halberstadt.[42] After the failure of an attempt to reconcile Ruothard to the imperial party, the antipope announced the sentence of the Roman church, deposing the archbishop and releasing his subjects from their obedience to him. 'The holy Roman church . . . has confirmed that another should be put in the place of him whom she has repudiated.'[43] The emperor, however, made no attempt to depose Ruothard from the archbishopric or to appoint a new archbishop.[44]

After his flight from Mainz Ruothard was exiled from the city for seven-and-a-half years. During this absence the emperor made fourteen visits to Mainz, staying in the city at least once every year in the period 1098–1105.[45] It was here that he held the impressive council of January 1103, in which he proclaimed the 'peace of God' throughout his kingdom. During the years 1098–1105 Henry IV's itinerary reverted to the pattern of 1077–80, when the

---

[39] Frutolf, *Chronica* 1097, p. 108.

[40] Clement III, *JL* 5336: *Codex Udalrici* 90, p. 175. See Meyer von Knonau (1904) 5:4–5; Kisch (1955) 57; Ziese (1982) 241.

[41] Frutolf, *Chronica* 1098, p. 110. See Meyer von Knonau (1904) 5:28–30; Schiffmann (1931) 49, 57; Rassow (1960) 257.

[42] *Epistolae Moguntinae* 31, pp. 374–6. Ruothard in Herrand's circle (1102): *Mainzer Urkundenbuch* p. 310; *Cronica Reinhardsbrunnensis* 1097, p. 528. See Meyer von Knonau (1904) 5:161–2; Fenske (1977) 141–6.

[43] Clement III, *JL* 5339: *Epistolae Moguntinae* 32, pp. 377–9. See Meyer von Knonau (1904) 5:67; Ziese (1982) 261–3.

[44] Ruothard's name continued to appear as arch-chancellor in imperial diplomas: *DD H IV* 463–6, 468, 470, 473–5, 479–80, 488–9, 491. See Gawlik (1978) xxiv.

[45] Kilian (1886) 150–2; Büttner (1973) 357–8; Kottje (1978) 140–1.

rebel Siegfried of Mainz had been expelled from the city and Henry visited Mainz on eight occasions. The chronicler Frutolf's account of the advantages that the emperor derived from Ruothard's absence explains why Henry did not hasten to replace him. 'The emperor placed all the revenues of the bishopric and the administration of its various affairs at his own disposal; he ordered the property of the fugitives to be confiscated and the city-walls to be demolished.'[46] In making himself master of the city and the archiepiscopal revenues, there is no doubt that he acted with the approval of the principal citizens.[47] No sooner had the emperor 'finally gained sole possession of the monarchy',[48] than the rebellion of Ruothard of Mainz threatened to undermine his newly restored authority over the German kingdom. While Henry profited from the archbishop's absence, living at his expense in his city, Ruothard's activity in Thuringia and eastern Saxony was likely to revive the fortunes of the Gregorian party and reanimate Saxon opposition to the emperor. Consequently in the years 1098–1104 Henry IV was no less active than his opponent, consolidating his power, maintaining the peace, assuring himself of the fidelity of the princes to himself and his new heir and filling vacant offices with suitably loyal candidates. He successfully intervened to suppress rebellions in Lower Lotharingia. The council which he held in Mainz in January 1103 'in order that peace and quiet might exist everywhere' decreed peace legislation that was the most significant innovation of his reign. Nevertheless the emperor and his advisers continued to be preoccupied with the threat presented by the Gregorian party under the leadership of Gebhard of Constance, despite that party's failure to rally any secular princes to their cause in the years 1098–1104. The death of the antipope in 1100 opened up the possibility of a rapprochement with the newly elected candidate of the reform papacy, Paschal II. Henry's failure to achieve this reconciliation was the decisive factor in the disintegration of his authority in the years 1105–6.

In the early months of 1099 the emperor was preoccupied with the installation of the young king. He made his first appearance in Lotharingia since his return to the German kingdom and witnessed the coronation of Henry V in Aachen on 6 January.[49] After leaving Lotharingia the emperor 'made for Bavaria and commended his son, whom he had made king, to those who were not present on that occasion, so that they might acknowledge him as king'.[50]

---

[46] Frutolf, *Chronica* 1098, p. 110.   [47] *Codex Udalrici* 123, pp. 234–5: see below p. 332.
[48] *Casus monasterii Petrishusensis* II.46, p. 648.
[49] Frutolf, *Chronica* 1099, p. 118. See Meyer von Knonau (1904) 5:30. Henry in the abbey of St Trond (30 January): Rudolf, *Gesta abbatum Trudonensium* v.7, p. 254. See Meyer von Knonau (1904) 5:57–8.
[50] Frutolf, *Chronica* 1099, p. 118; Cosmas of Prague, *Chronica Boemorum* III.8, p. 168. See Meyer von Knonau (1904) 5:60.

(The emperor may have considered this ceremony the more necessary because of the initial opposition to his proposal to raise his son to the kingship in 1098.) The emperor celebrated Easter (10 April) in Regensburg and it was perhaps on this occasion that Henry V received the homage of the Bavarians. During this imperial visit to Regensburg a sudden outbreak of sickness claimed many victims, including two of the emperor's most important adherents in the duchy, the count palatine Rapoto and his cousin, Count Udalric of Passau.[51] The Rapotones were a great loss to the emperor. The count palatine had been a most effective opponent of the Gregorian party in southern Germany.[52] The heir to his extensive property was Diepold III, margrave of the Bavarian Nordgau, who also succeeded to his titles of count of Cham and margrave of Vohburg. The property of Count Udalric of Passau (whom contemporaries nicknamed 'the very rich') passed, through the remarriage of his widow, Adelaide, into the hands of Count Berengar of Sulzbach, the kinsman of Diepold III. The consequence of the sudden extinction of the Rapotones, the emperor's faithful adherents, was, therefore, the aggrandisement of two families from the Bavarian Nordgau closely linked both with each other and with the house of Zähringen. Both Diepold and Berengar appeared in the ranks of the emperor's enemies in the final crisis of the reign.[53]

Henry IV's visit to Regensburg at Eastertide 1099 was the occasion for important transactions concerning the duchy of Bohemia: the investiture of a new bishop of Prague and the regulation of the succession to the duchy. Since his accession (1092) Duke Bretislav II had pursued a policy objectionable to the emperor: a war to compel the duke of the Poles to resume the payment of tribute to Bohemia. (Duke Vladislav-Herman of Poland had married Henry's sister Judith and his principal ally against the Bohemians was the king of Hungary, with whom the emperor likewise sought an alliance.) By 1099, however, Bretislav was eager for good relations with the emperor, for more and more of the Bohemian nobility were rallying to the duke's enemies within his own dynasty. When Henry 'celebrated Easter in Regensburg that year, Duke Bretislav was commanded to come there with his [bishop] elect [of Prague]' and on 19 April 'the emperor gave [the bishop elect] Herman the ring and episcopal staff'.[54] Like King Vratislav, Bretislav acknowledged that the bishop of Prague was an imperial bishop, subject to the authority of the emperor, from whom he must receive investiture. Bretislav submitted to imperial authority because he urgently needed the emperor's help in altering the succession to his duchy. The Bohemians accepted the principle not of hereditary succession but

---

[51] Ekkehard, *Chronica* I, 1100, p. 158. See Meyer von Knonau (1904) 5:60–1.

[52] Frutolf, *Chronica* 1099, p. 118; Bernold, *Chronicon* 1099, p. 466.

[53] Meyer von Knonau (1904) 5:61–2 and ns. 8–9.

[54] Cosmas, *Chronica Boemorum* III.8, p. 169. See Meyer von Knonau (1904) 5:65.

of seniority within the Przemyslid ducal family.[55] According to this principle, Bretislav II's successor should be his cousin Udalric of Brünn, whom Bretislav was determined to exclude from the succession in favour of his own younger brother, Borivoi. Bretislav had no doubt that the emperor possessed the authority to alter the Bohemian law of succession: he had after all conferred the title of king on Bretislav's father fourteen years before as a reward for his distinguished services. The duke 'gained his object: that [Henry] would confer a banner on [Bretislav's] brother Borivoi and would point him out [as his successor] to all the Bohemians who had come with him, so that after [Bretislav's] death they would place his brother Borivoi on the throne'.[56] It was not the first time that a duke of Bohemia had acknowledged the feudal superiority of the German monarch.[57] The novelty of the ceremony of 19 April 1099 was that the emperor identified Borivoi as the lawful successor to the Bohemian duchy by investing him with a banner. It was by this means that the German dukes were traditionally inducted into their office by the king: Borivoi was treated as a German prince, subject to the authority of his lord, the king.[58]

A similar investiture ceremony occurred two years later, after Borivoi's accession to the duchy. His cousin, Udalric of Brünn, determined to reverse the 1099 settlement, turned, as Bretislav II had done, to the emperor. In 1101 Udalric petitioned the emperor in Regensburg to invest him with the duchy in place of Borivoi. 'The emperor took his money and gave him the insignia of the duchy and a banner.'[59] The account of the ceremony of 1101 by the chronicler Cosmas of Prague makes the parallel with the investiture of a German duke even clearer: the ducal candidate received both a banner and the insignia of his office, presumably a sword, a sceptre and the ceremonial headgear of a duke. Evidently by the end of the eleventh century the duke of Bohemia was regarded in his own land and in the German kingdom as an imperial prince, who was invested with his duchy by the German monarch. This development originated in Henry III's efforts to compel Bohemia to become a vassal state of his empire. It was accelerated by the close relationship of Vratislav II and Henry IV and came to fruition because of the political needs of Bretislav II and Udalric of Brünn. At the end of Henry IV's reign Bohemia was regarded, not as German territory but yet as a duchy of the German kingdom. The king did not travel through Bohemia with his entourage in the same way that he visited the German duchies, but the duke of

[55] Cosmas, *Chronica* III.13, pp. 175–6.
[56] *Ibid.*, III.8, p. 169. See Meyer von Knonau (1904) 5:63–5, 102, 130–1; Wegener (1959) 55, 69, 165, 213–14, 233.
[57] Bretislav I (1041); Spitignev II (1055): Steindorff (1874) 1:106–12; (1881) 2:291.
[58] Deér (1972) 15.
[59] Cosmas, *Chronica* III.15, p. 176. Udalric was defeated by Borivoi at the battle of Malin.

Bohemia was undoubtedly his vassal and (like the Bohemian bishops of Prague and Olmütz) owed his office to royal investiture.

Henry IV's itinerary in the summer of 1099 took him from Bavaria to eastern Franconia, where he celebrated the feast of Peter and Paul (29 June) in Bamberg. His principal concern was to 'exhort the princes of that region faithfully to preserve the peace'. The emperor 'compelled them to take an oath to pursue without hesitation and to condemn highway-robbers and thieves'.[60] This account by the local historian Frutolf of Michelsberg is the only reference to Henry's concern with 'the peace of God' between the council of Mainz of 1085 and that of 1103.[61] It is not known whether the oath which he imposed on the princes was a peace initiative confined to the diocese of Bamberg, provoked by outbreaks of lawlessness in that locality, or whether the initiative extended to other dioceses. The maintenance of peace may also have been the reason for the impressive gathering of princes in the imperial entourage in Mainz in November 1099.[62] The majority of those present were Saxon princes – the archbishops of Bremen and Magdeburg, eight Saxon bishops, Cuno of Beichlingen (son of Otto of Northeim), Siegfried of Ballenstedt (a Saxon prince newly appointed Lotharingian count palatine) and perhaps Wiprecht of Groitzsch – so that it is likely that Saxon affairs were discussed.

There was perhaps a connection between this gathering in Mainz and a letter addressed by Henry V to his father (dated 1099 or 1100) concerning the young king's visit to Thuringia. 'I have decided to go to Saalfeld, which your diligence has often exhorted me to do, both in letters and in conversation.' Henry V undertook to do 'whatever is appropriate to your honour and is useful to you, according to your guidance and counsel' and hoped to celebrate Christmas with his father in Saalfeld. He therefore requested the emperor to obtain safe conduct for him from Count Henry 'the Fat' of Northeim (brother of Cuno of Beichlingen).[63] The reference to Henry V's responsibility for upholding his father's 'honour' in Thuringia has been interpreted as evidence of a return to a strategy attributed to Henry IV in December 1080, when he had allegedly proposed a separate kingdom of Saxony ruled by its own Salian king, his son Conrad. Perhaps the emperor contemplated such a project in 1099 or 1100, seeking to extend his influence over Saxony through the mediation of Henry V.[64] No such project was ever put into effect, however, and this interpretation of Henry V's letter of 1099/1100 is highly speculative. It is unlikely that the emperor would have considered any measure threatening the

---

[60] Frutolf, *Chronica* 1099, p. 118. See Meyer von Knonau (1904) 5:66.

[61] See above pp. 249–50 and below pp. 318–19.

[62] *Urkundenbuch . . . Speyer* 1:68. See Meyer von Knonau (1904) 5:70–1; Lange (1961) 90, 94; Fenske (1977) 148.   [63] *Codex Udalrici* 94, pp. 182–3. See Meyer von Knonau (1904) 5:120.

[64] Giese (1979) 184. See above pp. 205–6.

position of Count Henry of Northeim, who currently enjoyed viceregal status in the duchy. It is more probable that what was under consideration in the assembly of princes in Mainz in November 1099 and in Henry V's letter was a 'royal journey' in Saxony, intended, like the recent visit to Bavaria, to enable the young king to receive the homage of princes absent from his election and coronation. That journey seems, however, not to have taken place.

The emperor celebrated Christmas 1099 not in Saalfeld but in Speyer, where on 6 January 1100 he invested Frederick of Schwarzenburg as archbishop of Cologne.[65] This was the first of seven imperial visits to Speyer during the last seven years of the reign. The later visits were in March and April 1101, in February 1102, in March and September 1103, in October 1104 and finally in February 1105. During these final years of his reign Speyer, the principal burial place of the Salian dynasty, was Henry IV's most frequent residence after Mainz. His diploma of 7 January 1100 for the church of Speyer (confirming the gift of the abbey of Hornbach) was the first of a series of six privileges for the bishop and cathedral chapter.[66] Like the fifteen earlier privileges that Henry had bestowed on Speyer since coming of age, the six donations of 1100–5 reveal a generosity unparalleled elsewhere among the diplomas of Henry IV. This imperial generosity was a recognition of the fact that the bishop and chapter of Speyer incurred heavy expenses as the custodians of the imperial burial place: they must pay both for the continuous commemoration of the illustrious dead and for the rebuilding of the cathedral. The diploma of 7 January 1100 underlined the emperor's devotion to the patron saint of the episcopal church, the Virgin Mary: a devotion intimately linked with the commemoration of his ancestors.[67] Henry's veneration of the Virgin and his preoccupation with the memory of his ancestors, the two basic elements of his personal religion, were perhaps intensified by the unhappy experience of his recent Italian expedition.[68]

At Eastertide 1100 the emperor was again in Mainz, where he received the legate of Clement III, Bishop Robert of Faenza.[69] This legation was the last contact between the emperor and his antipope, who died on 8 September 1100.[70] Henry's response to Clement's death was 'to summon all the princes to a general assembly in Mainz on the Lord's Nativity, so that the Roman see may be ordered according to their advice and a plan devised to restore the unity of the Church, which has long been unhappily divided'.[71] The advice of the

---

[65] Frutolf, *Chronica* 1100, p. 118. See Meyer von Knonau (1904) 5:97.

[66] *DD H IV* 464, 466, 474–5, 480, 489.   [67] *D H IV* 464.

[68] So Heidrich (1988) 275. Cf. Heidrich (1991) 206, 221–2.

[69] Cosmas, *Chronica* III.10, pp. 170–1. See Meyer von Knonau (1904) 5:100; Ziese (1982) 263.

[70] Evidence of an incipient cult of Clement III: *Codex Udalrici* 108, pp. 194–6. See Servatius (1979) 70; Ziese (1982) 270–3.   [71] Henry IV, *Letter* 30, pp. 38–9.

Mainz assembly in December 1100 was that the emperor 'should send envoys to Rome concerning the unity of the Church and set up a pope according to the election of the Romans and all the churches'.[72] It is not known whether envoys were sent to Rome and, if so, what negotiations took place. The anti-Henrician chronicler Ekkehard of Aura reported another imperial assembly in Mainz at Christmastide 1101, likewise concerned with the question of the papacy. The assembly considered acknowledging the authority of the newly elected Paschal II. Henry 'announced that he would depart for Rome and summon a general council there around 1 February, to debate his case and that of the lord pope according to canon law and to establish catholic unity between the royal and the priestly power, which had been divided for so many years'. Ekkehard's account implies that the assembly of Mainz decided in favour of peace with the papacy, but that Henry defied their decision: 'he attempted to set up another pope in place of the lord Paschal, but failed in the attempt'.[73] There is no evidence to corroborate Ekkehard's version of Henry's motives.

The antipope had three successors: Theoderic of Albano (1100–1), Albert of Silva Candida (1102) and Maginulf, archpriest of S. Angelo (1105–11). Their election was the work of the cardinals of Clement III, assisted by the pro-imperial nobility of Rome and central Italy, especially the Roman families of the Corsi and Baruncii and Werner, margrave of Ancona and duke of Spoleto.[74] These families could make the city as dangerous for Paschal II as it had been for Urban II. Nevertheless their antipopes were incapable of challenging the Gregorian papacy as Clement had done, since they lacked the imperial support that he had enjoyed. Those who appointed the antipopes believed that they were acting in the emperor's interests.[75] Henry IV, however, showed no interest in these appointments: there is no evidence of any contact between him and any of Clement's successors. The message of the emperor's own letters and of his assemblies in Mainz was that he was now determined 'to restore the unity of the Church'.

Henry's preoccupation with peace and 'catholic unity' was proclaimed most emphatically in the council of Mainz on 6 January 1103. Here the emperor proclaimed the 'peace of God' throughout the kingdom.[76] Furthermore he 'caused

---

[72] *Würzburger Chronik* 1101, p. 57; Frutolf 1101, p. 120. See Meyer von Knonau (1904) 5:102–3.

[73] Ekkehard, *Chronica* I, 1102, pp. 178–80. See Meyer von Knonau (1904) 5:133; Servatius (1979) 150–2.

[74] *Liber Pontificalis* 3, 145; *Annales Romani* 1116, pp. 477–8. See Meyer von Knonau (1904) 5:110–11, 273–7; Servatius (1979) 69–72. Self-confidence of the Wibertine cardinals: *Cardinalium schismaticorum scripta* IV–X, pp. 403–21. See Ziese (1982) 241–52.

[75] Werner of Ancona, Letter: Sigebert, *Chronica* 1105, pp. 368–9. See Meyer von Knonau (1904) 5:273–4; Servatius (1979) 13; Zotz (1991) 48.   [76] See below p. 318.

Bishop Emehard [of Würzburg] to announce publicly that he would transfer the government to his son, King Henry, and visit the Lord's Sepulchre'.[77] This pilgrimage to Jerusalem, had it proved feasible, would have been the most spectacular of Henry IV's acts of penitence. The penances of 1074 in Nuremberg and 1077 in Canossa had been performed under the immediate pressure of a dangerous alliance between the papacy and a group of German princes. The penitential journey to the Holy Land was proposed in January 1103 in order to prevent the recurrence of such an alliance. Hostile commentators assumed that the emperor's promise of 6 January was simply a propaganda exercise, intended to silence his critics.[78] Henry's own view of the project is found in his letter to his godfather, Abbot Hugh of Cluny. He proposed to 'make good the ruin of the Church, which was caused by us, through the restoration of peace and justice'. 'If with God's grace we can reconcile kingship and priesthood, we are determined, once peace is established, to go to Jerusalem and see the Holy Land in which our Lord appeared in the flesh and dwelled among men.'[79]

This letter contains Henry's first unambiguous statement that his 'plan to restore the unity of the Church' meant reconciliation with the Gregorian papacy. His admission to Hugh of Cluny, Paschal II's prominent supporter,[80] of responsibility for 'the ruin of the Church' must be taken as an earnest of Henry's sincerity in seeking a reconciliation. Perhaps his intention was that Hugh of Cluny should once more play the role of mediator with the pope. The emperor's decision to seek reconciliation may be attributable to pressure from the princes in the assemblies of Mainz from 1100 to 1103. Perhaps, however, the decision was a personal one, linked with that intensification of his personal piety apparent in the visits to Speyer. The vicissitudes of his last Italian expedition may have heightened his sense of being the object of God's wrath, which must be appeased by the restoration of the unity of the Church. The emperor had last considered reconciliation with the Gregorian papacy during his negotiations with Welf IV in 1089–90 and 1091. The emperor had allegedly rejected this chance of reconciliation on the insistence of the episcopal supporters of Clement III.[81] By 1103 not only the antipope but also the principal bishops of his 'faction' were dead. Henry had lost the prelates who had been his principal advisers during the last two decades of the conflict with the papacy: Liemar of Bremen, Conrad of Utrecht, Rupert of Bamberg, Egilbert of Trier and Wido of Osnabrück.[82] The removal of these influential

---

[77] Ekkehard, *Chronica* I, 1103, pp. 182–4. Cf. *Annales Hildesheimenses* 1103, pp. 50–1. See Meyer von Knonau (1904) 5:173–4; Mikoletzky (1960) 263; Servatius (1979) 152–3.

[78] Ekkehard, *Chronica* I, 1103, pp. 182–4.   [79] Henry IV, *Letter* 31, pp. 39–40.

[80] Paschal II, *JL* 6181: 235BC. See Servatius (1979) 12.   [81] See above pp. 274, 282.

[82] Meyer von Knonau (1904) 5:67–8, 119, 121–4, 125–6, 156–7, 163. Wido of Osnabrück at Liemar's behest composed the polemic *Liber de controversia* pp. 461–70.

advisers made it easier for the emperor to contemplate reconciliation, as did the appearance at the imperial court of three bishops who had already submitted to the papacy: Emehard of Würzburg (who played an important role in the council of Mainz in 1103), Otto of Strasbourg and Herman of Augsburg. The position of these bishops apparently resembled that of Archbishop Hartwig of Magdeburg, who had become the emperor's 'most intimate friend' without acknowledging Clement III as pope. He had remained loyal to the emperor, while maintaining contact with the Gregorian party in Saxony and their pope, and was remembered as 'a tireless mediator between the two parties in the work of ending the schism'.[83]

Nothing is known of a direct response by Paschal II to any peace overtures in the years 1101–3. In January 1100 he bade Gebhard of Constance pay no heed to 'those who publish the tale that we are about to reach an agreement with Henry and his supporters'. He would 'labour to the utmost so that both their perversity and their power are overturned'.[84] Three years later his attitude was unchanged. In January 1103, a fortnight after the emperor's declaration in Mainz, Paschal wrote to congratulate Count Robert II of Flanders on his campaign against the imperial party in the diocese of Cambrai. 'You are to punish Henry, the chief of the heretics, and his supporters with all your strength not only in that region but wherever you can.' The war against Henry was as meritorious as the First Crusade from which Robert had recently returned and the count and his knights therefore received the 'remission of sins' granted to the crusaders.[85] The pope was unmoved by the emperor's peace initiatives. Paschal's view of the question of the reconciliation of empire and papacy was revealed in the Lateran synod of March 1102. The synod pronounced the excommunication of Henry IV and 'renewed the well-known decrees of our fathers forbidding any clerk to perform homage to a layman or to receive churches or ecclesiastical property from the hand of a layman'.[86] The sentence of excommunication was repeated in a ceremony in the Lateran basilica on 3 April, at which German pilgrims were present. They were expected, on their return to Germany, to spread the news of the sentence and reanimate the Gregorian party in the kingdom.[87]

The Lateran synod demonstrated that the effect of the imperial peace initiatives was to bring the issue of lay investiture to the forefront of papal–imperial relations. In the previous pontificate the issue of investiture resurfaced,

[83] Ekkehard, *Chronica* I, 1103, p. 180: see above p. 268. See Meyer von Knonau (1904) 5:156–7.

[84] Paschal II, *JL* 5817: *Acta pont. Rom. inedita* 2, 169.

[85] Paschal II, *JL* 5889: *MGH Libelli* 2, 451–2.

[86] Ekkehard, *Chronica* I, 1102, p. 180; Paschal II, *JL* 5908: *Anselmi Cantuariensis archiepiscopi Opera* 4, 125. See Meyer von Knonau (1904) 5:170–1; Minninger (1978) 90; Servatius (1979) 153–4; Beulertz (1991) 16, 132–3.   [87] Ekkehard, *Chronica* I, 1102, p. 180.

after a six-year silence, when Urban II became the ally of King Conrad in 1095. Urban II, like Gregory VII, assumed that the settlement of the investiture question depended on the existence of a legitimate secular authority sympathetic towards the reform papacy. Similarly, the resolution of the assemblies of Mainz of 1100 and 1101 'to restore the unity of the Church' prompted Paschal II to restate his predecessor's legislation concerning investiture. The Lateran synod of 1102 made clear to Henry IV that his reconciliation with the papacy was conditional upon the renunciation of the customs of investiture and homage. During this period in which he announced his desire to 'reconcile kingship and priesthood', however, the emperor continued to play his customary role in the appointment of bishops, investing seven candidates in 1100–2.[88] The emperor, pressed either by his conscience or by the princes, desired reconciliation with the papacy, but he had no intention of surrendering the traditional rights of the crown. When in 1102 the cathedral clergy of Magdeburg made their own election, the emperor 'declared that they had thereby defied the royal power'.[89] Henry refused to accept the papal argument that lay investiture was contrary to canon law. When the clergy of Bamberg challenged the authority of the bishop whom he had invested, the emperor wrote, 'I call upon God and both your and our consciences to witness that he came to his office according to secular and canon law.'[90] Henry IV was determined to retain the practice of investiture, which Paschal II declared to be 'the root of simoniacal wickedness'.[91] The conflict of empire and papacy had at last become truly an 'Investiture Contest', a conflict concerned principally with the rights of the monarch in the appointment of prelates, which was to continue for sixteen years after the death of Henry IV.

During these years in which the emperor was both seeking peace with the papacy and defending his right of investiture, he paid particular attention to his role of defender of the imperial churches, notably the monasteries of Lotharingia. A series of diplomas reveals the interweaving of two of the central preoccupations of Henry's last years: the duty of protecting the rights of his churches and that of commemorating his ancestors. The beneficiaries included the abbeys of Lobbes and Prüm and Abbot Anselm of Lorsch's foundation of St Stephen on the Heiligenberg. The emperor conferred privileges on them 'both for the sake of the eternal reward of [his] soul and of those of [his] ancestors'.[92] The diploma of 26 March 1101 for the monastery of St

---

[88] Frederick of Cologne, Burchard of Utrecht, Baldwin and Cuno of Strasbourg (1100); Humbert of Bremen, Bruno of Trier (1101); Otto of Bamberg (1102). See Meyer von Knonau (1904) 5:97–8, 68, 101, 125, 131–2, 169; Servatius (1979) 156–7.

[89] *Annales Patherbrunnenses* 1102, p. 107. See below p. 317.

[90] Henry IV, *Letter* 33, p. 42. See Erdmann (1939) 210–11.

[91] Paschal II, *JL* 5889: *Anselmi Opera* 4, 125.   [92] *DD H IV* 468, 471, 477.

Maximin in Trier, issued after Henry's recovery from a severe illness, depicts a conscience-stricken emperor, anxious to make reparation to the abbey. His offence was that he had formerly used two of the abbey's estates as a benefice for a vassal: it was conduct for which reformers had denounced him in the early years of his majority. He restored the estates as a memorial to himself, his parents and grandparents, his 'most beloved son King Henry' and his 'other ancestors'.[93] The monks of St Maximin were required for the rest of the emperor's life to mark the anniversary of his imperial coronation by providing food for three hundred poor people; thereafter the same provision was to be made on the anniversary of his death.[94] The obligation of commemorating the emperor and his family in perpetuity by feeding the poor reappears in other privileges of 1101–2, notably two for the church of Speyer.[95] These provisions explain the portrait in the anonymous *Life of Emperor Henry IV* of Henry as 'the emperor of the poor'. In his lament for the emperor's death the biographer addressed the poor of the empire: 'You, o poor, have the greatest cause for grief . . . since you have lost him who comforted your poverty.' The anonymous author described Henry's arrangements for his own commemoration. 'You are fortunate, Emperor Henry, in having prepared for yourself such vigils, such mediators: you now receive back from the Lord's hand with a manifold increase what you secretly placed in the hands of the poor.'[96]

A number of diplomas from the years 1101–4 reveal another aspect of the emperor's concern to defend the churches: the curbing of abuses of power by the advocates of religious houses. He had first demonstrated this concern during his visit to Bamberg in June 1099. There he 'forbade advocates to appoint other advocates, subordinate to themselves, to prey on the people and on the churches'. Immediately on his departure, however, 'the princes returned to their ancient custom, refusing to do without the troop of knights whom they recruited by offering benefices in this way'.[97] The grievance which the emperor attempted to correct was the abuse of their authority by secular advocates, entrusted with the defence of a church's property. The delinquent advocates of the Bamberg diocese were enfeoffing their vassals with the estates of the churches which they were pledged to defend. This was the offence with which Henry IV himself had been charged by the reformers in the years 1069–75, referring to his conduct in the dioceses of Constance and Bamberg.[98] A quarter of a century later the mature Henry IV campaigned to defend the

[93] See above p. 308.   [94] *D H IV* 465.
[95] *D H IV* 466, 475. Cf. *D H IV* 471 (Prüm). See Meyer von Knonau (1904) 5:113, 115–16, 178 n. 12; Feierabend (1913) 167–8, 171–2; Heidrich (1991) 206–8.
[96] *Vita Heinrici IV* c. 1, 13, pp. 10, 43. See Bornscheuer (1968) 157; Schmid (1984a) 706–12.
[97] Frutolf, *Chronica* 1099, p. 118. See Meyer von Knonau (1904) 5:66 and also above p. 307.
[98] See above pp. 120–1.

churches against such depredations. When he celebrated Easter (21 April) 1101 in Liège, many petitioners 'invoked . . . imperial justice against the injuries caused by advocates'. Henry upheld the claims of Abbot Stephen of St James in Liège in his case against the advocate of his monastery, Count Arnulf of Looz.[99] A diploma of 1102 records a similar intervention on behalf of the abbey of Weissenburg (in the diocese of Speyer).[100] Diplomas of 1103 for Prüm and Waulsort regulate the rights and duties of the advocate.[101] Finally, the conduct of the advocates of the church of Augsburg was the subject of a decision made by an imperial assembly in Regensburg in January 1104.[102] From the time of his visit to Bamberg in June 1099 the emperor exerted himself as never before to protect the churches against the depredations of the secular aristocracy, including the advocates appointed to protect them. While insisting that lay investiture was sanctioned by 'secular and canon law', the emperor during the final years of his reign both strove to preserve the rights and property of the churches over which he ruled and reiterated his desire to 'reconcile kingship and priesthood'. Henry IV, that is, sought to reconstruct the ecclesiastical regime of his father.

The emperor's intervention to protect Lotharingian abbeys was part of a wider preoccupation with suppressing disorder in the province in 1101–3. The duchy of Lower Lotharingia had been without a duke since the departure of Godfrey of Bouillon in August 1096 on the crusade of which he would ultimately become the leader. That he had no intention of returning was evident from his disposing of his family properties before his departure.[103] The emperor made no attempt to appoint a new duke, even after Godfrey's death in Jerusalem (18 July 1100), but a change was made in the office of Lotharingian count palatine. Count Henry I of Limburg was replaced by Count Siegfried of Ballenstedt.[104] In the years following his loss of the office of count palatine Henry of Limburg became a formidable enemy of the churches of Lotharingia, his victims including the church of Trier and the abbey of Prüm.[105] Henry of Limburg's seizure of the property of Prüm was condemned by 'the judgement of the princes', probably during the emperor's visit to Liège at Eastertide 1101. The princes who attended the ceremony of girding the young king Henry V with the sword (21 April) and heard the com-

[99] D H IV 470: see Gawlik (1978) XLVI n. 134, L.   [100] D H IV 473.

[101] DD H IV 476, 478: Gawlik (1978) XLIX. See Meyer von Knonau (1904) 5:60 n. 5, 117, 151, 179 n. 14; Feierabend (1913) 97–8, 168.

[102] D H IV 482 (MGH Constitutiones I, 126–7). See Meyer von Knonau (1904) 5:194–5; Feierabend (1913) 203.   [103] Mohr (1976) 2:73; Werner (1991) 445–6.

[104] Urkundenbuch . . . Speyer I, 68. See Meyer von Knonau (1904) 5:70, 115; Fenske (1977) 341.

[105] Gesta Treverorum, Continuatio 1.16, p. 189; D H IV 471; Rudolf, Gesta abbatum Trudonensium v.3–4, pp. 252–3.

plaints of the monks of St James of Liège against their advocate, the count of Looz, probably also judged the case of Prüm against Henry of Limburg.[106] Their judgement against him provoked Henry of Limburg to rebel against the emperor. By 16 May 1101 the emperor was laying siege to the rebel's fortress of Limburg, east of Liège.[107] Limburg and the rebel's other fortresses were captured and destroyed by the imperial army and Count Henry was compelled to submit. It was not easy, however, to make the defeated rebel comply with the judgement given by the princes in April and restore the property of the abbey of Prüm. An assembly of princes meeting in Cologne in July once more ruled that he must surrender the property; but when the imperial entourage moved to Kaiserswerth on 3 August, 'Count Henry denied that he had renounced the estate which he had surrendered in Cologne'. The emperor was obliged to assemble the princes yet again to overcome his opposition.[108]

In the light of Henry of Limburg's rebellion and his subsequent recalcitrance, it is surprising to find that on his next appearance at court, in Mainz during Christmastide 1101, he bore the title 'Duke Henry'. He had become duke of Lower Lotharingia in succession to Godfrey of Bouillon.[109] His principal qualification was his ancestry: he was the grandson of Frederick of Luxemburg, duke of Lower Lotharingia (1046–65), whose daughter Judith had married Count Walram I of Limburg. The descendant of Frederick of Luxemburg may have seemed the obvious candidate for the duchy after the departure of the Verdun dynasty from Lotharingia.[110] Henry of Limburg's career of violence, culminating in rebellion, was evidently not regarded as a disqualification for high office: perhaps it ensured his promotion, by demonstrating to the emperor that he was too dangerous to be ignored. In investing the count of Limburg with the duchy, Henry IV adopted a strategy which he had used twice before in Saxony: in 1075, when he had conferred 'his authority and the administration of public affairs' on Otto of Northeim, and in 1087, when he had offered 'the care of all [his] affairs in Saxony and Thuringia' to Ekbert II of Meissen. In the case of Henry of Limburg, the emperor must have calculated, firstly, that his lineage would make him acceptable to the Lotharingians and, secondly, that the ducal title would satisfy his ambitions and ensure his loyalty to his benefactor. In the cases of the two Saxon princes the emperor had miscalculated. Henry of Limburg, however, after a brief

---

[106] *D H IV* 471. See Meyer von Knonau (1904) 5:115.

[107] *D H IV* 468; Sigebert, *Chronica* 1101, p. 368. See Meyer von Knonau (1904) 5:115.

[108] *D H IV* 471. See Meyer von Knonau (1904) 5:118.

[109] *D H IV* 473: Gawlik (1970a) 97–8. See Meyer von Knonau (1904) 5:131–3; Mohr (1976) 2:72–5.

[110] Sigebert, *Chronica* 1101, p. 368: he 'repurchased the emperor's favour with a very large sum of money'.

flirtation with the emperor's enemies in 1105, became the foremost defender of the imperial cause in Lotharingia in the final year of the reign.

A second area of serious disorder in Lower Lotharingia in 1101–3 was the diocese of Cambrai on the western frontier of the duchy, where the imperialist bishop Walcher was hard-pressed by Count Robert II of Flanders. This conflict dated back to the partition of the diocese in 1092. The French church of Arras, at that time part of the diocese of Cambrai but formerly an independent diocese, regained its independence of the imperial bishopric through the joint initiative of its clergy, Pope Urban II, King Philip I of France and especially Count Robert I of Flanders, in whose territory Arras was situated. In 1093 the clergy and people of Cambrai elected a French cleric, Manasses, brother of the count of Soissons, as their bishop. The emperor, however, rejected their candidate in favour of Walcher, archdeacon of Brabant, who had distinguished himself in the struggle to retain Arras within the diocese of Cambrai. Once invested with the bishopric, Walcher faced continual opposition from a papalist faction in his diocese, determined to enthrone Manasses as bishop and supported by the metropolitan, the archbishop of Rheims, and the pope.[111] The real trial of strength between the rival factions in the diocese came with the return of Count Robert II of Flanders from the First Crusade (1100). The count, urged by the archbishop of Rheims and Pope Paschal II, made war on Walcher and his supporters. In spring 1101 Walcher appeared at court, seeking the emperor's help. Henry placed at his disposal a force of two hundred knights led by Count Godfrey of Louvain and three hundred under Bishop Otbert of Liège, promising to come in person to Cambrai. The emperor's expedition was delayed until October 1102, by which time Robert had laid siege to the city and laid waste the surrounding countryside. Henry ended the siege of Cambrai and carried the war into Flanders. The Flemish territory beyond the Scheldt was burned and plundered, Robert constantly retreating before the imperial advance, never venturing to give battle. The arrival of winter halted the campaign. The emperor withdrew to Cambrai and there dismissed his forces, after obtaining from them the promise on oath that they would resume the campaign the following spring.[112] After the emperor had returned to the Rhineland, however, Robert demonstrated that he could still inflict serious damage on Cambrai by carrying out a night attack. The citizens felt obliged to negotiate a truce, undertaking to surrender their city to Robert if the emperor failed to come to their assistance in the spring.[113]

---

[111] *Gesta Galcheri Cameracensis* c. 7–8, 14, 16–22, pp. 190–3, 198, 199–202. See Meyer von Knonau (1903) 4:407–11, 525–7; (1904) 5:8.

[112] Sigebert, *Chronica* 1102, p. 368; *Annales Patherbrunnenses* 1102, p. 107. See Meyer von Knonau (1904) 5:126–30, 153–5; de Moreau (1945) 92–5, 100–1; Servatius (1979) 161–2, 164.

[113] This was the context of Paschal II's letter to Robert (*JL* 5889: *MGH Libelli* 2, 451–2), which provoked Sigebert's *Epistola Leodicensium*. See Erdmann (1935) 244–5.

With the approach of spring Robert II began to dread a repetition of the destructive imperial campaign of 1102. On the advice of the Flemish magnates, he sent envoys to Henry to negotiate peace. The ceremony of reconciliation took place on 29 June 1103 in Liège 'in a very numerous assembly of princes from the whole kingdom'. The anonymous biographer of Walcher of Cambrai represented the ceremony as a renewal of homage and fealty on the part of the penitent rebel, who also guaranteed the future security of Walcher as bishop.[114] According to Walcher's biographer, Robert sought reconciliation with the emperor in the spring of 1103 because he 'was very much afraid of being disinherited of his property'. Robert II explained his conduct in a letter to his confidant, the papalist Bishop Lambert of Arras. 'I have performed homage to the German emperor because otherwise I could not obtain full possession of the fiefs that I ought to hold from him by right of ancestry and especially because I felt that it was impossible to restore peace to our fatherland except by this means.' He feared to lose 'imperial Flanders', that region of his county which belonged to the German kingdom and was held of the German monarch as a benefice. The count assured Lambert that his reconciliation with the emperor would not undermine his allegiance to the apostolic see.[115]

On the eve of the pacification of Cambrai Henry IV also 'calmed the seditions of the Saxons'.[116] There had been two distinct outbreaks of violence. The first, in Westphalia, was the result of a feud between Archbishop Frederick of Cologne and Count Frederick of Arnsberg (of the pro-Henrician dynasty of Werl). Since the archiepiscopate of Anno II the archbishops of Cologne had been extending their territorial interests in the Westphalian region of their archdiocese. The intervention of the energetic Archbishop Frederick seemed to Count Frederick to threaten the interests of the Werl family. His response was to pillage the lands of the church of Cologne, for which he was outlawed by the emperor. The outlawed count continued his intermittent harrying of the church until the end of the reign.[117] The beginning of this feud in 1102 coincided with the second of 'the seditions of the Saxons', the election of a Gregorian candidate to the archbishopric of Magdeburg against the will of the emperor. Henry of Assel was elected by the Gregorian party in Magdeburg, only to be compelled by the imperial party to flee from the city. He narrowly escaped capture by the

---

[114] *Gesta Galcheri* c. 22, p. 202; Sigebert of Gembloux, *Chronica* 1103, p. 368; *Annales Patherbrunnenses* 1103, pp. 107–8. See Meyer von Knonau (1904) 5:179.

[115] Lambert of Arras, *Epistolae* 76: 676D–677B. See Meyer von Knonau (1904) 5:199–200, 287–8.   [116] Sigebert, *Chronica* 1103, p. 368; *Annales Augustani* 1103, p. 135.

[117] *Annales Patherbrunnenses* 1102, p. 107. See Meyer von Knonau (1904) 5:162; Meier (1987) 91–4; Reuter (1991) 311.

Wettin prince Count Dedi, who had been ordered by the emperor to arrest him.[118]

'Once peace and calm existed everywhere, [the emperor] summoned the princes to the court and caused peace to be confirmed on oath throughout the whole kingdom and, in order to curb future evils, he decreed that transgressors should be severely punished.' Thus the anonymous biographer of Henry IV introduced what he believed to be the crowning achievement of the reign, the 'imperial peace' of the council of Mainz of January 1103.[119] It was during that council, on 6 January, that Henry announced his intention of going to Jerusalem 'for the sake of his transgressions'. The 'peace of God' was perhaps proclaimed on the same day. The juxtaposition of the pilgrimage to Jerusalem and the pacification of the kingdom was perhaps a deliberate imitation of the council of Clermont of 1095, in which Urban II preached the crusade and proclaimed the 'peace of God'. An anonymous report of the peace council specifies that the emperor and the ecclesiastical princes 'confirmed the peace with their own hands', while Henry V and the secular princes 'swore an oath' to preserve the peace 'until Whitsun and thereafter for four years'. 'They swore . . . [to preserve] the peace for the churches, clergy, monks and lay brethren; for merchants, women (lest they be forcibly abducted) and Jews.' The princes' oath prescribed the penalties for breaches of the 'peace of God'. The penalty of mutilation (blinding or the loss of a hand) was invoked for attacking or burning another's house; taking prisoner, wounding or killing a debtor; persistent theft or defending a peace-breaker. If a peace-breaker took refuge in a castle, it was permissible for those who had sworn the oath of January 1103 to destroy the castle; if he evaded justice, his benefice could be seized by his lord and his patrimony by his kinsmen.[120]

For almost all these detailed provisions there were precedents in the earlier peace councils of the reign: the episcopal peace councils in Lotharingia in 1082 and 1084, the imperial synod of Mainz in 1085 which they inspired and the peace councils held by the emperor's enemies in 1093–4 during his absence in Italy.[121] The single innovatory detail among the provisions of 1103 was the extension of the 'peace of God' to the Jewish community. In the light of the concern to protect the Jews which he had shown, especially after the pogroms of 1096, it is likely that this provision was the emperor's personal contribution

---

[118] *Annales Patherbrunnenses* 1102, p. 107; *Gesta archiepiscoporum Magdeburgensium* c. 23, p. 407. See Meyer von Knonau (1904) 5:158–9; Fenske (1977) 149 n. 288, 209–10; Meier (1987) 79.   [119] *Vita Heinrici IV* c. 8, p. 28.

[120] *MGH Constitutiones* I, 125–6, a report from a twelfth-century Augsburg manuscript, not an imperial document: Wadle (1973) 155 n. 69. Cf. *Vita Heinrici IV* c. 8, pp. 28–9. See Meyer von Knonau (1904) 5:175–7; Gernhuber (1952) 74–95; Wadle (1973) 153–7, 162–9, 172–3.

[121] See above pp. 249–50.

to the peace programme of Mainz. For the rest, the provisions of 1103 most closely resemble those of the Bavarian peace of 1094, instituted by Welf IV on the model of the peace sworn by his Swabian allies in Ulm the previous autumn.[122] The Bavarian peace similarly identified robbery as a breach of the peace demanding the severest penalty and sought to prevent feuds 'for the sake of money', that is, feuds waged by creditors against debtors. Most importantly, the Bavarian peace anticipated the 'imperial peace' of 1103 in prescribing a single penalty of mutilation, irrespective of the nature of the breach of the peace and irrespective of the social status of the offender. In one respect, however, the Bavarian peace was more ambitious than that of 1103. Those who swore that peace effectively renounced the feud: the oath of 1103 permitted the vendetta in certain circumstances. The noblemen who took the oath were permitted to pursue their private feuds, provided that this involved no attack on the property of a third party.[123]

The 'peace of God' proclaimed at the synod of Mainz in 1085 had been not an imperial but an episcopal initiative, inspired by the peace councils of Liège (1082) and Cologne (1084). By 1103 the 'peace of God' had ceased to be an exclusively episcopal institution and had begun to be regulated by the secular government. This development was already apparent in the peace movement initiated by the emperor's enemies in Ulm in 1093, which applied not to individual dioceses, but to the areas of jurisdiction of secular princes. These attempts to institute a 'territorial peace' (*Landfriede*) were presumably the models for the 'imperial peace' (*Reichsfriede*) of 1103.[124] The 'territorial' peace institutions of 1093–4 differed from that 'imperial peace', however, in one important respect. The objective of the south German princes in pacifying their territories was to enable themselves to concentrate more effectively on their war against the emperor. The 'imperial peace' of 1103 was intended to be a genuine pacification of the whole kingdom, from which no one was excluded.[125]

Henry IV has been identified as the 'creator' of the new institution of the 'imperial peace' and the peace of 1103 seen as 'the beginning of imperial legislation'.[126] It is clear that in 1103 (in contrast to the Mainz synod of 1085) Henry was reclaiming the preservation of the peace as a function of the crown, in the manner of Henry III's peace councils of 1043 and 1047. It is not clear, however, that Henry IV's role in January 1103 was that of legislator. The peace arrangements of the years 1082–94 had been binding not because of any

---

[122] Wadle (1973) 149.   [123] *MGH Constitutiones* I, 126.

[124] Bernold, *Chronicon* 1093, p. 458. See Wadle (1973) 150–2.

[125] The report of the imperial peace of 1103 specifically mentions that the former enemies Welf V, Berthold II of Zähringen and Frederick I of Swabia took the oath to preserve the peace.

[126] Gernhuber (1952) 81–2.

act of legislation but because of the oath by which the participants (*coniura-tores*) bound themselves to observe the peace. In the case of the 'imperial peace' of 1103 likewise 'the king's son swore an oath and the princes of the whole kingdom, the dukes, margraves, counts and many others'. Henry IV's anonymous biographer noted the central role of the oath: the emperor 'caused peace to be confirmed on oath throughout the whole kingdom'. Henry himself, however, did not take the oath: he 'confirmed and established the peace *with his own hand*'. This same formula was used to describe the adhesion of the prelates to the 'imperial peace': 'the archbishops and bishops confirmed [the peace] with their own hands.' Canon law forbade the clergy to swear oaths. According to a legal tradition first recorded in the thirteenth century, a similar prohibition applied to the king: once elected to the king-ship, he could no longer swear an oath but could only give his solemn word.[127] This tradition – a relic of 'sacral kingship', equating the legal status of the king with that of the episcopate – may explain why Henry IV did not swear the oath sworn by his son and by the secular princes in January 1103. The statement that Henry 'confirmed and established the peace with his own hand' need not imply, therefore, that the emperor acted as a legislator on this occasion; only that he gave his word to observe the peace, while the secular princes swore an oath. What gave authority to the 'imperial peace' of 1103 was not an imperial decree, but the action of those who either swore or promised to observe the peace.[128] The peace of 1103 differed from the earlier initiatives in that it was proclaimed by the emperor and applied to the whole kingdom, but in other respects it resembled the earlier models. It cannot be used as unambiguous evidence of a significant increase in the emperor's authority over his German kingdom or of the monarch's acknowledged right to alter or add to the laws of his kingdom.

[127] Wadle (1973) 166–8.

[128] The twelfth-century Augsburg manuscript containing 'the peace of Mainz' also contains a report of the Swabian 'territorial peace' of 1104 (*MGH Constitutiones* I, 614–15), an extended version of the 'imperial peace' of 1103. The additions suggest that Frederick I considered it permissible to adapt the 'imperial peace' to the circumstances of his own duchy. See Wadle (1973) 155–6.

10

The end of the reign, 1103–1106

The 'imperial peace' of January 1103 committed princes and nobility to
cooperation with the emperor in the task of eradicating crimes of violence.
Another harmonious scene was enacted six months later, when the rebellious
Count Robert II of Flanders was reconciled to the emperor in Liège 'in a very
numerous assembly of princes from the whole kingdom'.[1] A large number
of Saxon princes joined the imperial entourage in mid-July. They doubtless
came to discuss Saxon affairs: perhaps the implementation of the 'imperial
peace' in Saxony.[2] 'Many princes both of the Church and of the kingdom'
were similarly present in Regensburg during the imperial visit of December
1103 – February 1104.[3] It was during this visit to Regensburg that the political harmony that had prevailed during 1103 was disturbed by an act of violence which aroused the keenest interest throughout the kingdom and had
serious repercussions for the emperor. On 5 February 1104 Count Sigehard
of Burghausen was murdered in Regensburg by *ministeriales*. Sigehard and
his brother, Count Frederick of Tengling, had been present at the assembly
of 14 January in Regensburg, which dealt with the grievances of the church
of Augsburg. According to the chronicler Ekkehard of Aura, Sigehard
became an object of imperial suspicion when he voiced the feeling of the
Bavarian princes that 'the Saxons and Franconians received friendlier and
more honourable treatment from the emperor than the natives'. Sigehard
was regarded with increasing hostility by the emperor 'because he had
brought with him a larger force of knights than all the other princes who
were then present and he seemed to have armed himself so as to resist any
evil that might befall him from the court'. When Sigehard eventually dismissed his followers, he was attacked by a mob 'both of citizens of
Regensburg and of *ministeriales* from various regions', whom even the intervention of the young Henry V could not pacify. After laying siege to

---

[1] *DD H IV* 478–9: Gawlik (1978) XLIX. Cf. Sigebert, *Chronica* 1103, p. 368. See Meyer von
Knonau (1904) 5:179–80.   [2] *D H IV* 479. See Meyer von Knonau (1904) 5:180.
[3] *DD H IV* 482–4, 486: see above p. 314. See Meyer von Knonau (1904) 5:194–5.

Sigehard's lodgings for six hours, the insurgents broke down the doors and beheaded their victim.[4]

The more detailed accounts agree that the main perpetrators of this murder were unfree knights: 'members of princes' households, who are called *ministeriales*'.[5] A plausible explanation of the attack is offered by the *Annals of Hildesheim*, referring to 'a court in Regensburg . . . in which Count Sigehard gave an unjust judgement concerning retainers (*clientes*) and for this reason he was killed by them'.[6] Despite their servile birth and the resultant obligation to serve their lords, the *ministeriales* were also the hereditary possessors of benefices with important functions and carefully defined rights. The Hildesheim account of the death of Sigehard of Burghausen suggests that *ministeriales* were prepared to resort to violence in defence of their customary rights. The incident of 5 February 1104 is the best documented of a series of violent attacks by *ministeriales* on lords in the decade 1094–1105. Only in the reports of the death of Sigehard of Burghausen is the conduct of the *ministeriales* specifically linked with a violation of their customary rights; but it is possible that similar conflicts between lords and their retinues provoked the other outbreaks of violence in these years.[7]

'Vengeance and the other evils flowing from this crime are still before our eyes,' wrote Ekkehard late in 1105 or early in 1106, 'and what the end of it may be, we cannot know.'[8] His was one of a number of accounts implying that the emperor was responsible for the murder. The allegation is made explicit in the *Annals of Hildesheim*, which records that immediately after the murder the emperor was subject to 'a very great persecution by [Sigehard's] kinsmen and by all the princes of the kingdom'. They believed that 'if [Henry] had been willing to help [Sigehard], he would never have been killed'. Henry had failed

---

[4] Sigehard belonged to the family of Tengling-Burghausen-Peilstein, kinsmen of Henry IV's supporters, the Bavarian Aribones: Ekkehard, *Chronica* I, 1104, pp. 184–6. See Meyer von Knonau (1904) 5:195–8.

[5] Otto of Freising, *Chronica* VII.8, p. 318. See Arnold (1985) 35, 95, 102, 226; Zotz (1991) pp. 35–6. Cf. the uncorroborated *Annales Rosenveldenses* 1104, p. 102: the killers were 'the king's knights'.

[6] *Annales Hildesheimenses* 1104, p. 51. The narrative of 1103–6 interpolated here, 'Libellus de rebellione Heinrici V', perhaps originated in Mainz: Meyer von Knonau (1904) 5:196 n. 3, 353; Wattenbach and Holtzmann (1967) 451–2. Cf. *Annales Augustani* 1104, p. 136.

[7] Bernold of St Blasien, *Chronicon* 1094, p. 460 (murder of Herman, advocate of Reichenau); Frutolf of Michelsberg, *Chronica* 1099, p. 118; Bernold, *Chronicon* 1099, p. 466 (murder of Bishop Conrad of Utrecht); *Annales Einsidlenses* 1102, p. 146 (murder of Louis of Montbéliard);. Ekkehard of Aura, *Chronica* I, 1103, p. 184 (murder of Cuno of Beichlingen); *Anonymi Chronica imperatorum* II, 1105, p. 232 (murder of Bishop Gebhard IV of Regensburg). See Meyer von Knonau (1903) 4:428 n. 20; (1904) 5:67–8, 185 n. 21, 184, 237; Arnold (1985) 228 n. 17; Zotz (1991) 35.   [8] Ekkehard, *Chronica* I, 1103, p. 186.

to defend one who was in attendance on him and therefore under his protection. The annalist linked the murder in Regensburg with the rebellion that broke out at the end of the year. At the news of the rebellion, Diepold III of Cham-Vohburg, margrave of the Bavarian Nordgau 'rejoiced with all the princes of that region'. Diepold was the kinsman of Sigehard and one of the princes responsible for the 'very great persecution' of the emperor immediately after Sigehard's death.[9]

The Hildesheim annalist claimed that after Sigehard's death the emperor was so 'hemmed in on all sides by the plots' of his enemies that it was only with difficulty that he escaped from Regensburg. An imperial diploma of 28 February 1104, however, shows the emperor still in Regensburg three weeks after the murder, attended by 'archbishops, bishops, counts and many other faithful men'.[10] Soon after Easter (17 April) he returned to Liège, to protect the interests of two of his episcopal allies. He supported Otbert of Liège in a quarrel with his clergy[11] and restored Walcher of Cambrai to his city after his expulsion by the citizens.[12] In Liège the emperor awaited a delegation from the imperial faction in Magdeburg, led by Herman, burgrave of Magdeburg and brother of the late Archbishop Hartwig, and his nephew, the provost of Magdeburg, also called Hartwig. Their object was probably to secure Hartwig's investiture as his uncle's successor.[13] Before they could reach the imperial court, however, they were overtaken by the Saxon prince Count Theoderic III of Katlenburg, who accused them of planning to dispose of the archbishopric by simony and took them prisoner.[14] Theoderic's conduct prompted the emperor to mount a punitive expedition against him. At the end of November Henry, accompanied by his son, led his army to Fritzlar, his intention being to spend the winter in Saxony. During this sojourn in Fritzlar, however, on the night of 12 December 1104 the young king secretly left his father's camp with a few companions and fled to Bavaria. On learning of his flight, the emperor abandoned his expedition and returned to Mainz.[15]

[9] *Annales Hildesheimenses* 1104, p. 136.
[10] *Ibid.* 1104, p. 51; Ekkehard, *Chronica* I, 1104, pp. 184–6; but see *D H IV* 486.
[11] *Chronicon sancti Huberti Andaginensis* c. 96–7, pp. 628–9. See Meyer von Knonau (1904) 5:199.
[12] *Gesta Galcheri Cameracensis* c. 27, p. 204. See Meyer von Knonau (1904) 5:199–201.
[13] *Annales Hildesheimenses* 1104, p. 51; *Annales Patherbrunnenses* 1104, p. 108; *Gesta archiepiscoporum Magdeburgensium* c. 23, p. 408. See Meyer von Knonau (1904) 5:201; Fenske (1977) 151, 211.
[14] Ekkehard, *Chronica* III, 1106, p. 280; *Gesta archiepiscoporum Magdeburgensium* c. 23, p. 408. Theoderic, the nephew of Ekbert II of Meissen, was the emperor's kinsman: Fenske (1977) 150–2, 376.
[15] *Annales Hildesheimenses* 1104, p. 107; *Annales Patherbrunnenses* 1104, p. 108. See Meyer von Knonau (1904) 5:202–4.

In the months following his flight Henry V rapidly became the focus of a coalition of the emperor's enemies. First to associate themselves with the rebel king were the princes of the Bavarian Nordgau, alienated from the emperor by the murder of Sigehard of Burghausen. Diepold III of Cham-Vohburg hastened to meet Henry V and escorted him to Regensburg, where he celebrated Christmas. Ekkehard of Aura attributed responsibility for Henry V's rebellion to Diepold and his allies, Count Berengar of Sulzbach and Otto, count of Kastl-Habsberg.[16] Otto, Diepold and Berengar are probably to be identified as the evil counsellors of Henry V to whom responsibility for the rebellion is ascribed in the imperial propaganda of 1105–6.[17] According to Ekkehard's account, the three princes of the Bavarian Nordgau induced Henry V to rebel, just as Welf IV of Bavaria and Matilda of Tuscany had encouraged the rebellion of his elder brother Conrad. It is easy to believe that Henry V's plans were coordinated in advance with these princes, since Margrave Diepold was waiting on the frontier to welcome the young king only a matter of days after his secret departure from Fritzlar. Like Welf IV and Matilda, Diepold, Berengar and Otto had close links with the Gregorian party. All three princes had participated in the foundation of the monastery of St Peter in Kastl, which was placed under the authority of the abbey of Hirsau and received a privilege from Paschal II. When Bishop Gebhard of Constance, the leader of the Gregorian party, was expelled from Constance by the anti-bishop Arnold, he took refuge with Diepold, the son of his sister, Liutgard of Zähringen. Members of the Gregorian party were the earliest beneficiaries of the rebellion of Henry V. Gebhard was restored to Constance early in 1105. The refugee Abbot Theoderic of Petershausen returned to his abbey and was chosen by Henry V as his confessor. The close associate of Bishop Gebhard and Abbot Theoderic, Abbot Gebhard of Hirsau, rallied to the young king and was rewarded with the bishopric of Speyer and the abbey of Lorsch. Berengar of Sulzbach and Margrave Diepold put the young king into contact with the inveterate Gregorian enemies of his father in southern Germany who had refused reconciliation in 1098.[18]

Immediately after Christmas 1104 Henry V sent envoys to Paschal II. The young king's attempt at rapprochement came at a time when the pope had been seeking unsuccessfully to revive the Gregorian party in the German

[16] Ekkehard, *Chronica* I, 1105, pp. 188, 190. Cf. *Annales Hildesheimenses* 1104, pp. 51–2. Henry V was the grandson of Adelaide of Turin, Otto of Kastl-Habsberg the great-grandson of her sister Irmgard.

[17] Henry IV, *Letters* 34, 37, pp. 44, 47. Cf. *Vita Heinrici IV* c. 9, pp. 29–30.

[18] Doeberl (1894) 31–5; Meyer von Knonau (1904) 5:204–6; Schumann (1912) 71–2; Jakobs (1961) 217–19; Waas (1967) 10–11; Bosl (1972) 1133, 1143–4; Servatius (1979) 170–1; Wollasch (1987) 38.

kingdom.[19] The rebellion of Henry V, raising the possibility of a new papal anti-king on the model of Conrad, took Paschal II by surprise. There is no evidence that the pope had encouraged his rebellion. According to the paraphrase of their correspondence in the *Annals of Hildesheim*, the young king sought papal advice concerning his oath 'that he would never interfere during the [emperor's] lifetime and against [his] will and [his] command in matters concerning [his] kingship . . .' Paschal responded with a promise of absolution 'if he would be a just king in his government of the Church'. The pope 'conferred on him the apostolic blessing through Bishop Gebhard of Constance', his legate. The king was subsequently absolved by the legate, probably in February 1105, from the excommunication that he had incurred through his association with the emperor.[20] While he was still awaiting a response from Rome, Henry V had received envoys from his father, Duke Frederick I of Swabia, the archbishops of Cologne and Trier and Erlung, chancellor for the German kingdom. Their task was 'somehow to reconcile' the young king with his father. Henry V replied that he could have nothing to do with an excommunicate.[21]

Soon after his absolution by the legate, Henry V gained the support of further opponents of the emperor. 'Instructed by a letter from Pope Paschal and with the advice and help of Ruothard of Mainz and Bishop Gebhard of Constance, [Henry] reconciled the whole of Saxony to the communion of the Roman church.'[22] After his quarrel with the emperor in 1098 Archbishop Ruothard of Mainz had remained until 1105 a refugee in Thuringia, where he associated himself with the Gregorian party in Saxony. In spring 1105 Paschal II confirmed him in the office of archbishop of Mainz, despite his investiture with the archbishopric by Henry IV.[23] Simultaneously the young king's rebellion offered an opportunity of recovering Mainz from the emperor. Ruothard was probably among those princes who urged Henry V to come to Thuringia and Saxony. Letters in the name of the Saxon count palatine Frederick I of Sommerschenburg and other Saxon princes urged the young king to come to Saxony, where both secular and ecclesiastical affairs awaited his attention and where bishoprics and abbeys needed to be filled.[24] At an assembly in Quedlinburg in mid-March 1105 Henry V's envoys Margrave Diepold and

[19] Paschal II, *JL* 5970–3: 121AC, 121D–122C, 197C–198B, *Acta pontificum Romanorum inedita* I, 78. See Meyer von Knonau (1904) 5:185–7; Servatius (1979) 163.

[20] *Annales Hildesheimenses* 1104, p. 52. Cf. *Chronica monasterii Casinensis* IV.36, p. 502. See Meyer von Knonau (1904) 5:214–18; Servatius (1979) 173–8.

[21] *Annales Hildesheimenses* 1105, p. 52; *Vita Heinrici IV* c. 9, p. 30. See Meyer von Knonau (1904) 5:211.   [22] *Anonymi Chronica imperatorum* II, 1105, p. 228.

[23] Paschal II, *JL* 6050, 6057: 174D–175D, *Regesta pontificum Romanorum* I, 723. See Meyer von Knonau (1904) 5:218–20; Servatius (1979) 182.   [24] *Codex Udalrici* 116–17, pp. 227–8.

Count Berengar on the king's behalf promised 'all faith and all justice', while the Saxon princes promised fealty and service to the king and invited him to celebrate Easter with them.[25]

Accompanied by Gebhard of Constance and 'the princes of the Nordgau and noblemen from Swabia and eastern Franconia', Henry V travelled to Thuringia. In Erfurt, where he celebrated Palm Sunday (2 April) with Ruothard of Mainz, he received the homage of his Saxon supporters. The Saxons 'swore fealty to him against his father, on condition that he provided for God's Church in a fitting manner and gave just judgements to all men'. This insistence on 'faith', 'justice' and the rights of the Church was an echo of the demands of the Saxon rebels in the early 1070s. According to the Erfurt chronicler, 'the young man . . . was enthroned in the kingship by the Thuringians and Saxons'. The significance of the performance of homage and the alleged enthronement has been variously interpreted. If no Saxon princes were present at Henry V's election in Mainz (May 1098) or his coronation in Aachen (6 January 1099), the princes in Erfurt may have demanded the opportunity to give their consent to the new king's elevation. Alternatively the ceremony in Erfurt may have signified that Henry V was now considered by his adherents to be the sole king of the Germans and no longer the junior partner of the emperor.[26]

On Good Friday (7 April) 1105 the young king 'walked barefoot into Quedlinburg', a demonstration of his penitence for having associated with the excommunicate emperor, and he subsequently celebrated Easter there. During Eastertide he supported the efforts of Gebhard of Constance and Ruothard of Mainz to bring the Saxon Church into communion with the reform papacy. Meeting the Saxon princes and Gebhard of Constance in Goslar, Henry V discussed with them 'how . . . he should purify the Church . . . and restore it from schism to union'. The assembly decided to hold a synod on the royal estate of Nordhausen on 21 May.[27] 'The young king presided' at the synod, in which the papal legate Gebhard of Constance and Ruothard of Mainz condemned 'simoniacal heresy' and clerical marriage and proclaimed the 'peace of God'. The synod witnessed the submission to their metropolitan of the bishops of Halberstadt, Paderborn and Hildesheim. The chronicler Ekkehard of Aura wrote an eyewitness account. 'We saw that King Henry, through his great humility and equally great authority, awoke in all men great

---

[25] *Annales Patherbrunnenses* 1105, pp. 108–9.

[26] *Annales Hildesheimenses* p. 52; *Annales Patherbrunnenses* 1105, p. 109; *Cronica sancti Petri Erfordensis* 1105, p. 159. See Meyer von Knonau (1904) 5:219–21; Haider (1968) 47–50; Scheibelreiter (1973) 26–7; Fenske (1977) 152–3, 158–9; Giese (1979) 59–60.

[27] *Annales Hildesheimenses* 1105, pp. 52–3; *Annales Patherbrunnenses* 1105, pp. 109–10. See Meyer von Knonau (1904) 5:224–7; Fenske (1977) 160; Servatius (1979) 182, 187–8.

hopes of his good qualities' and 'showed a fitting reverence towards the priests of Christ'. Henry V declared that 'he did not usurp his father's authority out of lust for power and did not wish his father to be deposed from the Roman empire'. 'He promised that if [his father] would submit to St Peter and his successors according to Christian law, he would either withdraw from the kingship or submit to him like a servant.'[28]

Henry V declared to the synod of Nordhausen, as he had to the emperor's envoys four months before, that his rebellion was prompted by his father's failure to secure absolution from papal excommunication. Saxon chroniclers readily accepted this explanation of his motive for rebellion.[29] Authors sympathetic to Henry IV, however, suggested that the young king rebelled 'under the pretext of improving the commonwealth and restoring the Church' and 'furthered his own cause under the appearance of furthering the cause of God'.[30] He exploited for his own purposes the political grievances of the princes of the Nordgau and Saxony and the ecclesiastical grievances of the Gregorian party. The only detailed contemporary analysis of his motives is found in the Bamberg chronicle dedicated to Henry V. The chronicler mentioned rumours that the young king's rebellion originated in the emperor's ruse to simulate a family quarrel so as to inveigle the Saxons into supporting his son, thus averting the election of an anti-king. Dismissing such rumours, the chronicler declared that the young king's decision to rebel stemmed from his fears of the emperor's imminent death and its consequences. 'Contemplating the many troubles suffered by his father, for all his circumspection, and his frequent physical ailments, [Henry V] began to consider the fluctuations of fortune and the mutability of the world.' When he deserted his father, he was 'guarding against the possibility that his father's sudden death would find him not yet fully provided with friends and knights and with no special reputation in military affairs and so give rise to scruples about his becoming king'.[31]

When Conrad had acknowledged the authority of the reform papacy ten years before, Urban II had offered 'his advice and aid in obtaining the kingship and the crown of the empire' on condition that Conrad accepted the papal reform programme, including the prohibition of lay investiture.[32]

---

[28] Ekkehard, *Chronica* I, 1105, p. 192.

[29] *Annales Rosenveldenses* 1105, p. 102; *Annales sancti Disibodi* 1105, p. 19; *Cronica sancti Petri Erfordensis* 1105, p. 158.

[30] Sigebert, *Chronica* 1105, p. 368; *Vita Heinrici IV* c. 9, p. 30. Otto of Freising, *Chronica* VII.8, p. 318.

[31] *Anonymi Chronica imperatorum* 1105, p. 226. See Schmale-Ott (1971) 403–61: this chronicle was compiled by Bishop Otto of Bamberg. Henry V's motives: Meyer von Knonau (1904) 5:353–8; Rassow (1928) 451–65; Haefele (1954) 99–113; Waas (1967) 11–12, 33–9.

[32] See above p. 292.

Henry V, however, was absolved from excommunication and secured the support of the German Gregorian party without renouncing lay investiture. The synodal proceedings of Nordhausen included no reference to lay investiture. Far from demanding a renunciation of investiture from the young king, Gebhard of Constance and Ruothard of Mainz are known to have participated during 1105 in the appointment of bishops who had been invested with their sees by Henry V.[33] A letter of Paschal II accuses Gebhard of Constance of having 'assisted in the consecration of those who received investiture'.[34] It is clear that in his relations with the papacy and its German adherents in 1105, Henry V's purpose was precisely that of his father at the time of the council of Mainz in January 1103. The emperor had hoped to 'reconcile kingship and priesthood' while ignoring the renewal of the papal decrees against lay investiture at the Lateran synod of 1102. The young king similarly desired to end the schism without sacrificing the crown's right of investiture.

He was doubtless encouraged to believe that this was feasible by the acquiescence of the papal legate Gebhard of Constance and Ruothard of Mainz in his episcopal appointments of 1105. The leaders of the Gregorian party considered it more important to assist the young king to overthrow his father's regime than to ensure his adhesion to the programme of the reform papacy. The 'Investiture Contest' between Henry V and the reform papacy was consequently postponed until after the defeat and death of Emperor Henry IV. Henry V's rebellion was clearly not inspired by the 'regard for the rights of the [Roman] church and for the apostolic decrees' that Gregorian chroniclers attributed to his brother Conrad. Henry V had acknowledged the authority of Paschal II, firstly, because only the pope could absolve him from the oath that he had sworn not to imitate his brother's conduct and, secondly, because papal supporters in Germany provided him with a ready-made opposition faction. The rapidity with which these papal supporters came to Henry V's aid in 1105 reveals how vulnerable was his father's regime, despite the pacification of the kingdom in 1098–1103, and how necessary had been the emperor's attempts at rapprochement with the Roman church in 1101–3. Father and son in turn made their bids for the support of the reform papacy. Henry V's was the successful bid, since he offered the deposition of the emperor, 'Henry, the chief of the heretics'.[35]

Since mid-December 1104, when his son's desertion caused him to abandon the expedition to Saxony, the emperor had remained in the Rhineland. In

---

[33] Magdeburg, Minden, Speyer and Würzburg: Ekkehard, *Chronica* I, 1105, pp. 192, 194, 196, 198; *Annales Hildesheimenses* 1105, p. 53. See Schumann (1912) 71–4; Diebolder (1916) 202–3, 206–7; Servatius (1979) 180–5; Beulertz (1991) 133–5.

[34] Paschal II, *JL* 6143: 213C–214A. Cf. *JL* 6144: 214BC; *Annales Patherbrunnenses* 1107, pp. 117–18.

[35] Paschal II, *JL* 5889: *MGH Libelli* 2, 452.

February 1105 he made his last visit to Speyer. The last of the twenty-one privileges conferred on the church of Speyer during the years of Henry IV's maturity (15 February) emphasises the church's connection both with his special protector, the Virgin Mary, and with his imperial dignity.[36] He celebrated Easter (9 April) in Mainz with his kinsman Udalric, patriarch of Aquileia and abbot of St Gallen. Udalric 'came to reconcile [the emperor with his son], if it could be done', but he was no more successful than the envoys of the previous January.[37] After the failure of these efforts at reconciliation the emperor attempted to outmanoeuvre his son by making peace with Paschal II.[38] The principal evidence of this attempt is the imperial letter to Paschal II of spring or summer 1105. The emperor described this as a secret communication, to be brought to Rome by a 'most faithful envoy', to whom he had entrusted an oral message for the pope.[39] The letter begins by contrasting the 'peace and harmony' of Henry IV's relations with the popes Nicholas II and Alexander II with the discord of the pontificates of Gregory VII and Urban II, who 'seemed to persecute us out of hatred and anger rather than zeal for righteousness'. Echoing the language of the Henrician polemics of the 1080s, the letter recalled how those popes 'strove to stir up and arm the kingdom against us'. Now the emperor's son, 'infected by the same poison', had risen in rebellion, encouraged by evil counsellors anxious to 'plunder . . . both ecclesiastical and royal property'. Instead of avenging this treachery, on the advice of his princes, the emperor turned to the pope, seeking to know if he wished to be 'united in love and friendship' with him. This restoration of unity was without prejudice to 'the honour of our kingship and empire and all our dignity, as it was preserved by our grandfather and father and our other predecessors'.[40] Anxious though he now was for peace with the pope, the emperor was not prepared to sacrifice any of the traditional rights of the monarchy. He would not try to outmanoeuvre his son by offering to renounce lay investiture.

By midsummer all the Saxon bishops, with the exception of Burchard of Münster, had rallied to the young king.[41] Henry V now considered himself

---

[36] *D H IV* 489. See Meyer von Knonau (1904) 5:210.

[37] *Annales Hildesheimenses* 1105, p. 53. See Meyer von Knonau (1904) 5:210.

[38] Erlung of Würzburg, Letter to Otto of Bamberg: *Codex Udalrici* 118, pp. 228–30. See Meyer von Knonau (1904) 5:213.

[39] The fact that this secret letter survives in two twelfth-century letter collections suggests that after the failure of this initiative the emperor made the letter public, to demonstrate the sincerity of his peace efforts: Erdmann (1939) 222.

[40] Henry IV, *Letter* 34, pp. 43–4. See Meyer von Knonau (1904) 5:212–13; Erdmann (1939) 222; Koch (1972) 31–2, 54–5; Servatius (1979) 171–2; Beulertz (1991) 135.

[41] *Annales Patherbrunnenses* 1105, p. 112. Walram of Naumburg, author of *De causa Heinrici* pp. 286–7, announced his conversion to Anselm of Canterbury: *Anselmi Cantuariensis Opera* 2, 237.

strong enough to mount an expedition against his father in Mainz and restore Archbishop Ruothard to his church. In the last week of June the young king's Saxon army was drawn up on the bank of the Rhine opposite Mainz. The emperor succeeded in frustrating the enemy's attempts to cross the river. Henry V found that those who had promised him ships, notably Siegfried of Ballenstedt, had succumbed to his father's bribery. Negotiations between the two camps proved fruitless.[42] Recognising that the emperor was in an unassailable position, Henry V withdrew to eastern Franconia. His objective was Würzburg, the city which Henry IV had fought so hard to secure during his wars of 1077–88. Henry V's intention was to replace the imperial adherent Bishop Erlung. He appointed Rupert, provost of the cathedral of Würzburg, to the bishopric and Ruothard of Mainz consecrated him. The clergy and people of Würzburg, in rebellion against the reform papacy since 1077, were required to swear an oath promising fidelity and obedience to Paschal II. After a short stay in the city, the young king 'dismissed the Saxon forces and, with the Bavarians, turned back to lay siege to the fortress of Nuremberg'.[43]

Meanwhile, on 1 August the emperor at last left Mainz with his army and advanced to Würzburg, where he had no difficulty in expelling Rupert and restoring Erlung to his see. The emperor remained in Würzburg perhaps until late September, attempting to gather forces sufficient to come to relieve Nuremberg. That royal fortress (which since Henry III's reign had been the administrative centre of the crown lands in southern Germany) endured a siege of more than two months before surrendering to Henry V.[44] The emperor's difficulties in August and September are apparent from two letters which he sent to Otto of Bamberg. He urged Otto to join him in Würzburg with every available vassal, warned him against the young king's threats or flatteries and commanded prayers for the emperor to be said 'without interruption' in all the churches and monasteries of the diocese.[45] By September 1105, when Nuremberg surrendered to the young king, the emperor was rapidly losing control of southern Germany. His severest setback was the death during the summer of his son-in-law, Duke Frederick I of Swabia, who for more than a quarter of a century had proved loyal to him. Henry V took his sister Agnes, Frederick I's widow, under his protection, together with her

[42] Ekkehard, *Chronica* I, 1105, pp. 192–4. Cf. *Annales Hildesheimenses* 1105, pp. 52–3. See Meyer von Knonau (1904) 5:230–1.

[43] *Anonymi Chronica imperatorum* 1105, pp. 230–2. See Meyer von Knonau (1904) 5:231–2; Wendehorst (1962) 124–7.

[44] Ekkehard, *Chronica* I, 1105, pp. 192–4; *Vita Heinrici IV* c. 9, pp. 30–1. See Meyer von Knonau (1904) 5:234–5; Rieckenberg (1942) 110; Brühl (1968) 134 and n. 83, 141 n. 112, 158.

[45] Henry IV, *Letters* 35–6, pp. 45–6. See Meyer von Knonau (1904) 5:233–4.

fifteen-year-old son, Frederick II.[46] The new duke of Swabia was the protégé of the young king: the emperor's influence in the duchy was at an end. Gebhard of Constance was able once more to reside in his own diocese. On 21 October 1105 he was able to hold in Constance a synod proclaiming the 'peace of God' throughout the diocese.[47] This synod met in the presence of Paschal II's legate, Cardinal bishop Richard of Albano, newly arrived in Germany.[48] His German legation of 1105–6 was to witness the gradual recruitment to the obedience of Paschal II of almost all the German bishops, following the example of their Saxon brethren in the first half of 1105.[49]

After the surrender of Nuremberg the young king dismissed his army and returned to Regensburg at the end of September. Learning that his son had withdrawn to his winter quarters, the emperor immediately moved his forces from Würzburg into Bavaria. He intended by a surprise attack 'to seize his son either on the march or in the city' of Regensburg. This strategy was so far successful that an advance party of his knights had crossed the Danube and gained access to the city before Henry V had warning of them. The young king nevertheless escaped from Regensburg and fled northwards, presumably to his supporters in the Bavarian Nordgau. The emperor was able to demonstrate his mastery over Regensburg by appointing a new bishop to the vacant see. His army in Regensburg was now reinforced by the contingents of Margrave Leopold III of Austria and his brother-in-law, Duke Borivoi of Bohemia, whose forces were sufficient to permit an offensive against the young king.[50] The envoys of Henry V had meanwhile recruited an army in Bavaria and Swabia, enabling him to return to Regensburg. The two armies faced each other across the River Regen for three days without joining battle, although warriors from the opposing armies challenged each other to single combat in the gap between the hostile forces. (A prominent imperial supporter, Count Hartwig of Bogen, met his death in such a duel.) A pitched battle seemed imminent, but it was averted by the leading princes on both sides, who held peace talks among themselves.[51] When, after three days, the emperor came to make his dispositions for the battle, he learned that Leopold

---

[46] Otto of Freising, *Gesta Friderici* I.9, 10, pp. 25, 26. Cf. Ekkehard, *Chronica* I, 1105, p. 202. Frederick's first appearance as 'duke of the Swabians' (21 July 1105): Stälin (1847) 2, 37 n. 5, 74. See Meyer von Knonau (1904) 5:237–8.

[47] *MGH Constitutiones* I, 615–16. See Wadle (1989) 141–53.

[48] Schumann (1912) 79–81; Hüls (1977) 93; Servatius (1979) 190 n. 121.

[49] Meyer von Knonau (1904) 5:246, 247–9, 271–3, 283, 288; Schlechte (1934) 33–4; von Guttenberg (1937) 120–1; Neuss and Oediger (1964) 208–9; Servatius (1979) 181 n. 103, 199.

[50] Ekkehard, *Chronica* I, 1105, p. 194; *Annales Hildesheimenses* 1105, p. 53; *Vita Heinrici IV* c. 9, p. 32. See Meyer von Knonau (1904) 5:235–7, 239.

[51] Ekkehard, *Chronica* I, 1105, p. 196. See Meyer von Knonau (1904) 5:241–2.

of Austria and Borivoi of Bohemia had deserted to his son. Henry V had won Leopold over by the offer of marriage to his sister Agnes.[52] Without the Austrian and Bohemian reinforcements the emperor was no longer in a position to attack his son. Fearing further treachery within his own camp, Henry IV fled by night with a small group of his supporters. When the emperor's flight became known, the army of Henry V was at once disbanded. The young king received the submission of 'the bishops and princes of his father's army whom he found within the walls' of Regensburg.[53] Henry V proceeded to Würzburg where, undoing the work of his father, he deposed Bishop Erlung and restored his own candidate.[54]

After fleeing from his camp on the River Regen, the emperor entered Bohemia, where 'Duke Borivoi honourably received' him.[55] Borivoi, who (in the words of the emperor's anonymous biographer) 'had recently left [Henry] in the lurch', evidently now repented of his flight from the imperial camp.[56] He conducted Henry IV as far as the Erzgebirge and, bestowing many gifts, delivered him into the care of Count Wiprecht I of Groitzsch. Wiprecht, who had risen to princely rank in the service of Henry IV and Vratislav II of Bohemia, was now a prominent figure in Bohemian politics through his marriage to Judith, daughter of Vratislav II. He conducted the emperor safely through Saxony and brought him back to the Rhineland, reaching Mainz probably in the last days of October.[57] The emperor's return to Mainz was prompted by a letter sent to him over a month before by the citizens of Mainz. These well-wishers reminded the emperor of their devotion to the imperial cause and warned him of an imminent attack on Mainz. Henry V's intention was to take the city at the end of September 1105 and restore Ruothard to his cathedral. The citizens begged the emperor to come to Mainz in person or to send an army to their defence.[58]

The emperor learned on his return to the city that Henry V was preparing to attack not Mainz but Speyer. The emperor immediately attempted to intercept his son before he could cross the Rhine and enter Speyer, but he arrived too late. Henry V had crossed the river on 31 October and gained control both

[52] Otto, *Chronica* VII.9, p. 321.

[53] Ekkehard, *Chronica* I, 1105, p. 196. Cf. *Annales Hildesheimenses* 1105, p. 53; *Vita Heinrici IV* c. 9, pp. 31–2. See Meyer von Knonau (1904) 5:247; Boshof (1991) 143.

[54] *Anonymi Chronica imperatorum* 1105, p. 234. See Meyer von Knonau (1904) 5:247–8.

[55] Cosmas, *Chronicon Boemorum* III.18, pp. 182–3; *Annales Gradicenses* 1105, p. 648; Ekkehard, *Chronica* I, 1105, p. 198. See Meyer von Knonau (1904) 5:243–4.

[56] *Vita Heinrici IV* c. 9, pp. 444–6.

[57] Since *c.* 1090 Wiprecht had fallen under the influence of the Saxon Gregorians, his monastery of Pegau adopting the monastic customs of Hirsau: *Annales Pegavienses* pp. 242–7. See Hallinger (1950–1) 405–11; Fenske (1977) 260, 262, 264–9.

[58] *Codex Udalrici* 123, pp. 234–5. See Meyer von Knonau (1904) 5:245–6; Büttner (1973) 358.

of the city and of the treasure that his father had stored there. He crowned his success by installing Abbot Gebhard of Hirsau as bishop of Speyer on 1 November. The emperor was obliged to return to Mainz, 'hungry and utterly weary', on the same day that he had set out. The next day he sent an envoy to his son, begging him 'to remember that he was his father and not to persist in his desire to depose him from the kingship'. Henry V sent back the message that the emperor should leave Mainz immediately, if he wished to avoid being seized by his enemies. Despite the recent assurances of the loyalty of the citizens of Mainz, Henry IV now concluded that it was unsafe for him to remain in the city. He fled first to the royal castle of Hammerstein and then, late in November, to Cologne.[59] The last two surviving diplomas of the reign were issued in Cologne on 24 November and 3 December 1105, in favour of Archbishop Anno's foundation, the abbey of Siegburg, and the monastery of St Pantaleon in Cologne, reformed by Anno on the model of Siegburg.[60]

The earliest account of the events of December 1105 and January 1106 is found in three letters issued by the emperor in the last months of his life. The first is addressed to his godfather, Abbot Hugh of Cluny, whom he envisaged negotiating his reconciliation with the papacy. The other two letters, addressed to King Philip I of France and the young king Henry V, were probably never sent to their addressees: they are works of propaganda, intended to justify the imperial cause to the widest possible audience.[61] They describe how the emperor's determination to return to Mainz in December 1105 precipitated the young king's successful attempt to capture his father and to force his abdication. The emperor learned of his son's intention to hold an assembly of 'all the princes of the kingdom' in Mainz during Christmastide. Determined to defend his own cause before this assembly, Henry IV sent two envoys, the Lotharingian count palatine Siegfried of Ballenstedt and Count William of Luxemburg, to prepare the way for him.[62] Henry V feared that the loyalty of the citizens of Mainz towards the emperor might prove dangerous to him, should his father succeed in reaching the city.

Hastening to intercept the emperor, the young king's army first encountered his envoys, who had reached the Soonwald, the forest to the south-east

---

[59] Ekkehard, *Chronica* I, 1105, p. 198; *Annales Hildesheimenses* 1105, p. 54. See Meyer von Knonau (1904) 5:250–1.

[60] *DD H IV* 490–1. See Meyer von Knonau (1904) 5:251; Semmler (1959) 260; Schieffer (1991) 23.

[61] Henry IV, *Letters* 37, 39, 40, 41, pp. 116, 124–6, 132, 136: see Erdmann (1939) 223–9; Koch (1972) 54–5. Cf. *Vita Heinrici IV* c. 10, pp. 32–4. Anti-Henrician accounts: Ekkehard, *Chronica* I, 1105, pp. 198–200; *Annales Hildesheimenses* 1105, pp. 54–5. See Meyer von Knonau (1904) 5:256–63.

[62] *Vita Heinrici IV* c. 10, p. 32. But see Ekkehard, *Chronica* I, 1105, p. 198 and *Annales Hildesheimenses* 1105, p. 54. See Twellenkamp (1991) 497.

of the Hunsrück. The envoys could offer no resistance to the 'great army' raised by Henry V and fled under cover of night. The young king pressed on towards Koblenz and found his father on the opposite bank of the River Mosel. A meeting was then negotiated by envoys (on the initiative of Henry V, according to the emperor's letters; on the emperor's initiative, according to the Hildesheim account). When the young king appeared before his father, the latter threw himself at his son's feet, beseeching him 'to desist from his inhuman persecution'. Subsequently Henry V in turn abased himself before his father and promised to make peace with him 'if only [he] would be reconciled to the apostolic see'. The emperor replied that he would submit himself to the deliberations of the forthcoming assembly in Mainz. His son's promise to enable him to participate in this assembly is heavily underlined in the emperor's propaganda letter of 1106. On the strength of this guarantee the emperor dismissed the greater part of his army and left Koblenz on 21 December in the direction of Mainz, his son preceding him on the road.[63]

On that first day's march one of the emperor's vassals warned him that he was being 'deceived and betrayed by a false promise of peace and fidelity'. When the emperor called back his son, confronting him with the accusation, Henry V repeated his former promise. The next day's march (22 December) brought them at nightfall to Bingen, where 'the number of [Henry V's] armed men increased considerably'. According to the imperial letter to Hugh of Cluny, 'when morning came, [the young king] surrounded [the emperor] with the clash of weapons and threats of every kind, saying that he would bring [him] not to Mainz but to a certain castle'. Henry V declared that the archbishop of Mainz would not admit the emperor to his city as long as he was excommunicate and that, since Mainz was full of his enemies, it was unsafe for the emperor to go there. The emperor threw himself at his son's feet and at the feet of the young king's companions, begging to be conducted to Mainz. Henry V for the third time guaranteed his safety on oath but refused his request. The emperor was brought instead to the castle of Böckelheim, a Salian family property on the River Nahe, where Henry V's recent appointee, Bishop Gebhard II of Speyer, was deputed to guard him.[64] Henry V then hastened to the assembly in Mainz, where he heard the papal legate, Gebhard of Constance, confirm the excommunication pronounced 'so often by so many popes in succession against the elder Henry, the so-called emperor'. It was 'an assembly of the whole German kingdom, greater than had ever been seen for very many years' including 'fifty-two princes or more'. Despite this impressive demonstration of support for his actions, however, the young king felt inse-

---

[63] Henry IV, *Letter 39*, p. 54. Cf. *Letter 37*, p. 48.
[64] Henry IV, *Letter 37*, pp. 48–9; cf. *Letter 39*, pp. 54–5; *Vita* c. 10, pp. 33–4.

cure. The citizens of Mainz 'spread the rumour that the father had been captured by his son by means of a trick and imprisoned'. When, therefore, Gebhard of Speyer arrived in Mainz, bearing the emperor's request to appear before the assembly (27 December), the princes proposed instead to meet him in the royal residence of Ingelheim on the Rhine.[65]

The imperial letter to Hugh of Cluny and that to Philip I of France provide detailed accounts of Henry IV's privations in the castle of Böckelheim in the last week of December 1105. The emperor was a prisoner, 'placed under the closest confinement and delivered up to [his] mortal enemies'.[66] His gaolers deprived him of all his followers 'except for three laymen'. One deprivation is particularly emphasised in the letter to the king of France. 'This I shall never forget; of this I shall never cease to complain to all Christians: that during those most holy days [of Christmastide] I was in prison without Christian communion.' According to the Hildesheim annalist, the emperor 'remained without a bath and unshaven and deprived of any divine service throughout all the holy days.' The chronicler was describing here the conditions enforced by canon law upon a repentant sinner: Henry was compelled by his gaoler, Gebhard of Speyer, to adopt the demeanour of a penitent.[67] The emperor's treatment in Böckelheim has been ascribed solely to 'the hatred and malice' of the young king.[68] More important, however, than Henry V's personal animosity was his need to placate his allies in the Gregorian party. His treatment of his father must accord with what staunch Gregorians like Gebhard of Speyer considered appropriate for an offender excommunicated by the pope. Henry V was almost certainly aware of the letter of 11 November 1105 which Paschal II had sent to Ruothard of Mainz, containing the first reference to lay investiture in his German correspondence. Paschal insisted that investiture was a cause of simony and that the function of the secular ruler was to defend the Church, not to appoint her clergy.[69] The raising of this issue was particularly unwelcome for Henry V, whose conduct had already made clear that he had no intention of relinquishing the right of investiture. He could not respond positively to this papal initiative, but he could at least demonstrate his respect for the canon law concerning excommunication through his treatment of his father.

[65] Ekkehard, *Chronica* I, 1105, pp. 200–2; *Annales Hildesheimenses* 1105, p. 55; *Vita Heinrici IV* c. 10, p. 34. See Meyer von Knonau (1904) 5:263, 265–6. *Historia Hirsaugiensis monasterii* c. 6, p. 258, contradicts Ekkehard's claim that Richard of Albano participated in the assembly. See Schumann (1912) 84; Jakobs (1961) 33–4, 220–1; Servatius (1979) 184 n. 109, 190–1.

[66] Henry IV, *Letter* 37, p. 49; *Letter* 39, p. 55. One of these gaolers was Gebhard, bishop of Speyer: Meyer von Knonau (1903) 4:362–3; Heidrich (1991) 213–14.

[67] Henry IV, *Letters* 37, 39, pp. 49, 55–6; *Annales Hildesheimenses* 1105, p. 55. See Meyer von Knonau (1904) 5:264–5; Schmeidler (1922) 175–8, 191–2.   [68] Waas (1967) 15–17.

[69] Paschal II, *JL* 6050: 174D–175D. See Servatius (1979) 195–7; Beulertz (1991) 135–6.

There are two conflicting accounts of the concessions made by the emperor during his imprisonment in Böckelheim. According to the Hildesheim annalist, the emperor acknowledged that his present calamities 'happened as a consequence of his sins' and began to fear that 'he would suffer worse misfortunes at the hands of the princes'. He therefore entrusted Gebhard of Speyer with the message of submission for the assembly of Mainz which was delivered on 27 December. The emperor promised 'to deliver up to his son the royal insignia and the most strongly fortified castles that he possessed, so that [Henry V] would at least grant him the wherewithal to live'.[70] According to the imperial letters, however, these concessions were not the result of the emperor's penitence, but were wrung from him by the threats of Henry V's adherents. The emperor was forced to command the garrison of the castle of Hammerstein, where the insignia were kept, to surrender the cross, the lance and the other insignia to Henry V.[71] According to the imperial letter to Hugh of Cluny, the emperor was threatened with 'harsh captivity'. According to the letter to the king of France, the threat delivered by Henry V's envoy was not of captivity but death.[72]

On 31 December 1105 the emperor was conducted to Ingelheim, where, in the words of the imperial manifesto, he found 'a very large crowd of enemies and [his] son no better disposed towards [him] than the rest'. Henry V had ensured that only his own supporters were present. The princes sympathetic to the imperial cause remained in Mainz, under the mistaken impression that the emperor was to be brought to the city. Prominent among the 'crowd of enemies' was the papal legate, Cardinal bishop Richard of Albano. The hostile assembly required Henry IV to make a public renunciation of his claim to the kingship, in confirmation of his previous action of surrendering the royal insignia. According to the imperial letters of 1106, the emperor, realising that the assembly had prejudged his case, threw himself at the feet of his accusers. He sought permission to answer the accusations against him, but his request was refused. He was permitted only to make a prescribed confession 'that [he] had inflicted unjust persecution on the apostolic see and on the whole Church'. The emperor finally made the required statement of abdication and

---

[70] *Annales Hildesheimenses* 1106, p. 55.

[71] Henry IV, *Letter* 37, pp. 49–50. Cf. *Letter* 39, pp. 56–7. See Schramm (1954–6) 514, 633–4; Schramm (1958) 83.

[72] Henry IV, *Letter* 37, p. 49; *Letter* 39, p. 56. The same discrepancy appears in the account of proceedings in Ingelheim and the emperor's departure from Ingelheim: *Letter* 37, p. 50; *Letter* 39, p. 57. Schmeidler (1922) 168–85: *Letter* 39 was an imperial manifesto, intended to prove that the emperor renounced his authority under duress and his abdication was therefore illegal. The threat of 'perpetual captivity' that Henry V actually used (*Letter* 37) seemed inadequate for the polemicist's purpose. See Erdmann (1939) 223–6.

then sought from the cardinal legate absolution from his excommunication. 'The legate replied that he had no right to absolve [him].'[73]

Henry's conduct at the assembly of Ingelheim echoed that at Canossa, twenty-nine years before. The emperor sought to wring absolution from the reluctant legate by a demonstration of penitence as meticulous as that which had forced the hand of Gregory VII in January 1077. Imploring, weeping, prostrating himself at his enemies' feet, he was even prepared to adopt the legate's form of confession which he found so objectionable, if only the legate would absolve him on the spot. The emperor's strength of purpose and his skill as a tactician had not deserted him even in the parlous condition in which he found himself in December 1105. Betrayed and defeated, he could still struggle to gain the absolution which might yet enable him to reverse his enforced abdication.[74] Henry was foiled by Richard of Albano's insistence that he lacked the authority to absolve the emperor from papal excommunication: his case was reserved for the pope alone to decide. The bitterness of this failure to obtain absolution is reflected in the language of the imperial manifesto. The papacy, instead of bringing consolation and salvation, had launched against the emperor 'the scourges of persecution, excommunication and perdition'. The manifesto emphasised the emperor's fears of imminent murder or execution: readers would have known that the one occasion on which a priest was obliged to give absolution, whatever the circumstances, was the imminent death of a penitent (*in articulo mortis*).[75] The legate's refusal to absolve the penitent emperor was represented as the characteristic culmination of the papal persecution of Henry IV.

Having forced the emperor's abdication, the young king and his supporters returned to Mainz. On 5 January the royal insignia arrived in the city. In a ceremony held either on that day or on the next (the seventh anniversary of his coronation in Aachen) Ruothard of Mainz invested the young king with the crown, cross, lance, sceptre and orb. Bishops and princes then did homage to him. It was from this ceremony that Henry V henceforward dated the beginning of his reign.[76] Meanwhile the emperor had been left in Ingelheim.

---

[73] Henry IV, *Letters* 37, 39, pp. 49–50, 56–7; *Annales Hildesheimenses* 1106, p. 55. In *Letter* 39 (intended to gain the sympathy of the German princes) the suggestion that the emperor go to Rome came from the papal legate, while the emperor himself chose to plead his cause before an assembly of princes. *Letter* 37 to Hugh of Cluny avoided criticism of the legate and sought to convince Hugh of the emperor's willingness to be judged by the apostolic see. See Meyer von Knonau (1904) 5:267–70; Schmeidler (1922) 185–213; Waas (1967) 17–19; Servatius (1979) 190–4.   [74] *Casus monasterii Petrishusensis* III.36, p. 657.

[75] Schmeidler (1922) 186–9.

[76] *Annales Hildesheimenses* 1106, p. 55; Ekkehard, *Chronica* I, 1106, p. 204. See Meyer von Knonau (1904) 5:279–80; R. Schmidt (1961) 216–17; Haider (1968) 52; Scheibelreiter (1973) 29–31.

The imperial manifesto reports that, having remained 'for some time' in Ingelheim, awaiting his son's return, the emperor was warned by a message from his vassals that Henry V proposed either to imprison or to execute him. He immediately took ship and travelled down the Rhine to Cologne, where he arrived early in February.[77] Gravely shaken though he must have been by the events of late December, the emperor now resolutely devoted himself to the restoration of his authority.

The emperor spent the last six months of his life recruiting support in Lower Lotharingia. The citizens of Cologne were immediately won over by his tearful recital of his wrongs and remained loyal until his death, even though this involved conflict with their archbishop, Frederick, now an adherent of the young king. The citizens wished to welcome the emperor to Cologne with the ceremonies appropriate to a royal visit, but he declined these honours, wishing to be treated merely 'as a private person'. Similarly, when soon afterwards he visited Aachen, Henry conducted himself as a penitent and one deprived of his office.[78] From Aachen he proceeded to Liège, where he was welcomed by the citizens and Otbert of Liège, the only bishop in Lotharingia, indeed in the kingdom, who is known to have supported the emperor in the last months of his life. Otbert had sworn fealty to Henry V at the assembly of Mainz; but once the emperor escaped to Lotharingia, Otbert returned to his former allegiance. He was tireless in raising money for the imperial cause and ensuring that the Lotharingian nobility did not rally to Henry V. He settled the quarrel between his church and Henry of Limburg, duke of Lower Lotharingia, in order to recruit the latter to the imperial party.[79] The emperor himself negotiated peace between Duke Henry and Count Godfrey of Namur to secure the allegiance of both these rival princes. Count Robert II of Flanders was also drawn into this coalition.[80]

During February or March the emperor issued the two letters containing the imperial version of the events of December 1105. The letter to Abbot Hugh of Cluny, firstly, was a confidential communication intended only for him. It is clear evidence of the central role that his godfather played in Henry's plans in the final months of his life: the abbot was to negotiate peace with the pope. Henry's message was: 'whatever you decide should be done concerning our

---

[77] Henry IV, *Letter* 39, pp. 57–8; cf. *Letter* 37, p. 50. *Vita Heinrici IV* c. 10, p. 35: Henry V granted his father the single estate of Ingelheim to live on. See Meyer von Knonau (1904) 5:270, 286–7.

[78] *Chronicon sancti Huberti Andaginensis* c. 97, p. 629. See Meyer von Knonau (1904) 5:288–9.

[79] *Chronicon sancti Huberti* c. 97, p. 629. Cf. *Annales Hildesheimenses* 1106, p. 56. See Meyer von Knonau (1904) 5:287, 290.

[80] Rudolf of St Trond, *Gesta abbatum Trudonensium* VI.10, 15, 17, pp. 258–60; *Anonymi Chronica imperatorum* III, 1106, p. 242.

reconciliation with the pope and concerning the peace and unity of the holy Roman church, saving our honour, we promise you and God that we shall perform fully and without question.' The final sentence was a postscript written in a different hand: 'Our son proclaims everywhere in his letters that we surrendered all our royal rights willingly, which your holiness knows to be untrue.'[81] It was the necessity of refuting these letters of Henry V (no longer extant) that prompted the composition of the letter addressed to Philip I of France, which was in reality an imperial manifesto, intended for general circulation in Germany.[82] The anonymous author's dramatisation of the emperor's sufferings made a strong impact on twelfth-century readers. Henry IV's grandson, Otto of Freising, thought that 'the letter containing the tragedy of his misfortunes could soften minds of stone, making them contemplate and deplore the miseries of the changing world'.[83]

The emperor planned to celebrate Easter (25 March) in Liège. When he learned of his father's intention, Henry V summoned the princes to an assembly in Liège on that same day. He entered Lotharingia with 'a great army', intending to drive his father from his refuge. To defend the city against an attack from the east, all the crossings over the River Maas were destroyed except the bridge near the town of Visé. On Thursday in Holy Week (22 March) the news reached Liège that Henry V had sent a force of three hundred knights to seize that bridge. Immediately Duke Henry of Lower Lotharingia, his son, Walram, and Count Godfrey of Namur led a force, including citizens of Liège, to repel the attackers. The young king's force suffered severe losses, while the emperor's supporters were unscathed. Henry IV was able to celebrate Easter triumphantly in Liège. Meanwhile news of the encounter at Visé prompted his son to leave Aachen and return to Cologne. The citizens of Cologne, however, now refused him admittance and he was obliged to spend Easter in the fortress of Bonn before returning to Mainz.[84]

The *Life of Emperor Henry IV* cites part of a letter said to have been sent by Henry V to the German princes at this juncture, ordering an expedition to

---

[81] Henry IV, *Letter* 37, pp. 46–51. (This is one of the three Henrician letters, all addressed to Hugh, which survive as originals, preserved in the archive of Cluny.) See Meyer von Knonau (1904) 5:288–9; Erdmann (1939) 186–7.

[82] Henry IV, *Letter* 39, pp. 52–8. See Meyer von Knonau (1904) 5:291–2; Erdmann (1939) 187, 222–7.

[83] Otto, *Chronica* VII.12, p. 324. Cf. Herman of Tournai, *Historia restaurationis abbatiae Tornacensis* c. 84, pp. 314–15.

[84] *Annales Hildesheimenses* 1106, p. 56; Ekkehard, *Chronica* III, 1106, p. 278; *Vita Heinrici IV* c. 11–13, pp. 36–40; Rudolf, *Gesta abbatum Trudonensium* VI.15, p. 260; Sigebert of Gembloux, *Chronica* 1106, p. 371; *Chronicon sancti Huberti* c. 97, p. 629; Herman of Tournai, *Historia restaurationis* c. 84, p. 314. See Meyer von Knonau (1904) 5:296–9, 359–62; Stehkämper (1991) 120–1.

Lotharingia. The letter does not mention his father. The 'proud enemies of the commonwealth' whom he proposed to punish were Otbert of Liège, Henry of Lower Lotharingia and the citizens of Cologne. The king represented the reverse at Visé as an 'insult' to both king and princes. Henry 'had assumed the dignity of the kingship in obedience to [the princes'] commands': his enemies 'intend to depose the king whom you appointed.' 'This is an injury to the kingdom rather than to myself. For the deposition of a leader, even the supreme leader, is a loss to the kingdom that can easily be made good; but to despise the princes is to ruin the kingdom.' The princes must defend their rights as the electors of the king by participating in the Lotharingian expedition, assembling in Würzburg on 1 July.[85] Meanwhile Henry V initiated judicial proceedings against Henry of Lower Lotharingia (13 May). He was deprived of his duchy 'by the judgement of the princes, as one guilty of high treason and as an enemy of the commonwealth'. The king conferred the duchy on Count Godfrey of Louvain.[86]

After celebrating Easter in Liège, the emperor visited Cologne during April. Archbishop Frederick had lost control of his city and fled. Duke Henry of Lower Lotharingia, knowing himself to be the principal target of the young king's expedition, played the leading role in organising the fortifications in Cologne and Liège and in recruiting an army.[87] According to the emperor's anonymous biographer, it was the duke, together with the citizens of Cologne and Liège, who tried to persuade a reluctant Henry IV 'to resume the office of emperor, which he had renounced not of his own free will but as a result of violence and the threat of death'. The emperor 'neither fully consented nor entirely refused', but allowed himself to be carried along by the enthusiasm of his advisers.[88] The anonymous biographer interpreted Henry IV's declining imperial honours and his penitent conduct since his arrival in Lotharingia as a refusal to reclaim his royal office. The biographer chose to portray Henry in the last months of his life as free of all worldly ambition. The demonstration of penitence in Aachen was intended, however, to emphasise Henry's desire for absolution from his excommunication and for reconciliation with the papacy. Like the imperial manifesto, it was part of the campaign to reverse the enforced abdication at Ingelheim. The last four surviving letters of Henry IV were issued in the name of 'Henry, by God's grace, august emperor of the Romans'.[89] They

---

[85] *Vita Heinrici IV* c. 13, pp. 40–1 (*MGH Constitutiones* I, 132–3). Meyer von Knonau (1904) 5:299–300 with n. 39: an authentic letter, stylistically improved by the author of the *Vita*.

[86] *Anonymi Chronica imperatorum* 1106, p. 242. See Meyer von Knonau (1904) 5:300–1.

[87] *Annales Hildesheimenses* 1106, p. 56. See Meyer von Knonau (1904) 5:301–2; Stehkämper (1991) 122–4.

[88] *Vita Heinrici IV* c. 13, p. 41. But see Ekkehard, *Chronica* III, 1106, p. 278.

[89] Henry IV, *Letters* 39–42, pp. 52–64.

reveal not the Henry of the anonymous biography, broken-spirited and resigned to his fate, but an emperor bent on the recovery of his rights. The context of these last letters was Henry V's second Lotharingian expedition of 1106 and his three or four-week siege of Cologne. The young king began the siege at the beginning of July, but his army made no impact on the well defended city. Unexpectedly high casualties, the oppressive heat of the summer and lack of provisions eventually compelled the king's withdrawal to Aachen.[90]

The emperor had already returned to Liège before the siege of Cologne began. Here he issued the final letters of his reign, the first reiterating his request for help to the abbot of Cluny,[91] the other three continuing the propaganda war against the young king. During the siege of Cologne envoys arrived in Henry V's camp with letters from the emperor for the young king and for the princes. Both these letters have survived in a number of manuscripts, suggesting that the emperor sent copies not only to Cologne but also throughout the kingdom. The letter to Henry V was addressed 'to his son H[enry]' without any royal title and without a greeting. Rebuking the young king for his unfilial conduct, the emperor warned him that his treachery in December 1105 was now common knowledge. The young king had justified his actions on the grounds that his father had been excommunicated by the pope and was the enemy of the Church. This justification, however, was no longer valid: 'as far as the lord pope and the Roman church are concerned, you no longer have any pretext.' The emperor was willing, as he had been at Ingelheim, to declare his obedience to the papal legate. There was no reason, therefore, why his son should not restore to him all that he had unjustly taken away: otherwise the emperor would appeal for justice to the holy see.[92]

Henry IV's letter to the princes complains of Henry V's treachery and emphasises the emperor's desire for reconciliation with the papacy. The letter to Henry V had pointed out that the emperor's desire for reconciliation deprived his son of the pretext for rebellion. The letter to the princes declared that the young king's pretext had always been a false one. He had merely feigned devotion to the papacy and ecclesiastical reform to gain control of his father's kingdom. The emperor, however, intended to be a reformer in real earnest. He was 'prepared to take the decisions concerning the state of the Church and the honour of the kingdom, as far as this concern[ed him], on the advice of [the princes] and [his] spiritual father, Abbot Hugh of Cluny, and other religious men'.[93] The emperor and his advisers may well have known of Paschal II's letter of 11 November 1105 to the archbishop of Mainz,

---

[90] Ekkehard, *Chronica* III, 1106, p. 280; *Annales Hildesheimenses* 1106, pp. 56–7. See Meyer von Knonau (1904) 5:302–3.   [91] Henry IV, *Letter* 38, pp. 51–2.   [92] *Ibid.* 40, pp. 58–60.
[93] *Ibid.* 41, pp. 61–3.

introducing the issue of lay investiture into the relations of Henry V and the papacy. Since the young king had already invested four candidates with bishoprics, he seemed destined to come into conflict with the pope.[94] In expressing concern for 'the state of the Church', the emperor was angling for the support of disenchanted Gregorians in his son's party.

Henry V caused the two letters to be read to his assembled supporters before deciding what reply to make. The resultant letter, composed 'on the advice of the princes', was read to his army by Archbishop Henry of Magdeburg. Its main purpose was to reclaim for the young king the role of champion of Church and papacy. After nearly forty years of schism unity was now restored through the deposition of 'the incorrigible leader of schism, our so-called Emperor Henry' and the election of a 'catholic king'. Although he voluntarily renounced his authority, however, the emperor now 'complains to the whole world that he has suffered an injustice'.[95] To avert a resumption of the schism and clear themselves of any suspicion of injustice, Henry V and the princes invited the emperor to put his case before an assembly of the princes and the people at a place of his own choosing. The emperor's reply to his enemies was that they should at once dismiss their army and meet him in an assembly in due course. Soon after this exchange, probably towards the end of July, the deteriorating situation of his army outside Cologne compelled the young king to withdraw to Aachen.[96] Believing that the emperor and Duke Henry of Lower Lotharingia were raising an army, Henry V once more sent envoys to Liège. Their message was that the emperor should meet his son in Aachen to negotiate peace terms: otherwise a battle was inevitable.

These envoys carried back to Aachen the emperor's last letter, issued probably at the beginning of August. This letter contrasted the emperor's peaceful intentions with the belligerency of his opponents. He desired a peaceful discussion of his injuries and a peace settlement 'for the honour of the kingdom'; the young king wished 'under the pretext of a conference to march against [the emperor] and [his] vassals with an army, granting a truce of eight days'. Henry IV demanded that at least the truce should be extended to give him time to seek the advice of the princes who would play a leading role in any conference between the emperor and his opponents: the archbishops of Mainz, Trier and Bremen, the bishops of Freising, Augsburg, Chur and Basel, the dukes of Saxony, Upper Lotharingia and Bohemia, the count of Flanders, Count William of Burgundy 'and others'. The emperor appealed to the princes to persuade Henry V to participate in a peace conference. If he refused to desist

---

[94] Paschal II, *JL* 6050: 174D–175D. See above p. 328.

[95] Ekkehard, *Chronica* III, 1106, pp. 282–4. See Erdmann (1939) 228.

[96] Ekkehard, *Chronica* III, 1106, p. 286; *Annales Patherbrunnenses* 1106, p. 114. See Meyer von Knonau (1904) 5:307–11.

from his persecution of his father, let the princes at least not aid him. Once more the emperor proclaimed his intention of appealing to the pope against his son's treatment.[97]

Soon after receiving this letter, Henry V learned of the sudden death of his father, which removed at once the threat of civil war. Henry IV died after nine days of illness on 7 August 1106. Present at his deathbed in Liège were his faithful chamberlain, the *ministerialis* Erkenbold, and an illustrious prisoner, Bishop Burchard of Münster.[98] The dying emperor entrusted to them his ring and his sword. These were to be brought to Henry V, together with his father's last two requests: that the young king pardon all those who had stood by the emperor in his last months and arrange for the emperor to be buried among his forebears in the cathedral of Speyer.[99] The emperor's biographer ascribed to his hero a tranquil Christian death, as also did the author of the Bamberg chronicle. 'Those who were present report that he ended his life after making a good confession and not without great courage. After he had disposed of all his possessions and had sent envoys both to the pope and to his son the king, he received viaticum and died, like one falling asleep.'[100] The question of how the news of the emperor's death was received in the kingdom was answered by the chroniclers according to their personal sympathies. The hostile Ekkehard of Aura reported that 'the hearts and voices of all true Christians . . . were filled with boundless delight by the rumour of his death', like the children of Israel rejoicing at the death of Pharaoh (Exodus 15:1–4). The anonymous biographer wrote that, while Henry V's entourage rejoiced, elsewhere 'the princes lamented, the people wept'.[101]

The emperor's faithful adherent, Bishop Otbert of Liège, gave his lord a burial befitting his rank before the altar of St Mary in the cathedral of Liège, until such time as he could be buried, according to his last wish, in Speyer. When Henry V reported this burial to an assembly of princes in Aachen, the archbishops and bishops advised him to exhume the body at once. As the body of an excommunicate, it must remain in an unconsecrated place until the pope absolved the deceased emperor from his excommunication. On 15 August, therefore, the emperor's body was removed to an unconsecrated chapel outside

---

[97] Henry IV, *Letter* 42, pp. 63–4.
[98] Burchard abandoned the imperial cause at the end of 1105. Driven from his diocese by his *ministeriales*, allied with Count Frederick of Arnsberg, he took refuge in the Rhineland. He was recognised and delivered to the emperor: *Annales Patherbrunnenses* 1106, p. 114. See Meyer von Knonau (1904) 5:313.
[99] *Annales Hildesheimenses* 1106, p. 57; Ekkehard, *Chronica* III, 1106, p. 286; Sigebert, *Chronica* 1106, p. 371. See Meyer von Knonau (1904) 5:313–15.
[100] *Anonymi Chronica imperatorum* III, 1106, p. 244. Cf. *Vita Heinrici IV* c. 13, p. 43.
[101] Ekkehard, *Chronica* III, 1106, p. 286; *Vita Heinrici IV* c. 13, p. 43.

Liège, where it was reinterred without a religious service. On 24 August, however, the body was exhumed again and brought back to the city. Messengers had arrived from the king, who had now decided that, in accordance with his last request, his father's body should be brought to Speyer. The bier was now seized by the citizens of Liège, in an attempt to reinter it in the cathedral.[102] The Verdun manuscript of the chronicle of Sigebert of Gembloux records a number of instances of the reverence shown to the emperor's body by the people of the region, evidence of the sacral character ascribed to royal graves. They believed that contact with the bier brought a blessing and some placed seedcorn on the bier to ensure a good harvest, while others took earth from the grave and scattered it on their fields and through their houses. It was with difficulty that Henry V's envoys removed the emperor's body from Liège, since the populace was convinced that its departure would bring them ruin.[103]

On 25 August the king entrusted some of his father's faithful servants, notably the chamberlain Erkenbold, with the task of bringing the emperor's body in its stone sarcophagus to Speyer. The cortège was honourably received in the city on 3 September and the sarcophagus brought into the cathedral; but Bishop Gebhard of Speyer intervened, commanding the removal of the body to an unconsecrated chapel. His action provoked 'tumult and great lamentation among the people', who continued to visit and show reverence to the unburied body. Five years passed before Henry IV found his last resting-place in the cathedral which he had rebuilt and adorned. In 1111, the year of Henry V's triumph over the papacy, the new emperor obtained from Paschal II permission to place his father in consecrated ground. On the fifth anniversary of his death, 7 August 1111, Henry IV was buried next to his father in Speyer cathedral. The unusual splendour of the burial, attended by 'a very numerous assembly of bishops and other princes', was evidently planned by Henry V as a celebration of his recent victory in his conflict with Paschal II concerning lay investiture. Henry IV, 'the incorrigible leader of schism' was now transformed into Henry V's 'dear father, Emperor Henry of happy memory'.[104]

---

[102] *Annales Patherbrunnenses* 1106, p. 115; *Annales Hildesheimenses* 1106, p. 57; Ekkehard, *Chronica* III, 1106, p. 288; See Meyer von Knonau (1907) 6:7–10.

[103] Sigebert, *Chronica* 1106, p. 371, variant d. See above p. 98.

[104] *Annales Patherbrunnenses* 1111, p. 125; Ekkehard, *Chronica* III, 1111, pp. 304–6. See Meyer von Knonau (1907) 6:206–9; Heidrich (1991) 215–16. The opening of Henry IV's grave in 1900: Grauert (1900) 579–80.

Conclusion

'He governed the Roman empire for fifty years. Sometimes he dutifully took care of those Romans who were well-disposed towards him; sometimes he resisted, as was necessary, those ingrates who attempted to humble the royal power in Germany. He was vigorous and warlike, accustomed to give everyone his due, according to age and circumstances, and he could hardly bear to be ignorant of anything. Like his father, he wished to have clerks at his side, especially those who were learned. He treated them honourably and spent his time amicably among them, sometimes in singing psalms, sometimes in reading or conversation or in discussion of the scriptures or the liberal arts. We could also prove from the evidence of very many witnesses that no one in our times seemed more fitted for the office of emperor, by birth, intelligence, courage and boldness and also by stature and bodily grace.'[1] This is the obituary of Henry IV in the Bamberg chronicle dedicated to Henry V (1112/3). This work was subsequently used by Abbot Ekkehard of Aura as a source for his own chronicle. He retained the observation that 'no one in our times seemed more fitted for the office of emperor', but added a proviso which entirely negated the praise of the Bamberg chronicler: 'if only the inner man had not degenerated and surrendered in the battle with the vices!' The rest of Ekkehard's revised obituary is a catalogue of the anti-Henrician allegations of the past thirty years. Henry was 'called by catholics – that is, by all those preserving fealty and obedience to St Peter and his successors – [not emperor but] archpirate and heresiarch and apostate and persecutor of souls more than bodies'.[2] The contrast between these two obituaries of the emperor encapsulates the problem of drawing an objective portrait of Henry IV. On the subject of the emperor's personality the sources cancel each other out.

The anonymous biography of the emperor presents a Henry IV who 'sometimes bore the character of an emperor, sometimes that of a mere knight, providing, in the first instance, a model of dignified behaviour and, in the second,

---

[1] *Anonymi Chronica imperatorum* III, 1106, p. 244. Authorship: above p. 327 n. 31.
[2] Ekkehard of Aura, *Chronica* III, 1106, pp. 288–90.

a model of humility'. 'He presented such a subtle intellect and such great wisdom' that he could resolve judicial and political problems that defeated the ingenuity of the princes. Nevertheless 'he spoke little; he did not insist on giving his opinion first, but waited for that of others'.[3] This portrait of a ruler who 'crushed the oppressors of the poor, delivered up robbers to be plundered and defeated the insolent who rebelled against his power' echoes the portrayal of Henry IV in the narrative poem, *Song of the Saxon War*, composed thirty years before. The hero of this earlier work was a 'king second to none in his piety', 'whom no enemy encountered with impunity'. To the lawless Saxons 'he gave laws; he tamed them by force; he demanded the return of whatever had been violently seized from churches, widows and the poor. Hereafter no robber went unpunished.'[4]

The chroniclers who wrote in defence of the Saxon and Thuringian rebels described Henry IV in exactly opposite terms. Lampert of Hersfeld claimed that, as a result of Henry's misgovernment, 'the churches and monasteries were destroyed; provision for the servants of God was converted into income for knights. Zeal for religion and for the affairs of the Church was transferred to weapons and the building of fortresses, not to ward off the violent attacks of the barbarians but to disturb the peace of the fatherland and place on the necks of free men the yoke of harshest servitude. Nowhere was there comfort for widows and orphans, refuge for the oppressed and persecuted, reverence for the laws.' Henry IV had 'received from his ancestors a most peaceful kingdom, in every way flourishing, and had rendered it filthy, despicable, bloodstained, a prey to internal conflicts . . . The majesty of the empire was destroyed, the authority of the princes cancelled.'[5] The even more vituperative account of Bruno of Merseburg declared that Henry IV was guilty of every possible crime. 'He committed so many abominable murders that it is uncertain which was the greater infamy, that of his incestuous lust or that of his boundless cruelty. He was horribly cruel to all men, but to none more than to his confidants in his own household.'[6] The Swabian chroniclers of the Gregorian party, equally hostile, wrote that Henry 'assailed [his subjects] with robbery and plundering and every kind of affliction'[7] and 'ceaselessly defiled holy Church with simoniacal heresy'. 'His thoughts turned to tyranny and he planned to hold the kingship not by justice but by violence'.[8]

---

[3] *Vita Heinrici IV* c. 1, pp. 11–12.

[4] *Carmen de bello Saxonico* 1.8, 10, 22–4, pp. 1–2. Schluck (1979); Beumann (1984) 305–19: whether the *Vita* was the work of the poet of the *Carmen*.

[5] Lampert of Hersfeld, *Annales* 1076, pp. 277–9.

[6] Bruno of Merseburg, *Saxonicum bellum* c. 10, p. 18; cf. c. 5–9, 11–14, pp. 16–18, 19–22.

[7] Berthold of Reichenau, *Annales* 1077, p. 298.

[8] Bernold of St Blasien, *Chronicon* 1076, 1077, pp. 431, 434.

The bitter conflict in Saxony, the unprecedented excommunication of the king by the pope and the election of anti-kings by the 'deposition faction' of German princes produced a historical literature entirely polemical in character, the work of Henrician and anti-Henrician historians who viewed the conflicts of the last three decades of the reign entirely in black-and-white terms. The transition from chronicler to polemicist was easy enough, given that eleventh-century scholars, imitating the practice of ancient and patristic authors, treated history primarily as a source of *exempla*, examples of correct or incorrect behaviour. Historical personages were studied primarily as models of good or evil conduct. Eleventh-century historical method is well illustrated by the treatise composed by the Gregorian polemicist Manegold of Lautenbach *circa* 1085. The treatise contains a catalogue of wicked rulers who deservedly lost their thrones. Manegold represented Henry IV as the most recent example of a monarch whose private vices and public crimes necessitated his deposition.[9] The most important *exempla* of virtuous and wicked kings were to be found in the Old Testament. The historical books of the Old Testament provided eleventh-century chroniclers with their most influential model, reinforcing their tendency to attribute the upheavals of their times to the personal failings of their rulers. Contemporary authors readily compared Henry IV to Old Testament kings. Gregory VII and his supporters saw him as Saul, the king rejected by God; the pope himself being the prophet Samuel, whom God commanded to provide a new king (1 Samuel 16:1).[10] Henry IV's adherents saw him as David and the rebel Henry V as Absalom (2 Samuel 15:10–12).[11] Ekkehard of Aura preferred the parallels of Nebuchadnezzar and the wicked grand vizier Haman.[12] Lampert of Hersfeld juxtaposed a modern and an ancient *exemplum* in order to convey how Henry IV disappointed his subjects after he came of age. 'He promised that he would play the role of Charlemagne in his own age, but the role that he played was that of Rehoboam.'[13]

Henrician and anti-Henrician historians drew their political assumptions from a common fund of early medieval writings, of which the most influential were two seventh-century texts: the discussion of righteous kingship in the Irish treatise, *The Twelve Abuses* (falsely attributed in the manuscripts to Cyprian or Augustine) and the definition of kingship and tyranny given in the encyclopaedic works of Isidore of Seville, the *Etymologies* and the *Sentences*. The anonymous Irish author ('Pseudo-Cyprian') defined the duties of kingship as exercising power without oppressing others, judging impartially,

---

[9] Manegold of Lautenbach, *Liber ad Gebehardum* c. 29, pp. 361–5. See von Moos (1988) 67; Vollrath (1991) 292–6.   [10] See above pp. 141, 288.

[11] Henry IV, *Letter* 37, p. 47; *Vita* c. 9, p. 32.   [12] Ekkehard, *Chronica* III, 1106, p. 290.

[13] Lampert, *Libellus de institutione* p. 353 (1 Kings 12:12–20).

defending strangers, orphans and widows; he must prevent robbery, punish adultery and give alms to the poor. He must place the administration of the kingdom in the hands of good men, have as his counsellors only the old and wise and defend his kingdom justly and valiantly against enemies.[14] Isidore of Seville wrote that the principal virtues of a king were 'justice' and 'piety', by means of which he 'corrected' the people. Echoing the definition of Augustine, Isidore declared that 'kings are so called from the fact that they act righteously (*reges a recte agendo vocati sunt*). Thus the title of king is retained by righteous conduct, but is lost by sinning.' A ruler who governed without justice and piety was no king but a tyrant. While kings were 'moderate and sober', tyrants were 'cruel', 'impious and savage'.[15]

It was on these definitions that both Henrician and anti-Henrician historians based their portraits of Henry IV. The *Song of the Saxon War* and the anonymous *Life* of the emperor echoed Pseudo-Cyprian's description of the just king. Henry was the protector of 'churches, widows and the poor', 'second to none in his piety', who punished robbers and defeated his enemies.[16] Lampert of Hersfeld, however, adopted the language of Isidore. Henry 'attacked the innocent in his own kingdom with barbarous cruelty'; his conduct in Saxony and Thuringia was 'manifest tyranny'.[17] Bruno of Merseburg similarly justified the rebellion of the Saxons with the argument that Henry had 'ceased to be king' and was merely a 'cruel tyrant'.[18] Berthold of Reichenau interpolated Isidore's remarks on tyrants in his account of the events of 1077 in order to justify the actions of the 'deposition faction' of princes.[19] The failings of Henry IV most frequently mentioned in the anti-Henrician chronicles are public vices particularly emphasised in the descriptions of Pseudo-Cyprian and Isidore of the archetypal wicked king. He lacked the qualities of a warlord; he exploited, rather than defended the Church; he listened to the advice of evil counsellors. Tyrant that he was, he imposed on his subjects an innovatory style of government, rejecting 'the laws and the custom of his predecessors'. This portrait of Henry IV as a 'cruel tyrant' owes more to the political thought of Pseudo-Cyprian and Isidore of Seville than to objective commentary.

Concerning the first allegation, that Henry was ineffective as a military commander and was indeed a coward, the rival sources seem to cancel each other out. The earliest hostile reference is Berthold of Reichenau's account of the

[14] *De XII abusivis* [*saeculi*] ed. Hellmann pp. 43–5, 51–3. See also the study of Breen (1988).
[15] Isidore of Seville, *Etymologiae* IX.3.20; cf. 1.31, II.29.7; *Sententiae* III.48–9.
[16] *Carmen de bello Saxonico* I.8, 22–4, pp. 1–2; *Vita Heinrici IV* c. 1, p. 12.
[17] Lampert, *Annales* 1073, p. 141. Cf. 1076, p. 270. See Struve (1970) 95–101.
[18] Bruno, *Saxonicum bellum* c. 25, 84, 96, pp. 29, 80, 89. See Kost (1962) 43–65, 169–77, 181–3.
[19] Berthold, *Annales* 1077, p. 297.

battle of Mellrichstadt (7 August 1078), according to which 'the king shame-fully was the first to flee, together with his close friends'.[20] Bruno of Merseburg cited two different instances of Henry's cowardice in battle: at Flarchheim (27 January 1080) and at Hohenmölsen (15 October 1080).[21] The chronicler Bernold of St Blasien reported similar conduct at the battle of Pleichfeld (11 August 1086).[22] The pro-Henrician sources present a different picture. The anonymous poet of the *Song of the Saxon War* described how at the battle of Homburg (9 June 1075) 'the brave king rushed into the midst of the enemy'.[23] An anonymous poem of 1084 describes Henry's siege and capture of Rome in similar terms. 'King Henry the Terrible surrounded the walls of Rome, laid ambushes and destroyed very many of the citizens . . . Mounted on his lofty steed, he marshalled his wrathful forces and slaughtered the Roman ranks.'[24] In the Augsburg chronicler's version of the battle of Pleichfeld, Henry 'fero-ciously charged the well-prepared enemy', only to be endangered by the unex-pected retreat of his own army.[25] The anonymous biographer's account of the battle of Pleichfeld likewise places Henry in the thick of the battle and in great danger. 'Certain knights of the royal party, who had stayed close to the king's side like faithful followers, but who had actually been bribed, suddenly turned their weapons on him.' The biographer portrayed Henry IV as an emperor who was capable of assuming 'the character of . . . a mere knight' and of a warlord who 'defeated the insolent who rebelled against his power'.[26] The Bamberg chronicle of 1112/3 describes Henry as 'vigorous and warlike', well able to resist 'those ingrates who attempted to humble the royal power'.[27] Ekkehard of Aura (for whom the Bamberg chronicle was an important source) was the only anti-Henrician chronicler who did not portray the emperor as an ineffectual coward. Instead he chose to represent him as a bloodthirsty warlord like the heathen emperors who had persecuted the Church in ancient times.[28]

Henry IV was defeated in all the major battles which he fought on German soil, with the single exception of Homburg. At Mellrichstadt, Flarchheim, Hohenmölsen, Pleichfeld and the lesser engagement of Gleichen (2 December 1088) Henry's army was compelled to withdraw from the field. Even in the case of Homburg (9 June 1075), contemporaries ascribed the victory over the Saxon rebels to Rudolf of Rheinfelden and his

[20] *Ibid.*, 1078, p. 312. Cf. 1080, p. 325 (Flarchheim).
[21] Bruno, *Saxonicum bellum* c. 117, 122, pp. 110, 115. Cf. Bonizo of Sutri, *Ad amicum* IX, p. 613 (Hohenmölsen).   [22] Bernold, *Chronicon* 1086, p. 445.
[23] *Carmen de bello Saxonico* III.167–8, p. 19. Cf. III.44–5, 170–1, pp. 15, 19.
[24] *MGH Libelli* I, 433.
[25] *Annales Augustani* 1086, p. 132. Cf. *Mariani Chronici Continuatio* II, 1108(=1086), pp. 563–4.
[26] *Vita Heinrici IV* c. 1, 4, pp. 11, 12, 18.   [27] *Anonymi Chronica imperatorum* III, 1106, p. 244.
[28] Ekkehard, *Chronica* III, 1106, p. 290.

Swabian contingent rather than to Henry himself.[29] The only observation that can safely be made about Henry IV's military operations in Germany is that they were unprecedented in their scale and their intensity. In the eleven years between June 1075 and August 1086 Henry fought five pitched battles; while a sixth battle was fought on the same day as his battle of Mellrichstadt (7 August 1078) by the Franconian peasant army which he had stationed on the Neckar to prevent the junction of his Saxon and south German enemies. Eleventh-century commanders usually tried at all costs to avoid battles, because of the impossibility of controlling the outcome: 'In a fairly evenly balanced situation a few minutes of confusion or panic and the patient work of months or even years might be undone.' A battle was a 'perilous moment [at which] events were felt to move out of human control and into the hands of God'.[30] Commanders preferred instead the war of attrition: laying siege to castles, devastating the surrounding countryside, collecting plunder; vict-ualling and rewarding the army at the enemy's expense, until the enemy was forced to accept their terms.

Henry IV frequently fought such campaigns of attrition during the years 1077–88; but he was also prepared to risk battle far more often than other eleventh-century commanders. Perhaps the reason for this was the large number of non-noble warriors in his armies, whom he may have regarded as more expendable than knights.[31] Bruno of Merseburg described the force which Henry led against the anti-king Rudolf in the autumn of 1077 as 'an army neither great nor strong, for it was composed for the most part of mer-chants': a reminder of the contribution that the citizens of Worms, Mainz and Cologne made to Henry's military effort. Henry's Saxon opponents were willing to accept the repeated challenge of battle because their armies were swelled by large numbers of peasants.[32]

Only at Homburg was Henry's high risk strategy successful.[33] The five battles of 1078–86 explain why more prudent eleventh-century commanders preferred to avoid risking a pitched battle. At Mellrichstadt the anti-king Rudolf fled in the mistaken belief that his army was disintegrating and was consequently unable to exploit the success of his allies, Otto of Northeim and Frederick of Sommerschenburg, who drove the Henrician army from the battlefield.[34] At Flarchheim the royal army came near to success with a skilful encircling movement, only to falter on encountering much fiercer resistance than had been anticipated.[35] At Hohenmölsen the royal army twice began to celebrate a victory, believing the Saxons to be routed, only to be disappointed

---

[29] Schmeidler (1927) 374.   [30] Gillingham (1989) 145, 147, 149. Cf. Leyser (1994) 14.
[31] Bruno, *Saxonicum bellum* c. 95, p. 88; Bernold, *Chronicon* 1078, p. 435. See above p. 176.
[32] Bruno c. 31, p. 34; Lampert, *Annales* 1075, p. 216.   [33] See above pp. 100–1.
[34] See above pp. 181–2.   [35] See above p. 193.

by a counter-attack by Otto of Northeim.[36] At Pleichfeld panic among the Lotharingian contingent in the royal army contributed to a general flight.[37] Why Henry continued to pursue his unorthodox and unrewarding strategy during 1078–86 is impossible to determine. Perhaps he had been dazzled by the initial victory at Homburg in 1075 and dreamed of repeating it. Perhaps there was in his character a streak of reckless audacity which neither Henrician nor anti-Henrician chroniclers chose to record. Most probably he was desperate to solve the problem of the German anti-kings without participating in the 'conferences' demanded by the Gregorian papacy. Victory in battle seemed to be the easiest way out of his difficulties.

The polemicists' allegation that Henry IV was an impious despoiler of the Church has prompted more scholarly discussion than any other aspect of his reign. The anti-Henrician reports of the king's encounter with Gregory VII at Canossa emphasising Henry's 'pretended reconciliation' and 'pretence of unprecedented humiliation'[38] have inspired the interpretation of Henry's penance as a ruse to outmanoeuvre the German princes, evidence of his skill as a politician rather than of his anxiety to be absolved from excommunication.[39] Similarly, the Gregorian reports that he 'ceaselessly defiled holy Church with simoniacal heresy'[40] have prompted the view that Henry was unsympathetic to the ideas of ecclesiastical reformers, perhaps incapable of appreciating how influential such ideas could be.[41] The pro-Henrician sources, of course, portray their hero as 'the most pious emperor'.[42] The most famous example is the passage in the imperial letter to King Philip I of France, describing Henry's treatment in the castle of Böckelheim in December 1105. 'This I shall never forget; of this I shall never cease to complain to all Christians: that during the most holy days [of Christmastide] I was in prison without Christian communion.'[43] In the account of these events sent to his godfather, Abbot Hugh I of Cluny, the emperor complained that, although he had good reason to believe himself to be near death, he had no access to a priest who could give him viaticum or hear his confession.[44] The public expressions of Henry's piety during the great Christian festivals form the framework of the chronicles of the reign, even those written by hostile authors. These liturgical spectacles were demonstrations of royal authority as well as religious observances, especially when at Christmas, Easter and Whitsun they were marked by 'crown-wearings',

---

[36] See above pp. 203–4.   [37] See above p. 261.
[38] Berthold, *Annales* 1077, pp. 289, 291; Bernold, *Chronicon* 1077, p. 433; Bruno, *Saxonicum bellum* c. 90, p. 84.   [39] Von Giesebrecht (1890) 491.
[40] Bernold, *Chronicon* 1076, p. 431.   [41] Hampe (English translation: 1973) 68, 69.
[42] *Annales Aquenses* 1106, p. 37. Cf. *Mariani Chronici Continuatio* 1108(=1086) p. 564.
[43] Henry IV, *Letter* 39, pp. 55–6. See above pp. 335–6.   [44] Henry IV, *Letter* 37, p. 49.

involving a solemn procession in which the monarch appeared with all the insignia of his office.[45]

More significant is the fragmentary evidence of Henry's private devotions. An anecdote referring to his residence in Rome in April or May 1084 mentions incidentally that 'the emperor was accustomed frequently to go to prayer in the church of St Mary, which is on the Aventine hill'.[46] In June 1095, at a low ebb in his fortunes, the emperor 'was moved by devotion to come to Venice to show reverence to St Mark'. (The relics of the patron saint of the city had been translated eight months before to the newly built church of St Mark.)[47] Important evidence of the emperor's personal piety was preserved in the circle of Bishop Otto I of Bamberg. The Bamberg chronicle of 1112/3 recorded that 'like his father, [Henry] wished to have clerks at his side, especially those who were learned . . . and spent his time amicably among them, sometimes in singing psalms, sometimes in reading or conversation or in discussion of the scriptures or of the liberal arts'.[48] Bishop Otto's biographer described how the emperor 'spent his time with [Otto], apart from all the rest, singing psalms whenever he could escape from business'. Otto earned the emperor's gratitude by providing a new binding for his psalter after the old cover was worn-out from constant use.[49] Henry's delight in psalm-singing was also noticed by the anonymous clerk who, at the 'crown-wearing' in Liège at Easter 1101, observed that 'amidst the joyous applause of all the people, [the emperor] dwelled very diligently on the psalmody'.[50] Twelfth-century historians remembered Henry as 'so well instructed in letters that he could read for himself and understand any documents that were sent to him'.[51]

Sixty years after Henry's death the chronicler Helmold of Bosau recorded a legendary version of the emperor's last days, including an appeal which he made to the bishop of Speyer after his forced abdication. 'Give me a prebend in Speyer so that I may serve my lady, the mother of God, to whom I have always been devoted. For I know my letters and I can still serve in the choir.'[52] Despite its legendary character, this anecdote draws on authentic elements of

[45] Klewitz (1939) 54–5. Henry IV's 'crown-wearing' in Liège, Easter 1101: Dümmler (1900) 205–6; Morin (1910) 412–15. Date of this text: Meyer von Knonau (1904) 5:114 n. 3; Klewitz (1939) 55. See above pp. 14, 80, 149, 150, 151, 174, 242.

[46] Beno, *Gesta Romanae aecclesiae* i.5, p. 371. St Mary on the Aventine was the monastery where the abbot of Cluny resided when visiting Rome.   [47] *D H IV* 445. See above p. 294.

[48] *Anonymi Chronica imperatorum* iii, 1106, p. 244.

[49] Ebo of Michelsberg, *Vita Ottonis Babenbergensis* i.6, pp. 826–7.

[50] The author addressed to Henry a Latin commentary on the seven penitential psalms, with a request for employment: Dümmler (1900) 205–6; Morin (1910) 412–15.

[51] Ebo, *Vita Ottonis* i.6, p. 594. Cf. William of Malmesbury, *Gesta regum Anglorum* iii.289, p. 343. See Erdmann (1939) 246–7; Mikoletzky (1960) 250–65; Struve (1987) 338–42; Tellenbach (1988) 365–7.   [52] Helmold of Bosau, *Cronica Slavorum* i.33, pp. 64–5.

Henry IV's personal piety: his delight in psalmody, his devotion to the Virgin Mary, his attachment to the church of St Mary in Speyer. 'Of all the churches of his kingdom,' wrote the Bamberg chronicler, 'he cared especially for that of Speyer and rebuilt and adorned it with royal magnificence.'[53] The twenty-one royal and imperial privileges for Speyer provide the clearest insights into Henry's personal religion, in which his cultivation of the memory of the ancestors who lay buried in the cathedral was inseparable from his veneration for the Virgin Mary. He regarded her as his 'protectress' and the special patron of his dynasty. 'Our fathers found refuge in her mercy and we also, under her protection, seek succour in the church of Speyer, which is especially called by her name.'[54] The Speyer diplomas concentrate on the *memoria* of Henry himself and of the ancestors for whom the cathedral served as mausoleum.[55] Other diplomas, however, illustrate Henry's wider preoccupation with the commemoration of the dead. An imperial privilege of 15 May 1097 for the monastery of St Georgen was issued 'for the relief of our soul and of those of our father Emperor Henry, our mother Empress Agnes, our wife Bertha and our other kindred and of those of our vassals who were slain or met their deaths in our service'.[56] A privilege of 30 March 1079 for the church of Osnabrück stipulated 'that in perpetuity on every Tuesday a special mass is to be sung by the brethren in the choir for the soul of our dear servant Siegfried and for the souls of those who fell in battle, defending our honour'.[57] Henry IV's diplomas declare in an unprecedented manner the ruler's responsibility to care for the *memoria* of his vassals and servants (*fideles, milites, servientes*).[58] It was an acknowledgement of the loyalty of those who had died defending the royal honour, the victims of the great crisis of the German kingship.

'The cathedral churches have lost their protector, the monasteries their father', wrote the anonymous biographer after the emperor's death. 'The good that he did them, the honour that he conferred on them will at last be recognised, now that he is no more.'[59] The privileges which Henry bestowed on the churches of the empire, with a generosity equal to that of his predecessors, were linked with his preoccupation with his own *memoria* and that of his dynasty and his faithful followers. In the case of the Sabine abbey of Farfa, the property of which he restored and augmented in four privileges, he was received 'into the fraternity of perpetual prayer . . . His name and those of certain of his vassals were written in the memorial book.'[60] He was similarly

---

[53] *Anonymi Chronica* III, 1106, p. 244. See above pp. 202–3, 257–8, 308.
[54] *D H IV* 325. See above pp. 203, 258, 308.   [55] See above pp. 203, 258, 266, 308.
[56] *D H IV* 454.   [57] *D H IV* 310.
[58] Schmid (1984a) 713–16; Schmid (1984b) 247–58, 260–4.   [59] *Vita Heinrici IV* c. 1, p. 9.
[60] Gregory of Catino, *Historiae Farfenses* c. 8, p. 561. See Schwarzmaier (1968) 122; Wollasch (1984) 4–5. See also above p. 218.

received into the fraternity of the monastery of Subiaco, with which his mother had close connections.[61] In the German kingdom his name is found among 'the brethren of our congregation' in the memorial book of the abbey of Echternach.[62] There was perhaps an analogy between this commemoration of the monarch in the monastic brotherhood of prayer and the frequently studied but still mysterious institution of the honorary royal canonry. A royal diploma of 1063 describes the canons of SS. Simon and Jude in Goslar as the young king's 'brethren' (*confratres*).[63] The name of Henry IV appears in the memorial book of the cathedral of Speyer.[64] This representation of the monarch as a 'brother' of the cathedral chapter has been interpreted by some commentators as an expression of the king's sacrality, of the quasi-priestly status which he assumed after his coronation and consecration as 'the Lord's anointed'. The relatively sparse evidence for the reign of Henry IV has contributed little to the debate about the significance of the royal canonries in the eleventh century.[65] It is possible that for a monarch preoccupied, as Henry was, with his own *memoria*, the importance of being a 'brother' of the canons, as in being a 'brother' of the monks, was that he was received into 'the fraternity of perpetual prayer'.

Henry's reputation as an enemy of the churches and monasteries was the work of a group of monastic chroniclers: Lampert of Hersfeld, the anonymous monk of Stablo, author of *The Triumph of St Remaclus*, Berthold of Reichenau and Bernold of St Blasien. Their allegations that 'the churches and monasteries were destroyed' derived mainly from monastic grievances of 1063 and 1065 (when Henry was still under the tutelage of Archbishop Adalbert of Bremen) and of 1071 (the year of the synod of Mainz, in which the cathedral clergy of Constance accused their bishop of simony). Adalbert of Bremen persuaded the king to grant royal abbeys to him and other princes. The consequence of these transactions of 1063 and 1065 was that thirteen royal abbeys lost their *libertas*: that is, royal protection and the rights that went with it, including immunity from the intervention of secular officials and freedom to elect the abbot. Lampert dwelt on this deplorable loss of monastic freedom, but failed to report that these abbeys regained their *libertas* after Henry attained his majority.[66] *The Triumph of St Remaclus* by an anonymous monk of Stablo describes the long campaign of his abbey to wrest her sister-house of Malmédy from the control of Archbishop Anno of Cologne. On 8 May 1071, during a

[61] Schwarzmaier (1968) 120–1.   [62] Sackur (1890) 132.

[63] *D H IV* 117. See Fleckenstein (1966) 235.   [64] Schulte (1934) 170.

[65] Klewitz (1939) 134–9; Fleckenstein (1964) 71; Fleckenstein (1966) 151–5, 230–3; Fuhrmann (1984) 321–6.

[66] Lampert, *Annales* 1063, pp. 89–90. The experience of Hersfeld: *ibid.* 1064, p. 92; 1066, p. 101 (not mentioning that the abbey received compensation: *D H IV* 146).

royal banquet in Liège, the monks of Stablo arrived carrying the shrine of their patron saint, Remaclus, and dropped it on the king's table. The table split asunder, severely injuring a royal attendant, and the ensuing series of miracles compelled the king to grant the monks' request.[67] The author concealed a crucial fact: the monks of Malmédy resented their ancient association with, or rather subordination to, Stablo and preferred dependence on Cologne.

The principal monastic grievance in 1071 was the king's treatment of the abbey of Reichenau, where he had invested two abbots in succession against the will of the monks: Meinward and Rupert.[68] The resignation of Abbot Meinward (1071) was prompted by the visit to Reichenau of Liupold of Meersburg, a knight from the royal household, who asked, in the king's name, to be given one of the abbey's estates as a benefice.[69] Lampert of Hersfeld had complained of similar depredations by Adalbert of Bremen and the royal favourite Count Werner during the king's minority. 'They distributed the estates of the monasteries to their followers, just as they pleased.'[70] There is evidence that *circa* 1071 the young king attempted to use the property of certain churches to defray the expenses of his government.[71] There is also evidence that Henry made reparation to churches affected by such practices or overburdened by royal *servitia*.[72] In the later years of the reign the emperor was active in curbing the depredations of the advocates of monasteries. He intervened to prohibit advocates from conferring monastic estates on 'troops of knights whom they recruited by offering benefices'.[73] In his final years Henry IV adopted the demeanour of a reformer, concerned to protect the churches of his kingdom against the rapacity of the secular aristocracy.

Throughout his reign the preambles of Henry's diplomas proclaimed the king's duties towards the monasteries in language similar to that of the privileges of the reform-minded Henry III.[74] The beginning of Henry IV's personal government was accompanied by a sudden increase in the number of privileges conferred on religious houses.[75] Henry's privileges were conferred

---

[67] *Triumphus sancti Remacli* II.5–13, pp. 452–5. Cf. *D H IV* 192 (Rheinau); *Annales Altahenses* 1071, p. 81 (Niederaltaich).

[68] Berthold, *Annales* 1069, 1070, 1071, pp. 274–5; Bernold, *Chronicon* 1070, p. 429. See above p. 119.

[69] *Annales Altahenses* 1071, p. 83. Cf. Lampert, *Annales* 1071, p. 127; Berthold, *Annales* 1070, p. 275. See above p. 121.   [70] Lampert, *Annales* 1063, p. 89. Cf. 1066, p. 101.

[71] See above pp. 120–1.   [72] See above p. 121.

[73] Frutolf of Michelsberg, *Chronica* 1099, p. 118. See above p. 313.

[74] *DD H IV* 146, 153, 192. See Szabó-Bechstein (1985) 87–8; Seibert (1991) 535–58.

[75] *DD H IV* 145–6, 148, 153, 158, 160. 1056–65: nineteen diplomas for monasteries; seventy-eight for episcopal churches and cathedral chapters. 1065–75: forty-five privileges for monasteries, forty-eight for episcopal churches. 1076–1105: fifty-four privileges for monasteries, seventy-nine for episcopal churches.

not only on the imperial abbeys but also on reformed monasteries. St Blasien (of which Rudolf of Rheinfelden was a patron) and St Nicholas in Passau (the foundation of the reformer Bishop Altmann of Passau) were recipients of royal diplomas.[76] A royal diploma of 1075 approved the first version of the reform devised for his monastery by Abbot William of Hirsau.[77] Five of Henry's diplomas record his generosity towards the reformed monastery of Siegburg, founded by Archbishop Anno of Cologne. In 1100 the emperor can be found supporting Bishop John I of Speyer in his project of introducing the monastic reform of Siegburg into the monastery of Sinsheim.[78] The evidence of the diplomas suggests that, despite the complaints of royal depredations of monastic property, Henry IV did not ignore his duties as 'prince and defender of the churches'.[79]

The final complaint of the anti-Henrician chroniclers was that Henry preferred the evil counsel of men of inferior status to the sound advice of the princes. The chronicler of Niederaltaich commented in 1072 on the king's tendency 'to despise the magnates and bestow riches and power on lesser men and govern according to their advice. He rarely admitted any member of the nobility to his confidence. Since much that was done was irregular, the bishops, dukes and other princes of the kingdom withdrew from royal affairs.'[80] Henry IV's preference for low-born advisers was a favourite theme of Lampert of Hersfeld. It first appears in his account of Saxon grievances in 1073. The king 'neglected the princes and continually had only Swabians about him, from whom he chose his confidential advisers and the administrators of both private and public affairs'. The Saxon rebels in June 1073 demanded that Henry 'expel from the palace those most vile counsellors by whose advice he had brought both himself and the kingdom to destruction and permit the affairs of the kingdom to be administered by the princes, who are fit to perform them'. Lampert returned to this theme in his report of the accusations against the king at the assembly of Tribur (October 1076). Henry 'had excluded the princes from his friendship and he had raised up to the highest honours men of the humblest origins with no ancestors and spent his days and nights with them, discussing how he might achieve the extermination of the nobility'.[81] The earliest extant version of this complaint is found in the letter of 1074/5 in which Archbishop Werner of Magdeburg defended the conduct of the Saxon rebels. 'After he came of age the king rejected the advice of his

[76] *DD H IV* 240, 273.

[77] *D H IV* 280. See T. Mayer (1950) 50–82; Hallinger (1950–1) 564, 840–3; Cowdrey (1970a) 197–9.   [78] *DD H IV* 163, 204, 223, 244, 490–1. See Semmler (1959) 72, 259–60.

[79] *D H IV* 153 (Reichenau).   [80] *Annales Altahenses* 1072, p. 84.

[81] Lampert, *Annales* 1073, pp. 147–8, 151; 1076, p. 277; cf. 1076, p. 270. See Bosl (1950) 1:87 n. 1; Struve (1970) 42–5.

princes' and 'submitted to the tutelage of those who care nothing for what is just or good'. He sought to seize the Saxons' property 'and to grant it to his familiars . . . because they possessed little or nothing at home'.[82]

Modern scholarship has often linked these complaints with the increasingly important role of the *ministeriales*, the unfree knights bound to the king's service and entrusted with both military and administrative duties. It has long been recognised that the reign of Henry IV was an important phase in the development of the ministerial class and that Henry employed *ministeriales* in a wide variety of duties. In a royal diploma of 1064 the fourteen-year-old king commended 'the faithful service' of the *ministerialis* Cuno, 'the servant (*pedissequus*) of our youth'. This servant was described by the Niederaltaich chronicler as 'Cuno, servant and educator of the king'.[83] (In later generations the education of a royal prince was to become a well-attested duty of *ministeriales*.) Three royal diplomas of the 1060s record grants of land to 'our *ministerialis* Otnand' for his 'devoted service'. Otnand was responsible for the administration of crown lands in the Bavarian Nordgau during the reign of Henry III and the first decade of the reign of his son.[84] From the opening phase of the Saxon war comes evidence that Henry IV's *ministeriales* were placed in command of royal castles and were called on to act as gaolers.[85] *Ministeriales* provided the garrison of the royal fortress of Hammerstein.[86] The events of December 1105 revealed that it was to the *ministeriales* of Hammerstein that the emperor had entrusted the royal insignia.[87] The military services of the *ministeriales* during the Saxon war are recorded in a series of royal diplomas of 1079, rewarding the living and commemorating the fallen.[88] The most exalted office attained by a *ministerialis* during the reign of Henry IV was that of duke of Spoleto and margrave of Ancona, conferred in 1093 or 1094 on Werner. This important royal servant is described in the chronicle of Ekkehard of Aura as 'one of the king's *ministeriales*, who held the command of the march in the region of Ancona' and in a papal document as 'a household servant of the German king'.[89] Finally, in the imperial diplomas of the years 1101–5 appear the names of three *ministeriales* holding office at the imperial court: the chamberlains Erkenbold and Gundekar and the steward

---

[82] Bruno, *Saxonicum bellum* c. 42, p. 41.

[83] *D H IV* 137. Cf. *DD H IV* 21, 45; *Annales Altahenses* 1069, p. 76. See above p. 48.

[84] *DD H IV* 69, 72, 198. Otnand as a 'hell-hound': *Briefsammlungen* pp. 196–8. See Meyer von Knonau (1890) 1:204 n. 2, 212 n. 20, 272, 291, 569 n. 40.

[85] Lampert, *Annales* 1076, p. 274.   [86] *Codex Udalrici* 107, p. 193.

[87] *Annales Hildesheimenses* 1105, pp. 55–6. See above p. 336.

[88] *DD H IV* 317–19 (gifts to *ministeriales*). *DD H IV* 309, 310, 314 (commemoration).

[89] Ekkehard, *Chronica* III, 1106, p. 274; Paschal II, *JL* 6054: 179B. Cf. *DD H IV* 431–2, 434, 450, 458. See above p. 293.

Volcmar. An anti-Henrician chronicler also identified 'the very wicked Volcmar, who was [the emperor's] adviser and privy to all his crimes' and the emperor's 'most faithful chamberlain' Erkenbold, who 'always remained by his side in his difficulties'. He was at Henry's deathbed to receive his last commands and it was he, together with other servants from the imperial household, who brought the emperor's body to Speyer.[90] Of the *ministeriales* in the service of Henry IV, Cuno (in the earliest years of his personal rule) and Erkenbold, Gundekar and Volcmar (in the final years) are the most likely to have enjoyed his special confidence and to have served as his advisers.[91]

Modern scholarship has also claimed a ministerial origin for five churchmen who were among Henry's most influential advisers: Archbishop Anno of Cologne, his nephew Bishop Burchard II of Halberstadt, Archbishops Liemar of Bremen and Hildolf of Cologne and Bishop Benno II of Osnabrück. Anno of Cologne and his nephew were of the Swabian family of Steusslingen. The suggestion that they were *ministeriales* derives solely from Lampert of Hersfeld's description of Anno as 'of middling rank'.[92] His chronicle is also the source of the claim that Anno's successor, Hildolf, was 'of obscure birth'.[93] Lampert's assertions (like his disparaging remarks about the king's Swabian favourites)[94] do not constitute reliable evidence of social status. The chronicler was keenly aware of the contrast between Hildolf, Anno and their highborn predecessor, Archbishop Herman II, the Ezzonid grandson of Emperor Otto II. Compared with Herman II, Anno was certainly 'of middling rank' and Hildolf 'of obscure birth'; but that did not make them *ministeriales*. As for Liemar of Bremen, a thirteenth-century chronicler described him as 'a Bavarian, originating among the *ministeriales* of Henry IV'. This description is contradicted, however, by the evidence of Bremen diplomas of 1091 and 1092, which identify respectively the archbishop's brother, Mazelin, and his nephew, Adalbero, as 'knights' (*milites*) and 'noblemen' (*nobiles*).[95] Finally

[90] *Annales Hildesheimenses* 1106, pp. 55–6. Cf. *DD H IV* 470b, 476, 483–4, 491. See Gawlik (1970a) 58. See above pp. 343, 344.

[91] The royal adviser Moricho (Sigeboto, *Vita Paulinae* c. 1, p. 911) has been claimed as a *ministerialis*: Bosl (1950) 1:77. But his brother was Bishop Werner of Merseburg ('born of a most illustrious family': *Vita Wernheri episcopi Merseburgensis* c. 1, p. 245). He is identified in *D H IV* 213 as 'our knight (*miles*)': cf. Althoff (1981) 333. See Fenske (1977) 280–2; Fleckenstein (1988) 385–6.

[92] Lampert, *Annales* 1075, p. 242. See Lück (1970a) 9–31; Zielinski (1984) 22–3.

[93] Lampert, *Annales* 1076, p. 251. See Bosl (1950) 1:78; Zielinski (1984) 26.

[94] Lampert, *Annales* 1073, p. 147. The misleading nature of his assessments of social status appears in 1076, p. 260: two rebels 'disregarded by [the king] because of their obscure name' were members of the Wettin family. See above p. 82.

[95] *Annales Stadenses* 1072, p. 316; but see May (1937) nos. 388–9. See Bosl (1950) 1:78; Zielinski (1984) 25.

Henry's loyal adviser, Bishop Benno II of Osnabrück, has been identified as a *ministerialis* on the basis of his biographer's statement that Benno's parents (who lived in the Swabian village of Löhningen) 'were indeed not noble but yet were superior to the plebeian condition'.[96] The biographer's description is reminiscent of Lampert's assessment of Henry IV's Swabian advisers as 'men sprung from obscure or almost non-existent ancestry'. The comments of Benno's biographer and of Lampert illustrate the aristocratic Saxon attitude towards the Swabian lesser nobility in their midst: it would be unwise to interpret them as proof of ministerial status. There is indeed no firm evidence that any of the ninety-four bishops appointed during the four decades of Henry IV's personal rule were *ministeriales*. Henry IV's bishops were, like those of his father and grandfather, overwhelmingly noble, many of the highest nobility, including the kinsmen of the imperial family.[97]

In his account of the first decade of Henry IV's personal government, when the king's advisers were allegedly drawn from 'men of the humblest origin with no ancestors', Lampert emphasised the importance of Liupold, Regenger and Udalric. These three advisers have been identified by modern scholarship as *ministeriales*, but again there is no evidence to support this assumption. The Swabian Liupold of Meersburg was 'very dear to the king, who was accustomed to rely most familiarly on his aid and advice'. His accidental death in July 1071 'afflicted the king with unbearable grief and melancholy. He immediately caused him to be brought to Hersfeld and buried him inside the church with a funeral of pomp and magnificence. He also conferred on the monastery thirty hides of land in the place called Martinfeld for the sake of [Liupold's] soul.'[98] The royal diploma recording this donation (30 July 1071) identifies Liupold as 'our most faithful and most dear knight' (*miles*). Two of the interveners in the diploma were Liupold's brothers, the 'knights' Arnold and Berthold. The latter is described in Bruno of Merseburg's chronicle as 'Berthold, the king's adviser'.[99] It was presumably of the knights Liupold and Berthold that Lampert was thinking when he complained that the king 'had only Swabians about him, from whom he chose his confidential advisers'. They were not, however, *ministeriales*, but men of free and noble birth. The other advisers mentioned by Lampert – Regenger and Udalric of Godesheim – appear in his account of an assassination plot allegedly devised by the king against the dukes of Swabia and Carinthia in 1073. Regenger, 'who had long been honoured with [Henry's]

[96] *Vita Bennonis Osnabrugensis* c. 1, p. 374. See Bosl (1950) 1:79–80; Fenske (1977) 282 n. 370; Kaiser (1980) 1917–18; Zotz (1991) pp. 46–7.

[97] Zielinski (1984) 25–7. See also above pp. 248, 275–6.

[98] Lampert, *Annales* 1071, pp. 130–1. Cf. *D H IV* 243. See above p. 67.

[99] Bruno, *Saxonicum bellum* c. 81, p. 78 (probably the Berthold who accompanied Henry to Canossa, 1077: Lampert, *Annales* 1077, p. 301).

closest confidence', warned the dukes of their peril. Confronted with this accusation by 'a man of no small reputation in the palace', the king expressed his readiness to defend his honour in single combat. Udalric of Godesheim, 'one of those who were accused of advising the action and were intended to carry out the crime', intervened to challenge Regenger to trial by combat. 'A few days before the trial Regenger was seized by a terrible demon and died a dreadful death.'[100] There is no evidence to identify Regenger as a *ministerialis*: no chronicler refers to his family origins.[101]

Udalric of Godesheim is identified in a royal diploma of 1074 as a 'knight'.[102] Udalric (the ancestor of the counts of Raabs, castellans of Nuremberg) was one of the most influential royal advisers of the middle years of the reign. He was one of the five advisers excommunicated in 1073 by Pope Alexander II and again in 1075 by Gregory VII on the grounds that they 'wished to separate [the king] from the unity of the Church'.[103] Late in 1075 Henry invested Udalric with the benefices of the youthful Margrave Ekbert II of Meissen, presumably as a reward for his services in the Saxon war.[104] In October 1076 the papal legates in Oppenheim demanded that Henry dismiss Udalric from his counsels, a demand repeated at Canossa in January 1077. Soon after his absolution at Canossa, however, the king 'recalled to the former degree of his favour and intimacy both Udalric of Godesheim and the others whom he had removed from his company under the most severe anathema and he returned to his custom of consulting them exclusively about private and public business'.[105] His death in the king's service in Italy (1083) was interpreted by the chronicler Bernold of St Blasien as a divine judgement, since Udalric was 'the author and inciter of this schismatical conspiracy', that is, of the conflict of empire and papacy.[106] Of the five royal advisers who played so important a role in Henry IV's relations with the papacy in the years 1075–7, only three can be named. Lampert identified Udalric of Godesheim, Eberhard and Hartmann among 'the excommunicates on whose aid and counsels he used to depend most willingly'.[107] Hartmann is no more than a name: he is not identified in any other source. The adviser Eberhard, however, is identifiable as one of the most prominent royal servants of the decade 1068–78.

---

[100] Lampert, *Annales* 1073, 1074, pp. 166, 167, 174. See above p. 93.

[101] Berthold, *Annales* 1073, p. 276: 'one of the king's advisers'.

[102] *D H IV* 271. See Tellenbach (1988) 359–60.

[103] Lampert, *Annales* 1073, 1074, 1076, 1077, pp. 168, 170, 175, 255, 282, 294, 300, 301. Cf. Berthold, *Annales* 1073, p. 276. See above p. 125.

[104] Bruno, *Saxonicum bellum* c. 56, p. 52: 'he had the surname "hatred-of-God" (*Godeshaz*)'.

[105] Lampert, *Annales* 1077, p. 300.

[106] Bernold, *Chronicon* 1083, p. 438. See above pp. 225, 226.

[107] Lampert, *Annales* 1076, p. 282.

This Count Eberhard 'the Bearded'[108] is to be distinguished from two other contemporary Count Eberhards. He is not to be identified with Count Eberhard of Nellenburg, kinsman of the imperial family and founder of the monastery of Schaffhausen, nor with his son of the same name. The younger Eberhard of Nellenburg served the king in the responsible post of commander of the garrison of the castle of Lüneburg in 1073. He fell, together with his brother Henry, in the battle of Homburg (9 June 1075).[109] Eberhard 'the Bearded' served the king both in the Saxon wars and in the kingdom of Italy. In 1071 he negotiated the surrender of Otto of Northeim after the latter's first rebellion. 'At that time,' wrote Lampert, 'the king made particular use of the advice of Count Eberhard, an extremely wise man.'[110] Most importantly, Eberhard was responsible for that mission of 1075 to Lombardy and southern Italy which Gregory VII interpreted as evidence that Henry IV no longer wished for peace with the papacy.[111] Reporting Eberhard's death in the battle of Mellrichstadt (7 August 1078), Bruno of Merseburg described him as 'the very savage inciter of this war'.[112] The evidence of the royal diplomas suggests that Eberhard was also a figure of considerable influence at the royal court. No other secular prince was so frequently named as intervener in the diplomas of this decade.[113]

The student of Henry IV's reign is continually aware of the significance of the intervention clauses of diplomas in identifying the politicians who were most frequently in the king's presence and had the best opportunity of exercising influence at court. The interveners named in a diploma were those personages who had supported the petitioner's efforts to obtain the privilege from the monarch. The petitioner usually enlisted the help of those whom he believed to have influence with the monarch. In some of the later diplomas of the reign the intervention clause is replaced by a list of witnesses, as an additional guarantee of authenticity. The same persons appeared as witnesses and interveners, the essential qualification being influence at court. The cumulative evidence of the intervention clauses and witness lists offers a series of snapshots of those persons most frequently at court and in a position to serve as royal advisers. In the absence of any permanent formal body of counsellors, Henry IV's advisers are presumably to be found among the interveners who were present at court at times other than those occasions when many princes assembled there (for example, the great festivals of the Christian year) and who remained at the court for long periods.

---

[108] Bruno, *Saxonicum bellum* c. 99, p. 90.
[109] Lampert, *Annales* 1073, 1075, pp. 160, 219. See Hils (1967) 75.
[110] Lampert, *Annales* 1071, p. 119. Cf. 1073, p. 145. Cf. Adam of Bremen, *Gesta* III.49, p. 192.
[111] Bonizo, *Ad amicum* VII, p. 605. Cf. Lampert, *Annales* 1076, pp. 255, 282; 1077, p. 301. See above pp. 139–40.   [112] Bruno, *Saxonicum bellum* c. 102, pp. 91–2.
[113] *DD H IV* 205, 207, 214, 245, 265, 286, 291–2.

In the diplomas of the early years of the reign the appearance of the Empress Agnes as by far the most frequent intervener accurately reflects her dominant role in government.[114] During the years 1062–5 the most frequent interveners are unsurprisingly the two leading politicians of the last years of the minority, Anno of Cologne and Adalbert of Bremen.[115] In the first decade of his personal rule Henry IV continued to be advised by prominent politicians of his minority. Anno of Cologne figured prominently again in the years 1066–75.[116] Anno's nephew Burchard of Halberstadt was a frequent intervener in diplomas of the years 1068–72.[117] In 1068 Burchard distinguished himself in a campaign against the Liutizi on the borders of eastern Saxony.[118] This success perhaps accounts for his prominence at court during the next four years. For the last fifteen years of his life, however, Burchard was Henry IV's bitterest enemy in Saxony, 'the leader of the whole Saxon rebellion and the originator and inciter of everything that had followed'.[119]

Two other rebels, members of the 'deposition faction' of princes in 1076 and subsequently adherents of the anti-kings, had likewise regularly appeared as interveners in diplomas of Henry IV's minority and of the first decade of his personal rule: Siegfried of Mainz and Otto of Northeim. Siegfried's principal preoccupation during this period was to vindicate the rights of the church of Mainz by ending the 'Thuringian freedom from tithes', in which (the Thuringian nobility believed) he enjoyed the active support of the king.[120] Siegfried acted as the king's faithful lieutenant in the synod of Worms in January 1076, but by the following autumn he had joined the 'deposition faction', whose anti-kings he crowned in 1077 and 1081.[121] The opening years of Henry's personal rule witnessed close cooperation between Otto of Northeim, duke of Bavaria, and the king.[122] In 1070, however, this cooperation came to an abrupt end: accused of treason and deprived of his duchy, Otto began that career of rebellion which, with two brief intervals of reconciliation, he would pursue for the rest of his life.[123] The principal purpose of his rebellions was to compel the king to restore him to the duchy from which

---

[114] Seventy-one interventions in the diplomas of 1056–62; sixteen in the diplomas of 1062–70. See Black-Veldtrup (1995) 85–96.

[115] Anno intervened in twenty-eight diplomas during 1062–5, Adalbert in twenty-six. See above pp. 45–6, 53, 57.

[116] DD H IV 177, 199, 200, 203, 215, 221, 229, 233, 242, 247, 254, 264. See Gawlik (1970a) 135–6, 142, 166–7.

[117] DD H IV 204, 209–11, 215, 227–31, 246, 254. See Gawlik (1970a) 132, 169.

[118] See above pp. 46, 78.   [119] Lampert, Annales 1076, p. 265.

[120] DD H IV 176, 180, 185–6, 204, 221, 264, 284. In the months following Adalbert's fall (January 1066) Siegfried was the most frequent intervener. See Gawlik (1970a) 130, 166.

[121] See above pp. 143, 167, 210.   [122] DD H IV 198, 209–10, 215. See Gawlik (1970a) 150.

[123] See above pp. 65–6.

he had been deposed in 1070. As for Siegfried of Mainz and Burchard of Halberstadt, Gregorian sources represent them as adherents of the reform papacy whose motive for rebellion was to protect the imperial Church against the depredations of Henry IV.

The royal advisers of the first decades of the reign also included three royal servants of exemplary loyalty: Bishops Herman I of Bamberg, Eberhard of Naumburg and Benno II of Osnabrück. All three appeared at court for the first time after Henry's coming of age. Herman, forced on the church of Bamberg against the will of the clergy and deposed through the combined efforts of the Bamberg clergy and the pope (1075), 'always stood by the king most readily in peace and war'. The assistance that he gave the king in financial matters was interpreted by his opponents as evidence of simony.[124] The most frequent intervener of the first decade of Henry IV's personal government (excepting only Queen Bertha) was Eberhard of Naumburg.[125] A former chaplain of Henry III, Eberhard had been appointed bishop in 1045. His support for Henry IV in the Saxon rebellion resulted in his expulsion from his diocese in 1073. He was one of the small group of bishops who advised Henry at Oppenheim (October 1076) and at Canossa (January 1077) and remained at the king's side until Henry gave him the task of administering the bishopric of Würzburg after the expulsion of the pro-papal Bishop Adalbero.[126] Lampert of Hersfeld coupled Eberhard's name with that of Benno of Osnabrück, reporting that the king 'ordered all things according to their advice now in this time of disturbance' (that is, the outbreak of the Saxon rebellion), 'just as he had done in previous quiet times'.[127] Benno, formerly steward of the palace of Goslar and perhaps also a royal chaplain, had long enjoyed the king's confidence. 'King Henry IV, when still a boy, found him extremely agreeable and all the affairs of the palace were regulated almost entirely by his will.'[128] Like Eberhard of Naumburg, Benno was expelled from his diocese because of his loyalty to the king, and he was at the king's side at Oppenheim and at Canossa.[129]

In the years immediately following the outbreak of the conflict with the reform papacy four long-serving prelates appeared with particular frequency as interveners: Bishops Burchard of Lausanne, Conrad of Utrecht and Rupert of Bamberg and Archbishop Liemar of Bremen. Burchard, one of the small

---

[124] *DD H IV* 211–12, 214, 221, 224, 235, 240, 242, 264, 267. See Gawlik (1970a) 131, 168. See also above pp. 119, 132.

[125] *DD H IV* 174, 187–8, 191, 193, 197–8, 201–2, 207, 215, 247, 264–5, 267–9, 283–4, 293, 295–7, 299. See Gawlik (1970a) 144, 171.   [126] See above pp. 161, 177.

[127] Lampert, *Annales* 1073, p. 153. Cf. *ibid.* 1074, p. 182.

[128] *Vita Bennonis Osnabrugensis* c. 9, p. 388.

[129] *DD H IV* 215, 247, 264–5, 293, 295–7, 299. See Gawlik (1970a) 138, 170.

group of royal advisers at Oppenheim and Canossa, played two major roles in Henry's struggle against the papacy and the anti-kings: that of royal agent in the duchy of Swabia and that of chancellor for the Italian kingdom. The most frequent intervener of 1081–2, when the king was in Italy, Burchard was evidently an important adviser on the second Italian expedition.[130] Equally prominent was Conrad of Utrecht, who was employed in particular in negotiating a peace with the Saxons. 'Clearsighted in matters of difficulty and active in many affairs',[131] he participated in the talks in the forest of Kaufungen in February 1081 and in the conference of Gerstungen-Berka in January 1085.[132] Rupert of Bamberg was considered by Lampert of Hersfeld 'harsher and fiercer than [the king's] other familiars and of proven loyalty towards [Henry] in adversity'. The chronicler coupled Rupert's name with that of Udalric of Godesheim as the men 'through whose advice [the king] had ruined both himself and the commonwealth' and whose society Henry was forced to abjure at Canossa.[133] His close association with the imperial court is also demonstrated by the seven imperial letters sent to the bishop between 1084 and 1102. Henry IV's letter of 1099 thanked him for having 'always been faithful to [his lord] according to [his] duty and, like a man of wisdom and excellent loyalty, striven to preserve and increase [Henry's] honour'.[134] A royal diploma of 22 June 1083 described Liemar of Bremen in even more exalted terms. He was 'the foremost lover of our name and very greatly deserving of our favour'. 'In the Saxon war he stood by [the king] in the greatest danger in two very fierce battles; he once acted as [Henry's] envoy at the apostolic see, opposing Hildebrand, the disturber of the world, amidst great difficulties and anxieties; three times he came with [the king] to attack and capture the city of Rome.'[135]

The principal interveners and witnesses in the imperial diplomas of the last years of the reign were four churchmen – Bishops John I of Speyer, Widelo of Minden and Burchard of Münster and Archbishop Frederick of Cologne – and two secular princes, Duke Frederick I of Swabia and Margrave Burchard of Istria. Duke Frederick (the emperor's son-in-law) and Margrave Burchard were the most frequent secular interveners and witnesses in the diplomas of

---

[130] DD H IV 293, 321, 327, 334–5, 337–9, 342–4, 373, 382, 394, 397. See Gawlik (1970a) 145, 171.
[131] Altercatio inter Urbanum et Clementem p. 171. But see Berthold, Annales 1076, p. 284; Bernold, Chronicon 1099, p. 466.
[132] DD H IV 284, 299, 324, 327, 356, 377, 390, 394, 405, 410, 414. See Gawlik (1970a) 138–9, 170–1.   [133] Lampert, Annales 1076, 1077, pp. 265, 294. Cf. ibid., 1075, p. 240.
[134] Henry IV, Letter 24, p. 34. Cf. Letters 20, 25–9, pp. 30, 34–8. DD H IV 283–4, 319, 325, 377, 392, 402, 407, 424, 426, 463. See Gawlik (1970a) 131, 168–9.
[135] D H IV 351. Cf. DD H IV 264–5, 267–9, 283, 299; in 1080–9: 323, 325, 350, 373, 390, 394, 402. See Gawlik (1970a) 142–3, 167.

Henry IV.[136] Like these two secular princes, Bishop John I of Speyer accompanied the emperor on his third Italian expedition. It was in the years following that expedition that Henry IV's visits to Speyer became most frequent (seven visits in the period 1099–1105) and his generosity towards the church of Speyer most pronounced. It was the emperor's devotion to the burial-place of his forebears that elevated Bishop John to a prominent role in his counsels.[137] Widelo of Minden[138] and Burchard of Münster[139] were the only Saxon bishops who remained faithful to the emperor after the outbreak of Henry V's rebellion. Both were consequently deposed from their sees in 1105 by papal legates. Widelo remained loyal to Henry IV (he was restored to his see only in 1113), but Burchard submitted to the young king and the legates. He was later captured by the emperor's adherents and it was as a prisoner in the imperial entourage that he came to be present at Henry IV's deathbed.[140] Archbishop Frederick I of Cologne, the emperor's most active supporter in the final years of the reign, was also the most frequent intervener and witness.[141] Suspended from his office by the papal legate in 1105, he eventually submitted to Henry V when the young king succeeded in taking the emperor prisoner.

In the imperial diplomas of 1101–5 there appear in the witness lists the names of *ministeriales* holding office at the imperial court: the chamberlains Erkenbold and Gundekar, the steward Volcmar and the otherwise unknown 'Henry of the emperor's household'.[142] Their inclusion in these witness-lists is undoubtedly evidence of influence at court during these years, but their importance must not be exaggerated. Their names appear only in five diplomas from the last years of the reign: they constituted an exception to the general picture presented by the intervention clauses and witness-lists of the Henrician diplomas. That general picture contradicts the claim made by hostile chroniclers about Henry IV's regime, that the king governed according to the advice of 'lesser men' and 'rarely admitted any member of the nobility to his confidence'. In fact the evidence of Henry IV's diplomas suggests a regime that differed little from that of his father or his grandfather. As in the diplomas of Conrad II and Henry III, the largest single category of interveners is that of members of the imperial family. In the diplomas of Conrad, his consort Gisela and his son Henry were the most frequently

---

[136] Frederick: *DD H IV* 377, 390, 424, 426, 485, 463–4, 468–71, 473, 476, 479. Burchard: *DD H IV* 426, 430–2, 434, 447, 450, 452, 485, 458, 463–4, 468, 470–1. See Gawlik (1970a) 151, 153–4.   [137] *DD H IV* 424, 466, 473, 476–7, 479–80, 483–4. See Gawlik (1970a) 133, 169.

[138] *DD H IV* 458, 464, 472–3, 479, 483–4, 490–1. See Gawlik (1970a) 137, 169–70.

[139] *DD H IV* 458, 468, 470–1, 473, 476–7, 479, 483–4, 490. See Gawlik (1970a) 138, 170.

[140] See above p. 343.

[141] *DD H IV* 464, 468, 470–1, 473, 476–7, 479, 483–4, 490–1. See Gawlik (1970a) 136, 167.

[142] *DD H IV* 470, 476, 483–4, 491. See above pp. 357–8. See Gawlik (1970a) 163–4.

named interveners; in the case of Henry III, the empress-mother Gisela and the consort Agnes appeared most often. These diplomas suggest a regime dominated by the dynastic principle of concentrating influence as far as possible in the monarch's immediate family.[143]

A similar principle is apparent in the diplomas of the years of Henry IV's majority. Bertha, queen and empress was by far the most frequent intervener of the period of her husband's personal rule.[144] The appearances of Henry's elder son King Conrad as intervener or witness were more sporadic, since he spent much of his young career in the Italian kingdom as his father's representative.[145] His younger brother Henry V appeared as intervener or witness between 1099 and 1103.[146] For the rest, the interveners and witnesses in Henry IV's diplomas were overwhelmingly princes, and above all ecclesiastical princes. Not all the archbishops and bishops of his empire figure in his diplomas and many made only sporadic appearances. The evidence of his diplomas suggests that Henry IV preferred to rely on a small number of ecclesiastical advisers: above all, Archbishops Liemar of Bremen and Frederick of Cologne and Bishops Eberhard of Naumburg, Benno II of Osnabrück, Herman I and Rupert of Bamberg, Burchard of Lausanne, Conrad of Utrecht, John I of Speyer, Widelo of Minden and Burchard of Münster.

The anti-Henrician chroniclers complained that the tyrant Henry IV and his 'most vile counsellors' created an innovatory form of government, calculated to eradicate 'the laws and the customs of his predecessors'. By 1076 'the commonwealth was turned upside-down, the peace of the churches disturbed, the majesty of the empire destroyed, the authority of the princes cancelled, morality overthrown, the laws abolished'.[147] The 'innovations' denounced by the king's critics were already in existence before the outbreak of the conflict with the papacy: these 'innovations' were characteristic of the first decade of Henry IV's personal rule. The 'policy of recuperation' of royal property and rights in eastern Saxony in 1069–72 was the 'innovation' particularly emphasised by Lampert of Hersfeld and Bruno of Merseburg. Lampert represented the recuperation policy as 'a great design such as none of his predecessors had ever attempted: namely to reduce all the Saxons and Thuringians to slavery and to add their estates to the crown lands'.[148] The king's harsh treatment of Otto of Northeim, suddenly toppled from power and deprived of his ducal office in 1070, seemed to confirm these fears. Henry IV's apologist, the anonymous author of the *Song of the Saxon War*, offered the royal view of the policy of recuperation. 'As long as the lord king was still a child, the fierce people [of

---

[143] Schetter (1935) 18–25, 126.   [144] Gawlik (1970a) 128–9, 165–6. See above p. 266.

[145] *DD H IV* 318, 322, 338–9, 345, 394, 396–7, 421, 426–7. See Gawlik (1970a) 128, 166.

[146] *DD H IV* 458, 469, 471–2, 476, 479. See Gawlik (1970a) 128, 166.

[147] Lampert, *Annales* 1076, p. 279.   [148] *Ibid.*, 1073, p. 147.

Saxony] escaped from the control of government. . . But once the king had grown out of his tender years . . . he gave them laws; he tamed them by force; he demanded the return of whatever had been violently seized from churches, widows and the poor.' Henry was compelled to proceed against the Saxons because they 'denied him his rights'.[149] According to this propagandist, the king's purpose was simply to restore order in Saxony and recover royal rights usurped during his minority.

Another characteristic of this first decade of Henry's personal government was the intensification of royal control over the imperial Church. Royal appointees, notably members of the imperial chapel, were placed in vacant bishoprics without consulting cathedral chapters and sometimes against fierce resistance by the canonical electors.[150] In each case the king 'determined on the appointment of a successor whose pliable disposition he could use to achieve all his purposes'.[151] This insistence on appointing bishops whose principal qualification was loyalty to the crown, like the sporadic royal encroachments on ecclesiastical property in this decade,[152] testified to the king's determination to regain control over the imperial Church after the laxer regime of his minority. To reform-minded contemporaries who sympathised with the programme of the reform papacy, with its insistence on the canonical election of bishops, free from secular pressure, and on the sanctity of ecclesiastical property, it seemed that 'Henry was ceaselessly defiling holy Church with simoniacal heresy'.[153] Affronted canonical electors – the cathedral chapters of Constance and Bamberg, the monks of Reichenau – appealed to the papacy to defend their rights and the interests of reform.[154] By 1075 the king found himself openly opposed by the pope in his attempts to assert his authority over the Church in his Italian and German kingdoms. The radical measure which he took in the synod of Worms of January 1076 to end this opposition unleashed a conflict with the papacy and its allies that lasted for the rest of his reign.[155] Conscious that the authority of the crown had been eroded during the minority, the royal government of 1066–76 vigorously set about the work of restoration. The chronicles of the 1070s reveal that many contemporaries regarded these endeavours not as restoration but as innovation, detecting a tendency towards tyranny and a disregard for the rights both of the nobility and of the churches. The king 'wished there to be no lords in his kingdom, so that he might be the sole lord over all men'.[156] These suspicions provoked the two crises of the Saxon rebellion and the more widespread rebellion arising from the dispute with Pope Gregory VII. The two successive rebellions

---

[149] *Carmen de bello Saxonico* I.2, II–14, 20–3, pp. I–2. See above pp. 84–5.
[150] Fleckenstein (1973) 125–33.   [151] Lampert, *Annales* 1076, p. 251.
[152] Schieffer (1972) 19–60.   [153] Bernold, *Chronicon* 1076, p. 431.   [154] See above p. 119.
[155] See above pp. 143–6.   [156] Bruno, *Saxonicum bellum* c. 60, p. 55.

revealed how fragile was Henry's regime. Eleventh-century kings could exert their authority only through the active cooperation of their vassals, the secular princes and bishops. The experience of Henry IV shows how this cooperation would be withheld from a king suspected of caring nothing for the rights of his princes.

Henry IV survived the crisis of 1076–7 by demonstrating qualities which had been far less apparent in the previous decade: flexibility, willingness to compromise. It was during this crisis that he acquired his most effective political technique: that of conciliating opponents in order to win time for himself. 'An incontestable characteristic of Henry IV's politics was the "dilatory" adroitness which contemporaries rightly attributed to him.'[157] Henry IV learned how to make timely concessions in order to divide his intransigent enemies from his more moderate opponents. This was how he outmanoeuvered the 'deposition faction' in 1076–7 and how he limited the damage inflicted on his regime by the party of the anti-kings. The divisions created by the conflicts of the 1070s were, however, never fully healed. In the 1080s, with the prestige derived from the success of his second Italian expedition and the acquisition of the imperial crown, Henry enjoyed considerable support in the German kingdom. There survived, however, an irreconcilable group of Gregorian bishops and their small but formidable band of princely allies, led by Welf IV of Bavaria. Reconciliation with the Gregorian party was only possible if the emperor was prepared to sacrifice Clement III, the antipope Wibert of Ravenna, elected at the synod of Brixen in 1080 and enthroned in Rome in 1084. Henry felt that it was impossible to repudiate the antipope who had crowned him emperor without impugning his own imperial title.[158] The proceedings of the synod of Brixen, like those of the council of Worms in 1076, were inspired by the conduct of Henry III in 1046. Henry IV claimed to be exercising the traditional right of the emperor elect to regulate the affairs of the Church, to remove an unsatisfactory pope and to replace him by a more suitable candidate.[159] In the changed circumstances of the 1080s, however, the appointment of the antipope seemed a shocking innovation, and this perpetuated the divisions created in 1076. The continuance of those divisions ensured that when the emperor's sons rebelled, Conrad in 1093 and Henry V in 1105, they immediately found ready-made opposition factions to assist them.

When the death of the antipope in 1100 seemed to prepare the way for reconciliation between empire and papacy, the issue of lay investiture at once

---

[157] Erdmann (1939) 247, citing Henry V's letter (Ekkehard, *Chronica* III, 1106, p. 284) denouncing his father's 'custom' of requesting 'long delays' before enacting necessary improvements in 'the condition of the Church and kingdom'.   [158] See above p. 274.

[159] See above pp. 198–200.

emerged to hinder efforts at peace. The emperor's last years were dominated by his desire to 'reconcile kingship and priesthood', but also by his conviction that his practice of investing bishops was 'according to secular and canon law'.[160] Even in 1105, when he might have tried to outmanoeuvre his rebellious son by agreeing to Pope Paschal II's demands concerning investiture, the emperor continued to insist on his customary right. Henry's letter of 1105 to Paschal II emphasises his determination to maintain the integrity of his royal and imperial office. He wished to be united with the pope 'in love and friendship', but this reconciliation must be without prejudice to 'the honour of our kingship and empire and all our dignity, as it was preserved by our grandfather and father and our other predecessors'.[161] Henry IV had preserved his throne in the past by making timely concessions, but he could never give up the hereditary 'honour of [his] kingship and empire', of which his rights over the imperial Church were so vital a part.

---

[160] Henry IV, *Letter* 33, p. 42. See above p. 312.
[161] Henry IV, *Letter* 34, p. 44. See above p. 329.

BIBLIOGRAPHY

ABBREVIATIONS

DA   Deutsches Archiv für Erforschung des Mittelalters
DD H III   Diplomata Heinrici III
DD H IV   Diplomata Heinrici IV
FS   Frühmittelalterliche Studien. Jahrbuch des Instituts für
                Frühmittelalterforschung der Universität Münster
HJ   Historisches Jahrbuch
HZ   Historische Zeitschrift
Investiturstreit   Investiturstreit und Reichsverfassung ed. J. Fleckenstein (Vorträge
                und Forschungen 17: Sigmaringen, 1973)
JK/JL   P. Jaffé, Regesta pontificum Romanorum ed. W. Wattenbach, S.
                Loewenfeld, F. Kaltenbrunner and P. Ewald, 2 volumes (second
                edition, Leipzig, 1885)
MGH   Monumenta Germaniae Historica
  Briefe   Die Briefe der deutschen Kaiserzeit
  Constitutiones   Constitutiones et acta publica imperatorum et regum
  DD   Diplomata
  Libelli   Libelli de lite imperatorum et pontificum
  SS   Scriptores (in Folio)
  SS rer. Germ. Scriptores rerum Germanicarum in usum scholarum separatim editi
MIÖG   Mitteilungen des Instituts für Österreichische Geschichtsforschung
NA   Neues Archiv der Gesellschaft für ältere deutsche Geschichtskunde
QFIAB   Quellen und Forschungen aus italienischen Archiven und
                Bibliotheken
Salier   Die Salier und das Reich ed. S. Weinfurter, 3 volumes (Sigmaringen,
                1991)
ZGO   Zeitschrift für die Geschichte des Oberrheins
ZSSRG   Zeitschrift der Savigny-Stiftung für Rechtsgeschichte
  GA   Germanistische Abteilung
  KA   Kanonistische Abteilung

PRIMARY SOURCES

Acta pontificum Romanorum inedita ed. J. Pflugk-Harttung 1, 2 (Tübingen-Stuttgart, 1880)

Adam of Bremen, *Gesta Hammaburgensis ecclesiae pontificum, MGH SS rer. Germ.* [2] (1917)

Alfanus, *I carmi di Alfano I, archivescovo di Salerno* ed. A. Lentini and F. Avagliano (Miscellanea cassinese 38, 1974)

Amatus of Monte Cassino, *Historia Normannorum* ed. V. de Bartholomaeis (Fonti per la Storia d'Italia 76: Rome, 1935)

Andrea Dandolo, *Chronicon Venetum* ed. E. Pastorello, *Rerum Italicarum Scriptores* 12 (Bologna, 1938)

Andreas of Strumi, *Vita sancti Arialdi, MGH SS* 30/2, 1049–75

Altercatio inter Urbanum et Clementem, MGH Libelli 2 (Hanover, 1892), 169–72

Anna Comnena Porphyrogenita, *Alexias* ed. A. Reifferscheid 1, 2 (Leipzig, 1884)

Annales Altahenses maiores, MGH SS rer. Germ. [4] (1891)

Annales Aquenses, MGH SS 24, 33–9

Annales Augustani, MGH SS 3, 123–36

Annales Brunwilarenses, MGH SS 16, 724–8

Annales Einsidlenses, MGH SS 3, 145–9

Annales Gradicenses, MGH SS 17, 643–52

Annales Hildesheimenses, MGH SS rer. Germ. [8] (1878)

Annales Leodienses, Continuatio, MGH SS 4, 28–30

Annales Magdeburgenses, MGH SS 16, 105–96

Annales Mellicenses, MGH SS 9, 479–501

Annales Palidenses, MGH SS 16, 48–96

Annales Patherbrunnenses. Eine verlorene Quellenschrift des 12. Jahrhunderts ed. P. Scheffer-Boichorst (Innsbruck, 1870)

Annales Pegavienses, MGH SS 16, 232–70

Annales Romani, MGH SS 5, 468–80

Annales Rosenveldenses, MGH SS 16, 99–104

Annales sancti Disibodi, MGH SS 17, 4–30

Annales sancti Iacobi Leodiensis minores, MGH SS 16, 632–45

Annales sancti Stephani Frisingenses, MGH SS 13, 50–60

Annales Spirenses, MGH SS 17, 80–5

Annales Stadenses, MGH SS 16, 271–379

Annales Weissenburgenses, in: *Lamperti Opera, MGH SS rer. Germ.* [38] (1894) pp. 9–57

Annales Wirziburgenses (Annales Sancti Albani Moguntini), MGH SS 2, 238–47

Annalista Saxo, MGH SS 6, 542–777

Annalium Ratisbonensium maiorum fragmentum, MGH SS rer. Germ. [4] (1891) pp. 87–91

Anonymi Chronica imperatorum Heinrico V dedicata ed. F.-J. Schmale and I. Schmale-Ott (Ausgewählte Quellen zur deutschen Geschichte des Mittelalters 15: Darmstadt, 1972) pp. 48–120

Anselm of Lucca, *Liber contra Wibertum*, MGH Libelli I, 519–28

Anselmi Cantuariensis archiepiscopi Opera Omnia ed. F.S. Schmitt 2, 4 (Edinburgh, 1946, 1949)

Arnulf of Milan, *Liber gestorum recentium, MGH SS rer. Germ.* 67 (1994)

Beno, *Gesta Romanae aecclesiae contra Hildebrandum, MGH Libelli* 2 (1892), 369–80

Benzo of Alba, *Ad Heinricum IV. imperatorem Libri VII, MGH SS rer. Germ.* 65 (1996)

Bernard of Hildesheim, *Liber canonum contra Heinricum quartum, MGH Libelli* 1 (1891), 471–516

Bernold of St Blasien, *Chronicon, MGH SS* 5, 385–467

Bernold of St Blasien, *De damnatione schismaticorum, MGH Libelli* 2 (1892), 26–58

Bernold of St Blasien, *Pro Gebhardo episcopo Constantiensi epistola apologetica, MGH Libelli* 2 (1892), 108–11

Berthold of Reichenau, *Annales* [first version]: *Herimanni Augiensis Chronici Continuatio . . . auctore, ut videtur, Bertholdo, MGH SS* 13, 730–2

Berthold of Reichenau, *Annales* [second version], *MGH SS* 5, 264–326

Bonizo of Sutri, *Liber ad amicum, MGH Libelli* 1 (1891), 568–620

Briefsammlungen der Zeit Heinrichs IV. ed. C. Erdmann and N. Fickermann, *MGH Briefe* 5 (1950)

Bruno of Merseburg, *Saxonicum bellum: Brunos Buch vom Sachsenkrieg, MGH Deutsches Mittelalter* 2 (1937)

Brunwilarensis monasterii fundatorum actus, MGH SS 14, 121–44

Burchard of Worms, *Decretum, MPL* 140, 337A–1058C

Cardinalium schismaticorum contra Gregorium VII. et Urbanum II. scripta, MGH Libelli 2 (1892), 366–422

Carmen de bello Saxonico, MGH SS rer. Germ. [17] (1889) pp. 1–23

Casus monasterii Petrishusensis, MGH SS 20, 621–82

Casuum Sancti Galli Continuatio II, MGH SS 2, 148–63

Chronica monasterii Casinensis: Die Chronik von Montecassino, MGH SS 34 (1980)

Chronica regia Coloniensis, MGH SS rer. Germ. [18] (1880)

Chronicon Ebersheimense, MGH SS 23, 427–53

Chronicon episcoporum Hildesheimensium, MGH SS 7, 845–73

Chronicon Gozecense, MGH SS 10, 140–57

Chronicon Lippoldesbergense, MGH SS 20, 546–56

Chronicon sancti Huberti Andaginensis, MGH SS 8, 565–630

Chronicon Wirziburgense, MGH SS 6, 17–31

Codex Laureshamensis ed. K. Glöckner 1 (Darmstadt, 1929)

Codex Udalrici ed. P. Jaffé, *Bibliotheca rerum Germanicarum* 5 (Berlin, 1869), 17–469

Collectio in LXXIV titulos digesta ed. J.T. Gilchrist (Monumenta Iuris Canonici B.1, Vatican City, 1973)

Conquestio Heinrici IV. imperatoris ad Heinricum filium, MGH SS rer. Germ. [17] (1889) pp. 24–8

Constitutum Constantini (Konstantinische Schenkung), MGH Fontes iuris Germanici antiqui 10 (1968)

Cosmas of Prague, *Chronica Boemorum: Die Chronik der Böhmen des Cosmas von Prag, MGH SS rer. Germ., nova series* 2 (1923)

Cronica Reinhardsbrunnensis, MGH SS 30/1, 515–656

Decretales Pseudo-Isidorianae et Capitula Angilramni ed. P. Hinschius (Leipzig, 1863)

Deusdedit, *Collectio canonum: Die Kanonessammlung des Kardinal Deusdedit* ed. V. Wolf von Glanvell 1 (Paderborn, 1905)

Deusdedit, *Libellus contra invasores et symoniacos et reliquos scismaticos*, MGH *Libelli* 2 (1892), 292–365

Die falschen Investiturprivilegien, MGH *Fontes iuris Germanici antiqui* 13 (1986)

Die Ordines für die Weihe und Krönung des Kaisers und der Kaiserin, MGH *Fontes iuris Germanici antiqui* 9 (1960)

Donizo of Canossa, *Vita Mathildis comitissae metrica*, MGH SS 12, 348–40

Ebo of Michelsberg, *Vita Ottonis episcopi Babenbergensis*, MGH SS 12, 822–83

Ekkehard of Aura, *Chronica* ed. F.-J. Schmale and I. Schmale-Ott (Ausgewählte Quellen zur deutschen Geschichte des Mittelalters 15: Darmstadt, 1972) pp. 124–208, 268–376

Epistolae Moguntinae ed. P. Jaffé, *Bibliotheca rerum Germanicarum* 3 (Berlin, 1866), 317–421

Epistolae Romanorum pontificum genuinae ed. A. Thiel 1 (Braunsberg, 1868)

Frutolf of Michelsberg, *Chronica* ed. F.-J. Schmale and I. Schmale-Ott (Ausgewählte Quellen zur deutschen Geschichte des Mittelalters 15: Darmstadt, 1972) pp. 48–121

Gebhard of Salzburg, *Epistola ad Herimannum Mettensem episcopum*, MGH *Libelli* 1 (1891), 261–79

Genealogia Welfonum, MGH SS 13, 733–4

Genealogia Zaringorum, MGH SS 13, 735–6

Geoffrey Malaterra, *De rebus gestis Rogerii Calabriae et Siciliae comitis et Roberti Guiscardi ducis fratris eius* ed. E. Pontieri, *Rerum Italicarum Scriptores* ser. 2, 5 (Bologna, 1926)

Gesta archiepiscoporum Magdeburgensium, MGH SS 14, 376–416

Gesta episcoporum Cameracensium, MGH SS 7, 393–489

Gesta episcoporum Halberstadensium, MGH SS 23, 73–123

Gesta Galcheri episcopi Cameracensis, MGH SS 14, 186–210

Gesta Treverorum, Continuatio I, MGH SS 8, 175–200

Gilles of Orval, *Gesta episcoporum Leodiensium*, MGH SS 25, 1–129

Gilles of Orval, *Gesta episcoporum Leodiensium abbreviata*, MGH SS 25, 129–35

Gregory VII, *Registrum*, MGH *Epistolae selectae* 2 (Berlin, 1920, 1923)

Gregory VII, *The Epistolae Vagantes of Pope Gregory VII* ed. H. E. J. Cowdrey (Oxford, 1972)

Gregory of Catino, *Historiae Farfenses*, MGH SS 11, 519–90

Gregory of Catino, *Il Regesto di Farfa, compilato da Gregorio di Catino* ed. I. Giorgi and U. Balzani 1–5 (Rome 1914, 1879–92)

Heinrici III Diplomata: Die Urkunden Heinrichs III., MGH *Diplomata* 5 (1931)

Heinrici IV Diplomata: Die Urkunden Heinrichs IV., MGH *Diplomata* 6/1–3 (1941, 1959, 1978)

Helmold of Bosau, *Cronica Slavorum: Helmolds Slavenchronik*, MGH SS rer. Germ. [32] (1921)

Henry IV, *Letters: Die Briefe Heinrichs IV., MGH Deutsches Mittelalter* 1 (Leipzig, 1937)

Herman of Reichenau, *Chronicon, MGH SS* 5, 67–133

Herman of Tournai, *Liber de restauratione sancti Martini Tornacensis, MGH SS* 14, 274–317

Herrand of Halberstadt, *Epistola de causa Heinrici regis, MGH Libelli* 2 (1892), 287–91

Historia monasterii Hirsaugiensis, MGH SS 14, 254–61

Historia Welfonum Weingartensis, MGH SS 21, 454–71

Hugh of Flavigny, *Chronicon, MGH SS* 8, 280–502

Humbert of Silva Candida, *Libri III adversus simoniacos, MGH Libelli* 1 (1891), 95–253

I Placiti del 'Regnum Italiae' ed. C. Manaresi 3 (Fonti per la Storia d'Italia 97: Rome, 1960)

Il Regesto di Farfa 5, ed. I. Giorgi and U. Balzani (Rome, 1892)

Isidore of Seville, *Etymologiarum sive Originum libri XX* ed. W. M. Lindsay (Oxford, 1911)

Isidore of Seville, *Sententiarum libri III, MPL* 83, 537–738

Italia Sacra ed. F. Ughelli (second edition: Venice, 1717–22)

Ivo of Chartres, *Epistola ad Hugonem,* MGH Libelli 2, 640–7

John of Mantua, *In Cantica Canticorum Tractatus* ed. B. Bischoff and B. Taeger (Freiburg, 1973)

Lambert of Arras, *Epistolae, MPL* 162, 647C–702A

Lampert of Hersfeld, *Annales,* in: *Lamperti monachi Hersfeldensis Opera, MGH SS rer. Germ.* [38] (1894) pp. 3–304

Lampert of Hersfeld, *Libellus de institutione Herveldensis ecclesiae,* in: *Lamperti Opera* pp. 343–54

Landulf Junior de sancto Paulo, *Historia Mediolanensis, MGH SS* 20, 17–49

Landulf Senior, *Historia Mediolanensis, MGH SS* 8, 32–100

Lanfranc: *Letters of Archbishop Lanfranc of Canterbury* ed. H. Clover and M. Gibson (Oxford, 1979)

Laurence of Liège, *Gesta episcoporum Virdunensium et abbatum sancti Vitoni, MGH SS* 10, 486–516

Liber concambiorum monasterii Eberspergensis ed. A.E. von Oefele, *Rerum Boicarum Scriptores* 2 (Augsburg, 1763)

Liber de unitate ecclesiae conservanda, MGH Libelli 2 (1892), 173–284

Liber pontificalis ed. L. Duchesne, C. Vogel 1–3 (Bibliothèque des Ecoles françaises d'Athènes et de Rome 2e série: Paris, 1886–1957)

Lorenzo Valla, *De falso credita et ementita Constantini donatione, MGH Quellen zur Geistesgeschichte des Mittelalters* 10 (1976)

Lupus Protospatarius, *Annales, MGH SS* 5, 52–3

Mainzer Urkundenbuch ed. M. Stimming (Darmstadt, 1932)

Manegold of Lautenbach, *Liber ad Gebehardum, MGH Libelli* 1 (1891) 308–430

Manegold of Lautenbach, *Liber contra Wolfelmum, MGH Quellen zur Geistesgeschichte des Mittelalters* 8 (1972)

Mariani Scotti Chronici Continuatio II, MGH SS 5, 563–4

Marianus Scottus, *Chronicon, MGH SS* 5, 481–562

Monumenta Erphesfurtensia saec. XII. XIII. XIV, MGH SS rer. Germ. [42] (1899)

Monumenta Historica Ducatus Carinthiae ed. A. von Jaksch 3 (Klagenfurt, 1904)

Notitiae fundationis et traditionum sancti Georgii in Nigra silva, MGH SS 15, 1005–23

Orthodoxa defensio imperialis, MGH Libelli 2 (1892), 534–42

Otto of Freising, *Chronica sive Historia de duabus civitatibus, MGH SS rer. Germ.* [45] (1912)

Otto of Freising and Rahewin, *Gesta Friderici I. imperatoris, MGH SS rer. Germ.* [46] (1912)

Paschal II, *Epistolae et Privilegia, MPL* 163, 31A–444A

Paul of Bernried, *Vita Gregorii VII papae* ed. J.M. Watterich, *Pontificum Romanorum Vitae* 1 (Leipzig, 1862), 474–546

Peter Damian, *Letters: Die Briefe des Petrus Damiani, MGH Briefe* 4 (1–4) (1983–93)

Petrus Crassus, *Defensio Heinrici IV, regis, MGH Libelli* 1 (1891), 432–53

Pseudo-Cyprian, *De XII abusivis saeculi* ed. S. Hellmann, Texte und Untersuchungen zur Geschichte der altchristlichen Literatur series 4, 3 (Leipzig, 1909) pp. 1–62

Rainald of Vézelay, *Vita sancti Hugonis abbatis, MPL* 159, 893B–906C

Rangerius of Lucca, *Vita metrica sancti Anselmi Lucensis episcopi, MGH SS* 30/2, 1155–1307

Regesta pontificum Romanorum ed. P. Jaffé (second edition: Leipzig, 1885)

Rudolf of St Trond, *Gesta abbatum Trudonensium, Libri I-VII, MGH SS* 10, 213–72

Rupert of Deutz, *Chronicon sancti Laurentii Leodiensis, MGH SS* 8, 261–79

Sigebert of Gembloux, *Chronica, MGH SS* 6, 268–374

Sigebert of Gembloux, *Leodicensium epistola adversus Paschalem papam, MGH Libelli* 2 (1892), 449–64

Sigeboto, *Vita Paulinae, MGH SS* 30/2, 910–38

Theoderic of Tholey, *Vita et passio Conradi archiepiscopi Treverensis, MGH SS* 8, 212–19

Thietmar of Merseburg, *Chronicon: Die Chronik des Bischofs Thietmar von Merseburg und ihre Korveier Überarbeitung, MGH SS rer. Germ., nova series* 9 (1935)

Triumphus sancti Remacli Stabulensis de coenobio Malmundariensi, MGH SS 11, 433–61

Udalschalk of Augsburg, *De Eginone abbate SS. Udalrici et Afrae et Herimanno episcopo Augustano, MGH SS* 12, 429–447

Urban II, *Epistolae et Privilegia, MPL* 151, 283A–552C

Urkundenbuch des Hochstifts Halberstadt und seiner Bischöfe ed. G. Schmidt 1 (Leipzig, 1883)

Urkundenbuch zur Geschichte der Bischöfe zu Speyer ed. F. X. Remling 1 (Mainz, 1852)

Vetera Analecta ed. J. Mabillon 1 (Paris, 1675)

Vita Adalberonis episcopi Wirziburgensis, MGH SS 12, 127–36

Vita Altmanni episcopi Pataviensis, MGH SS 12, 226–43

Vita Annonis archiepiscopi Coloniensis, MGH SS 11, 462–514

Vita Anselmi Lucensis, MGH SS 12, 1–35

Vita Bennonis II. episcopi Osnabrugensis ed. H. Kallfelz, *Lebensbeschreibungen einiger Bischöfe des 10.-12. Jahrhunderts* (Ausgewählte Quellen zur deutschen Geschichte des Mittelalters 22: Darmstadt, 1973) pp. 372–440

Vita Gebehardi archiepiscopi [*Salisburgensis*], *MGH SS* 11, 25–8

Vita Gebehardi archiepiscopi Salisburgensis et successorum eius, MGH SS II, 33–49

Vita Heinrici IV. imperatoris, MGH SS rer. Germ. [58] (1899)

Vita Theogeri abbatis sancti Georgii in Nigra silva et episcopi Mettensis, MGH SS 12, 449–79

Vita Wernheri episcopi Merseburgensis, MGH SS 12, 244–8

Vita Willihelmi abbatis Hirsaugiensis, MGH SS 12, 209–25

Walram of Naumburg, *Epistola de causa Heinrici regis, MGH Libelli* 2 (1892), 286–7

Wenrich of Trier, *Epistola sub Theoderici episcopi Virdunensis nomine composita, MGH Libelli* 1 (1891), 280–99

Wibert of Ravenna (Clement III), *Decretum Wiberti vel Clementis papae, MGH Libelli* 1 (1891), 621–6

Wido of Ferrara, *De scismate Hildebrandi, MGH Libelli* 1 (1891), 529–67

Wido of Osnabrück, *Liber de controversia inter Hildebrandum et Heinricum imperatorem, MGH Libelli* 1 (1891), 461–70

William of Apulia, *Gesta Roberti Wiscardi* ed. M. Mathieu (Istituto Siciliano di Studi Bizantini e Neoellenici. Testi e Monumenti. Testi 4: Palermo, 1961)

William of Malmesbury, *Gesta regum Anglorum* ed. W. Stubbs, *Rerum Britannicarum medii aevi Scriptores* 90 (London, 1887–9)

Wipo, *Gesta Chuonradi II. imperatoris* in *Wiponis Opera, MGH SS rer. Germ.* [61] (1915) pp. 3–62

Würzburger Chronik: G. Buchholz, *Die Würzburger Chronik. Eine quellenkritische Untersuchung* (Leipzig, 1879)

SECONDARY WORKS

Affeldt, W. (1969), 'Königserhebung Pippins und Unlösbarkeit des Eides im Liber de unitate ecclesiae conservanda', *DA* 25, 313–46

Althoff, G. (1981), 'Nunc fiant Christi milites, qui dudum extiterunt raptores', *Saeculum* 32, 317–33

(1986), 'Die Zähringerherrschaft im Urteil Ottos von Freising' in *Die Zähringer* ed. K. Schmid 1 (Sigmaringen), 43–58

(1989), 'Königsherrschaft und Konfliktbewältigung im 10. und 11. Jahrhundert', *FS* 23, 265–90

(1991), 'Die Billunger in der Salierzeit' in *Salier* 1: 309–29

Anton, H. H. (1988), 'Beobachtungen zur heinrizianischen Publizistik: die *Defensio Heinrici IV regis*' in *Historiographia Mediaevalis. Festschrift für Franz-Josef Schmale* ed. D. Berg and H.-W. Goetz (Darmstadt) pp. 149–67

Arnold, B. (1985), *German Knighthood, 1050–1300* (Oxford)

(1991), *Princes and Territories in Medieval Germany* (Cambridge)

Arquillière, H.-X. (1950), 'Le sens juridique de l'absolution de Canossa (1077)', *Actes du Congrès de Droit Canonique, 1947* (Paris) pp. 157–64

(1952a), 'Grégoire VII, à Canossa, a-t-il réintégré Henri IV dans sa fonction royale?' *Studi Gregoriani* 4, 1–25

(1952b), 'La IIe lettre de Grégoire VII à Herman de Metz (1081): ses sources patristiques', *Recherches de science religieuse* 40, 231–42

Baaken, G. (1961), 'Königtum, Burgen und Königsfreie. Studien zu ihrer Geschichte in Ostsachsen', *Vorträge und Forschungen* 6 (Constance-Stuttgart) pp. 9–95

Baethgen, F. (1941), 'Zur Tribur-Frage', *DA* 4, 394–411

Bannasch, H. (1969), 'Zur Gründung und älteren Geschichte des Benediktinerklosters Selz im Elsaß', *ZGO* 117, 97–160

Bauch, K. (1976), *Das mittelalterliche Grabbild* (Berlin and New York)

Bauernfeind, G. (1929), *Anno II., Erzbischof von Köln* (dissertation, Munich)

Becker, A. (1964), *Papst Urban II.* 1 (Schriften der MGH 19/1, Stuttgart)

(1973), 'Urban II. und die deutsche Kirche' in *Investiturstreit* pp. 241–75

Berges, W. (1947), 'Gregor VII. und das deutsche Designationsrecht', *Studi Gregoriani* 2, 189–209

Berges, W. (1963), 'Zur Geschichte des Werla-Goslarer Reichsbezirks vom 9. bis zum 11. Jahrhundert' in: *Deutsche Königspfalzen. Beiträge zu ihrer historischen und archäologischen Erforschung* 1 (Göttingen) pp. 113–57

Berschin, W. (1972), *Bonizo von Sutri. Leben und Werke* (Berlin and New York)

Bernhardt, J.W. (1993), *Itinerant Kingship and Royal Monasteries in Early Medieval Germany c. 936–1075* (Cambridge)

Bertolini, M. G. (1965), 'Beatrice di Lorena', *Dizionario Biografico degli Italiani* 7, 352–63

Beulertz, S. (1991), *Das Verbot der Laieninvestitur im Investiturstreit* (MGH Studien und Texte 2, Hanover)

Beumann, H. (1973), 'Tribur, Rom und Canossa' in *Investiturstreit* pp. 33–60

(1977), 'Reformpäpste als Reichsbischöfe in der Zeit Heinrichs III.' in *Festschrift Friedrich Hausmann* ed. H. Ebner (Graz, 1977) pp. 21–37

(1984), 'Zur Verfasserfrage der Vita Heinrici IV' in *Institutionen, Kultur und Gesellschaft im Mittelalter* ed. L. Fenske (Sigmaringen) pp. 305–19

Beumann, H. and W. Schlesinger (1955), 'Urkundenstudien zur deutschen Ostpolitik unter Otto III. Exkurs I', *Archiv für Diplomatik* 1, 236–50

Beyerle, K. (1925), 'Von der Gründung bis zum Ende des freiherrlichen Klosters (724–1427)' in *Die Kultur der Abtei Reichenau.* ed. K. Beyerle 1 (Munich), 55–212

Bischoff, B. (1948), 'Der Canticumkommentar des Johannes von Mantua für die Markgräfin Mathilde' in *Lebenskräfte in der abendländischen Geistesgeschichte.* ed. W. Stammler (Marburg) pp. 22–36

Black-Veldtrup, M. (1995), *Kaiserin Agnes (1043–1077). Quellenkritische Studien* (Cologne, Weimar and Vienna)

Bloch, H. (1986), *Monte Cassino in the Middle Ages* 1–3 (Rome)

Böhme, W. (1970), *Die deutsche Königserhebung im 10. bis 12. Jahrhundert* 1 (Göttingen)

Böhmer, J. F. and C. Will (1877), *Regesta archiepiscoporum Maguntinensium. Regesten zur Geschichte der Mainzer Erzbischöfe* 1 (Innsbruck)

Böhmer, J. F. and T. Struve, (1984), *Regesta Imperii* 3, 2: *Die Regesten des Kaiserreiches unter Heinrich IV.* 1 (Cologne-Vienna)

Borino, G. B. (1948), 'L'arcidiaconato di Ildebrando', *Studi Gregoriani* 3, 463–516

(1952), 'Cencio del prefetto Stefano l'attentatore di Gregorio VII', *Studi Gregoriani* 4, 373–440

(1956a), 'Perché Gregorio VII non annunciò la sua elezione ad Enrico IV e non ne richiese il consenso', *Studi Gregoriani* 5, 313–43

(1956b), 'Il monacato e l'investitura di Anselmo vescovo di Lucca', *Studi Gregoriani* 5, 361–74

(1958), 'Odelrico vescovo di Padova (1064–1080) legato di Gregorio VII in Germania (1079)' in *Miscellanea in honore di Roberto Cessi* I (Storia e Letteratura 71, Rome) pp. 63–79

(1959), 'La lettera di Walone abate di S. Arnolfo di Metz e di S. Remigio di Reims a Gregorio VII (1073)' in *Studi ricerche nella biblioteca e negli archivi Vaticani in memoria del Cardinal Giovanni Mercati* (Florence) pp. 28–33

(1959–61a), 'Le lettere di Gregorio VII e di Sigfrido archivescovo di Magonza', *Studi Gregoriani* 6, 265–75

(1959–6b), 'La lettera di Enrico IV alla madre Agnese imperatrice (1074)', *Studi Gregoriani* 6, 297–310

(1959–61c), 'Il decreto di Gregorio VII contro le investiture fu "promulgato" nel 1075', *Studi Gregoriani* 6, 329–48

Bornscheuer, L. (1968), *Miseriae Regum* (Arbeiten zur Frühmittelalterforschung 4, Berlin)

Boshof, E. (1978), 'Köln, Mainz, Trier', *Jahrbuch des kölnischen Geschichtsvereins* 49, 19–48

(1979a), *Heinrich IV. Herrscher an einer Zeitenwende* (Persönlichkeit und Geschichte 108–109, Göttingen)

(1979b), 'Das Reich in der Krise. Überlegungen zum Regierungsausgang Heinrichs III.', *HZ* 228, 265–87

(1981), 'Bischof Altmann, St. Nikola und die Kanonikerreform. Das Bistum Passau im Investiturstreit' in *Tradition und Entwicklung. Gedenkschrift für J. Riederer* ed. K.-H. Pollok (Passau) pp. 317–45

(1986), 'Das Reich und Ungarn in der Zeit der Salier', *Ostbairische Grenzmarken* 28, 178–94

(1987), *Die Salier* (Stuttgart, Berlin, Cologne and Mainz)

(1991) 'Bischöfe und Bischofskirchen von Passau und Regensburg' in *Salier* 2, 113–54

Bosl, K. (1950), *Die Reichsministerialität der Salier und Staufer* (Schriften der MGH 10/1, Stuttgart)

(1971), 'Adel, Bistum, Klöster Bayerns im Investiturstreit' in *Festschrift für Hermann Heimpel zum 70. Geburtstag* 2 (Göttingen), 1121–46

Brackmann, A. (1912), 'Heinrich IV. und der Fürstentag von Tribur', *Historische Vierteljahrschrift* 15, 135–93

(1927), 'Heinrich IV. als Politiker beim Ausbruch des Investiturstreits', *Sitzungsberichte der Preußischen Akademie der Wissenschaften, phil.-hist. Klasse* 32, 393–411

(1939), 'Tribur', *Abhandlungen der Preußischen Akademie der Wissenschaften 1939, phil.-hist. Klasse* 9, 3–37

Breen, A. (1988), *De XII abusivis. A critical edition with translation and introduction* (dissertation, Dublin)

Bresslau, H. (1879, 1884), *Jahrbücher des Deutschen Reiches unter Konrad II.* 1, 2 (Leipzig)

Brooke, Z. N. (1939), 'Lay investiture and its relation to the conflict of empire and papacy', *Proceedings of the British Academy* 25, 217–47

Brühl, C. (1954), 'Die Kaiserpfalz bei St. Peter und die Pfalz Ottos III. auf dem Palatin', *QFIAB* 34, 1–30

(1968), *Fodrum, Gistum, Servitium regis* 1 (Cologne-Graz)

Brüske, W. (1955), *Untersuchungen zur Geschichte des Lutizenbundes* (Münster)

Buchner, R. (1963), 'Der Titel rex Romanorum in deutschen Königsurkunden des 11. Jahrhunderts', *DA* 19, 327–38

Bücking, J. (1968), 'Zur Grabinschrift Rudolfs von Rheinfelden', *ZGO* 116, 393–5

Büttner, H. (1949), 'Das Erzstift Mainz und die Klosterreform im 11. Jahrhundert', *Archiv für mittelrheinische Kirchengeschichte* 1, 30–64

(1952), 'Die Anfänge der Stadt Kreuznach und die Grafen von Sponheim', *ZGO* N.F. 61, 433–44

(1973), 'Die Bischofsstädte von Basel bis Mainz in der Zeit des Investiturstreites' in *Investiturstreit* pp. 351–61

Bulst-Thiele M. L. (1933), *Kaiserin Agnes* (dissertation, Göttingen)

Capitani, O. (1970), 'Storiografia e riforma della Chiesa in Italia' in *La storiografia alto-medievale* (Settimane di studio del Centro italiano di Studi sull' Alto Medioevo 17, Spoleto) pp. 557–629

Chalandon, F. (1907), *Histoire de la domination normande en Italie et en Sicile* 1 (Paris)

Classen, P. (1964), 'Heinrichs IV. Briefe im Codex Udalrici', *DA* 20, 115–29

Claude, D. (1972), *Geschichte des Erzbistums Magdeburg bis in das 12. Jahrhundert* 1 (Cologne-Vienna)

Cowdrey, H. E. J. (1966), 'Archbishop Aribert II of Milan', *History* 51, 1–15

(1968a), 'The papacy, the Patarenes and the church of Milan', *Transactions of the Royal Historical Society* fifth series, 18, 25–48

(1968b), 'The succession of the archbishops of Milan in the time of Pope Urban II', *English Historical Review* 83, 285–94

(1970a), *The Cluniacs and the Gregorian Reform* (Oxford)

(1970b), 'The peace of God and the truce of God in the eleventh century', *Past and Present* 46, 42–67

(1972), 'Pope Gregory VII and the Anglo-Norman church and kingdom', *Studi Gregoriani* 9, 77–114

(1978), 'Memorials of Abbot Hugh of Cluny (1049–1109)', *Studi Gregoriani* 11, 11–176

(1982), 'Pope Gregory VII's "crusading" plans of 1074' in *Outremer. Studies in the History of the Crusading Kingdom of Jerusalem* (Jerusalem) pp. 27–40

(1983), *The Age of Abbot Desiderius. Montecassino, the Papacy and the Normans in the Eleventh and Early Twelfth Centuries* (Oxford)

Cram, K.-G. (1955), *Iudicium belli. Zum Rechtscharakter des Krieges im deutschen Mittelalter* (Münster-Cologne)

Dahlhaus, J. (1991), 'Zu den Anfängen von Pfalz und Stiften in Goslar' in *Salier* 2: 373–428

Dasberg, L. (1965), *Untersuchungen über die Entwertung des Judenstatus im 11. Jahrhundert* (Paris-La Haye)

Deér, J. (1936), 'Die Anfänge der ungarisch-kroatischen Staatsgemeinschaft', *Archivum Europae Centro-Orientalis* 2

(1972), *Papsttum und Normannen* (Cologne and Vienna)

Dempf, A. (1929), *Sacrum Imperium* (Munich and Berlin)

Despy, G. (1958), 'La date de l'accession de Godefroid de Bouillon au duché de Basse-Lothringie', *Revue belge de philologie et d'histoire* 36, 1275–84

Diebolder, P. (1916), 'Bischof Gebhard III. von Konstanz (1084–1100) und der Investiturstreit in der Schweiz', *Zeitschrift für Schweizerische Kirchengeschichte* 10, 81–101, 187–208

Diener, H. (1959), 'Das Itinerar des Abtes Hugo von Cluny' in *Neue Forschungen über Cluny und die Cluniacenser* ed. G. Tellenbach (Freiburg) pp. 353–426

Doeberl, M. (1894), *Die Markgrafschaft und die Markgrafen auf dem bayerischen Nordgau* (Munich)

Dressler, F. (1954), *Petrus Damiani. Leben und Werke* (Studia Anselmiana 34, Rome)

Dümmler, E. (1900), 'Ein Brief an König Heinrich IV.', *NA* 25, 205–6

Eckhardt, K. A. (1964), *Eschwege als Brennpunkt thüringisch-hessischer Geschichte* (Marburg)

Eichmann, E. (1938), 'Der sog. Salische Kaiserordo', *ZSSRG KA* 27, 1–26

(1942), *Die Kaiserkrönung im Abendland* 2 (Würzburg)

Elze, R. (1980), 'Über die Leistungsfähigkeit von Gesandtschaften und Boten im 11. Jahrhundert' in *Histoire comparée de l'administration (IVe-XVIIIe siècles)* ed. W. Paravicini and K. F. Werner (Beihefte der Francia 9, Munich) 3–10

Erdmann, C. (1932), 'Die Briefe Meinhards von Bamberg', *NA* 49, 332–431

(1934), 'Kaiserliche und päpstliche Fahnen im hohen Mittelalter', *QFIAB* 25

(1935), *Die Entstehung des Kreuzzugsgedankens* (Stuttgart). English translation: *The Origins of the Idea of Crusade* (Princeton, 1977)

(1936a), 'Die Anfänge der staatlichen Propaganda im Investiturstreit', *HZ* 154, 491–512

(1936b), 'Die Bamberger Domschule im Investiturstreit', *Zeitschrift für bayerische Landesgeschichte* 9, 1–46

(1937), 'Tribur und Rom. Zur Vorgeschichte der Canossafahrt', *DA* 1, 361–88

(1938), *Studien zur Briefliteratur Deutschlands im elften Jahrhundert* (Schriften der MGH 1, Leipzig)

(1939), 'Untersuchungen zu den Briefen Heinrichs IV.', *Archiv für Urkundenforschung* 16, 184–253

Erdmann, C. and D. von Gladiss (1939), 'Gottschalk von Aachen im Dienste Heinrichs IV.', *DA* 3, 115–74

Erkens, F.-R. (1987), 'Die Kanonikerreform in Oberlothringen', *HJ* 107, 1–43

Faußner, H. C. (1973), 'Die Verfügungsgewalt des deutschen Königs über weltliches Reichsgut', *DA* 29, 345–449

Feierabend, H. (1913), *Die politische Stellung der deutschen Reichsabteien während des Investiturstreites* (Breslau)

Feine, H. E. (1965), 'Zum Papstwahldekret Nikolaus' II. "In nomine domini" von 1059 nach neueren Forschungen' in *Etudes d'histoire du droit canonique dédiées à G. Le Bras* 1 (Paris), 541–51

Fenske, L. (1977), *Adelsopposition und kirchliche Reformbewegung im östlichen Sachsen* (Göttingen)

Fichtenau, H. (1977), *Beiträge zur Mediävistik* 1, 2 (Stuttgart)

Ficker, J. (1874), *Forschungen zur Reichs- und Rechtsgeschichte Italiens* 4 (Innsbruck)

Fleckenstein, J. (1957), 'Über die Herkunft der Welfen und ihre Anfänge in Süddeutschland' in *Studien und Vorarbeiten zur Geschichte des großfränkischen und frühdeutschen Adels* (Freiburg/Br.) pp. 71–136

(1964), 'Rex canonicus. Über Entstehung und Bedeutung des mittelalterlichen Königskanonikates' in *Festschrift Percy Ernst Schramm* ed. P. Classen and P. Scheibert 1 (Wiesbaden), 57–71

(1966), *Die Hofkapelle der deutschen Könige* 2 (Schriften der MGH 16/2, Stuttgart)

(1968), 'Heinrich IV. und der deutsche Episkopat in den Anfängen des Investiturstreites' in *Adel und Kirche. Festschrift für Gerd Tellenbach* ed. J. Fleckenstein and K. Schmid (Freiburg-Basel-Vienna) pp. 221–36

(1973), 'Hofkapelle und Reichsepiskopat unter Heinrich IV.' in *Investiturstreit* pp. 117–40

(1985), 'Problematik und Gestalt der ottonisch-salischen Reichskirche' in *Reich und Kirche vor dem Investiturstreit* ed. K. Schmid (Sigmaringen) pp. 83–98

(1988), 'Über den engeren und weiteren Begriff von Ritter und Rittertum (*miles und militia*)' in *Person und Gemeinschaft im Mittelalter* ed. G. Althoff, D. Geuenich, O. G. Oexle, J. Wollasch (Sigmaringen) pp. 379–92

Fliche, A. (1912), *Le règne de Philippe I roi de France (1060–1108)* (Paris)

(1924, 1926), *La réforme grégorienne* (Louvain, Paris)

(1947), 'Grégoire VII, à Canossa, a-t-il réintégré Henri IV dans sa fonction royale?' *Studi Gregoriani* 1, 373–86

Fornasari, G. (1979), 'Prospettive del pensiero politico di S. Pier Damiano' in *Fonte Avellana nella società dei secoli XI e XII. Atti del II Convegno del Centro di Studi Avellaniti 1978* pp. 117–22

Forni, P. (1964), 'Studi sulla tavola genealogica ascendentale della contessa Matilde di Canossa' in *Studi Matildici. Atti e Memorie del Convegno di Studi Matildici* (Modena) pp. 259–83

Fraeys de Veubeke, A.-C. (1976), 'Les *Annales Sancti Iacobi Leodiensis* seraient-elles originaires de Gembloux?' in *Hommage à André Boutemy* ed. G. Cambier (Collection Latomus 145, Brussels) pp. 117–28

Franke, T. (1987), 'Studien zur Geschichte der Fuldaer Äbte im 11. und frühen 12. Jahrhundert', *Archiv für Diplomatik* 33, 55–238

Freytag, H.-J. (1951), *Die Herrschaft der Billunger in Sachsen* (Göttingen)

Fuhrmann, H. (1975), '"Volkssouveranität" und "Herrschaftsvertrag" bei Manegold von Lautenbach' in *Festschrift für Hermann Krause* ed. S. Gágner, H. Schlosser, W. Wiegand (Cologne-Vienna) pp. 21–42

(1982), 'Pseudoisidor, Otto von Ostia (Urban II.) und der Zitatenkampf von Gerstungen (1085)', *ZSSRG KA* 68, 52–69

(1984), 'Rex canonicus – Rex clericus?' in *Institutionen, Kultur und Gesellschaft im Mittelalter* ed. L. Fenske, W. Rösener, T. Zotz (Sigmaringen) pp. 321–6

Gaettens, R. (1962), 'Das Geburtsjahr Heinrichs V. 1081 oder 1086?', *ZSSRG GA* 79, 52–71

Gawlik, A. (1970a), *Intervenienten und Zeugen in den Diplomen Kaiser Heinrichs IV. (1056–1105)* (Kallmünz)

(1970b), 'Bischof Adalbero von Trient und Bischof Oger von Ivrea als Leiter der italienischen Kanzlei unter Heinrich IV.', *DA* 26, 208–19

(1975), 'Analekten zu den Urkunden Heinrichs IV.', *DA* 31, 370–419

(1978), *Die Urkunden Heinrichs IV.* 3 (*MGH Diplomata* 6/3, Hanover) [Einleitung]

Gericke, H. (1955), 'Die Wahl Heinrichs IV. Eine Studie zum deutschen Königswahlrecht', *Zeitschrift für Geschichtswissenschaft* 3, 735–49

Gernhuber, J. (1952), *Die Landfriedensbewegung in Deutschland bis zum Mainzer Reichslandfrieden von 1235* (Bonn)

Giese, W. (1979), *Der Stamm der Sachsen und das Reich in ottonischer und salischer Zeit* (Wiesbaden)

(1991), 'Reichsstrukturprobleme unter den Saliern – der Adel in Ostsachsen' in *Salier* 1: 273–308

(1993), 'Venedig-Politik und Imperiums-Idee bei den Ottonen' in *Herrschaft, Kirche, Kultur. Festschrift für Friedrich Prinz* (Stuttgart) pp. 219–43

Giesebrecht, W. von (1866), 'Die Gesetzgebung der römischen Kirche zur Zeit Gregors VII.', *Münchner Historisches Jahrbuch für 1866* (Munich)

(1890), *Geschichte der deutschen Kaiserzeit* 3 (fifth edition, Leipzig)

Gilchrist, J. (1965), '*Simoniaca haeresis* and the problem of orders from Leo IX to Gratian', *Proceedings of the Second International Congress of Medieval Canon Law* ed. S. Kuttner and J. J. Ryan (Monumenta Iuris Canonici C.1, Vatican City) pp. 209–35

Gillingham, J. (1989), 'William the Bastard at war' in *Studies in Medieval History presented to R. Allen Brown* ed. C. Harper-Bill, C. J. Holdsworth, J. L. Nelson (Woodbridge)

(1991), 'Elective kingship and the unity of medieval Germany', *German History* 9, 124–35

Gladel, N. (1932), *Die trierischen Erzbischöfe im Investiturstreit* (dissertation, Cologne)

Glaesener, H. (1947), 'Un mariage fertile en conséquences (Godefroid le Barbu et Béatrice de Toscane)', *Revue d'histoire ecclésiastique* 42, 379–416

Glaeske, G. (1962), *Die Erzbischöfe von Hamburg-Bremen als Reichsfürsten (937–1258)* (Hildesheim)

Goetz, H.-W. (1991), 'Das Herzogtum im Spiegel der salierzeitlichen Geschichtsschreibung' in *Salier* 1: 253–71

Goez, E. (1995), *Beatrix von Canossa und Tuszien. Eine Untersuchung zur Geschichte des 11. Jahrhunderts* (Sigmaringen)

(1996), 'Der Thronerbe als Rivale: König Konrad, Kaiser Heinrichs IV. älterer Sohn', *HJ* 116, 1–49

Goez, W. (1962), *Der Leihezwang. Eine Untersuchung zur Geschichte des deutschen Lehnrechts* (Tübingen)

(1968), 'Zur Erhebung und ersten Absetzung Papst Gregors VII.', *Römische Quartalschrift für christliche Altertumskunde und Kirchengeschichte* 63, 117–44

(1973), 'Reformpapsttum, Adel und monastische Erneuerung in der Toscana' in *Investiturstreit* pp. 205–39

(1974), 'Rainald von Como. Ein Bischof des 11. Jahrhunderts zwischen Kurie und Krone' in *Historische Forschungen für Walter Schlesinger* ed. H. Beumann (Cologne-Vienna) pp. 462–94

(1980), 'Gebhard I., Bischof von Eichstätt, als Papst Viktor II.', *Fränkische Lebensbilder* 9, 11–21

(1983), *Gestalten des Hochmittelalters* (Darmstadt)

Gottlob, T. (1936), *Der kirchliche Amtseid der Bischöfe* (Bonn)

Grauert, H. (1900), 'Die Kaisergräber im Dom zu Speyer', *Sitzungsberichte der Bayerischen Akademie der Wissenschaften, phil.-hist. Klasse* (Munich)

Gussone, N. (1978), *Thron und Inthronisation des Papstes von den Anfängen bis zum 12. Jahrhundert* (Bonn)

Guttenberg, E. von (1937), *Das Bistum Bamberg* 1 (Germania Sacra 2/1, Berlin)

Haase, K. (1901), *Die Königskrönungen in Oberitalien und die 'eiserne' Krone* (dissertation, Strasbourg)

Haefele, H. F. (1954), *Fortuna Heinrici IV. Imperatoris* (Vienna)

Hägermann, D. (1970a), 'Zur Vorgeschichte des Pontifikats Nikolaus' II.', *Zeitschrift für Kirchengeschichte* 81, 352–61

(1970b), 'Untersuchungen zum Papstwahldekret von 1059', *ZSSRG KA* 56, 157–93

Hagenmeyer, H. (1877), *Ekkehardi Uraugiensis abbatis Hierosolymita* (Tübingen)

Haider, S. (1968), *Die Wahlversprechen der römisch-deutschen Könige bis zum Ende des zwölften Jahrhunderts* (Vienna)

Haller, J. (1906), 'Canossa', *Neue Jahrbücher für das klassische Altertum, Geschichte und deutsche Literatur* 17, 102–47

(1939), 'Der Weg nach Canossa', *HZ* 160, 229–85

(1951), *Das Papsttum. Idee und Wirklichkeit* 2 (second edition, Stuttgart)

Hallinger, K. (1950–1), *Gorze-Kluny. Studien zu den monastischen Lebensformen und Gegensätzen im Hochmittelalter* (Rome)

Hampe, K. (1912), *Deutsche Kaisergeschichte in der Zeit der Salier und Staufer* (Leipzig) English translation: *Germany under the Salian and Hohenstaufen Emperors* (Oxford, 1968)

Hauck, A. (1952), *Kirchengeschichte Deutschlands* 3 (sixth edition, Leipzig)

Hauck, K. (1959), 'Pontius Pilatus aus Forchheim', *Jahrbuch für fränkische Landesforschung* 19, 171–92

Heidrich, I. (1984), *Ravenna unter Erzbischof Wibert (1073–1100)* (Sigmaringen)

(1988), 'Beobachtungen zur Stellung der Bischöfe von Speyer im Konflikt zwischen Heinrich IV. und den Reformpäpsten', *FS* 22, 266–85

(1991), 'Bischöfe und Bischofskirche von Speyer' in *Salier* 2: 187–224

Heinrichsen, A. (1954), 'Süddeutsche Adelsgeschlechter in Niedersachsen im 11. und 12. Jahrhundert', *Niedersächsisches Jahrbuch für Landesgeschichte* 26, 24–116

Heinzelmann, K. (1904), *Die Farfenser Streitschriften* (dissertation, Strasbourg)

Herberhold, F. (1934), 'Die Beziehungen des Cadalus von Parma (Gegenpapst Honorius II.) zu Deutschland', *HJ* 54, 84–104

(1947), 'Die Angriffe des Cadalus von Parma (Gegenpapst Honorius II.) auf Rom in den Jahren 1062 und 1063', *Studi Gregoriani* 2, 477–503

Heyck, E. (1891), *Geschichte der Herzöge von Zähringen* (Freiburg)

Hils, K. (1967), *Die Grafen von Nellenburg im 11. Jahrhundert* (Freiburg)

Hirsch, H. (1922), *Die hohe Gerichtsbarkeit im deutschen Mittelalter* (Prague)

Hlawitschka, E. (1974), 'Zwischen Tribur und Canossa', *HJ* 94, 25–45

(1990), 'Zum Geburtsdatum Kaiser Heinrichs V.', *HJ* 110, 471–5

(1991), 'Zur Herkunft und zu den Seitenverwandten des Gegenkönigs Rudolf von Rheinfelden' in *Salier* 1: 175–220

Höss, I. (1945), *Die deutschen Stämme im Investiturstreit* (dissertation, Jena)

Hoffmann, H. (1959), 'Ivo von Chartres und die Lösung des Investiturproblems', *DA* 15, 393–440

(1964), *Gottesfriede und Treuga Dei* (Schriften der MGH 20, Stuttgart)

Hofmann, E. (1931), 'Die Stellung der Konstanzer Bischöfe zu Papst und Kaiser während des Investiturstreits', *Freiburger Diözesan-Archiv* 58, 181–242

Holder-Egger, O. (1894), 'Studien zu Lampert von Hersfeld' *NA* 19, 141–213, 369–430, 507–74

(1906), 'Fragment eines Manifestes aus der Zeit Heinrichs IV.', *NA* 31, 183–93

Holtzmann, R. (1941), *Geschichte der sächsischen Kaiserzeit (900–1024)* (Munich)

Holtzmann, W. (1924–25), 'Studien zur Orientpolitik des Reformpapsttums und zur Entstehung des ersten Kreuzzuges', *Historische Vierteljahresschrift* 22, 167–99

(1963), 'Maximilla regina, soror regis Rogerii', *DA* 19, 149–67

Hóman, B. (1940), *Geschichte des ungarischen Mittelalters* 1 (Berlin)

Hucke, R. G. (1956), *Die Grafen von Stade 900–1144* (Stade)

Hübinger, P. E. (1973), *Die letzten Worte Papst Gregors VII.* (Opladen)

Hüls, R. (1977), *Kardinäle, Klerus und Kirchen Roms 1049–1130* (Tübingen)

Hyde, J. K. (1973), *Society and Politics in Medieval Italy* (London)

Jakobs, H. (1961), *Die Hirsauer* (Cologne-Graz)

(1964), 'Das Papstwahldekret von 1059. Bericht über ein neues Buch', *HJ* 83, 351–9

(1968), *Der Adel in der Klosterreform von St. Blasien* (Cologne and Graz)

(1973), 'Rudolf von Rheinfelden und die Kirchenreform' in *Investiturstreit* pp. 87–115

Jäschke, K.-U. (1963–4, 1965–6), 'Studien zu Quellen und Geschichte des Osnabrücker Zehntstreits unter Heinrich IV.' I, II, *Archiv für Diplomatik* 9/10, 112–285; 11/12, 280–402

Jasper, D. (1986), *Das Papstwahldekret von 1059* (Sigmaringen)

Jenal, G. (1974, 1975), *Erzbischof Anno II. von Köln (1056–75) und sein politisches Wirken* 1, 2 (Stuttgart)

Johanek, P. (1991), 'Die Erzbischöfe von Hamburg-Bremen und ihre Kirche im Reich der Salierzeit' in *Salier* 2: 79–112

Joranson, E. (1928), 'The great German pilgrimage of 1064–65' in *The Crusades and other Historical Essays* ed. L.J. Paetow (New York) pp. 3–43

Jordan, K. (1938a), 'Ravennater Fälschungen aus den Anfängen des Investiturstreites', *Archiv für Urkundenforschung* 15, 426–48

(1938b), 'Der Kaisergedanke in Ravenna zur Zeit Heinrichs IV.', *DA* 2, 85–128

(1964), 'Investiturstreit und frühe Stauferzeit (1056–1197)' in *Handbuch der deutschen Geschichte* ed. H. Grundmann 1 (seventh edition, Stuttgart), 242–339

(1970), 'Sachsen und das deutsche Königtum im hohen Mittelalter', *HZ* 210, 529–59

Joris, A. (1961–62), 'Observations sur la proclamation de la Trêve de Dieu à Liège à la fin du XIe siècle' in *La Paix* 1 (Recueils de la société Jean Bodin 14, Brussels) pp. 503–45

Kaiser, R. (1980), 'Benno II., Bischof von Osnabrück, 1068–1088', *Lexikon des Mittelalters* 1 (Munich-Zürich), 1917–18

Kehr, P. (1921), 'Zur Geschichte Wiberts von Ravenna (Clemens III.), *Sitzungsberichte der Preußischen Akademie der Wissenchaften, Jahrgang 1921* (Berlin) pp. 355–68, 973–88

(1930), 'Vier Kapitel aus der Geschichte Kaiser Heinrichs III.' *Abhandlungen der Preußischen Akademie der Wissenschaften, phil.-hist. Klasse* 3, pp. 1–61

Keller, H. (1970), 'Die soziale und politische Verfassung Mailands in den Anfängen des kommunalen Lebens', *HZ* 211, 34–64

(1973), 'Pataria und Stadtverfassung, Stadtgemeinde und Reform: Mailand im "Investiturstreit"' in *Investiturstreit* pp. 321–50

(1982), 'Reichsstruktur und Herrschaftsauffassung in ottonisch-frühsalischer Zeit', *FM* 16, 74–128

(1983), 'Schwäbische Herzöge als Thronbewerber: Hermann II. (1002), Rudolf von Rheinfelden (1077), Friedrich von Staufen (1125)', *ZGO* 131, 123–62

Kempf, F. (1964), 'Pier Damiani und das Papstwahldekret von 1059', *Archivum Historiae Pontificiae* 2, 73–89, 157–93

(1982), [review of R. Schieffer (1981)], *Archivum Historiae Pontificiae* 20, 409–15

Kern, F. (1914), *Gottesgnadentum und Widerstandsrecht im früheren Mittelalter* (Münster, Cologne) English translation: *Kingship and Law in the Middle Ages* (Oxford, 1939)

Keunecke, H. O. (1978), *Die Münzenberger* (Darmstadt)

Kieft, C. van de (1955), 'Bisschop Willem en de Utrechtse synode van 1076', *Tijdschrift voor Geschiedenis* 68, 70–9

Kienast, W. (1965), 'Der Herzogtitel in den deutschen Königsurkunden' in *Festschrift Hermann Aubin* ed. O. Brunner (Wiesbaden) pp. 563–82

(1968), *Der Herzogtitel in Frankreich und Deutschland (9. bis 12. Jahrhundert)* (Munich and Vienna)

Kilian, E. (1886), *Itinerar Kaiser Heinrichs IV.* (Karlsruhe)

Kimpen, E. (1955), 'Zur Königsgenealogie der Karolinger- bis Stauferzeit', *ZGO* 103, 35–115

Kisch, G. (1955), *Forschungen zur Rechts- und Sozialgeschichte der Juden in Deutschland während des Mittelalters* (Zürich)

Kittel, E. (1931), 'Der Kampf um die Reform des Domkapitels in Lucca im 11. Jahrhundert' in *Festschrift A. Brackmann* ed. L. Santifaller (Weimar) pp. 220–35

Klaar, K.-E. (1966), *Die Herrschaft der Eppensteiner in Kärnten* (Klagenfurt)

Klebel, E. (1955), 'Alemannischer Hochadel im Investiturstreit' in *Grundfragen der alemannischen Geschichte* (Vorträge und Forschungen 1, Lindau-Constance) pp. 209–42

Klewitz, H.-W. (1939a), 'Die Festkrönungen der deutschen Könige', *ZSSRG KA* 28, 48–96

(1939b), 'Königtum, Hofkapelle und Domkapitel im 10. und 11. Jahrhundert', *Archiv für Urkundenforschung* 16, 102–53

(1957), *Reformpapsttum und Kardinalkolleg* (Darmstadt)

(1971), *Ausgewählte Aufsätze zur Kirchen- und Geistesgeschichte des Mittelalters* (Aalen)

Knabe, L. (1936), *Die gelasianische Zweigewaltentheorie bis zum Ende des Investiturstreits* (Berlin)

Koch, G. (1972), *Auf dem Wege zum Sacrum Imperium* (Vienna, Cologne and Graz)

Köbler, G. (1971), *Das Recht im frühen Mittelalter* (Cologne and Vienna)

Köhncke, O. (1888), *Wibert von Ravenna (Papst Clemens III.)* (Leipzig)

Kolmer, L. (1991), 'Regensburg in der Salierzeit' in *Salier* 3: 191–213

Kost, O.-H. (1962), *Das östliche Niedersachsen im Investiturstreit* (Göttingen)

Kottje, R. (1978), 'Zur Bedeutung der Bischofsstädte für Heinrich IV.', *HJ* 97–98, 131–57

Kraus, A. (1972), *Civitas Regia. Das Bild Regensburgs in der deutschen Geschichtsschreibung des Mittelalters* (Kallmünz)

Krause, H. (1965), 'Consilio et iudicio' in *Speculum historiale* ed. C. Bauer, L. Boehm, M. Müller (Freiburg-Munich) pp. 416–38

Krause, H.-G. (1960), *Das Papstwahldekret von 1059 und seine Rolle im Investiturstreit* (Studi Gregoriani 7, Rome)

Krautheimer, R. (1980), *Rome. Profile of a City, 312–1308* (Princeton)

Ladewig, P. and T. Müller, (1895), *Regesten zur Geschichte der Bischöfe von Constanz* 1 (Innsbruck)

Lange, K.-H. (1961), 'Die Stellung der Grafen von Northeim in der Reichsgeschichte des 11. und 12. Jahrhunderts', *Niedersächsisches Jahrbuch für Landesgeschichte* 33, 1–107

(1969), *Der Herrschaftsbereich der Grafen von Northeim 950 bis 1144* (Göttingen)

Leccisotti, T. (1947), 'L'incontro di Desiderio di Montecassino col re Enrico IV ad Albano', *Studi Gregoriani* 1, 307–19

Lechner, K. (1976), *Die Babenberger. Markgrafen und Herzöge von Österreich 976–1246* (Vienna, Cologne and Graz)

Lehmgrübner, H. (1887), *Benzo von Alba. Ein Verfechter der kaiserlichen Staatsidee unter Heinrich IV.* (Berlin)

Leidinger, P. (1969), 'Westfalen im Investiturstreit', *Westfälische Zeitschrift* 119, 267–314

Lewald, U. (1979), 'Die Ezzonen. Das Schicksal eines rheinischen Fürstengeschlechtes', *Rheinische Vierteljahrsblätter* 43, 120–68

Leyser, K. (1968), 'The German aristocracy from the ninth to the early twelfth century', *Past and Present* 41, 25–53

(1979), *Rule and Conflict in an Early Medieval Society. Ottonian Saxony* (London)

(1981), 'Ottonian government', *English Historical Review* 96, 721–53

(1983), 'The crisis of medieval Germany', *Proceedings of the British Academy* 69, 409–43

(1991), 'Gregory VII and the Saxons', *La Riforma Gregoriana e l'Europa* 2 (Studi Gregoriani 14/2) pp. 231–8

(1994), *Communications and Power in Medieval Europe. The Gregorian Revolution and Beyond* (London)

Liebermann, F. (1901), 'Lanfranc and the antipope', *English Historical Review* 16, 328–32

Lintzel, M. (1929), 'Der Ursprung der deutschen Pfalzgrafschaften', *ZSSRG GA* 49, 233–63

Löffler, K. (1903), *Die westfälischen Bischöfe im Investiturstreit und in den Sachsenkriegen unter Heinrich IV. und Heinrich V.* (Paderborn)

Loud, G. A. (1979), 'Abbot Desiderius of Montecassino and the Gregorian papacy', *Journal of Ecclesiastical History* 30, 305–26

(1985), *Church and Society in the Norman Principality of Capua, 1058–1197* (Oxford)

Lück, D. (1970a), 'Erzbischof Anno II. von Köln. Standesverhältnisse, verwandtschaftliche Beziehungen und Werdegang bis zur Bischofsweihe', *Annalen des Historischen Vereins für den Niederrhein* 172, 7–112

(1970b), 'Die Kölner Erzbischöfe Hermann II. und Anno II. als Erzkanzler der Römischen Kirche', *Archiv für Diplomatik* 16, 1–50

Lynch, J. (1976), *Simoniacal Entry into Religious Life from 1000 to 1260* (Columbus, Ohio)

(1985), 'Hugh I of Cluny's sponsorship of Henry IV: its Context and consequences', *Speculum* 60, 800–26

Maccarrone, M. (1974), 'La teologia del primato romano del secolo XI' in *Le istituzioni ecclesiastiche della 'societas christiana' dei secoli XI–XII* 1 (Milan) pp. 21–122

Märtl, C. (1991), 'Die Bamberger Schulen – ein Bildungszentrum des Salierreiches' in *Salier* 3: 327–45

Martens, W. (1894), *Gregor VII., sein Leben und Wirken* 1, 2 (Leipzig)

Maurer, H. (1970), 'Ein päpstliches Patrimonium auf der Baar', *ZGO* 118, 53–6

(1978), *Der Herzog von Schwaben* (Sigmaringen)

(1991), 'Die Konstanzer Bischofskirche in salischer Zeit' in *Salier* 2: 155–86

May, O.-H. (1937), *Regesten der Erzbischöfe von Bremen* 1 (Hanover-Bremen)

Mayer, H.-E. (1959), 'Zwei Fragmente des Chartulars des Bistums Lausanne', *Schweizerische Zeitschrift für Geschichte* 9, 465–88

Mayer, T. (1950), *Fürsten und Staat* (Weimar)

Meier, G. (1987), *Die Bischöfe von Paderborn und ihr Bistum im Hochmittelalter* (Paderborn, Munich, Vienna and Zürich)

Methuen, E. (1966–67), 'Die Aachener Pröpste bis zum Ende der Stauferzeit', *Zeitschrift des Aachener Geschichtsvereins* 78, 5–95

Metz, W. (1971), 'Tafelgut, Königsstrasse und Servitium regis in Deutschland vornehmlich im 10. und 11. Jahrhundert', *HJ* 91, 257–91

Meyer, W. (1882), 'Ein Gedicht und ein Brief aus Freising von den Jahren 1084 und 1085 und ein Labyrinth mit Versen', *Sitzungsberichte der königlich bayerischen Akademie der Wissenschaften, phil.-hist. Klasse* 2, 3 (Munich) pp. 253–300

Meyer von Knonau, G. (1890, 1894, 1900, 1903, 1904, 1907), *Jahrbücher des Deutschen Reiches unter Heinrich IV. und Heinrich V.* 1–6 (Leipzig)

Miccoli, G. (1956), 'Il problema delle ordinazioni simoniache e le sinodi Lateranensi del 1060 e 1061', *Studi Gregoriani* 5, 57–72

(1960), *Pietro Igneo. Studi sull'età gregoriana* (Studi storici 40–41, Rome)

(1966), *Chiesa gregoriana* (Florence)

Michel, A. (1936), *Papstwahl und Königsrecht oder das Papstwahl-Konkordat von 1059* (Munich)

(1939), 'Das Papstwahlpactum von 1059', *HJ* 59, 291–351

Mikoletzky, H. L. (1960), 'Der "fromme" Kaiser Heinrich IV.', *MIÖG* 68, 250–65

Minninger, M. (1978), *Von Clermont zum Wormser Konkordat* (Cologne and Vienna)

Mitteis, H. (1927), *Politische Prozesse des früheren Mittelalters in Deutschland und Frankreich* (Sitzungsberichte der Heidelberger Akademie der Wissenschaften, phil.-hist. Klasse, 1926/27, 3. Abhandlung, Heidelberg)

(1944), *Die deutsche Königswahl* (second edition, Brünn, Munich and Vienna)

(1953), *Der Staat des hohen Mittelalters*. English translation: *The State in the Middle Ages* (Amsterdam and Oxford, 1975)

Mohr, W. (1976), *Geschichte des Herzogtums Lothringen* 2 (Saarbrücken)

Mommsen, T. E. and K. F. Morrison, (1962), *Imperial Lives and Letters of the Eleventh Century* (Columbia)

Moos, P. von (1988), *Geschichte als Topik. Das rhetorische Exemplum von der Antike zur Neuzeit* (Hildesheim, Zürich and Vienna)

Moreau, E. de (1945), *Histoire de l'Eglise en Belgique* 2 (second edition, Brussels)

Morin, G. (1910), 'Un épisode inédit du passage de l'empereur Henri IV à Liège en MCIII', *Revue Bénédictine* 27, 412–15

Morrison, K. F. (1962), 'Canossa. A revision', *Traditio* 18, 121–48

Müller, E. (1901), *Das Itinerar Kaiser Heinrichs III.* (Berlin)

Müller-Mertens, E. (1970), *Regnum Teutonicum* (Vienna, Cologne and Graz)

Naumann, H. (1967), 'Die Schenkung des Gutes Schluchsee an St. Blasien', *DA* 23, 358–404

Neuss, W. and F. W. Oediger, (1964), *Geschichte des Erzbistums Köln* 1 (Cologne)

Nicol, D. M. (1988), *Byzantium and Venice. A Study in Diplomatic and Cultural Relations* (Cambridge)

Nitschke, A. (1971), 'Adelheid (Eupraxia, Praxedis)', *Neue Deutsche Biographie* 1 (Berlin), 58

Ortmanns, K. (1972), *Das Bistum Minden in seinen Beziehungen zu König, Papst und Herzog bis zum Ende des 12. Jahrhunderts* (Bensberg)

Ott, H. (1986), 'Die Burg Zähringen und ihre Geschichte' in *Die Zähringer* ed. K. Schmid 1 (Sigmaringen), 11–15

Overmann, A. (1895), *Gräfin Mathilde von Tuscien. Ihre Besetzungen* (Innsbruck)

Panofsky, E. (1924), *Die deutsche Plastik des 11. bis 13. Jahrhunderts* 1 (Munich)

Partner, P. (1972), *The Lands of St Peter* (London)

Patze, H. (1962), *Die Entstehung der Landesherrschaft in Thüringen* 1 (Cologne)
(1963), 'Die Pegauer Annalen, die Königserhebung Wratislaws von Böhmen und die Anfänge der Stadt Pegau', *Jahrbuch für die Geschichte Mittel- und Ostdeutschlands* 12, 1–62

Perst, O. (1956), 'Eschwege, Speyer und das Reich', *Zeitschrift des Vereins für hessische Geschichte* 67, 76–97

Peyer, H. C. (1955), *Stadt und Stadtpatron im mittelalterlichen Italien* (Zürich)
(1972), 'Frühes und hohes Mittelalter' in *Handbuch der Schweizer Geschichte* 1 (Zürich), 93–160

Pidoux de la Maduère, A. (1935), 'Bernard de Menthon (saint)', *Dictionnaire d'histoire et de géographie ecclésiastique* 8, 690–6

Previté-Orton, C.W. (1912), *The Early History of the House of Savoy (1000–1233)* (Cambridge)

Ranke, L. von (1888), 'Zur Kritik fränkisch-deutscher Reichsannalisten 2. Über die Annalen des Lambertus von Hersfeld' in *Sämtliche Werke* 51–52 (Leipzig), 125–49

Rassow, P. (1928), 'Der Kampf Kaiser Heinrichs IV. mit Heinrich V.', *Zeitschrift für Kirchengeschichte* 47, 451–65
(1960), *Die geschichtliche Einheit des Abendlandes* (Cologne-Graz)

Reinecke, K. D. (1969), *Studien zur Vogtei- und Territorialentwicklung im Erzbistum Bremen (937–1184)* (Marburg)

Reinhardt, U. (1975), *Untersuchungen zur Stellung der Geistlichkeit bei den Königswahlen im Fränkischen und Deutschen Reich (751–1250)* (dissertation, Marburg)

Reinke, M. (1987), 'Die Reisegeschwindigkeit des deutschen Königshofes im 11. und 12. Jahrhundert nördlich der Alpen', *Blätter für deutsche Landesgeschichte* 123, 225–51

Renn, H. (1941a), *Das erste Luxemburger Grafenhaus (963–1136)* (Rheinisches Archiv 39, Bonn)
(1941b), 'Die Luxemburger in der lothringischen Pfalzgrafschaft', *Rheinische Vierteljahrsblätter* 11, 102–18

Reuter, T. (1982), 'The "Imperial Church System" of the Ottonian and Salian rulers: a reconsideration', *Journal of Ecclesiastical History* 33, 347–74
(1991a), *Germany in the Early Middle Ages c. 800–1056* (London)
(1991b), 'Unruhestiftung, Fehde, Rebellion, Widerstand' in *Salier* 3: 297–325

Rieckenberg, H. J. (1942), 'Königsstrasse und Königsgut in liudolfingischer und frühsalischer Zeit (919–1056)', *Archiv für Urkundenforschung* 17, 32–154

Riley-Smith J., (1984), 'The First Crusade and the persecution of the Jews', *Studies in Church History* 21 (Oxford), 51–72

(1986), *The First Crusade and the Idea of Crusading* (Philadelphia)

Robinson, I. S. (1973), 'Gregory VII and the soldiers of Christ', *History* 58, 169–92

(1976), 'The "colores rhetorici" in the Investiture Contest', *Traditio* 32, 209–38

(1978a), *Authority and Resistance in the Investiture Contest* (Manchester)

(1978b), 'Zur Arbeitsweise Bernolds von Konstanz und seines Kreises', *DA* 34, 51–122

(1978c), '"Periculosus homo": Pope Gregory VII and episcopal authority', *Viator* 9, 103–31

(1979), 'Pope Gregory VII, the princes and the pactum, 1077–1080', *English Historical Review* 94, 721–56

(1989), 'Bernold von Konstanz und der gregorianische Reformkreis um Bischof Gebhard III.' in *Die Konstanzer Münsterweihe von 1089 in ihrem historischen Umfeld* ed. H. Maurer (Freiburg) pp. 155–88

(1990), *The Papacy 1073–1198* (Cambridge)

Rörig, F. (1948), *Geblütsrecht und freie Wahl in ihrer Auswirkung auf die deutsche Geschichte* (Abhandlungen der deutschen Akademie der Wissenschaften zu Berlin, 1945/46, phil.-hist. Klasse, no. 6, Berlin)

Rothe, E. (1940), *Goslar als Residenz der Salier* (Dresden)

Ryan, J. J. (1956), *Saint Peter Damiani and his Canonical Sources* (Toronto)

Sackur, E. (1890), 'Handschriftliches aus Frankreich', *NA* 15, 115–39

Salloch, S. (1931), *Hermann von Metz* (Frankfurt a.M.)

Saltet, L. (1907), *Les réordinations. Etude sur le sacrement de l'ordre* (Paris)

Sandberger, G. and A. (1964), 'Frauenchiemsee als bayerisches Herzogskloster', *Zeitschrift für bayerische Landesgeschichte* 27, 55–73

Sander, P. (1893), *Der Kampf Heinrichs IV. und Gregors VII. von der zweiten Exkommunication bis zu seiner Kaiserkrönung* (Berlin)

Santifaller, L. (1957), *Quellen und Forschungen zum Urkunden- und Kanzleiwesen Papst Gregors VII.* 1 (Studi e Testi 190, Vatican City)

(1964), *Zur Geschichte des ottonisch-salischen Reichskirchensystems* (Österreichische Akademie der Wissenschaften, phil.-hist. Klasse, Sitzungsberichte 229/1, Graz, Vienna and Cologne)

Scharnagl, A. (1908), *Der Begriff der Investitur in den Quellen und der Literatur des Investiturstreits* (Stuttgart)

Schebler, A. (1936), *Die Reordinationen in der 'altkatholischen' Kirche* (Bonn)

Scheffer-Boichorst, P. (1879), *Die Neuordnung der Papstwahl durch Nikolaus II.* (Strasbourg)

Scheibelreiter, G. (1973), 'Der Regierungsantritt des römisch-deutschen Königs (1056–1138)', *MIÖG* 81, 1–62

Schetter, R. (1935), *Die Intervenienz der weltlichen und geistlichen Fürsten in den deutschen Königsurkunden von 911–1056* (dissertation, Berlin)

Schieffer, R. (1971), 'Die Romreise deutscher Bischöfe im Frühjahr 1070', *Rheinische Vierteljahrsblätter* 35, 152–74

(1972), 'Spirituales latrones. Zu den Hintergründen der Simonieprozesse in Deutschland zwischen 1069 und 1075', *HJ* 92, 19–60

(1975), 'Hermann I., Bischof von Bamberg', *Fränkische Lebensbilder* 6, 55–76

(1981), *Die Entstehung des päpstlichen Investiturverbots für den deutschen König* (Schriften der MGH 28, Stuttgart)

(1989), 'Der ottonische Reichsepiskopat zwischen Königtum und Adel', *FS* 23, 291–301

(1991), 'Erzbischöfe und Bischofskirche von Köln' in *Salier* 2:1–29

Schiffmann, S. (1931), *Heinrich IV. und die Bischöfe in ihrem Verhalten zu den deutschen Juden zur Zeit des ersten Kreuzzugs* (dissertation, Berlin)

Schlechte, H. (1934), *Erzbischof Bruno von Trier* (dissertation, Leipzig)

Schlesinger, W. (1967), 'Pfalz und Stadt Ulm bis zur Stauferzeit', *Ulm und Oberschwaben* 38, 9–30

(1973), 'Die Wahl Rudolfs von Schwaben zum Gegenkönig 1077 in Forchheim' in *Investiturstreit* pp. 61–85

Schluck, M. (1979), *Die Vita Heinrici IV. imperatoris* (Vorträge und Forschungen, Sonderband 26, Sigmaringen)

Schmale, F.-J. (1957), 'Fiktionen im Codex Udalrici', *Zeitschrift für bayerische Landesgeschichte* 20, 434–74

Schmale-Ott, I. (1971), 'Untersuchungen zu Ekkehard von Aura und zur Kaiserchronik', *Zeitschrift für bayerische Landesgeschichte* 34, 403–61

Schmeidler, B. (1920), 'Lampert von Hersfeld und die Ehescheidungsangelegenheit Heinrichs IV. im Jahre 1069', *Historische Vierteljahrschrift* 20, 141–9

(1922), 'Heinrichs IV. Absetzung 1105/06 kirchenrechtlich und quellenkritisch untersucht', *ZSSRG KA* 12, 168–221

(1927), *Kaiser Heinrich IV. und seine Helfer im Investiturstreit* (Leipzig)

Schmid, K. (1973), 'Adel und Reform in Schwaben' in *Investiturstreit* pp. 295–319

(1984a), 'Die Sorge der Salier um ihre Memoria' in *Memoria. Der geschichtliche Zeugniswert des liturgischen Gedenkens im Mittelalter* ed. K. Schmid and J. Wollasch (Munich) pp. 666–726

(1984b), 'Salische Gedenkstiftungen für *fideles*, *servientes* und *milites*' in *Institutionen, Kultur und Gesellschaft im Mittelalter* ed. L. Fenske, W. Rösener, T. Zotz (Sigmaringen) pp. 245–64

(1988), 'Frutolfs Bericht zum Jahr 1077 oder der Rückzug Rudolfs von Schwaben' in *Historiographia Mediaevalis. Festschrift für Franz-Josef Schmale* ed. D. Berg and H.-W. Goetz (Darmstadt) pp. 181–98

(1989), 'Zu den angeblichen Konstanzer Gegenbischöfen während des Investiturstreites' in *Die Konstanzer Münsterweihe von 1089 in ihrem historischen Umfeld* ed. H. Maurer (Freiburg) pp. 189–212

Schmidinger, H. (1952), 'Die Besetzung des Patriarchenstuhls von Aquileia bis zur Mitte des 13. Jahrhunderts', *MIÖG* 60, 335–54

(1954), *Patriarch und Landesherr. Die weltliche Herrschaft der Patriarchen von Aquileia bis zum Ende der Staufer* (Graz-Cologne)

Schmidt, G. (1917), *Erzbischof Siegfried I. von Mainz* (dissertation, Berlin)

Schmidt, R. (1961), 'Königsumritt und Huldigung in ottonisch-salischer Zeit', *Vorträge und Forschungen* 6 (Konstanz-Stuttgart), 97–233

Schmidt, T. (1977), *Alexander II. (1061–1073) und die römische Reformgruppe seiner Zeit* (Stuttgart)

Schmidt, U. (1987), *Königswahl und Thronfolge im 12. Jahrhundert* (Cologne-Vienna)

Schneider, C. (1972), *Prophetisches Sacerdotium und heilsgeschichtliches Regnum im Dialog 1073–1077* (Munich)

Schneider, F. (1926), 'Canossa', *Zeitschrift für Kirchengeschichte* 45, 163–75

Schölkopf, R. (1957), *Die sächsischen Grafen (919–1024)* (Göttingen)

Schramm, P.E. (1929), *Kaiser, Rom und Renovatio* 1 (Leipzig-Berlin)

(1937), 'Der "Salische Kaiserordo" und Benzo von Alba', *DA* 1, 389–407

(1954, 1955, 1956), *Herrschaftszeichen und Staatssymbolik* (Schriften der MGH 13/1–3, Stuttgart)

(1958), *Sphaira, Globus, Reichsapfel* (Stuttgart)

(1968), 'Böhmen und das Regnum. Die Verleihungen der Königswürde an die Herzöge von Böhmen' in *Adel und Kirche. Festschrift für Gerd Tellenbach* ed. J. Fleckenstein and K. Schmid (Freiburg, Basel and Vienna) pp. 221–36

Schramm, P. E. and F. Mütherich, (1962), *Denkmale der deutschen Kaiser und Könige* (Munich)

Schreiner, K. (1977), 'Die Staufer als Herzöge von Schwaben' in *Die Zeit der Staufer. Geschichte, Kunst, Kultur* 3 (Stuttgart), 7–19

Schrod, K. (1931), *Reichsstraßen und Reichsverwaltung im Königreich Italien* (Stuttgart)

Schulte, A. (1934), 'Deutsche Könige, Kaiser, Päpste als Kanoniker an deutschen und römischen Kirchen', *HJ* 54, 137–77

(1935), 'Anläufe zu einer festeren Residenz der deutschen Könige im Hochmittelalter', *HJ* 55, 131–42

Schumann, O. (1912), *Die päpstlichen Legaten in Deutschland zur Zeit Heinrichs IV. und Heinrichs V. (1056–1125)* (dissertation, Marburg)

Schwartz, G. (1913), *Die Besetzung der Bistümer Reichsitaliens unter den sächsischen und salischen Kaisern* (Leipzig-Berlin)

Schwarzmaier, H. (1968), 'Der Liber Vitae von Subiaco', *QFIAB* 48, 80–147

Schwineköper, B. (1977), *Königtum und Städte bis zum Ende des Investiturstreits* (Vorträge und Forschungen, Sonderband 11, Sigmaringen)

Sdralek, M. (1890), *Die Streitschriften Altmanns von Passau und Wezilos von Mainz* (Paderborn)

Seegrün, W. (1967), *Das Papsttum und Skandinavien bis zur Vollendung der nordischen Kirchenorganisation, 1164* (Neumünster)

(1982), 'Erzbischof Adalbert von Hamburg-Bremen und Gottschalk, Grossfürst der Abodriten (1043–1066/72)' in *Beiträge zur mecklenburgischen Kirchengeschichte* ed. B. Jähnig (Cologne-Vienna) pp. 1–14

Seibert, H. (1991), 'Libertas und Reichsabtei. Zur Klosterpolitik der salischen Herrscher' in *Salier* 2:503–69

Semmler, J. (1959), *Die Klosterreform von Siegburg* (Bonn)

Servatius, C. (1979), *Paschalis II. (1099–1118)* (Stuttgart)

Simeoni, L. (1947), 'Il contributo della contessa Matilde al papato nella lotta per le investiture', *Studi Gregoriani* 1, 353–72

Somerville, R. (1970), 'The French councils of Pope Urban II: some basic considerations', *Annuarium Historiae Conciliorum* 2, 56–65

—— (1977), 'Cardinal Stephan of S. Grisogono' in *Law, Church and Society* ed. K. Pennington and R. Somerville (University of Pennsylvania) pp. 157–66

Spangenberg, H. (1899), 'Die Königskrönung Wratislaws von Böhmen und die angebliche Mainzer Synode des Jahres 1086', *MIÖG* 20, 382–96

Spier, H. (1962), 'Die Harzburg als salische Residenz', *Harz-Zeitschrift* 14, 31–7

—— (1967–8), 'Die Harzburg Heinrichs IV. Ihre geschichtliche Bedeutung und ihre besondere Stellung im Goslarer Reichsbezirk', *Harz-Zeitschrift* 19–20, 185–204

Stadtmüller, G. and B. Pfister, (1971), *Geschichte der Abtei Niederaltaich 741–1971* (Munich)

Stälin, C. F. (1847), *Württembergische Geschichte* 2 (Stuttgart)

Stehkämper, H. (1991), 'Die Stadt Köln in der Salierzeit' in *Salier* 3: 75–152

Steinbach, F. (1964), 'Die Ezzonen' in *Das erste Jahrtausend. Kultur und Kunst im werdenden Abendland an Rhein und Ruhr*, Textband ed. V. H. Elbern 2 (Düsseldorf), 848–66

Steinböck, W. (1972), *Erzbischof Gebhard von Salzburg (1060–1088)* (Vienna-Salzburg)

Steindorff, E. (1874, 1881), *Jahrbücher des Deutschen Reiches unter Heinrich III.*, 1, 2 (Leipzig)

Stenzel, G. A. H. (1827), *Geschichte Deutschlands unter den fränkischen Kaisern* 1 (Leipzig)

Stenzel, K. (1936), *Waiblingen in der deutschen Geschichte* (Waiblingen)

Stimming, M. (1922), *Das deutsche Königsgut im 11. und 12. Jahrhundert* 1 (Berlin)

Störmer, W. (1991), 'Bayern und der bayerische Herzog im 11. Jahrhundert' in *Salier* 1:503–47

Strait, P. (1974), *Cologne in the Twelfth Century* (Gainesville, Florida)

Straus, R. (1937), 'Die Speyerer Judenprivilegien von 1084 und 1090', *Zeitschrift für die Geschichte der Juden in Deutschland* 7, 234–9

Struve, T. (1969, 1970), 'Lampert von Hersfeld. Persönlichkeit und Weltbild', *Hessisches Jahrbuch für Landesgeschichte* 19, 1–123; 20, 32–142

—— (1982), 'Die Intervention Heinrichs IV. in den Diplomen seines Vaters', *Archiv für Diplomatik* 28, 190–222

—— (1984), 'Zwei Briefe der Kaiserin Agnes', *HJ* 104, 411–24

—— (1985), 'Die Romreise der Kaiserin Agnes', *HJ* 105, 1–29

—— (1987), 'Heinrich IV. Die Behauptung einer Persönlichkeit im Zeichen der Krise', *FS* 21, 317–45

—— (1991a), 'Die Stellung des Königtums in der politischen Theorie der Salierzeit' in *Salier* 3:217–44

—— (1991b), 'Gregor VII. und Heinrich IV. Stationen einer Auseinandersetzung', *Studi Gregoriani* 14/2, 29–60

—— (1995), 'Mathilde von Tuszien-Canossa und Heinrich IV.', *HJ* 115, 41–84

Stürner, W. (1968), '"Salvo debito honore et reverentia". Der Königsparagraph im Papstwahldekret von 1059', *ZSSRG KA* 54, 1–56

—— (1972), 'Der Königsparagraph im Papstwahldekret von 1059', *Studi Gregoriani* 9, 37–52

Szabó-Bechstein, B. (1985), *Libertas Ecclesiae. Ein Schlüsselbegriff des Investiturstreits und seine Vorgeschichte* (Studi Gregoriani 12, Rome)

Tangl, G. (1967), 'Schwaben' in *Deutschlands Geschichtsquellen im Mittelalter. Die Zeit der Sachsen und Salier* ed. W. Wattenbach and R. Holtzmann; new edition by F.-J. Schmale 2 (Cologne and Graz) 507–39

Tellenbach, G. (1940), 'Zwischen Worms und Canossa (1076/77)', *HZ* 162, 316–25

(1943), 'Vom karolingischen Reichsadel zum deutschen Reichsfürstenstand' in *Adel und Bauern im deutschen Staat des Mittelalters* ed. T. Mayer (Leipzig) pp. 22–73. English translation: *The Medieval Nobility* ed. T. Reuter (Amsterdam, 1978) pp. 203–42

(1988a), *Die westliche Kirche vom 10. bis zum frühen 12. Jahrhundert* (Göttingen). English translation: *The Church in Western Europe from the Tenth to the Early Twelfth Century* (Cambridge, 1993)

(1988b), 'Der Charakter Kaiser Heinrichs IV.' in *Person und Gemeinschaft im Mittelalter* ed. G. Althoff, D. Greuenich, O. G. Oexle, J. Wollasch (Sigmaringen) pp. 345–67

Thomas, H. (1970), 'Erzbischof Siegfried I. von Mainz und die Tradition seiner Kirche', *DA* 26, 368–99

Tondelli, L. (1952), 'Scavi archeologici a Canossa. Le tre mura di cinta', *Studi Gregoriani* 4, 365–71

Toubert, P. (1973), *Les structures du Latium médiéval* (Rome)

Twellenkamp, M. (1991), 'Das Haus der Luxemburger' in *Salier* 1:475–502

Ulmann, H. (1886), 'Zum Verständnis der sächsischen Erhebung gegen Heinrich IV.' in *Historische Aufsätze dem Andenken an Georg Waitz gewidmet* (Hanover) pp. 119–29

Ullmann, W. (1959–61), 'Romanus pontifex indubitanter effectus sanctus', *Studi Gregoriani* 6, 229–64

(1970), *The Growth of Papal Government in the Middle Ages* (third edition, London)

Vehse, O. (1929–30), 'Die päpstliche Herrschaft in der Sabina bis zur Mitte des 12. Jahrhunderts', *QFIAB* 21, 120–75

Violante, C. (1952), 'La politica italiana di Enrico III prima della sua discesa in Italia (1039–46)', *Rivista storica italiana* 64, 157–76, 293–314

(1955–57)), 'I movimenti patarini e la riforma e la riforma ecclesiastica', *Annuario del l'Università Cattolica* pp. 207–33

(1961), 'Anselmo II da Baggio', *Dizionario Biografico degli Italiani* 3, 399–407

(1968), 'I laici nel movimento patarino' in *I laici nella 'societas christiana' dei secolo XI e XII* (Milan) pp. 597–687

Vogel, J. (1982a), 'Gregors VII. Abzug aus Rom und sein letztes Pontifikatsjahr in Salerno' in *Tradition als historische Kraft* ed. N. Kamp and J. Wollasch (Berlin and New York) pp. 341–9

(1982b), 'Zur Kirchenpolitik Heinrichs IV. nach seiner Kaiserkrönung', *FS* 16, 74–128

(1983), *Gregor VII. und Heinrich IV. nach Canossa* (Berlin and New York)

(1984), 'Rudolf von Rheinfelden, die Fürstenopposition gegen Heinrich IV. im Jahr 1072 und die Reform des Klosters St. Blasien', *ZGO* 132, 1–30

Vogelsang, T. (1954), *Die Frau als Herrscherin im hohen Mittelalter. Studien zur 'consors regni Formel'* (Göttingen)

Vogtherr, T. (1991), 'Die Reichsklöster Corvey, Fulda und Hersfeld' in *Salier* 2:429–64

Volkert, W. and F. Zoepfl, (1974), *Die Regesten der Bischöfe und des Domkapitels von Augsburg* 1/3 (Augsburg)

Vollrath, H. (1974), 'Kaisertum und Patriziat in den Anfängen des Investiturstreits', *Zeitschrift für Kirchengeschichte* 85, 11–44

(1991), 'Konfliktwahrnehmung und Konfliktdarstellung in erzählenden Quellen des 11. Jahrhunderts' in *Salier* 3: 279–96

Volpini, R. (1967), 'Bernardo d'Aosta, santo', *Dizionario biografico degli Italiani* 9 (Rome), 259–6

Waas, A. (1967), *Heinrich V. Gestalt und Verhängnis des letzten salischen Kaisers* (Munich)

Wadle, E. (1973), 'Heinrich IV. und die deutsche Friedensbewegung' in *Investiturstreit* pp. 141–73

(1989), 'Die Konstanzer Pax und Bischof Gebhard III.' in *Die Konstanzer Münsterweihe von 1089 in ihrem historischen Umfeld* (Freiburg) pp. 141–53

Waley, D. (1969), *The Italian City-Republics* (London)

Wattenbach, W., and R. Holtzmann (1967), *Deutschlands Geschichtsquellen im Mittelalter. Die Zeit der Sachsen und Salier* ed. F.-J. Schmale (Cologne and Graz)

Wegener, W. (1959), *Böhmen/Mähren und das Reich im Hochmittelalter* (Cologne and Graz)

Weinfurter, S. (1991), 'Herrschaftslegitimation und Königsautorität im Wandel: Die Salier und ihr Dom zu Speyer' in *Salier* 3: 55–96

Weisweiler, H. (1937), 'Die vollständige Kampfschrift Bernolds von St. Blasien gegen Berengar', *Scholastik* 12, 58–92

Wendehorst, A. (1962), *Das Bistum Würzburg* I, *Die Bischofsreihe bis 1254* (Germania Sacra N.F. 1, Berlin)

Werle, H. (1956), 'Titelherzogtum und Herzogsherrschaft', *ZSSRG GA* 73, 225–99

Werner, M. (1991), 'Der Herzog von Lothringen in salischer Zeit' in *Salier* 1: 367–473

Wilke, S. (1970), *Das Goslarer Reichsgebiet und seine Beziehungen zu den territorialen Nachbargewalten* (Göttingen)

Williams, J. R. (1948–49), 'Archbishop Manasses I of Rheims and Pope Gregory VII', *American Historical Review* 54, 804–24

Wolf, A. (1991), 'Königskandidatur und Königsverwandtschaft', *DA* 47, 45–117

Wollasch, H.-J. (1964), *Die Anfänge des Klosters St. Georgen im Schwarzwald* (Freiburg)

Wollasch, J. (1968), 'Die Wahl des Papstes Nikolaus II.' in *Adel und Kirche. Festschrift für Gerd Tellenbach* ed. J. Fleckenstein and K. Schmid (Freiburg) pp. 205–20

(1984), 'Kaiser und Könige als Brüder der Mönche', *DA* 40, 1–20

(1987), 'Markgraf Hermann und Bischof Gebhard III. von Konstanz' in *Die Zähringer in der Kirche des 11. und 12. Jahrhunderts* ed. K. S. Frank (Munich-Zürich) pp. 27–53

Woody, K. M. (1970), '*Sagena piscatoris*. Peter Damiani and the Papal Election Decree of 1059', *Viator* 1, 33–54

Zafarana, Z. (1966a), 'Ricerche sul' *Liber de unitate ecclesiae conservanda'*, *Studi medievali* 3. ser., 7, 617–700

(1966b), 'Sul "conventus" del clero romano nel maggio 1082', *Studi medievali* 3. ser., 7, 399–403

Zema, D. B. (1941–2), 'Reform legislation in the eleventh century and its economic import', *Catholic Historical Review* 27, 16–38

(1944), 'The houses of Tuscany and Pierleone in the crisis of Rome in the eleventh century', *Traditio* 2, 155–75

Zey, C. (1996), 'Die Synode von Piacenza und die Konsekration Tedalds zum Erzbischof von Mailand im Februar 1076', *QFIAB* 76, 496–509

Zielinski, H. (1984), *Der Reichsepiskopat in spätottonischer und salischer Zeit (1002–1125)* 1 (Stuttgart)

Ziese, J. (1982), *Wibert von Ravenna, der Gegenpapst Clemens III. (1084–1100)* (Stuttgart)

Zimmermann, H. (1968), *Papstabsetzungen des Mittelalters* (Graz-Vienna-Cologne)

(1970), 'Wurde Gregor VII. 1076 in Worms abgesetzt?', *MIÖG* 78, 121–31

(1975), *Der Canossagang von 1077* (Akademie der Wissenschaften und der Literatur, Mainz, 1975, no. 5)

Zoepfl, F. (1952), 'Die Augsburger Bischöfe im Investiturstreit', *HJ* 71, 305–33

Zotz, T. (1982), 'Pallium et alia quaedam archiepiscopatus insignia' in *Festschrift für Berent Schwineköper* ed. H. Maurer and H. Patze (Sigmaringen) pp. 155–75

(1991), 'Die Formierung der Ministerialität' in *Salier* 3: 3–50

INDEX

Aachen, royal palace of, 8 n.31, 22–3, 26, 151, 262, 263, 292, 301, 304, 326, 337, 338, 339, 340, 341, 342, 343
Adalbero IV, bishop of Metz, 276, 277
Adalbero, bishop of Worms, 55–6, 116, 117
Adalbero, bishop of Würzburg, 102, 145, 152 n.46, 153, 156, 167 n.123, 170, 176, 247, 260, 261, 275, 282, 363
'Adalbero C', see Gottschalk, provost of Aachen
Adalbero, canon of Metz, German chancellor, 11 n.40
Adalbero, nephew of Liemar of Bremen, 358
Adalbert, archbishop of Bremen, 5, 61, 74, 116, 181; and Henry IV, 7, 45, 46, 50, 51, 52, 53, 54–5, 56, 57, 58, 59–60, 66, 69–70, 71, 72, 85–6, 354, 355, 362
Adalbert, bishop of Worms, 93, 94, 117, 145, 152 n.46, 153, 156, 167 n.123, 181, 182, 247, 248, 275
Adalbert, count of Ballenstedt, 64, 66, 74, 81
Adalbert, count of Calw, 127, 239 n.2
Adalbert, count of Schauenburg, 67, 68
Adalbert, margrave in Italy, 197
Adalbert Azzo II, margrave of Este, 70, 134, 161, 165, 295, 297
Adaldag, archbishop of Bremen, 57–8
Adam of Bremen, historian, 7, 46, 53, 56, 57, 58–9, 116
Adela of Louvain, wife of Dedi of Lower Lusatia, 64, 74, 87
Adelaide, abbess of Quedlinburg, 19, 270, 272
Adelaide, daughter of Henry IV, 111, 266
Adelaide, margravine of Turin, 25, 60, 111, 134, 160, 161, 221, 287, 324 n.16
Adelaide of Susa, wife of Rudolf of Swabia, 34, 110
Adelaide, wife of Udalric, count of Passau, 305
Adelgaud, abbot of Ebersheimmünster, 167
Adelpreth, royal adviser, 138, 140, 141, 142, 147
advocates, 6–7, 117, 257, 259, 301, 313–14, 315, 355
Agnes, daughter of Henry IV: wife of Frederick I of Swabia, 189, 223, 266, 330; wife of Leopold III of Austria, 332
Agnes, empress: in Henry III's reign: 19–20, 23, 25, 61, 266, 366; as regent, 27–37, 42–4, 115, 116, 189, 200, 362; after 1062, 44–5, 53, 92, 108, 125, 126, 127, 128, 129, 130, 132, 134, 148–9, 154, 159, 167, 169, 178, 353
Albert, cardinal bishop of Silva Candida, antipope, 309
Albert III, count of Namur, 148, 253, 254, 262
Albert, royal envoy in Constantinople, 214
Albuin, bishop of Merseburg, 276
Alexander II, pope, 33, 42, 44, 49–50, 51, 54, 64, 89, 107, 108, 109, 110, 111, 112, 117, 118, 120, 123, 124, 125, 129, 132, 155, 200, 225, 329, 360
Alexius I Comnenus, Byzantine emperor, 214, 215, 222, 223, 224, 227, 294
Almus, duke in Hungary, 294
Altmann, bishop of Passau, 145, 148, 149, 152 n.46, 153–4, 155, 156, 167 n.123, 170, 174, 185, 207, 211, 247, 260, 275, 282, 356
Altwin, bishop of Brixen, 57, 174, 283
Amadeus II, count of Savoy, 134, 160, 161
Ambrose, St, 123
Anastasia, queen, wife of Andreas I of Hungary, 53
Andreas I, king of Hungary, 20, 21, 34–5, 53
Andreas-Wezel, bishop of Olmütz, 251 n.71, 283
Anna Comnena, historian, 214
Anno II, archbishop of Cologne: early career, 30, 41, 88, 358; during Henry IV's minority, 43–4, 45, 46–8, 49, 50–1, 52, 56, 116, 362; later career, 54, 55, 57, 59, 61, 89, 91, 93, 94, 96, 100, 108, 116–17, 126, 127, 131, 144, 275, 317, 333, 354, 356
Anonymi Chronica imperatorum, see Bamberg chronicle
Anselm, abbot of Lorsch, 312
Anselm III, archbishop of Milan, 278 n.18, 281, 287

Anselm I, bishop of Lucca, *see* Alexander II
Anselm II, bishop of Lucca, 129, 215, 221
Anzo, bishop of Brixen, 297
Ariald, deacon, Patarine leader, 122
Aribones, family, 173–4, 322 n.4
Arnold, anti-bishop of Constance, 248 n.49, 276,
    284, 324
Arnold, brother of Liupold of Meersburg, 359
Arnulf, count of Looz, 314, 315
Arnulf of Milan, chronicler, 135, 137, 139
Arpo, bishop of Feltre, 293
Attila, sword of, 53, 66, 67
Atto, archbishop of Milan, 124, 140
Augsburg, annals of, 199, 259, 263, 264, 268, 349

Babenberg family, 4
Baldwin, bishop of Strasbourg, 312
Baldwin V, count of Flanders, 24, 31, 70
Baldwin VI, count of Flanders and Hainault, 31
Bamberg chronicle, 327, 343, 345, 349, 352, 353
Baruncii, Roman family, 309
Bavarian Nordgau, march of, 4, 305, 323, 324, 331,
    357
Bavarian Ostmark, march of, 4, 190, 211, 222, 251
Beatrice, abbess of Quedlinburg and
    Gandersheim, daughter of Henry III, 19
Beatrice, margravine of Tuscany, 24, 25, 32, 33, 37,
    43, 49, 50, 109, 130, 134, 138
Bela I, king of Hungary, 34–5, 53, 70
Benedict X, pope, 37, 38, 39, 42
Benno I, bishop of Meissen, 243, 247
Benno II, bishop of Osnabrück, 74, 86, 89, 118,
    155, 161, 178, 179, 186, 188, 199, 205, 222, 223,
    358, 359, 363, 366
Beno, cardinal priest of SS. Martino e Silvestro,
    227
Benzo, bishop of Alba, polemicist, 14, 54 n.131,
    139, 199, 221, 230
Berard, abbot of Farfa, 219
Berengar, count of Sangerhausen, 75
Berengar, count of Sulzbach, 305, 324, 326
Bernard, abbot of St Victor in Marseilles, 166, 168,
    169, 171, 172, 177, 178
Bernard, cardinal deacon, 166, 168, 169, 171, 172,
    177, 178, 179, 181
Bernard, master of the cathedral school of
    Hildesheim, 242 n.25
Bernard of Menthon, archdeacon of Aosta, 211 n.4
Bernard II Billung, duke of Saxony, 63
Bernold, monk of St Blasien, chronicler, 121, 174,
    185 n.68, 261, 262, 264, 269, 274, 275, 288,
    290, 293, 349, 354, 360
Bertha, empress, 19, 25, 34, 60–1, 89, 95, 108, 109,

110, 111, 159, 160, 229, 256, 266, 287, 290, 353,
    363, 366
Berthold, anti-archbishop of Salzburg, 248, 257,
    259
Berthold, brother of Liupold of Meersburg, 359
Berthold, monk of Reichenau, chronicler, 31, 96,
    155, 156, 159, 175, 177, 180, 192, 194, 348, 354
Berthold of Rheinfelden, anti-duke of Swabia,
    189, 190, 260, 262, 274, 282, 286
Berthold I of Zähringen, duke of Carinthia, 127,
    181, 188, 245; in the service of the crown,
    35–6, 59, 67, 73, 91, 92, 93, 96, 98, 99, 126,
    130, 131, 132, 359; rebellion: 13, 152, 153, 156,
    160, 166, 167, 173, 174, 176, 177, 182
Berthold II of Zähringen, anti-duke of Swabia,
    181, 188, 189, 259, 260, 274, 286, 298, 299, 319
    n.125
Billungs, family, 3, 58, 61, 69, 70, 72, 82, 87, 97,
    103
Billungs, march of, 3
Boleslav II, duke of Poland, 35, 72
Boniface of Canossa, margrave of Tuscany, 24
Boniface I, margrave of Vasto, 287 n.69
Bonizo, bishop of Sutri, polemicist, 108, 125, 129,
    195, 235
Borivoi II, duke of Bohemia, 211, 252, 306, 331,
    332, 342
Boso, count in Italy, 197
Bretislav I, duke of Bohemia, 20, 252, 306 n.57
Bretislav II, duke of Bohemia, 252, 305, 306
Brixen, council of (1080), 144, 198–201, 212, 213,
    217, 227, 228, 368
Bruno, archbishop of Trier, 276, 312, 325, 342
Bruno, clerk of Merseburg, chronicler, 74, 75, 76,
    77, 82, 83, 88, 89, 95, 96, 97, 99, 100, 101,
    102, 168, 170, 172, 202, 204, 205, 207, 209,
    359, 361; on Henry IV, 1, 13, 67, 72, 73, 78, 81,
    176, 193, 206, 346, 348, 349, 350, 366; on
    Otto of Northeim, 67, 68, 103, 210
Bruno, count of Brunswick, 64
Brunones, family, 4, 34 n.49, 64, 80, 81, 272
Burchard, bishop of Basel, 95, 147, 155, 181, 342
Burchard I, bishop of Halberstadt, 41
Burchard II, bishop of Halberstadt: in the service
    of the crown, 29, 30, 46, 47, 48–9, 51, 78, 88,
    89, 90, 358, 362; rebellion, 74, 87, 91, 99, 100,
    103, 131, 146, 152, 167 n.123, 243, 247, 255,
    260, 265, 267, 268, 293, 363
Burchard, bishop of Lausanne, 155, 188, 271,
    363–4, 366
Burchard, bishop of Münster, 329, 343, 364, 365,
    366
Burchard, bishop of Utrecht, 276, 312

Burchard, count of Nellenburg, 260
Burchard, count, royal envoy in Constantinople, 214
Burchard, margrave of Istria, 281, 293, 364

Cadalus, bishop of Parma, antipope Honorius II, 42, 43, 44, 49, 50, 54, 107, 109, 116, 128, 145
Canossa, absolution at (1077), 136, 157 n.71, 159, 160–4, 169, 174, 175, 178, 184, 199, 212, 223, 226, 310, 337, 351, 360, 363, 364
Canossa, family of, 11, 30, 37, 108, 212, 215, 281, 282, 288, 289, 291, 300
Carmen de bello Saxonico, see Song of the Saxon War
Casimir, king of Poland, 20
Celestine I, pope, 118
Cencius Johannis, Roman prefect, 178
Cencius Stephani, Roman nobleman, 147
chancery, royal, 10–13, 29–30, 130, 158, 231, 276, 293 n.106, 364
chapel, royal, 11, 117, 140, 175, 187, 363
Charlemagne, 96, 151, 204, 206, 224 n.77, 241 n.19, 246, 255, 347
Charles, bishop of Constance, 118, 119, 121, 354
Châtenois, family, 3, 32
Childeric III, king, 155, 208
Clement II, pope, 36, 200
'Clement III', antipope, *see* Wibert, archbishop of Ravenna
clerical marriage, papal prohibition of, 136, 145, 200, 326
Cluny, abbey of, 20, 127, 339 n.81
Coloman, king of Hungary, 294, 305
Cono, anti-bishop of Mantua, 282 n.41
Conrad, archbishop of Trier, 47, 116, 117, 119
Conrad, bishop of Utrecht, 175, 207 n.177, 243, 257, 273, 310, 322 n.7, 363, 364, 366
Conrad I, count of Luxemburg, 208
Conrad, count of Reinhausen, 244, 271
Conrad I, duke of Bavaria, 21–2, 23–4, 25, 35
Conrad III, duke of Carinthia, 3, 31, 35
Conrad II, emperor, 2, 8, 9, 12, 19, 23, 36, 57, 79, 80, 87, 123, 124, 174, 218, 266, 269 n.174, 359, 365, 369
Conrad, king, son of Henry IV, 13, 23 n.13, 95, 104, 143, 148, 159, 166, 205, 206, 214, 233, 253, 262, 263, 266, 307, 366; as anti-king, 279, 286–8, 289, 290, 291–2, 295, 297, 300, 301, 312, 325, 327, 328, 368
Conrad, margrave of Moravia, 246, 247
Conrad, *ministerialis*, adviser of King Conrad, 288
Conrad of Staufen, brother of Frederick I, duke of Swabia, 281, 286

Conrad, son of Henry III, 19 n.3, 22, 28, 98
Constantine, Byzantine envoy, 222
Constantine I, emperor, 231–2, 291; *Donation of Constantine*, 231
Corsi, Roman family, 232, 309
Corvey, abbey of, 56
Cosmas, bishop of Prague, 283
Cosmas of Prague, chronicler, 251, 283, 306
count, office of, 4–5
count palatine, office of, 5
Crescentii, Roman family, 36, 37
crown lands, 3, 5, 8–9, 80, 81, 84–5, 86, 87
'crown-wearings', 14, 80, 149, 150, 151, 174, 242, 351–2
Cunigunde, empress, 28 n.28, 61
Cuniza, wife of Adalbert Azzo II of Este, 70
Cuno, bishop of Strasbourg, 312
Cuno, count of Beichlingen, 267, 296, 307, 322 n.7
Cuno, count of Wülflingen, 261
Cuno, royal *ministerialis*, 48, 66, 357, 358

Damasus II, pope, 36, 200
Dedi, count, 318
Dedi I, margrave of Lower Lusatia, 4, 64–5, 66, 67, 74, 75, 83, 85, 87, 102
Dedi II, son of Dedi I, 66, 67
Denis, bishop of Piacenza, 42, 135, 165, 166, 199
Desiderius, abbot of Monte Cassino, *see* Victor III
Diepold III, margrave of the Bavarian Nordgau, 305, 323, 324
Donizo, monk of Canossa, historian, 284 n.56, 293
duke, office of, 2–3, 306

Eberhard, archbishop of Trier, 52, 95
Eberhard, bishop of Eichstätt, 276
Eberhard, bishop of Naumburg, 74, 86, 89, 95, 155, 161, 177, 363, 366
Eberhard, bishop of Parma, 233
Eberhard, count of Nellenburg, 82, 90, 101, 125 n.85, 127, 361
Eberhard, son of Eberhard of Nellenburg, 82, 90, 101, 125 n.85, 361
Eberhard 'the Bearded', count, royal adviser, 71, 125, 139, 140, 147, 155, 165, 182, 360–1
Egeno, accuser of Otto of Northeim, 65, 66, 67, 68
Egilbert, archbishop of Trier, 187, 197, 207 n.177, 240, 242, 243, 251, 252, 254, 257, 292, 310
Einhard, bishop of Speyer, 29 n.31, 31 n.40, 57
Ekbert I, count of Brunswick, margrave of Meissen, 4, 43, 44, 61, 80

Ekbert II, count of Brunswick, margrave of
Meissen, 4, 13, 75, 80, 102, 153, 175, 192, 244,
256–7, 258, 260, 262, 264–5, 266, 267, 268,
269, 270, 271–2, 273, 283, 315, 323 n.14, 360
Ekbert, count of Formbach, 178
Ekkehard, abbot of Aura, chronicler, 288, 309, 321,
322, 324, 326, 343, 345, 347, 349
Ekkehard, abbot of Reichenau, 119
Ellenhard, bishop of Freising, 57, 95, 174
Embrico, bishop of Augsburg, 95, 102, 171, 174
n.20
Emehard, bishop of Würzburg, 276, 292, 310, 311
Emicho, count of Leiningen, 302
Engelbert, count, casualty at Homburg (1075), 101
Engelbert, count of Spanheim, 257, 259, 260
Eppenstein family, 3, 166, 175, 248, 259
Eppo, bishop of Worms, 241 n.16
Erkenbold, chamberlain, 343, 344, 357, 358, 365
Erlung, bishop of Würzburg, 276, 325, 330, 332
Ernest I, duke of Swabia, 36
Ernest, margrave of the Bavarian Ostmark, 101
Erpo, bishop of Münster, 241, 270
Ethelinde, daughter of Otto of Northeim, 65, 70
Eupraxia-Adelaide, empress, 266, 269, 270,
289–91
Eustace, count of Boulogne, 148
exceptio spolii, 225, 243, 244
Ezzonid family, 3, 22 n.8, 23, 35, 66 n.10, 208
n.183, 210, 358

Farfa, abbey of, 218, 219, 224, 353
Felix, anti-bishop of Meissen, 248
First Crusade, 294, 300, 302, 311, 314, 316
Flarchheim, battle of (1080), 193, 194, 349, 350
fodrum, 212
Folcmar, bishop of Minden, 205, 255, 270
Folcmar, Saxon nobleman, 101
Forchheim, assembly of (1077), 13, 166, 167–70,
172, 173 n.11, 209, 210, 255
Formbach, family of, 173, 297
Frederick, abbot of Goseck, abbot of Hersfeld,
277, 278
Frederick, archbishop of Bremen, 342
Frederick I, archbishop of Cologne, 276, 308, 312,
317, 325, 338, 340, 364, 365, 366
Frederick, bishop of Halberstadt, 277, 326
Frederick, bishop of Münster, 11, 29, 73, 241
Frederick, count of Arnsberg, 317, 343 n.98
Frederick II, count of Goseck, Saxon count
palatine, 5, 74, 75, 82, 87, 90, 99, 255
Frederick, count of Montbéliard, 287
Frederick I, count of Sommerschenburg, Saxon
count palatine, 5, 181, 296, 325, 350

Frederick, count of Tengling, 321
Frederick *de Monte*, Saxon rebel, 100
Frederick, duke of Lower Lotharingia, 32, 55, 315
Frederick I, duke of Swabia, 3, 34, 173, 188, 189,
190, 203, 223, 246, 257, 260, 281, 286, 292,
296, 298, 299, 319 n.125, 320 n.128, 325, 330,
364
Frederick II, duke of Swabia, 331
Frederick of Liège, abbot of Monte Cassino,
cardinal priest of S. Grisogono, *see* Stephen
IX
Frederick of Putelendorf, Saxon count palatine,
255
Frutolf of Michelsberg, chronicler, 33 n.48, 249,
250, 303, 304, 307
Fruttuaria, abbey of, 29, 44, 45, 126, 127
Fulco, margrave of Este, 297

Gebhard, abbot of Hirsau, bishop of Speyer, 324,
328 n.33, 333, 334, 335, 344, 352
Gebhard, archbishop of Salzburg, 11, 29, 59, 102,
145, 152 n.46, 167 n.123, 170, 174, 206, 207,
239, 242, 243, 247, 259, 260, 268
Gebhard III, bishop of Constance, 127, 245, 259,
260, 261; leader of the German Gregorian
party, 275, 278, 284, 286, 290, 292–3,
299–300, 304, 311, 324, 325, 326, 328, 331, 334
Gebhard, bishop of Eichstätt, *see* Victor II
Gebhard III, bishop of Regensburg, 21, 22, 26
Gebhard IV, bishop of Regensburg, 174, 277, 322
n.7
Gebhard, count of Supplinburg, 101
Gebhard-Jaromir, bishop of Prague, 11, 250, 251
Geisa, king of Hungary, 53, 70, 99
Gelasius I, pope, 107, 134, 151
Gerald, cardinal bishop of Ostia, 132, 133, 161, 178
Gerard II, bishop of Cambrai, 137
Gerard, bishop of Florence, *see* Nicholas II
Gerard, duke of Upper Lotharingia, 32
Gero, count of Brehna, 74, 152, 192
Gerstungen, peace of (1074), 75, 77, 82, 95–6, 97,
98, 99, 100, 131, 249
Gerstungen-Berka, conference of (1085), 242–4,
245, 263, 364
Gertrude, wife of Henry, count of Northeim, 272,
273
Gisela, empress, wife of Conrad II, 19, 23, 34, 36,
61, 80, 81, 266, 365, 366
Giselbert, count of Luxemburg and Salm, 208
Giso, count of Gudensberg, 67, 68
gistum, 9
Gleiberg, counts of, 301
Godfrey, archbishop of Milan, 122, 124, 125, 140

Godfrey, count of Louvain, duke of Lower
Lotharingia, 316, 340
Godfrey, count of Namur, 338, 339
Godfrey 'the Bearded' of Verdun, margrave of
Tuscany, duke of Lower Lotharingia, 20, 24,
25, 31–3, 37, 42, 49, 50, 54, 55, 56, 108, 109
Godfrey III ('the Hunchback'), duke of Lower
Lotharingia, 32, 91, 99, 100, 102, 134, 138, 143,
144, 147–8, 253, 254, 263
Godfrey IV of Bouillon, margrave of Antwerp,
duke of Lower Lotharingia, 148, 253, 254,
262, 263, 271 n.187, 314, 315
Godschalk, bishop of Minden, 328 n.33
Goslar, palace of, 8 n.31, 10, 19, 25, 59, 63, 68, 70,
71, 73, 77, 79, 80, 83, 86, 89, 93, 95, 103, 104,
143, 172, 187, 202, 205, 209, 245 n.35, 249,
267, 363
Gotebald, patriarch of Aquileia, 26
Gottschalk, provost of Aachen, monk of
Klingenmünster, 11, 150, 151, 154 n.55, 175, 217
n.35, 224, 231
Gregory, bishop of Vercelli, 42, 128, 139, 161
Gregory I, pope, 129 n.105
Gregory VI, pope, 146
Gregory VII, pope, 128–9, 144, 235, 251; and
Henry IV, 1, 13, 15, 112, 113, 114, 120, 125, 128,
130, 131, 132, 133, 134, 135, 139, 140, 141, 142,
143, 145, 146, 148, 149, 154, 155, 156, 157, 158,
159, 160, 161–5, 172, 178, 179, 180–1, 182, 185,
186, 191, 194, 195, 196, 208, 211, 212, 215, 221,
223, 224, 225, 226, 227, 229, 243, 264, 274,
283, 288, 329, 337, 347, 351, 360, 361, 367; and
German princes, 28, 127, 150, 153, 154, 155,
156, 157, 159, 160, 161, 162, 163, 164, 166, 168,
171, 172, 177, 184, 206, 207, 255; and imperial
bishops, 90, 110, 133, 134, 137, 145, 146, 179,
184, 187, 200, 201, 210, 245, 247; and Milan,
123, 135, 138, 139, 141, 145, 160; and Normans,
40, 178, 214, 219, 232–4; and Rudolf of
Swabia, 127, 130, 166–7, 169, 171, 172, 179,
194, 196, 205, 207, 209, 216, 229; concept of
kingship, 13, 14–15, 27, 107, 132, 178, 207–8,
244; reform programme, 29, 136, 138, 145,
183–4, 194–5, 220, 278, 279, 312; polemics
against, 11, 128–9, 144–5, 146, 147, 150, 151,
169, 197, 198–9, 205, 213, 216, 217, 220, 221
n.60, 224, 229, 232, 235, 241, 364
Gundechar, bishop of Eichstätt, 29, 30, 95
Gundekar, chamberlain, 357, 358, 365
Gunhild, first wife of Henry III, 19
Gunther, bishop of Bamberg, 29–30, 44 n.82, 51
Gunther, bishop of Naumburg, 74, 187 n.76, 202,
243, 247, 248–9, 267, 270, 277

Hadrian I, pope, 241 n.19, 247 n.46
Hamezo, anti-bishop of Halberstadt, 248, 270
Hammerstein, royal fortress, 336, 357
Hartmann II, count of Dillingen and Kyburg, 302
Hartmann, royal adviser, 125, 155, 360
Hartwig, abbot of Hersfeld, archbishop of
Magdeburg (Henrician), 95, 247, 255, 278
Hartwig, archbishop of Magdeburg (Gregorian),
187, 207 n.177, 243, 245, 247, 255, 259, 260,
261, 265, 267; in the service of Henry IV,
268, 270, 271, 275, 307, 311, 323
Hartwig, bishop of Regensburg, 323
Hartwig, bishop of Verden, 243, 247
Hartwig, count of Bogen, 331
Harzburg, royal fortress, 72, 73, 74, 78, 82, 83, 90,
93, 97, 98, 99, 100, 103, 152
Helmold of Bosau, chronicler, 352
Henry, archbishop of Ravenna, 109
Henry, bishop of Augsburg, 30–1, 42, 43
Henry, bishop of Chur, 132
Henry, bishop of Freising, 276, 342
Henry, bishop of Liège, 142, 249, 253, 254
Henry, bishop of Speyer, 117, 118
Henry, bishop of Trent, 108
Henry I, count of Eilenburg, margrave of Lower
Lusatia and Meissen, 4, 267, 269–70, 272,
296
Henry II, count of Laach, Lotharingian count
palatine, 5, 203, 204, 269
Henry I, count of Limburg, duke of Lower
Lotharingia, 314, 315–16, 338, 339, 340, 342
Henry III, count of Stade, margrave of the Saxon
Nordmark, 269
Henry II, emperor, 35, 211 n.4
Henry III, emperor, 5 n.19, 9, 12, 19–26, 28, 32, 34,
35, 36, 37, 38, 39, 40, 45, 57, 63, 69, 79, 80,
85, 87, 111, 112, 115, 117, 118, 123, 124, 132, 140,
145, 146, 170, 174, 187, 198, 200, 216, 218,
240, 241, 246, 248, 249, 250, 252, 266, 276,
306, 314, 319, 330, 353, 355, 357, 359, 363, 365,
366, 368, 369
Henry IV, emperor: and Bavaria, 22, 27, 28, 34, 65,
68, 70–1, 96, 98, 166, 172, 173–4, 178, 182,
190, 192, 239, 257, 259–60, 262, 266, 280,
282, 283, 297–8, 304–5, 308, 321–3, 331; and
Lotharingia, 55, 147–8, 180, 187, 242, 253–4,
263, 304, 312–13, 314–17, 323, 338–42; and
Saxony, 10, 63–104, 131, 132, 138, 143, 148,
152–3, 156, 175, 176, 179–80, 182, 188, 192, 193,
202, 205–7, 210, 224, 239, 241, 242, 243, 246,
249, 254–7, 258–9, 262, 264–5, 267–74, 304,
307–8, 317–18, 321, 323, 328, 346, 347, 348,
350, 356, 357, 360, 361, 362, 363, 366–7; and

Henry IV, emperor (*cont.*)
 Swabia, 172–3, 176, 177, 182, 183, 185, 188–9,
  190, 280, 298–9, 331, 364; and the Italian
  kingdom, 54, 55, 107, 108–9, 124, 139, 140,
  147, 159, 160–6, 197, 201, 206, 207, 211–33,
  241, 253, 254, 263, 280–9, 293–5, 308, 310, 364,
  365, 366, 367, 368; and southern Italy, 40,
  108, 214, 218, 219, 223, 227, 233; and Bohemia,
  4, 100, 102, 104, 153, 181, 202, 203, 211, 222,
  241, 246, 248, 250–2, 283–4, 305–7, 331, 332;
  and Byzantium, 214–15, 222–3, 224, 227; and
  Mainz, 176, 193, 197, 198, 202, 217, 240, 246,
  300, 301, 302, 303–4, 307, 309, 310, 311,
  318–19, 323, 329 330, 332, 333, 334, 335, 336,
  350; and Milan, 122, 123, 130, 133, 135, 138, 139,
  140, 141, 201, 211, 287; and Regensburg, 172,
  173, 239, 296, 305, 306, 314, 321, 322, 323, 331;
  and Rome, 41–2, 54, 159, 201, 212, 213–14,
  216–18, 220, 221, 222, 223–5, 226–32, 235, 364,
  368; and Speyer, 86, 117, 139, 156, 202–3,
  257–8, 263, 276, 282, 302, 308, 310, 313, 329,
  332–3, 343, 344, 352–3, 354, 358, 365; and
  Venice, 281, 289, 293–4, 352; and Worms, 52,
  80, 93–4, 95, 97, 99, 143, 156, 175, 176, 257,
  297, 302, 350; and Würzburg, 176, 177, 191,
  192, 260, 261, 330, 332, 363; advisers, 52, 53,
  56, 59–60, 61, 67, 68, 69–70, 71, 74, 82, 86,
  92, 93, 96, 102, 107–8, 114, 120, 125, 127, 128,
  129, 130, 131, 132, 133, 135. 136, 138, 139, 141,
  143, 146, 147, 149, 154, 155, 158, 159, 174, 177,
  178, 182, 224, 225, 271, 276, 285, 295, 310, 340,
  348, 356–63, 366; and Jewish communities,
  302–3, 318; and 'peace of God', 249–50, 302,
  303, 308, 318–20, 321; as patrician of the
  Romans, 36, 41–2, 144, 200, 228; attitude
  towards the imperial Church, 15, 56, 114–15,
  119, 120, 121–2, 128, 132, 141, 145, 146, 164, 174,
  175, 184, 187, 192, 195, 198, 202, 240–1, 245,
  246–9, 279, 312, 329, 355, 356, 367, 369;
  concern with *memoria*, 47, 258, 266, 301, 308,
  312–13, 353, 354; devotion to Virgin Mary, 151,
  174, 203, 224, 232, 258, 285, 308, 329, 352–3;
  diplomas, 11, 12–13, 27, 44–6, 51, 52–3, 60–1,
  85, 88, 94–5, 109, 111, 121, 131, 151, 165, 174,
  175, 191, 192, 201, 202–3, 218, 224, 231, 233,
  251, 264, 266, 282, 285, 290, 293, 301, 308,
  312–13, 314, 333, 355, 356, 357, 359, 361–6;
  emperorship, 50, 54, 109, 111, 112, 130, 134,
  138, 141, 146, 212, 213, 216, 220, 223, 224–5,
  226, 228, 229–32, 239, 242, 244, 313, 329;
  episcopal appointments, 114–5, 116, 117–18,
  119, 137, 139, 140, 175, 186–7, 205, 240–1,
  247–8, 253, 255, 275–8, 312; itinerary, 9–10,

79, 93–4, 173, 176, 289, 293, 296, 303–4, 306,
  307; letters, 10, 11, 114, 120, 121, 130–1, 133
  n.125, 144, 145, 147, 150–1, 156, 205, 213,
  216–17, 228, 229–30, 231, 232, 233, 239, 254,
  268, 297, 300, 308, 330, 333, 334, 335, 336, 337,
  338–9, 340–1, 342–3, 364; piety, 131–2, 151, 161,
  202–3, 224, 230 n.116, 232, 258, 285, 294, 308,
  310, 312–13, 324, 329, 337, 338, 340, 343, 345,
  351–4; polemics against, 1, 113, 114 n.40, 152,
  195, 233, 247, 277, 288–9, 290, 328, 345, 346,
  347, 348, 349, 351, 356, 365, 366; portrayed as
  divinely ordained ruler, 14, 132, 134, 144, 149,
  150, 164, 205, 216, 247; propaganda in favour
  of, 136, 142, 144–5, 150, 182, 193, 197, 198, 199,
  205, 213, 216–17, 224, 225, 227 n.95, 232, 244,
  246, 300, 301, 329, 333, 339, 346, 348, 349, 351
Henry V, emperor, 13, 23 n.13, 241 n.19, 266, 273
  n.197, 294 n.111, 298 n.14, 300, 301, 304, 305,
  307–8, 310, 313, 314, 318, 321, 366; rebellion,
  288, 323, 324–36, 347, 365, 368; accession,
  337–44
Henry, first-born son of Henry IV, 98, 111, 266
Henry I, king of the Germans, 24, 34 n.49, 208
  n.183, 231 n.117
Henry I, Lotharingian count palatine, 5
Henry, *ministerialis*, 365
Henry of Assel, bishop of Paderborn, archbishop
  of Magdeburg, 317–18, 328 n.33, 342
Henry of Eppenstein, duke of Carinthia, 259, 281,
  289, 297
Henry of Werl, bishop of Paderborn (Henrician),
  241, 326
Henry, patriarch of Aquileia, 137, 175, 186, 190,
  198, 215
Henry, son of Dedi II of Lower Lusatia, 102
Henry, son of Eberhard of Nellenburg, 101, 361
Henry 'the Black', son of Welf IV, 297
Henry 'the Fat', count of Northeim, 272, 273, 307,
  308
Herlembald Cotta, Patarine leader, 122–3, 124
Herman, advocate of Reichenau, 322 n.7
Herman, anti-bishop of Passau, 248, 259
Herman II, archbishop of Cologne, 19, 22, 23, 30,
  50, 358
Herman III, archbishop of Cologne, 11, 269, 275,
  276
Herman, bishop of Augsburg, 276, 277, 300 n.19,
  311, 342
Herman I, bishop of Bamberg, 91, 95, 116, 118, 119,
  121, 132, 135, 137, 145, 363, 366
Herman, bishop of Metz, 91, 95, 145, 152, 154 n.55,
  180, 185, 208, 209, 241–2, 247, 253, 254, 261,
  275, 282

Herman, burgrave of Magdeburg, 323
Herman, count of Salm, anti-king, 13, 208–9, 210, 221, 222, 241, 245, 246–7, 255, 257, 262, 267, 268–9, 270, 362
Herman, count of Werl, 35
Herman II, duke of Swabia, 166 n.115
Herman II, Lotharingian count palatine, 5
Herman I, margrave of Baden, 127
Herman, monk of Reichenau, chronicler, 21, 22
Herman of Cannae, nephew of Robert Guiscard, 227
Herman Billung, count, 58, 69, 74, 75, 90, 182, 192
Herrand, bishop of Halberstadt, 267 n.159, 293, 303
Hersfeld, abbey, 41, 43, 64, 65, 67, 74, 75, 76, 78, 90, 95, 100, 121, 264, 266, 278, 354 n.66, 359
Hersfeld, anonymous polemicist of, 246, 265, 267
Hezelid family, 5, 22 n.8, 31
Hezilo, bishop of Hildesheim, 61, 85, 131, 134, 146
Hildebrand, archdeacon, *see* Gregory VII
Hildesheim, annals of, 322 and n.6, 323, 325, 334, 335, 336
Hildolf, archbishop of Cologne, 118, 155, 275, 358
Hirsau, abbey, 127, 245, 324, 332 n.57
Hochstaden, family, 275
Hohenmölsen, battle of (1080), 202, 203–4, 212, 258, 349, 350
homage, performance by bishops, 220; papal prohibition of, 279, 311, 312
Homburg, battle of (1075), 101, 102, 132, 138, 203, 204, 258, 349, 350, 351, 361
'Honorius II', antipope, *see* Cadalus, bishop of Parma
Hubert, cardinal bishop of Palestrina, 132, 133, 161
Hugh I, abbot of Cluny, 20, 29 n.32, 34 n.51, 92, 126, 158–9, 161, 223, 226, 310, 333, 335, 336, 337 n.73, 338–9, 341, 351
Hugh, margrave of Este, 297
Hugh Candidus, cardinal priest of S. Clemente, 145, 146, 147, 198
Hugo-Ugiccio I, duke of Spoleto, 215
Humbert, archbishop of Bremen, 276, 312
Humbert, cardinal bishop of Silva Candida, 115, 116, 120, 244
Huzman, bishop of Speyer, 137, 147, 155, 197, 207 n.177, 258

Ida, wife of Thimo of Brehna, 75
idoneitas, Gregorian concept of, 169, 208
Imad, bishop of Paderborn, 74, 100
Imiza, wife of Welf II, 70, 209
Imola, counts of, 201

immunities, ecclesiastical, 5–7, 56
'imperial Church system', 6–7, 114, 115, 126, 184
intervenientes in diplomas, 12, 23, 27, 45, 46, 52–3, 60, 109, 111, 266, 301, 361–6
investiture of bishops, 29, 114–15, 116, 117, 122, 129, 139, 140, 141, 187, 195, 276, 278, 312, 314, 328, 329, 342, 344, 368; papal prohibition of, 135–8, 141, 183–4, 186, 194–5, 220, 256, 277, 278–9, 292, 311–12, 327, 335, 369; Henrician defence of, 241, 247 n.46, 279
'Investiture Contest', 194–5, 279, 312, 328
Isidore of Seville, 113, 347, 348
iter, royal, 2, 8–10, 55, 109, 171, 172, 308; imperial, 233

Jewish communities in the Rhineland, 302–3, 318
John, abbot of S. Apollonio di Canossa, 284 n.55
John I, bishop of Olmütz, 251
John, bishop of Osnabrück, 276
John I, bishop of Speyer, 275, 276, 302, 356, 364, 365, 366
John II, cardinal bishop of Porto, 232
John II, cardinal bishop of Velletri, *see* Benedict X
John Comnenus, nephew of Alexius I Comnenus, 214, 223
John of Fécamp, 29, 125
John of Mantua, exegete, 284 n.55
Jordan I, prince of Capua, 139, 214, 218, 219, 220, 227, 234
Judith, daughter of Vratislav II of Bohemia, 332
Judith, wife of Welf IV, 70
Judith (Sophia), daughter of Henry III: queen of Hungary, 19, 35, 53, 152; wife of Duke Vladislav-Herman of Poland, 276, 305

Ladislaus I, king of Hungary, 190, 263, 286, 294
Lambert, bishop of Arras, 317
Lampert, monk of Hersfeld, chronicler, 10, 28, 31, 33, 44, 45, 46, 47, 52, 53, 56–7, 59, 63, 64, 65, 66, 71, 74, 75, 76, 77, 80, 83, 87 n.77, 89, 91, 92, 93, 94, 95, 97, 98, 99, 100, 102, 112, 116, 121, 125, 126, 128, 129, 144, 152, 156, 157, 160, 167, 354, 355, 358, 359, 360, 361, 363, 364; on Henry IV, 1, 43, 60, 72, 78, 79, 80, 82, 88, 111, 159, 346, 347, 348, 356, 366; on Otto of Northeim, 67, 68, 101, 103, 153
Landulf Cotta, Patarine leader, 122
Lanfranc, archbishop of Canterbury, 235
Lechsgemünd-Graisbacher, family of, 173
Leo VIII, pope, 241 n.19, 247 n.46
Leo IX, pope, 20, 21, 25, 32, 36, 37, 39–40, 50, 110, 200
Leopold II, margrave of Austria, 190, 211, 222

Leopold III, margrave of Austria, 331–2

Liber de unitate ecclesiae conservanda, see Preservation of the Unity of the Church

Liemar, archbishop of Bremen, 89, 95, 133, 134, 135, 138, 145 n.14, 161, 194, 195, 197, 224, 243, 245, 257, 270, 271, 295, 307, 310, 358, 363, 364, 366

Life of Emperor Henry IV, anonymous, 113, 163, 205, 288, 301, 313, 318, 320, 332, 339, 340, 341, 343, 345, 348, 349, 353

Liupold of Meersburg, knight, adviser of Henry IV, 67, 68, 69, 121, 355, 359

Liutgard, daughter of Berthold I of Zähringen, 324

Liutizi, Slav confederation, 4, 24, 46, 63, 72, 77, 78, 88, 90, 362

Liutold of Eppenstein, duke of Carinthia and margrave of Verona, 3, 166, 173, 175, 221, 222, 246, 259, 265

Liutpold, archbishop of Mainz, 23, 30

Lorsch, abbey of, 56, 57, 59, 121

Lothar, count of Supplinburg (Emperor Lothar III), 101, 271 n.185, 298 n.14

Louis, count of Montbéliard, 322 n.7

Lower Lusatia, march of, 4, 102, 153, 211, 251

Luder-Udo I, count of Stade, margrave of the Saxon Nordmark, 4

Ludwig 'the Leaper', Thuringian count, 248, 255

Lüneburg, fortress of, 72, 81, 82, 86, 90

Luxemburg, family of, 32, 208, 209

Maginulf, archpriest of S. Angelo, antipope 'Silvester IV', 309

Magnus Billung, duke of Saxony, 69, 70, 71, 72, 74, 75, 90, 167 n.123, 182, 192, 262, 272 n.195, 342

maiestas, concept of, 229, 258

Mainz, council of (1103), 302, 303, 307, 309, 318–20, 328

Mainz, synod of (1085), 246–51, 255, 258, 267, 276, 307, 319

Malmédy, abbey of, 56, 354, 355

Manasses II, archbishop of Rheims, 316

Manasses, bishop of Cambrai (papalist), 316

Manegold, count of Veringen, 260

Manegold of Lautenbach, polemicist, 113 n.32, 170 n.132, 347

Manfred, count of Padua, 293

margrave, office of, 3–4

Markward, bishop of Osnabrück, 276 n.7

Markward IV, count of Eppenstein, 35

Matilda, daughter of Henry III, 19, 33, 34

Matilda, margravine of Tuscany, 32, 134, 138, 160, 161, 165, 197; rebellion, 212, 215, 216, 221, 225, 233, 234, 253, 254, 279–80, 281, 282, 283, 284, 285, 287, 288, 290, 291, 292, 293, 295, 300, 324

Matilda, wife of the *ministerialis* Cuno, 48

Maximilla, daughter of Roger I of Sicily, 292, 300

Mazelin, brother of Liemar of Bremen, 358

Mazo, bishop of Verden, 241 n.16

Meginward, bishop of Freising, 174, 187, 257 n.98, 259, 260

Meinfried, burgrave of Magdeburg, 75

Meinhard, cardinal bishop of Silva Candida, 54

Meinhard of Bamberg, anti-bishop of Würzburg, 135, 248, 257, 260, 261, 276

Meinward, abbot of Reichenau, 119, 121, 355

Meissen, march of, 4, 153, 211, 251, 256, 264, 265, 269, 270, 272

Mellrichstadt, battle of (1078), 181–2, 184, 192, 193, 348, 349, 350, 361

ministeriales (unfree knights), 4–5, 48, 81, 82, 267, 288, 321, 322, 343, 357–60, 365

Monte Cassino, abbey, 32, 218, 219, 220

Monte Cassino chronicle, 33, 264

Moosburg, family, 248, 256

Moricho, royal adviser, 358 n.91

Nicholas II, pope, 33, 37–9, 40–1, 42, 200, 329

Niederaltaich, abbey, 57, 192

Niederaltaich chronicle, 19, 21, 37, 43, 44, 48, 49, 65, 66, 68, 92, 109, 121, 356, 357

Nordhausen, synod of (1105), 326–7, 328

Northeim, family, 35, 69, 267, 270, 272, 296, 307

Nortpert, bishop of Chur, 187

Obodrite Slavs, 3

Oddo, bishop of Asti, 287 n.70

Odo I, cardinal bishop of Ostia, *see* Urban II

Ogerius, bishop of Ivrea, 263

Olmütz, bishopric of, 134

Oppenheim, Promise of, 156, 157–8, 159, 160, 163, 164, 185

Ordulf Billung, duke of Saxony, 58, 69, 70, 72, 75, 85 n.67

Otakars, family, 4

Otbert, bishop of Liège, 276, 277, 316, 323, 338, 340, 343

Otbert, margrave in Italy, 285

Otnand, *ministerialis*, 357

Otto I, bishop of Bamberg, 276, 277, 278, 312, 327 n.31, 330, 352

Otto, bishop of Constance, 119, 155 n.64, 245

Otto, bishop of Freising, historian, 189, 298, 339

Otto, bishop of Regensburg, 29 n.31, 30 n.37, 51, 174

Otto, bishop of Strasbourg, 292, 311

Otto, count of Kastl-Habsberg, 324

Otto, count of Northeim, duke of Bavaria: in the service of the crown, 34, 35, 36, 43, 44, 45, 46, 53–4, 57, 59, 78, 103, 108, 152, 273, 315, 362; rebellion, 65–6, 67, 68, 69, 70, 71–2, 73, 74, 75, 76, 83, 85, 86, 92, 96, 97, 98, 99, 100, 101, 104, 153, 167 n.123, 168, 181, 204, 206, 207, 209, 210, 211, 222, 243, 257, 265, 350, 351, 361, 366

Otto, count of Savoy, 25, 60

Otto, count of Weimar-Orlamünde, margrave of Meissen, 4, 64–5, 85, 86

Otto I, emperor, 2, 6, 58, 241 n.19, 294

Otto II, emperor, 35, 210, 358

Otto III, emperor, 6, 28, 36, 224 n.77, 231, 294

Otto, half-brother of William, margrave of the Saxon Nordmark, 63–4

Otto-William, count of Burgundy, 20

Papal Election Decree (1059), 38–9, 40, 41, 42, 128, 129, 130, 198, 200, 228 n.101

Paschal II, pope, 279, 299–300, 304, 309, 310, 311, 312, 316, 324, 325, 328, 329, 330, 331, 335, 341, 342, 344, 369

Patarini, Milanese, 122–4, 139, 145, 160, 281 n.30

'patrician of the Romans', office of, 36, 39, 41–2, 144, 200, 228

'peace of God', 249–50, 253, 258, 302, 303, 307, 309, 318–20, 321, 326, 331

Peter, anti-bishop of Lucca, 216

Peter, cardinal bishop of Albano, 186, 190, 191, 192, 194, 196, 229

Peter, son of Frederick, count of Montbéliard, 287

Peter Damian, cardinal bishop of Ostia, 15, 27, 29, 36, 39, 40–1, 48, 49, 54, 107, 111, 112, 125

Petershausen chronicle, 299

Petrus Crassus, polemicist, 197, 229

Philip I, king of France, 316, 333, 335, 336, 339, 351

Pibo, bishop of Toul, 11, 117, 119–20, 134, 149

Pippin III, king, 155

Pleichfeld, battle of (1086), 260–1, 262, 349, 351

Poppo, bishop of Metz, 277

Poppo, bishop of Paderborn, 207 n.177

Prague, bishopric of, 134, 250, 251, 305

Praxedis, *see* Eupraxia-Adelaide

Preservation of the Unity of the Church, The, polemic, 212 n.12, 246

Przemyslid, Bohemian ruling dynasty, 252, 306

'Pseudo-Cyprian', *The Twelve Abuses*, 347, 348

Pseudo-Isidorean Decretals, 243

Rabbodi, royal adviser, 138, 140, 141, 142, 147

Rainald, bishop of Como, 129, 130, 132

Rainer II, margrave of Fermo, duke of Spoleto, 215

Rangerius, bishop of Lucca, historian, 215

Rapoto IV, count of Cham, 125, 203, 204

Rapoto of Cham and Vohburg, Bavarian count palatine, 5, 246, 260, 283, 284, 295, 305

Rapotones, family, 305

Regenger, royal adviser, 93, 359, 360

Regensburg chronicle, 256, 259

Reichenau, abbey, 119, 126, 188, 355, 367

Rheinfelden, family, 33, 188, 189, 190, 298

Richard, cardinal bishop of Albano, 331, 335 n.65, 336, 337

Richard of Aversa, prince of Capua, 38, 39, 40, 42, 108, 218–19

Richer, bishop of Verdun, 277

Richenza, wife of Otto of Northeim, 35, 66 n.10, 210

Richwara, wife of Berthold, duke of Carinthia, 36

Robert, bishop of Faenza, 308

Robert I, count of Flanders, 316

Robert II, count of Flanders, 311, 316, 317, 321, 338, 342

Robert Guiscard, duke of Apulia and Calabria, 38, 39, 139, 178, 214, 215, 219, 223, 227, 232–4, 293

Roger I, count of Sicily, 288 n.72, 292

Roland, canon of Parma (bishop of Treviso), 147, 148

Rudolf of Rheinfelden, duke of Swabia, anti-king: in the service of the crown, 3, 33–4, 36, 56, 57, 59, 67, 71, 91, 92, 93, 96, 97, 99, 100, 101, 110, 125–6, 127, 128, 130, 131, 145, 349, 356, 359; rebellion, 13, 104, 152, 153, 156, 160, 165, 166–7; as anti-king, 168–9, 170, 171, 172, 173, 175, 176, 177, 178, 179, 180, 181, 182, 185, 186, 187, 188, 189, 190, 191, 192, 193, 194, 195, 196, 202, 204–5, 207, 209, 229, 258, 261, 292, 351, 362; Henrician propaganda against, 33 n.48, 169, 173 n.11, 204–5, 216, 229

Rudolf II, king of Burgundy, 34

Rudolf III, king of Burgundy, 34

Rumold, bishop of Constance, 57

Ruotger, count of Bilstein, 69, 75, 103

Ruothard, archbishop of Mainz, 302, 303, 304, 325, 326, 328, 330, 332, 334, 335, 337, 342

Ruozelin, abbot of Fulda, 121

Rupert, abbot of Reichenau, 119, 127, 355

Rupert, bishop of Bamberg, 103, 117, 137, 155, 174, 195, 197, 207 n.177, 250, 257, 271, 273, 297, 310, 363, 364, 366

Rupert, bishop of Würzburg, 328 n.33, 330, 332

Rusticus, nephew of Gregory VII, 232
Rusticus Crescentii, Roman nobleman, 218

St Blasien, abbey, 29, 126, 127, 356
St Gallen, abbey, 188, 248 n.49, 259
St Maximin, Trier, abbey, 121, 312–13
SS. Simon and Jude, Goslar, 29, 30, 61, 79, 80,
     117, 118, 119, 187, 241 n.16, 354
'Salian imperial *ordo*', 230–1
Salomon, king of Hungary, 34, 35, 53, 66, 99, 152
Saul, king, 141, 288, 347
Savoy-Turin, family, 25, 108, 111, 287
Saxon Nordmark, 3
servitium, 9, 321, 355
Siegfried I, archbishop of Mainz: in the service of
     the crown, 29, 41, 45, 46, 51, 52, 56–7, 59, 64,
     65, 76, 91, 92, 98, 99, 102, 110, 112, 118, 119,
     126, 127, 131, 132, 134, 135, 138, 143–4, 155, 362;
     rebellion, 167, 168, 176, 181, 190, 207 n.177,
     210, 240 n.9, 304, 363
Siegfried II, bishop of Augsburg, 73, 175, 239, 240
Siegfried, canon of Constance, 118
Siegfried, count of Ballenstedt, Lotharingian
     count palatine, 5, 301, 307, 314, 330, 333, 334
Siegfried III, count of Boyneburg, 267, 270
Siegfried, *serviens*, 353
Sigebert I, count of Saarbrücken, 248
Sigebert, monk of Gembloux, chronicler, 205,
     229, 272, 279 n.23, 344
Sigehard, count of Burghausen, 321–2, 324
Sigehard, patriarch of Aquileia, 11, 152 n.46, 155,
     156, 166, 174
Sigewin, archbishop of Cologne, 187, 207 n.177,
     243, 249, 250, 255, 262, 275, 276
simony, 114, 118, 119, 120, 122, 125, 130, 132, 135,
     136, 145, 146, 149, 168, 170, 184, 198, 200,
     247, 277, 312, 323, 326, 335, 346, 351, 354, 363
Sizzo, count of Schwarzburg-Käfernburg, 75
Song of the Saxon War, 84, 91, 92, 96, 100, 101, 102,
     346, 348, 349, 366
Sophia, wife of Magnus Billung, 70
Speyer, cathedral, 9, 26, 86, 117, 156, 158, 202–3,
     257–8, 266, 276, 308, 313, 329, 343, 344, 352,
     353, 354, 358, 365
Spitignev II, duke of Bohemia, 35, 252, 306 n.57
Stablo, abbey, 354–5
Staufen, family, 189, 299
Stephen, abbot of St James, Liège, 314
Stephen, cardinal priest of S. Grisogono, 40
Stephen IX, pope, 32–3, 36–7, 38 n.60, 108, 200,
     219
Steusslingen family, 30, 47, 88, 358
Suidger, Saxon nobleman, 101

Svatabor-Frederick, patriarch of Aquileia, 241
Swein Estrithson, king of Denmark, 72, 86

Tedald, archbishop of Milan, 139, 140, 166, 198,
     222
Tengling-Burghausen-Peilstein, family, 321–2
Theoderic, abbot of Petershausen, 324
Theoderic, abbot of St Maximin, Trier, 121
Theoderic, bishop of Verdun, 95, 134, 158, 178,
     179, 197, 233, 239, 240, 241, 253, 254
Theoderic, burgrave of Trier, 117
Theoderic, cardinal bishop of Albano (Wibertine),
     antipope, 309
Theoderic, count of Holland, 144
Theoderic II, count of Katlenburg, 75, 81, 244,
     254–5
Theoderic III, count of Katlenburg, 323
Theoderic II, duke of Upper Lotharingia, 100, 342
Theoderic, margrave of Lower Lusatia, 11
Theoderic, son of Gero of Brehna, 74, 152, 192
Theophanu, empress, 28, 61
Thiebald, bishop of Strasbourg, 175, 181
Thietmar Billung, count, 63
Thimo, count of Brehna, 74
Thuringian tithes dispute, 64–5, 76–7, 91, 110, 111,
     362
Tostig, earl of Northumbria, 70
Tribur-Oppenheim, assembly of (1076), 136, 153,
     155–8, 162, 163, 177, 178, 356, 360, 363, 364
Triumph of St Remaclus, 354, 355
'truce of God', 250
Tusculani, Roman family, 36, 37

Ubald, bishop of Mantua, 282
Udalric, bishop of Eichstätt, 174
Udalric, bishop of Padua, 186, 190, 191, 192, 194
Udalric, bishop of Passau (Gregorian), 286, 293
Udalric, count of Passau, 277, 305
Udalric of Brünn (Przemyslid), 306
Udalric of Eppenstein, abbot of St Gallen,
     patriarch of Aquileia, 175, 188, 248, 259, 284,
     285–6, 289, 297, 329
Udalric of Godesheim, royal adviser, 102, 125, 155,
     225, 360, 359, 360, 364
Udalschalk, royal adviser, 140, 141, 142, 147
Udo, archbishop of Trier, 82, 117, 120, 134, 143,
     151–2, 156, 159, 178, 179, 183
Udo, bishop of Hildesheim, 187 n.76, 207 n.177,
     243, 244, 245, 246, 255, 257, 270, 271, 326
Udo II, count of Stade, margrave of the Saxon
     Nordmark, 7, 34 n.49, 74, 101, 167 n.123, 269
Udo III, count of Stade, margrave of the Saxon
     Nordmark, 271 n.185

Ugiccio, count in Tuscany, 216
Unwan, archbishop of Bremen, 58
Urban II, pope: as Odo I, cardinal bishop of Ostia, 226, 229, 242, 243, 244–5; as pope, 275, 278–9, 280, 281, 290, 291, 292, 293, 299, 300, 309, 312, 316, 318, 327, 329

Verdun, family, 3, 32, 33, 253, 263, 315
vicarius Christi, king as, 13–14, 149
Victor II, pope, 24–5, 26–7, 32, 36, 37, 40, 112, 132, 155, 200
Victor III, pope: as Desiderius, abbot of Monte Cassino, 219, 220; as pope, 219, 233, 263–4
Viehbach-Eppensteiner, family, 173
Vita Heinrici IV, see *Life of Emperor Henry IV*
Vitalis Falieri, doge of Venice, 294
Vladislav II, duke of Bohemia, king, 252
Vladislav-Herman, duke of Poland, 276, 305
Volcmar, imperial steward, 358, 365
Vratislav II, duke of Bohemia, king: as duke, 4, 11, 100, 102, 104, 153, 181, 202, 203, 211, 222, 241, 246, 248; as king, 250–2, 264, 265, 269, 283, 284, 305, 306, 332
Vsevolod, grand prince of Kiev, 269

Walbruno, bishop of Verona, 293
Walcher, bishop of Cambrai, 276, 316, 317, 323
Walo, abbot of St Arnulf in Worms, anti-bishop of Metz, 248, 253, 254, 276
Walram, bishop of Naumburg, 276, 277, 278, 329 n.41
Walram I, count of Limburg, 315
Walram, son of Henry of Limburg, duke of Lower Lotharingia, 339
Waltolf, bishop of Padua, 29 n.31, 31 n.40
Weilheimer, family, 173
Weimar-Orlamünde, family, 4, 64
Weissenburg annals, 56, 59
Welf family, 65, 70, 209, 280, 281, 289, 291, 298, 299, 300
Welf II, count, 70, 209
Welf III, duke of Carinthia, margrave of Verona, 24, 70
Welf IV, duke of Bavaria, 65, 70; in the service of the crown, 71, 96, 98, 100, 127, 130, 145; rebellion, 13, 152, 153, 156, 167 n.123, 168, 173, 174, 176, 177, 181, 182, 184, 188, 189, 190, 209, 210, 211, 239, 240, 259, 260, 261, 262, 274, 280, 282, 283, 286, 294, 310, 319, 324; later career, 295, 296, 297, 298, 299, 300, 368
Welf V, duke of Bavaria, 280, 281, 284, 286, 287, 290, 295, 297, 319 n.125

Wenceslas, abbot of Niederaltaich, 49
Wenrich of Trier, bishop of Piacenza, polemicist, 205, 241, 276, 293
Werl, family, 317
Werner, archbishop of Magdeburg, 13, 47, 74, 84, 88–9, 90, 91, 99, 100, 152, 167 n.123, 181, 182, 356
Werner, bishop of Merseburg, 29, 74, 76, 89, 90, 100, 152, 181, 243, 247, 255, 267, 270, 358 n.91
Werner II, bishop of Strasbourg, 56, 116, 118, 155, 174, 175
Werner, count, confidant of Henry IV, 56, 355
Werner, count of Habsburg, 127
Werner, margrave of Ancona, duke of Spoleto, 293, 309, 357
Wettin family, 4, 29, 74, 153, 241, 248–9, 358 n.94
Wezilo, archbishop of Mainz, 135, 240, 243, 245, 247–8, 252, 255, 257, 276
Wibert of Parma, archbishop of Ravenna, antipope Clement III: earlier career, 11, 30, 38, 128, 151, 198, 199, 200; as antipope, 201, 202, 211, 212, 216, 217, 220, 221, 223, 227, 228, 229, 230, 231, 232, 233, 234, 240, 241, 245, 252, 264, 267, 274, 278, 279, 280, 281, 282, 283, 284, 285, 286 n.65, 289, 291, 295, 303, 304, 308, 309, 310, 311, 368
Widelo, bishop of Minden, 364, 365, 366
Widerad, abbot of Fulda, 61, 100
Wido, archbishop of Milan, 124
Wido, bishop of Chur, 342
Wido, bishop of Ferrara, polemicist, 113, 241, 279 n.23
Wido, bishop of Osnabrück, polemicist, 14, 276, 310
Wido II, margrave of Sezze, 221
Widones, family, 215
Widukind, clerk of Cologne, 135
Wigold, bishop of Augsburg (Gregorian), 187 n.76, 239
William, abbot of Hirsau, 222 n.63, 282, 356
William, bishop of Utrecht, 51, 144, 145, 149, 151
William, count of Burgundy, 159, 160, 342
William, count of Luxemburg, 333, 334
William, count of Weimar-Orlamünde, margrave of Meissen, 4, 64
William V, duke of Aquitaine, 19
William, margrave of the Saxon Nordmark, 4, 24, 63
William of Lodersleben, Saxon rebel, 76, 87
William, son of Gero of Brehna, 74, 152
Winither, abbot of Lorsch, anti-bishop of Worms, 248

Winither, bishop of Merseburg, 29
Wipo, imperial chaplain, 2, 8
Wiprecht I, count of Groitzsch, 192, 202, 296,
    307, 332
witness lists in diplomas, 266 n.155, 361, 365
Worms, council of (1076), 128–9, 143–6, 148,
    150, 158, 167, 195, 198, 217, 246, 362, 367,
    368

Wulfhilde, wife of Ordulf Billung, 70
Würzburg chronicle, 26

Yaroslav 'the Wise', grand prince of Kiev, 269
    n.174

Zacharias, pope, 155, 208
Zähringen, family, 190, 245, 298, 299, 305, 324